Book Marketing Opportunities

A Directory

A Directory of Book Wholesalers, Distributors, Chain Stores, Catalogs, Book Clubs, Mailing Lists, Marketing Services, Reviewers, and other Book Marketing Channels

John Kremer

Book Marketing Opportunities

A Directory

A Directory of Book Wholesalers, Distributors, Chain Stores, Catalogs, Book Clubs, Mailing Lists, Marketing Services, Reviewers, and other Book Marketing Channels

---

John Kremer

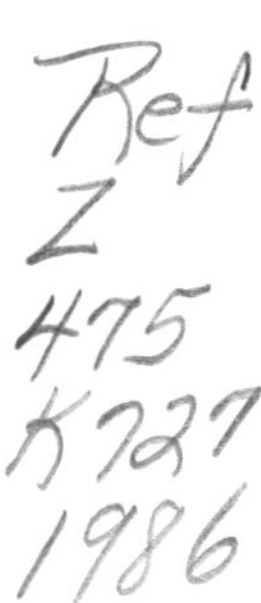

Copyright 1986 by John Kremer

Published by: Ad-Lib Publications
                51 N. Fifth Street
                P. O. Box 1102
                Fairfield, IA 52556-1102
                (515) 472-6617

Printed and bound in the United States of America.

Library of Congress Cataloging-in-Publication Data

Kremer, John, 1949-
   Book marketing opportunities.

   Bibliography: p.
   Includes index.
   1. Book industries and trade--United States--
Directories. 2. Books--Marketing--Directories.
I. Kiefer, Marie, 1945-   . II. McIlvride, Bob.
III. Title.
Z475.K727 1986   070.5'025'73   86-7994
ISBN 0-912411-10-4 (pbk.)

TABLE OF CONTENTS

Table of Contents

INTRODUCTION

Book Marketing Opportunities: A Directory is a directory of
the key contacts for marketing books. It includes the following:

```
 900 Wholesalers and Distributors
  75 Book Sales Representatives
 300 Chain and Department Stores
 215 Book Clubs
 220 Catalogs which Feature Books
  45 Remainder Dealers
  75 Mailing List Sources for Book Publishers
  50 Card Packs (or Decks)
  20 Foreign Sales Representatives and Exporters
  30 Book Fairs and Conventions
  17 Exhibit Services
  17 Cooperative Marketing Programs
  17 Fulfillment and Marketing Services
  75 Publicity and Public Relations Services
  80 Publicity and Marketing Directories
  70 Bibliographies and Other Publisher Listings
 420 Daily Newspapers (and approximately 800 editors)
 135 Weekly Newspapers (and approximately 200 editors)
1235 Magazine Editors and Book Reviewers
1200 Radio Stations, Networks, and Syndicated Shows
 575 TV Stations, Networks, and Syndicated Shows
=====
5771 total (or 6200, including individual newspaper editors)
```

While this list is obviously not all-inclusive, it does
cover most of the major book marketing contacts. The publicity
file (newspapers, magazines, radio and television) includes the
key book reviewers and interviewers to allow you to set up a
national publicity campaign or author tour.

Some of you might ask why we put together this directory
when the Literary Market Place directory already exists. While
it is true that some of the material in this directory duplicates
material in the LMP, this directory includes much more. For
example, the LMP only lists a hundred or so of the wholesalers
and distributors in the U.S. and Canada; the BMO (this directory)
lists 900 of them--and with more detailed information important
to any book marketer.

The publicity file of newspapers, magazines, radio and TV
stations is much more extensive than anything offered by the LMP.
Plus the BMO includes a listing of the major chain stores and
catalogs which feature books (data which is unavailable in any
form in the LMP).

Within the listings themselves, this directory provides more details than the LMP. The most important added details, in my way of looking at things, are the Categories listings. For every contact listed in this directory, we have indicated (where known) what kind of books they are interested in reviewing or handling. These category codes should allow you to target your contacts more precisely for each new book you publish.

For example, if you publish children's books, the category codes you would be interested in tracking are as follows:

    21 (Children's Books -- Non-Fiction)
    31 (Education and Child Development)
    76 (Children's Stories -- Fiction)
    89 (Young Adult -- Fiction)

If, in addition, you publish these books in Spanish editions, you could also look for the following category codes:

    45 (Languages -- Spanish or SP)
    78 (Ethnic/Minority Literature)
    80 (Foreign Literature)

A complete listing of the category codes may be found on the following pages: page 10, page 122, page 196, and page 258.

Note that many listings have a general category code, either 10 (indicating general non-fiction), 75 (indicating general fiction), or 99 (indicating all categories, both general non-fiction and general fiction). The code 99 was assigned to any company which indicated no special interests or so many special interests that for all practical purposes they are interested in everything.

How This Directory Was Developed

This directory began as an offshoot of my _Directory of Short-Run Book Printers_. Many publishers, after seeing the work I did on that directory, began asking me for information on other book publishing resources. Hence, about two years ago I began systemizing the information I already had accumulated. Then last fall (while working on my other two books in the Ad-Lib Book Marketing Library -- _Book Marketing Made Easier_ and _101 Ways to Market Your Books -- For Publishers and Authors_), I began entering the data into a computer database program. At this point, Bob McIlvride joined me. In February, Marie Kiefer also joined the project.

Most of the material in this directory has been recently updated. In March and April, 1986, we sent out survey forms to all the book wholesalers, sales representatives, major magazines and newspapers, and radio and TV stations. Most of the responses came back in late April and early May. While not all of the

companies responded to the survey, well over 30% did. Even among
those who did not respond to the survey, we did confirm the
accuracy of their addresses (by requesting address corrections
through the Post Office).

Obviously, as with any directory, the moment it is published
it is already out of date. We've already added over 100 new
listings since the printed directory was formated for printing.
This is one of the drawbacks of any printed directory.

Since printed directories cannot be updated every other day,
we are also offering a database version of this directory which
will be updated daily so when you order it, you will get the very
latest information. (See page 283 for a more detailed descrip-
tion of this database, <u>Book Marketing Opportunities: A Database</u>.)

<u>Specific Notes -- The Various Listings</u>

<u>WHOLESALERS</u>

Besides wholesalers, these listings also include book
distributors (both exclusive and non-exclusive) and publishers
who distribute other publishers books. The major difference
between a wholesaler and a distributor is that a distributor has
sales representatives who sell direct to the specific markets
they serve while wholesalers rely solely on catalogs and other
promotions for their sales.

As part of each listing (where known), we have provided the
following details (besides the name of company, person to contact, address, and phone number):

    * the categories of books they are interested in handling,
    * their designation (wholesaler, distributor, publisher),
    * the territory they serve (US, Canada, etc.),
    * the markets they serve (bookstores, libraries, etc.),
    * the items they carry (hardcovers, calendars, etc.),
    * the year they started (how long in business),
    * the number of representatives they have,
    * the number of accounts they serve,
    * the number of titles they carry, and
    * the number of publishers they carry.

This information should help you to target those wholesalers
or distributors who can best serve your needs. For example, if
you publish a regional title, you can target all the wholesalers
who carry regional titles for your area. (You can also contact
all wholesalers in your region by referring to the wholesaler
index on page 59.)

Or you can target only those wholesalers serving libraries
or schools; those wholesalers carrying trade paperbacks, calendars, or whatever; or those carrying few titles or many titles.

<u>SALES REPRESENTATIVES</u>

If you decide to form a network of commissioned sales representatives for your books, these listings will help you to select representatives based on how long they've been in the business, how many publishers they serve, what territories they cover, etc.

<u>BOOK STORE CHAINS</u>

This list includes all chains of four or more book stores (or department stores with book departments). In most cases the name of the person responsible for buying books is included. Since this list was not updated this past spring, you may want to call ahead to verify the name of the book buyer (especially for the most important chains). [This list will be updated later this summer (1986).]

Note that we have also provided a list of these book store chains sorted by state and city, so you can personally visit those chains headquartered in your region, or target them for special promotions.

<u>BOOK CLUBS AND CATALOGS</u>

We've included all the book clubs we could locate. And where known, we've also included the name of the book buyer or editor.

The list of catalogs which carry books is obviously incomplete. Depending on whose count you use, there are anywhere from 6000 to 10,000 catalogers, some with small circulations of as little at 1000, others with circulations in the millions. While many of these catalogs do not carry books, we still hope to increase the listings in this category in future editions.

Book clubs and catalogs can sell many books for you. Though both require large discounts (anywhere from 50% to 85% of the retail price), they usually buy on a no-return basis.

<u>REMAINDER DEALERS</u>

If all else fails, you can remainder your books to one of these companies. In most cases, they won't pay you more than the estimated cost of production, but at least you will recover some of your money which would otherwise be tied up in inventory.

<u>MISCELLANEOUS SERVICES</u>

For those of you interested in marketing by direct mail, we've provided a listing of some reputable brokers and compilers who will be able to provide you with mailing lists of people and businesses responsive to buying books by mail. Select the source or sources which can provide the lists you require.

We've also include a brief listing of card packs featuring books (this listing includes about 50 of the 650 card packs currently being published). We will be expanding this listing in future editions of the directory (many of these new listings will be available in the database by September).

If you are interested in marketing your books overseas, we've provided a short list of companies and individuals who can help you either by providing rights representation or by actually distributing your books overseas. You might also want to exhibit your books at one or more of the international book fairs we've listed (or use an exhibit service to represent you).

Finally, we've provided a short list (clearly not complete) of co-op marketing programs, marketing services, and fulfillment services. We highly recommend the co-op marketing programs as being a cost-effective way to reach certain audiences. Before, however, you use one of these co-op programs, be sure to ask for the names of some publishers who have used the program before (and then call some of these publishers to see how well the co-op program worked for them). Also, be sure to see a sample package.

<u>PUBLICITY</u> <u>AND</u> <u>PROMOTION</u>

Besides the listings of magazines, newspapers, radio, and television, we've also included three other lists which will be useful to you in your promotional campaigns. If you'd rather use a professional publicity service, check out the listing of 75 such services, many of whom specialize in authors and books. To supplement the listings in this directory, we've also included a bibliography of 80 other directories which you might find useful in your promotional campaigns (everything from a directory of minority publications to a listing of literary bookstores). Finally, we've listed 70 major reference works used by book buyers when trying to locate books or publishers. Obviously, you should be listed in as many of these directories as appropriate for your company and books.

For more information on the newspaper, magazine, radio and TV files, see page 121, "How to Use the Review Files."

Future Editions

Help us help you. We've tried our best to make these listings complete and up-to-date. Nonetheless, if you do find any listing which is incomplete, out-of-date, or misspelled, please let us know. We'll be sure to update it for the next edition.

Also, please send us information on any company or review media which we've omitted that you feel should be in this directory. We'll be happy to add them to future editions. As far as we are concerned, the more, the merrier.

<u>**CATEGORIES**</u> -- coded by number

10 General Nonfiction
11 Art/Music/Photography/Dance
13 Alternative Issues
15 Animals/Pets
17 Biographies/Autobiographies
19 Business/Economics
21 Children's Books
23 Computers/Technology
25 Consumer Issues and Guides
27 Cookbooks/Nutrition
29 Crafts/Hobbies/How-to
31 Education/Child Development
33 Entertainment/Movies/Humor
35 Family/Marriage/Retirement
37 Gay/Lesbian
39 Health/Medicine/Diet/Exercise
41 History

43 House/Garden/Automobiles
45 Languages:________________
47 Literature/Humanities
49 Minority Studies
51 Nature/Ecology/Conservation
53 New Age/Astrology/Occult
55 Politics/Government/Military
57 Psychology/Self-Help
59 Reference Books
61 Regional Titles
63 Religions/Philosophy
65 Scholarly Titles
67 Science/Mathematics
69 Sports/Games/Recreation
71 Travel/Geography
73 Women's Issues

75 General Fiction
76 Children's Stories
77 Contemporary Novels
78 Ethnic/Minority Literature
79 Folklore/Fairy Tales
80 Foreign Literature
81 Historical
82 Horror/Occult

83 Literary
84 Mystery/Detective
85 Romance/Gothic
86 Science Fiction/Fantasy
87 Suspense/Adventure
88 Westerns
89 Young Adult
90 Short Stories/Anthologies

95 Poetry
97 News

98 Other:________________________
99 All subjects and categories

===

<u>**WHOLESALERS**</u> -- codes

<u>Markets</u>

BK = Bookstores
CO = Colleges
JB = Jobbers
MM = Mass Markets
NS = Newsstands
PL = Public Libraries
RO = Retail Outlets
SC = Schools
SL = Special Libraries

<u>Items</u>

CA = Calendars
CO = Comics
GC = Greeting Cards
GI = Gifts
HC = Hardcovers
MA = Maps and Atlases
MG = Magazines, General
ML = Magazines, Literary
MM = Mass Market Books
NP = Newspapers

OT = Other:___________
PB = Trade Paperbacks
PO = Posters
RC = Records
RM = Remainders
SB = Stickers/Bookmarks
ST = Stationery
TA = Tapes, Audio
TV = Tapes, Video
TX = Textbooks

Territories: US = United States   CN = Canada   IT = International
              other abbreviations indicate states or provinces

Designations: DE = Distributor, Exclusive   DN = Distributor, Nonexclusive   WH = Wholesaler
               PD = Publisher who distributes books

Numbers: #R = # of Representatives   #A = # of Accounts   #T = # of Titles   #P = # of Publishers

21st Century Antiques
Peter Rakelbush, Owner
11 1/2 Main Street
P O Box 70
Hatfield MA 01038
413-247-9396
Categories: 29(antiques)
WH

21st Century Publications
Tony Kulvinskas, Manager
401 N 4th Street
Fairfield IA 52556-0702
515-472-5105
Categories: 39
PD -- Territory: US-CN
Markets: BK-JB-SC-CO-MM-PL
Items: HC-PB-MM
Year started: 1975
#T 80; #P 15

A & B Smith
Stuart J Smith, President
P O Box 1776
Pittsburgh PA 15230-1776
412-242-5400
Categories: 99
WH

A B & T Marketing
Tom E Chrisp, Marketing
P O Box 854
Minneapolis MN 55440
612-341-8531
Categories: 27
WH

A-Betta Book Service
Fred A Montella, Manager
50 Oser Avenue
Hauppauge NY 11787
516-582-3131
Categories: 99
WH

ABC School Supply
I W Ross, Owner
240 - 9th Street N
Saint Petersburg FL 33705
813-822-7921
Categories: 21-31-76-99
WH

Abner Schram Ltd
Frances Schram, President
36 Park Street
Montclair NJ 07042
201-744-7755
Categories: 99
WH

Abranovic Associates
Mark Abranovic, Manager
140 S Jefferson Street

Kittanning PA 16201
412-543-2005
Categories: 99
WH

Academic Book Caravans
Donald Geraghty, Manager
459 Burlington Street E
P O Box 768
Hamilton L8N 3N2 ON Canada
416-529-9575
Categories: 31-65-99
WH

Academic Book Center
Daniel P Halloran, V.P.
5600 NE Hassalo Street
Portland OR 97213-3640
503-287-6657; 800-547-7704
Categories: 65-99
WH -- Territory: US
Markets: CO-PL-SL
Items: HC-TX-PB
Year started: 1974
#R 2

Adair Distributors
Bryan Weiner, Owner
208 S Mulanix Street
Kirksville MO 63501
816-665-4662
Categories: 99
WH

Adams Book Company
Carl Raymond, Manager
537 Sackett Street
Brooklyn NY 11217
718-875-5464; 800-221-0909
Categories: 99
WH -- Territory: part(NY)
Markets: BK-SC
Items: TX-PB-SW
Year started: 1940

Adams News Company
Genevieve Lofgren, Buyer
1555 W Galer Street
Seattle WA 98119
206-284-7617
Categories: 99
WH -- Territory: part(Northwest)
Markets: BK-CO-SC-PL-SL
Items: PB-MM-MG-NP-games, puzzles)
Year started: 1929
#R 28

Advanced Marketing Services
Alan Orso, Buyer
   Basic and Bestselling Books
Ann Fontanesi, Buyer
   Juvenile and Mass Market Books
Cindy Tellenghast, Buyer
   Regional Books and Cookbooks

R Craig Schafer, Buyer
   Promotional Books
Categories: 21-26-31-61
            71-76-89-99
WH -- Territory: US
Markets: BK
Items: HC-PB-MM-RM
Year started: 1982
#T 175

Advent Books
C Kumble, President
141 East 44th Street
New York NY 10017
212-697-0887
Categories: 99
WH

Affiliated Book Distributors
Steve Keen, Manager
415 N Wolf Road
Wheeling IL 60090
312-537-0554
WH

Affiliated Medical Book
Attn: Book Buyer
1335 Nostrand Avenue
Brooklyn NY 11226
718-856-1173
Categories: 39
WH

AG Access Corporation
Michael Arciero, Manager
P. O. Box 2008
Davis CA 95617-6994
Categories: 99
WH

Alaska News Agency
Russ Riemann, President
325 W Potter Drive
Anchorage AK 99502
907-563-3251
Categories: 61(AK)-99
WH -- Territory: AK
Markets: BK-CO-SC-PL-MM
Items: HC-PB-MM-RM-MG-NP
Year started: 1953
#R 10; #P all

Alberta Book & Novelty
Hal Whyte, Book Buyer
7140 Fairmont Drive SE
Calgary T2H 0X4 AB Canada
403-252-4426
Categories: 99
WH -- Territory: CN(western)
             part(Pacific NW)
Markets: SC-CO-PL-SL
Items: HC-PB-SW-TA
Year started: 1940
#R 1; #A 1000; #T 5000

Alchemy Books
Ken Cameron, Book Buyer
717 Market Street #514
San Francisco CA 94103
415-777-2197
Categories: 10-75-90-95
PD -- Territory: US-CN-IT
Markets: BK-JB-SC-CO-MM-PL-SL
Items: HC-PB-CO
Year started: 1976
#T 50; #P 20

Alfonsi Enterprises
Rebecca Umberger, Manager
10 Airlawn Street
P.O. Box 100
Taylorville IL 62568-0100
217-824-9871
Categories: 99
WH

Alico International
Edward Ryan, President
990 Greentree Road
Pittsburgh PA 15220
412-928-9999
Categories: 99
WH

All America Distributors
Marian O'Farrell, Manager
8431 Melrose Place
Los Angeles CA 90069
213-651-2650
Categories: 49-99
WH -- Territory: (western US)
Markets: BK-CO-SC-PL
Items: MM-MG-NP
Year started: 1960
#R 4

Allied Books
Janet R Hall, Owner
933 Tewa Loop
Los Alamos NM 87544
505-662-2162
Categories: 21-31-45(Spanish)-89
        61(Southwest)-76-80
WH -- Territory: US
Markets: SC-PL
Items: HC-PB-MM-TA-TV
Year started: 1968
#R 5; #T 10M; #P 60

Alonso Book & Periodical Service
Al Alonso, Manager
7670 Richmond Highway
Alexandria VA 22306
Categories: 99
WH

Alpic Library Company
Linda Jackson, Manager
2211 Church Street
Greensboro NC 27405
919-275-6497
Categories: 99
WH

Alpine News Distributors
0105 Marand Road
Glenwood Springs CO 81601
303-945-2269
Categories: 99
WH -- Territory: part(CO)
Markets: BK
Items: HC-MM-RM-MG
#R 5

Altarinda Books
Phil Thayer
13 Estates Drive
Orinda CA 94563
415-254-3830
Categories: 29(food, wine)
PD -- Territory: US
Markets: BK-PL
Items: HC-PB

Ambassador Book Service
Kaye Manson, Buyer
42 Chasner Street
Hempstead NY 11550
516-489-4011; 800-431-8913
Categories: 19-23-41-47-55-57
           59-63-65-67-99
WH -- Territory: US
Markets: CO-PL-SL
Items: HC-PB-MM-TX
Year started: 1973
#R 4; #T 100M; #P all

American Book Distributors
Robert Sennholz, Manager
Spring Mills PA 16875
814-422-8554
Categories: 55(conservative)-99
WH -- Territory: US
Markets: BK
Items: HC-PB-MM

American Overseas Book Company
Carmine C Lepore, Book Buyer
550 Walnut Street
Norwood NJ 07648
201-767-7600
Categories: 10-75
WH -- Territory: US-CN-IT
Markets: BK-SC-CO-PL-SL
Items: HC-TX-PB-MM-MG-ML
        MA-SW-NW-TV
Year started: 1969
#R 2; #A 2000; #T 25M; #P 10M

American Society of Agronomy
Book Distribution
677 S Segoe Road
Madison WI 53711
608-274-1212
Categories: 98(agriculture)
WH -- Territory: US
Markets: BK
Items: HC-TX-PB

American Toy & Book Distributors
Larry Granet, President
P O Box 530512

Miami FL 33153-0051
305-634-8500
Categories: 21-76
WH -- Territory: part(Southeast)
Markets: BK-RO(toy stores)
Items: HC-PB-MM-toys
#R 5

Ames News Agency
Gary Hurlbut, Manager
2110 E 13th Street
Ames IA 50010
515-232-1788
WH

Anderson News Company
Frank Stockard, Manager
Helton Drive
P. O. Box 219
Florence AL 35630
205-766-3789
WH

Andich Brothers News Company
Hyman Andich, Manager
2115 4th Avenue
Rock Island IL 61201
309-788-9393
WH

Andrzejewski's Religious Goods
Attn: Book Buyer
1304 Kosciuszko Avenue
Bay City MI 48706
517-892-8511
Categories: 63
WH

Annex Book Distributors
Sandra H Weiss, President
1889 Wantagh Avenue
Wantagh NY 11793
516-781-3324
Categories: 99
DN

Apollo Book
Glenn B Opitz, Owner
5 School House Lane
Poughkeepsie NY 12603
914-462-0040
Categories: 11(architecture)-17
        29(collectibles,
        antiques)-43-33-59
PD -- Territory: US-CN-IT
Markets: BK-JB-NS-SC-CO-MM-PL-SL
Items: HC-PB-RM
Year started: 1977
#A 10000; #T 250; #P 50

Appalacian Bible & Books
H Thomas Torbett, President
604 Rolling Hills Drive
P. O. Box 1573
Johnson City TN 37601
615-926-0128
Categories: 63
WH

Book Wholesalers and Distributors

Apple Book Company
Carrie Boyko, V.P.
P. O. Box 2111
Charlotte NC 28211
704-527-4030
Categories: 99
WH -- Territory: part(Southeast)
Markets: SC
Items: PB-MM
Year started: 1982
#R 2; #A 300+; #T 1500; #P 30

Apt Books
C Kumble, President
141 East 44th Street #511
New York NY 10017
212-697-0887
WH

Arabic & Islamic Univ. Press
Ben Chaban, Manager
4283 Fountain Avenue
Los Angeles CA 90029
213-665-1000
WH

Arbit Books
Joseph Steinberg, Manager
8050 N Port Washington Road
Milwaukee WI 53217
414-352-4404
WH

Arbuta House
V Kerry Inman
P O Box 48
1040 Arbuta Road
Abington PA 19001
215-576-8270
Categories: 63(Protestant)
PD -- Territory: US-IT
Markets: OT(churches,
        organizations)
Items: HC-PB
#P 5

Ardic Book Distributors
Richard Sargeaunt
Montgomery Center
Skillman NJ 08558
609-924-2121
Categories: 71
DN -- Territory: US
Markets: BK-CO-SC-PL-SL
Items: HC-PB-MM-RM-MG-MA
Year started: 1980
#R 4; #T 200; #P 4

Arkansas Book Company
Jerry Wilkins, Manager
2101 Bond Street
Little Rock AR 72203-1657
501-375-1184
WH

Arlington Card Company
David Leduersis, Owner
Book Department

140 Gansett Avenue
Cranston RI 02910
401-942-3188
WH

Armchair Sailor Publishing
Jane Parfet, Book Buyer
Lee's Wharf
Newport RI 02840
401-847-4252
Categories: 69(marine, sailing)
PD -- Territory: US
Markets: BK-CO-PL-consumer mail
Items: HC-PB-MM-MA-TX
Year started: 1979
#A 15000; #T 10M

Arthur J Viders Company
Arthur J Viders, President
7906 Hopi Place
Tampa FL 33614
813-888-8484
Categories: 99
WH -- Territory: US
Markets: SC-CO-PL-SL
Items: HC-PB-RM-MA-TA
Year started: 1974
#R 0; #A 150; #T 5000; #P 300

Arthur Vanous Company
Arlene Rudd, Manager
P. O. Box 650279
Vero Beach FL 32965
305-562-9186
Categories: 27-29-45-59-71
WH -- Territory: US
Markets: BK-JB-SC-CO-PL-SL
Items: TX-MM-MA
Year started: 1960
European imports only

ASI Distributors
Henry Weingarten, Owner
63 West 38th Street #505
New York NY 10018
212-719-2919
Categories: 39-53
PD -- Territory: IT
Markets: BK-RO(metaphysical)
Items: HC-TX-PB-CA-SW-TA-TV
Year started: 1970
#R 0; #A 400; #T 40; #P 6

Associated Booksellers
Alex M Yudkin, President
P O Box 38
Greens Farms CT 06436
203-366-5494
Categories: 21-29-47-53-83
DE -- Territory: US
Markets: BK-JB-SC-CO-PL
Items: HC-PB-RM-MM-CA-SB-TA
Year started: 1949
#R 15; #A 4000; #T 800; #P 15

Associated Libraries
Kenneth Hunn, President
229 N 63rd Street

Philadelphia PA 19139
215-476-3200
Categories: 21-31-76
WH -- Territory: part(PA-NJ)
Markets: SC-PL
Items: HC-PB-MM
Year started: 1944
#R 38; #A 2000+
prebound children's books

Associated News
Chris Swanzy, Buyer
914 Winbern
Houston TX 77002
713-528-3351
Categories: 21-31-76-89-99
WH -- Territory: part(TX)
Markets: BK
Items: HC-PB-MM-RM
Year started: 1977
#R 4

Astrology & Spiritual Center
Darlene M Enber, Owner
4535 Hohman Avenue
Hammond IN 46327
219-931-8050
Categories: 21-27-39-53-57-63
          73-82-84
WH -- Territory: US-CN-IT
Markets: BK-SC-CO-PL
Items: HC-TX-PB-RM-MM-CA-TA-TV
Year started: 1973
#T 6000; #P 40

Atlas Publishing Company
Klaus D Gurgel, Manager
1464 - 36th Street
Ogden UT 84403
801-627-1043
WH

Augsburg Publishing House
426 S 5th Street
P O Box 1209
Minneapolis MN 55440
612-330-3300; 800-752-8153
Categories: 63(Protestant)-99
PD -- Territory: US
Markets: BK-CO-PL
Items: HC-PB-MM-religious goods
Year started: 1890
#R 7

Auromere
Vanzetti & Zucker, Directors
1291 Weber Street
Pomona CA 91768
714-629-8255
WH

Austin News Agency
2830 Real Street
P O Box 2133
Austin TX 78768
512-474-8023
Categories: 99
WH -- Territory: part(TX)

Markets: BK
Items: HC-MM-MG-NP
Year started: 1935
#R 15

Austin Periodical Services
Ruth Austin, Owner
Route 4, Fayetteville Highway
Shelbyville TN 37160
615-684-7591
Categories: 99
WH -- Territory: part(TN, KY)
Markets: BK-CO-SC
Items: HC-PB-MM-MG
#R 14

Austin Periodical Services
Garry Ratcliffe, Manager
701 E Princeton
P O Box 31
Springfield IL 62705
217-525-1417
Categories: 99
WH -- Territory: part(midwest)
Markets: BK-CO-SC-PL-RO
Items: HC-PB-MM-MG-NP
Year started: 1942
#R 6

Auto-Bound
Andrew DeFrancesco, Book Buyer
2313 Santa Clara Avenue
Alameda CA 94501
415-521-8630
Categories: 98(auto, motorcycles)
WH -- Territory: part(West)
Markets: BK-JB-SC-CO-PL
        OT(auto parts)
Items: HC-PB-MM-CA-PO
Year started: 1978
#R 3; #A 300; #T lots; #P 12

Avanti Enterprises
Dr Sudhir Kumar, Director
18901 Springfield
Flossmoor IL 60422
312-799-9382
WH

Aviation Book Company
Walter P Winner, President
1640 Victory Boulevard
Glendale CA 91201
818-240-1771
Categories: 69(aviation only)
WH -- Territory: US-IT
Markets: BK-SC-PL
Items: HC-PB-SW-GI
Year started: 1964
#T 1600; #P 350

B Broughton Company
Mr Joe Rizza, Book Buyer
2105 Danforth Avenue
Toronto M4C 1K1 ON Canada
416-690-4777
Categories: 21-35-57-61-63-65
DE -- Territory: CN

Markets: BK-SC-PL-SL
Items: HC-TX-PB-CA-GI-GC-ML-RC
       TA-TV
Year started: 1970
#R 2; #A 1000; #T 5000; #P 13
offers direct mail

B L Winch & Associates
B L Winch, President
45 Hitching Post Drive #2
Rolling Hills Ests CA 90274
213-547-1240
Categories: 31-35-57
DN -- Territory: US-IT
Markets: SC-CO-PL-individuals
Items: HC-PB-TA-TV
Year started: 1971
#R 5; #A 75,000; #T 100; #P 5
creative parenting, self-esteem

Back-to-Basics Books
Ted K Black, Director
105 Stoney Mountain Road
P. O. Box 70
Hendersonville NC 28791
704-693-0211
WH

Baggins Books
W David Lewis, Manager
15 Unity
Bellingham WA 98225
206-671-2667
WH

Baker & Taylor Company
Jackie Kelly, Buying Manager
Western Division
380 Edison Way
Reno NV 89564
702-786-6700
Categories: 99
WH -- Territory: US
Markets: BK-SC-CO-PL-SL
Items: HC-PB-MM-TX-RM
Year started: 1828
#R 0; #A 15,000; #T 110M; #P all

Baker & Taylor Company
R. Cancelliere, Buying Manager
Eastern Division
50 Kirby Avenue
Somerville NJ 08876
201-722-8000
Categories: 99
WH -- Territory: US
Markets: BK-SC-CO-PL-SL
Items: HC-PB-MM-TX-RM
Year started: 1828
#R 0; #A 15,000; #T 110M; #P all

Baker & Taylor Company
Jill Bartholomew, Buying Manager
Southeastern Division
Mount Olive Road
Commerce GA 30599
404-335-5000
Categories: 99

WH -- Territory: US
Markets: BK-SC-CO-PL-SL
Items: HC-PB-MM-TX-RM
Year started: 1828
#R 0; #A 15,000; #T 110M; #P all

Baker & Taylor Company
Donna Lippold, Buying Manager
Midwest Division
501 S Gladiolas Street
Momence IL 60954
815-472-2444
Categories: 99
WH -- Territory: US
Markets: BK-SC-CO-PL-SL
Items: HC-PB-MM-TX-RM
Year started: 1828
#R 0; #A 15,000; #T 110M; #P all

Ballen Booksellers
337 N San Pedro Road
Irvine CA 92714
714-559-1742
Categories: 23-39-59-65-67-99
WH -- Territory: US-IT
Markets: CO-PL-SL
Items: HC-TX-PB-MM-TV
#R 5; #T 150M; #P all

Ballen Booksellers
Barry Bernstein, Buyer
66 Austin Boulevard
Commack NY 11725
516-543-5600; 800-645-5237
Categories: 23-39-59-65-67-99
WH -- Territory: US-IT
Markets: CO-PL-SL
Items: HC-TX-PB-MM-TV
Year started: 1969
#R 5; #T 150M; #P all

Balzekas Museum
Mary Podolak, Manager
Book Department
4012 Archer Avenue
Chicago IL 60632
312-847-2441
WH

Barrett Bookstore
Michael Coates, Manager
Goodwives Shopping Center
Old Kings Highway N
Darien CT 06820
203-322-8270
Categories: 99
WH
Markets: BK-SC-CO-PL-SL
Items: HC-TX-PB-RM-MM
Year started: 1945

Bayou News Agency
Fred Miller, Manager
10641 N Dual
P O Box 15639
Baton Rouge LA 70895
504-275-5670
Categories: 99

WH -- Territory: part(South)
Markets: BK-CO-SC-PL
Items: HC-PB-MM-MG-NP
Year started: 1953
#R 31

Beekman Publishers
K Peters, Book Buyer
Mill Hill Road
P O Box 888
Woodstock NY 12498
914-679-2301
Categories: 19-23-39-41-55-57
          59-65-75-81-83
DN -- Territory: US
Markets: BK-JB-SC-CO-PL-SL
Items: HC-TX-PB-RM
Year started: 1972
#T 1500; #P 20

Before Columbus Foundation
Gundars Strads, Manager
1446 6th Street #D
P O Box 2370, Station A
Berkeley CA 94702
415-527-1586
Categories: 11-47-83-90-95
WH -- Territory: US
Markets: BK-CO-PL
Items: HC-PB-ML
Year started: 1977
#R 5

Benjamin News
R Legault, Manager
0160 Jean Milot
La Salle H8R 1X7 PQ Canada
514-364-1780
WH

Berkeley Educational Paperbacks
Edward J Hunolt, Manager
2480 Bancroft Way
Berkeley CA 94704
415-848-7907
WH

Bernan Associates
Jerome M Frumkin, Director
9730 E George Palmer Highway
Lanham MD 20706
301-459-7666
Categories: 19-55(International)
WH -- Territory: US-IT
Markets: BK-SC-CO-PL
Items: HC-PB-TX-reports
Year started: 1952
government publications

Bernard H. Hamel - Spanish Books
Bernard H Hamel, Manager
2326 Westwood Boulevard
Los Angeles CA 90064
213-475-0453
Categories: 99
WH -- Territory: part(western)
Markets: BK-SC-CO-PL
Items: HC-TX-PB-MM-RC-TA-TV

Year started: 1957
#A 150; #T 7000; #P 125
all Spanish

Bernhard DeBoer Inc
113 E Centre Street
Nutley NJ 07110
201-667-9300
Categories: 75-83-99
WH -- Territory: US
Markets: BK-SC-CO
Items: MG-ML-NP
periodicals

Best Continental Book Company
Harry Eckstein, Owner
P. O. Box 615
Merrifield VA 22031
703-280-1400
WH

Better Book Fairs
Virginia A Chapman, President
6821 SW 81st Street
South Miami FL 33143
305-665-5875
WH

Beverly Books
M Sedacca
36 E Price Street
Linden NJ 07036
201-486-6500
Categories: 23-67
WH -- Territory: US
Markets: PL-SL
Items: HC-TX-PB-MG
Year started: 1972
#A 7500; #T 5000

Beyda & Associates
Morris Beyda
6943 Valjean Avenue
Van Nuys CA 91406
818-988-3102
Categories: 21-31-76-89-99
DN -- Territory: US
Markets: BK-SC-PL-RO(toy stores)
Items: HC-PB-MM-TA
Year started: 1974
#R 7; #A many; #P 135

Biblio & Tannen Bookseller
Margaret B Moser
P O Box 302
Cheshire CT 06410
PD

Biddy Books
Ben R Biddy, Owner
Rte 2, Box 2775
Manchester TN 37353
615-728-6967
WH

Big Country Books
David Hencock, President
1431 Harrison Avenue

Blaine WA 98230
604-538-1114
Categories: 61(Northwest US)-99
WH -- Territory: US-CN
Markets: BK-JB-NS-SC-CO-MM-PL-SL
Items: HC-PB-RM-CA-MA
Year started: 1938
#R 10; #A 1000; #T 5000

Big Country Books
Brent Jolliffe, Manager
19313 Zero Avenue
Surrey V3S 5J9 BC Canada
604-531-3557
WH

Bilingual Books
Kris Kershul, President
5903 Seaview Avenue NW
Seattle WA 98107
206-789-7544
Categories: 45(Spanish)-71-80-99
WH -- Territory: US
Markets: BK-SC-CO-MM
          RO(travel agencies)
Year started: 1981

Bilingual Educational Services
Joann Baker, Manager
2514 S Grand Avenue
Los Angeles CA 90007-2688
213-749-6213
Categories: 45(Spanish)-71-80-99
WH -- Territory: US
Markets: SC-CO-PL
Items: HC-TX-PB-MA-PO-OT(games)-TV
Year started: 1971
#T 5000

Bilingual Publications
Linda E Goodman, President
1966 Broadway
New York NY 10023
212-873-2067
Categories: 45(Spanish)-71-80-99
PD -- Territory: US
Markets: BK-SC-PL
Items: HC-PB-MA-TA
Year started: 1974
#T 10M

Bill Dean Books
Bill Dean, President
151-49 Seventh Avenue
Whitestone NY 11357
718-767-6632
Categories: 41-55(aviation,
          naval)
DN -- Territory: US
Markets: BK-RO(hobby)
Items: HC-PB-MG
Year started: 1970
#R 0; #A 1000; #T 5000; #P 300

Blackburn News Agency
Robert Sayman, Owner
125 Regional Park Drive
P. O. Box 1039

Kingsport TN 37662
615-349-7145
WH

Blackwell North America
Oliver Sitea, Publisher Contact
6024 SW Jean Road
Building G
Lake Oswego OR 97034
503-684-1140
Categories: 99
WH -- Territory: US
Markets: PL-SL
Items: HC-PB-MM
Year started: 1975
#R 15; #T 25M

Blackwell North America
Bob Sochurek, Eastern Division
1001 SW Jean Road
Blackwood NJ 08012
609-629-0700
Categories: 99
WH -- Territory: US
Markets: PL-SL
Items: HC-PB-MM
Year started: 1975
#R 15; #T 25M

Bloomington News Agency
Anthone J Saluto, Owner
304 S Mason Street
Bloomington IL 61701
309-829-9405
WH

BMI Educational Services
Gerald Wagner, V.P.
Hay Press Road
Dayton NJ 08810-0707
201-329-6991
Categories: 21-31-76-89
WH -- Territory:
Markets: SC-CO-PL-SW
Items: TX
Year started: 1963
#T 6000

Bomber Joe's Bookstore Ltd
Ingred Schossleitner, Owner
P. O. Box 23440
Vancouver V7B 1W1 BC Canada
604-278-8021
WH

Book & Tape Gallery Association
Norman Kretz, Owner
1104 - 96th Street
Edmonton T5G 1S7 AB Canada
403-474-7252
WH

Book Caboose
Alice Schafer, President
94 Compark Road
Centerville OH 45459
513-434-9217
WH

Book Carrier
Dana Marsden, Buyer
19434 Club House Road
Gaithersburg MD 20879
301-670-9555; 800-231-4469
Categories: 23-41-49-71-78-99
WH -- Territory:
        part(mid-Atlantic)
Markets: BK-CO
Items: HC-PB-MM-SW
Year started: 1981
#R 5

Book Center
E Kalles, President
1140 Beaulac Street
Montreal H4R 1R8 PQ Canada
514-332-4154
Categories: 99
WH -- Territory: CN
Markets: BK-SC-CO-PL-SL
Items: HC-TX-PB-RM
Year started: 1944
#R 9

Book Clearing House
Nancy Smoller, Manager
2089 Boston Post Road
Larchmont NY 10538
914-834-4933
WH -- Territory: US
Markets: SL
Year started: 1940
#P all

Book Dynamics
Michael Gourley, Buyer
836 Broadway
New York NY 10003
212-254-7798
Categories: 11-27-39-53-57-84
WH -- Territory: US
Markets: BK
Items: PB-MM
Year started: 1978
#R 2
small press titles as well as MM

Book Fare
Claudia W Veilkanowitz - Pres
12-J Wendy Court
P. O. Box 18006
Greensboro NC 27419
919-292-0151
WH

Book House
James Marsh, V.P.
208 W Chicago Street
Jonesville MI 49250
517-849-2117
Categories: 23-67-99
WH -- Territory: US
Markets: PL-SL
Items: HC-PB-TX
Year started: 1962
#R 4; #T 20M; #P all
any book in print

Book Inventory Systems
Kathleen Richardson, Buyer
  Small Press Books
Robin Wagner, Purchasing Manager
5451 S State Road
Ann Arbor MI 48104
313-995-7262
Categories: 99
WH -- Territory: US
Markets: BK
Items: HC-PB-MM-CA-MA-TA-TV
Year started: 1976
#R 1

Book Jobbers Hawaii
Colin Miyabara, Manager
287 Kalihi Street
Honolulu HI 96819
808-845-2656
Categories: 61(HI)-99
WH -- Territory: part(HI)
Markets: BK-SC-CO-PL
Items: HC-TX-PB-MG-NP

Book Service California
Woody Woodard, Buyer
2620 Del Monte Street
West Sacramento CA 95691
916-371-0359; 800-457-4424
Categories: 99
WH -- Territory: US
Markets: MM(chain stores)
Items: HC-PB-MM-TA
Year started: 1962
#R 50; #P all

Book Service Company
Edwin Stewart, Owner
P. O. Box 5418
Spring Hill FL 33526
904-596-3009
WH

Book Service Unlimited
Norm Woodard, President
Barbara Redick, Buyer
  Backlist Titles
15030 Highway 99 South
Lynnwood WA 98037
206-743-6444; 800-457-4424
Categories: 99
WH -- Territory: US
Markets: MM(chain stores)
Items: HC-PB-MM-TA
Year started: 1962
#R 50; #P all

Book Services International
Martin B Berke, Director
425 Asylum Street
Bridgeport CT 06610-9990
203-334-2165
WH

Bookazine Company
Bob Hochman, Hardcover Buyer
Harold Krausher, Paperback Buyer
303 West 10th Street

New York NY 10014
212-675-8877
Categories: 99
WH -- Territory: US-IT
Markets: BK-SC-CO-MM-PL-SL
Items: HC-TX-PB-RM-MM-CA-CO
       GI-MA-TA-TV
Year started: 1932
#R 5; #A 11,000; #T 100M; #P 500

Bookcraft
Marvin W Wallin, Manager
1848 West 2300 South
Salt Lake City UT 84119
801-972-6180
WH

Booklink Distributors
Lachlan P MacDonald, Owner
3430-B Sacramento Drive
San Luis Obispo CA 93406
805-543-5404
Categories: 27-51-61(Western)
            71-99
PD -- Territory: part(CA, NV)
Markets: BK-SC-CO-PL
Items: HC-PB
Year started: 1982
#R 2; #T 1000

Bookmailer
Marcy Silverman, Manager
77 Wild Gingerway
North York M3H 5W9 ON Canada
416-635-7707
WH

Bookmarket Inc
Don Searer, Book Buyer
P O Box 20248
Bloomington MN 55420
612-884-1985
Categories: 10(adult non-fiction)
WH -- Territory: part(midwest)
Markets: SC-CO-PL
Items: HC-PB

Bookpeople
Gene Taback, Trade Buyer
Randy Beek, Small Press Buyer
2929 Fifth Street
Berkeley CA 94710
415-549-3030; 800-227-1516
Categories: 13-51-75-83-95
            99(small press)
WH -- Territory: US
Markets: BK-PL-SL-RO
Items: HC-PB-MM
Year started: 1968
#R 3; #A 5000; #T 7M; #P 300

Books & Research
Naseem Jamali, President
400 Riverside Drive
New York NY 10025
212-662-0400
WH

Books and Periodicals
R David Neal, Manager
3863 S W Loop 820, #200
P. O. Drawer 16549
Fort Worth TX 76133
817-292-4270
WH

Books Unlimited
Charles W Silverman, Manager
23 Gardenia Lane
Hicksville NY 11801
516-935-5777
WH

Books West
P. O. Box 10207
Albuquerque NM 87184
505-897-3144
WH

Bookslinger
Bobbi Rix, Buyer
213 East 4th Street
Saint Paul MN 55101
612-221-0429
Categories: 11-37-47-53-65-73
            77-79-81-83-90-95
DN -- Territory: US
Markets: BK-JB-SC-CO-PL-SL
Items: HC-TX-PB-ML
Year started: 1976
#A 600+; #T 3M+; #P 190
small press literary presses

Bookworm
Betty Mills, Owner
7901 Queenair Drive
Gaithersburg MD 20879
301-840-9372
WH

Bookworm Bookfairs
Ed Stubbs, Owner
968 Farmington Avenue W
West Hartford CT 06107
203-523-9460
WH

Bound to Stay Bound Books
Robert L Sibert, V.P.
West Morton Road
Jacksonville IL 62650-2697
217-245-5191
Categories: 21(K-12)
WH -- Territory: US
Markets: SC-PL
Items: OT(prebound)
Year started: 1920
#R 8; #A 8000; #T 15M; #P 125

Bowers & Merena
Raymond N Merena, President
P. O. Box 1224
Wolfboro NH 03894-1224
603-569-5095
WH

Bradt Enterprises
George N Bradt, President
93 Harvey Street #8
Cambridge MA 02140
617-492-8776
Categories: 69-71
PD -- Territory: US-CN-IT
Markets: BK-PL
Items: HC-PB-MA
Year started: 1978
#R 3; #T 500

Bright Horizons
E Bright, Book Buyer
138 Springside Road
Asheville NC 28803
704-684-8840
Categories: 21-27-29-41-33-51-61
DN -- Territory: part(Southern
                     Appalacians)
Markets: BK-RO(gift)
Items: HC-PB-RM-CA-MA-RC
Year started: 1977
#R 2; #A 300+; #T 1400; #P 40

Bro-Dart Industries
R Hulcoup, Manager
109 Roy Boulevard
Brantford N3T 5M3 ON Canada
519-759-4350; 800-265-8470
Categories: 99
WH -- Territory: CN
Markets: SC-CO-PL
Items: HC-PB-MM
Year started: 1950
#R 2

Brodart
Sandra L Rose, Book Buyer
500 Arch Street
Williamsport PA 17705
717-326-2461
Categories: 10-75-90
WH -- Territory: US-CN-IT
Markets: BK-RO-SC-CO-MM-PL-SL
Items: HC-TX-PB-MM-SW-TV
Year started: 1956
#R 15; #T 100M; #P 10M

Brookfield Publishing Company
James W Gerard, President
Old Post Road
Brookfield VT 05036
802-276-3162
Categories: 19-23-47-49-55-57
            59-63-65-67
DE -- Territory: US-CN
Markets: BK-JB-SC-CO-PL-SL
Items: HC-TX-PB
Year started: 1978
#R 0; #T 1350; #P 10

Brotherhood of Life
Graham Dodd, V.P.
110 Dartmouth SE
Albuquerque NM 87106
505-255-8980

Categories: 53-63-79
PD -- Territory: US-OT(Europe,
                Australia)
Markets: BK-JB
Items: HC-PB-MG-GI-GC-TA
Year started: 1969
#R 0; #A 300; #T 60; #P 8

Brown & Connolly
William J Brown, President
2 Keith Way
Hingham MA 02043
617-749-8570; 800-225-8233
Categories: 39-59
WH -- Territory: part(New
                England)
Markets: BK-CO-SL
Items: HC-PB
Year started: 1947
#R 5

Brown Book Company
Joseph Altmann, Manager
P. O. Box 69-3883
Miami FL 33269-0883
WH

Brunner News Agency
James J Brunner, President
217 Flanders Avenue
P. O. Box 598
Lima OH 45801
419-225-5826
WH

Bud Plant
Paul Blair, Book Buyer
13393 Grass Valley Avenue #7
P. O. Box 1886
Grass Valley CA 95945-1886
916-273-9588
Categories: 11-17-21-29-33-82-86
DN -- Territory: US-CN-IT
Markets: BK-RO(comics, games)
Items: HC-PB-RM-CA-CO-GI(toys)-PO
Year started: 1978
#R 0; #A 500; #T 3000; #P 200
Comics are their specialty.

Burlington News Agency
T F Murphy, Owner
P. O. Box 638
257 Pine Street
Burlington VT 05402
802-863-4533
WH

Byrd Enterprises
Willard Williams, President
1126 Cedardale Lane
Alexandria VA 22308
703-765-5626
WH

C & W Zabel Company
Andrew Zabel
345 Commercial Avenue
Palisades Park NJ 07605

201-947-3300
Categories: 99
WH -- Territory: part(Northeast)
Markets: SC-CO-PL-SL
Items: HC-RM-TV
Year started: 1975
#R 3; #A 1000; #T 750; #P all

C W Associates
C T Williams, Manager
12221 Parklawn Drive
P.O. Box 34099
Bethesda MD 20852
301-881-4411
WH

Cal Wilson Fine Numismatic
Calvin O Wilson, Owner
38228 Glenmoor Drive
Fremont CA 94536
415-792-4133
WH

Cal-West Periodicals
Attn: Book Buyer
2400 Filbert Street
Oakland CA 94607
415-444-3570
WH

Cambridge Company
Benita Somerfield, President
888 Seventh Avenue
New York NY 10106
212-957-5300
WH

Can-Ed Media Ltd
Jack Geddes, Manager
185 Spadina Avenue #1
Toronto M5T 2C6 ON Canada
416-593-0737
Categories: 11-69-98(physical
                education)
PD -- Territory: US-CN
Markets: SC-CO-PL-SL
Items: HC-TX-PB-PO-RC-SW-TA-TV

Canadian News Company
M Mousseau, Owner
1530 Erin Street
Winnipeg R3E 3K5 MB Canada
204-786-3465
WH

Cannon Book Distribution Ltd
Ian Rhind, V.P.
25-2 Connell Court
Toronto M8Z 1E8 ON Canada
416-252-5207
Categories: 10-75
DN -- Territory: US-CN
Markets: BK-JB-NS-SC-CO-MM-PL
                RO(gift)
Items: HC-PB-RM-MM-CA-CO-GI-MA
                RC-TA-TV
Year started: 1975
#R 10; #A 2000; #T 4000; #P 60

Cape News Company
Kenneth A Martin, Owner
49 Potomska Street
P.O. Box 3051
New Bedford MA 02741
617-997-9346
WH

Cape News Company
James T Coppage, Owner
700 Clearlake Road
P. O. Box 3466
Cocoa FL 32924-3466
305-636-5909
WH

Capital City Distribution
Milton Griepp
2827 Perry Street
Madison WI 53713
608-274-8987
Categories: 33
WH -- Territory: US
Markets: BK-RO(game stores)
Items: PB-MM-CO-GI-PO-SB-TV
offices in TX,CA,IL,LA,CT,OH,MI

Capital Distributing Company
Edward Handi, Director
Charlton Building
Derby CT 06418
203-735-3381
Categories: 99
WH -- Territory: US
Markets: BK-MM
Items: MM-MG-CO
Year started: 1954
#R 21

Capital Library Wholesale
David Dollin, Manager
1427 Ogilvie Road
Ottawa K1J 8M7 ON Canada
613-749-5949
Categories: 99
WH -- Territory: CN-IT
Markets: BK-CO-SC-PL
                OT(business, govt.)
Items: HC-PB
Year started: 1979

Cariad Limited
Barbara McInnes, Director
1103-89 Isabella Street
Toronto M4L 1N8 ON Canada
416-924-1918
WH

Carl Fischer Music Distributor
Tomas Mormile, Manager
54 Cooper Square
New York NY 10003
212-777-0900
Categories: 11
WH -- Territory: US-CN-IT
Markets: JB-SC-CO-MM-SL
                RO(music stores)
Items: HC-TX-PB-MG-CA-GI-PO

Items continued: RC-ST-TA
Year started: 1979
#R 2

Carmel Book Company
David L Harvey, Manager
P O Box 3130
Glen Ellyn IL 60138
312-668-0400
WH

Carolina News Company
Harry Page, Manager
245 Tillinghast Street
P O Drawer 10
Fayetteville NC 28302
919-483-4135
WH

Carrier Pigeon
Sasha Alyson, Manager
P O Box 2783
Boston MA 02208
617-542-5679
Categories: 13-37-41-49-55-73
WH -- Territory: US
Markets: BK-SC-CO-PL
Items: PB-MG-ML
Year started: 1977

Carroll Book Service
J & G Carroll, Owners
140 Hunter Avenue
P O Box 1776
North Tarrytown NY 10591
914-631-1776
Categories: 99
WH -- Territory: mid-Atlantic
Markets: Co-SC-PL
Items: HC-PB-TX
Year started: 1972
#R 20

Casa Escobar
John S Escobar, Manager
721 W Roosevelt Road
Chicago IL 60607
312-226-1334
WH

Cassette Book Company
Robert E Dempster, Owner
235 Bellefontaine
Pasadena CA 91109
818-799-4139
WH

Catholic Book & Supply Company
Francis J Mahsem, Manager
1234 Milwaukee Avenue
South Milwaukee WI 53172
414-762-1087
Categories: 63(Catholic)-99
WH -- Territory: US
Markets: CO-SC
Items: HC-TX-RM-GI
Year started: 1935
#R 1

Catholic Bookrack Service
Mary McMahon, Manager
194 Akenside Road
Riverside IL 60546
312-447-4374
Categories: 17-41-47-49-57-59
           63-76-77-81-83-86
           87-89-90-95
WH -- Territory: Chicago IL
Markets: SC
Items: PB-MM
Year started: 1955
#R 2; #A 50

Central Arizona Distributing
Tom Lieberman, Manager
4932 W Pasadena Avenue
Glendale AZ 85301
602-939-6511
Categories: 21-31-76-89-99
WH -- Territory: AZ
Markets: SC
Items: HC-PB-MM-MG-NP
Year started: 1982

Central Illinois Periodicals
Craig Havp, Manager
501 Kenyon Road
Champaign IL 61820
217-351-7047
WH

Central Kentucky Books
Judy Warrix, Book Buyer
P O Box 500
Jct. 1862 Welch Hill Road
Mayking KY 41837
606-633-0634
Categories: 99
WH -- Territory: KY-OH-TN-VA-WV
Markets: SC-CO-PL-SL
Items: HC-RM-MA-SW
Year started: 1977
#R 3; #A 500; #T 500M; #P all

Central Kentucky News Company
Curtis Sharff, V.P.
1236 Versailles Road
Lexington KY 40508
606-254-2765
Categories: 99
WH -- Territory: KY
Markets: NS-SC-CO-MM-PL-SL
Items: HC-PB-RM-MM-MG-ML
      CA-CO-MA-SB
Year started: 1948
#R 10; #A 750; #T 5000; #P all

Chapter & Cask
Art Ballant, President
P O Box 3604
Glyndon MD 21071
301-833-7172
Categories: 99
DN -- Territory: MD-DE-DC-VA
Markets: BK
Items: HC-PB-MG
#P 7

Cheng & Tsui Company
J T Cheng, President
25 West Street
Boston MA 02111
617-426-6074
Categories: 11-19-27-41
           45(Chinese, Japanese)
           49-55-59-63-69-71-90
PD -- Territory: US-CN-IT
Markets: BK-JB-SC-CO-MM-PL-SL
Items: HC-TX-PB
Year started: 1979
#R 8

Chicago Law Book Company
Bernadine Dziedzic, Manager
4814 S Pulaski Road
Chicago IL 60632
312-376-1713
Categories: 17-19-25-41-47-55-57
           59-63-73-84-87
DN -- Territory: US
Markets: CO-SL
Items: HC-TX-PB-RM-MM-GI-PO-SB
Year started: 1942
#R 3; #A 20000; #T 15M; #P 620

Children's Small Press Collection
Kathleen Baxter, Trade Department
719 N Fourth Avenue
Ann Arbor MI 48104
313-668-8056
Categories: 21-31-76-89
WH -- Territory: US
Markets: BK-SC-PL
Items: HC-PB-CA-OT(games)
Year started: 1985

Chile Coin, Stamp & Supply
Norman R Boughton, President
1356 Buffalo Road
Rochester NY 14624-1873
716-235-2830
Categories: 21-27-29-59-61-77-79
           81-82-84-85-86-87-88-89
WH -- Territory: US
Markets: BK-SC-PL-RO(cooking,toy)
Items: HC-PB-RM-MM-CA-MA-SB
Year started: 1976
#R 1; #A 500; #T 1000; #P 25

China Books & Periodicals
Nancy Ippolito, Manager
2929 24th Street
San Francisco CA 94110
415-282-2994
Categories: 45(Chinese)
           99(on China)
PD -- Territory: US
Markets: BK-SC-CO-PL-SL
Items: HC-PB-MG-CA-GI-GC-MA
      NW-TA-TV
Year started: 1960
#R 3; #A 5000; #T 500; #P 20

China House Gallery
Anita Christy, Director
125 East 65th Street

New York NY 10021
212-744-8181
WH

Chinese American Company
May C Yee, President
83 Harrison Avenue
Boston MA 02111
617-423-2264
WH

Christian Book Distributors
David Neuenschwander, Manager
2934 E Las Hermanas
Compton CA 90221-5509
213-537-6296
Categories: 63
WH

Christian Literature Crusade
Leonard Buck, Manager
701 Pennsylvania Avenue
Fort Washington PA 19034-8449
215-542-1240
Categories: 63
WH

Cicero Bible Press
Glenda Ruble, Book Buyer
1901 Airport Road
P. O. Box 160
Harrison AR 72601
501-741-3400
Categories: 63-99
PD -- Territory: US-IT
Markets: BK-SC-CO
Items: HC-TX-PB-MM-CA-CO-GC-MA
    SB-TA-TV
Year started: 1952
#R 0; #A 6000; #T 25M; #P 100

Circa Publications
I Anthony Valente, President
415 Fifth Avenue
Pelham NY 10803
914-738-5570
Categories: 19-23-39-59-67
WH -- Territory: US
Markets: SC-PL-SL
Items: HC-PB
Year started: 1960
#R 2; #T 10M

Circle Book Service
Fred M Banks, V.P.
303 Wells Fargo Drive, #16
P. O. Box 73265
Houston TX 77273
713-320-9141
WH

City News Agency
Willian Solomon, Owner
220 Cherry Avenue NE
Canton OH 44702-1198
216-456-7179
Categories: 99
WH

City News Stand Book World
R & J Feuer, Owners
316 N 3rd Street
P.O. Box 466
Lafayette IN 47902
317-742-1051
WH

City Wide Book Company
Robert Chalfin, Owner
159 Manhatten Avenue
P. O. Box 211
Brooklyn NY 11221-0211
718-388-0037
WH

Clergy Book Service
Nancy Spangler, Book Buyer
12855 W Silver Spring Drive
Butler WI 53007
414-781-1234
Categories: 63
WH -- Territory: US-CN-IT
Markets: SC-CO-OT(religious
    institutions)
Items: HC-TX-PB-RM-MM-CA-MA-RC
    SW-TA-TV
Year started: 1968
#R 0; #A 21000; #T 25M+; #P 80+

CNS Judaica
Attn: Jane, Book Buyer
111 Lakeview Avenue
Clifton NJ 07011
201-772-3141
Categories: 45(Hebrew)
        63(Jewish)-99
WH -- Territory: Eastern US
Markets: SC-PL-SL-RO(religious)
Items: HC-TX-PB-MM-GI-GC-RC-ST
    SB-TA
Year started: 1965
#R 0; #A 200; #T 600

Cogan Books
Nancy Cogan, Manager
4332 W Artesia Avenue
Fullerton CA 92633
213-941-5017; 800-556-book
Categories: 21-27-59-61
WH -- Territory: US
Markets: BK-RO(gift, gourmet)-PL
Items: HC-PB
Year started: 1971
#R 9; #T 4000; #P 35

Collegedale Distributors
Gerald Fleming, Manager
6101 Mountain View Road
Ooltewah TN 37363
615-238-4121
WH

Colorado News
4841 Warehouse Drive
Pueblo CO 81008
303-543-0928
Categories: 99

WH -- Territory: CO
Markets: BK-SC-CO
Items: HC-TX-PB-MM-MG-NP
#R 8

Columbine Distributing
Rob Putmaner, Manager
1671 Valtec Lane
P O Box 9050
Boulder CO 80301
303-449-1973
WH

Comics Unlimited Ltd
Walter Wang, Book Buyer
6833 Amboy Road
Staten Island NY 10308
718-948-2222
Categories: 13-21-29-33-69
        79-82-86-87-89
DN -- Territory: US
Markets: BK-JB-NS-SC-CO-MM-PL
    SL-RO games·
Items: HC-PB-RM-MM-CA-CO
    OT(games & toys)
Year started: 1975
#R 3; #A 200; #T 1000; #P 100+

Computer Book Service
Paul Byron, V.P.
4201 Raymond Drive
Hillside IL 60162
312-547-4400
Categories: 99
WH -- Territory: US
Markets: BK-SC-CO
Items: HC-PB-MM-RM
Year started: 1968
#R 10; #A 1000; #T 7000

Concord Books
Evelyn Davis, Manager
419 Opal Cove Way
P. O. Box 2707
Seal Beach CA 90740
213-596-3260
Categories: 17-19-27-29-31-33-35
        39-41-43-55-57-59-67
DN -- Territory: US-IT(Australia,
        NZ, and Europe)
Markets: BK-JB-SC-CO-PL-RO
Items: HC-PB-MM-TA
Year started: 1972
#R 0; #T 120; #P 100
conservative subjects

Connemara Trading Company
R Davis, Owner
409 W Rosemary Street
Chapel Hill NC 27514
919-967-1157
WH

Contemporary Arts Press
Carl Loeffler or Anna Couey
70 12th Street
P. O. Box 3123, Rincon Annex
San Francisco CA 94119-3123

415-431-7672
Categories: 11-23-47-59-65-73
PD -- Territory: US-CN-IT
Markets: BK-JB-SC-CO-PL-SL
Items: HC-PB-SW-TV
       OT(online databases)
Year started: 1975
#A 1000; #T 40+; #P 27+

Continental Book Company
Mr Hayat, Manager
11-03 46th Avenue
Long Island City NY 11101
718-937-4868
WH

Coopers Shoppe The Distlefink
Pat Cooper, Owner
471-375 Singletree Lane
Susanville CA 96130
916-257-4640
WH

Copeland Distributors
842 Goodale Boulevard
Columbus OH 43212
Categories: 11-29
WH -- Territory: US
Markets: RO(craft stores)
Items: HC-PB-craft supplies

Cornwall News Distributors
Irvine Leger, Manager
840 Campbell Street
P. O. Box 787
Cornwall K6H 5T7 ON Canada
613-932-8453
WH

Corvallis Periodicals
Lisa Crook, Book Buyer
350 Wake Robin Avenue
P. O. Box 830
Corvallis OR 97333
503-758-0315
Categories: 99
DN -- Territory: part(OR)
Markets: BK-NS-SC-CO-MM-PL
Items: HC-PB-RM-MM-MG-CA
       CO-MA-PO-SW-TA
Year started: 1983
#R 3; #A 148; #T 1M+; #P 200+

Council On Interracial Books
Anita Stark, Manager
1841 Broadway, 5th Floor
New York NY 10023
212-757-5339
Categories: 49-99
WH

County News Agency
A & R Welkowitz, Owners
221 N Queen Street
Lancaster PA 17603
717-393-3911
Categories: 99
WH

Coutts Library Services
John K Coutts, President
736 Cayuga Street
Lewiston NY 14092
716-754-4304
Categories: 99
WH -- Territory: US
Markets: CO-PL-SL
Items: HC-TX-PB
Year started: 1969
#R 3

Cowley Distributing
John Cowley II, Manager
732 Heisinger Road
Jefferson City MO 65101
314-636-6511
WH

Craft Wholesalers
4555 Groves Road
Columbus OH 43232
800-248-6112; OH:800-633-2828
Categories: 11-29
WH -- Territory: US
Markets: RO(craft stores)

Creative Homeowner Press
Bernard J Conlee, Sales Director
24 Parkway
Upper Saddle River NJ 07458
201-934-7100; 800-631-7795
Categories: 29-43
PD -- Territory: US
Markets: BK-RO
Items: HC-PB
Year started: 1927
#R 155

Crescent Imports & Publications
Ashfag Ibrahim, Owner
P O Box 7827
Ann Arbor MI 48107-7827
313-971-1404
Categories: 27-29-39-45(Arabic,
            Asian, African)-49
            57-63-71
DN -- Territory: US
Markets: BK-PL-SL
Items: HC-PB-MM-CA-GI-ST-SB-TA
Year started: 1978
#R 0; #A 29

Cromland
Lars Cromsjo, Manager
4417 - 18th Avenue #312
Brooklyn NY 11204
718-851-4219
Categories: 19-23-65-67
WH -- Territory: US-CN-IT
Markets: BK-RO(computer)
Items: HC-TX-PB-SW
Year started: 1982
#T 5000

Cuban Boy's Spanish Books
Luis Tigera, Owner
1225 W 18th Street

Chicago IL 60608
312-243-5911
Categories: 45(Spanish)-99
WH

Cucumber Bookshop
Eugene E Hansch, Manager
5611 Kraft Drive
Rockville MD 20852
301-881-2722
WH

Cultural Hispana
Jose M Guerricagoitia, Manager
1413 Crestridge Drive
Silver Spring MD 20910
301-585-0134
Categories: 10-75-95-90
DN
Markets: BK-NS-SC-PL
Items: HC-PB-MM-CO-MA
Year started: 1982 .
#R 10+; #A 25; #T 4000; #P 50+

Cummings Distributing
John Kocan, Manager
1745 23rd Street SE
Salem OR 97302
503-399-7731
WH

Cupress Canada Limited
J. Michael Bailey, Book Buyer
10 Falconer Drive #8
MississaugaL5N 1K8 ON Canada
416-826-5081
Categories: 11-15-21-27-29-33-39
            43-45-47-59-69-71
DE -- Territory: US-CN
Markets: BK-SC-CO-MM-PL
Items: HC-RM-SB
Year started: 1983
#R 25; #P 20

Dakota News
George Mitchel, Manager
828 N Main Avenue
Sioux Falls SD 57102
605-336-7271
WH

Darcy Williamson Distributor
Darcy Williamson, Owner
P. O. Box 1528
McCall ID 83638
208-325-8606
Categories: 13-27-51-61
WH -- Territory: US
Markets: BK-CO-MM-PL-RO(health
         food, gift)
Items: PB
Year started: 1978
#A 1200; #T 16; #P 2

Darian Books
Donald Lilly, Owner
3008 W Angela Drive
Phoenix AZ 85023

602-866-1068
Categories: 99
WH

David Enterprises
Henry DuBose, President
18 N Mill Street
Manning SC 29102
803-435-4149
WH

Dawn Sign Press
Joe W Dannis, President
2490 Channing Way #501
Berkeley CA 94704
415-845-7715
Categories: 21-31-45(sign lang
          & deaf culture)-90
          98(flashcard games)
PD -- Territory: US-CN
Markets: BK-JB-SC-CO-PL-SL
          RO(serving deaf)
Items: TX-PB-PO
Year started: 1983
#R 2; #A 23; #T 15; #P 8

De Wolfe & Fiske
James A Scott, V.P.
300 Turnpike Street
Canton MA 02021
617-828-8300
Categories: 99
WH -- Territory: US-IT
Markets: BK-SC-CO-PL
Items: HC-PB-MM-MG
Year started: 1872
wholesale and retail (Lauriats)

Delmar News Agency
Joseph P Byrne, Manager
848 Church Street
Box 945
Wilmington DE 19899
302-654-9921
WH

Deltiologists of America
James Lewis Lowe, Owner
10 Felton Avenue
Ridley Park PA 19078
215-521-1092
WH

Demonet
Carolyn Jones, Buyer
7310 C Adams Street
Paramount CA 90701
213-408-1966
WH

Denver News Company
Loraine French, Owner
3601 East 46th Avenue
Denver CO 80216
303-321-1111
WH

Deru's Fine Art Books
Kenneth F Jones, Manager
9100 E Artesia Boulevard
Bellflower CA 90706
213-920-1312
WH

Deseret Book Distribution
Pat Harrison, Manager
2150 West 1500 South
Salt Lake City UT 84104
Categories: 99
WH

Desert News Company
Leith J Bergier, Book Buyer
206 East Ave #K-4
P. O. Box 2197
Lancaster CA 93535
805-945-4571
Categories: 99
WH -- Territory: southern CA
Markets: BK-NS-SC-CO-MM-MM
          RO(own)-OT(USAF)
Items: HC-PB-MM-MG-CA-CO-MA-SW
          NW-TA-TV
Year started: 1968
#R 7; #A 150; #T 2M+; #P 25+

Devorss Book Distributors
Hedda G Lark, Book Buyer
1046 Princeton Drive
P O Box 550
Marina Del Rey CA 90294-0550
213-870-7478
Categories: 13-27-39-53-57-63
PD -- Territory: US-CN-IT
Markets: BK-JB-MM-OT(churches)
Items: HC-PB-MM-CA-TA-OT(Tarot
          cards)
Year started: 1929
#R 0; #A 4000; #T 3000; #P 300

Diamond Comic Distributors
1720 C Belmont Avenue
Baltimore MD 21207
800-638-7873
Categories: 33
DN -- Territory: US
Markets: BK-MM-RO(toy stores)
Items: PB-CO
9 warehouses around the U.S.

Dicmar Trading
P O Box 3533, Georgetown Station
Washington DC 20007
202-338-2049
Categories: 29(quilting)
WH -- Territory: US
Markets: RO(craft stores)
Items: HC-PB-OT(craft supplies)
Year started:
#T 200

Diffusion Prologue
Francine Paquehe, Owner
2975 Sartelon
Quebec H4R 1E6   PQ Canada
514-332-5860
WH

Dillon Book Company
Reynold Akison, Trade Buyer
Mark Miller, Paperback Buyer
3640 Walnut
P O Drawer J
Boulder CO 80306
303-442-5323
Categories: 21-23-31-76-99
WH -- Territory: Mountain States
Markets: BK-SC-CO-PL
          RO(computers, toys)
Items: HC, PB
Year started: 1939
#R 1; #A 1100; #T 25M

Dimondstein Book Express
Sandy Rose, Hardcover Buyer
Jim Bobak, Paperback Buyer
500 Arch Street
Williamsport PA 17705
717-326-2461; 800-233-8467
Categories: 99
WH -- Territory: US
Markets: BK-PL
Items: HC-PB-backlist specialists
Year started: 1960
#A 10,000; #T 100M; #P all

Dinosaur Discounts
Paul Schneider, Manager
5068-B W Chester Pike
Edgemont PA 19028
215-353-5166
WH

Directional Learning Canada
Gail P Thorpe, Owner
480 Washington Street
Elora N0B 1S0   ON Canada
519-846-5398
WH

==

Items: HC = Hardcover   TX = Textbooks   RM = Remainders   MG = Magazines, General
         PB = Softcover   MM = Mass-Markets   NP = Newspapers   ML = Magazines, Literary
         CA = Calendars   CO = Comics   GC = Greeting Cards   PO = Posters   TA = Tapes, Audio
         SW = Software   GI = Gifts   MA = Maps & Atlases   RC = Records   TV = Tapes, Video
         ST = Stationery   SB = Stickers/Bookmarks   OT = Other items (games, toys, etc.)

Discount Book Distributors
1812 Highway 7
Charleston SC 29407
803-556-6582
WH

Displays For Schools
Sherry and Herbert DuPree
P O Box 163
Gainesville FL 32602
904-373-2030
Categories: 21-76
PD -- Territory: US
Markets: SC-PL-SL
Items: GC-MA-PO-OT(workbooks)
Year started: 1976
#R 5

Distrib-U-Toys
901 Avenue S
Grand Prairie TX 75050
800-527-3682; TX:800-442-1630
Categories: 21-29-69-76
WH -- Territory: West, Southwest
Markets: BK-RO(toy & hobby)-MM
Items: HC-PB-TA-TV-toys, games

Distribution Ariane
Marc Vallee, President
45 Boulevard D'anjou Chateauquay
Quebec J6N 1T4   PQ Canada
514-429-2171
Categories: 39-51-53-63
DN -- Territory: CN
Markets: BK-CO-PL
Items: PB-MG-PO-TA
Year started: 1983
#T 90; #P 8

Distributors International
Dennis & Landman, Owners
1150 18th Street
Santa Monica CA 90403
213-453-4643
Categories: 11
WH -- Territory: US
Markets: BK-SC-CO-PL
Items: HC-PB-MM-GI
Year started: 1972

Distributors Nueva Vida
Tony Mendoza, Owner
605 N Saint Vrain
El Paso TX 79902
915-565-6215
Categories: 45(FR-Port-SP-IT)-63
WH -- Territory: US
Markets: BK-RO(gift, religious)
Items: HC-PB-GI

DMR International
5748 Commerce Lane
Miami FL 33143-3641
305-661-8950
WH

Dog Museum of America Shop
Barry Neuman, Manager
51 Madison Avenue, Main Floor
New York NY 10010
212-696-8350
Categories: 15
WH

Don & Linda's Suitcase of Books
Linda L Sass, Owner
18993 S Forest Grove Loop
Oregon City OR 97045
503-656-6823
WH

Donars Spanish Books
Yolanda Faggioni, Manager
407 N Lincoln Avenue
P O Box 24
Loveland CO 80539-0024
303-669-0586
Categories: 45(Spanish)-99
WH -- Territory:
Markets: BK-SC-PL-SL
Items: HC-PB
Year started: 1968

Dot Gibson Distributors
Dot Gibson
P O Box 117
Waycross GA 31502
912-285-2848
Categories: 27 (community)
DN -- Territory: US
Markets: BK-RO(gift stores)
#T 225

Downtown Book Center
Jose M Rabade, Manager
245 SE 1st Street #236
Miami FL 33131
305-377-9941
WH

DreamHaven Books & Art
Greg Ketter, Owner
1300 Fourth Street SE
Minneapolis MN 55414
612-379-8924
Categories: 11-76
WH -- Territory: US
Markets: BK-JB-PL-individuals
Items: HC-PB-PO-CA

Duval News
James L White III, Owner
5700 Commonwealth Avenue
P O Box 61297
Jacksonville FL 32236
904-783-2350
WH

Eagle's View Publishing
Sue K Smith, Manager
706 W Riverdale Road
Ogden UT 84405
801-393-3991
Categories: 17-21-29-41-49-51
         45(American Indian)
         55-57-63-69-81-88
PD -- Territory: US-IT
Markets: BK-JB-SC-CO-PL
Items: HC-PB-RM-CA-GC
Year started: 1976
#R 0; #A 1200; #T 3600; #P 200

EAL Enterprises
Leona Carbone, Buyer
22700 Shore Center Drive
Cleveland OH 44123
216-731-2500
Categories: 21-23-39-59-67-75-76
WH -- Territory: part(OH)
Markets: SC-CO-PL-SL
Items: HC-PB-MM
Year started: 1970
#R 4

Early Childhood Bookhouse
J Lybecker, Book Buyer
724 NW 23rd Avenue
P O Box 2791
Portland OR 97208
503-224-6372
Categories: 99
DN -- Territory: US-CN-IT
Markets: BK-SC-CO-PL-SL-RO
Items: HC-PB-RM-MM-CA-GC-PO-RC
       SB-TA-TV
Year started: 1977
#R 4; #A 400+; #T 8M+; #P 300+

East Coast Christian Distributor
35 Readington Road
P O Box 4200
Somerville NJ 08876
201-722-5050
WH

East Kentucky News
Robin T Cooper, Manager
229 Broadway
P O Box 510

===

Markets: BK = Bookstore   SC = Schools   PL = Public Libraries   MM = Mass Markets and Chain Stores
           JB = Jobbers   CO = Colleges   SL = Special Libraries   NS = Newsstands
           RO = Other Retail Outlets   OT = Other (organizations, churches, etc.)

Territories: US = entire United States   CN = Canada   IT = International
               Others indicate parts of United States or abbreviations for states

Paintsville KY 41240
606-789-8169
Categories: 99
WH

East Texas Distributing
7171 Grand Boulevard
Houston TX 77054
713-748-2520; 800-231-6648
Categories: 99(videotapes only)
DN -- Territory: Southwest
Markets: BK-RO(video stores)
Items: TV

East Texas Periodicals
7171 Grand Boulevard
Houston TX 77054
713-748-8120
WH

Eastern Book Company
David H Foshey, Buyer
131 Middle Street
P O Box 4540
Portland ME 04112-4540
207-774-0331
Categories: 99
WH -- Territory: East Coast
Markets: BK-SC-CO-PL-SL
Items: HC-TX-PB
Year started: 1957
#R 2; #T 15M; #P all

Eastern News Distributors
Ira Cohen, Manager
250 West 55th Street
New York NY 10019
212-262-7474; 800-221-3148
Categories: 99
WH -- Territory: US
Markets: BK-RO-MM
Items: MG-NP
Year started: 1948
#R 6

Eastview Editions
N Glenn, Manager
1185 Morris Avenue
Union NJ 07083
201-964-9485
Categories: 10-11-15-29-43-45
DE -- Territory: US-CN-IT
Markets: BK-JB-NS-SC-CO-PL-SL
Items: HC-PB-MG-MA
Year started: 1979

Eastwind Books & Arts
Doroteo Ng, Manager
1435-A Stockton Street
San Francisco CA 94133
415-781-3331
WH

EBS Book Service
Lucious McFalling, Buyer
290 Broadway
Lynbrook NY 11563
516-593-1195

Categories: 23-39-41-55-59-67-99
WH -- Territory: US
Markets: CO-PL
Items: HC-PB-MM
Year started: 1949
#R 5; #T 425M; #P all

Econo-Clad Books
Richard A Crawford, President
2101 N Topeka Boulevard
P O Box 1777
Topeka KS 66608
913-233-4252
WH

Economical Wholesale Company
Joseph J Fortier, Owner
6 King Philip Road
Worcester MA 01606
617-853-3127
WH

Ediciones Universal
P O Box 450353
Shenandoah Station
Miami FL 33145
Categories: 45(Spanish)-78-80-99
WH -- Territory: US
Markets: BK-PL

Ediciones Vitral
Armando Garcia, President
P O Box 701394
Trainsmeadow NY 11370
718-424-9408
Categories: 45(Spanish)-99
DE -- Territory: US
Markets: BK-CO-PL
Items: HC-PB-MM-MA-RC-TA
Year started: 1980
#R 3+; #A 500+; #T 600+; #P 3+

Editions Champlain Ltd
Berthe Arsenault, Book Buyer
107 Church Street
Toronto M5C 2G5 ON Canada
416-364-4345
Categories: 45(French)-80-99
PD -- Territory: US-CN
Markets: BK(French)-SC-CO-PL-SL
Items: HC-TX-PB-MM-MG
      CA-ML-MA-PO-RC-SW
Year started: 1960
#R 2; #T many
French language only

Editions Nouvelle Frontiere
Brian O'Keefe, Manager
185 E Ontario
Montreal H2X 1H5 PQ Canada
514-844-3242
Categories: 11-21-41-47-49
         51-55-67-71-73
DE -- Territory: CN-US(sometimes)
Markets: BK-RO(book fairs)
Items: HC-TX-PB-MM
Year started: 1970
#R 0; #A 135; #T 1400; #P 15

Editorial Cernuda
Ramon Cernuda, Owner
7175 SW 8th Street #214
Miami FL 33144
305-264-9397
Categories: 45(Spanish, ESL)-99
WH

Editorial Excelsior
Hector Pereyra-Suarez, Owner
P. O. Box 710771
San Jose CA 95171
408-293-3734
WH

Editorial Services Company
Jacqueline Thompson, President
10 Bay Street Landing #7K
Staten Island NY 10301
718-723-3229
WH

Editorials International
Kenneth P Smith, Manager
3446 SW 8th Street #201
Miami FL 33135
305-447-9388
Categories: 31-45(Spanish)-59
DN -- Territory: US
Markets: BK-SC-CL-PL
Items: HC
Year started: 1977
#R 10

Edmonds Book Sales
James Edmonds, Manager
P.O. Box 143
Ledbetter KY 42058-0143
502-898-6716
WH

Edu-Tech Corporation
Miriam Caston, V.P. Sales
65 Bailey Road
Fairfield CT 06430
203-374-4212
Categories: 99
WH
Markets: PL-SL
Items: HC-PB-RM
Year started: 1979

Education Guide
Bob Pastman, Manager
10 Bayberry Lane
Randolph MA 02368
617-961-2217
Categories: 31-45-59
PD -- Territory: US
Markets: SC-CO-PL-SL
Items: HC-TX-PB
Year started: 1971
#T 300; #P 4

Educational Book Distributors
Robert Toms, President
P O Box 551
San Mateo CA 94939

415-344-8458
Categories: 21-31-76
WH -- Territory: western
Markets: BK-CO-RO(teacher supply)
Items: HC-PB-TX
Year started: 1979
#R 6

Educational Book Service
P O Box 4869 Hato Rey Station
San Juan PR 00918
809-753-6586
Categories: 99
WH -- Territory: PR
Markets: BK-SC-CO-MM-PL-SL
Items: HC-TX-PB-MM
Year started: 1980
#A 10

Educational Reading Service
M Schecter
320 Route 17
Mahwah NJ 07430
201-529-4000
Categories: 21-31-76
WH -- Territory: US
Markets: SC-PL
Year started: 1958

Educator Supplies Ltd
William T Webster, President
2323 Trafalgar Street
London N5W 5H2   ON Canada
519-451-8840
WH

Edward Weston Graphics
Edward Weston, President
19355 Business Center Drive
Northridge CA 91324
818-885-1044
WH

Eisenbrauns
J & M Eisenbraun, Owners
P O Box 275
Winona Lake IN 46590-0275
219-269-2011
WH

El Qui-Jote Book
Jose Obelleiro, Owner
12651 Monarch
Houston TX 77047
713-433-3388
WH

ElecTech Book Service
W Evdokimoff, Manager
3223 Broadwater Road
Castlegar V1N 3H3   BC Canada
604-365-3223
Categories: 10-23-59-67
DN -- Territory: CN
Markets: BK-SC-CO-PL-SL
Items: HC-TX-PB
Year started: 1972
#R 2; #A 1800; #T 2600; #P 10

Eliseo Torres
Daniel Torres
1164 Garrison Avenue
Bronx NY 10474
Categories: 45(Spanish,
             Portuguese)-99
WH -- Territory: US

Elkhart City News
W & G Forman, Managers
519 S Main Street
Elkhart IN 46516
219-293-2521
WH

Emerald Marketing
Jack Gaughan, Manager
116 Sandpiper Circle
Corte Madera CA 94925
415-692-8677
Categories: 11-19-21-23-59-67
DN -- Territory: US
Markets: MM-RO(photo, electronic)
Items: HC-PB-RM-SW-TA-TV
Year started: 1976
#R 60; #A 2000; #T 60

Emery-Pratt Company
Mrs Cathy Witte, Book Buyer
1966 W Main Street
Owosso MI 48867-1372
516-723-5291
Categories: 99
WH -- Territory: US-CN
Markets: PL-SL
Items: HC-TX-PB
Year started: 1873
#R 8; #P 40M

Empire State News
Robert Scheur, Owner
125 McKesson Parkway
Cheektowaga NY 14225
716-681-7177
WH

Enrica Fish Medical Books
Enrica Fish, Owner
814 Washington Avenue SE
Minneapolis MN 55414
612-623-0707
Categories: 39-59
WH -- Territory: part(midwest)
Markets: BK-CO-SC-PL-SL
Items: HC-PB-TX-MM
Year started: 1978
#R 3

European Book Company
925 Larkin Street
San Francisco CA 94109
415-474-0626
WH

Excalibur Hobbies Ltd
William F Murphy, President
170 Massachusetts Avenue
Arlington MA 02174

617-643-0180
Categories: 29-41-55-69
DN -- Territory: US
Markets: RO(hobby & game)
Items: HC-TX-PB-RM-MG-CO-ML-SW
Year started: 1977
#R 2; #A 400; #T 1000; #P 10

Executive Books
Charles Jones, President
4280 Carlisle Pike
Camp Hill PA 17011
717-763-1950
Categories: 17-19-21-31-35-41-33
         47-57-59-63-81-83-89-90
PD -- Territory: US-CN-IT
Markets: JB-SC-MM-PL
Items: HC-PB-RM-MM-TA-TV
Year started: 1965
#R 1; #A 500+; #T 550; #P 25

EZ Cookin' Book Company
Dede Napoli, Book Buyer
9925 Currant Avenue
Fountain Valley CA 92708
714-968-9102
Categories: 27
DN -- Territory: US
Markets: BK-RO
Items: HC-PB

F & SF Book Company
Frank Preito Jr, V.P.
740 Delafield Avenue
P O Box 415
Staten Island NY 10302
718-981-3526
Categories: 86
WH -- Territory: US
Markets: BK-SC-CO-PL
Items: HC-PB-MM-MG-NP
Year started: 1973
#T 25M

Fairbanks News Agency
Bill Foltz, Book Buyer
307 Ladd Avenue
Fairbanks AK 99701
907-452-4589
Categories: 61(AK)-99
WH -- Territory: AK
Markets: BK-JB-NS-SC-CO-MM-PL
Items: PB-RM-MM-MG-CA-CO-MA-SB
Year started: 1949
#R 5; #A 170; #T 700

Fairfield County News
Joel Rottman, Owner
387 Warren Street
P O Box 1981
Bridgeport CT 06601
203-335-4161
WH

Falkynor Communications
Gail C Watson, Manager
4950 SW 70th Avenue
Davie FL 33314

305-791-1562
Categories: 23-27-39-43-53-57-71
PD -- Territory: US
Markets: BK-JB-CO-PL
Items: HC-PB-SW-TA-TV
Year started: 1976
#R 0; #T 20+; #P 4

Family Reading Service
L Alan Greer, V.P.
1209 Toledo Drive
Albany GA 31705
912-439-2279
WH

Fantaco Company
Thomas D Skulan, Book Buyer
21 Central Avenue
Albany NY 12210-1391
518-463-3367
Categories: 33-69-82-86
PD -- Territory: US-CN-IT
Markets: BK-CO-MM-PL-SL-RO
Items: HC-PB-MM-CA-CO-PO
Year started: 1978
#R 4; #A 100; #T 50; #P 12

Far West Book Service
Rosalie Nicholson, Manager
3515 NE Hassalo
Portland OR 97232
503-234-7664
WH

Fine Associates
B & M Fine, Owners
One Farragut Square S
Washington DC 20006
202-628-2609
WH

Finn News Agency
Arnold Finn, President
116 N Cowen Street
P O Box 300
Garrett IN 46738-0300
219-357-3760
WH

Firefly Books
Martin Waxman, Director
3520 Pharmacy Avenue, Unit 1-C
Scarborough M1W 2T8 ON Canada
416-499-8412
Categories: 11-21-27-29-39-76
            99(small press)
DN -- Territory: CN
Markets: BK-PL
Items: HC-PB-CA
Year started: 1978

Flannery Company
Bud Sparks, Book Buyer
13106 S Avalon Boulevard
Los Angeles CA 90061
213-324-1179
Categories: 13-21-31-35-41-47-55
            57-59-63-65-67-71

WH -- Territory: Western
Markets: BK-SC-RO(religious)
Items: HC-TX-PB-GI-OT(Bibles)
Year started: 1938
#R 2; #A 4000+; #T 25M+; #P 300+

Fleming Museum
Lillain Kerr Haversat, Manager
Colchester Avenue
University of Vermont
Burlington VT 05405
802-656-2090
WH

5405 Boran Place
Tampa FL 33610
813-621-6085
Categories: 21-31-76-89-99
WH -- Territory: Southeast
Markets: BK-CO-SC-PL
Items: HC-PB-TX
Year started: 1971
#R 2; #T 8500; #P 150

Follett Library Book Company
Lewis Wingard, Manager
4506 NW Highway
Route 14 & 31
Crystal Lake IL 60014
815-455-1100
Categories: 21-31-45(bilingual
            books)-76-89
WH -- Territory: Midwest
Markets: SC-PL
Items: HC-PB
Year started: 1948
#R 29; #T 40M; #P all

Forest Sales & Distributing Comp
Joseph A Arrigo, President
2616 Spain Street
New Orleans LA 70117
504-947-2107
Categories: 11-17-21-41-33-55
            61(southern LA)
WH -- Territory: LA
Markets: BK-NS-SC-CO
        RO(gift, department)
Items: HC-PB-MM
Year started: 1967
#R 3; #A 300+; #T 400+; #P 40

Forsyth Travel Library
Ms Pat Gilgannon, Book Buyer
9154 W 57th Street
Shawnee Mission KS 66201
913-384-3440
Categories: 45-71
DN -- Territory: US-CN
Markets: SC-CO-PL-SL
        OT(travel industry)
Items: HC-TX-PB-RM-MM-MA
Year started: 1976
#R 0; #A 2000+; #T 5M+; #P 300+

Franklin Book Company
Manny Deckter, President
7804 Montgomery Avenue

Elkins Park PA 19117
215-635-5252
WH

Franklin County News
Paul Barrett, Manager
99 Elm Street
Greenfield MA 01301
413-773-7164
WH

Fraser Publishing Company
Karla R Ferrelli, Manager
309 South Willard
P. O. Box 494
Burlington VT 05402
802-658-0322
WH

Fred Biermann Bookseller
Route 7, Box 414
Springfield MO 65802
417-866-6983
WH

French & Spanish Book Corporation
Emanuel Molho, Manager
115 Fifth Avenue
New York NY 10003
212-673-7400
Categories: 45(FR-SP)-59
WH -- Territory: US
Markets: BK-JB-NS-SC-CO-PL-SL
Items: HC-TX-PB-RM-MG
       CA-CO-MA-NW-TA-TV
Year started: 1928
#R 0; #A 10000; #T 30M; #P 1000

French & Spanish Book Corporation
652 S Olive Street
Los Angeles CA 90014
Categories: 45(FR-SP)-59
WH -- Territory: US
(see above specifics)

Friends of Terpsichore
Robert Williams, Owner
569 1/2 Yonge Street
P O Box 563, Station Q
Toronto M5P 3H9 ON Canada
416-960-5817
Categories: 11(dance)
WH -- Territory: US-CN
Markets: BK-JB-SC-CO-PL-SL
Items: HC-TX-PB-RM-MM-MG
Year started: 1981

Fulmont News Company
Kenneth Daly, Manager
182 Division Street
P O Box 389
Amsterdam NY 12010
518-843-2421
WH

G H Arrow Company
Louis Kohn, Owner
P O Box 16558

Book Wholesalers and Distributors

Philadelphia PA 19123
215-922-3211
Categories: 99
WH

G Paulsen Company
Harold Paulsen, Manager
27 Sheep Davis Road
Concord NH 03301-1596
603-225-9787
WH

Galahad Books
Lawrence D Alexander, President
166 5th Avenue 4th Floor
New York NY 10010-5909
212-725-4970
WH

Gardner's Book Service
Eileen Gardner, President
4335 W Van Buren
Phoenix AZ 85043
602-233-9424
WH

Garrett Book Company
John Garrett, V.P.
130 E 13th
P. O. Box 1588
Ada OK 74820
405-332-6884
WH

Gay Bowles Sales
P O Box 1060
Janesville WI 53547
800-356-9438; WI:800-362-8466
Categories: 11-29
WH -- Territory: US
Markets: RO(craft stores)
Items: HC-PB-craft supplies

Genealogical Institute
JoAnn Jackson, Book Buyer
P. O. Box 22045
Salt Lake City UT 84122-0045
801-532-3327
Categories: 17-29-41-59
          98(geneology)
PD -- Territory: US-CN-IT
Markets: BK-SC-CO-PL-SL
          OT(direct)
Items: TX
Year started: 1972
#R 1; #T 36; #P 3

Genealogy Digest Club
Scott Barlow, Manager
420 South 425 West
P. O. Box 886
Bountiful UT 84010
Categories: 25-98(genealogy)
WH

General News
Paul Ganger, Book Buyer
2907 - 2nd Avenue S

P O Box 3004
Lethbridge T1J 4A9   AB Canada
403-327-4220
Categories: 99
WH -- Territory: CN
Markets: BK-JB-NS-SC-CO-MM-PL-SL
Items: HC-PB-MM-MG-ML-NW
          CA-CO-MA-TA-TV
Year started: 1940
#R 6; #A 300; #T 4000; #P all

George Kurian Reference Books
George Kurian, Manager
P O Box 519
Baldwin Place NY 10505
914-962-3687
Categories: 17-19-21-31-41-45
          47-49-55-59-65
PD -- Territory: US
Markets: SC-CO-PL-SL
Items: HC-PB-MA
Year started: 1976
#A 200; #T 1500; #P

German & International Bookstore
Celeste Hutchinson, Owner
1767 N Vermont Avenue
Los Angeles CA 90027
213-660-0313
Categories: 45-71
WH -- Territory: Western US
Markets: BK-CO-SC-PL
Items: HC-PB-MM
Year started: 1973
#R 1

German News Company
Fred Hoefer, Manager
220 East 86th Street
New York NY 10028
212-288-5500
WH

Gessler Publishing Company
Seth C Levin, Book Buyer
900 Broadway
New York NY 10003-1291
212-673-3113
Categories: 21-23-27-41-45(Fr,Sp,
          Gm,It,ESL,Lt)-47-59
PD -- Territory: US-CN-IT
Markets: BK-SC-CO-PL
Items: TX-GC-MA-PO-RC-SW-ST-TA-TV
Year started: 1932
#R 0; #A 0; #T 1100; #P 23

Gilmore-Howard
Vern R Gilmore, Owner
604-J Doug Russell Road
Arlington TX 76010
817-265-0351
WH

Girol Books
Leslie Roster, Manager
120 Somerset Street W
P. O. Box 5473, Station F
Ottawa K2C 3M1   ON Canada

613-233-9044
Categories: 45(SP-Port)-99
PD -- Territory: US-CN-IT
Markets: BK-JB-SC-CO-PL-SL
Items: HC-TX-PB-MM-MG-NW-GC-RC
Year started: 1975
#R 1; #A 300; #T 10M+; #P 300+

Glenwood Distributors
Mr Phillips, Manager
3491 Ten Mile Road
Warren MI 48091-1308
WH

Global Library Services
Fran M Secor, Manager
3712 Commercial Street NE
Albuquerque NM 87107
505-345-8163
Categories: 99
WH -- Territory: US
Markets: PL-SL
Items: HC-PB
Year started: 1979
see also Yankee Book Peddler

Golden Lee Book Distributors
Erika Weinman, Hardcover Buyer
Carol Phittard, Trade Paperbacks
Eileen O'Neil, Buyer
   Mass Market Books & Calendars
Ron Petrusha, Buyer
   Business and Computer Books
Mike Nicita, Buyer
   Audio and Video Tapes
1000 Dean Street
Brooklyn NY 11238
718-357-6333; 800-221-0960
Categories: 19-23-99
WH -- Territory: mid-Atlantic
Markets: BK-SC-CO-PL
Items: HC-MM-CA-TA-TV
Year started: 1960
#R 3; #A 7000; #T 12M

Good Reading Book Distributors
A F Whitehead Jr
P O Box 21788
Chattanooga TN 37421
615-238-4963
Categories: 99
WH

Gordon's Books
William Brown, Senior Buyer
   Hardcover Books
Paul Downing, Buyer
   Mass Market Books
Lisa Knudsen, Buyer
   Children's Books
Larry Eson & Randy Rick, Buyers
   Small Press and Regional Books
2323 Delgany
Denver CO 80216
303-296-1830; 800-525-6979
Categories: 21-31-61(CO, Western
          Americana)-76-99
WH -- Territory: Mountain states

Markets: BK-SC-CO-MM-PL-RO
Items: HC-PB-MM
Year started: 1972
#R 2; #T 35M; #P 300

Gospel Mission
Christopher Garramon, Manager
316 - 1st Street NW
P. O. Box M
Choteau MT 59422
406-466-2311
Categories: 63
WH

Gould Athletic Supply Company
Marguerite D Gould, Manager
3156 N 96th Street
Milwaukee WI 53222-3499
414-871-3943
Categories: 69
WH

Goyescas Corporation of Florida
Attn: Book Buyer
2155 NW 26th Avenue
Miami FL 33142
305-635-5321
Categories: 45(Spanish)-99
WH

Graham Maughan Company
David Christensen, Manager
50 East 500 South
Provo UT 84601
801-377-3335
WH

Graham News Company
Gilbert J Brechter, Manager
924 Kenner Avenue
Kenner LA 70063
504-241-9480
WH

Great Tradition
Jim Tate, Director
750 Adrian Way #111
San Rafael CA 94903
415-492-9382
Categories: 53-63
DN -- Territory: US-CN
Markets: ALL
Items: HC-PB-MM
Year started: 1985
#T 300; #P 30

Green Gate Books
Karen M Nester, Manager
1162 Latham Avenue
P O Box 934
Lima OH 45802
419-225-3816
Categories: 19(how-to)
            29(collectibles)
PD -- Territory: US
Markets: RO(antique trade)
Items: HC-PB-RM-OT(labels)
Year started: 1977

Green Mountain Book Company
Jean R Jones, Owner
P. O. Box 338
Main & Montgomery
Markleville CA 96120
916-694-2141
WH

Grenoble Books
Robert R Tyler, President
1931 Vernier
Grosse Pointe Wood MI 48236
313-884-5255
WH

Gryphon House
Larry Rood, President
3706 Otis Street
P O Box 275
Mount Rainier MD 20712
301-779-6200
Categories: 21-31-76
PD -- Territory: US-CN-IT
Markets: BK-SC-PL-child care
Items: HC-PB
Year started: 1971
#R 0; #A 1400; #T 800; #P 85

Guardian Book Company
N Black, Owner
1045 Northville Drive
Toledo OH 43612
419-476-7624
Categories: 21-27-29-76-99
WH -- Territory: OH-MI
Markets: SC-PL
Items: HC-PB-MM-RM
Year started: 1969
#R 4

Gulf Coast Periodicals
David Moskow, Owner
1954 Whitfield Avenue
Sarasota FL 33580
813-755-4145
WH

Gulf States Book Fairs
Philip Smith, Owner
2901 Mill Street
P. O. Box 7422
Mobile AL 36607
205-471-1227
WH

Gull Book Shop
Everett V Cunningham, Owner
1547 San Pablo Avenue
Oakland CA 94612
415-834-8108
WH

Gundy's News Supply Ltd
Helen Hladchuk, Book Buyer
1722 Ogilvie Street, #3
Prince George BC Canada
604-564-5414
Categories: 99

WH -- Territory: CN
Markets: BK-NS-SC-CO-MM-PL-SL-R
Items: HC-PB-RM-MM-MG
       CA-CO-ML-MA-NW
Year started: 1976
#A 105; #T most; #P most

H Foxman Publications Ltd
H Foxman, President
6635 Mackle Road #506
Dollard des Orm.   PQ Canada
514-684-8041
WH

H H Marshall Ltd
E R Schimpf, Manager
3731 Mackintosh Street
P. O. Box 9301, Station A
Halifax B3K 5N5   NS Canada
902-454-8381
WH

H P Kopplemann
Allan Hartley, Marketing Manage
140 Van Block Avenue
Hartford CT 06141-0145
203-549-6210; 800-243-7724
Categories: 21-31-76-89
WH -- Territory: US
Markets: SC-PL
Items: PB-MM
Year started: 1910
#T 20M

Ham Radio's Bookstore
J C Clark, Manager
Main Street
Greenville NH 03048
603-878-1441
WH

Hamakor Judaica
Herschel Strauss, Owner
6112 N Lincoln
Chicago IL 60659
312-463-6186
WH

Handelman Company
Ken Vastic, Manager
9700 Bell Ranch Drive
Santa Fe Springs CA 90670
213-946-4431
WH

Harmony Book Company
Kenneth J Kuzma, V.P.
1795 3rd Street
Beaver PA 15009
412-728-6621
WH

Harrisburg News Company
Daniel M Adolt, Manager
2244 N 7th Street
Harrisburg PA 17105
717-232-9981
WH

Harry Young Publication Services
Harry Young Kim, Book Buyer
880 South Norton Avenue
Los Angeles CA 90005
213-381-1310
Categories: 99
WH -- Territory: US-IT
Markets: BK-JB-SC-CO-PL-SL
Items: HC-TX-MG-ML-MA
Year started: 1978
#P 1M+

Harvard Art Museums Sales Shop
Amanda Marshall, Manager
32 Quincy Street
Cambridge MA 02138
617-495-7768
WH

Harvard Associates
Bill Glass, Manager
260 Beacon Street
Somerville MA 01243
617-492-0660
WH

Hawaii Geographic Books & Info
Willis Moore, Manager
217 S King Street #308
P O Box 1698
Honolulu HI 96806-1698
808-538-3952
Categories: 61(HI)-71-99
WH -- Territory: HI

Herr's Inc
70 Eastgate Drive
Danville IL 61832
217-442-4121; 800-637-2647
Categories: 11-29
WH -- Territory: US
Markets: RO(craft stores)
Items: HC-PB-craft supplies

Hertzberg - New Method
Benson R Maugum, Manager
617 E Vandalia Road
Jacksonville IL 62650
217-243-5451
WH

Heyden & Son
Nina Sammon, V.P.
P. O. Box 230 / IPS
Accord MA 02018-0230
WH

Hilgard News Agency
Bill Cooper, Owner
2609 - 17th Street NE
P. O. Box 338
Great Falls MT 59414
406-453-7867
WH

Hillsboro News
Robert Falo, Manager
P. O. Box 25738

Tampa FL 33622-5738
813-877-5351
Categories: 99
WH

Himalaya Books
George Deshpande, Book Buyer
P. O. Box 2112, Station B
Brampton L6T 3S3 ON Canada
416-793-8007
Categories: 10-75-95-90(many
                   Indian languages)
WH -- Territory: US-CN
Markets: SC-PL
Items: HC-PB
Year started: 1975
#R 1; #A 45+; #T 2000

Himber's Books
David Himber, Manager
1380 W 2nd Avenue
Eugene OR 97402
503-686-8003
Categories: 10-75-90-95
WH -- Territory: US
Markets: BK-JB-NS-SC-CO-MM-PL-SL
Items: HC-PB-MM-MG-CA-CO-MA-SB
Year started: 1928
#R 0; #A 750+; #T 25M; #P 150+

Hispania Books Distributors
Lois Atley, Director
2116 - 18th Street NW
P O Box 11441
Washington DC 20008
202-265-2325
Categories: 45(Spanish)-78-80-99
WH -- Territory: US
Markets: BK-CO-SC-PL
Items: HC-PB
Year started: 1983

Hispano - American Publications
Herman Mendoza, President
45-57 Davis Street
Long Island City NY 11101
718-937-2330
Categories: 45(Spanish)-99
WH

Historic Aviation
James B Horne, Owner
3850 Coronation Road
Eagan MN 55122-1896
612-454-2493
Categories: 69(aviation)
WH -- Territory: US
Markets: BK-SC-CO-PL-RO
Items: HC-PB-RM-CA-TV
Year started: 1968
#R 0; #T 1200; #P 125

Historic Cherry Hill
Anne Ackerson, Director
523 1/2 Pearl Street
Albany NY 12202
518-434-4806
WH

Holiday Enterprises
James Rochester, Manager
Easley Highway 123
Greenville SC 29602
803-269-4311
WH

Holyoke News Company
Michael Pitera, Manager
720 Main Street
P.O. Box 990
Holyoke MA 01041
413-534-4537
WH

Homestead Book
David Tatelman, President
6101 - 22nd Avenue NW
Seattle WA 98107
206-782-4532; 800-426-6777
Categories: 11-13-23-27-29-33
              43-51-69-71-76-99
WH -- Territory: US'
Markets: BK-CO
Items: HC-PB-MG-NP-GC
Year started: 1972
#R 5; #T 1500; #P 60

Horizon Publishers & Distributor
Duane S Crowther, President
50 South 500 West
P O Box 490
Bountiful UT 84010-0490
801-275-9451; 800-453-0812
Categories: 11-27-29-35-43-63
WH -- Territory: US
Markets: BK-SC-PL-craft stores
Items: HC-PB-MM
Year started: 1971
#R 8; #T 3500

Hotchkiss House
James Panosian, Owner
18 Hearthstone Road
Pittsford NY 14534
716-381-4735
WH

Hudson Valley News
Bryon Waters, Manager
175 Overlook Place
Newburgh NY 12550
914-562-3399
WH

Huntington News Agency
Thomas P Schamder, V.P.
121 Erskine Lane
Scott Depot WV 25560
304-757-8831
WH

Husker News Company
Don Albert, Manager
1st & Locust Streets
Atlantic IA 50022
712-243-5557
WH

I-Am-I Books
Suzanne Kaftal, Owner
474 Orange Center Road
Orange CT 06477
203-795-5382
WH

Iaconi Book Imports
Mariuccia Iaconi, Owner
300 Pennsylvania Avenue
San Francisco CA 94107
415-285-7393
Categories: 45(many)-78-80-99
WH -- Territory: US
Markets: SC-PL
Items: HC-PB-TA-TV
Year started: 1955

Ian MacDonald Library Services
R & P MacDonald, Owners
198 Pemberton Avenue
North Vancouver BC Canada
604-986-1578
WH

Idaho News Agency
Ron Edinger, Manager
1825 N 15th
Coeur D'Alene ID 83814
208-664-3444
WH

Ideal Foreign Books
Andre A Fetaya, Owner
132-10 Hillside Avenue
Richmond Hill NY 11418
718-297-7477
WH

IEEE Computer Society
C G Stockton, Director
1730 Massachusetts Avenue NW
Washington DC 20036-1903
202-371-0101
Categories: 23-67
PD -- Territory: US

Illinois News Service
David R Myers, Manager
1301 SW Washington Street
Peoria IL 61602
309-673-4549
WH

Imperial News Company
Irwin Salbe, Manager
225 Pinelawn Road
Melville NY 11747
516-752-9330
WH

Imported Publications
Mark Almberg, Book Buyer
320 W Ohio Street
Chicago IL 60610-4175
312-787-9017
Categories: 99
DE -- Territory: US
Markets: BK-JB-RO-MM-PL-SL
Items: HC-TX-PB-MG-NW
Year started: 1970
#R 3; #T 1500; #P 50

Indiana Periodicals Distributors
Donald L Parish, Manager
2120 S Meridian Street
Indianapolis IN 46225-1923
317-786-1488
Categories: 99
WH -- Territory: US
Markets: BK-NS-SC-MM-PL-SL
Items: HC-PB-RM-MM-MG
       CA-CO-ML-MA-SB
Year started: 1950
#R 8; #A 700; #T 3000; #P 40

Info 21 Booksellers
Hisayuke Ishimatsu, Manager
1376 Hearst Street
El Cerrito CA 94530
415-540-0821
WH

Ingram Book Company
Susan Moffat, Buyer
  Mass Market Books
Cathey Clark, Buyer
  new companies (A to L)
Jim Batte, Buyer
  new companies (M to Z)
Jay Moench, Trade Buyer
P O Box 17266
Nashville TN 37217
615-361-5000; 800-251-5900
Categories: 99
WH -- Territory: US
Markets: BK-SC-CO-PL-SL-RO-MM
Items: MM
Year started: 1933
#R 0; #T 35M; #P most

Ingram Book Company -- West
16175 Stephens Street
City of Industry CA 91744
213-961-3385
Categories: 99
WH -- Territory: US
Markets: BK-SC-CO-PL-SL-RO-MM
Items: HC-TX-PB-MM-CA-PO-SW-TA-TV
Year started: 1933
#R 0; #T 35M; #P most

Ingram Book Company
Eastern Distribution Center
8201 B Slayton Drive
Jessup MD 20794
301-725-7110
Categories: 99
WH -- Territory: US
Markets: BK-SC-CO-PL-SL-RO-MM
Items: HC-TX-PB-MM-CA-PO-SW-TA-TV
Year started: 1933
#R 0; #T 35M; #P most

Inland Book Company
David Wilk, President
22 Hemingway Avenue
East Haven CT 06512
203-467-4257; 800-243-0138
Categories: 13-37-41-49-53-55
            73-99(small press)
WH -- Territory: US
Markets: BK-PL-SL
Items: PB
Year started: 1981
#T 5000; #P 100

Inland Empire Periodicals
Duane Friesen, Manager
4800 N Yellowstone Avenue
Idaho Falls ID 83401
208-523-0183
Categories: 21-31-76-89
WH -- Territory: mountain states
Markets: BK-CO-SC-PL
Items: HC-PB-MM-MG-NP
Year started: 1938
#R 4

Instructional Products Services
Herman Berke, Manager
1287 Combermere
P O Box 95
Troy MI 48099
313-540-4540
WH

Interbook Inc
Matt A Gouig, Sales Manager
859 Lawrence Drive
P O Box 456
Newbury Park CA 91320
805-498-6703; 415-352-9221
Categories: 99
DE -- Territory: US
Markets: BK
Items: HC-PB
#P 12

Intermountain Periodical Dist.
Lettie Marquis, Mike Majerek
812 W 17th Street

==

Items: HC = Hardcover   TX = Textbooks   RM = Remainders   MG = Magazines, General
          PB = Softcover   MM = Mass-Markets   NP = Newspapers   ML = Magazines, Literary
          CA = Calendars   CO = Comics   GC = Greeting Cards   PO = Posters   TA = Tapes, Audio
          SW = Software   GI = Gifts   MA = Maps & Atlases   RC = Records   TV = Tapes, Video
          ST = Stationery   SB = Stickers/Bookmarks   OT = Other items (games, toys, etc.)

Ogden UT 84404
801-394-6681
Categories: 99
WH -- Territory: UT
Markets: BK-NS-SC-CO-MM-PL-SL
Items: PB-RM-MM-MG-CA
       CO-ML-MA-SB-TV
Year started: 1980
#R 1; #A 300; #P 100

International Book Centre
Claude J Mukalla, Manager
2007 Laurel Drive
Troy MI 48099
313-879-8436
WH

International Circulation
Richard Dooda, Book Distribution
250 West 55th Street
New York NY 10019
212-262-8653
DE -- Territory: US-CN
Markets: JB
#R 38; #A 397; #P 3

International Imports
Dorothy Spencer, Owner
8050 Webb Avenue
North Hollywood CA 91605-1504
818-768-0069
WH

International Periodical Distr.
Gary D Judy, V.P.
11760 Sorrento Valley Road #B
San Diego CA 92121
619-481-5928; 800-621-5461
Categories: 11-19-23-29-39-75-83
DN
Markets: BK-RO
Items: MG-ML

International Service Company
Katherine Swanberg, Manager
333 - 4th Avenue
Indialantic FL 32903
305-724-1443
WH

International Specialized Books
Jeannette Bokma, Book Buyer
5602 NE Hassalo St
Portland OR 97213
503-287-3093
Categories: 11(architecture)
DE -- Territory: US-CN-IT
Markets: BK-SC-CO-MM-PL-SL-RO
Items: HC-TX-PB-SW-TA-TV
Year started: 1967
#R 20; #T 3000; #P 75

International Univ. Booksellers
Max J Holmes, President
30 Irving Place
New York NY 10003
212-254-4100
WH

Interstate Books
Ron Surface
P O Box 113B
Locust Grove OK 74352
918-598-3149
Categories: 99
WH discount book distributor

Interstate Distributors
David A Jacobs, Manager
199 Commander Shea Boulevard
Quincy MA 02171
617-328-9500
WH

Interstate Periodical Distrs.
Amy Tobias, Manager
201 E Badger Road
P O Box 2237
Madison WI 53701
608-271-3600
Categories: 99
WH -- Territory: Midwest
Items: MG-NP

Islamic Book Service
Kamal I Shaarawy, Manager
10900 W Washington
Indianapolis IN 46231
317-839-8150
WH

Island Heritage Distribution
Lynne Madden, Manager
550 N Nimitz Highway
Honolulu HI 96817-5030
808-531-0133
WH

J & L Book Company
Terry L Smith, Owner
P. O. Box 3548
E 1710 Trent
Spokane WA 99220
509-535-3360
Categories: 21(K-9)-89
WH -- Territory: Northwest US-CN
Markets: SC-PL
Items: HC-PB-RM-MM
Year started: 1979
#R 1; #A 500; #T 10M; #P 250

J A Majors Medical Book Company
1851 Diplomat Drive
P O Box 819074
Dallas TX 75061-9074
214-247-2929; 800-527-3492
Categories: 39-67
WH -- Territory: US
Markets: BK-CO-PL-SL
Items: HC-TX-PB
Year started: 1909
#R 2; #A 10,000; #T 127M; #P all

J A Majors Medical Book Company
1806 Southgate
Houston TX 77030
713-526-5757; 800-527-3492

Categories: 39-67
WH -- Territory: US
Markets: BK-CO-PL-SL
Items: HC-TX-PB
Year started: 1909
#R 2; #A 10,000; #T 127M; #P all

J A Majors Medical Book Company
3909 Bienville
Atlanta GA 70119
504-486-5956
Categories: 39-67.
WH -- Territory: US
Markets: BK-CO-PL-SL
Items: HC-TX-PB
Year started: 1909
#R 3; #T 127M; #P

J A Majors Medical Book Company
3770-A Zip Industrial Boulevard
Atlanta GA 30354
404-768-4956; 800-527-3492
Categories: 39-67
WH -- Territory: US
Markets: BK-CO-PL-SL
Items: HC-TX-PB
Year started: 1909
#R 3; #T 127M; #P all

J Levine Religious Supplies
Seymour Levine, President
58 Eldridge Street
New York NY 10002
212-966-4460
Categories: 45(Hebrew, Yiddish)
        98(Judaica)
WH -- Territory: US
Markets: SC-SL-RO(gift)-synagogue
Items: HC-PB-RM-MM-CA-CO
       GI-MA-PO-RC-TA
Year started: 1890
#A 3000; #T 100M; #P 200

J S Latta
Thomas B Pafford, Manager
1502 - 4th Avenue
Huntington WV 25726
304-523-9433
WH

Jack Martin News Agency
Casey N Martin, Manager
Rt 1, Box 910
Tyler TX 75708-9801
214-597-1378

James & Law Company
David C Carpenter, Book Buyer
217 W Main Street
Clarksburg WV 26302-2468
304-624-7401
Categories: 61(WV)-99
WH -- Territory: WV
Markets: SC-CO-PL-SL
Items: HC-PB-RM-MM-MG-CA
       GI-MA-RC-SB-TA
Year started: 1899
#R 5; #A 900; #T 5000; #P all

Janway Company
W & J Stebbins, Owners
Academy Road
RD 3, Box 211
Cogan Station PA 17728
717-494-1239
WH

Jean Karr & Company
C Lee, Buyer
5656 - 3rd Street NE
Washington DC 20011
202-529-6789
Categories: 21-31-76-89
WH -- Territory: US
Markets: SC-CO-PL
Items: HC-PB
Year started: 1938
#R 13; #T 25M; #P all

Jech Distributing
Bill Jech, Owner
11760 Sorrento Valley Road
San Diego CA 92115
619-452-7251
Categories: 75
WH

JJV Associates
Joseph J Villeneuve, Manager
107 S Lowell Avenue
Syracuse NY 13204
315-475-9725
WH

John Coutts Library Services
John K Coutts, President
4290 Third Avenue
Niagara Falls L2E 4K7   ON Canada
416-356-6382
Categories: 99
WH -- Territory: CN
Markets: BK-CO-SL
Items: HC-TX-PB

John Justice Book Wholesalers
John P Justice, Owner
107 W Main Street
Route 9
Hedgesville WV 25427
304-754-3232
Categories: 10-17-41(military,
          American)-55
WH -- Territory: US
Markets: BK-JB-SL
Items: HC-PB-RM
Year started: 1978
#R 0; #A 500; #T 1000

John W Lewis Enterprises
John W Lewis, President
168 Perez Street
Santurce PR 00936
809-725-1014
Categories: 21-31-76-89
DN -- Territory: PR-VI
Markets: SC-PL
Items: HC-PB

Johnson News Agency
Karl Johnson, Owner
1320 Mountain View Road
P. O. Box 9009
Moscow ID 83843
208-882-7088
WH

Johnson Safari Bookshop
Sondra Alden, Director
16 S Grant
Chanute KS 66720
316-431-2730

Jonathan David Company
Marvin Sekler, V.P.
68-22 Eliot Avenue
Middle Village
Flushing NY 11379
718-456-8611
WH

Josten's
Wholesale Book Division
5501 Norman Center Drive
Bloomington MN 55437
612-830-3300
WH

Judaic Specialties
Sally Thor, Owner
P. O. Box 1884
Jupiter FL 33468-1884
WH

Junius Book Distributors
Michael V Cordasco, President
P. O. Box 85
Fairview NJ 07022
201-868-7725
WH

Kable News Company
David Abramowitz, V.P.
777 Third Avenue
New York NY 10017
212-371-5321
Categories: 99
WH -- Territory: US
Markets: BK-MM
Items: PB-MM-MG-CA
Year started: 1933
#R 34

Kalispell News Agency
Leigh Johnson, Owner
1500 Airport Road
Kalispell MT 59901
406-755-5430
WH

Kampmann & Company
Eric Kampmann, President
9 East 40th Street
New York NY 10016
212-685-2928
Categories: 99
DE -- Territory: US

Markets: ALL
Items: HC-PB-MM
#T 300; #P 40
small and medium size presses

Kaplan School Supply Corporation
Leon Kaplan, Owner
600 Jonestown Road
Winston-Salem NC 27103
919-768-4450
Categories: 21-31-76-89
WH -- Territory: Southeast
Markets: SC-PL-OT(day care)
Items: HC-PB-TX
Year started: 1969
#R 6

Kartes Video Communciations
Jim Kartes, President
7225 Woodland Drive
Indianapolis IN 46278
800-582-2000
Categories: 99   .
DN -- Territory: US
Markets: BK-RO-PL-MM
Items: TV videotapes only

Kazi Publications
L Ali, President
1215 W Belmont
Chicago IL 60657
312-327-7598
Categories: 21(Islamic)
          45(Arabic, Urdu)-63
PD -- Territory: US-CN-IT
Markets: BK-JB-SC-CO-MM
          PL-SL-RO(Islamic)
Items: HC-TX-PB-CA-GI-GC
          MA-PO-SW-TA-TV
Year started: 1970
#R 5; #A 100; #T 500; #P 10

Keltie News
Gene & Josephine Davids, Owners
518 Washington Street
Cape May NJ 08204
609-884-7797
WH

Kent News Agency
Douglas & Norman Kent, Owners
1402 Avenue B
P. O. Box 661
Scottsbluff NE 69361
308-635-2225
WH

Kent News Service Ltd
Cor Vreugdenhil, Manager
195 Sandys Street
P. O. Box 487
Chatham N7M 5K6   ON Canada
519-352-3440
WH

Keramos
Marjorie E Uren, Manager
P.O. Box 7500

Ann Arbor MI 48107-7500
313-429-7864
WH

Ketab
Sohrab, Book Buyer
16661 Ventura Boulevard #111
Encino CA 91436
818-995-3822
Categories: 45(Persian)
             99(Persian only)
PD -- Territory: US-CN
Markets: BK-SC-CO-PL-SL
Items: HC-TX-PB-MG-CA-GI
       ML-MA-PO-NW-TA
Year started: 1981
#R 3; #A 250; #T 2000; #P 50

Key Book Service
Melody Merola, Buyer
425 Asylum Street
Bridgeport CT 06610-9990
203-334-2165
Categories: 99
WH -- Territory: US-IN
Markets: PL-SL
Items: HC-TX-PB-MM
Year started: 1952
#R 5

Key News Agency
Stanley G Budner, Owner
P O Box 1318
Marathon FL 33050-1318
305-743-6448
Categories: 99
WH -- Territory: FL
Markets: BK-SC-CO-PL
Items: HC-TX-PB-MM-MG-NP
#R 4

KidsBooks
Julie Chase V.P.
Stamford Industrial Park
737 Canal Street, Building 22
Stamford CT 06902
203-323-1819
Categories: 15-17-21-23-27-29
             31-41-43-59-69-89
WH -- Territory: Northeast
Markets: BK-SC-PL
Items: HC-PB-RM-CA-PO-SB-TA
Year started: 1978
#A 100; #T 4000

King Electronics Distributing
Jeanne Laughlin, Manager
1711 Southeastern Avenue
Indianapolis IN 46201-3990
317-639-1484
WH

King News
Dennis G Fode, Book Buyer
1013 N 5th Street
P. O. Box 160
Grand Forks ND 58206-0160
701-775-0182

Categories: 21-27-33-69-75
WH -- Territory: ND-MN
Markets: NS-SC-MM-PL
Items: PB-MM-MG-CA-CO
Year started: 1940
#R 6; #A 125; #T 3M+; #P 15

Kinokuniya Bookstores America
Kotaro Hishiguchi, Manager
1581 Webster Street
San Francisco CA 94115
415-567-7625
WH

Kitchen Table: Women of Color
Barbara Smith
593 Park Avenue
New York NY 10021
212-308-5389
Categories: 49-73
PD -- Territory: US
Items: PB-MM

Kitchener News Company
Paula Cosgrove, Book Buyer
455 Dutton Drive
P. O. Box 274
Waterloo N2J 4A4   ON Canada
519-884-3710
Categories: 10-75
WH -- Territory: CN
Markets: NS-SC-CO-MM-PL-SL
Items: PB-MM
Year started: 1929
#R 4; #A 2000; #P 100

Koala Books of Canada Ltd
Vera Lech, Book Buyer
14327 - 95 A Avenue
Edmonton T5N 0B6   AB Canada
403-452-5149
Categories: 99
WH -- Territory: US-CN
Markets: BK-JB-SC-CO-PL-SL
Items: HC-TX-PB-MA-PO-RC-TA
Year started: 1974
#T 500; #P 19

Koen Book Distributors
Keith McCabe, Mass Market Buyer
Sally Lindsay, Buyer
514 N Read Avenue
P O Box 223
Cinnaminson NJ 08077
609-786-1111; 800-257-8381
Categories: 99
WH -- Territory: East Coast
Markets: BK-SC-PL
Items: HC-PB-MM
Year started: 1972
#R 4; #T 18M; #P 300
small presses

Kokomo News Agency
Jack Adams, Owner
3926 Mobile Avenue
Fort Wayne IN 46805-1088
WH

Kraus Reprint & Periodicals
Herbert Cohen, President
Route 100
Millwood NY 10546
914-762-2200
Categories: 41-47-55-57-65-67
WH -- Territory: US
Markets: PL-SL
Items: HC-PB-MG-microform
Year started: 1985

Kuykendall's Press
Frances K Owen, Manager
506 Chandler Street
Athens AL 35611-0627
205-232-1754
WH

L & L Company
Freda Leiss, Manager
20 Lakeshore Drive
Newport News VA 23602
804-877-2939
WH

L & M News Company
Dennis Boucher, Manager
1301 Highway 70E
New Bern NC 28560
919-633-2179
WH

L L Company
Marlin S Wallace, Manager
1647 Manning Avenue
Los Angeles CA 90024
213-475-3664
WH

L-S Distributors
Richard Seifert, Buyer
  Magazines and Newspapers
Bob Belmont and Norman Gover
  Buyers, Trade Books
Ronald Shoop, Buyer
  Mass Market Books
480 Ninth Street
San Francisco CA 94103
415-861-6300
Categories: 99
WH -- Territory: Northern CA
Markets: BK
Items: HC-PB-MM-MG-ML-NP
Year started: 1957
#R 4; #A 600+; #T 15M; #P 300+
formerly Ellis News Co.

L-W Book Sales
Jane Condor, Book Buyer
5243 S Adams
Marion IN 46953
317-674-6450
Categories: 11-29-59(art,
             collectibles)
PD -- Territory: US-CN
Markets: BK-JB-PL-antique dealers
Year started: 1972
#T 1M+; #P 100+

La Crosse News Agency
Robert Butterfield, Manager
620 State Street
P. O. Box 85
La Crosse WI 54601
608-784-4210
WH

La Moderna Poesia
J E Lopez-Serrano, Owner
5246 SW 8th Street
Miami FL 33134
305-446-9884
Categories: 41-45(Spanish)
47-78-80-99
WH -- Territory: US-FL

Landau Book Company
Louis Landau, Owner
272 W Park Avenue
P O Box 570
Long Beach NY 11561
516-889-0616
Categories: 11-31-45-53-55
WH -- Territory: US
Markets: BK
Items: HC-PB
Year started: 1929
#R 1; #T 400

Lanson's Inc
Paul Tremaine, President
12566 SW Main Street
Portland OR 97223
503-639-4852
Categories: 99
WH -- Territory: US
Items: HC-PB
Year started: 1962
#A 6000

Larousse Company
Gerard Hamon, Manager
572 Fifth Avenue
New York NY 10036
212-575-9515
WH

Larry Smith Books
710 Grand Avenue
North Bergen NJ 07047
201-864-2586
WH

Las Vegas News Agency
Jim Snape, Ron Dewey, Buyers
333 W St Louis
Las Vegas NV 89102
702-384-1888
Categories: 99
WH

Lash Distributors
John Gray, Manager
3636 Pennsy Drive
Landover MD 20785
301-937-4900
WH

Lectorum Publications
Teresa Mlawer, Buyer
  Children's Books
Alberto Romo, Buyer
  Literature Books
Hilda Loayza, Buyer
  Science Fiction and Romance
137 West 14th Street
New York NY 10011
212-929-2833
Categories: 45(Spanish)-21-31-47
              76-78-80-85-86-89
WH -- Territory: US
Markets: BK-JB-SC-CO-MM-PL-SL
Items: HC-TX-PB-MM
Year started: 1960
#R 5; #A 700; #T 10M; #P 100
Spanish language

Lentz Enterprises
Ginny Lentz, Owner
310 Broad Street
P O Box 1021
Charleston SC 29402-1021
803-723-7231; 800-845-2568
Categories: 27-71
PD -- Territory: US
Markets: BK-CO-PL
Items: HC-PB-GI-TV
Year started: 1979
#R 10

Les Editions Francaises
Daniel Johnson, Book Buyer
1411 rue Ampere / C P 395
Boucherville J4B 5W2 PQ Canada
514-641-0514
Categories: 10-75-90-95
PD -- Territory: US-CN
Markets: BK-SC-CO-MM-PL-SL
Items: HC-TX-PB-MM-MA
Year started: 1951
#R 7; #T 5M+; #P 4

Les Editions Heritage
Luc Payette, V.P.
300 Arran
Saint Lambert PQ Canada
514-672-6710
WH

Les Editions Levesque
Rodrigue Levesque, Owner
Chemin Dufresne, RR 3
Gatineau J8P 7G7 PQ Canada
819-663-6748
WH

Les Editions Un Monde Dif Ltee
Louise M Laurin, Director
3400 Losch, Local 8
Saint Hubert PQ Canada
514-656-2660
WH

Lescron Enterprises
Bert Rosenbaum, President
80-90 Arch Street

P. O. Box B
Johnson City NY 13790
607-729-6281

Liberation Distributors
Gary Sanders, Manager
P O Box 5341
Chicago IL 60680
312-987-0004
Categories: 13-41-47-49-73
WH -- Territory: US-CN
Markets: BK-CO-PL-SL
Items: HC-TX-PB
Year started: 1979
#R 2; #A 200; #T 200; #P 12

Librairie La Liberte
Lucius Laliberte, Owner
3020 Chemin Sainte-Foy
Sainte Foy G1X 3V6 PQ Canada
418-658-3763
WH

Librairie Lemeac
371 Laurier W
Montreal H2V 2K6 PQ Canada
514-273-2841
WH

Library Book Selection Services
Larry Efaw, Manager
2714 McGraw Drive
P. O. Box 277
Bloomington IL 61701
309-663-1411
WH

Library Systems & Services
Judy Huffman, Manager
General Motors Building
1395 Piccard Drive
Rockville MD 20850
301-258-0200
WH

Libreria Bereana
Ronald Lundin, Manager
1825 San Alejandro
Urb San Ignacio
Rio Piedras PR 00927
809-764-6175
WH

Libros de Espana Y America
Angel Capellan, Owner
170-23 83rd Avenue
Jamaica Hills NY 11432
718-291-9891
Categories: 45(Spanish)
            99(Spanish imports)
DN -- Territory: US-Spain
Markets: BK-NS-SC-CO-MM-PL
Items: HC-TX-RM-SW
Year started: 1978

Libros Espanoles SA
Rafael Ruiz, Manager
1898 SW 8th Street

Miami FL 33135
305-541-2223
Categories: 45(Spanish)-99
WH

Libros International
Larry Downs, Manager
7214 SW 41st Street
Miami FL 33155
305-262-2023
Categories: 45(SP-IT)-99
WH

Life Unlimited
Tim Torian, Owner
8125 Sunset #204
Fair Oaks CA 95628
916-967-8442
Categories: 13-19-23-39-51-57-63
            98(self-improvement)
WH -- Territory: US-CN-IT
Markets: BK-SC-CO-RO(religious)
Items: HC-TX-PB-RM-MM-CA
       GC-PO-SW-TA-TV
Year started: 1972
#R 1; #A 500; #T 350; #P 30

Lifespring Books
Arlene Schulz, Manager
517 Springfield
Winnipeg R2G 0S1   MB Canada
204-667-5315
WH

Light Impressions Corporation
William Edwards, President
439 Monroe Avenue
P O Box 940
Rochester NY 14603
716-271-8960
Categories: 11(photography,
            graphic arts)
WH -- Territory: US
Markets: BK-CO-SC-PL-SL
Items: HC-PB
Year started: 1969

Ling's International Books
David Ling, Manager
7531 Convoy Court
P. O. Box 82684
San Diego CA 92138
619-292-8104
Categories: 45(Fr, Sp)-47-65
            83(Fr & Sp mainly)
DN -- Territory: US
Markets: BK-SC-CO-PL
Items: HC-PB
Year started: 1974
#T 3000

Lion Services Company
Lee Saalinger, Owner
P. O. Box 667
Coronado CA 92118
805-323-8255
WH

Living Books
Nora Murphy, Buyer
12155 Magnolia Avenue
Riverside CA 92503
714-354-7330
WH

Livraria Freebook Ltda
Caixa Postal 7983
Sao Paulo CEP 01051 Brasil
Categories: 99 (USA books)
DN -- Territory: IT(Brazil)
Markets: BK-PL

Login Brothers Book
1450 W Randolph
Chicago IL 60607
312-733-6424; 800-621-4249
Categories: 39
WH -- Territory: US
Markets: BK-CO-PL-SL
Items: HC-TX
Year started: 1967
#R 10; #T 10M; #P all

Login Brothers Book - Ohio
1550 Enterprise Road
Twinsburg OH 44087
216-439-7500; 800-321-8778
Categories: 39
WH -- Territory: US
Markets: BK-CO-PL-SL
Items: HC-TX
Year started: 1979
#R 10; #T 10M; #P all

Login Brothers New Jersey
135 New Dutch Lane
Fairfield NJ 07006
201-882-0440; 800-526-3025
Categories: 39
WH -- Territory: US
Markets: BK-CO-PL-SL
Items: HC-TX
Year started: 1982
#R 8; #T 8000; #P all

Lone Star School Book Depot
Jeff Falke, V.P.
4640 Harry Hines Boulevard
Dallas TX 75235
214-631-7160
WH

Longman Trade USA
Charles Wenk, Marketing
5 S 250 Frontenac Road
Naperville IL 60540
312-983-6400; 800-245-book
Categories: 10
DE -- Territory: US
Markets: BK-PL
Items: HC-PB-MM
#P 50

Lord's Line
Betty A Grissom, V.P.
1734 Armour Lane
Redondo Beach CA 90278
213-542-5575
Categories: 63
WH

Louis Goldberg Book Supply
Katherine Hoadley, Manager
139 Main Street
Nazareth PA 18064
215-759-9458
WH

Louisiana Periodicals
Woody Taylor, Manager
8201 Wyngate Boulevard
P.O. Box 3723
Shreveport LA 71133
318-688-9560
WH

Louisville News Company
Ivan Ludington Jr, President
2106 Production Drive
P.O. Box 99008
Louisville KY 40299
502-491-1950
Categories: 99
WH

LTO Enterprises
Walnut Press
6036 N 10th Way
Phoenix AZ 85014
602-265-7765
Categories: 21-31-45(Vietnamese)
            76-89
PD -- Territory: US
Markets: BK-PL
Items: HC-PB

Ludington News Company
Ivan Ludington Jr, Manager
1600 E Grand Boulevard
Detroit MI 48211
313-925-7600
WH

===

Items: HC = Hardcover   TX = Textbooks   RM = Remainders   MG = Magazines, General
          PB = Softcover   MM = Mass-Markets   NP = Newspapers   ML = Magazines, Literary
          CA = Calendars   CO = Comics   GC = Greeting Cards   PO = Posters   TA = Tapes, Audio
          SW = Software   GI = Gifts   MA = Maps & Atlases   RC = Records   TV = Tapes, Video
          ST = Stationery   SB = Stickers/Bookmarks   OT = Other items (games, toys, etc.)

M S News Company
Robert L Hampton, Manager
901 E Morris
Wichita KS 67202
316-263-9002
Categories: 99
WH -- Territory: KS
Markets: BK-NS-SC-CO-MM-PL
Items: PB-RM-MM
Year started: 1928
#R 16; #A 495; #T 10M; #P 24

Ma'Ayan
Ms Bregman, Book Buyer
P.O. Box 246
Sudbury MA 01776
617-877-5128
Categories: 63-99(Judaica)
WH -- Territory: US
Markets: BK-SC-PL-SL-RO(gift)
         book fairs
Items: HC-TX-PB-RM-MM
Year started: 1975
#R 2; #P 50

Macalester Park Bookstore
Patricia Olsen, Manager
1571 Grand Avenue
Saint Paul MN 55105
612-698-8877
WH

MacGregor News Agency
G Moutsatson, Manager
1733 Industrial Park
Mount Pleasant MI 48858
517-773-3888
Categories: 99
Items: MG-ML
WH magazine subscription agency

MacRae's Indian Book Distributor
Ken MacRae, Owner
P O Box 652
Enumclaw WA 98022
206-825-3737
Categories: 98(American Indian)
PD -- Territory: US
Markets: SC-CO-PL-SL-OT(museums)
Year started: 1965

Magazines Inc.
Ralph Foss, Manager
1135 Hammond Street
Bangor ME 04401
207-942-8237
WH

Magickal Childe
Herman Slatter, Owner
35 West 19th Street
New York NY 10011
212-242-7182
Categories: 53-57
WH -- Territory: US
Markets: BK
Items: HC-PB-RM
Year started: 1968

Main Court Book Fair
Susan Church, Manager
240 Main
White Plains NY 10601
914-428-0330
WH

Main Line Book Company
Paul Schneider, Manager
P. O. Box 914
Bryn Mawr PA 19010
215-353-5166
WH

Main Street News & Bookstore
Hal Levine, Manager
255 Royal Poinciana Way
P. O. Box 788
Palm Beach FL 33480
305-833-4027
WH

Maine Writers & Publishers
P O Box 7542
Portland ME 04112
207-774-8451
Categories: 61(ME)-83
              99(small press)
WH -- Territory: US
Markets: BK-PL
Items: HC-PB-ML
#T 500; #P 100

Mangelsen's
Attn: Book Buyer
P O Box 3314
Omaha NE 68103
402-339-3922; 800-642-9040
Categories: 11-29
WH -- Territory: US
Markets: RO(craft stores)
Items: HC-PB-OT(craft supplies)

Manson News
Attn: Book Buyer
634 South Avenue
P O Box 1211
Rochester NY 14620
716-244-3880
Categories: 99
WH -- Territory: NY
Markets: NS-SC-CO-RO(drug, food)
         OT(business, industry)
Items: PB-RM-MM-MG-CA-CO
       ML-MA-PO-NW-SB
#R 6

Many Feathers Southwestern Books
Diane M Fessler, Owner
5738 N Central
Phoenix AZ 85012
602-266-1043
Categories: 99-61(AZ & Southwest)
WH -- Territory: AZ
Markets: BK-SC-CO-PL-SL-RO(gift)
Items: HC-TX-PB-MA
Year started: 1947
#R 2; #A 400; #T 1000; #P 100

Marco Company
M Penn, Owner
739 E New York Avenue
P. O. Box 108
Brooklyn NY 11203
718-773-0005
WH

Marshall-Mangold Distributors
Marsha Goldberg, Book Buyer
4805 Nelson Avenue
Baltimore MD 21215
301-542-7214
Categories: 19-21-31-43-33-75
WH -- Territory: MD-DC-VA
Markets: BK-MM(supermarkets,
         drugstores)
Items: PB-MM-CO-MA-RC
Year started: 1947
#R 2; #A 300; #P 12

Marston's
Martha Marston, Owner
483 Main Street
P.O. Box 789
Presque Isle ME 04769
207-764-6761
WH

Matagiri Sri Aurobindo Center
Julian Lines, Manager
P O Box 372
Highfalls NY 12440
914-687-9222
Categories: 10-63-95
DN -- Territory: US-CN
Markets: BK-SC-PL-SL
         RO(Oriental, occult)
Items: HC-PB-OT(incense)
Year started: 1971
#A 1000; #T 400; #P 4

Matthews Medical Books
John Marcus, Owner
11559 Rock Island
Saint Louis MO 63043
314-432-1400
Categories: 39
WH -- Territory: MO
Markets: BK-CO-PL-SL
Items: HC-PB
Year started: 1889
#R 1; #T 16M; #P all

Maxwell Scientific International
Fairview Park
Elmsford NY 10523
914-592-7700
Categories: 39-59-67
WH -- Territory: US
Markets: SC-CO-PL-SL
Year started: 1948

McAinsh & Company
J M Rogers, Manager
2760 Old Leslie Street
Willowdale M2K 2X5 ON Canada
416-499-2500

Categories: 39-67
DN -- Territory: CN
Markets: BK-CO-SL-hospitals, MDs
Items: MG - subscription agency
Year started: 1885
#R 2; #T 10M; #P 12

McCoy Church Goods Company
Casimir J Norton, President
2432 Mission Avenue
Carmichael CA 95608
916-481-8770

Meader Book Distributing
1686 Gervais Avenue
Saint Paul MN 55109
612-777-8343
WH

Medical & Technical Books
Frederick Ruby, V.P.
11511 Tennesee Avenue
Los Angeles CA 90064
213-879-1607; 800-421-7149
Categories: 23-39-59-67
WH -- Territory: US
Markets: BK-CO
Items: HC-TX-PB
Year started: 1968
#R 1

Melton Book Company
Morris Melton, President
111 Leslie Street
Dallas TX 75207
214-748-0564
WH

Menasha Ridge Press
Holland Wallace, Marketing
Route 3, Box 450
Hillsborough NC 27278
919-732-6661
Categories: 15-51-71
PD -- Territory: US

Mercedes Book Distributors
Joel Goldstein, President
62 Imlay Street
Brooklyn NY 11231
718-522-7110
Categories: 99
WH -- Territory: US
Markets: BK-CO-SC-PL-SL
Items: HC-TX-PB-RM
#R 3

Merchandise Dynamics
Joanna Sztabaluk, Manager
184 Fifth Avenue
New York NY 10010
212-929-0090
WH

Merle Distributing Company
Kevin Lentz, Book Buyer
Joyce Clisch, Juvenile Buyer
27222 Plymouth Road
Detroit MI 48239
313-937-8400; 800-233-9380
Categories: 21-31-76-89-99
WH -- Territory: MI
Markets: BK-SC-CO-MM-PL
Items: HC-PB-MM-CA-CO-MA
        PO-ST-SB-TA-TV
Year started: 1962
#A 1000; #T 25M; #P 150

Merry Thoughts
L Kahn, President
380 Adams
Bedford Hills NY 10507-0002
914-241-0447
WH

Metro Toronto News Company
120 Sinnott Road
Scarborough M1L 4N1   ON Canada
416-752-8720
Categories: 21-31-76-99
WH -- Territory: CN
Markets: BK-SC-CO-PL
Items: HC-TX-PB-MG-NP
#T 23M

Michiana News Service
Tad Majerek, Book Buyer
3926 Mobile Avenue
Fort Wayne IN 46805
219-484-0571
Categories: 99
WH -- Territory: IN-MI
Markets: BK-NS-SC-CO-MM-PL-SL
Items: HC-PB-RM-MM-MG-CA
        CO-ML-MA-NW-TA
Year started: 1956
#R 6; #A 500; #T 2000; #P most
formerly Summit News Agency

Michiana News Service
Jeff Majerek, Book Buyer
2232 S 11th Street
Niles MI 49120
616-684-3013
Categories: 99
WH -- Territory: US
Markets: BK-SC-CO-MM-PL
Items: HC-PB-RM-MM-MG-CA-CO
Year started: 1955
#R 10; #A 1300; #T 20M

Michigan Church Supply Company
Leo F Flynn, President
P. O. Box 23
Mount Morris MI 48458-0023
313-686-8877
WH

Mid-Pacific Book Distributors
John F Kooistra, President
150 Haili Street
Hilo HI 96720
808-935-5622
Categories: 99
DN -- Territory: US- HI
Markets: RO-SC-CO-PL-SL
Items: HC-TX-PB-RM-MM-MA-PO-SB-AT
Year started: 1975

Mid-Penn Magazine Agency
Allen Deemel, President
100 Eck Circle
Williamsport PA 17701
717-323-8471
WH

Mid-Western News Agency
Bob Palmer, Book Buyer
334 Portage Avenue
Saskatoon S7K 3J4   SK Canada
306-934-4414
Categories: 99
WH -- Territory: CN(Sasketchewan)
Markets: BK-JB-NS-SC-CO
          MM-PL-SL-RO
Items: PB-MM-CA-CO-MA
Year started: 1930
#A 750; #T 7000; #P 150

Middletown News Agency
B C Annenberg, Book Buyer
1223 Hook Drive
P. O. Box B
Middletown OH 45042
513-422-7876
Categories: 99
WH -- Territory: OH
Markets: BK-NS-SC-CO-MM-PL
Items: HC-PB-MM-MG-CA-CO-MA-NW
Year started: 1942
#R 4; #A 120; #T 2000

Midtown Auto Books
M Ray, Owner
212 Burnet Avenue
Syracuse NY 13203
315-476-9421
Categories: 43(automobiles)
WH

Midwest European Publications
Jery Root, Buyer
915 Foster Street
Evanston IL 60201-3199
312-866-6262
Categories: 45(SP-IT-FR-GR)-99
WH -- Territory: US
Markets: BK-CO-SC-PL
Items: HC-PB
Year started: 1971
#R 2

===

#R = # of representatives   #A = # of accounts   #T = # of titles   #P = # of publishers

----

Midwest Library Service
Evelyn Smith, Book Buyer
11443 St Charles Rock Road
Bridgeton MO 63044-9986
314-739-3100
Categories: 23-39-59-65-67
WH -- Territory: Midwest
Markets: CO-PL-SL
Items: HC-TX-PB-MM
Year started: 1959
#R 6; #T 75M; #P all

Midwest Natural Foods
David Davis, Manager
170 April Drive
Ann Arbor MI 48103
313-769-8444
Categories: 27-39-53-69
WH -- Territory: MI
Markets: BK-RO(natural food)
Items: HC-PB-MM-MG-NP
Year started: 1972
#R 4

Miller Harness Company
Michael Diamond, Manager
235 Murray Hill Parkway
East Rutherford NJ 07073
201-460-1200
Categories: 15(horses)
          69(horse riding)
WH -- Territory: US
Markets: BK-RO(riding shops)
Items: HC-PB-RM-gifts, supplies
#R 7

Milligan News Company
Jim Barton, Book Buyer
150 N Autumn Street
San Jose CA 95110
408-298-3322
Categories: 99
WH -- Territory: US-CA
Markets: BK-JB-NS-SC-CO-MM
       PL-SL-RO(toy)
Items: HC-PB-RM-MM-MG-CA
       CO-ML-MA-TA-TV
Year started: 1936
#R 23; #A 1200; #T 18M; #P 300

Mississippi Library & Media
John C Conner, Owner
P. O. Box 41-51
Brandon MS 39042
601-939-7571
WH

MLES, Inc
W Johnson, Manager
Lower Village
Gilsum NH 03448
603-357-0236
Categories: 99
WH -- Territory: US
Markets: SC-CO-PL-SL
Items: HC-TX-PH-MM
Year started: 1976
#R 13; #A 1000+; #P all

Mobile News Company
Guy Moman, Owner
3001 Mill Street
Mobile AL 36607
205-479-1435
WH

Modesto News Company
H W Harrison, Manager
1035 Reno Avenue
P. O. Box 5038
Modesto CA 95352
209-577-5551
WH

Monahan Agencies Ltd
Tom J Monahan, Owner
2506 - 41st Street
Vernon V1T 6J9 BC Canada
604-545-3235
WH

Montgomery News Company
Nancy S Johnson, Manager
874 Martha Street
Montgomery AL 36102
205-262-6681
WH

Mook & Blanchard
Jerry J Mook, Book Buyer
546 S Hofgaarden
P O Box 1295
La Puente CA 91749-1295
818-968-6424
Categories: 21-31-76-89
WH -- Territory: US
Markets: SC-PL
Items: HC-OT(prebound)-SW
Year started: 1970
#R 6; #A 1000; #T 15M; #P all

Moshy Brothers
M J Moshy, President
127 W 25th Street
New York NY 10001-7207
212-227-6267
WH

Mother Lode Distributing Company
Dick Nelson, Owner
119 E Theall Street
Sonora CA 95370-5798
209-532-4224
WH

Motorbooks International
Rick Seymour, Manager
729 Prospect Avenue
Osceola WI 54020-0002
715-294-3345; 800-826-6600
Categories: 43(automobiles)
          69(aviation)
PD -- Territory: US
Markets: BK-PL-SL
Items: HC-PB
Year started: 1972
#T 8000; #P 30

Moving Books
Frank F Kroger, Owner
1214 10th Avenue
Seattle WA 98122-4210
206-325-9077
Categories: 53-57-63-95
          98(alcholism)
WH -- Territory: US
Markets: BK-PL-RO(health,
       self-help)
Items: PB-RM-MM-CA-GC-PO-RC-TA-TV
Year started: 1979
#R 1/2; #A 200; #T 2000; #P 100
formerly Holistic Health Center

Moza Publications
Jeris E Strain, Director
5010 Austin Road
Chattanooga TN 37443
615-875-5443
WH

Mumford Library Book Sales
Sue Mumford, V.P.
Route 2, Box 135
Plano TX 75074
214-422-7083
WH

Mumford Library Book Sales
Douglas McNamara, V.P.
7847 Bayberry Road
Jacksonville FL 32216
904-737-2649
WH

Murr's Library Service
Jane Murr, Owner
6512 E Jean Drive
Scottsdale AZ 85254
602-948-2425
Categories: 99
WH -- Territory: Southwest
Markets: SC-PL-SL
Items: RM-OT(library bound)
Year started: 1981
#R 5; #A 467; #T 30M; #P 15

Musicart West
J Jackman, Book Buyer
1815 S State Street
P. O. Box 1900
Orem UT 84057
801-225-0859
Categories: 11-19-98(music antho-
          logies & sheet music)
DN -- Territory: US
Markets: BK-RO(music stores)
Items: HC-TX-PB-RC-TA
Year started: 1975
#R 3; #A 2700; #T 1500; #P 110

Muskoka Educational Supply
William Curell, President
11 Manitoba Street
Bracebridge P0B 1C4 ON Canada
705-645-6515
WH

Book Wholesalers and Distributors

Najarian Music Company
Robert Najarian, V.P.
269 Lexington Street
Waltham MA 02154
617-899-2200
Categories: 11(music only)
WH -- Territory: New England
Markets: RO(music)
Items: PB-MM
Year started: 1980
#R 0; #A 300; #T 1MM; #P 250

NASCORP Inc
Gary Swisher, Manager
  Book Merchandising
Susan Hiesser, Buyer
  Mass Market Books
Marybeth Albert and Susan Mason
  Trade Books
528 E Lorain Street
Oberlin OH 44074-1238
216-775-7777; 800-321-3883
Categories: 99
WH -- Territory: US
Markets: BK-CO
Items: HC-PB-MM-CA
Year started: 1960
#T 25M; #P 165

National Association of Deaf
Barbara Olmert, Manager
Book Distribution
814 Thayer Avenue
Silver Spring MD 20910
301-587-6282
WH

National Book Centre
Joanne Marler, Book Buyer
66 Northline Road
Toronto M4B 3E6   ON Canada
416-751-3530
Categories: 99
WH -- Territory: CN
Markets: CO-SC-PL-SL
Items: HC-TX-PB
Year started: 1954
#R 4

National Book Distributors
Mark Neddy, Manager
1055 West Maple Road
Clawson MI 48017
313-435-3100
Categories: 99(promotional)
WH -- Territory: Midwest
Markets: BK-MM(chain stores)
Items: HC-PB-MM-RM
Year started: 1976
#R 150

National Book Distributors
Samuel Yudkin, Manager
1125 King Street
Alexandria VA 22314-2993
703-549-9330
Categories: 99
WH -- Territory: East Coast
Markets: BK
Items: HC-PB-RM
Year started: 1954
#R 1

National Catholic Reading Dists
John P Twomey, Manager
545 Island Road
Ramsey NJ 07446
201-825-7300
WH

National Learning Corporation
M Peters, Manager
212 Michael Drive
Syosset NY 11791
516-921-8888
Categories: 31-55
WH -- Territory: US
Markets: SC-PL-OT(business,
              government)
Items: HC-PB
Year started: 1967
#T 5400

National Library Resources Ltd
P J Boyle, Manager
530 McNicoll Avenue
Willowdale M2H 2E1   ON Canada
416-499-5166
WH

National Magazine Service
Holly Jones, Manager
535 Linden Way
P. O. Box 4200
Pittsburgh PA 15202
412-766-7734
Categories: 99
Items: MG
WH - magazine subscription agency

Naturegraph Publishers
Barbara Brown
3543 Indian Creek Road
P O Box 1075
Happy Camp CA 96039
916-493-5353
Categories: 15-27-29-39-43
              49(American Indian)
              51-61(Western)-71
PD -- Territory: US
Year started: 1946

Nebraska Book Company
George Culwell, Manager
6400 Cornhusker Highway
P. O. Box 80529
Lincoln NE 68501
402-464-9161
Categories: 99
WH -- Territory: NE
Items: HC-PB-MM

Negev Importing Company
Morty Kaplan, Buyer
3509 Bathurst Street
Toronto M6A 2C5   ON Canada
416-781-9356
Categories: 63-99(Israel, Jewish)
DN -- Territory: CN
Markets: BK-SC-CO-MM-PL-SL
Items: HC-TX-PB-RM-MM-ML
            NP-CA-CO-TA-TV
Year started: 1963
#R 0; #A 500; #T 10M; #P 50

Ner Tamid Book Distributors
Herbert Wilkenfeld, Owner
P. O. Box 10401
Riviera Beach FL 33404
305-686-9095
Categories: 10-75-90-98(Judaica)
WH -- Territory: US-CN-IT
Markets: RO(Judaica gifts)
            SC-CO-PL-SL
Items: HC-TX-PB-RM-MM-SW-TA-TV
Year started: 1968
#R 0; #A 13000

New England Book Service
Gayle Lane, Manager
Church Hill
Charlotte VT 05445
802-425-2461
Categories: 23-67-99
WH -- Territory: New England
Markets: CO-PL-SL
Items: HC-PB
Year started: 1959
#R 2

New England Mobile Book Fair
Stephen Cleary
82 Needham Street
P O Box 340
Newton MA 02161
617-527-5817; 800-225-4264
Categories: 99
WH -- Territory: New England
Markets: BK-SC-CO-PL-SL
Items: HC-PB-RM-MM-CA-MA-TA-TV
Year started: 1958
#R 2; #A 800; #T 200M; #P 400+

==

```
Items:   HC = Hardcover    TX = Textbooks     RM = Remainders    MG = Magazines, General
         PB = Softcover    MM = Mass-Markets  NP = Newspapers    ML = Magazines, Literary
         CA = Calendars    CO = Comics    GC = Greeting Cards    PO = Posters    TA = Tapes, Audio
         SW = Software     GI = Gifts     MA = Maps & Atlases    RC = Records    TV = Tapes, Video
         ST = Stationery   SB = Stickers/Bookmarks   OT = Other items (games, toys, etc.)
```

New Era Press
Joseph Altmann, Director
P O Box 29
Farmingdale NY 11735
516-277-9708
Categories: 39-53
PD -- Territory: US
Markets: BK-PL
Items: HC-PB
Year started: 1983

New Era Publications
Donna Barancewicz, Manager
221 Felch Street #2
P O Box 8139
Ann Arbor MI 48107
313-663-1929
Categories: 63(Islam and
          Middle East)-99
DE -- Territory: US-CN-IT
Markets: OT(direct order)
Items: HC-TX-PB-RM-MG-CA
       GI-ML-MA-PO-TA
Year started: 1980
#R 5; #A 150; #T 1680; #P 50

New Jersey Book Agency
Linton Segal, Owner
59 Leamoor Drive
P. O. Box 144
Morris Plains NJ 07950
201-267-7093
Categories: 19-23-39-59-67
WH -- Territory: US-IT
Markets: BK-SL
Year started: 1979
#R 0; #A 100; #T 0; #P 0
no stock--special orders only

New Jersey Books
Terry Flynn, Manager
59 Market Street
Newark NJ 07102
201-624-7987
WH

New Jersey State News
Arnold Lyner, Book Buyer
Canal Drive & Delihla
Pleasantville NJ 08232
609-646-4165
WH

New Leaf Distributing
Halin Provo-Thompson, Buyer
  Major Publishers
Judith Hawkins, Buyer
  Metaphysical Books
Ann Crutcher, Health Books

1020 White Street SW
Atlanta GA 30310
404-755-3454; 800-241-3829
Categories: 21-29-39-53-63
WH -- Territory: US
Markets: BK-RO(metaphysics)
         OT(health & church)
Items: HC-PB-MM-MG-CA
       GI-PO-RC-TA-TV
Year started: 1975
#R 0; #A 1400; #T 13M; #P 800+

New Life Foundation
Murray Oxman, Manager
700 Wyoming Street
P. O. Box 684
Boulder City NV 89005-0684
702-293-4444
Categories: 53-57-63(books by
            Vernon Howard only)
PD -- Territory: US-IT
Markets: BK-RO(health food)
         CO-MM-PL
Items: HC-PB-MM-TA-TV-booklets
Year started: 1973
#T 26; #P 4

New London News Company
Albert B Blassenberg, Owner
374 Broad Street
P O Box 711
New London CT 06320
203-442-4394
Categories: 99
WH -- Territory: New England
Items: PB-MM-MG-NP

New York Astrology Center
Henry Weingarten, Owner
63 West 38th Street #505
New York NY 10018
212-719-2919
Categories: 39-53
WH -- Territory: US
Items: HC
Year started: 1968
#T 40

Newark Book Center
Norman B Lehrman, Owner
162 Washington Street
Newark NJ 07102
201-642-7956
Categories: 19-23-59-67
DN -- Territory: US
Markets: SL
Items: HC-TX-PB
Year started: 1959
#R 1; #A 500+; #T 10M+; #P all

Newborn Enterprises
808 Green Avenue
Altoona PA 16603
814-944-3593
WH

Newman Communications Corp.
2700 Broadbent Parkway NE
Albuquerque NM 87107
505-345-1843; 800-545-6260
PD -- Territory: US
Markets: BK-RO-MM
Items: TA audiotapes only

Newsdealers Supply Company
5800 W Main
Dothan AL 36301
205-792-3811
WH

Niagara Publishers
A M Krar, Manager
Church Street & Webber Road
Fenwick L0S 1C0 ON Canada
416-892-5759
WH

Nicholas Hoare Ltd
Graham Courtnell, Buyer
2165 Madison Avenue
Montreal H4B 2T2 PQ Canada
514-489-9341
Categories: 99
WH -- Territory: CN
Markets: BK-CO-SC-PL
Items: HC-TX-PB
Year started: 1971
#R 2

Noll's Educational Books
Matgaret E Noll, Owner
P.O. Box 55
Arthur IA 51431
712-367-2422
WH

Nor-Cal News Company
Robert Erwin, Manager
2040 Petaluma Boulevard
Petaluma CA 94953
707-763-2606
WH

North Carolina News
Clayborne Evans Jr, Manager
1207 Angier Avenue
Durham NC 27701
919-683-2795
WH

==

Markets: BK = Bookstore   SC = Schools   PL = Public Libraries   MM = Mass Markets and Chain Stores
           JB = Jobbers   CO = Colleges   SL = Special Libraries   NS = Newsstands
           RO = Other Retail Outlets   OT = Other (organizations, churches, etc.)

Territories: US = entire United States   CN = Canada   IT = International
              Others indicate parts of United States or abbreviations for states

North Carolina School Book Depot
O W Overton, Manager
811 W Hargett Street
Raleigh NC 27602
919-833-6615
WH

North Country Book Express
Pat Hart, Buyer
112 W 4th Street
P O Box 9223
Moscow ID 83843
208-882-0888
Categories: 27-41-51-61(ID, Rocky
          Mountains)-69-71
WH -- Territory: Northwest
Markets: BK-CO
Items: HC-PB
Year started: 1976
#R 1

North Country Books
Robert Igoe, Owner
18 Irving Place
Utica NY 13501
315-735-4877

North Shore News Company
Mulkern & Gardner, Owners
150 Blossom Street
Lynn MA 01902
617-592-1300
WH

Northern Arizona News Company
Allen McCracker, Manager
1709 N East Street
P. O. Box 1947
Flagstaff AZ 86002
602-774-6171
WH

Northern News Company
Arthur C Foster Sr, Manager
Harbor-Petoskey Road
P. O. Box 543
Petoskey MI 49770
616-347-3936
WH

Nutri-Books
Daniel A Nidess, Book Buyer
790 W Tennessee Avenue
Denver CO 80014
303-778-8383
Categories: 21-27-39-53-57-59
WH -- Territory: US
Markets: RO(health, maternity,
          gyms, pharmacies)
Items: HC-PB-RM-MM-CA
       GC-MG-PO-TA-TV
Year started: 1955
#R 0; #A 8000+; #T 2000; #P 200+

Odyssey Book Company
Alan Shih, Manager
2 Fernwook Road
P. O. Box 4186
Warren NJ 07060
201-668-1593
WH

Odyssey Distributing Company
Mike Smriga, Manager
717 Grant Street #200
Santa Monica CA 90405
213-392-9793
WH

Oklahoma City News Company
Jay Robben, Manager
7000 N Robinson
P. O. Box 25489
Oklahoma City OK 73125
405-843-9383
Categories: 99
WH

Oklahoma School & Office Supply
Budo Perry, Owner
1305 N Main Street
P. O. Box 1549
Muskogee OK 74401
918-683-7746
Categories: 19-21-31-76-99
WH -- Territories: OK
Markets: SC-RO(Office)

Ollis Book Corporation
Kenneth E Ollis, President
28 East 35th Street
Steger IL 60475
312-755-5151
Categories: 21-31-76-89
WH -- Territory: Midwest
Markets: SC-PL
Year started: 1965
#R 10

Omnibooks
Medina & Howe, Owners
456 Vista Del Mar
Aptos CA 95003-4832
408-688-4098
Categories: 99
WH

Orange News Company
Dave Arnold, Book Buyer
3840 Vineland Road
Orlando FL 32811
305-841-8738
Categories: 17-19-21-27-59-75
WH -- Territory: FL
Markets: BK-NS-SC-MM
Items: HC-PB-RM-MM-MG-CO-GC
#R 25; #A 1000; #P most

Orbit Books Corporation
Olga Grilli, Manager
43 Timberline Drive
Poughkeepsie NY 12603
914-462-5653
WH

Original Publications
2486 Webster Avenue
Bronx NY 10458
Categories: 53(occult)
PD -- Territory: US
Items: HC-PB
Year started: 1986

Osiander Book Trade Limited
Ingrid Risop, Manager
35 W 38th Street #3W
New York NY 10018
212-730-0518
Categories: 99
WH -- Territory: IT(W Europe)
Markets: BK-SC-CO-PL-SL
Items: HC-TX-PB-MM-MG
       CA-CO-GC-ML-MA
Year started: 1981
#P all

Ottawa Valley News Company
Ron Grenier, Manager
44 MacDonald Street N
P. O. Box 157
Arnprior K7S 3H4   ON Canada
613-623-3197
WH

Ozark News Agency
Marshall & Kroeger, Owners
397 W Poplar
P. O. Box 1150
Fayetteville AR 72701
501-442-6441
WH

Pacific Northwest Agencies
John A Lewis-Kingsley, Owner
1437 - 129A Street
Ocean Park V4H 3Y8   BC Canada
604-531-0129
Categories: 99
WH -- Territory: Western CN
Markets: BK
Items: HC-PB
#R 8; #P 7

Pacific Periodical Services
G Scranton and D Kruse, Buyers
4630 - 95th Street SW
P O Box 98907
Tacoma WA 98499
206-581-1940
Categories: 99
WH -- Territory: WA

===

    #R = # of representatives   #A = # of accounts   #T = # of titles   #P = # of publishers

----

Markets: BK-SC-PL
Items: HC-PB-MM-RM-MG-NP-SW
Year started: 1980
#R 13

Pacific Pipeline
Roberta Dyer, Calendar Buyer
Michael Brasky, Senior Buyer
Valorie Tutt, Mass Market Buyer
Pennie Clark, Small Press Buyer
19215 - 66th Avenue S
Kent WA 98032
206-872-5523; 800-521-0714
Categories: 61(Northwest)
            99(small press)
WH -- Territory: Northwest US
Markets: BK-SC-CO-PL
         RO(department store)
Items: CA
Year started: 1974
#R 1; #T 12M+; #P all

Pacific Trade Group
Richard E Pultz, President
P O Box 1227
Kailua HI 96734
808-671-6735
Categories: 21-27-41-61(HI)
            69-71-99
DN -- Territory: HI
Markets: BK-NS-SC-CO-MM
         PL-SL-RO(gift)
Items: HC-PB-RM-CA-GC-MA-PO-SB-TV
Year started: 1977
#R 8; #A 1500; #T 2000; #P 200

Palmetto News Company
Robert Alexander, Manager
307 Fall Street
Greenville SC 29601
803-232-8751
WH

Palo Alto Book Service
Hessen & Austin, Managers
200 California Avenue
Palo Alto CA 94306
415-327-7781
WH

Pannonia Books
P O Box 1017
Postal Station B
Toronto M5T 2T8 ON Canada
Categories: 45(European)-99
WH -- Territory: CN

Paperback Books
Harvey D Eluto, President
4617 N Witchduck Road
Virginia Beach VA 23455
804-480-1211
Categories: 21-31-59-76
WH -- Territory: mid-Atlantic
Markets: SC
Items: HC-PB-MM
Year started: 1974
#R 2

Paperback Sales
425 N Michagan Avenue #760
Chicago IL 60611
312-943-6300

Paperback Supply
Gerry Flavin, Buyer
Jim Mathews, Regional Book Buyer
4121 Forest Park
Saint Louis MO 63108
314-652-1000; 800-325-8404
Categories: 21-31-61(MO)-76-99
WH -- Territory: Midwest
Markets: BK-CO-SC-PL
Items: HC-PB-MM-OT(study aids)
Year started: 1974
#R 1; #T 12M

Paperbacks for Educators
Dave Craig, President
Route 2, Box 80
1240 Ridge Road
Ballwin MO 63021
314-027-2590
Categories: 19(careers)-21-31-35
            57-98(counseling,
            human development)
DN -- Territory: US
Markets: SC-CO-PL-SL
Items: HC-TX-PB-MM-SW
Year started: 1978
#R 0; #A 20000; #T 2400; #P 128

Para Research
Frank Molinski, Trade Buyer
Carol R Coles, Paperback Buyer
Emily McKeigue, Text Buyer
85 Eastern Avenue
Gloucester MA 01930
617-283-3438
Categories: 39-53-57
PD -- Territory: US
Markets: BK-CO-PL
Items: HC
Year started: 1972
#A 50,000; #T 100; #P

Paris Paperbacks French Books
L Plauzoles, President
2306 Westwood Boulevard
Los Angeles CA 90064-2186
213-475-0095
WH

Parliament News Company
Tony Stoor, Marketing Director
12011 Sherman Road
North Hollywood CA 91605
818-982-4000
WH

Patrice Press
P O Box 42
Gerald MO 63037
314-764-2801
Categories: 41
PD -- Territory: US
Markets: BK-PL

Pekin News Agency
Maurice B Smith, Owner
522 Court Street
Pekin IL 61554
309-347-2560
WH

Pen Notes
Lorette Konezny, Manager
134 Westside Avenue
Freeport NY 11520
516-868-5753
Categories: 11-21-29-31
PD -- Territory: US-CN-IT(Europe)
Markets: BK-SC-CO-MM-PL
         OT(child care)
Items: HC-OT(calligraphy)
Year started: 1979
#R 50; #A 2000; #T 5; #P 1

Periodical Services
Ernest T Bronsveld, Owner
P. O. Box 367
Stockton NJ 08559
201-782-2969
WH

Perry Enterprises
Coni Brownlow, Book Buyer
1403 Iron Spring Road
Prescott AZ 86301
602-445-5673
Categories: 15-21-27-29-31-35
            39-41-45-71-73
PD -- Territory: US-CN(limited)
Markets: BK-JB
Items: HC-PB-MM
Year started: 1980
#R 3; #A 600; #T 350

Personal Goals
Bob Love, Manager
3721 W Main Street
P O Box 135
Rapid City SD 57709
605-348-3722
Categories: 19(financial
            planning)-31-35-39-57
DN -- Territory: SD
Markets: BK-PL-RO(office supply)
Items: TA-TV
Year started: 1982
#R 3; #A 500; #T 1000; #P 2

Peterborough Distribution
Raymond G Cote, Manager
837 Greenfield Road
Peterborough NH 03458-0458
603-547-8855
WH

Peton Corp
Donald Peterson, Owner
50 S Main
P. O. Box 11925
Salt Lake City UT 84147
801-363-1399
WH

Book Wholesalers and Distributors

Plough Publishing House
Martin Johnson, Manager
Hutterian Brethren, Route 213
Rifton NY 12471
914-658-3141
Categories: 31-35-63-98(community
             life, Christian)
PD -- Territory: US-CN
Markets: BK-JB-SC-CO-PL-SL
Items: HC-PB-CA-RC
Year started: 1938
#R 0; #A 0; #T 100; #P 6

PMG International
Tom Brown, President
1104 Summit Avenue #100B
Plano TX 75074
214-423-0312
Categories: 99
DE -- Territory: US
Markets: BK-PL

Polybook Distributors
Joshua H Makanoff, Owner
30 S 6th Avenue
P. O. Box 109
Mount Vernon NY 10550
914-664-1935
Categories: 98(book reviews)-99
WH -- Territory: US
Markets: BK-SC-CO-MM-PL-SL
Items: HC-PB-MM-CA-MA-SB-TA-TV
Year started: 1966
#R 2; #A 500; #T 20M+; #P 100

Pomona Valley News Agency
Jay Bogg, Manager
10736 Fremont Avenue
Ontario CA 91762
714-591-3885
WH

Pop-M Company
Paul Gross, President
65 Richards Road
Ivyland PA 18975
215-364-1373
WH

Portland News Company
270 Western Avenue
P.O. Box 1728
South Portland ME 04104
207-774-2633

Potter Library Services
A & G Potter, Owners
223 S 60th Street
Milwaukee WI 53214
414-453-2984
WH

Pottstown News Company
557 W High Street
Pottstown PA 19464
215-326-2450
WH

Prairie News Agency
Nancy Singham, Buyer
2404 W Hirsch
Chicago IL 60622
312-384-5350; 800-621-1605
Categories: 23-75-83-99
WH -- Territory: US
Markets: BK-SC-CO-RO(computer)
Items: MG-ML-NP
Year started: 1980
#R 1

Printed Matter
Susan Wheeler, Director
7 Lispenard Street
New York NY 10013
212-925-0325
Categories: 11
WH -- Territory: US-IT
Markets: BK-CO-SC-PL
Items: BK-PB
Year started: 1976
#R 1; #T 2000; #P 20

Professional Book Distributors
James E Dockter, President
200 Hembree Park Drive
Roswell GA 30076
614-442-8633
Categories: 10
DE -- Territory: US-CN-IT
Markets: OT(individual orders)
Items: HC-TX-PB-OT(anything)
Year started: 1976
#R 3; #A 25; #T 1500; #P 20

Progress Books
71 Bathurst Street, 3rd Floor
Toronto M5V 2P6 ON Canada
416-368-5336
WH

Prometheus Books
700 E Amherst Street
Buffalo NY 14215
716-837-2475
WH

Provincial News Company
Bill Hall, Manager
14436 - 121 A Avenue
P. O. Box 2378
Edmonton T5J 2R8 AB Canada
403-454-0306
WH

Publisher's Group
Emil N Spehar, Director
50 Mungertown Road
Madison CT 06443
203-245-0748
Categories: 10
DE -- Territory: New England
Markets: SC-PL
Items: HC-PB-RM
Year started: 1982
#R 6; #T 500; #P 10

Publisher's Group West
Charlie Winton, Buyer
5855 Beaudry Street
Emeryville CA 94608
415-658-3453
Categories: 10
DE -- Territory: US
Markets: BK-JB-SC-CO-PL-SL
Items: HC-PB-MM
Year started: 1976
#R 17; #A 5300; #T 1500; #P 250

Publishers Media
Harry Neuman, Owner
5507 Morella Avenue
North Hollywood CA 91607
818-760-0700
Categories: 10-45-59-83-90
WH -- Territory: US
Markets: SC-CO-PL-SL
Items: HC-PB-MM-MA
Year started: 1974
#R 3; #A 1200; #T 2000; #P 300

Puski-Corvin Hungarian Books
251 East 82nd Street
New York NY 10028
Categories: 45(Hungarian)-80-99
WH -- Territory: US

Quality Books
Tom Drewes, President
918 Sherwood Drive
Lake Bluff IL 60044-2204
312-498-4000
Categories: 10
WH -- Territory: US
Markets: PL-SL
Items: HC-TX-PB-RM
Year started: 1964
#R 21; #P many smaller presses
non-fiction only

Quebec Livres
Paul Decoste, Manager
4435 des Grandes Prairies
Quebec H1R 3N4 PQ Canada
514-327-6900
WH

===

Markets: BK = Bookstore   SC = Schools   PL = Public Libraries   MM = Mass Markets and Chain Stores
          JB = Jobbers   CO = Colleges   SL = Special Libraries   NS = Newsstands
          RO = Other Retail Outlets   OT = Other (organizations, churches, etc.)

Quiltworks
2920 N Second Street
Minneapolis MN 55411
612-588-5345; 800-328-8414
Categories: 29(quilting)
WH -- Territory: US
Markets: RO(craft stores)
Items: HC-PB-OT(craft supplies)

R & A Book Distributors
Mark Binstoek, Manager
P. O. Box 1266
Canoga Park CA 91304
818-992-1301
WH

R G Mitchell Family Books
Bob Wood, Manager
565 Gordon Baker Road
Willowdale M2H 2W2 ON Canada
416-499-4615
WH

Raincoast Book Distributors
Tom Best, Director
112 East 3rd Avenue
Vancouver V5T 1C8 BC Canada
604-873-6581
Categories: 99
DN -- Territory: CN
Markets: BK-PL
Items: HC-PB
Year started: 1980
#R 13

Rainier News Company
Linda S Tonning, Book Buyer
1122 - 80th Street SW
Everett WA 98203
206-355-5350
Categories: 99
WH -- Territory: WA
Markets: BK-NS-SC-CO-MM-PL-SL
Items: HC-PB-RM-MM-MG-CA
        CO-ML-MA-TA-TV
Year started: 1952
#R 18; #A 350; #T M's; #P 50+

Randall Book Company
Doyle Mortimer, President
9500 South 500 West, #103
Sandy UT 84070
801-562-5481; 800-453-1356
Categories: 17-19-21-27-29-31-33
            35-39-61-63-69-73-76
            77-81-85-88-89
PD -- Territory: Rocky Mountain
Markets: BK-RO(office supply,
        children)-PL
Items: HC-PB-RM-GI-SB-TA-TV
Year started: 1979
#R 4; #A 700; #T 100; #P 5

Read News Agency
1110 14th Street
Tuscaloosa AL 35403
205-752-3515
WH

Reading Peddler Book Fairs
Sharon Hearn, Manager
10580 3/4 W Pico Boulevard
Los Angeles CA 90064
213-559-2665
Categories: 21-31-76-89
WH -- Territory: Los Angeles CA
Markets: SC
Items: HC-PB-RM-MM-CA
        GC-MA-RC-SB-TA
Year started: 1979
#R 2; #A 60; #T 2000; #P 70

Redwing Book Company
Martha Fielding, President
44 Linden Street
Brookline MA 02146
617-738-4664
WH

Regal Books
William T Greig, President
2300 Knoll Drive
P O Box 3875
Ventura CA 93003
805-644-6869
Categories: 63-99
PD -- Territory: US

Regent Book Company
Morton & Doris Levin, Managers
101 A Route 46
Saddlebrook NJ 07662
201-368-2208
Categories: 21-31-43-45-76
WH -- Territory: US
Markets: BK-SC-PL
Items: HC-PB-RM-TA
Year started: 1938
#R 1; #T 100M

Reid Michener Company
Reid Michener, Owner
5321 S Kimbark
Chicago IL 60615
312-493-6872
WH

Reprint Distribution
Robert G Davis, Manager
P O Box 249
Kent CT 06757
203-927-3938
Categories: 99
WH -- Territory:
Markets: SC-CO-PL
Items: HC-reprints
Year started: 1971
#R 15

Research Books
John F Vance, President
1200 Boston Post Road
P O Box 573
Guilford CT 06437
203-453-5117
Categories: 19-23-59-67
WH -- Territory: East Coast

Markets: SL
Items: HC-PB
Year started: 1963
#R 1

Research Books
John Vance, President
38 Academy Street
Madison CT 06443
Categories: 19-23-65-67
WH -- Territory: US
Markets: PL-SL
Items: HC-TX-PB
Year started: 1963
international publishers

Richard Maher Sales
Larry White, Manager
P. O. Box 531
Salt Lake City UT 84054
801-298-7506
WH

Richardson's Educators
John Richardson, General Buyer
2014 Lou Ellen Lane
Houston TX 77018
713-688-2242; 800-231-0568
Categories: 61(TX)-99
WH -- Territory: US
Markets: BK-SC-PL-RO(specialty)
Items: HC-PB
Year started: 1968
#R 1; #T 24M; #P all

Rio Grande Book Company
Vinson McLeod, Manager
1101 Upas Avenue
McAllen TX 78501
512-682-7531
WH

Rittenhouse Book Distributors
Timothy Foster, Manager
511 Feheley Drive
King of Prussia PA 19406
215-277-1414
Categories: 39-59
WH -- Territory: US-CN-IT
Markets: BK-JB-RO(medical,
        professional, government)
Items: HC-TX
Year started: 1946
#R 6; #T 17M; #P 80
medical jobber

Ritter Book Company
Amamae Henderson, Manager
111 N Wabash Avenue
Chicago IL 60602
312-236-7960
WH

Riverside Book & Bible House
Alan Fitz, Manager
1500 Riverside Drive
P O Box 370
Iowa Falls IA 50126-9989

515-648-4269; 800-247-5111
Categories: 63-99
WH -- Territory: US
Markets: BK-RO(churches)
Items: HC-PB-MM-RM
Year started: 1962
#R 32

Roadrunner Library Service
L & A Kerbs, Owners
1221 E Washington
Phoenix AZ 85034-1101
602-252-8897
WH

Roanoke News Agency
Grant Spaulding, Manager
1714 - 9th Street SE
Roanoke VA 24013
703-345-4977
WH

Rochester News Agency
Richard Nelson, Manager
421 First Avenue NW
Rochester MN 55091
507-282-8641
Categories: 99
WH -- Territory: MN-IA
Markets: BK-CO-SC-PL
Items: PB-MM-MG-NP
#R 2

Rockbottom Learning Express
Jill Abdo, Owner
P. O. Box 36036
Minneapolis MN 55435
612-944-5522
WH

Roig Spanish Books
Vincent A Mahiques Sr, Manager
29 West 19th Street
New York NY 10011
212-675-1047
WH

Rose-Zell Books
Estelle and Bruce von Zellen
136 Illehamwood
DeKalb IL 60115
815-756-2801
Categories: 21-31-76-89
WH -- book fairs
Markets: SC-PL
Items: HC-PB-MM

Roy Derstine Book Company
Roy Derstine, Owner
14 Birch Road
Kinnelon NJ 07405
201-838-1109
Categories: 10-86-90
WH -- Territory: NJ-NY-PA
Markets: SC-PL
Items: HC-RM
Year started: 1965
#R 2; #A 1500; #T 1000; #P vary

Royce Wholesale Distributors
302 Old Mill Lane
Exton PA 19341
215-363-5550; 800-232-5550
Categories: 11-29
WH -- Territory: US
Markets: RO(craft stores)
Items: HC-PB-OT(craft supplies)

Rushmore News
Michael Freese, Manager
924 E Saint Andrew Street
Rapid City SD 57701
605-342-2617
Categories: 99
WH -- Territory: SD-WY
Markets: BK-NS-SC-MM
Items: HC-PB-RM-MM-MG-CA-CO-TA
Year started: 1956
#A 305

Rutland News Company
Ronald P Fletcher, Manager
207 N Main Street
P. O. Box 579
Rutland VT 05701
801-773-2920
WH

S & L Sales Company
Rickey L Perritt, Manager
Industrial Boulevard
P. O. Box 2067
Waycross GA 31501
912 283-0252
Categories: 99
WH -- Territory: US
Markets: BK-NS-SC-CO-MM
Items: PB-RM-MM-CO-MA-PO-SB-TA
Year started: 1965
#R 5; #A 350; #T 10M; #P 150+

S Goldman - Otzar Hasefarim
Jack Goldman, President
33 Canal Street
New York NY 10002
212-674-1707
WH

Saint John News Company
Leslie Armstrong, President
P. O. Box 2148, Station C
Saint John E2L 3T5 NB Canada
506-672-2064
WH

Saks News
W E Schmitke, V.P.
2210 E Broadway
P. O. Box 1857
Bismark ND 58502
701-223-0818
WH

Samson International Book Distr.
Richard Gray, Manager
1004 Grand Boulevard
Deer Park NY 11729

516-595-2235
Categories: 47-65-67
WH -- Territory: US
Markets: CO-SL
Items: HC-PB
Year started: 1980
#R 3

Samuel Weiser Inc
97 Raydon Road
P O Box 612
York Beach ME 03910
207-363-4393
Categories: 53-63
PD -- Territory: US
Markets: BK-PL-SL-RO
Items: HC-PB-MM-CA-GI
       PO-TA-OT(games)
Year started: 1955
#T 2000; #P 250

San Diego Museum of Art
David W Hewitt, Manager
P O Box 2107
San Diego CA 92112
619-232-7931
Categories: 11
WH
Items: HC-PB

Sandpiper Book Service
Wellington B Hay Jr, Owner
39 Danbury Road
Wilton CT 06897
203-762-5400
WH

Saunders Books
John Saunders, Manager
199 Campbell Street
P. O. Box 308
Collingwood L9Y 3Z ON Canada
705-445-4777
WH

Schnell's Book Service
Lynn & Mary Merle, Owners
529 Maurice River Boulevard
Vineland NJ 08360-2698
609-692-8078
WH

Schoenhofs Foreign Books
David Leyenson, Manager
76 A Mount Auburn Street
Cambridge MA 021138
617-547-8855
Categories: 45(European)-59
WH -- Territory: US
Year started: 1856
#T 50M from foreign publishers

Scholar's Choice Ltd
L E DeBoer, President
P. O. Box 4214
Stratford N5W 5W3 ON Canada
519-453-7470
WH

Book Wholesalers and Distributors

Scholarly Book Center
Robert Mastejulia, Manager
3828 Hawthorn Court
Waukegan IL 60087
312-249-3180; 800-323-9382
Categories: 65-99
WH -- Territory: US
Markets: CO-PL-SL
Items: HC-TX-PB
Year started: 1975
#R 3; #T 8000

Scholium International
Author L Candido, Book Buyer
265 Great Neck Road
Great Neck NY 11021
516-466-5181
Categories: 19-23-27-39-51-59-67
PD -- Territory: US-CN
Markets: BK-JB-SC-CO-PL-SL
Items: HC-TX
Year started: 1973
#R 3; #T 1500; #P 7

School Aid Company
Lisa Long, Manager
911 Colfax
Danville IL 61832
217-442-6854
WH

School Book Fairs Ltd
Ronald I Grant, Manager
2201 Dunwin Drive
Mississauga L5L 1A ON Canada
416-828-6620
WH

School Book Service
John Kuehne, Manager
2030 SW 71st Terrace C-9
Davie FL 33317
305-472-0824
WH

School Products Company
1201 Broadway
New York NY 10001
212-679-3516
Categories: 29
DE -- Territory: US
Markets: RO(needlework & craft)
Year started: 1949
#R 5; #A 150; #T 100+; #P 2
formerly Basic Crafts Company

Schroeder's Book Haven
Bert or Faye Schroeder, Owners
Route 1, Box 2820
Dickinson TX 77539

713-337-1002
Categories: 10-61(Texana)-83
WH -- Territory: TX
Markets: SC-CO-PL-SL
Items: HC-PB-RM
Year started: 1968
#A 100

Schulze News
Robert H Schulze, Owner
2907 Palma Drive
Ventura CA 93003
805-642-9759
WH

Scott Kraus News Agency
Ron Scherer, President
777 W Goodale
P. O. Box 193
Columbus OH 43216
614-224-4901
WH

Second Genesis Ltd
Richard Finn, President
1112 NE 21st Street
Portland OR 97232
503-281-1821
WH

Select Magazines
8 East 40th Street
New York NY 10016
212-696-7300
Categories: 99
DE -- Territory: US
Markets: BK-RO-MM
Items: MG

Selections Book Fairs
Sally R Oddi, Manager
4505 N High Street
Columbus OH 43214-2637
614-263-1624

Serials Management Systems
Book Division
P. O. Box 2382
London N6A 5A7 ON Canada
519-472-1072
Categories: 99
WH
Items: MG-ML

Servatius News Agency
F & R Servatius, Owners
601 - 2nd Street
Clarkston WA 99403
509-758-7592
WH

Service News Company
Dennie Heck, Manager
1306 N 23rd Street
Wilmington NC 28406
919-762-5542
WH

Seven Hills Books
Ion Itescu, President
49 Central Ave #300
Cincinnati OH 45202
513-381-3889
Categories: 11-17-21-29(antiques)
        27-41-33-51-55-59-65-71
PD -- Territory: US-CN-IT
Markets: BK-PL-SL
        RO(camera,antique)
Items: HC-PB-MA-SW
Year started: 1975
#R 27; #A 3500; #T 850; #P 22

Sharon News Agency
Toby Abrutz, Manager
527 Silver Street
Sharon PA 16146
412-342-7331
WH

Shelter Publications
Lloyd Kahn, President
P. O. Box 279
Bolinas CA 94924
415-868-0280
WH

Shirley Lewis Information Servic
Miles Stanley, Manager
196 North Queen Street
Etobicoke M9C 4Y1 ON Canada
416-622-3336
WH

Sierra News Company
David Munroe, Manager
21 Locust Street
Reno NV 89520
702-329-1714
WH

Siler's Library Distributors
W A Pierce Jr, Manager
2737 Bienville Avenue
New Orleans LA 70119
504-822-3686
Categories: 99
WH -- Territory: South
Markets: CO-PL-SL
Items: HC-PB-MM
Year started: 1906
#R 1; #P all

===

Markets: BK = Bookstore   SC = Schools   PL = Public Libraries   MM = Mass Markets and Chain Stores
          JB = Jobbers   CO = Colleges   SL = Special Libraries   NS = Newsstands
          RO = Other Retail Outlets   OT = Other (organizations, churches, etc.)

Territories: US = entire United States   CN = Canada   IT = International

Book Wholesalers and Distributors

Silver Burdett Company
250 James Street
Morristown NJ 07960
201-285-7758
WH

Slawson Communications
Leslie Smith
3719 Sixth Avenue
San Diego CA 92103
619-291-9126
Categories: 15-17-19-21-23
          27-29-51-55
PD -- Territory: US
Markets: BK-JB-NS-SC-CO
      MM-PL-SL-RO
Items: HC-PB
Year started: 1983
#R 60; #T 67; #P 6

Sleuth Publications
Gary Grady, Book Buyer
689 Florida Street
San Francisco CA 94110
415-821-2912
Categories: 69-84
PD -- Territory: US
Markets: BK-JB-RO(game &
          department stores)
Items: PB-RM-MG-OT(games)
Year started: 1981
#R 3; #A 200; #T 50; #P 10

Slingerland-Comstock Company
John A Gustafson, Owner
5881 Cold Brook Road, RR 1
Homer NY 13077
607-749-3655
WH

Small Changes
Sherry Basom
3443 Twelfth Avenue W
Seattle WA 98119
206-282-3665
Categories: 21-31-76-89
WH -- Territory: Northwest US
Markets: BK-SC-PL
Items: HC-PB-MG

Small Press Distribution
Jean T Day, Director
1814 San Pablo Avenue
Berkeley CA 94702-1624
415-549-3336
Categories: 75-83-95
WH -- Territory: US
Markets: BK-SC-CO-PL
Items: HC-PB-MG-ML
Year started: 1969
#T 5000; #P 325

SMS Publishing Corporation
Sara M Schreiner, President
P O Box 2276
Glenview IL 60025
312-724-1427
Categories: 31(learning disabled)
          39-67
PD -- Territory: US
Markets: BK-PL
Items: HC-PB

Social Studies School Service
Weiner & Levin, Owners
10000 Culver Boulevard
P O Box 802
Culver City CA 90232-0802
213-839-2436
Categories: 10
DN -- Territory: US
Markets: SC-CO-PL
Items: HC-PB-MM-MA-PO-SW-TV
Year started: 1965
#T 6000; #P 700

Solidarity Publications
David Loeb, Manager
3410 - 19th Street
P. O. Box 40874
San Francisco CA 94140
415-626-6626
WH

Sonshine Harbor
Attn: Book Buyer
825 Glen Arden Way
Altamonte Springs FL 32701-6844
305-339-0401
WH

South Carolina Bookstores
Manager, Wholesale Division
523 Jasper Street
P. O. Box 4767
West Columbia SC 29171
803-796-8200
WH

South Central Books
R & P Lynam, Owners
613 W Benedict
Shawnee OK 73801
405-275-4522
WH

South Sky Book Company
Mrs Sylvia Lee, Book Buyer
5501 University Way N E
Seattle WA 98105
206-523-4904
Categories: 10-45(Chinese)-75
PD -- Territory: US-CN-IT

Markets: BK-SC-CO-MM-PL
        SL-RO(Chinese)
Items: HC-TX-PB-MM
Year started: 1957
all Chinese

Southeast Periodical & Book Sales
Jose Bohorques, V.P.
10100 NW 25th Street
P. O. Box 520155
Biscayne Annex FL 33152
305-592-8260
WH

Southern Book Service
Barbara Franzen, Buyer
3625 E 10th Court
Hialeah FL 33013
305-836-4140; FL: 800-432-3356
Categories: 61(FL-South)-99
WH -- Territory: South
Markets: BK-SC-CO-PL
Items: HC-PB-MM
Year started: 1968
#R 1; #T 10M

Southern California Book Company
Ray Gonzales, Manager
2219 S Union Avenue
Los Angeles CA 90007
213-747-9563
Categories: 63(Jewish)-76-99
WH -- Territory: CA
Markets: BK-CO-SC
Items: HC-PB-MM-RM-MG-NP-TA
Year started: 1948
#R 3

Southern Michigan News Company
Richard Stoll, President
5601 Enterprise Drive
Lansing MI 48910
517-393-2213; 800-248-2213
Categories: 99
WH -- Territory: US-MI
Markets: BK-CO-SC-PL
Items: HC-PB-MM
Year started: 1956
#R 4; #T 15M

Southern News Company
Alton Lewis, Owner
202 - 14th Street NW
Atlanta GA 30318
404-874-6392
Categories: 99
WH -- Territory: GA
Markets: BK-CO-SC-PL
Items: PB-MM-RM-MG-NP
Year started: 1973
#R 2

===

Items: HC = Hardcover   TX = Textbooks   RM = Remainders   MG = Magazines, General
          PB = Softcover   MM = Mass-Markets   NP = Newspapers   ML = Magazines, Literary
          CA = Calendars   CO = Comics   GC = Greeting Cards   PO = Posters   TA = Tapes, Audio
          SW = Software   GI = Gifts   MA = Maps & Atlases   RC = Records   TV = Tapes, Video

Southern Tier News Company
Jeff Rubin, Manager
3465 Upper Oakwood Avenue
Elmira NY 14903
607-734-7108
WH

Southwest Book Company
John Dorroh, Manager
13955 Murphy Road
Stafford TX 77477
713-499-7113
WH

Southwestern Publishing Company
5101 Madison Road
Cincinnati OH 45227
Categories: 45(Spanish)-78-80-99
PD

Spanish International Books
Nancy Perez Crispo, Owner
4635 SW 89th Place
Miami FL 33165
305-552-9780
Categories: 45(Spanish)-99
WH

Sparks & Company
Lee Sparks
898 Summer Street
Stamford CT 06905
203-697-3617
Categories: 11-45-99
DE -- Territory: US
Markets: BK-PL
Items: HC-PB
#P 12

Specialized Book Service
Howard Hirsh, Book Buyer
1418 Barnum Avenue
Stratford CT 06497-5403
203-337-6510
Categories: 23-55-67-99
WH -- Territory: US-IT
Markets: CO-SL-OT(industry)
Items: HC-TX-PB-MM-SW-TA-TV
Year started: 1956
#R 2; #A 300+; #T 2000; #P all

Specialty Book Services
Stanley Ritland, Owner
3535 N Monte Vista
Flagstaff AZ 86002
602-774-0629
WH

Specialty Promotions
Abdul Salaam, Owner
6841 S Gregier Avenue
Chicago IL 60619
312-488-0833
WH

Speedimpex USA
Bernadette Scheller, Book Buyer
45-45 39th Street
Long Island City NY 11104
718-392-7477
Categories: 11-17-21-27-31-33-41
          45(Italian,Spanish)
          47-59-65-71-77-79-81
          83
DN -- Territory: US
Markets: BK-SC-CO-PL-SL
Items: HC-TX-PB-RM-MM-MG
       CA-CO-ML-MA-TV
Year started: 1963
#R 1; #A 1000
importer (Spanish and Italian)

Sports & Fitness Book Service
Robin Roach, Buyer
B1001 Lakeshore Road
Jacksons Point L0E 1L0 ON Canada
416-722-8529
Categories: 39-69
WH -- Territory: CN
Markets: BK-CO-SC-PL-consumers
Items: HC-PB-MM-GI
Year started: 1977

Spring Arbor Distributors
Melissa Helfers, Buyer
  Adult Trade Books
Susan Heuser, Buyer
  Children's Books
John Topliff, Buyer
  Religious Titles
10885 Textile Road
Belleville MI 48111
313-481-0900; 800-521-3690
Categories: 17-21-27-31-35-39-57
          59-63-69-73-76-77-87-89
DE -- Territory: US-CN-IT
Markets: BK-MM-RO
Items: HC-PB-MM-MG-CA-GI
       GC-RC-ST-TA-TV
Year started: 1978
#A 5000+; #T 40M+; #P 500

Spring Arbor Distributors
Texas Distribution Center
909 Avenue S
Grand Prairie TX 75050
214-988-1144; 800-521-3690
Categories: 63-99
DE -- Territory: US-CN-IT
Markets: BK-MM-RO
Items: HC-PB-MM-MG-CA-GI
       GC-RC-ST-TA-TV
Year started: 1978
#A 5000+; #T 40M+; #P 500

Spring Arbor Distributors
California Distribution Center
2934 E Las Hermanas
Compton CA 90221

800-521-3690
Categories: 63-99
DE -- Territory: US-CN-IT
Markets: BK-MM-RO
Items: HC-PB-MM-MG-CA-GI
       GC-RC-ST-TA-TV
Year started: 1978
#A 5000+; #T 40M+; #P 500

Spring Arbor Distributors West
Vern Haas, Manager
5600 NE Hassalo Street
Portland OR 97213
503-288-6931
Categories: 17-21-27-31-35-39-57
          59-63-73-77-87-89
DE -- Territory: US-CN-IT
Markets: BK-MM-RO
Items: HC-PB-MM-MG-CA-GI
       GC-RC-ST-TA-TV
Year started: 1972
#A 5000+; #T 40M+; #P 500

St. Maries Gopher News
Craig Traviss, Book Buyer
9000 N 10th Avenue
Minneapolis MN 55427
612-546-5300
Categories: 17-21-27-29-59-77
          82-84-85-86-87-89
WH -- Territory: MN
Markets: NS-SC-MM
Items: RM-MM-MG-CO-ML-MA
Year started: 1904

Stan V Wright Ltd
Wayne Wright, Book Buyer
2120 Quadra Street
P. O. Box 970
Victoria V8W 2R9 BC Canada
604-384-0597
Categories: 99
WH -- Territory: CN-BC
Markets: BK-NS-SC-CO-MM-PL-SL
Items: HC-PB-MM-MG-CA-CO
       ML-MA-NW-TA-TV
Year started: 1922
#R 10; #A 590; #T 15M; #P 50

Starkmann Book Service
H Biggs, V.P.
15 Thompson Street
Winchester MA 01890
617-721-1537
WH

Starlite Distributors
Thomas Anderson, President
P O Box 20729
Reno NV 89515
702-359-5676
Categories: 10-13-27-31-35
          39-53-57-63
DN -- Territory: US-CN-IT

==

#R = # of representatives   #A = # of accounts   #T = # of titles   #P = # of publishers

Markets: BK-NS-CO-PL
        RO(metaphysical)
Items: HC-PB-RM-MM-MG-CA-TA
Year started: 1975
#R 0; #A 300; #T 2000; #P 200+

State News Company
George O'Rourke, Manager
610 Industrial Avenue
Greensboro NC 27406
919-274-2459
WH

Steiner Book Centre
Steven Roboz, Manager
151 Carisbrooke Crescent
North Vancouver BC Canada
604-986-2444
WH

Sterling Rock Falls News Agency
David Hand, Manager
30 West 3rd Street
Sterling IL 61081
815-625-0241
WH

Story House Corporation
Sigurd Rahmus, President
Bindery Lane
Charlotteville NY 12036-0010
607-397-8725
Categories: 15-21-29-31-39-41-33
            47-49-59-69-79-81-84
            85-86-87-88-89-90
DN -- Territory: US
Markets: BK-SC-CO-PL
         SL(military bases)
Items: HC-PB-MM
Year started: 1951
#R 1; #T 4000; #P 50

Studio & Book Sales
D Miller, Manager
335 W Pender
Vancouver V6B 1T3 BC Canada
604-684-1620
WH

Subterranean Company
Craig Broadley, Manager
1327 W 2nd Avenue
P O Box 10233
Eugene OR 97440
503-343-6324
Categories: 13-75-83-90-95
DN -- Territory: US
Markets: BK-CO-PL
Items: HC-PB
Year started: 1977
#R 15

Sudbury News Service
George Martin, Manager
309 Douglas Street W
Sudbury P3E 4S6 ON Canada
705-673-3643
WH

Sun News Company
David H Wiggins, Manager
3600 - 75th Terrace N
P. O. Box 2050
Pinellas Park FL 33565
813-577-6808
WH

Sundance Distribution
Anne Sterling, Buyer
Newtown Road
P O Box 1326
Littleton MA 01460
617-486-9201
Categories: 21-31-76-89
WH -- Territory: US
Markets: SC-PL
Items: PB-MM
Year started: 1971

Supermart Book Distributors
Greg Oviatt, V.P.
12 S Middlesex Avenue
Cranbury NJ 08512
609-655-8335
Categories: 10-75
WH -- Territory: East Coast
Markets: MM
Items: HC-PB-RM-MM-CA
        MA-OT(imports)
Year started: 1981
#R 6; #A 165; #T 1350; #P 66

Swift News Agency
Kevin Swift, Manager
338 E Highway 50
Poncha Springs CO 81242
303-539-2121
Categories: 99
WH -- Territory: CO
Markets: BK-SC-CO
Items: HC-PB-MM-NP
Year started: 1949
#R 6

Symmes Systems
Ed Symmes, President
P O Box 8101
Atlanta GA 30306
404-876-7260
Categories: 11(photography)-43-51
PD -- Territory: US
Markets: SL-RO (horticultural)
Items: HC-PB-PO-TA-TV
Year started: 1972
#R 1

T-V Library Associates
R & L Verlaine, Owners
1216 Henry Ruff
Garden City MI 48135
313-427-9074
WH

Talman Company
Marilee Talman
150 Fifth Avenue
New York NY 10011

212-620-3182
Categories: 27-53-63-99
DE -- Territory: US
Markets: BK-PL
Items: HC-PB
Year started: 1984
#T 200; #P 25

Taunton News Company
Lisa Carvalho, Manager
37 Adams Street
Quincy MA 02169
WH

Taylor & Francis
Joel Packman, President
242 Cherry Street
Philadelphia PA 19106-1906
215-238-0939
Categories: 31-39-41-55-59-67
WH -- Territory: US
Markets: BK-PL-OT(research,
            institutions)
Items: HC-TX
Year started: 1955

Taylor-Carlisle
Barry Fast, President
245 - 7th Avenue
New York NY 10001
212-255-8702; 800-223-4442
Categories: 23-39-59-65-67
WH -- Territory: US
Markets: SC-PL-SL
Items: HC-PB-MM
Year started: 1951
#R 2; #T 10M

Ted Thompson Distributors
Carla Hicks, Manager
1001 Navaho Drive
Raleigh NC 27609
919-878-0020
WH

Tesla Book Company
1580 Magnolia Avenue
Millbrae CA 94030
415-697-4903
WH

Texas Art Supply
John Gilbreath, V.P.
2001 Montrose Boulevard
Houston TX 77006
713-526-5221
WH

Texas Library Book Sales
Raymond A Williams, Buyer
1002 Springdale Road
Austin TX 78762
512-926-4903
Categories: 21-31-76
WH -- Territory: TX
Markets: SC-PL
Items: HC-PB-MM
Year started: 1963

Book Wholesalers and Distributors

Thames Book Company
Beatrice Schuman, Owner
34 Truman Street
P O Box 97
New London CT 06320
203-443-1293
Categories: 21-31-76-75
WH -- Territory: New England
Markets: SC-PL
Items: HC-TX
Year started: 1946

Thatcher Distributing Group
Avice R Wilson
17 Robinson Street
New Brunswick NJ 08901
201-246-1357
Categories: 98(English
           local history)
DE -- Territory: US
Markets: BK-SC-CO-SL
Items: HC
Year started: 1984
#T 400; #P 1
distributes for Phillimore & Co.

The Book Fiend
T Anno, Manager
549 Mount Pleasant Road
Toronto M4S 2M5 ON Canada
416-487-2672
Categories: 99
DN -- Territory: CN
Markets: SC-CO-PL-SL
Items: HC-TX-PB-MM
Year started: 1973

The Book Mart
1153 E Hyde Park Boulevard
Inglewood CA 90302
213-673-5470
WH

The Bookery
Cal Barksdale, Ivan Colon-Morales
Dewitt Building
Ithaca NY 14850
607-273-5055
Categories: 45(FR-SP-GM-IT)
DN -- Territory: US-CN
Markets: BK-SC-CO-PL-SL
        RO(foreign lang)
Items: HC-TX-PB-MA
Year started: 1982
#R 0; #A 500; #T 9000; #P 100

The Booklegger
Director
12693 Oak Drive
Grass Valley CA 95495
WH

The Bookmen
Norton Stillman, Manager
525 N 3rd Street
Minneapolis MN 55401
612-341-3333; 800-328-8411
Categories: 21-31-76-89

WH -- Territory: Midwest
Markets: BK-SC-PL
Items: HC-TX-PB-MM-CA
Year started: 1972
#R 10; #T 10M

The Collection
Larry L Eveler, Manager
2101 Kansas City Road
Olathe KS 66061-1220
913-764-1811
Categories: 27 community
WH -- Territory: US
Markets: BK-PL
Items: HC-PB
Year started: 1982
#T 275

the distributors
Linda Speckman, Buyer
702 S Michigan
South Bend IN 46618
219-232-8500; 800-348-5200
Categories: 99(small press)
DN -- Territory: US
Markets: BK-CO
Items: HC-PB-MM-MG-ML-NP
Year started: 1972
#R 3; #T 15M; #P 1200

The Dream Workshop
2117 W Bentrup
Chandler AZ 85224
602-831-5308
WH

The Handicraft Press
G H DeNorman, Director
Commerce Building
Grant Park IL 60940-0248
815-465-6046
Categories: 11-27-29-63
PD -- Territory: US-CN-IT
Markets: BK-JB-NS-SC-CO
        PL-SL-MM-OT
Items: HC-PB-RM-MM-MG-CA
        CO-SW-NW-TA-TV
Year started: 1978
#A 300; #T 20M; #P 22

The Homing Pigeon
William Kelsey, Owner
Route 1, Box 813
Elgin TX 78621
512-276-7962
WH

The Jewish Bookshelf
Doris Orenstein, Owner
P O Box 434
Teaneck NJ 07666
201-833-1244
Categories: 21-63(Jewish)-76-99
WH -- Territory: US
Markets: SC-PL
Items: HC-PB
Year started: 1978

The Joyce Book Shops
Everett V Cunningham, Owner
P. O. Box 310
Martinez CA 94553
415-228-4462
WH

The Last Gasp of San Francisco
Keith Pullium, Manager
2180 Bryant
P. O. Box 212
San Francisco CA 94107
415-824-6636
WH

The Other Publishers
Dick Higgins
P O Box 35
Barrytown NY 12507
914-758-8163
Categories: 99
DE -- Territory: US
Markets: BK-PL
Items: HC-PB
#P 10
coop marketing and fulfillment

The Outdoorsman
Charles Hall, Manager
P O Box 268
Allston Station
Boston MA 02215
617-277-4054
Categories: 51-69(canoeing)
WH -- Territory: US
Markets: BK-PL
Items: HC-PB-MG-NP
Year started: 1956

The Reading Circle
Jack Davis, President
1456 N High Street
P. O. Box 8458
Columbus OH 43201
614-299-9673
Categories: 99
WH

The Scholar's Bookshelf
Kathy Easton, Manager
51 Everett Drive #G-5
Princeton Junction NJ 08550
609-799-7233
WH

The Tatnuck Bookseller
Lawrence Abramoff, President
647 Chandler Street
Worcester MA 01602
617-756-7644
WH

The Word For Today
2230 Anne Street
P. O. Box 8000
Santa Ana CA 92728
714-979-0706
WH

Thieme - Stratton
Jutta Grosser, V.P.
381 Park Avenue S
New York NY 10016
212-683-5088
WH

Thomas Brothers Maps
David P Tsoneff, President
17731 Cowan
Irvine CA 92714
714-863-1984
Categories: 71
WH -- Territory: US
Items: HC-PB-MM-MA
Year started: 1915

Thomas Brothers Maps
Dorothy Gilkey, Manager
550 Jackson Street
San Francisco CA 94133
415-981-7520
Categories: 71
WH -- Territory: US
Items: HC-PB-MM-MA
Year started: 1915

Thomas Law Book Company
1909 Washington Avenue
St. Louis MO 63103
314-621-2236
Categories: 19-55(law)
PD -- Territory: US
Markets: BK-PL
Items: HC-PB
Year started: 1885

Thomas More Association
John Sprague, Book Buyer
223 W Erie Street
Chicago IL 60610
312-951-2100
Categories: 63(Catholic)
WH -- Territory: US
Markets: BK-RO(churches)
Items: HC-PB-MM
Year started: 1938

Thomas Slatner & Company
Jamie Treggett, Manager
401 Baldwin Avenue
Jersey City NJ 07405
201-656-1100
WH

TIS Wholesale
Michael R Fulk, Manager
1928 Arlington Road
Bloomington IN 47402
812-332-3307
WH

Title Books
Nellie Simpson, Manager
3013 2nd Avenue
Birmingham AL 35233
205-324-2596
WH

Total Information
Gary DeWitt, Manager
844 Dewey Avenue
Rochester NY 14613
716-254-0621
Categories: 19-23-67-61(Europe)
WH -- Territory: US
Markets: BK-SC-PL
Items: HC-SW-TV
Year started: 1975
#R 1
import titles from UK and Japan

Toys 'n Things Press
Dan Goodenough, Deb Fackler
906 N Dale
Saint Paul MN 55103
612-488-7284
Categories: 21-27-31-35-73
PD -- Territory: US-IT
Markets: BK-PL-SL
        OT(child professionals)
Items: HC-TX-PB-MM-PO-RC
      TA-OT(filmstrips)
Year started: 1980
#A 12000; #T 350; #P 30

TransAmerican & Export News
Thomas Hollander, Manager
591 Camino de la Reina #200
San Diego CA 92126
619-297-8033
Categories: 21-29-41-43-33
       59-67-69-71-75
DN -- Territory: US-CN-OT(NZ,
       Australia)
Markets: BK-NS-SC-CO-MM
Items: HC-PB-RM-MM-MG
      CA-SO-MA-SB-TV
Year started: 1932
#R 3; #A 630; #T 150; #P 6

Transbooks
Stanley Salmen, Owner
611 Broadway #227
New York NY 10012
212-677-9201
WH

Tree Frog Trucking Company
Bill Kloster, Buyer
Katie Radditz, Juvenile Buyer
318 SW Taylor Street
Portland OR 97204
503-227-4760
Categories: 21-27-29-31-39-76-79
WH -- Territory: US
Markets: BK-RO(natural foods)
Items: HC-PB-MG-NP
Year started: 1970
#R 2

Tri-State Newsdealers Supply
Jay Fusciardi, Manager
P. O. Box 189A
East Stroudsburg PA 18301
717-421-3990
WH

Tri-State Periodicals
Tom Rademacher, Manager
Box 3503
Evansville IN 47734
812-423-4261
WH

Triangle News Company
B J Morton, Owner
301 Munson Avenue
McKees Rocks PA 15136
412-771-4433
WH

Troyka Ltd
Stanley Nazarec, Manager
799 A College Street
Toronto M6G 1C7 ON Canada
416-535-6693
WH

Tulare County News Agency
Richard A Manning, Owner
637 S Lover's Lane
P. O. Box 831
Visalia CA 93279
209-734-9206
WH

Twin City News Agency
R & J Feuer, Owners
316 N 3rd Street
P.O. Box 466
Lafayette IN 47902
317-742-1051
WH

U S Games Systems
Stuart R Kaplan, President
38 East 32nd Street
New York NY 10016
212-685-4300
WH

UBC Book Company
George Rumsey, Owner
2517 San Pablo Avenue
Oakland CA 94612
415-452-4980
WH

Unipub
Director
P O Box 1222
Ann Arbor MI 48106
313-761-4700; 800-521-8110
Categories: 19-23-45(Japanese)
PD -- Territory: US
Markets: BK-PL
Items: HC-PB

United News Wholesalers Ltd
Gene Skokowski, Book Buyer
5716 Burbank Road SE
Calgary T2H 1Z4 AB Canada
403-253-8856
Categories: 10-75
WH -- Territory: Western CN

Markets: NS-SC-CO-MM-PL-SL
Items: HC-PB-MM-MG-CA-CO
       ML-MA-PO-SB-TA
Year started: 1936
#R 25; #A 2500; #T 2000; #P 200

United Publishers Reps
Stella Broderick, Manager
50A Wynford Drive
Don Mills M3C 1J8 ON Canada
416-441-3112
WH

Univelt
Robert H Jacobs, V.P.
740 Metcalf Street #13
P. O. Box 28130
San Diego CA 92128
619-746-4005
Categories: 23-41-55-59-67
            98(astronomy, space)
PD -- Territory: US-IT
Markets: BK-CO-PL-SL-aerospace
Items: HC-PB
Year started: 1970
#R 0; #A 50; #T 200; #P 20

University Press Books
Timothy R Blondell, Director
11 W Main Street
Middletown NY 10940
914-343-8811
Categories: 65-99
WH -- Territory: US-IT
Markets: BK-CO-SC-PL
Items: HC-PB
Year started: 1984
#R 4; #T 15M
university press books

V & L Enterprises
Lali Bhatia, President
920 Alness Street #4
Downsview M3J 2H7 ON Canada
416-663-7425
WH

Val Publishing Company
D Allai, Owner
P. O. Box 731
Mount Vernon NY 10551
914-664-7077
WH

Valley Distributors
Sidney Handler, Owner
2947 Felton Road
Norristown PA 19401
215-279-7651
WH

Valley News Agency Ltd
Doug Smith, Manager
801 - 30th Street
P. O. Box 3249
Courtenay V9N 5N4 BC Canada
604-338-1366
WH

Valley News Company
Judy Hecht, Manager
1305 Stadium Road
Mankato MN 56001
507-345-4819
WH

Valley News Service
Dan S Stephan, Manager
1919 Garfield Avenue
Parkersburg WV 26101
304-428-1441
WH

Van Dyke News Company
William R Van Dyke, Owner
5671 E Fountain Way
Fresno CA 93727
209-291-7768
WH

Van Khoa Book Store
Do Dinh Tuan, Manager
9393 Bolsa Avenue #E
Westminster CA 92683
714-531-6591
WH

Vancouver Magazine Services
Nick Kavak, Manager
2500 Vauxhall Place
Richmond V6V 1Y8 BC Canada
604-278-4841
WH

Video Trend
5490 Milton Parkway
Rosemont IL 60018
312-678-3700; 800-451-7185
Categories: 99
DN -- Territory: US
Markets: BK-RO(video stores)-MM
Items: TV video tapes only

Video Trend
6103 Johns Road
Tampa FL 33614
813-884-405; 800-523-04790
Categories: 99
DN -- Territory: US
Markets: BK-RO(video stores)-MM
Items: TV video tapes only

Video Trend
12900 Richfield Court
Livonia MI 48150
313-591-0200; 800-521-0242
Categories: 99
DN -- Territory: US
Markets: BK-RO(video stores)-MM
Items: TV video tapes only

VistaBooks
William R Jones, President
217 Kimball Avenue
Golden CO 80401
303-279-4070
Categories: 15-17-27-29-39-41
            43-51-61-69-71
PD -- Territory: US
Markets: BK-PL-RO(museums,
         gift, sports)
Items: HC-PB-RM-MM-CA-GI-MA-PO-VT
Year started: 1972
#R 0; #A 1000; #T 5000; #P 300

Vitality Distributors
D & L Scarborough, Owners
1010 NW 51st Place
Fort Lauderdale FL 33309
305-771-0445
WH

Voyles News Agency
Tom Maurer, Manager
310 N 8th Street
Richmond IN 47374
317-962-3718
WH

W E Falk Books
Jennifer Robertson, Book Buyer
140 NE 123rd Street
P. O. Box 610937
North Miami FL 33161-0937
305-688-3252
Categories: 23-51-55-59-65-67
WH -- Territory: US
Markets: SL
Items: HC-PB
Year started: 1945
#R 1; #A 100+; #P all

W H Smith Wholesale
E C Hoare, Manager
3808 Victoria Park Avenue
Willowdale M2H 3H7 ON Canada
416-497-1372
WH

Wallace's College Book Company
Kevin McKiernan, Manager
928 Nandino Boulevard

==

Markets: BK = Bookstore   SC = Schools   PL = Public Libraries   MM = Mass Markets and Chain Stores
          JB = Jobbers   CO = Colleges   SL = Special Libraries   NS = Newsstands
          RO = Other Retail Outlets   OT = Other (organizations, churches, etc.)

Territories: US = entire United States   CN = Canada   IT = International

Book Wholesalers and Distributors

P.O. Box 11518
Lexington KY 40576-1518
606-254-8861
WH

Washington Toy Company
Walt Kiner, Manager
220 - 9th Street
San Francisco CA 94103
415-863-5965
Categories: 21-29-45(Spanish)-76
WH -- Territory: US
Markets: BK
Items: HC-TX-PB-GI-TA

Wausau News Agency
J Kass Jr, Owner
601 - 3rd Street
Wausau WI 54401
715-842-5224
Categories: 99
WH

Weidner Associates
James H Weidner
Floris Publications
P O Box C-50
Riverton NJ 08077
609-829-6830
Categories: 31-39-45(linguistics)
        51-65-55(law)
DE -- Territory: US-CN-S America
Markets: BK-JB-SC-CO-PL-SL
Items: TX
Year started: 1976
#T 200+; #P 3

Wenatchee News Agency
Jack L Davis, President
814 S Wenatchee Avenue
Wenatchee WA 98801
509-662-3511
Categories: 99
WH -- Territory: WA
Markets: BK-NS-SC-CO-MM-PL-SL
Items: HC-PB-RM-MM
Year started: 1930
#R 3; #A 100; #P 40

Western Book Distributors
Matt Wyse, President
2970 San Pablo Avenue
Berkeley CA 94702
415-849-2929
Categories: 99
WH -- Territory: US
Markets: BK-JB-CO-MM
Items: HC-PB-RM
Year started: 1976
#R 2; #A 1000; #T 3000; #P 120

Western Illinois News Company
Ron Flanagan, Manager
Route 4
P.O. Box 376
Macomb IL 61455
309-833-2890
WH

Western Merchandisers
Ed Perry, Manager
421 E 34th Street
P. O. Box 32270
Amarillo TX 79120
806-376-6251
WH

Western Michigan News
Ronald Lankerd, V.P.
3810 Roger Chaffee Boulevard
Grand Rapids MI 49508
616-241-4453
WH

Westland Book Wholesale
Sandy Cobb, Sales Manager
1004 Hamilton Street
Vancouver V6B 2&5 BC Canada
604-681-3021
Categories: 99
WH -- Territory: CN
Markets: BK-SC-P
Items: HC-PB
Year started: 1978

Whitaker House
Earl Whitaker, V.P.
Pittsburgh & Colfax Streets
Springdale PA 15144
412-274-4440
WH

Whiting News Company
Jay Chrustowski, President
1417 - 119th Street
Whiting IN 46394
219-659-0775
WH

Wholesale Distributors
John Sandell, V.P.
RR 3, P.O. Box 126
Burlington IA 52601
319-753-1683
WH

Wilcor International
Shawn Corrigan, Manager
Book Department
333 Lafayette Street
Utica NY 13502
315-733-3542
WH

Wilderness Books
Clayton Klein, Manager
320 Garden Lane
P.O. Box 968
Fowlerville MI 48836
517-223-9581
Categories: 51-71-81
            98(wilderness)
PD -- Territory: US-CN
Markets: BK-SC-CO-PL
Items: HC-PB
Year started: 1983
#R 1; #T 13; #P 3

William S Hein & Company
Kevin Marmion, Director
1285 Main Street
Buffalo NY 14209
716-882-2600
WH

Wilson & Company
1760 Hillhurst Avenue
Los Angeles CA 90027
213-669-1055
WH

Wilson & Sons
Dave Wilson, Owner
P. O. Box 996
Bellevue WA 98009
206-392-1965
Categories: 10-67
WH -- Territory: West
Markets: SC-CO-PL-SL
        business, government
Items: HC-TX-PB-MA-SW-TV
Year started: 1974
#R 1; #A 450

Wine Appreciation Guild
Maurice Sullivan, Director
155 Connecticut Street
San Francisco CA 94107
415-566-3532
Categories: 27(wine)
PD -- Territory: US
Markets: BK-PL
Items: HC-PB

Winebaum News
Douglas Bates, Manager
145 Heritage Avenue
Portsmouth NH 03801
603-431-2020
WH

Wit 'N Wisdom
Judy Greene, Manager
870 N Lake Street
Aurora IL 60506
312-892-2545
WH

Womwrath Bookshops & Libraries
John Martin, Manager
180 Varick Street
New York NY 10014
212-255-1211
WH

Word of Life Distributors
Soon Park, Manager
1828 W 9th
Los Angeles CA 90006
213-382-4538
WH

World Book Marketing
Jeffrey and Gail Press, Managers
99 Fremont Street
Bridgewater MA 02324

617-580-4528
Categories: 99
WH -- Territory: US-CN-IT
Markets: BK-JB-MM
Items: HC-TX-PB-RM-MM-CA-CO-MA
Year started: 1976
#R 5; #A 50

World Wide Media Service
S Joseph, Manager
386 Park Avenue S
New York NY 10016
212-686-1520
WH

Writers & Books
Joseph Flaherty, Manager
892 S Clinton Avenue
Rochester NY 14620
716-473-2590
Categories: 11-47-65-83
WH -- Territory: US
Markets: BK-CO-SC-PL-SL
Items: HC-PB-ML
Year started: 1980
#R 2

Wyoming News Company
Sal Bartlett, Manager
1212 Big Horn Avenue
Worland WY 82401
307-347-2381
WH

Wyoming Periodical Distributors
Alan C Olsen, Manager
P. O. Box 2340
Casper WY 82601
307-266-5328
WH

Yankee Book Peddler
John Secor, President
Maple Street
Contoocook NH 03229
603-746-3102; 800-258-3774
Categories: 99
WH -- Territory: US
Markets: PL-SL
Items: HC-PB
Year started: 1971

Yankee News Company
Charles L Pastorino Jr, Manager
62 Harper Avenue
P O Box 2689
Waterbury CT 06723-2689
203-757-9606
Categories: 21-31-76-99
WH -- Territory: New England
Markets: BK
Items: HC-PB
Year started: 1972
#R 3

Yarn Tree Designs
P O Box 724
Ames IA 50010
800-247-3952; IA:800-247-5500
Categories: 11-29
WH -- Territory: US
Markets: RO(craft stores)
Items: HC-PB-craft supplies

York News Agency
Gail Matson, Book Buyer
1141 S Edgar Street
P. O. Box 1187
York PA 17403
717-845-2739
Categories: 10-75
WH -- Territory: US
Markets: BK-NS-SC-CO-MM-PL-RO
Items: HC-PB-RM-MM-MG-CA
        CO-MA-NW-TA-TV
Year started: 1930
#A 250; #P 250

York News Company
Lyle F York, Owner
P.O. Box 1030
Anderson IN 46015
317-642-9911
WH

York Promotional Books Ltd
Harvey Low, President
25 Connell Court
Toronto M5V 2P8 ON Canada
416-252-2253
WH

Yuma Magazine Distributors
Moe Pepple, Manager
P. O. Box 5780
Yuma AZ 85364
602-782-1822
WH

LATE ENTRIES

Giovanni's Room
Edwin Hermence
345 S 12th Street
Philadelphia PA 19107
215-923-2960
Categories: 37
WH -- Territory: US-IT

W W Distributing
2161 Graming Lane
Dousman WI 53118
414-965-3666
Categories: 11-29
WH -- Territory: US
Markets: RO(craft stores)
Items: HC-PB-craft supplies

Klein Arts and Crafts
7556 Watson Road
St. Louis MO 63119
314-961-2600
Categories: 11-29
WH -- Territory: US
Markets: RO(craft stores)
Items: HC-PB-craft supplies

Lee Enterprises
655 Montgomery Avenue
Lexington KY 40505
606-253-4889; 800-354-9085
Categories: 11-29
WH -- Territory: US
Markets: RO(craft stores)
Items: HC-PB-craft supplies

Pickering's Inc
1644 Clara Street
Columbus OH 43211
614-291-8888
Categories: 11-29
WH -- Territory: US
Markets: RO(craft stores)
Items: HC-PB-craft supplies

Robert James Distributors
504 East 48th
Holland MI 49423
616-396-4651; 800-253-1838
Categories: 11-29
WH -- Territory: US
Markets: RO(craft stores)
Items: HC-PB-craft supplies

R & S Supply
P O Box 2774
Amarillo TX 79105
806-376-4301; 800-858-4386
Categories: 11-29
WH -- Territory: US
Markets: RO(craft stores)
Items: HC-PB-craft supplies

Edward M Hopper & Associates
P O Box 11243
Charlotte NC 28220
704-523-8141; 800-438-1242
Categories: 11-29
WH -- Territory: US
Markets: RO(craft stores)
Items: HC-PB-craft supplies

Eugene Chernin Company
1401 Germantown Avenue
Philadelphia PA 19122
215-235-2700; 800-523-0115
Categories: 11-29
WH -- Territory: US
Markets: RO(craft stores)
Items: HC-PB-craft supplies

==

#R = # of representatives   #A = # of accounts   #T = # of titles   #P = # of publishers

Abraham-Welch Associates
Stu Abraham
2020 W Shakespeare
Chicago IL 60647
312-276-8309
Categories: 99
Territory: part(Midwest)
Markets: BK
Items: HC-PB
#R 4; #P 12

Belfour R McMillen
4 Lombardy Terrace
Fort Worth TX 76132
817-731-4413
Categories: 99
Territory: part(AR-LA-TX-OK)
Markets: BK

Book Professionals
Stanley H Siegel
P O Box 5075
208 Abalone Avenue
Balboa Island CA 92662
714-675-5696
Categories: 99
Territory: part(13 Western)
Markets: BK-JB-SC-CO-RO(museums)
Items: HC-PB-RM-MM-CA-TA
Year started: 1981
#R 3; #A 500; #T 2M; #P 14

Book Travelers West
C Thomas Fritzinger
9551 Landfall Drive
Huntington Beach CA 92646
714-968-2301
Categories: 99
Territory: part(13 Western)
Markets: BK
Items: HC-PB
#R 5; #P 10

Books Alive
Paul D Tracy, President
P O Box 791
Montclair NJ 07042
201-783-3988
Categories: 99
#P 7

Borthwick Associates
James K Borthwick
6462 Xenium Lane
Maple Grove MN 55369
612-559-0505; 800-328-3349
Categories: 99
Territory: part(Midwest)
Markets: BK
#R 3

Brent Lovell Associates
Brent Lovell, President
3811 Pinot Court

Pleasanton CA 94566
415-846-6330
Categories: 10-21-27-29-43
Territory: US-part(CA, NV)
Markets: SC-CO-PL-SL-RO(many)
Items: PB-SW(educational)-TV
Year started: 1975
#R 3; #A 350; #T 70; #P 4

Carroll, Oleary & Wems Associate
George Carroll
P O Box 4240
Seattle WA 98104
206-340-0359
Categories: 99
Territory: part(13 Western)
Markets: BK-CO-OT(museums,
            specialty stores)
Items: CA-GC-MA-SB-TA
Year started: 1984
#R 4; #A 500; #P 12
formerly I-5 Associates

Chapin-West Associates
Larry West
945 First Street S
Kirkland WA 98003
206-822-5562
Categories: 99
Territory: part(West Coast)

Charles Gregg, Representative
1558 Tremont Street
Duxbury MA 02332
617-934-2701
Categories: 99
Territory: part(New England)
Markets: BK
Items: HC-PB

Colbourne-Siddall Associates
Frank Colbourne
1134 Homer Street #301
Vancouver V6B 2X6   BC Canada
604-662-3511
Categories: 99
Territory: CN(Western Canada)
Markets: BK-JB-RO(computers, etc)
            MM-PL
Items: HC-TX-PB-CA-SW
Year started: 1980
#R 4; #P 7

Como Sales Company
Jock Moore
799 Broadway
New York NY 10003
212-677-1720
Categories: 99
Territory: part(New England,
            mid-Atlantic)
Markets: BK
Items: HC-PB-CA
#P 14

Connors Associates
Kevin Connors, President
15 Lilac Terrace
Boston MA 02131
617-323-7029
Categories: 99
Territory: part(New England)
Markets: BK
Items: HC-PB

Crandall Associates
Richard N Crandall
5518 Hialeah
Houston TX 77092
713-681-4376
Categories: 99
Territory: part(Southwestern US)
Markets: BK
Items: HC-PB
#P 3

**Culinary & Hospitality
Industry Publications Services**
Harry K and Janet Noe
12550 Westerley Lane
Houston TX 77077
713-531-0216
Categories: 27
Territory: US
Markets: OT(food service,
            hospitality companies)
Items: HC-TX-PB

Damon L Webb, Representative
Damon L Webb
2446 Jonesboro
Dallas TX 75228
214-327-0409
Categories: 99
Territory: part(AR, LA, TX, OK)
Markets: BK
Items: HC-PB
#P 12

Dan Wedge, Representative
RD1, Box 538
Sussex NJ 07461
201-875-8646
Categories: 99
Territory: part(mid-Atlantic)
Markets: BK
Items: HC-PB
#P 9

Ed Shearer Associates
Ed Shearer
P O Box 126
Jewel IA 50130
515-827-5089
Categories: 99
Territory: part(IA, MN, MO)
Markets: BK
Items: HC-PB-MM
#R 2

Book Sales Representatives

Educational Resources
Pat Benning, Account Executive
John P Walsh Inc
3024 Springboro West
Dayton OH 45439
513-299-8777; 800-531-3456
Categories: 99
Territory: US
Markets: SC
Items: HC-TX-PB-TA-TV
#P 30

Errett Stuart Associates
Terre Stuart
3118 Old Coach Drive
Camarillo CA 93010
805-482-8755
Categories: 99
Territory: part(Western)
Markets: BK
Items: HC-PB
#R 4

Eugene Rotenberg & Associates
Gene Rotenberg
6532 N Trumbull
Lincolnwood IL 60635
312-677-2411
Categories: 99
Territory: part(Midwest)
Markets: BK
Items: HC-PB
#R 3

Faherty & Associates
Tom Faherty
1670 S Amphlett #203
San Mateo CA 94402
415-571-1277; 800-325-8478
Categories: 99
Territory: part(Western)
Markets: BK
Items: HC-PB
#R 6

Floyd L Nourse, Representative
Floyd Nourse
Quail Hill Apartments
1480 Creekside Drive #23
Walnut Creek CA 94596
415-932-7845
Categories: 99
Territory: part(northern CA)
Markets: BK-JB-RO-CO
Items: HC-PB
Year started: 1943
#R 1; #A 50; #P 4

Fujii Associates
Jerry L Stroud, President
2740 N Pine Grove, #15D
Chicago IL 60614
312-549-0300
Categories: 99
Territory: part(Midwest)
Markets: BK
Items: HC-PB
#R 5; #P 10

Fuller Associates
Alan E Fuller
P O Box 957
Golden CO 80402
303-582-5822
Categories: 99
Territory: part(Rocky Mountain)
Markets: BK-JB
Items: HC-PB
Year started: 1973
#P 3

G R Welch Company
David Cole
960 Gateway
Burlington L7L 5K7 ON Canada
416-681-2760
Categories: 99
Territory: CN
Markets: BK
Items: HC-PB

Gary Trim Associates
Gary Trim
2643 N Burling Street
Chicago IL 60614
312-871-1249
Categories: 99
Territory: part(Midwest)
Markets: BK
Items: HC-PB
#P 15

Genesis Marketing Group
R Dana Sullivan, President
16 Wellington Avenue
Greenville SC 29609
803-233-2651
Categories: 63-99
Territory: US
Markets: BK
Items: HC-PB
#R 20; #P 2

George Dawson, Representative
P O Box 317
Wellesley Hills MA 02181
617-449-5508
Categories: 99
Territory: part(New England, NY)
Markets: BK
Items: HC-PB
#P 12

George Scheer Associates
George F Scheer
918 Kings Mill Road
Chapel Hill NC 27514
919-967-1088
Categories: 99
Territory: part(South, Southwest)
Markets: BK
Items: HC-PB
#R 4; #P 9

Hand Associates
Richard Sybenga
1238 Campus Drive

Berkeley CA 94708
415-848-1064
Categories: 99
Territory: part(13 Western)
Markets: BK
Items: HC-PB
#R 6; #P 20

Harold Dillon, Representative
3882 S Newport Way
Denver CO 80237
303-758-0494
Categories: 99
Territory: part(Rocky Mountain)
Markets: BK
Items: HC-PB

Harold Torbert, Representative
1510 Live Oak
Irving TX 75061
214-254-9736
Categories: 99
Territory: part(LA, OK, TX, AR)
Markets: BK-JB-CO
Items: HC-PB-CA-TA
#P 12

Heinecken & Associates
Ted Heinecken
1733 N Mohawk Street
Chicago IL 60614
312-649-9181
Categories: 99
Territory: part(14 Midwest)
Markets: BK-JB-RO(museums)-MM
Items: HC-PB-RM-CA-MA-SW-TA
Year started: 1978
#R 7; #A 500; #P 20

Hopkins Bagot
George D Hopkins
30 Eldwick Court
Potomac MD 20854
301-299-2567
Categories: 99
Territory: part(South, Southwest)
Markets: BK
Items: HC-PB-MG
#R 4; #P 20

Intl Specialized Book Service
Cliff Martin, Marketing Director
P O Box 1632
Beaverton OR 97075
503-292-2606
Categories: 19-27-29-43
          45(many)-71-99
Territory: US-IT
Markets: BK-CO-PL-RO(many)
Items: HC-PB-TV
Year started: 1963
#R 5; #T 10M; #P 56

Irish Books and Media
Ethna McKiernan, Manager
683 Osceola Avenue
St Paul MN 55105
612-647-5678

Book Sales Representatives

Categories: 45(Irish)-71-99
Territory: US
Markets: BK-PL-consumers
Items: HC-PB

J S Ide Associates
Jay Ide
50 N Ela Street
Barrington IL 60010
312-382-4500
Categories: 99
Territory: part(14 Midwest)
Markets: BK-JB-MM
Items: HC-PB-RM-CA-MA-TA
Year started: 1968
#R 4

James W Beardsley, Sales Rep
13 Patriots Road
Acton MA 01720
617-263-2582
Categories: 99
Territory: part(New England)
Markets: BK
Items: HC-PB
#P 12

John C Murray Associates
John Murray
P O Box 488
Canby OR 97013
503-678-2621
Categories: 99
Territory: part(Western)
Markets: BK
Items: HC-PB
#P 5

John M Lovejoy Company
P O Box 158
Wilbraham MA 01095
413-596-3735
Categories: 99
Territory: part(New England)
Markets: BK
#P 15

Knight-Ward Associates
Christopher Ward
68 E Hartsdale Avenue
Hartsdale NY 10530
914-681-0508
Categories: 99
Territory: part(mid-Atlantic)
Markets: BK
Items: HC-PB
#R 3

Krikorian-Miller Associates
Helen Krikorian
59 Middlesex Turnpike
  Center 422G
Bedford MA 01730
617-275-6236
Categories: 99
Territory: part(New England)
Markets: BK-RO(gift trade)
#P 30

Lee R Collins Associates
Lee R Collins
4910 St Louis Court
Culver City CA 90230
213-838-4362
Categories: 99
Territory: part(Western US)
Markets: BK
Items: HC-PB
#R 7

Leibfried and Eickemeyer
John E Leibfried, Jr
942 Black Rock Road
Gladwyne PA 19035
215-649-9174
Categories: 99
Territory: part(mid-Atlantic)
Markets: BK

Mac S Albert, Representative
3515 Henry Hudson Parkway
Riverdale NY 10463
212-548-2514
Categories: 99
Territory: part(NY, NJ)
Markets: BK
Items: HC-PB
#P 5

Melman/Moster
Ned Melman
25 Quacker Bridge Road
Ossining NY 10562
914-762-5353
Categories: 11-29-99
Territory: part(East Coast)
Markets: BK
Items: HC-PB
#P 7

Miller Trade Book Marketing
Bruce Miller
2930 N Sheridan Road, #1502
Chicago IL 60657
312-975-7619
Categories: 99
Territory: part(Midwest)
#P 10

New England Book Sales Company
Arnold A Nickelsberg
2 Wedgewood Road
Westport CT 06880
203-226-9262
Categories: 99
Territory: part(New England)
#P 6

New England Books & Arts
Ralph Woodward
P O Box 2436
Framingham MA 01701
617-877-5328
Categories: 99
Territory: part(New England)
Markets: BK
Items: HC-PB-MG

Nicholas H Alwerger & Company
Nicholas H Altwerger, President
35375 Northmoat Drive
Farmington Hills MI 48018
313-553-7678
Categories: 99
Territory: part(Midwest)
Markets: BK
Items: HC-PB

Publishing Resources
Ronald J Chevako, President
P O Box 41307
San Juan PR 00940
809-724-0318
Categories: 99
Territory: IT(Caribbean)
Markets: BK-PL
Items: HC-PB

Richard D Cole
Hal Wilson
9 Elm Drive
Easton CT 06612
203-236-1303
Categories: 99
Territory: part(New England, NY)
Markets: BK
Items: HC-PB
#R 3; #P 6

Robert Silver Associates
Robert M Silver
307 East 37th Street
New York NY 10016
212-686-5630
Categories: 11
Territory: part(NY)
Markets: BK-PL
Items: HC-PB
#R 4; #P 15

Roghaar Associates
Linda Roghaar
11800 Sunrise Valley Drive #320
Reston VA 22091
703-476-5710
Categories: 99
Territory: part(Southeast)
Markets: BK
Items: HC-PB
#R 3; #P 7

Ron Doussard & Associates
Ron Doussard
2020 Chestnut #409
Glenview IL 60025-1651
312-998-1827
Categories: 99
Territory: part(Midwest)
Markets: BK-JB-RO-CO-MM
Year started: 1976
#R 4; #A 800+; #P 15

Ron Erickson & Associates
Ron Erickson
15445 Ventura Boulevard #10-350
Los Angeles CA 91413

818-992-1425
Categories: 99
Territory: part(West Coast)
Markets: BK
Items: HC-PB

Ronald Columbus, Representative
320 West 76th Street
New York NY 10023
212-873-0524
Categories: 99
Territory: part(New England
        mid-Atlantic)
Markets: BK
Items: HC-PB
#R 5; #P 4

Ryen, Evans Associates
Robert Evans
585 Seminole Street
Oradell NJ 07649
201-261-7450
Categories: 99
Territory: part(mid-Atlantic)
Markets: BK
Items: HC-PB
#R 3; #P 10

School Media Associates
Tom Kenworthy, Director
2620 Caladium Drive
Atlanta GA 30345
404-939-4717
Categories: 21-31-76
Territory: part(South)
Markets: SC-PL
Items: BK-PB-MM
#P 6

Scott Billyou, Representative
P O Box 555
West Hartford CT 06107
203-521-7645
Categories: 99
Territory: part(New England, NY)
Markets: BK
Items: HC-PB-RM
#P 12

Sirak & Sirak Associates
Lincoln Gardens #38B
Madison Avenue
Lake Hiawatha NJ 07034
201-299-0085
Categories: 99
Territory: part(mid-Atlantic)
Markets: BK-JB-CO
        RO(museum shops)
Items: HC-PB-RM-CA-SB
Year started: 1980
#R 2; #A 200+; #P 12

Southern Territory Associates
James Shepherd
P O Box 13447
Arlington TX 76013
817-277-3199

Categories: 99
Territory: part(South)
Markets: BK
Items: HC-PB
#R 6

Stephen Wilson, Representative
168 Chestnut Street
Cambridge MA 02139
617-354-0785
Categories: 99
Territory: part(New England)
Markets: BK
Items: HC-PB
#P 9

Taber/Hicks/Montgomery
Terry A Hicks
318 Fry Branch Road
Lynnville TN 38472 ·
615-527-3657
Categories: 99
Territory: part(South)
Markets: BK
Items: HC-PB

The Southern Traveller
John W Moss
201 Doe Run
Peachtree City GA 30269
404-487-8646
Categories: 99
Territory: part(South)
Markets: BK
Items: HC-PB
#R 4

Theron Palmer Associates
Theron Palmer
1503 West 29th Street
Austin TX 78703
512-478-9148
Categories: 99
Territory: part(Southwest)
Markets: BK
Items: HC-PB
#R 2

University Marketing Group
Horace Coward, Director
2405 Whitney Avenue #704
Hamden CT 06518
203-248-6598
Categories: 65-99(university
        press titles)
Territory: part(New England
        mid-Atlantic)
Markets: BK
Items: HC-PB
#P 9

Vantage Sales & Marketing
William C Kohler, President
27 Bucknell Drive
Hazlet NJ 07730
201-739-3313
Categories: 99

Territory: US-part(mid-Atlantic)
Markets: BK-MM
Items: HC-PB-MM
#R 3+; #P 15

Walck Rikhoff Strauss
John Rikhoff
4484 Church School Road
Doylestown PA 18901
215-794-7326
Categories: 99
Territory: part(mid-Atlantic)
Markets: BK
Items: HC-PB-MM-CA-GC
#R 5

Wilbur Toll, Representative
44 Huntington Avenue
Scarsdale NY 10583
914-723-4246
Categories: 99

Wilcher Associates
Roger Moss
1668 San Lorenzo Avenue
Berkeley CA 94707
415-525-7570
Categories: 99
Territory: part(Western)
Markets: BK
Items: HC-PB
#R 5; #P 15

William J Whitaker Associates
William J Whitaker Jr
9920 Maple Leaf Drive
Gaithersburg MD 20879
301-258-0564
Categories: 99
Territory: part(mid-Atlantic
        states, NYC)
Markets: BK-JB-CO-MM
Items: HC-PB-CA
Year started: 1971
#R 1; #A 250; #T 500; #P 12

William Stumm
2499 Howard Road
N Bellmore NY 11710
516-781-8604
Categories: 99
Territory: part(New England
        mid-Atlantic)
Markets: BK
Items: HC-PB
#P 4

Wybel Marketing Group
Terry Wybel
101 S Hough Street
Barrington IL 60010
312-381-7622
Categories: 99
Territory: part(Midwest)
Markets: BK
Items: HC-PB
#R 6

Wholesalers/Distributors -- Sorted by State and City

ST	CITY	WHOLESALER OR DISTRIBUTOR
AK	Anchorage	Alaska News Agency
AK	Fairbanks	Fairbanks News Agency
AL	Athens	Kuykendall's Press
AL	Birmingham	Title Books
AL	Dothan	Newsdealers Supply Company
AL	Florence	Anderson News Company
AL	Mobile	Gulf States Book Fairs
AL	Mobile	Mobile News Company
AL	Montgomery	Montgomery News Company
AL	Tuscaloosa	Read News Agency
AR	Fayetteville	Ozark News Agency
AR	Harrison	Cicero Bible Press
AR	Little Rock	Arkansas Book Company
AZ	Chandler	The Dream Workshop
AZ	Flagstaff	Northern Arizona News Company
AZ	Flagstaff	Specialty Book Services
AZ	Glendale	Central Arizona Distributing
AZ	Phoenix	Darian Books
AZ	Phoenix	Gardener's Book Service
AZ	Phoenix	LTO Enterprises
AZ	Phoenix	Many Feathers Southwestern Books
AZ	Phoenix	Roadrunner Library Service
AZ	Prescott	Perry Enterprises
AZ	Scottsdale	Murr's Library Service
AZ	Yuma	Yuma Magazine Distributors
CA	Alameda	Auto-Bound
CA	Aptos	Omnibooks
CA	Balboa Island	Book Professionals
CA	Bellflower	Deru's Fine Art Books
CA	Berkeley	Before Columbus Foundation
CA	Berkeley	Berkeley Educational Paperbacks
CA	Berkeley	Bookpeople
CA	Berkeley	Dawn Sign Press
CA	Berkeley	Hand Associates
CA	Berkeley	Small Press Distribution
CA	Berkeley	Western Book Distributors
CA	Berkeley	Wilcher Associates
CA	Bolinas	Shelter Publications
CA	Camarillo	Errett Stuart Associates
CA	Canoga Park	R & A Book Distributors
CA	Carmichael	McCoy Church Goods Company
CA	CityofIndustry	Ingram Book Company
CA	Compton	Christian Book Distributors
CA	Compton	Spring Arbor Distributors
CA	Coronado	Lion Services Company
CA	Corte Madera	Emerald Marketing
CA	Culver City	Lee R Collins Associates
CA	Culver City	Social Studies School Service
CA	Davis	AG Access Corporation
CA	El Cerrito	Info 21 Booksellers
CA	Emeryville	Publisher's Group West
CA	Encino	Ketab
CA	Fair Oaks	Life Unlimited
CA	FountainValley	EZ Cookin' Book Company
CA	Fremont	Cal Wilson Fine Numismatic
CA	Fresno	Van Dyke News Company
CA	Fullerton	Cogan Books
CA	Glendale	Aviation Book Company
CA	Grass Valley	Bud Plant
CA	Grass Valley	The Booklegger
CA	Happy Camp	Naturegraph Publishers
CA	Huntington Bch	Book Travelers West

ST	CITY	WHOLESALER OR DISTRIBUTOR
CA	Inglewood	The Book Mart
CA	Irvine	Ballen Booksellers
CA	Irvine	Thomas Brothers Maps
CA	La Puente	Mook & Blanchard
CA	Lancaster	Desert News Company
CA	Los Angeles	All America Distributors
CA	Los Angeles	Arabic & Islamic Univ. Press
CA	Los Angeles	Bernard H. Hamel - Spanish Books
CA	Los Angeles	Bilingual Educational Services
CA	Los Angeles	Flannery Company
CA	Los Angeles	French & Spanish Book Corp.
CA	Los Angeles	German & International Bookstore
CA	Los Angeles	Harry Young Publication Services
CA	Los Angeles	L L Company
CA	Los Angeles	Medical & Technical Books
CA	Los Angeles	Paris Paperbacks French Books
CA	Los Angeles	Reading Peddler Book Fairs
CA	Los Angeles	Ron Erickson & Associates
CA	Los Angeles	Southern California Book Company
CA	Los Angeles	Wilson & Company
CA	Los Angeles	Word of Life Distributors
CA	MarinaDelRey	Devorss Book Distributors
CA	Markleville	Green Mountain Book Company
CA	Martinez	The Joyce Book Shops
CA	Millbrae	Tesla Book Company
CA	Modesto	Modesto News Company
CA	Newbury Park	Interbook Inc
CA	N Hollywood	International Imports
CA	N Hollywood	Parliament News Company
CA	N Hollywood	Publishers Media
CA	Northridge	Edward Weston Graphics
CA	Oakland	Cal-West Periodicals
CA	Oakland	Gull Book Shop
CA	Oakland	Sierra Club SF Bay Bookstore
CA	Oakland	UBC Book Company
CA	Ontario	Pomona Valley News Agency
CA	Orinda	Altarinda Books
CA	Palo Alto	Palo Alto Book Service
CA	Paramount	Demonet
CA	Pasadena	Cassette Book Company
CA	Petaluma	Nor-Cal News Company
CA	Pleasanton	Brent Lovell Associates
CA	Pomona	Auromere
CA	Redondo Beach	Lord's Line
CA	Riverside	Living Books
CA	Rolling Hills	B L Winch & Associates
CA	San Diego	Advanced Marketing Services
CA	San Diego	International Periodical Distr.
CA	San Diego	Jech Distributing
CA	San Diego	Ling's International Books
CA	San Diego	San Diego Museum of Art
CA	San Diego	Slawson Communications
CA	San Diego	TransAmerican & Export News
CA	San Diego	Univelt
CA	San Francisco	Alchemy Books
CA	San Francisco	China Books & Periodicals
CA	San Francisco	Contemporary Arts Press
CA	San Francisco	Eastwind Books & Arts
CA	San Francisco	European Book Company
CA	San Francisco	Iaconi Book Imports
CA	San Francisco	Kinokuniya Bookstores America
CA	San Francisco	L-S Distributors

ST	CITY	WHOLESALER OR DISTRIBUTOR
CA	San Francisco	Sleuth Publications
CA	San Francisco	Solidarity Publications
CA	San Francisco	The Last Gasp of San Francisco
CA	San Francisco	Thomas Brothers Maps
CA	San Francisco	Washington Toy Company
CA	San Francisco	Wine Appreciation Guild
CA	San Jose	Editorial Excelsior
CA	San Jose	Milligan News Company
CA	SanLuisObispo	Booklink Distributors
CA	San Mateo	Educational Book Distributors
CA	San Mateo	Faherty & Associates
CA	San Rafael	Great Tradition
CA	Santa Ana	The Word For Today
CA	SantaFeSprgs	Handelman Company
CA	Santa Monica	Distributors International
CA	Santa Monica	Odyssey Distributing Company
CA	Seal Beach	Concord Books
CA	Sonora	Mother Lode Distributing Company
CA	Susanville	Coopers Shoppe The Distlefink
CA	Van Nuys	Beyda & Associates
CA	Ventura	Regal Books
CA	Ventura	Schulze News
CA	Visalia	Tulare County News Agency
CA	Walnut Creek	Floyd L Nourse, Representative
CA	W Sacramento	Book Service California
CA	Westminster	Van Khoa Book Store
CO	Boulder	Columbine Distributing
CO	Boulder	Dillon Book Company
CO	Denver	Denver News Company
CO	Denver	Gordon's Books
CO	Denver	Harold Dillon, Representative
CO	Denver	Nutri-Books
CO	Glenwood Sprgs	Alpine News Distributors
CO	Golden	Fuller Associates
CO	Golden	VistaBooks
CO	Loveland	Donars Spanish Books
CO	Poncha Sprgs	Swift News Agency
CO	Pueblo	Colorado News
CT	Bridgeport	Book Services International
CT	Bridgeport	Fairfield County News
CT	Bridgeport	Key Book Service
CT	Cheshire	Biblio & Tannen Bookseller
CT	Darien	Barrett Bookstore
CT	Derby	Capital Distributing Company
CT	East Haven	Inland Book Company
CT	Easton	Richard D Cole
CT	Fairfield	Edu-Tech Corporation
CT	Greens Farms	Associated Booksellers
CT	Guilford	Research Books
CT	Hamden	University Marketing Group
CT	Hartford	H P Kopplemann
CT	Kent	Reprint Distribution
CT	Madison	Publisher's Group
CT	Madison	Research Books
CT	New London	New London News Company
CT	New London	Thames Book Company
CT	Orange	I-Am-I Books
CT	Stamford	KidsBooks
CT	Stamford	Sparks & Company
CT	Stratford	Specialized Book Service
CT	Waterbury	Yankee News Company
CT	West Hartford	Bookworm Bookfairs
CT	West Hartford	Scott Billyou, Representative
CT	Westport	New England Book Sales Company
CT	Wilton	Sandpiper Book Service
DC	Washington	Dicmar Trading
DC	Washington	Fine Associates
DC	Washington	Hispania Books Distributors
DC	Washington	IEEE Computer Society
DC	Washington	Jean Karr & Company
DE	Wilmington	Delmar News Agency
FL	AltamonteSprgs	Sonshine Harbor
FL	Biscayne Annex	Southeast Periodical & Book Sale
FL	Cocoa	Cape News Company
FL	Davie	Falkynor Communications
FL	Davie	School Book Service
FL	Ft Lauderdale	Vitality Distributors
FL	Gainesville	Displays For Schools
FL	Hialeah	Southern Book Service
FL	Indialantic	International Service Company
FL	Jacksonville	Duval News
FL	Jacksonville	Mumford Library Book Sales
FL	Jupiter	Judaic Specialties
FL	Marathon	Key News Agency
FL	Miami	American Toy & Book Distributors
FL	Miami	Brown Book Company
FL	Miami	DMR International
FL	Miami	Downtown Book Center
FL	Miami	Ediciones Universal
FL	Miami	Editorial Cernuda
FL	Miami	Editorials International
FL	Miami	Goyescas Corporation of Florida
FL	Miami	La Moderna Poesia
FL	Miami	Libros Espanoles SA
FL	Miami	Libros International
FL	Miami	Spanish International Books
FL	North Miami	W E Falk Books
FL	Orlando	Orange News Company
FL	Palm Beach	Main Street News & Bookstore
FL	Pinellas Park	Sun News Company
FL	Riviera Beach	Ner Tamid Book Distributors
FL	St Petersburg	ABC School Supply
FL	Sarasota	Gulf Coast Periodicals
FL	South Miami	Better Book Fairs
FL	Spring Hill	Book Service Company
FL	Tampa	Arthur J Viders Company
FL	Tampa	Florida Educational Paperbacks
FL	Tampa	Hillsboro News
FL	Tampa	Video Trend
FL	Vero Beach	Arthur Vanous Company
GA	Albany	Family Reading Service
GA	Atlanta	J A Majors Medical Book Company
GA	Atlanta	New Leaf Distributing
GA	Atlanta	School Media Associates
GA	Atlanta	Southern News Company
GA	Atlanta	Symmes Systems
GA	Commerce	Baker & Taylor Company
GA	Peachtree City	The Southern Traveller
GA	Roswell	Professional Book Distributors
GA	Waycross	Dot Gibson Distributors
GA	Waycross	S & L Sales Company
HI	Hilo	Mid-Pacific Book Distributors
HI	Honolulu	Book Jobbers Hawaii
HI	Honolulu	Hawaii Geographic Books & Info
HI	Honolulu	Island Heritage Distribution
HI	Kailua	Pacific Trade Group
IA	Ames	Ames News Agency
IA	Ames	Yarn Tree Designs
IA	Arthur	Noll's Educational Books
IA	Atlantic	Husker News Company
IA	Burlington	Wholesale Distributors
IA	Fairfield	21st Century Publications

ST	CITY	WHOLESALER OR DISTRIBUTOR
IA	Iowa Falls	Riverside Book & Bible House
IA	Jewel	Ed Shearer Associates
ID	Coeur D'Alene	Idaho News Agency
ID	Idaho Falls	Inland Empire Periodicals
ID	McCall	Darcy Williamson Distributor
ID	Moscow	Johnson News Agency
ID	Moscow	North Country Book Express
IL	Aurora	Wit 'N Wisdom
IL	Barrington	J S Ide Associates
IL	Barrington	Wybel Marketing Group
IL	Bloomington	Bloomington News Agency
IL	Bloomington	Library Book Selection Services
IL	Champaign	Central Illinois Periodicals
IL	Chicago	Abraham-Welch Associates
IL	Chicago	Balzekas Museum
IL	Chicago	Casa Escobar
IL	Chicago	Chicago Law Book Co
IL	Chicago	Cuban Boy's Spanish Books
IL	Chicago	Fujii Associates
IL	Chicago	Gary Trim Associates
IL	Chicago	Hamakor Judaica
IL	Chicago	Heinecken & Associates
IL	Chicago	Imported Publications
IL	Chicago	Kazi Publications
IL	Chicago	Liberation Distributors
IL	Chicago	Login Brothers Book
IL	Chicago	Miller Trade Book Marketing
IL	Chicago	Paperback Sales
IL	Chicago	Prairie News Agency
IL	Chicago	Reid Michener Company
IL	Chicago	Ritter Book Company
IL	Chicago	Specialty Promotions
IL	Chicago	Thomas More Association
IL	Crystal Lake	Follett Library Book Company
IL	Danville	Herr's Inc
IL	Danville	School Aid Company
IL	DeKalb	Rose-Zell Books
IL	Evanston	Midwest European Publications
IL	Flossmoor	Avanti Enterprises
IL	Glen Ellyn	Carmel Book Company
IL	Glenview	Ron Doussard & Associates
IL	Glenview	SMS Publishing Corporation
IL	Grant Park	The Handicraft Press
IL	Hillside	Computer Book Service
IL	Jacksonville	Bound to Stay Bound Books
IL	Jacksonville	Hertzberg - New Method
IL	Lake Bluff	Quality Books
IL	Lincolnwood	Eugene Rotenberg & Associates
IL	Macomb	Western Illinois News Company
IL	Momence	Baker & Taylor Company
IL	Naperville	Longman Trade USA
IL	Pekin	Pekin News Agency
IL	Peoria	Illinois News Service
IL	Riverside	Catholic Bookrack Service
IL	Rock Island	Andich Brothers News Company
IL	Rosemont	Video Trend
IL	Springfield	Austin Periodical Services
IL	Steger	Ollis Book Corporation
IL	Sterling	Sterling Rock Falls News Agency
IL	Taylorville	Alfonsi Enterprises
IL	Waukegan	Scholarly Book Center
IL	Wheeling	Affiliated Book Distributors
IN	Anderson	York News Company
IN	Bloomington	TIS Wholesale
IN	Elkhart	Elkhart City News
IN	Evansville	Tri-State Periodicals
IN	Fort Wayne	Kokomo News Agency
IN	Fort Wayne	Michiana News Service
IN	Garrett	Finn News Agency
IN	Hammond	Astrology & Spiritual Center
IN	Indianapolis	Indiana Periodicals Distributors
IN	Indianapolis	Islamic Book Service
IN	Indianapolis	Kartes Video Communciations
IN	Indianapolis	King Electronics Distributing
IN	Lafayette	City News Stand Book World
IN	Lafayette	Twin City News Agency
IN	Marion	L-W Book Sales
IN	Richmond	Voyles News Agency
IN	South Bend	the distributors
IN	Whiting	Whiting News Company
IN	Winona Lake	Eisenbrauns
KS	Chanute	Johnson Safari Bookshop
KS	Lawrence	Spencer Museum Bookstore
KS	Olathe	The Collection
KS	Shawnee Mission	Forsyth Travel Library
KS	Topeka	Econo-Clad Books
KS	Wichita	M S News Company
KY	Ledbetter	Edmonds Book Sales
KY	Lexington	Central Kentucky News Company
KY	Lexington	Lee Enterprises
KY	Lexington	Wallace's College Book Company
KY	Louisville	Louisville News Company
KY	Mayking	Central Kentucky Books
KY	Paintsville	East Kentucky News
LA	Baton Rouge	Bayou News Agency
LA	Kenner	Graham News Company
LA	New Orleans	Forest Sales & Distributing Comp
LA	New Orleans	Siler's Library Distributors
LA	Shreveport	Louisiana Periodicals
MA	Accord	Heyden & Son
MA	Acton	James W Beardsley, Sales Rep
MA	Arlington	Excalibur Hobbies Ltd
MA	Bedford	Krikorian-Miller Associates
MA	Boston	Carrier Pigeon
MA	Boston	Cheng & Tsui Company
MA	Boston	Chinese American Company
MA	Boston	Connors Associates
MA	Boston	The Outdoorsman
MA	Bridgewater	World Book Marketing
MA	Brookline	Redwing Book Company
MA	Cambridge	Bradt Enterprises
MA	Cambridge	Harvard Art Museums Sales Shop
MA	Cambridge	Schoenhofs Foreign Books
MA	Cambridge	Stephen Wilson, Representative
MA	Canton	De Wolfe & Fiske
MA	Duxbury	Charles Gregg, Representative
MA	Framingham	New England Books & Arts
MA	Gloucester	Para Research
MA	Greenfield	Franklin County News
MA	Hatfield	21st Century Antiques
MA	Hingham	Brown & Connolly
MA	Holyoke	Holyoke News Company
MA	Littleton	Sundance Distribution
MA	Lynn	North Shore News Company
MA	New Bedford	Cape News Company
MA	Newton	New England Mobile Book Fair
MA	Quincy	Interstate Distributors
MA	Quincy	Taunton News Company
MA	Randolph	Education Guide
MA	Somerville	Harvard Associates
MA	Sudbury	Ma'Ayan
MA	Waltham	Najarian Music Company

ST	CITY	WHOLESALER OR DISTRIBUTOR
MA	WellesleyHills	George Dawson, Representative
MA	Wilbraham	John M Lovejoy Company
MA	Winchester	Starkmann Book Service
MA	Worcester	Economical Wholesale Company
MA	Worcester	The Tatnuck Bookseller
MD	Baltimore	Diamond Comic Distributors
MD	Baltimore	Marshall-Mangold Distributors
MD	Bethesda	C W Associates
MD	Gaithersburg	Book Carrier
MD	Gaithersburg	Bookworm
MD	Gaithersburg	William J Whitaker Associates
MD	Glyndon	Chapter & Cask
MD	Jessup	Ingram Book Company
MD	Landover	Lash Distributors
MD	Lanham	Bernan Associates
MD	Mount Rainier	Gryphon House
MD	New Windsor	Craft World
MD	Potomac	Hopkins Bagot
MD	Rockville	Cucumber Bookshop
MD	Rockville	Library Systems & Services
MD	Silver Spring	Cultural Hispana
MD	Silver Spring	National Association of Deaf
ME	Bangor	Magazines Inc.
ME	Portland	Eastern Book Company
ME	Portland	Maine Writers & Publishers
ME	Presque Isle	Marston's
ME	S Portland	Portland News Company
ME	York Beach	Samuel Weiser Inc
MI	Ann Arbor	Book Inventory Systems
MI	Ann Arbor	Children's Small Press Collectio
MI	Ann Arbor	Crescent Imports & Publications
MI	Ann Arbor	Keramos
MI	Ann Arbor	Midwest Natural Foods
MI	Ann Arbor	New Era Publications
MI	Ann Arbor	Unipub
MI	Bay City	Andrzejewski's Religious Goods
MI	Belleville	Spring Arbor Distributors
MI	Clawson	National Book Distributors
MI	Detroit	Ludington News Company
MI	Detroit	Merle Distributing Company
MI	Farmington	Nicholas H Alwerger & Company
MI	Fowlerville	Wilderness Books
MI	Garden City	T-V Library Associates
MI	Grand Rapids	Western Michigan News
MI	Grosse Pointe	Grenoble Books
MI	Holland	Robert James Distributors
MI	Jonesville	Book House
MI	Lansing	Southern Michigan News Company
MI	Livonia	Video Trend
MI	Mt Morris	Michigan Church Supply Company
MI	Mt Pleasant	MacGregor News Agency
MI	Niles	Michiana News Service
MI	Owosso	Emery-Pratt Company
MI	Petoskey	Northern News Company
MI	Troy	Instructional Products Services
MI	Troy	International Book Centre
MI	Warren	Glenwood Distributors
MN	Bloomington	Bookmarket Inc
MN	Bloomington	Josten's
MN	Duluth	Purple Unicorn Books
MN	Eagan	Historic Aviation
MN	Mankato	Valley News Company
MN	Maple Grove	Borthwick Associates
MN	Minneapolis	A B & T Marketing
MN	Minneapolis	Augsburg Publishing House
MN	Minneapolis	DreamHaven Books & Art

ST	CITY	WHOLESALER OR DISTRIBUTOR
MN	Minneapolis	Enrica Fish Medical Books
MN	Minneapolis	Quiltworks
MN	Minneapolis	Rockbottom Learning Express
MN	Minneapolis	St. Maries Gopher News
MN	Minneapolis	The Bookmen
MN	Rochester	Rochester News Agency
MN	Saint Paul	Bookslinger
MN	Saint Paul	Irish Books and Media
MN	Saint Paul	Macalester Park Bookstore
MN	Saint Paul	Meader Book Distributing
MN	Saint Paul	Toys'n' Things Press
MO	Ballwin	Paperbacks for Educators
MO	Bridgeton	Midwest Library Service
MO	Gerald	Patrice Press
MO	JeffersonCity	Cowley Distributing
MO	Kirksville	Adair Distributors
MO	Saint Louis	Matthews Medical Books
MO	Saint Louis	Paperback Supply
MO	Springfield	Fred Biermann Bookseller
MO	St. Louis	Klein Arts and Crafts
MO	St. Louis	Thomas Law Book Company
MS	Brandon	Mississippi Library & Media
MT	Choteau	Gospel Mission
MT	Great Falls	Hilgard News Agency
MT	Kalispell	Kalispell News Agency
NC	Asheville	Bright Horizons
NC	Chapel Hill	Connemara Trading Company
NC	Chapel Hill	George Scheer Associates
NC	Charlotte	Apple Book Company
NC	Charlotte	Edward M Hopper & Associates
NC	Durham	North Carolina News
NC	Fayetteville	Carolina News Company
NC	Greensboro	Alpic Library Company
NC	Greensboro	Book Fare
NC	Greensboro	Craft and Hobby Supplies
NC	Greensboro	S & W Distributors
NC	Greensboro	State News Company
NC	Hendersonvil	Back-to-Basics Books
NC	Hillsborough	Menasha Ridge Press
NC	New Bern	L & M News Company
NC	Raleigh	North Carolina School Book Depot
NC	Raleigh	Ted Thompson Distributors
NC	Rocky Mount	Rocky Mountain News Agency
NC	Wilmington	Service News Company
NC	Winston-Salem	Kaplan School Supply Corporation
ND	Bismark	Saks News
ND	Grand Forks	King News
NE	Lincoln	Nebraska Book Company
NE	Omaha	Mangelsen's
NE	Scottsbluff	Kent News Agency
NH	Concord	G Paulsen Company
NH	Contoocook	Yankee Book Peddler
NH	Gilsum	MLES, Inc
NH	Greenville	Ham Radio's Bookstore
NH	Peterborough	Peterborough Distribution
NH	Portsmouth	Winebaum News
NH	Wolfboro	Bowers & Merena
NJ	Blackwood	Blackwell North America
NJ	Cape May	Keltie News
NJ	Carlstadt	X-S Books
NJ	Cinnaminson	Koen Book Distributors
NJ	Clifton	CNS Judaica
NJ	Cranbury	Supermart Book Distributors
NJ	Dayton	BMI Educational Services
NJ	E Rutherford	Miller Harness Company
NJ	Fairfield	Login Brothers New Jersey

ST	CITY	WHOLESALER OR DISTRIBUTOR
NJ	Fairview	Junius Book Distributors
NJ	Hazlet	Vantage Sales & Marketing
NJ	Jersey City	Thomas Slatner & Company
NJ	Kinnelon	Roy Derstine Book Company
NJ	Lake Hiawatha	Sirak & Sirak Associates
NJ	Linden	Beverly Books
NJ	Mahwah	Educational Reading Service
NJ	Montclair	Abner Schram Ltd
NJ	Montclair	Books Alive
NJ	Morris Plains	New Jersey Book Agency
NJ	Morristown	Silver Burdett Company
NJ	New Brunswick	Thatcher Distributing Group
NJ	Newark	New Jersey Books
NJ	Newark	Newark Book Center
NJ	North Bergen	Larry Smith Books
NJ	Norwood	American Overseas Book Company
NJ	Nutley	Bernhard DeBoer Inc
NJ	Oradell	Ryen, Evans Associates
NJ	Palisades Pk	C & W Zabel Company
NJ	Pleasantville	New Jersey State News
NJ	Princeton	The Scholar's Bookshelf
NJ	Ramsey	National Catholic Reading Dists
NJ	Riverton	Weidner Associates
NJ	Saddlebrook	Regent Book Company
NJ	Skillman	Ardic Book Distributors
NJ	Somerville	Baker & Taylor Company
NJ	Somerville	East Coast Christian Distributor
NJ	Stockton	Periodical Services
NJ	Sussex	Dan Wedge, Representative
NJ	Teaneck	The Jewish Bookshelf
NJ	Union	Eastview Editions
NJ	Upper Saddle	Creative Homeowner Press
NJ	Vineland	Schnell's Book Service
NJ	Warren	Odyssey Book Company
NM	Albuquerque	Books West
NM	Albuquerque	Brotherhood of Life
NM	Albuquerque	Global Library Services
NM	Albuquerque	Newman Communications Corp.
NM	Los Alamos	Allied Books
NV	Boulder City	New Life Foundation
NV	Las Vegas	Las Vegas News Agency
NV	Reno	Baker & Taylor Company
NV	Reno	Sierra News Company
NV	Reno	Starlite Distributors
NY	Albany	Fantaco Company
NY	Albany	Historic Cherry Hill
NY	Amsterdam	Fulmont News Company
NY	Baldwin Place	George Kurian Reference Books
NY	Barrytown	The Other Publishers
NY	Bedford Hills	Merry Thoughts
NY	Bronx	Eliseo Torres
NY	Bronx	Original Publications
NY	Brooklyn	Adams Book Company
NY	Brooklyn	Affiliated Medical Book
NY	Brooklyn	City Wide Book Company
NY	Brooklyn	Cromland
NY	Brooklyn	Golden Lee Book Distributors
NY	Brooklyn	Marco Company
NY	Brooklyn	Mercedes Book Distributors
NY	Brooklyn	Saphogragh Corporation
NY	Brooklyn	Sepher-Hermon Press
NY	Buffalo	Prometheus Books
NY	Buffalo	William S Hein & Company
NY	Charlottevil	Story House Corporation
NY	Cheektowaga	Empire State News
NY	Commack	Ballen Booksellers

ST	CITY	WHOLESALER OR DISTRIBUTOR
NY	Deer Park	Samson International Book Distr.
NY	Elmira	Southern Tier News Company
NY	Elmsford	Maxwell Scientific International
NY	Farmingdale	New Era Press
NY	Flushing	Jonathan David Company
NY	Freeport	Pen Notes
NY	Great Neck	Scholium International
NY	Hartsdale	Knight-Ward Associates
NY	Hauppauge	A-Betta Book Service
NY	Hempstead	Ambassador Book Service
NY	Hicksville	Books Unlimited
NY	Highfalls	Matagiri Sri Aurobindo Center
NY	Homer	Slingerland-Comstock Company
NY	Ithaca	The Bookery
NY	Jamaica Hills	Libros de Espana Y America
NY	Jamestown	Empire News of Jamestown
NY	Johnson City	Lescron Enterprises
NY	Larchmont	Book Clearing House
NY	Lewiston	Coutts Library Services
NY	Long Beach	Landau Book Company
NY	Long Island	Continental Book Company
NY	Long Island	Hispano - American Publications
NY	Long Island	Speedimpex USA
NY	Lynbrook	EBS Book Service
NY	Melville	Imperial News Company
NY	Middletown	University Press Books
NY	Millwood	Kraus Reprint & Periodicals
NY	Mount Vernon	Polybook Distributors
NY	Mount Vernon	Val Publishing Company
NY	N Bellmore	William Stumm
NY	New York	Advent Books
NY	New York	Akiwa Information Access
NY	New York	Apt Books
NY	New York	ASI Distributors
NY	New York	Bilingual Publications
NY	New York	Book Dynamics
NY	New York	Bookazine Company
NY	New York	Books & Research
NY	New York	Cambridge Company
NY	New York	Carl Fischer Music Distributor
NY	New York	China House Gallery
NY	New York	Como Sales Company
NY	New York	Council On Interracial Books
NY	New York	Dog Museum of America Shop
NY	New York	Eastern News Distributors
NY	New York	French & Spanish Book Corp.
NY	New York	Galahad Books
NY	New York	German News Company
NY	New York	Gessler Publishing Company
NY	New York	International Circulation
NY	New York	International Univ. Booksellers
NY	New York	J Levine Religious Supplies
NY	New York	Kable News Company
NY	New York	Kampmann & Company
NY	New York	Kitchen Table: Women of Color
NY	New York	Larousse Company
NY	New York	Lectorum Publications
NY	New York	Magickal Childe
NY	New York	Merchandise Dynamics
NY	New York	Mod-Ad Agency
NY	New York	Moshy Brothers
NY	New York	New York Astrology Center
NY	New York	Osiander Book Trade Limited
NY	New York	Philipp Feldheim
NY	New York	Printed Matter
NY	New York	Puski-Corvin Hungarian Books

ST	CITY	WHOLESALER OR DISTRIBUTOR
NY	New York	ReadMore Publications
NY	New York	Robert Silver Associates
NY	New York	Roig Spanish Books
NY	New York	Ronald Columbus, Representative
NY	New York	S Goldman - Otzar Hasefarim
NY	New York	School Products Company
NY	New York	Select Magazines
NY	New York	Talman Company
NY	New York	Taylor-Carlisle
NY	New York	Thieme - Stratton
NY	New York	Transbooks
NY	New York	U S Games Systems
NY	New York	Womwrath Bookshops & Libraries
NY	New York	World Wide Media Service
NY	Newburgh	Hudson Valley News
NY	N Tarrytown	Carroll Book Service
NY	Ossining	Melman/Moster
NY	Pelham	Circa Publications
NY	Pittsford	Hotchkiss House
NY	Poughkeepsie	Apollo Book
NY	Poughkeepsie	Orbit Books Corporation
NY	Richmond Hill	Ideal Foreign Books
NY	Rifton	Plough Publishing House
NY	Riverdale	Mac S Albert, Representative
NY	Rochester	Chile Coin, Stamp & Supply
NY	Rochester	Light Impressions Corporation
NY	Rochester	Manson News
NY	Rochester	Total Information
NY	Rochester	Writers & Books
NY	Scarsdale	Wilbur Toll
NY	Staten Island	Comics Unlimited Ltd
NY	Staten Island	Editorial Services Company
NY	Staten Island	F & SF Book Company
NY	Syosset	National Learning Corporation
NY	Syracuse	JJV Associates
NY	Syracuse	Midtown Auto Books
NY	Trainsmeadow	Ediciones Vitral
NY	Utica	North Country Books
NY	Utica	Wilcor International
NY	Wantagh	Annex Book Distributors
NY	White Plains	Main Court Book Fair
NY	Whitestone	Bill Dean Books
NY	Woodstock	Beekman Publishers
OH	Canton	City News Agency
OH	Centerville	Book Caboose
OH	Cincinnati	Seven Hills Books
OH	Cincinnati	Southwestern Publishing Company
OH	Cleveland	EAL Enterprises
OH	Columbus	Copeland Distributors
OH	Columbus	Craft Wholesalers
OH	Columbus	Pickering's Inc
OH	Columbus	Scott Kraus News Agency
OH	Columbus	Selections Book Fairs
OH	Columbus	The Reading Circle
OH	Dayton	Educational Resources
OH	Lima	Brunner News Agency
OH	Lima	Green Gate Books
OH	Middletown	Middletown News Agency
OH	Oberlin	NASCORP Inc
OH	Toledo	Guardian Book Company
OH	Twinsburg	Login Brothers Book - Ohio
OK	Ada	Garrett Book Company
OK	Locust Grove	Interstate Books
OK	Muskogee	Oklahoma School & Office Supply
OK	Oklahoma City	Crafts Distributing
OK	Oklahoma City	Oklahoma City News Company

ST	CITY	WHOLESALER OR DISTRIBUTOR
OK	Shawnee	South Central Books
OR	Beaverton	Intl Specialized Book Service
OR	Canby	John C Murray Associates
OR	Corvallis	Corvallis Periodicals
OR	Eugene	Himber's Books
OR	Eugene	Subterranean Company
OR	Lake Oswego	Blackwell North America
OR	Lebanon	Lifespring Christian Bookstore
OR	Oregon City	Don & Linda's Suitcase of Books
OR	Portland	Academic Book Center
OR	Portland	Early Childhood Bookhouse
OR	Portland	Far West Book Service
OR	Portland	International Specialized Books
OR	Portland	Lanson's Inc
OR	Portland	Second Genesis Ltd
OR	Portland	Spring Arbor Distributors West
OR	Portland	Tree Frog Trucking Company
OR	Salem	Cummings Distributing
PA	Abington	Arbuta House
PA	Altoona	Newborn Enterprises
PA	Beaver	Harmony Book Company
PA	Bryn Mawr	Main Line Book Company
PA	Camp Hill	Executive Books
PA	Cogan Station	Janway Company
PA	Doylestown	Walck Rikhoff Strauss
PA	E Stroudsburg	Tri-State Newsdealers Supply
PA	Edgemont	Dinosaur Discounts
PA	Elkins Park	Franklin Book Company
PA	Exton	Royce Wholesale Distributors
PA	Farrell	Boycan's Craft and Art Supplies
PA	Ft Washington	Christian Literature Crusade
PA	Gladwyne	Leibfried and Eickemeyer
PA	Harrisburg	Harrisburg News Company
PA	Ivyland	Pop-M Company
PA	KingofPrussia	Rittenhouse Book Distributors
PA	Kittanning	Abranovic Associates
PA	Lancaster	County News Agency
PA	McKees Rocks	Triangle News Company
PA	Nazareth	Louis Goldberg Book Supply
PA	Norristown	Valley Distributors
PA	Philadelphia	Associated Libraries
PA	Philadelphia	Eugene Chernin Company
PA	Philadelphia	G H Arrow Company
PA	Philadelphia	Giovanni's Room
PA	Philadelphia	Taylor & Francis
PA	Pittsburgh	A & B Smith
PA	Pittsburgh	Alico International
PA	Pittsburgh	National Magazine Service
PA	Pottstown	Pottstown News Company
PA	Ridley Park	Deltiologists of America
PA	Sharon	Sharon News Agency
PA	Spring Mills	American Book Distributors
PA	Springdale	Whitaker House
PA	Williamsport	Brodart
PA	Williamsport	Dimondstein Book Express
PA	Williamsport	Mid-Penn Magazine Agency
PA	York	York News Agency
PR	Rio Piedras	Libreria Bereana
PR	San Juan	Educational Book Service
PR	San Juan	Publishing Resources
PR	Santurce	John W Lewis Enterprises
RI	Cranston	Arlington Card Company
RI	Manville	Creative Crafts Distributor
RI	Newport	Armchair Sailor Publishing
SC	Charleston	Discount Book Distributors
SC	Charleston	Lentz Enterprises

ST	CITY	WHOLESALER OR DISTRIBUTOR	ST	CITY	WHOLESALER OR DISTRIBUTOR
SC	Greenville	Genesis Marketing Group	UT	SaltLakeCity	Bookcraft
SC	Greenville	Holiday Enterprises	UT	SaltLakeCity	Deseret Book Distribution
SC	Greenville	Palmetto News Company	UT	SaltLakeCity	Genealogical Institute
SC	Manning	David Enterprises	UT	SaltLakeCity	Peton Corp
SC	West Columbia	South Carolina Bookstores	UT	SaltLakeCity	Richard Maher Sales
SD	Rapid City	Personal Goals	UT	Sandy	Randall Book Company
SD	Rapid City	Rushmore News	VA	Alexandria	Alonso Book & Periodical Service
SD	Sioux Falls	Dakota News	VA	Alexandria	Byrd Enterprises
TN	Chattanooga	Good Reading Book Distributors	VA	Alexandria	National Book Distributors
TN	Chattanooga	Moza Publications	VA	Merrifield	Best Continental Book Company
TN	Johnson City	Applacian Bible & Books	VA	Newport News	L & L Company
TN	Kingsport	Blackburn News Agency	VA	Reston	Roghaar Associates
TN	Lynnville	Taber/Hicks/Montgomery	VA	Roanoke	Roanoke News Agency
TN	Manchester	Biddy Books	VA	VirginiaBeach	Paperback Books
TN	Nashville	Ingram Book Company	VT	Brookfield	Brookfield Publishing Company
TN	Ooltewah	Collegedale Distributors	VT	Burlington	Burlington News Agency
TN	Shelbyville	Austin Periodical Services	VT	Burlington	Fleming Museum
TX	Amarillo	R & S Supply	VT	Burlington	Fraser Publishing Company
TX	Amarillo	Western Merchandisers	VT	Charlotte	New England Book Service
TX	Arlington	Gilmore-Howard	VT	Rutland	Rutland News Company
TX	Arlington	Southern Territory Associates	WA	Bellevue	Wilson & Sons
TX	Austin	Austin News Agency	WA	Bellingham	Baggins Books
TX	Austin	Texas Library Book Sales	WA	Blaine	Big Country Books
TX	Austin	Theron Palmer Associates	WA	Clarkston	Servatius News Agency
TX	Dallas	Damon L Webb, Representative	WA	Enumclaw	MacRae's Indian Book Distributor
TX	Dallas	J A Majors Medical Book Company	WA	Everett	Rainier News Company
TX	Dallas	Lone Star School Book Depot	WA	Kent	Pacific Pipeline
TX	Dallas	Melton Book Company	WA	Kirkland	Chapin-West Associates
TX	Dickinson	Schroeder's Book Haven	WA	Lynnwood	Book Service Unlimited
TX	El Paso	Distributors Nueva Vida	WA	Seattle	Adams News Company
TX	Elgin	The Homing Pigeon	WA	Seattle	Bilingual Books
TX	Fort Worth	Belfour R McMillen	WA	Seattle	Carroll, Oleary & Wems Associate
TX	Fort Worth	Books and Periodicals	WA	Seattle	Homestead Book
TX	Grand Prairie	Distrib-U-Toys	WA	Seattle	Moving Books
TX	Grand Prairie	Spring Arbor Distributors	WA	Seattle	Small Changes
TX	Houston	Associated News	WA	Seattle	South Sky Book Company
TX	Houston	Circle Book Service	WA	Spokane	J & L Book Company
TX	Houston	Crandall Associates	WA	Tacoma	Pacific Periodical Services
TX	Houston	Culinary & Hospitality	WA	Wenatchee	Wenatchee News Agency
TX	Houston	East Texas Distributing	WI	Butler	Clergy Book Service
TX	Houston	East Texas Periodicals	WI	Dousman	W W Distributing
TX	Houston	El Qui-Jote Book	WI	Janesville	Gay Bowles Sales
TX	Houston	J A Majors Medical Book Company	WI	La Crosse	La Crosse News Agency
TX	Houston	Richardson's Educators	WI	Madison	American Society of Agronomy
TX	Houston	Texas Art Supply	WI	Madison	Capital City Distribution
TX	Irving	Harold Torbert, Representative	WI	Madison	Interstate Periodical Distrs.
TX	Marble Falls	Texas Hill Country Cookbook	WI	Milwaukee	Arbit Books
TX	McAllen	Rio Grande Book Company	WI	Milwaukee	Gould Athletic Supply Company
TX	Plano	Mumford Library Book Sales	WI	Milwaukee	Potter Library Services
TX	Plano	PMG International	WI	Osceola	Motorbooks International
TX	San Antonio	Scylax Press	WI	S Milwaukee	Catholic Book & Supply Company
TX	Stafford	Southwest Book Company	WI	Wausau	Wausau News Agency
TX	Tyler	Jack Martin News Agency	WV	Clarksburg	James & Law Company
UT	Bountiful	Genealogy Digest Club	WV	Hedgesville	John Justice Book Wholesalers
UT	Bountiful	Horizon Publishers & Distributor	WV	Huntington	J S Latta
UT	Ogden	Atlas Publishing Company	WV	Parkersburg	Valley News Service
UT	Ogden	Eagle's View Publishing	WV	Scott Depot	Huntington News Agency
UT	Ogden	Intermountain Periodical Dist.	WY	Casper	Wyoming Periodical Distributors
UT	Orem	Musicart West	WY	Worland	Wyoming News Company
UT	Provo	Graham Maughan Company			

Canadian Wholesalers/Distributors

ST	CITY	WHOLESALER OR DISTRIBUTOR
AB	Calgary	Alberta Book & Novelty Ltd
AB	Calgary	United News Wholesalers Ltd
AB	Edmonton	Book & Tape Gallery Association
AB	Edmonton	Provincial News Company
AB	Edmonton	Koala Books of Canada Ltd
AB	Lethbridge	General News
AB	Saint Albert	Book Order Service of Canada
BC	Castlegar	ElecTech Book Service
BC	Courtenay	Valley News Agency Ltd
BC	N Vancouver	Ian MacDonald Library Services
BC	N Vancouver	Steiner Book Centre
BC	Ocean Park	Pacific Northwest Agencies
BC	Prince George	Gundy's News Supply Ltd
BC	Richmond	Vancouver Magazine Services
BC	Surrey	Big Country Books
BC	Vancouver	Raincoast Book Distributors
BC	Vancouver	Westland Book Wholesale
BC	Vancouver	Studio & Book Sales
BC	Vancouver	Colbourne-Siddall Associates
BC	Vancouver	Williams Books
BC	Vancouver	Bomber Joe's Bookstore Ltd
BC	Vernon	Monahan Agencies Ltd
BC	Victoria	Stan V Wright Ltd
MB	Winnipeg	Lifespring Books
MB	Winnipeg	Canadian News Company
NB	Saint John	Saint John News Company
NS	Halifax	H H Marshall Ltd
ON	Arnprior	Ottawa Valley News Company
ON	Bracebridge	Muskoka Educational Supply
ON	Brampton	Himalaya Books
ON	Brantford	Bro-Dart Industries
ON	Burlington	G R Welch Company
ON	Chatham	Kent News Service Ltd
ON	Collingwood	Saunders Books
ON	Cornwall	Cornwall News Distributors
ON	Don Mills	United Publishers Reps
ON	Downsview	V & L Enterprises
ON	Elora	Directional Learning Canada
ON	Etobicoke	Shirley Lewis Information Service
ON	Fenwick	Niagara Publishers
ON	Hamilton	Academic Book Caravans
ON	London	Educator Supplies Ltd
ON	London	Serials Management Systems
ON	Mississauga	School Book Fairs Ltd
ON	Mississauga	Cupress Canada Limited
ON	North York	Bookmailer
ON	Ottawa	Capital Library Wholesale
ON	Ottawa	Girol Books
ON	Scarborough	Firefly Books
ON	Scarborough	John Coutts Library Services
ON	Scarborough	Metro Toronto News Company
ON	Scarborough	Sports & Fitness Book Service
ON	Stratford	Scholar's Choice Ltd
ON	Sudbury	Sudbury News Service
ON	Toronto	Pannonia Books
ON	Toronto	Negev Importing Company
ON	Toronto	National Book Centre
ON	Toronto	B Broughton Company
ON	Toronto	Cariad Limited
ON	Toronto	The Book Fiend
ON	Toronto	Editions Champlain Ltd
ON	Toronto	Friends of Terpsichore
ON	Toronto	Can-Ed Media Ltd
ON	Toronto	Progress Books
ON	Toronto	York Promotional Books Ltd
ON	Toronto	Troyka Ltd
ON	Toronto	Cannon Book Distribution Ltd
ON	Waterloo	Kitchener News Company
ON	Willowdale	National Library Resources Ltd
ON	Willowdale	R G Mitchell Family Books
ON	Willowdale	W H Smith Wholesale
ON	Willowdale	McAinsh & Company
PQ	Boucherville	Les Editions Francaises
PQ	Dollard des	H Foxman Publications Ltd
PQ	Gatineau	Les Editions Levesque
PQ	La Salle	Benjamin News
PQ	Montreal	Nicholas Hoare Ltd
PQ	Montreal	Book Center
PQ	Montreal	Librairie Lemeac
PQ	Montreal	Editions Nouvelle Frontiere
PQ	Quebec	Quebec Livres
PQ	Quebec	Diffusion Prologue
PQ	Quebec	Distribution Ariane
PQ	Saint Hubert	Les Editions Un Monde Dif Ltee
PQ	Saint Lambert	Les Editions Heritage
PQ	Sainte Foy	Librairie La Liberte
SK	Saskatoon	Mid-Western News Agency

20th Century Christian Bookstore
2809 Granny White Pike
P O Box 678
Nashville TN 37204
615-383-3842
Categories: 63(Protestant)-99
Number of stores: 5

A Clean Well-Lighted Place
Sonya Blackman, Children's Books
or Trade Book Buyer
2417 Larkspur Landing Circle
Larkspur CA 94939
415-461-0171
Categories: 21-31-76-89-99
Number of stores: 4

Abraham & Straus Stores
Robert Elterstein, Manager
Book Department
420 Fulton Street
Brooklyn NY 11201
718-875-7200
Categories: 99
Number of stores: 4
(department stores)

Abranovic Associates
Mark Abranovic, Manager
140 Jefferson Street
Kittanning PA 16201
412-543-2005
Categories: 99
Number of stores: 6

Agape Christian Bookstore
Arthur & Ann Richmond, Managers
4417 Roosevelt Boulevard
Jacksonville FL 32210
904-384-1242
Categories: 63(Christian)-99
Number of stores: 7

**Alaska Natural History
Association Bookstores**
2525 Gambell Street
Anchorage AK 99503
907-274-8440
Categories: 11-29-41-51-61(AK)
71-99
Number of stores: 13

Alfonsi Reading Centers
Rebecca Umberger, Book Buyer
1446 Ashby Road
St. Louis MO 63132
314-428-3111
Categories: 99
Number of stores: 7

American Opinion Bookstore
Sally Humphries, Book Buyer
395 Concord Avenue
Belmont MA 02178

617-489-0604
Categories: 55(conservative)
Number of stores: 132

Ann Ar Bookshoppes
Anna Rodale, Book Buyer
827 Linden Street
Allentown PA 18101
215-433-5070
Categories: 11-27-29-39-99
Number of stores: 3

Annie's Book Stop
Annie Adams, Book Buyer
15 Lackey Street
Westborough MA 01581
617-366-5840
Categories: 21-76-99
Number of stores: 56
(used paperbacks, juveniles)

Army & Air Force Exchange
Attn: Book Buyer
Ohio Valley Exchange Region
IAAP Bldg 2501
Charlestown IN 47111-9670
812-283-1647
Categories: 55-99
Number of stores: 8

Associated Dry Goods
Mike Jacobson, Buyer
Book Department
417 Fifth Avenue
New York NY 10016
212-679-8700
Categories: 99
Number of stores: many
(department stores)

Association of Logos Bookstores
P O Box 197
Bolton MA 01704
617-779-6967
Categories: 63(Protestant,
Jewish)-99
Number of stores: 56 franchises

Atlantic Bookshops
1036 Bethlehem Pike, Route 309
Montgomeryville PA 18936
215-628-2583
Categories: 99
Number of stores: 8
(primarily remainders)

Augsburg Publishing, Retail
Roderick Olson, Book Selector
426 S 5th Street
P O Box 1209
Minneapolis MN 55440
612-330-3300
Categories: 63(Lutheran)-99
Number of stores: 10

B Altman and Company
Winifred Apt, Book Buyer
Fifth Avenue and 34th Street
New York NY 10016
212-679-7800
Categories: 99
Number of stores: 5
(department stores)

B Dalton Bookseller
Mike Hejny, Buying Supervisor
Felicia McCann, Business Buyer
Shelley Hurley, Cookbook Buyer
Sallie Neal, Fiction Book Buyer
One Corporate Center
7505 Metro Boulevard
Minneapolis MN 55435
612-893-7000
Categories: 99
Number of stores: 750+

Baker Book House
Gary Popma, Book Buyer
2768 E Paris Road
P O Box 6287
Grand Rapids MI 49506
616-957-3110
Categories: 63(Protestant)-99
Number of stores: 9

Baptist Book Stores
Phil Fortenberry, Book Buyer
127 Ninth Avenue N
Nashville TN 37234
615-251-2011
Categories: 63(Baptist)-99
Number of stores: 65

Barbara's Bookstore
Pat Peterson, Book Buyer
1434 N Wells Street
Chicago IL 60610
312-642-5045
Categories: 84-99
Number of stores: 5

Barnes & Noble Bookstores
Janine von Juergensonn, Trade
Maureen Golden, Juveniles
Ronda Wanderman, Paperbacks
105 Fifth Avenue
New York NY 10003
212-206-8800
Categories: 21-76-99
Number of stores: 130+
(retail and college stores)

Belk Stores Corporate Offices
308 East Fifth Street
Charlotte NC 28231
701-372-8900
Categories: 99
Number of stores: 46
(department stores)

Benjamin Books
Judith Guerra, Book Buyer
47 Murray Street
New York NY 10007
212-406-3550
Categories: 99
Number of stores: 7
(5 airport locations)

Berean Bookstores
8121 Hamilton Avenue
P O Box 31150
Cincinnati OH 45231
513-931-4050
Categories: 63-99
Number of stores: 24

Bethany Fellowship Bookshop
6820 Auto Club Road
Minneapolis MN 55438
612-944-2121
Categories: 63(Protestant)-99
Number of stores: 6

Black Bond Books Headquarters
15531 - 24th Avenue #9
Surrey V4A 2J4 BC Canada
604-536-4444
Categories: 99
Number of stores: 6

Bloomingdales Department Stores
Janet Markovits, Buyer
Book Department
1000 Third Avenue
New York NY 10022
212-705-2173
Categories: 99
Number of stores: 13
(department stores)

The Bon Department Stores
Cindy Policvka, Buyer
Book Department
Third and Pine Streets
Seattle WA 98118
206-344-2121
Categories: 99
Number of stores: 15
(department stores)

Book & Game Company
Paul Wilson, Manager
Merlyn's Science Fiction/Fantasy
621 W Mallon
Spokane WA 99201
509-325-3358
Categories: 33-39-61(Western)
            69-75-86
Number of stores: 3

The Book & Record
Georgia Kustas, Book Buyer
Main Office, Commerce Street
Poughkeepsie NY 12603
914-471-2740
Categories: 99
Number of stores: 11

Book & Supply Stores
Hollis Mattraw, Book Buyer
University Center
University of Tennessee
Knoxville TN 37996
615-974-3361
Categories: 99
Number of stores: 5
(college stores)

Book 'N Card Inc
Warwick Village South
Newport News VA 23601
804-595-1141
Categories: 99
Number of stores: 8
(card shoppes)

The Book Bag Stores
Jim Goolsby, Book Buyer
P O Drawer 40
Charleston SC 29402
803-744-1611
Categories: 99
Number of stores: 11

Book Corner
Michael Joachim, Book Buyer
Headquarters
50 Shrewsbury Street
Boylston MA 01505
617-869-2779
Categories: 99
Number of stores: 8

Book Peddler
122 Avondale Drive
P O Box 317
Hendersonville TN 37077
615-822-0263
Categories: 99
Number of stores: 12

Book Rack Management
2703 E Commercial Boulevard
Fort Lauderdale FL 33308
305-771-4310
Categories: 99
Number of franchises: 187
(new and used paperbacks)

The Book Stall
Cathy Ball, Manager
1110 W Main
Norman OK 73069
405-329-6787
Categories: 11-17-41-95-99
Number of stores: 6
(used books)

Book Town
General Offices
3733 W University
Jacksonville FL 32217
904-733-8510
Categories: 99
Number of stores: 8
(primarily paperbacks)

Book World Inc
Bill Streur, Book Buyer
2420 West 4th
Appleton WI 54914
414-731-9521
Categories: 99
Number of stores: 11

Bookland Inc
1135 S Edgar Street
York PA 17403
717-843-0179
Categories: 99
Number of stores: 7

Bookland Stores
Sarah Jones, Book Buyer
202 N Court Street
Florence AL 35630
205-764-6150
Categories: 99
Number of stores: 36

Bookmania
Josephine Fox, Book Buyer
Corporate Offices
25590 Seaboard Lane
Hayward CA 94545
415-786-1919
Categories: 99
Number of stores: 7
(discount stores)

Books Et Cetera
Michael Smriga, Book Buyer
General Offices
717 Grant Street #200
Santa Monica CA 90405
213-392-9791
Categories: 99
Number of stores: 5

Books Inc
Michael Grant, Book Buyer
120 Park Lane
San Mateo CA 94005
415-468-6111
Categories: 99
Number of stores: 9

Bookstop Stores
Sesselee Hensley, Book Buyer
4521 Westgate Boulevard #124
Austin TX 78745
512-892-1824
Categories: 99
Number of stores: 12
(discount stores)

The Bookstore Inc
John Kearns, Buying Supervisor
Peter Rossi, Book Buyer
808 Green Avenue
Altoona PA 16601
814-944-3593
Categories: 99
Number of stores: 9
(also wholesale news agencies)

BookWorld
Reba T Hornsby, Buyer
417 Church Street
Nashville TN 37219
615-256-7144
Categories: 99
Number of stores: 4
(see also Readmore Books)

Borders Bookshop
Tom Borders, President
303 State Street
Ann Arbor MI 48104
313-668-7652
Categories: 99
Number of stores: 14

Boscov's Department Stores
Attn: Buyer
Book Department
4500 Perkiomen Avenue
Reading PA 19605
215-779-2000
Categories: 99
Number of stores: 10
(department stores)

Brauninger News Company
P O Box 438
Trenton NJ 08638
609-396-1546
Categories: 99
Number of stores: 5

Brennan College Service
Thomas Foy, Book Buyer
45 Island Pond Road
Springfield MA 01118
413-781-2296
Categories: 99
Number of stores: 35
(college stores)

Burrows Brothers
Diane Franz, Manager
210 Hayes Drive
Brooklyn Heights OH 44131
216-398-8000
Categories: 99
Number of stores: 34

Bush Stationers
Cotswald Mall
Charlotte NC 28211
704-366-6715
Categories: 99
Number of stores: 6
(stationers)

Caldor's Department Stores
Paul H Blumenthal, Buyer
Book Department
20 Glover Avenue
Norwalk CT 06852
203-846-1641
Categories: 99
Number of stores: 109
(department stores)

Campus Books
9150 Rumsey Road
Columbia MD 21045
301-596-0807
Categories: 99
Number of stores: 16
(college stores)

Campus Store Queens College
65-30 Kissena Boulevard
Flushing NY 11367
718-268-7252
Categories: 99
Number of stores: 6
(college stores)

Cara Operations
238 Bloor Street W
Toronto M5J 1T8   ON Canada
416-962-4571
Categories: 99
Number of stores: 6

Carson Pirie Scott & Company
Lucy Swan, Manager
Book Department
1 S State Street
Chicago IL 60603
312-744-2000
Categories: 99
Number of stores: 12
(department stores)

Castner-Knott Department Stores
Donna Carter, Manager
Book Department
618 Church Street
Nashville TN 37219
615-256-6411
Categories: 99
Number of stores: 3
(department stores)

Century Bookstores
Louis Page, Book Buyer
Headquarters
3028 Greene
P O Box 788
Fort Worth TX 76101
817-927-5811
Categories: 99
Number of stores: 6

Children's Book Mark
Mark Hyman, Book Buyer
420 West 14 Mile Road
Troy MI 48084
313-589-1544
Categories: 21-76-89
Number of stores: 5

Christian Armory
Betty Willke, Book Buyer
2250 Morse Road
Columbus OH 43232
614-476-2600
Categories: 63(Christian)-99
Number of stores: 4

Christian Book & Gift Shop
John Snyder, Book Buyer
107 N Jefferson Street
Kittanning PA 16201
412-548-4521
Categories: 11-63(Christian)
Number of stores: 5

Christian Discount Book Center
734 - 28th Street SE
P O Box 8549
Grand Rapids MI 49508
616-247-8262
Categories: 63(Christian)-99
Number of stores: 5

Christian Light Bookstore
P O Box 226
158 E Market
Nappanee IN 46550
Categories: 63(Christian)-99
Number of stores: 15

Christian Supply Centers
10209 SE Division Street
Portland OR 97266
503-256-4520
Categories: 63(Christian)-99
Number of stores: 8

Church of God Publishing House
Buyer, Pathway Bookstores
922 Montgomery Avenue
Cleveland TN 37311
615-476-4512
Categories: 63(Christian)-99
Number of stores: 10

Church of Scientology
Rick Nelson, Book Buyer
Washington Bookstore Offices
2004 Westlake
Seattle WA 98121
206-622-6344
Categories: 31-57-99
Number of stores: 5

Claremont Newsstand
380 W Foothill Boulevard
Claremont CA 91711
714-626-0040
Categories: 99
Number of stores: 7

Cokesbury - Retail Division
201 Eighth Avenue S
Nashville TN 37202
615-749-6352
Categories: 63(Methodist)-99
Number of stores: 38

Colborn School Supply Stores
999 S Jason
P O Box 9348
Denver CO 80209
303-778-1220
Categories: 21-31-76-89
Number of stores: 3

Coles, The Book People
Peter Lavin, Book Buyer
90 Ronson Drive
Rexdale M9W 1C1   ON Canada
416-249-9121
Categories: 99
Number of stores: 231
(Canada and the U.S.)

College Management Service
3000 N Atlantic Avenue
P O Drawer 400
Cocoa Beach FL 32931
305-783-3100
Categories: 99
Number of stores: 9
(college stores)

Comics & Comix
2461 Telegraph Avenue
Berkeley CA 94704
415-845-4091
Categories: 33-84-86-87
Number of stores: 7
(comics and paperbacks)

Community News Center
5601 Enterprise Drive
Lansing MI 48910
517-393-0272
Categories: 99
Number of stores: 6

Crossroads Bookstore
Mark Knecht, Book Buyer
1998 W Pullman Road
Moscow ID 83843
208-882-1140
Categories: 63(Protestant)-99
Number of stores: 6

Crown Books
John Sutton, Book Buyer
Corporate Offices
12th and K Streets NW
Washington DC 20005
202-289-7170
Categories: 99
Number of stores: 183
(discount stores)

D H Holmes Department Stores
Ed Wear, Buyer
Book Department
819 Canal Street
P O Box 60160
New Orleans LA 70160
504-561-6611
Categories: 99
Number of stores: 4
(department stores)

Dawn Horse Book Depot
750 Adrian Way
San Rafael CA 94903
415-492-9382
Categories: 63(spiritual)-57
Number of stores: 4

Dayton-Hudson Department Stores
Jim Jenson, Buyer
Book Department
700 Nicollet Mall
Minneapolis MN 55402
612-375-2200
Categories: 99
Number of stores: 20
(department stores)

Deseret Book Company, Retail
James Asay, Book Buyer
40 E South Temple
P O Box 30178
Salt Lake City UT 84130
801-534-1515
Categories: 35-63(Mormons)-99
Number of stores: 17

Diamond's Department Stores
Attn: Buyer, Book Department
1616 S Priest Drive
Tempe AZ 85281
602-829-5100
Categories: 99
Number of stores: 9
(department stores)

Dick Blick Company
Highway 150 East
P O Box 1267
Galesburg IL 61401
309-343-6181
Categories: 11
Number of stores: 3
(art supply stores and catalog)

Dickson's Bookstores
1315 S Woodward Avenue
Royal Oak MI 48067
313-543-7444
Categories: 63(Christian)-99
Number of stores: 5

Dightman's Bible Book Centers
3816 S Yakima Avenue
Tacoma WA 98408
206-475-0990
Categories: 63(Christian)-99
Number of stores: 4

Dillard's Department Store
Attn: Buyer, Book Department
900 West Capitol
Little Rock AR 72203
501-376-5200
Categories: 99
Number of stores: 4
(department stores)

DMI Industries
Myrna Horne, Book Buyer
1201 Whitcomb
Madison Heights MI 48071
313-585-1490
Categories: 11-23(engineering)
Number of stores: 3
(art supply stores)

Doubleday Book Shops
Sidney Gross, Buyer
673 Fifth Avenue
New York NY 10022
212-953-4828
Categories: 99
Number of stores: 25

Du Bey's News Centers
115 S Monroe Street
Tallahassee FL 32301
904-222-1920
Categories: 99
Number of stores: 9
(books, cards, and gifts)

Eastern Mountain Sports
Bill Houlihan, Book Buyer
One Vose Farm Road
Peterborough NH 03458
603-924-9571
Categories: 39-51-69-71
Number of stores: 26
(stores and mail order catalog)

**Eastern National Park and
Monument Association Bookstores**
339 Walnut Street
Philadelphia PA 19106
215-597-7129
Categories: 11-41-51-71
                61(Eastern US)
Number of stores: 88

Eden Books Corporate Offices
13703 Eureka Road
Southgate MI 48195
313-281-6610
Categories: 63(Protestant)-99
Number of stores: 9

Elder Beerman Department Stores
Kathy Reno, Buyer
Book Department
3155 El Bee Road
Morraine OH 45439
513-296-2700
Categories: 99
Number of stores: 10+
(department stores)

Emporium Capwell Stores
Barbara Perolini, Buyer
Book Department
835 Market Street
San Francisco CA 94105
415-764-3090
Categories: 99
Number of stores: 20+
(department stores)

Encore Books
Pat Johnson, Book Buyer
34 S 17th Street
Philadelphia PA 19103
215-567-6115
Categories: 99
Number of stores: 27

Epic Bookstores
313 Supertest Road
Downsview M3J 2M4 ON Canada
416-661-0428
Categories: 99-45(French)
Number of stores: 16

F A O Schwarz Stores
Ian McDermott, Book Buyer
745 Fifth Avenue
New York NY 10151
212-644-9400
Categories: 21-31-76-89
Number of stores: 25
(toy stores)

Famous Barr Department Stores
Carol McMurran, Buyer
Book Department
601 Olive Street
St. Louis MO 63101
314-444-3111
Categories: 99
Number of stores: 4
(department stores)

Fantastic Worlds Bookstores
Bob Wayne, Owner
3011 Lackland Road
Fort Worth TX 76116-4121
817-731-6222
Categories: 33-69(games)-86
Number of stores: 5

Farm Fresh Bookstore
7530 Tidewater Drive
Norfolk VA 23505
804-587-9980
Categories: 99
Number of stores: 12

Foley's Department Stores
Kim Bradley, Buyer
Book Department
1110 Main Street
Houston TX 77001
713-651-6924
Categories: 99
Number of stores: 14
(department stores)

Follett College Stores
Coleen Sherburne, Book Buyer
103 Myrtle Street
P O Box 268
Elmhurst IL 60126
312-279-2330
Categories: 99
Number of stores: 76
(college stores)

Fortress Church Supply Store
2900 Queen Lane
Philadelphia PA 19129
215-848-6800
Categories: 63(Lutheran)-99
Number of stores: 20
(church supply stores)

Frederick & Nelson Stores
Mary Malmassari, Buyer
Book Department
Fifth and Pine Streets
Seattle WA 98111
206-682-5500
Categories: 99
Number of stores: 4
(department stores)

French & Spanish Book Corp.
115 Fifth Avenue
New York NY 10003
212-673-7400
Categories: 45(FR, SP)-59-80
Number of stores: 5

Friar Tuck Bookshop
7 Van Dam Street
Saratoga Springs NY 12866
518-587-9447
Categories: 99
Number of stores: 6

Front Page Bookstore
947 Joslyn
Pontiac MI 48055
313-338-9718
Categories: 21-45-59-76-80-99
Number of stores: 5
(paperbacks)

Gallery Book & Magazine Shop
222 E Market
Indianapolis IN 46204
317-638-2062
Categories: 99
Number of stores: 6

Garland & Grace
P O Box 218
West Barnstable MA 02668
Categories: 99
Number of stores: 8 stores

Gateway Books
6305 Baum Drive
P O Box 2684
Knoxville TN 37901
615-584-6141
Categories: 63-99
Number of stores: 74

Georgia Bookstore
124 Edgewood Avenue NE
Atlanta GA 30303
404-659-0959
Categories: 99
Number of stores: 5
(college stores)

Geppi's Comic World
Hetchinger's Square Mall
701-921 Security Boulevard
Baltimore MD 21207
301-298-1727
Categories: 33-98(comics)
Number of stores: 6

German & International Bookstore
1767 N Vermont Avenue
Los Angeles CA 90027
213-660-0313
Categories: 45(German)-59-80
Number of stores: 5

Gifts of Praise General Offices
Tom and Pam Parker, Book Buyers
821 NW 27th Street
Moore OK 73160
405-793-7013
Categories: 63(Christian)-99
Number of stores: 7

Godard Stationary Stores
704 Iroquois Drive
Cornwall K6H 5S7 ON Canada
613-938-9119
Categories: 99
Number of stores: 6
(stationery stores)

Godchaux's Department Stores
Attn: Buyer, Book Department
828 Canal Street
P O Box 53069
New Orleans LA 70153
504-528-3700
Categories: 99
Number of stores: 3
(department stores)

**Golden Gate National Parks
Association Bookstores**
Fort Mason, Building 201
San Francisco CA 94123
415-556-0693
Categories: 11-41-51-71
            61(Eastern US)
Number of stores: 5

Gordon's Booksellers
Margery Heymann, Book Buyer
8 E Baltimore Street
Baltimore MD 21202
301-685-7313
Categories: 99
Number of stores: 6

Graham's Book and Stationery
460 Second Street
Lake Oswego OR 97034
503-636-5676
Categories: 11-19-23-27
            69-71-95-99
Number of stores: 4
(stationery stores)

Guelph Campus Co-Op Bookstores
Jim Sauder, Manager
Physical Science Complex
University of Guelph
Guelph N1H 6N5 ON Canada
519-821-2050
Categories: 99
Number of stores: 6
(college stores)

Chain and Department Stores

The Guild
400 Wyoming Avenue
Scranton PA 18503
717-342-8246
Categories: 63(Catholic)-99
Number of stores: 6

Guzzardo's
George Guzzardo, Book Buyer
111 N Main Street
Kewanee IL 61443
309-852-5621
Categories: 99
Number of stores: 5

Half Price Books
4811 Swiss Avenue
Dallas TX 75204
214-826-4781
Categories: 99
Number of stores: 19
(used paperbacks)

Hall of Cards & Books
Jeff Majerek, Book Buyer
2232 S 11th Street
Niles MI 49120
616-684-3013
Categories: 99
Number of stores: 12
(greeting cards)

Hammett's Learning World
South Shore Plaza
250 Granite Street
Braintree MA 02184-2801
617-848-4096
Categories: 21-31-35-76-89
Number of stores: 14
also Hammett's Teachers Stores

Harry W Schwartz, Booksellers
David Schwartz, Buyer
209 E Wisconsin Avenue
Milwaukee WI 53203
414-272-2700
Categories: 99
Number of stores: 5

Harvard Bookstores
Carole Horne, Book Buyer
Chester Clayton, Law Buyer
12 Plympton Street
Cambridge MA 02138
617-661-0494
Categories: 19-55(law)-99
Number of stores: 4
(college stores)

Harvard Cooperative Society
George Stevens, Book Buyer
Irma Ford, Business Text Buyer
1400 Massachussetts Avenue
Cambridge MA 02238
617-492-1000
Categories: 19-99
Number of stores: 5
(college stores)

Hastings Books & Records
2101 S Western Street #15
Amarillo TX 79109-3267
806-355-0061
Categories: 99
Number of stores: 19
(books and records)

Hatch's
15677 East 17th Avenue
Aurora CO 80011
303-341-7234
Categories: 99
Number of stores: 9

Hess's Department Stores
Karen McGimpsy, Buyer
Book Department
831 Hamilton Street
Allentown PA 18101
215-821-4377
Categories: 99
Number of stores: 12
(department stores)

Higbee Company
Irene Sullivan, Buyer
Book Department
100 Public Square
Cleveland OH 44113
216-579-3553
Categories: 99
Number of stores: 11
(department stores)

Hinkle's Bookstores
Eunice Vogler, Buyer
5 West Fourth Street
P O Box 2109
Winston-Salem NC 27102
919-725-0213
Categories: 99
Number of stores: 5

House of Christian Books
113 E Jefferson
Dallas TX 75208
214-942-3344
Categories: 63(Christian)-99
Number of stores: 4
(religious book stores)

Hudson's Bay General Merchandise
Martha Newbold, Buyer
Book Department
2000 Yonge Street
Toronto M4S 2C6 ON Canada
416-964-5000
Categories: 99
Number of stores: 25
(department stores)

Huguley's
269 King Street
Charleston SC 29401
803-577-2721
Categories: 61(Southern)-99
Number of stores: 9

Hunter's Bookstores
Larry Todd, General Manager
463 N Rodeo Drive
Beverly Hills CA 90210
213-274-7301
Categories: 99
Number of stores: 6

Hutzler's Department Stores
Paula Shelley, Book Buyer
222 N Howard Street
Baltimore MD 21201
301-727-1234
Categories: 99
Number of stores: 5
(department stores)

J A Majors Medical Book Company
1851 Diplomat
P O Box 819074
Dallas TX 75061-9074
214-247-2929
Categories: 39
Number of stores: 10

J B Ivey Department Stores
Nellaine Ward, Book Buyer
127 N Tyron Street
PO Box 34799
Charlotte NC 28234
704-372-3511
Categories: 99
Number of stores: 4
(department stores)

J K Gill
10983 Via Frontera
San Diego CA 92127
619-451-0250
Categories: 11-99
Number of stores: 9
(stationers, Staceys Bookstores)

Jefferson Store Book Department
Kim Williams, Buyer
15800 NW 13th Avenue,
P O Box 693410
Miami FL 33169
305-620-2833
Categories: 99
Number of stores: 17
(department stores)

John Wanamaker Department Stores
David A Reh, Book Buyer
13th and Market Streets
Philadelphia PA 19101
215-422-2194
Categories: 99
Number of stores: 14
(department stores)

Kaufer-Stadler
1834 Market Street
San Francisco CA 94102
415-431-6827
Categories: 11-63(Catholic)-99
Number of stores: 5 art stores

Kaufmann Department Stores
Bill Blick, Buyer
Book Department
400 Fifth Avenue
Pittsburgh PA 15219
412-232-2560
Categories: 99
Number of stores: 3
(department stores)

Kent State University Bookstores
Mike Rogers, Textbook Buyer
Jack Clemons, Trade Buyer
Kenneth Anderson, Juvenile Buyer
Kent Student Center
Kent State University
Kent OH 44242
216-672-2762
Categories: 21-31-76-89-99
Number of stores: 8
(college stores)

Kinko's Publishing Group
Charles Williams, Vice President
4141 State Street
Santa Barbara CA 93110
800-235-6919
Categories: 65
Number of stores: 300
(college quick print shops)

Kroch's & Brentano's
William Rickman, Trade Buyer
Ray Carrol, Paperback Buyer
Harlan Smith, Business/Science
Philip Anderson, Remainder Buyer
General Offices
29 S Wabash Avenue
Chicago IL 60603
312-332-7500
Categories: 19-23-67-99
Number of stores: 17

L S Ayres and Company
Steve James, Buyer
Book Department
1 W Washington Street
Indianapolis IN 46204
317-262-4411
Categories: 99
Number of stores: 4
(department stores)

Lancaster Office Supply
150 W Main Street
Lancaster OH 43130
614-654-0824
Categories: 19-23-99
Number of stores: 4
(office supply stores, colleges)

Lauriat's Books
10 Pequot Way
Canton MA 02021
617-828-8300
Categories: 99
Number of stores: 8
(see also Royal Discount Books)

Law Books Ltd
Edward Frushon, Book Buyer
1981 Moreland Parkway
P O Box 6565
Annapolis MD 21401
301-269-6395
Categories: 19, 55(law)
Number of stores: 3

Law Distributors
14415 S Main Street
Gardena CA 90248
213-321-3275
Categories: 19, 55(law)
Number of stores: 5
(also wholesalers)

Lazarus Department Stores
Joe Kapps, Buyer
Book Department
Town and High Streets
Columbus OH 43215
614-463-2855
Categories: 99
Number of stores: 10
(department stores)

Lemstone Book Branch
999 North Main #205
Glen Ellyn IL 60137
312-790-0600
Categories: 63(Protestant)-99
Number of stores: 12

Les Librairies Boyer
Marie Boyer Grefford, Book Buyer
10 Nicholson
Valleyfield J6T 4M2 PQ Canada
514-373-6211
Categories: 21-31-76-89
Number of stores: 4

Librairie DeMarc Headquarters
1691 est rue Fleury
Montreal H2C 1T1 PQ Canada
514-384-8760
Categories: 99-45(French)
Number of stores: 7

Librairie Du Scorpion
2150 boul Lapiniere
Brossard J4W 2T5 PQ Canada
514-465-2242
Categories: 99
Number of stores: 4

Libreria Giron
Gladys Giron, Book Buyer
3547 West 26th Street
Chicago IL 60623
312-521-5651
Categories: 45(Spanish)-80-99
Number of stores: 6

Lichtman's News and Books
Marlene Daley, Juvenile Buyer
Val Butler, Paperback Buyer
16 Temperance Street, 2nd Floor

Toronto M5H 1Y4 ON Canada
416-365-1750
Categories: 21-31-76-89-99
Number of stores: 6

Linn Benton College Bookstore
6500 SW Pacific
Albany OR 97321
503-928-2361
Categories: 99
Number of stores: 6

Little Professor Book Centers
21333 Haggerty Road
Novi MI 48050
313-348-6700
Categories: 99
Number of stores: 70
(franchised stores)

Little Red School House
5110 E Holt Boulevard
Montclair CA 91763
714-626-1130
Categories: 21-31-76-89
Number of stores: 4

Lone Star Comics/Science Fiction
Nancy Simons, Buyer
511 E Abram Street
Arlington TX 76010
817-265-0491
Categories: 33-69(games)-86
Number of stores: 4

Los Angeles City College Stores
Charlotte Saldick, Book Buyer
4301 Monroe Street
Los Angeles CA 90029
213-664-2987
Categories: 99
Number of stores: 9
(college stores)

Madcats Corporate Offices
P O Box 5722
Little Rock AR 72215
501-224-3792
Categories: 99
Number of stores: 7

Marjen Books
Marshall Miller, Buyer
150 Greenleaf Avenue
Portsmouth NH 03801
603-430-8400
Categories: 11-99
Number of stores: 4

Marshall Field, Book Department
Sharon Roth, Senior Book Buyer
Chales Dansereau, Paperbacks
111 N State Street
Chicago IL 60690
312-781-4285
Categories: 99
Number of stores: 14
(department stores)

McAlpin Company
William Martin, Buyer
Book Department
12 West 4th Street
Cincinnati OH 45201
513-352-4236
Categories: 99
Number of stores: 5
(department stores)

McCurdy & Company
William Stoltze, Buyer
Book Department
E Main Street
Rochester NY 14645
716-232-1000
Categories: 99
Number of stores: 5
(department stores)

McLeod's
Grant McLeod, Book Buyer
506 S Edgemore
P O Box 18484
Wichita KS 67218
316-685-9251
Categories: 19-23-99
Number of stores: 4
(office supply stores)

McRae's Department Stores
Jean Marie Rough, Buyer
Book Department
P O Box 20080
Jackson MS 39209
601-968-4400
Categories: 99
Number of stores: 5
(department stores)

**Mesa Verde Museum
Association Bookstores**
P O Box 38
Mesa Verde Natl Pk CO 81330
303-529-4445
Categories: 11-41-51-61(CO)-71
Number of stores: 3

Mike's Bookstores
PH 21, 296 Mill Road
Etobicoke M9Z 4X8 ON Canada
416-626-6315
Categories: 99
Number of stores: 8

Miller & Paine Department Stores
Martha Hoppe, Buyer
Book Department
P O Box 81408
Lincoln NE 68501
402-474-2111
Categories: 99
Number of stores: 3
(department stores)

The Missouri Store
Adminstrative Offices
908 Woodson Way

Columbia MO 65201
314-442-3171
Categories: 99
Number of stores: 14
(college stores)

Moody Bookstores
B J Goodwin, Book Buyer
150 W Chicago Avenue
Chicago IL 60610
312-329-4352
Categories: 63(Protestant)-99
Number of stores: 5

Mr Paperback
Pamela Williams, Book Buyer
1135 Hammond Street
Bangor ME 04401
207-942-8237
Categories: 99
Number of stores: 15
(paperbacks)

Mustard Seed Bible Book Store
3139 S Broadway
Englewood CO 80110
303-761-2743
Categories: 63(Protestant)-99
Number of stores: 5
(religious stores)

Nebraska Book Company
6400 Cornhusker Highway
P O Box 80529
Lincoln NE 68501
402-467-4481
Categories: 99
Number of stores: 12
(college stores)

**New Hampshire College
Campus Bookstores**
2500 N River Road
Manchester NH 03104
603-668-2211
Categories: 99
Number of stores: 5
(college stores)

New Haven News Agency
P O Box 1624
New Haven CT 06506
203-777-5545
Categories: 99
Number of stores: 8
(newsstands)

News 'N Novels
Kevin Costello, Book Buyer
2220 Golden Gate Drive
Greensboro NC 27405
919-275-2220
Categories: 75-99
Number of stores: 4

News Center West
224 West Shore Plaza
Lemoyne PA 17043

717-761-2900
Categories: 99
Number of stores: 3
(paperbacks, news centers)

Newsland
215 Washington Street
P O Box 126
Burlington IA 52601
319-754-4457
Categories: 99
Number of stores: 10+
(newsstands)

Newstand
North King Street
Northampton MA 01060
413-584-3534
Categories: 99
Number of stores: 11
(newsstands)

Northwestern Products
Paul R Cutshall, Book Buyer
3255 Spring Street NE
Minneapolis MN 55413
612-331-9384
Categories: 63(Protestant)-99
Number of stores: 8
(religious supply stores)

Oakland Community College
Jan Hatcher, Book Buyer
College Bookstores
2480 Opdyke Road
Bloomfield Hills MI 48013
313-540-1558
Categories: 99
Number of stores: 5
(college stores)

Old West Book & News Center
123 Front Street
Salida CO 81201
303-539-4515
Categories: 99
Number of stores: 5
(newsstands)

Orr's Department Stores
Dereen Templeton, Buyer
Book Department
306 Northhampton
P O Box 111
Easton PA 18042
215-253-2701
Categories: 99
Number of stores: 3
(department stores)

OSU Bookstores
1315 Kinnear Road
Ohio State University
Columbus OH 43212
614-422-9400
Categories: 99
Number of stores: 10
(college stores)

Chain and Department Stores

Otto Ulbrich Company
Al Fox, Book Buyer
1517 Kenmore
Kenmore NY 14217
716-874-3996
Categories: 99
Number of stores: 10

The Owl Bookshops
Morris Ave & Yarrow Street
Bryn Mawr PA 19010
215-525-6117
Categories: 00
Number of stores: 9

**Pacific Northwest National Parks
and Forest Association Bookstore**
2001 Sixth Avenue #1920
Seattle WA 98121
206-442-7958
Categories: 11-41-51-71
          61(Northwest US)
Number of stores: 17

Palmer News Company
Attn: Book Buyer, Retail Section
1050 Republican Avenue
Topeka KS 66601
913-234-6679
Categories: 99
Number of stores: 6
(Town Crier Bookstores)

Paperback Booksmith
Edward A Hardy, Book Buyer
Cape Cod Mall, Route 132
Hyannis MA 02601
617-775-6566
Categories: 99
Number of stores: 5
(paperbacks)

Paperback Outlet
Patricia Franks, Book Buyer
55555 Jewell
Washington MI 48094
313-781-4151
Categories: 99
Number of stores: 5
(paperbacks)

**Parks and History
Association Bookstores**
P O Box 40929
Washington DC 20016
202-472-3083
Categories: 11-41-51-71
          61(Eastern US)
Number of stores: 16

Paul Rudd's Christian Supply
Paul Rudd, Book Buyer
208 West 6th Street
Oxnard CA 93030
805-487-5540
Categories: 63(Protestant)-99
Number of stores: 5
(religious supply stores)

People's News and Book Mart
406 Market Street
Parkersburg WV 26101
304-422-3842
Categories: 99
Number of stores: 4

Periodical Management Group
1011 N Frio
P O Box 7609
San Antonio TX 78207
512-226-6820
Categories: 99
Number of stores: 8
(Readmore Stores in Indiana)

Peter's Campus Services
Cheryl L Hall, Book Buyer
19 Harvey Road
Bedford NH 03102
603-668-1326
Categories: 99
Number of stores: 24
(college stores)

Play & Learn Achievement Place
116 - 103rd Street
Saskatoon S7N 1Y7 SK Canada
306-477-0160
Categories: 21-31-76-89
Number of stores: 9
(education stores)

Pomeroy's Book Department
David Taylor, Book Buyer
4th & Market Streets
Harrisburg PA 17105
717-238-1661
Categories: 99
Number of stores: 5
(department stores)

Pomeroy's Book Department
Jean Casullo, Book Buyer
500 Leviton South Center
Levittown PA 19059
215-945-5000
Categories: 99
Number of stores: 6
(department stores)

Portland News Company
Attn: Book Buyer, Retail Section
270 Western Avenue
P O Box 1728
Portland ME 04104
207-774-2633
Categories: 61(New England)-99
Number of stores: 12

Powers Department Stores
Brenda Bergquist, Book Buyer
429 Nicollet Mall
Minneapolis MN 55401
612-332-2141
Categories: 99
Number of stores: 5
(department stores)

Printer's Ink
Jeannie Polloway, Manager
Main Office
112 E Van Buren Street
Joliet IL 60432
815-727-1180
Categories: 21-76-99
Number of stores: 4

Promises Bookstores
Lana Morris, Book Buyer
General Offices
1425 N Dallas Avenue #303
Lancaster TX 75134
214-227-2326
Categories: 63(Christian)-99
Number of stores: 4

Provident Bookstores
Dorothy Cutrell, Book Buyer
Corporate Headquarters
616 Walnut Avenue
Scottsdale PA 15683
412-887-8500
Categories: 63(Mennonite)-99
Number of stores: 15

Quest Bookshops
306 W Geneva Road
P O Box 270
Wheaton IL 60189-0270
312-665-0123
Categories: 53-57-63(theosophy)
Number of stores: 6

R M Mills Bookstores
1817 - 21st Avenue S
Nashville TN 37212
615-383-5520
Categories: 99
Number of stores: 5

Rainbow West Christian Store
Dave Adams, Book Buyer
142 Candelaria Boulevard S
Salem OR 97302
503-399-1971
Categories: 63(Protestant)-99
Number of stores: 6
(religious supply stores)

Rainy Day Books
Vivian Lee Jennings, Book Buyer
2812 West 53rd Street
Shawnee Mission KS 66205
913-384-3126
Categories: 99
Number of stores: 5
(paperbacks)

Ratcliffe's Book & Office Supply
Lee Ratcliff, Book Buyer
724 N Custer
Weatherford OK 73096
405-772-3387
Categories: 19-23-99
Number of stores: 7
(office supply stores)

Readmor Bookstores
Janet Schmidt, Book Buyer
1131 West 5th Avenue
Columbus OH 43212
614-294-7526
Categories: 99
Number of stores: 5

Readmore Books
P O Box 9127
Paducah KY 42002
502-442-1372
Categories: 99
Number of stores: 17
(Austin Periodicals;
see also Bookworld stores)

Readmore Books - Hallmark Cards
James Brunner, Manager and Buyer
217 Flanders Avenue
P O Box 598
Lima OH 45802
419-225-5826
Categories: 99
Number of stores: 7

Readmore Corporation
Tom Maurer, Book Buyer
901 Promenade
P O Box 399
Richmond IN 47374
317-962-0212
Categories: 99
Number of stores: 4
(see Periodical Management Group)

Red House Books
Margaret Jackson, Book Buyer
1413 S Oats
Dothan AL 36301
205-792-1475
Categories: 99
Number of stores: 5
(paperbacks)

Remington Bookstores
508 St. Paul Place
Baltimore MD 21202
301-752-3121
Categories: 99
Number of stores: 3

Revelations Christian Books
Jan Blackwell, Manager
Nowthwest Arkansas Mall
Fayetteville AR 72701
501-521-0070
Categories: 63(Christian)-99
Number of stores: 4
(religious supply stores)

Revolution Books
Liberation Distributors
3449 N Sheffield
Chicago IL 60657
312-528-5353
Categories: 13-41-49-55
Number of stores: 14

Rich's Department Stores
Faith Brunson, Trade Book Buyer
Betty Fowler, Paperback Buyer
P O Box 4539
Atlanta GA 30302
404-586-2687
Categories: 99
Number of stores: 9
(department stores)

Rizzoli International Bookstores
Cynthia Conigliaro, Book Buyer
31 West 57th Street
New York NY 10119
212-759-2424
Categories: 99
Number of stores: 11
(also Scribner Bookstores)

Robinson's Department Stores
Ann Sahey, Book Buyer
600 West 7th Street
Los Angeles CA 90017
213-488-6800
Categories: 99
Number of stores: 13
(department stores)

Royal Discount Bookstores
10 Pequot Way
Canton MA 02021
617-828-8300
Categories: 99
Number of stores: 11
(see also Lauriat's Books)

Rudd Christian Bookstore
Lucian Rudd, Manager
12 Meta Drive
Midland TX 79701
915-683-3231
Categories: 63(Christian)-99
Number of stores: 4

Salvation Army Supply Purchasing
George Larson, Book Buyer
145 West 15th Street
New York NY 10011
212-620-4550
Categories: 63(Christian)
Number of stores: ?
serves 11 Eastern states

Sam Flax Inc
111 Eighth Avenue
New York NY 10011
212-620-3000
Categories: 11-19(advertising)
Number of stores: 5
(art supplies)

School of Metaphysics Bookstores
Jerry Rothermel, Book Buyer
Star Route, Box 15
Windyville MO 65783
417-831-0955
Categories: 53-63(metaphysics)
Number of stores: 28

Scrantom's Book & Stationery
Lynne Burns, Book Buyer
334 E Main Street
Rochester NY 14604
716-454-6060
Categories: 99
Number of stores: 11
(stationery stores)

Sears, Roebuck & Company
Wade Anderson, Manager
Book Department
General Offices, Sears Towers
Chicago IL 60684
312-875-2500
Categories: 99
Number of stores: many
(department stores, catalog)

Shillito-Rike's Department Store
Lynne Pacella, Buyer
Book Department
7th and Race Streets
Cincinnati OH 45202
513-369-6167
Categories: 99
Number of stores: 7
(department stores)

Shinder's Readmore Bookstores
Steve Kupetz, Paperback Buyer
628 Hennepin Avenue
Minneapolis MN 55403
612-333-3628
Categories: 75-82-84-85
           86-87-88-99
Number of stores: 4
(paperbacks)

Shopko Stores
Skip Carlson, Buyer
Book Department
2800 S Ashland
P O Box 19060
Green Bay WI 54307-9060
414-497-2211
Categories: 99
Number of stores: 10
(variety stores)

Simpson Department Stores
Mark Coffery, Buyer
Book Department
401 Bay Street
Toronto M5H 3K2 ON Canada
416-861-9111
Categories: 99
Number of stores: 23
(department stores)

Smithsonian Institution Museum
Attn: Book Buyer, Museum Shops
600 Maryland Avenue SW #295
Washington DC 20560
202-287-3563
Categories: 11-29-41-51-55-67
Number of stores: 9
(museum shops)

**Southwest Parks and Monuments
Association Bookstores**
221 N Court
Tucson AZ 85701
602-662-1999
Categories: 11-41-51-71
          61(Southwestern US)
Number of stores: 40

St Leo College Campus Stores
St Leo College
Saint Leo FL 33574-2096
904-588-8344
Categories: 63(Catholic)-99
Number of stores: 15
(college stores)

St Paul Catholic Book Center
172 Tremont Street
Boston MA 02111
617-426-5464
Categories: 63(Catholic)-99
Number of stores: 23

Stone & Thomas Department Stores
Jeff Norton, Manager
Book Department
1030 Main Street
Wheeling WV 26003
304-232-3344
Categories: 99
Number of stores: 3
(department stores)

Strand Book Stores
828 Broadway
New York NY 10003
212-473-1452
Categories: 99
Number of stores: 4
(2 stores, 2 outdoor stalls)

Strawbridge and Clothier
Catherine Moore, Buyer
Book Department
Market and 8th Streets
Philadelphia PA 19105
215-629-6258
Categories: 99
Number of stores: 10
(department stores)

Sun Wa Bookstore
421 Dundas Street W
Toronto M5T 2W4 ON Canada
416-596-8887
Categories: 45(Chinese)-80-99
Number of stores: 6

T Eaton Company
Jean Sawicki, Buyer
Book Department
1 Dundas Street W
Toronto M5B 1C8 ON Canada
416-591-3563
Categories: 99
Number of stores: 40+
(department stores)

Taylors Bookstores
Michael Taylor, Book Buyer
5455 Beltline Road
Dallas TX 75240
214-934-1500
Categories: 99
Number of stores: 4

Temple University Student Stores
Ken Wallick, Book Buyer
13th & Montgomery Avenues
Temple University
Philadelphia PA 19122
215-787-7384
Categories: 99
Number of stores: 5
(college stores)

Tex's Toys
Cindy Harris, Buyer
Book Department
655 S San Antonio Road
Mountain View CA 94040
415-941-1018
Categories: 21-31-76-89
Number of stores: 3

The Book Cache
Jan Westfall, Book Buyer
325 W Potter Drive
Anchorage AK 99502
907-561-1438
Categories: 61(AK)-99
Number of stores: 20

The Book Emporium
Deb Rogers, Book Buyer
1301 SW Washington Street
Peoria IL 61602
309-673-2327
Categories: 99
Number of stores: 11

The Book Trader
Dave Voss, Book Buyer
111 E Army Post Road
Southridge Mall
Des Moines IA 58315
515-287-2774
Categories: 82-84-85-86-87-88
Number of stores: 6
(primarily used paperbacks)

The Compleat Strategist
Danny Klibert, Book Buyer
11 East 33rd Street
New York NY 10016
212-685-3880
Categories: 55(military)-86-87
Number of stores: 5

The Love Shops
2301 E Lamar #230
Arlington TX 76011
817-633-2410
Categories: 63(Christian)-99
Number of stores: 25+
(franchises)

The Nature Company
Jolaine Munck, Buyer
Corporate Offices
750 Hearst Avenue
Berkeley CA 94710
415-524-9811
Categories: 15-51-69-71
Number of stores: 12
(gifts & books, also a catalog)

**Theodore Roosevelt Nature and
History Association Bookstores**
P O Box 167
Medora ND 58645
701-623-4466
Categories: 11-41-51-71
          61(ND, SD)
Number of stores: 4

Thompson Book & Supply
Lowell Thompson, Book Buyer
2627 NE Expressway
P O Box 1160
Oklahoma City OK 73136
405-478-3963
Categories: 21-31-65-76-99
Number of stores: 4

Time Warp Inc
Kent Cordray, Manager
1717 Pearl
Boulder CO 80302
303-443-4500
Categories: 86
Number of stores: 3
(comics)

Titles Unlimited
P O Drawer T
Rocky Hill NJ 08553
609-924-8280
Categories: 99
Number of stores: 5

Tower Books
Albert Chow, Book Buyer
2538 Watt Avenue
Sacramento CA 95821
916 481-6600
Categories: 99
Number of stores: 8

Toys-R-Us Stores
395 W Passaic Street
Rochelle Park NJ 07662
201-845-5033
Categories: 21-76-89
Number of stores: many
(toy stores)

TPA Books
Frances D Keilty, Book Buyer
254 College Street
New Haven CT 06510
203-787-3986
Categories: 99
Number of stores: 9
(Atticus Bookstore Cafes)

Twig Bookshops
Susanna Nawrocki, Book Buyer
6995 Blanco Road
San Antonio TX 78216
512-342-1401
Categories: 99-45(Spanish)
Number of stores: 4
(L & M Bookstore)

United College Bookstores
Carl Rosendorf, Book Buyer
1590 Concord Street
Framingham MA 01701
617-877-7583
Categories: 99
Number of stores: 67
(college stores)

Univ. of Cincinnati Bookstore
Mail Location 9
University of Cincinnati
Cincinnati OH 45221
513-475-6966
Categories: 99
Number of stores: 6
(college stores)

Univ. of Connecticut Co-operative
Madeline Dolengewicz, Manager
81 Fairfield Road
P O Box U-19
Storrs CT 06268
203-486-3537
Categories: 99
Number of stores: 6
(college stores)

University of Minnesota Bookstore
Mr. Breer, Book Buyer
231 Pillsbury Drive SE
Minneapolis MN 55455
612-373-3236
Categories: 99
Number of stores: 5
(college stores)

University Bookstores
West Virginia University
College Avenue
Morgantown WV 26505
304-293-2711
Categories: 99
Number of stores: 8
(college stores)

University of Hawaii Bookstores
Shoso C Sueda, Trade Buyer
2465 Campus Road
University of Hawaii
Honolulu HI 96822
808-948-8252
Categories: 99
Number of stores: 7
(college stores)

University of Oklahoma Bookstore
731 Elm Street
Norman OK 73019

405-325-3511
Categories: 99
Number of stores: 4
(college stores)

University of Toronto Bookroom
Koffler Student Services Center
214 College Street
Toronto M5S 1A6 ON Canada
416-978-2248
Categories: 99
Number of stores: 5
(college stores)

University of Wisconsin
Book Purchasing Office
149 N Francis Street
Madison WI 53703
608-263-7972
Categories: 99
Number of stores: 13
(college stores)

Upstart Crow & Company Books
Kelly Cannon, Book Buyer
150 North Hill Drive
Brisbane CA 94005
415-626-9840
Categories: 99
Number of stores: 12

Utrecht Gift Shops
33 - 35th Street
Brooklyn NY 11232
718-768-2525
Categories: 11
Number of stores: 5
(gift shops)

W H Smith Bookstores
N Berrisford, Buying Manager
113 Merton Street
Toronto M4S 1A8 ON Canada
416-485-6660
Categories: 99
Number of stores: 190
(Classic and Evergreen Books)

Waldenbooks
Paul Kolker, Business Buyer
Maureen McMahon, Cookbook Buyer
Corporate Headquarters
201 High Ridge Road
Stamford CT 06904
203-356-7500
Categories: 19, 27, 99
Number of stores: 932
(also Readers Market, Brentano's,
and Waldenbooks and More)

Wallace's Bookstores
928 Nandino Boulevard
P O Box 11518
Lexington KY 40576
606-255-0886
Categories: 99
Number of stores: 12
(college stores)

Walt's Gift Shops
2110 East 13th Street
Ames IA 50010
515-232-1788
Categories: 99
Number of stores: 5
(gift shops)

Western Christian Bookstores
1618 Franklin Street
Oakland CA 94612
415-823-2040
Categories: 63(Protestant)-99
Number of stores: 7
(religious supply stores)

Wieboldt Department Stores
Attn: Buyer, Book Department
7601 S Cicero
Chicago IL 60652
312-581-5400
Categories: 99
Number of stores: 5
(department stores, catalog)

Wilderness Equipment Company
638 Westbury Square
Houston TX 77035
713-721-1530
Categories: 51-69(camping,
            hiking)-71
Number of stores: 3

Wilkie News
Eric S Oda, General Manager
101 S Ludlow Street
Dayton OH 45202-1891
513-223-2541
Categories: 99
Number of stores: 4
(newsstands)

Wills Book & Stationary
Ethel Allen, Book Buyer
103 Longale Road
P O Box 19239
Greensboro NC 27419
919-299-1411
Categories: 99
Number of stores: 9

Winebaum News Shop
72 Congress Street
Portsmouth NH 03801
603-436-1226
Categories: 99
Number of stores: 6
(newsstands)

Woodward Stores Ltd.
Attn: Buyer, Book Department
101 West Hastings Street
P O Box 8600
Vancouver V6B 4G1 BC Canada
604-684-5231
Categories: 99
Number of stores: 19
(department stores)

Chain and Department Stores

Woolco Department Stores
Anna Agostino, Juvenile Buyer
Don Cameron, Adult Buyer
Books Department
33 Adelaide Street W
Toronto M5H 1N1 ON Canada
416-361-2111
Categories: 21-31-76-89
Number of stores: 70+
(variety stores)

Younkers Department Stores
Attn: Buyer, Book Department
701 Walnut Street
Des Moines IA 50306
515-244-1112
Categories: 99
Number of stores: 10+
(department stores)

Zayre Corporation
Everett Tillinghast, Buyer
Book Department
770 Cochituate Road
Framingham MA 01701
617-620-5403
Categories: 99
Number of stores: 275
(department stores)

ZCMI Department Stores
Duane Taylor, Buyer
Book Department
2200 South 900 West
Salt Lake City UT 84137
801-321-6179
Categories: 99
Number of stores: 10
(department stores)

**Zion Natural Historical
Association Bookstore**
Visitor Center
Zion National Park
Springdale UT 84767
801-772-3256
Categories: 41-51-61(AZ-UT)-71
Number of stores: 3

Zondervan Family Bookstores
Maury Lehman, Buyer
Corporate Headquarters
1420 Robinson Road SE
Grand Rapids MI 49506
616-459-7294
Categories: 63(Christian)-99
Number of stores: 80

Chain Stores -- Sorted by State and City

ST	CITY	COMPANY
AK	Anchorage	Alaska Natural History
AK	Anchorage	The Book Cache
AL	Dothan	Red House Books
AL	Florence	Bookland Stores
AR	Fayetteville	Revelations Christian Books
AR	Little Rock	Dillard's Department Store
AR	Little Rock	Madcats
AZ	Tempe	Diamond's Department Stores
AZ	Tucson	Southwest Parks and Monuments
CA	Berkeley	Comics & Comix
CA	Berkeley	The Nature Company
CA	Beverly Hills	Hunter's Bookstores
CA	Brisbane	Upstart Crow & Company Books
CA	Claremont	Claremont Newsstand
CA	Gardena	Law Distributors
CA	Hayward	Bookmania Inc
CA	Larkspur	A Clean Well-Lighted Place
CA	Los Angeles	German & International Bookstore
CA	Los Angeles	Los Angeles City College Stores
CA	Los Angeles	Robinson's Department Stores
CA	Montclair	Little Red School House
CA	Mountain View	Tex's Toys
CA	Oakland	Western Christian Bookstores
CA	Oxnard	Paul Rudd's Christian Supply
CA	Sacramento	Tower Books
CA	San Diego	J K Gill
CA	San Francisco	Banana Republic Stores
CA	San Francisco	Emporium Capwell Stores
CA	San Francisco	Golden Gate National Parks
CA	San Francisco	Kaufer-Stadler
CA	San Mateo	Books Inc
CA	San Rafael	Dawn Horse Book Depot
CA	Santa Barbara	Kinko's Publishing Group
CA	Santa Monica	Books Et Cetera
CO	Aurora	Hatch's
CO	Boulder	Time Warp Inc
CO	Denver	Colborn School Supply Stores
CO	Englewood	Mustard Seed Bible Book Store
CO	Mesa Verde	Mesa Verde Museum Assn Bookstore
CO	Salida	Old West Book & News Center
CT	New Haven	New Haven News Agency
CT	New Haven	TPA Books
CT	Norwalk	Caldor's Department Stores
CT	Stamford	Waldenbooks
CT	Storrs	Univ of Connecticut Co-operative
CT	Trumbull	D M Read
DC	Washington	Crown Books
DC	Washington	Parks and History Association
DC	Washington	Smithsonian Institution Museum
FL	Cocoa Beach	College Management Service
FL	Ft Lauderdale	Book Rack Management
FL	Jacksonville	Agape Christian Bookstore
FL	Jacksonville	Book Town
FL	Miami	Jefferson Stores
FL	Saint Leo	St Leo College Campus Stores
FL	Tallahassee	Du Bey's News Centers
GA	Atlanta	Georgia Bookstore
GA	Atlanta	Rich's Department Stores
HI	Honolulu	University of Hawaii Bookstores
IA	Ames	Walt's Gift Shops
IA	Burlington	Newsland
IA	Des Moines	The Book Trader
IA	Des Moines	Younkers Department Stores
ID	Moscow	Crossroads Bookstore
IL	Chicago	Barbara's Bookstore
IL	Chicago	Carson Pirie Scott & Company
IL	Chicago	Kroch's & Brentano's
IL	Chicago	Libreria Giron
IL	Chicago	Marshall Field, Book Department
IL	Chicago	Moody Bookstores
IL	Chicago	Revolution Books
IL	Chicago	Sears, Roebuck & Company
IL	Chicago	Wieboldt Department Stores
IL	Elmhurst	Follett College Stores
IL	Galesburg	Dick Blick Company
IL	Glen Ellyn	Lemstone Book Branch
IL	Joliet	Printer's Ink
IL	Kewanee	Guzzardo's
IL	Peoria	The Book Emporium
IL	Wheaton	Quest Bookshop
IN	Charlestown	Army & Air Force Exchange
IN	Indianapolis	Gallery Book & Magazine Shop
IN	Indianapolis	L S Ayres and Company
IN	Nappanee	Christian Light Bookstore
IN	Richmond	Readmore Corporation
KS	Shawnee Msn	Rainy Day Books
KS	Topeka	Palmer News Company
KS	Wichita	McLeod's
KY	Lexington	Wallace's Bookstores
KY	Paducah	Readmore Books
LA	New Orleans	D H Holmes Department Stores
LA	New Orleans	Godchaux's Department Stores
MA	Belmont	American Opinion Bookstore
MA	Bolton	Association of Logos Bookstores
MA	Boston	St Paul Catholic Book Center
MA	Boylston	Book Corner
MA	Braintree	Hammett's Learning World
MA	Cambridge	Harvard Bookstores
MA	Cambridge	Harvard Cooperative Society
MA	Canton	Lauriat's Books
MA	Canton	Royal Discount Bookstores
MA	Framingham	United College Bookstores
MA	Framingham	Zayre Corporation
MA	Hyannis	Paperback Booksmith
MA	Northampton	Newstand
MA	Springfield	Brennan College Service
MA	W Barnstable	Garland & Grace
MA	Westborough	Annie's Book Stop
MD	Annapolis	Law Books Ltd
MD	Baltimore	Geppi's Comic World
MD	Baltimore	Gordon's Booksellers
MD	Baltimore	Hutzler's Department Stores
MD	Baltimore	Remington Bookstores
MD	Columbia	Campus Books
ME	Bangor	Mr Paperback
ME	Portland	Portland News Company
MI	Ann Arbor	Borders Bookshop
MI	Bloomfield	Oakland Community College
MI	Grand Rapids	Baker Book House
MI	Grand Rapids	Christian Discount Book Center
MI	Grand Rapids	Zondervan Family Bookstores
MI	Lansing	Community News Center
MI	Madison Hghts	DMI Industries
MI	Niles	Hall of Cards & Books

Chain Stores -- Sorted by State and City

ST	CITY	COMPANY
MI	Novi	Little Professor Book Centers
MI	Pontiac	Front Page Bookstore
MI	Royal Oak	Dickson's Bookstores
MI	Southgate	Eden Books
MI	Troy	Children's Book Mark
MI	Washington	Paperback Outlet
MN	Minneapolis	Augsburg Publishing, Retail
MN	Minneapolis	B Dalton Bookseller
MN	Minneapolis	Bethany Fellowship Bookshop
MN	Minneapolis	Dayton-Hudson Department Stores
MN	Minneapolis	Northwestern Products
MN	Minneapolis	Powers Department Stores
MN	Minneapolis	Shinder's Readmore Bookstores
MN	Minneapolis	Univ. of Minnesota Bookstores
MO	Columbia	The Missouri Store
MO	St. Louis	Alfonsi Reading Centers
MO	St. Louis	Famous Barr Department Stores
MO	Windyville	School of Metaphysics Bookstores
MS	Jackson	McRae's Department Stores
NC	Charlotte	Belk Stores
NC	Charlotte	Bush Stationers
NC	Charlotte	J B Ivey Department Stores
NC	Greensboro	News 'N Novels
NC	Greensboro	Wills Book & Stationary
NC	Winston-Salem	Hinkle's Bookstores
ND	Medora	Theodore Roosevelt Nature and
NE	Lincoln	Miller & Paine Department Stores
NE	Lincoln	Nebraska Book Company
NH	Bedford	Peter's Campus Services
NH	Manchester	New Hampshire College
NH	Peterborough	Eastern Mountain Sports
NH	Portsmouth	Marjen Books
NH	Portsmouth	Winebaum News Shop
NJ	Rochelle Park	Toys-R-Us Stores
NJ	Rocky Hill	Titles Unlimited
NJ	Trenton	Brauninger News Company
NY	Brooklyn	Abraham & Straus Stores
NY	Brooklyn	Utrecht Gift Shops
NY	Flushing	Campus Store Queens College
NY	Kenmore	Otto Ulbrich Company
NY	New York	Associated Dry Goods
NY	New York	B Altman and Company
NY	New York	Barnes & Noble Bookstores
NY	New York	Benjamin Books
NY	New York	Bloomingdales Department Stores
NY	New York	Doubleday Book Shops
NY	New York	F A O Schwarz Stores
NY	New York	French & Spanish Book Corp.
NY	New York	Rizzoli International Bookstores
NY	New York	Salvation Army Supply Purchasing
NY	New York	Sam Flax Inc
NY	New York	Strand Book Stores
NY	New York	The Compleat Strategist
NY	Poughkeepsie	The Book & Record
NY	Rochester	McCurdy & Company
NY	Rochester	Scrantom's Book & Stationery
NY	Saratoga Sprgs	Friar Tuck Bookshop
OH	Brooklyn Hghts	Burrows Brothers
OH	Cincinnati	Berean Bookstores
OH	Cincinnati	McAlpin Company
OH	Cincinnati	Shillito-Rike's Department Store
OH	Cincinnati	Univ of Cincinnati Bookstore
OH	Cleveland	Higbee Company
OH	Columbus	Christian Armory
OH	Columbus	Lazarus Department Stores
OH	Columbus	OSU Bookstores
OH	Columbus	Readmor Bookstores
OH	Dayton	Wilkie News
OH	Kent	Kent State University Bookstores
OH	Lancaster	Lancaster Office Supply
OH	Lima	Readmore Books - Hallmark Cards
OH	Morraine	Elder Beerman Department Stores
OK	Moore	Gifts of Praise
OK	Norman	The Book Stall
OK	Norman	University of Oklahoma Bookstore
OK	Oklahoma City	Thompson Book & Supply
OK	Weatherford	Ratcliffe's Book & Office Supply
OR	Albany	Linn Benton College Bookstore
OR	Lake Oswego	Graham's Book and Stationery
OR	Portland	Christian Supply Centers
OR	Salem	Rainbow West Christian Store
PA	Allentown	Ann Ar Bookshoppes
PA	Allentown	Hess's Department Stores
PA	Altoona	The Bookstore Inc
PA	Bryn Mawr	The Owl Bookshops
PA	Easton	Orr's Department Stores
PA	Harrisburg	Pomeroy's
PA	Kittanning	Abranovic Associates Inc
PA	Kittanning	Christian Book & Gift Shop
PA	Lemoyne	News Center West, Offices
PA	Levittown	Pomeroy's
PA	Montgomeryvil	Atlantic Bookshops
PA	Philadelphia	Eastern National Park and
PA	Philadelphia	Encore Books
PA	Philadelphia	Fortress Church Supply Store
PA	Philadelphia	John Wanamaker Department Stores
PA	Philadelphia	Strawbridge and Clothier
PA	Philadelphia	Temple University Student Stores
PA	Pittsburgh	Kaufmann Department Stores
PA	Reading	Boscov's Department Stores
PA	Scottsdale	Provident Bookstores
PA	Scranton	The Guild
PA	York	Bookland Inc
SC	Charleston	The Book Bag Stores
SC	Charleston	Huguley's
TN	Cleveland	Church of God Publishing House
TN	Hendersonville	Book Peddler
TN	Knoxville	Book & Supply Stores
TN	Knoxville	Gateway Books
TN	Nashville	20th Century Christian Bookstore
TN	Nashville	Baptist Book Stores
TN	Nashville	BookWorld
TN	Nashville	Castner-Knott Department Stores
TN	Nashville	Cokesbury - Retail Division
TN	Nashville	R M Mills Bookstores
TX	Amarillo	Hastings Books & Records
TX	Arlington	Lone Star Comics/Science Fiction
TX	Arlington	The Love Shop
TX	Austin	Bookstop Stores
TX	Dallas	Half Price Books
TX	Dallas	House of Christian Books
TX	Dallas	J A Majors Medical Book Company
TX	Dallas	Taylors Bookstores
TX	Fort Worth	Century Bookstores, Headquarters
TX	Fort Worth	Fantastic Worlds Bookstores
TX	Houston	Foley's Department Stores
TX	Houston	Wilderness Equipment Company
TX	Lancaster	Promises Bookstores
TX	Midland	Rudd Christian Bookstore
TX	San Antonio	Periodical Management Group
TX	San Antonio	Twig Bookshops
UT	SaltLakeCity	Deseret Book Company, Retail

Chain Stores -- Sorted by State and City

ST	CITY	COMPANY
UT	SaltLakeCity	ZCMI Department Stores
UT	Springdale	Zion Natural Historical Assn.
VA	Newport News	Book 'N Card Inc
VA	Norfolk	Farm Fresh Bookstore
WA	Seattle	The Bon Department Stores
WA	Seattle	Church of Scientology
WA	Seattle	Frederick & Nelson Stores
WA	Seattle	Pacific Northwest National Parks
WA	Spokane	Book & Game Company
WA	Tacoma	Dightman's Bible Book Centers
WI	Appleton	Book World Inc
WI	Green Bay	Shopko Stores
WI	Madison	University of Wisconsin
WI	Milwaukee	Harry W Schwartz, Booksellers
WV	Morgantown	University Bookstores
WV	Parkersburg	People's News and Book Mart
WV	Wheeling	Stone & Thomas Department Stores

CANADA

ST	CITY	COMPANY
BC	Surrey V4A 2J4	Black Bond Books
BC	Vancouver V6B 4G1	Woodward Stores Ltd.
ON	Cornwall K6H 5S7	Godard Stationary Stores
ON	Downsview M3J 2M4	Epic Bookstores
ON	Etobicoke M9Z 4X8	Mike's Bookstores
ON	Guelph N1H 6N5	Guelph Campus Co-Op Bookstores
ON	Rexdale M9W 1C1	Coles, The Book People
ON	Toronto M4S 1A8	W H Smith Bookstores
ON	Toronto M4S 2C6	Hudson's Bay General Merchandise
ON	Toronto M5B 1C8	T Eaton Company
ON	Toronto M5H 1N1	Woolco Department Stores
ON	Toronto M5H 1Y4	Lichtman's News and Books
ON	Toronto M5H 3K2	Simpson Department Stores
ON	Toronto M5J 1T8	Cara Operations
ON	Toronto M5S 1A6	University of Toronto Bookroom
ON	Toronto M5T 2W4	Sun Wa Bookstore
PQ	Brossard J4W 2T5	Librairie Du Scorpion
PQ	Montreal H2C 1T1	Librairie DeMarc
PQ	Valleyfield J6T4M2	Les Librairies Boyer
SK	Saskatoon S7N 1Y7	Play & Learn Achievement Place

Book Clubs

Academic Book Club
Guy Gelinas, Vice President
P O Box 1507
11 Princess Street #20
Kingston K7L 1A1 ON Canada
613-547-7666
Categories: 31-65-99

**Advertising, Marketing, and
Sales Promotion Book Club**
Gary R Alexander, Editor
The Putter Building
Middle Island NY 11953
516-924-8555
Categories: 19(marketing)

American Artist Book Club
Glorya Hale, Editor
Watson-Guptill Publications
1515 Broadway
New York NY 10036
212-764-7300
Categories: 11

American Life Foundation
John Crosby Freeman, Director
P O Box 349
Watkins Glen NY 14891
607-535-4737
Categories: 11-29-41-65

Antares SF Book Club
W H Wheeler Associates
2697 Lavery Court #23A
Newbury Park CA 91320
Categories: 86

Aquarian Agent Book Club
Henry Weingarten, Director
ASI Publishers
63 West 38th Street #505
New York NY 10018
212-719-2919
Categories: 39-53

**Architects & Planners
  Book Service**
Howard Gordon, Director
Macmillan Book Clubs
866 Third Avenue
New York NY 10022
212-702-2000
Categories: 11(architecture)
           55(planning)

Architects' Book Club
Leonard Josephson, Editor
McGraw-Hill Book Clubs
1221 Avenue of the Americas
New York NY 10020
212-512-2000
Categories: 11(architecture)

Arrow Book Club
Molly Harrington, Editor
Scholastic Book Services
730 Broadway
New York NY 10003
212-505-3000
Categories: 21-76
some reprints, grades 4-6

ASI Healing Arts Book Club
Henry Weingarten, Director
ASA Publishers
63 West 38th Street #505
New York NY 10018
212-719-2919
Categories: 39-53

Astronomy Book Club
Richard Kelley, Director
Macmillan Book Clubs
866 Third Avenue
New York NY 10022
212-702-2000
Categories: 67(astronomy)

Augsburg Reading Club
Roderick Olson, Director
P O Box 1209
426 S Fifth Street
Minneapolis MN 55440
612-330-3319
Categories: 63

Auraria Book Club
Auraria Book Center
Lawrence and 9th Streets
Denver CO 80204
303-629-3230
Categories: 31-99

Automobile Quarterly Book Club
Kevin Bitz, Manager
Automobile Quarterly
P O Box 348
Kutztown PA 19530
215-683-8352
Categories: 41-43(automobiles)

Aviators Guild
R Collins, Editor
TAB Books
Blue Rdg Summit PA 17214
217-794-2191
Categories: 69(aviation)

Avicultural Book Club
Pat Sutherland, Editor
Avicultural Book Company
P O Box 446
East Elmhurst NY 11369
718-779-0541
Categories: 15(birds)-29
           69(bird watching)

B'nai B'rith Book Club
Arthur Kurzweil, Editor
Jason Aronson Company
111 Eighth Avenue
New York NY 10011
212-924-6663
Categories: 63(Jewish)

Behavioral Books Institute
Dwight Wardell, Editor
Prentice-Hall Book Clubs
Sylvan Avenue
Englewood NJ 07632
201-592-2477
Categories: 31-57

Behavioral Science Book Service
Lilian Schein, Director
Macmillan Book Clubs
866 Third Avenue
New York NY 10022
212-702-2000
Categories: 31-57-65

**Better Homes and Gardens
Family Book Service**
1716 Locust Street
Des Moines IA 50309
Categories: 27-29-35-39-43-69

**Better Homes and Gardens
Cook Book Club**
Blair Brown Hoyt, Editor
750 Third Avenue
New York NY 10017
212-557-6600
Categories: 27-29-39

Birding Book Society
Richard Platt, Editor
North American Book Clubs
51 Washington Street
Dover NH 03820
603-742-4662
Categories: 15(birds)-29
           69(bird watching)

BMOC Cooking & Crafts Club
Pat Adrian, Director
485 Lexington Avenue
New York NY 10017
212-767-4300
Categories: 27-29-39

Book Club for Martial Arts
Chuck Reeves, Editor
Seven Putter Building
Middle Island NY 11953
516-924-8555
Categories: 39-69(martial arts)

Book Club Northwest
Ken Bushnell or Jack Eldridge
80 S Jackson Street #308
Seattle WA 98104
206-622-4200
Categories: 61(OR, WA, ID, AK)
206-937-5996

Book Collector's Book Shelf
William Burton, Director
Moretus Press
274 Madison Avenue
New York NY 10016
212-685-2250
Categories: 59(bibliographies)
98(books)

Book-of-the-Month Club
Nancy Evans, Editor-in-Chief
485 Lexington Avenue
New York NY 10017
212-767-4300
Categories: 17-75-99
the largest U.S. book club

Book-of-the-Month Club/Science
Spencer Smith, Director
485 Lexington Avenue
New York NY 10017
212-767-4300
Categories: 23-51-67

Books for Accountants
Dwight Wardell, Director
Prentice-Hall Book Clubs
Sylvan Avenue
Englewood NJ 07632
201-592-2477
Categories: 19(accounting)

Books of Light
Chris Kurtz, Editor
3391 Edenbrook Court
Columbus OH 43220
614-876-0211
Categories: 39-53-57-86

Buddy Paperback Book Club
Susan LaBella, Editor
Field Publications
245 Long Hill Road
Middletown CT 06457
203-347-7251
Categories: 21-76
quality paperbacks and reprints
grades K-1

**Builder's and Contractor's
Book Service (Prentice-Hall)**
Dwight Wardell, Director
Sylvan Avenue
Englewood NJ 07632
201-592-2477
Categories: 11(architecture)-19

BYTE Book Club
Leonard Josephson, Editor
McGraw-Hill Book Clubs

1221 Avenue of the Americas
New York NY 10020
212-997-4128
Categories: 23

Catholic Book Club
Thomas H Stahel, Editor
The America Press
106 West 56th Street
New York NY 10019
212-581-4640
Categories: 63(Catholic)

Catholic Digest Book Club
Henry Lexau, Editor
815 Second Avenue
New York NY 10017
212-867-9766
Categories: 63(Catholic)

Century Book Club
Mary Gabriel, Editor
1560 N La Brea Avenue
Los Angeles CA 90028
213-466-8989
Categories: 37

Chemical Engineers' Book Club
Leonard Josephson, Editor
McGraw-Hill Book Clubs
1221 Avenue of the Americas
New York NY 10020
212-512-2000
Categories: 23(engineering)-67

**China Book Club and
Far East Book Society**
Fredric M Kaplan, Editor
302 Fifth Avenue
New York NY 10001
212-564-4099
Categories: 11-19-41-45(Chinese)
55-71-80
books related to China

Choice Reader Service
John Biagini, Editor
Harlequin Enterprises
300 East 42nd Street
New York NY 10017
212-682-6080
Categories: 75(women's fiction)

Christian Bookshelf
Mary Risley, Editor
Christian Herald Association
40 Overlook Drive
Chappaqua NY 10514
914-769-9000
Categories: 63(Christian)

**Christian Quality Paperback
Book Club**
Leonard George Goss, Editor
1000 E Huron Street
Milford MI 48042
313-685-8773
Categories: 63(Christian)

Civil Engineers' Book Club
Leonard Josephson, Editor
McGraw-Hill Book Clubs
1221 Avenue of the Americas
New York NY 10020
212-512-2000
Categories: 23(engineering)

Classics Club
Pamela Kennedy, Editor
Walter J Black Company
Flower Hill
Roslyn NY 11576
516 627-4920
Categories: 75-99(classics)

Club del Libro
Denise Crowell, President
AIMS International
3216 Montana Avenue
Cincinnati OH 45211
513-661-9200
Categories: 45(Spanish)-59-63
80(Spanish)-95

Club del Libro, Ninos y Juvenile
Mariano Domingo, Purchasing
AIMS International
3216 Montana Avenue
Cincinnati OH 45211
513-661-9200
Categories: 21-45(Spanish)-76

Coaches' Book Club
Dwight Wardell, Director
Prentice-Hall Book Clubs
Sylvan Avenue
Englewood Cliffs NJ 07632
201-592-2477
Categories: 31-57-69(coaching)

Computer Book Club
Lawrence Jackel, President
TAB Books
Blue Rdg Summit PA 17214
217-794-2191
Categories: 23

Conservative Book Club
Maureen McCaffrey, Editor
15 Oakland Avenue
Harrison NY 10528
914-835-0900
Categories: 19-55-63

Cookery Book Club
Kristie Beard, Editor
P O Box 768
Port Washington NY 11050
516-883-2227
Categories: 27-39-43-98
(fashion and beauty)

Cosmopolitan Book Club
225 Park Avenue S, 17th Floor
New York NY 10003
Categories: 19(careers)-27
98(beauty)

Dance Book Club
Charles Woodford, Director
Princeton Book Company
P O Box 109
Princeton NJ 08540
609-737-8178
Categories: 11(dance)-39

Data Processing Book Service
Dwight Wardell, Director
Prentice-Hall Book Clubs
Sylvan Avenue
Englewood Cliffs NJ 07632
201-592-2477
Categories: 23

Designers Book Club
Glorya Hale, Editor
Watson-Guptill Publications
1515 Broadway
New York NY 10036
212-764-7300
Categories: 11(graphic design)

Detective Book Club
Pamela Kennedy, Editor
Walter J Black Company
Flower Hill
Roslyn NY 11576
516-627-4920
Categories: 84

Direct Mail Book Service
Terri Castillo, Editor
Guideposts Book Club
757 Third Avenue
New York NY 10017
212-371-6060
Categories: 57(inspirational)-63

Discover California Book Club
Chronicle Books
One Hallidie Plaza #806
San Francisco CA 94102
415-777-7240
Categories: 61(CA)-71-99

Discovering Book Club
Sally Lodge, Editor
245 Long Hill Road
Middletown CT 06457
203-347-7251
Categories: 21-76
quality paperbacks, grades 4-6

Dolphin Book Club
Nancy Donaldson, Director
485 Lexington Avenue
New York NY 10017
212-767-4300
Categories: 69(nautical, boating)

Doubleday Book Club
Sam Blum, Editor
245 Park Avenue
New York NY 10167
212-953-4561
Categories: 99

Early Learning Book Club
Elizabeth Cater, Director
Macmillan Book Clubs
866 Third Avenue
New York NY 10022
212-935-2000
Categories: 31

Ebony Book Club
Ebony Magazine
820 S Michigan Avenue
Chicago IL 60605
Categories: 99-49(Black)

Ecological Book Club
Claudine de la Belle Issue, Ed.
6 N Water Street
Greenwich CT 06830
203-531-7755
Categories: 13-39-51

Educator's Book Club
Dwight Wardell, Director
Prentice-Hall Book Clubs
Sylvan Avenue
Englewood Cliffs NJ 07632
201-592-2477
Categories: 31-69

Electrical and Electronics
Engineering Book Club
Howard Gordon, Director
866 Third Avenue
New York NY 10022
212-702-2000
Categories: 23(electronics)

Electronics and Control
Engineers' Book Club
Leonard Josephson, Editor
1221 Avenue of the Americas
New York NY 10020
212-512-2000
Categories: 23(electronics,
              engineering)

Electronics Book Club
Lawrence Jackel, President
TAB Books
Blue Rdg Summit PA 17214
717-794-2191
Categories: 23(electronics)

Electronics Book Service
Dwight Wardell, Director
Prentice-Hall Book Clubs
Sylvan Avenue
Englewood Cliffs NJ 07632
201-592-2477
Categories: 23(electronics)

Engineers' Book Society
Leonard Josephson, Editor
McGraw-Hill Book Clubs
1221 Avenue of the Americas
New York NY 10020
212-512-2000
Categories: 23(engineers)-67

Episcopal Book Club
James B Simpson, Director
P O Box 153
Shrewsbury NJ 07701
Categories: 17-41
              63(Episcopalian)

Erotic Art Book Society
Ralph Ginzburg, Editor
Avant-Garde Media
251 West 57th Street
New York NY 10019
212-581-2000
Categories: 11-35-33

Evangelical Book Club
Leonard George Goss, Editor
Mott Media
1000 E Huron Street
Milford MI 48042
313-685-8773
Categories: 63(Christian)

Executive Program
Eileen Concannon, Director
Macmillan Book Clubs
866 Third Avenue
New York NY 10022
212-935-2000
Categories: 19(management)

Family Bookshelf
Mary Risley, Editor
Christian Herald Association
40 Overlook Drive
Chappaqua NY 10514
914-769-9000
Categories: 17-35-63
              75(religious)

Farm Journal Family Bookshelf
Mary Risley, Editor
Farm Journal Magazine
40 Overlook Drive
Chappaqua NY 10514
914-769-9000
Categories: 99
wholesome reading for family

Field and Stream Book Club
1225 S Market
Camp Hill PA 17011
Categories: 51-69(fishing and
              hunting)

Fireside Theatre
Robert Main, Editor
245 Park Avenue
New York NY 10167
212-953-4561
Categories: 11-33

Fortune Book Club
Pat Adrian, Director
485 Lexington Avenue
New York NY 10017
212-767-4300
Categories: 19

Book Clubs

Gambler's Book Club
Howard Schwartz, Editor
630 S 11th Street
P O Box 4115
Las Vegas NV 89127
702-382-7555
Categories: 17-33-57-69-75

Garden Book Club
Rachel Asher, Editor
Readers Garden
250 West 57th Street
New York NY 10107
212-757-8070
Categories: 43

Get Rich Book Club
Gayle Geisert, Editor
Seven Putter Building
Middle Island NY 11953
516-924-8555
Categories: 19(opportunity)

Global Church Growth Book Club
Ralph Winter, Director
P O Box 40129
1705 N Sierra Bonita Avenue
Pasadena CA 91104
818-798-0819
Categories: 63(Christian
                missions)

Goodtime Paperback Book Club
Susan LaBella, Editor
Field Publications
245 Long Hill Road
Middletown CT 06457
203-347-7251
Categories: 21-76
quality paperbacks, grades 2-3

Graphic Artist's Book Club
Mert Ransdell, Director
F & W Publications
9933 Alliance Road
Cincinnati OH 45242
513-984-0717
Categories: 11(graphics, art)
                19(advertising)

Grit Family Bookshelf
Philip March, Director
40 Overlook Drive
Chappaqua NY 10514
914-769-9000
Categories: 99

Health & Vitality Book Guild
Dwight Wardell, Director
Prentice-Hall Book Clubs
Sylvan Avenue
Englewood Cliffs NJ 07632
201-592-2477
Categories: 27-39-53

Herald Book Club
Mark Hegener, Manager
Franciscan Herald Press

1434 West 51st Street
Chicago IL 60609
312-254-4462
Categories: 63(Catholic)-99

History Book Club
Nancy R M Whitin, Director
P O Box 790
40 Guernsey Street
Stamford CT 06904
203-359-4250
Categories: 41-65

How-To Book Club
Lawrence Jackel, President
TAB Books
Blue Ridge Summit PA 17214
717-794-2191
Categories: 29-43

Instructor Book Club
Judith K Wathen, Director
P O Box 790
40 Guernsey Street
Stamford CT 06904
203-359-4250
Categories: 31

Interior Design Book Club
Christine K Duffy, Director
Interior Design Magazine
475 Park Avenue, 3rd Floor
New York NY 10016
212-576-8068
Categories: 11(interior design)
                43

International Collectors Library
Tom Davis, Editor
Doubleday Book Clubs
245 Park Avenue
New York NY 10167
212-953-4561
Categories: 80-99

Irish-American Book Society
Roger Lourie, Manager
Devin-Adair Publishing
P O Box A
Old Greenwich CT 06870
203-531-7755
Categories: 71-78-79
                95(anything Irish)

Jewelers' Book Club
Cynthia B Pearlman, Coordinator
Chilton Way
Radnor PA 19089
215-964-4480
Categories: 29(jewelry)

Judaica Book Club
Florence Weissman, Editor
Jonathan David Publishers
68-22 Eliot Avenue
MIddle Village NY 11379
718-456-8611
Categories: 63(Jewish)-99

Junior Literary Guild
Marjorie Jones, Director
245 Park Avenue
New York NY 10167
212-953-4768
Categories: 21-31-76-89
hardcover, grades K-12

Large Print Home Library
Marjorie Goldstein, Manager
Doubleday Book Clubs
245 Park Avenue
New York NY 10167
212-953-4561
Categories: 99(large print)

Lawyer's Book Clubs
Dwight Wardell, Director
Prentice-Hall Book Clubs
Sylvan Avenue
Englewood Cliffs NJ 07632
201-592-2477
Categories: 19-55(law)

Lawyers' Book Society
Andrew Sussman, Director
51 Washington Street
Dover NH 03820
603-742-4662
Categories: 19-55(law)

Le Cercle du Livre de France
David Hayat, President
French Book Guild
8000 Cooper Avenue, Building 29
Glendale NY 11385
718-326-0577
Categories: 45-80(French)

Let's Read Book Club
Norman Finkelstein, Director
P O Box 3064
Framingham MA 01701
617-879-6756
Categories: 21-31-76-89

Library of Computers and
Information Sciences
Richard Kelley, Director
866 Third Avenue
New York NY 10022
212-702-2000
Categories: 23

Library of Human Behavior
Martin V Azarian, Director
315 Fifth Avenue
New York NY 10016
212-684-7900
Categories: 57

Library of Science
Lilian Schein, Director
Macmillan Book Clubs
866 Third Avenue
New York NY 10022
212-935-2000
Categories: 67

Book Clubs

Library of Special Education
Elizabeth Cater, Director
Macmillan Book Clubs
866 Third Avenue
New York NY 10022
212-935-2000
Categories: 31-39

Libro Club
Rose Balzowski, Manager
Nixell's Inc
P O Box 21231
Concord CA 94521
415-827-3609
Categories: 45(Spanish)-78-80-99
books in Spanish

Limited Editions Club
Sidney Shiff, Director
551 Fifth Avenue
New York NY 10017
212-682-7115
Categories: 11-75
new illustrated editions of
classic literature

Literary Guild of America
Maureen Mahon Egen, Editor
Doubleday Book Clubs
245 Park Avenue
New York NY 10167
212-953-4561
Categories: 99
second largest U.S. book club

Lucky Book Club
Eva Moore, Editor
Scholastic Book Services
730 Broadway
New York NY 10003
212-505-3000
Categories: 21-76
some reprints, grades 2-3

Management Books Institute
Dwight Wardell, Director
Prentice-Hall Book Clubs
Sylvan Avenue
Englewood Cliffs NJ 07632
201-592-2477
Categories: 19(management)

Mechanical Engineers' Book Club
Leonard Josephson, Editor
McGraw-Hill Book Clubs
1221 Avenue of the Americas
New York NY 10020
212-997-4128
Categories: 23(engineering)

Media Books
Stephen J Rechner, Director
Westwood Enterprises
Perrin Road
Woodstock CT 06281
203-974-1050
Categories: 19(marketing,
      publicity)

Military Book Club
Tom Davis, Editor
Doubleday Book Clubs
245 Park Avenue
New York NY 10167
212-953-4561
Categories: 55(military)-87

Minister's Personal Library
Linda Stephenson, Editor
Word Books
4800 W Waco Drive
Waco TX 76703
817-772-7650
Categories: 63(Christian)

Movie Entertainment Book Club
Maureen McCaffrey, Editor
15 Oakland Avenue
Harrison NY 10528
914-835-0900
Categories: 11-17-33

Music Book Society
Andrew Sussman, Director
North American Book Clubs
51 Washington Street
Dover NH 03820
603-742-4662
Categories: 11-17(composers)

Music Educators' Book Society
Dwight Wardell, Director
Prentice-Hall Book Clubs
Sylvan Avenue
Englewood Cliffs NJ 07632
201-592-2477
Categories: 11-31-41(music)

Mystery Guild
Ellen Asher, Editor
Doubleday Book Clubs
245 Park Avenue
New York NY 10167
212-953-4561
Categories: 84

Mystic Arts Book Society
Robert Salomon, President
Lyle Stuart Inc
120 Enterprise Avenue
Secaucus NJ 07094
201-866-0490
Categories: 39-53

Natural Science Book Club
Lilian Schein, Director
Macmillan Book Clubs
866 Third Avenue
New York NY 10022
212-935-2000
Categories: 15-51-67

Neighborhood Book Clubs
P O Box 20880
Long Beach CA 90801
Categories: 99(for families)
still in business?

New Professional Chef Book Club
Van Nostrand Reinhold
135 West 50th Street
New York NY 10020
212-265-8700
Categories: 27-39

Nostalgia Book Club
Gail Kinn, Editor
One Park Avenue
New York NY 10016
212-532-9200
Categories: 11-33-41(nostalgia)

Nurse's Book Society
Jennefer Marmaduke, Director
Macmillan Book Clubs
866 Third Avenue
New York NY 10022
212-935-2000
Categories: 39(nursing)

Organic Gardening Book Club
Anne Halpin, Acquisitions Editor
33 E Minor Street
Emmaus PA 18049
215-967-5171
Categories: 27-43-51

Outdoor Life Book Club
Grace Mishkin, Editorial
Outdoor Life Magazine
380 Madison Avenue
New York NY 10017
212-687-3000
Categories: 51-69(recreation)

Performing Arts Book Club
Lynne Mazza, Editor
27 Union Square W #505
New York NY 10017
212-924-6666
Categories: 11(classical music)
      17-41

Personal Achievement Association
Dwight Wardell, Director
Prentice-Hall Book Clubs
Sylvan Avenue
Englewood Cliffs NJ 07632
201-592-2477
Categories: 19-57

Personal Computer Book Club
Dwight Wardell, Director
Prentice-Hall Book Clubs
Sylvan Avenue
Englewood Cliffs NJ 07632
201-592-2477
Categories: 23

Photography Book Club
David E Lewis, Editor
Watson-Guptill Publications
1515 Broadway
New York NY 10036
212-764-7300
Categories: 11(photography)

Book Clubs

Popular Science Book Club
Grace Mishkin, Editorial
Popular Science Magazine
380 Madison Avenue
New York NY 10017
212-687-3000
Categories: 29-43

Practical Homeowner's Book Club
Ray Wolf, Acquisitions Editor
33 E Minor Street
Emmaus PA 18049
215-967-5171
Categories: 43-51

Preferred Choice Bookplan
Gail Kinn, Editor
Crown Publishers
One Park Avenue
New York NY 10016
212-532-9200
Categories: 99

Prevention Book Club
Charles Gerras, Editor
33 E Minor Street
Emmaus PA 18049
215-967-5171
Categories: 27-35-39

Print/Graphic Design Book Club
Jean Kofoed, Book Buyer
6400 Goldsboro Road
Bethesda MD 20817-9969
301-229-9040
Categories: 11(graphics)
            19(printing)

Printing & Publishing Book Club
Joanne Concannon, Manager
North American Publishing
401 N Broad Street
Philadelphia PA 19108
215-238-5300
Categories: 19(printing)

Professional Civil Engineering Book Club
Howard Gordon, Director
866 Third Avenue
New York NY 10022
212-702-2000
Categories: 23(engineering)-67

Professional Mechanical Engineering Book Club
Howard Gordon, Director
866 Third Avenue
New York NY 10022
212-702-2000
Categories: 23(engineering)-67

Psychotherapy and Social Science Book Club
111 Eighth Avenue
New York NY 10011
212-924-6663
Categories: 57

Public Relations Book Club
Michael M Smith, Editor
Larimi Communications
246 West 38th Street
New York NY 10018
212-819-9310
Categories: 19(marketing,
              publicity)

Quality Paperback Book Club
Martin Asher, Director
Book-of-the-Month Club
485 Lexington Avenue
New York NY 10017
212-867-4300
Categories: 99
trade paperback books only

Reader's Digest Condensed Books
Barbara J Morgan, Editor
Reader's Digest Association
Pleasantville NY 10570
914-769-7000
Categories: 99

Reader's Subscription Book Club
Arthur Goldwag, Editor
Readers Garden
250 West 57th Street
New York NY 10107
212-757-8070
Categories: 47-75

Real Estate Books Institute
Dwight Wardell, Director
Prentice-Hall Book Clubs
Sylvan Avenue
Englewood Cliffs NJ 07632
201-592-2477
Categories: 19(real estate)

Real Estate Pros Book Club
Sandra Goodwin, Editor
Union Square Books (Crittenden)
P O Box 1150
Novato CA 94948
415-883-8771
Categories: 19(real estate)

Registered Nurse Book Club
Carla R Nelson, Editor
Jason Aronson Company
111 Eighth Avenue
New York NY 10011
212-924-6663
Categories: 39(nursing)

Religious Book Club
Kenneth Bazyn, Editor
Iverson-Norman Associates
5 S Buckhout Street
Irvington NY 10533
914-591-6505
Categories: 63(Protestant)

Romance Book Club
Ofelia Delgadillo, President
2401 Perimeter Mall

4400 Ashford Dunwoody Road
Atlanta GA 30346
404-394-6748
Categories: 85

Sales Book Club
Dwight Wardell, Director
Prentice-Hall Book Clubs
Sylvan Avenue
Englewood Cliffs NJ 07632
201-592-2477
Categories: 19(marketing)

Science Fiction Book Club
Ellen Asher, Editor
Doubleday Book Clubs
245 Park Avenue
New York NY 10167
212-953-4561
Categories: 86

See-Saw Book Club
Ellen Miles, Editor
Scholastic Book Services
730 Broadway
New York NY 10003
212-505-3000
Categories: 21-76
some reprints, grades K-1

Semantodonics
Jim Rhode, Director
4925 E Thomas Road
P O Box 15668
Phoenix AZ 85060
602-955-5662
Categories: 19-27(nutrition)
            39-57

Small Computer Book Club
Richard Kelley, Manager
Macmillan Book Clubs
866 Third Avenue
New York NY 10022
212-935-2000
Categories: 23

Small Press Book Club
Ellen Ferber, Editor
P O Box 100
Paradise CA 95969
916-877-6110
Categories: 10-75-83-90-95

Speakers & Toastmasters Bk Club
Dwight Wardell, Director
Prentice-Hall Book Clubs
Sylvan Avenue
Englewood Cliffs NJ 07632
201-592-2477
Categories: 19-33-57

Spiritual Book Associates
Kenneth W Peters, Editor
Ave Maria Press
Notre Dame IN 46556
219-287-2838
Categories: 63(Catholic)-99

Book Clubs

Spiritual Growth Book Club
Jeffrey Japinga, Director
Guideposts Book Club
757 Third Avenue
New York NY 10017
212-371-6060
Categories: 57(inspirational)-63

Teacher Book Club
Elizabeth Cater, Director
Macmillan Book Clubs
866 Third Avenue
New York NY 10022
212-935-2000
Categories: 31

Teen Age Book Club
Ellen Miles, Editor
Scholastic Book Services
730 Broadway
New York NY 10003
212-505-3000
Categories: 21-76-89
some reprints, grades 7-12

Thomas More Book Club
John L Sprague, Director
223 W Erie Street
Chicago IL 60610
312-951-2108
Categories: 63(Catholic)

Troll Book Club
Roy Wandelmaier, Editor
Troll Associates
320 Route #17
Mahwah NJ 07430
201-529-4000
Categories: 11-33-99

Trumpet Club
Dell Publishing Company
245 East 47th Street
New York NY 10017
212-605-3122
Categories: 21-31-76
grades 4-6

Twenty One Bookclub
Gail Kinn, Editor
Crown Publishers
One Park Avenue
New York NY 10016
212-532-9200
Categories: 99(books for adults)

Verbatim Book Club
Laurence Urdang, Editor
P O Box 668
Essex CT 06426
203-767-8248
Categories: 45(linquistics)-59

Veritas Book Club
Claudine Lourie, Editor
Devin-Adair Publishing
6 N Water Street
Greenwich CT 06830
203-531-7755
Categories: 41-55(conservative)

Weekly Reader Children's Books
Jacqueline Ball, Editor
Field Publications
245 Long Hill Road
Middletown CT 06457
203-638-2400
Categories: 21-31-76-89
hardcover books, grades K-6

Word Book Club
Linda Stephenson, Editor
Word Books
4800 W Waco Drive
Waco TX 76703
817-772-7650
Categories: 63(Christian)

Writer's Digest Book Club
Mert Ransdell, Director
9933 Alliance Road
Cincinnati OH 45242
513-984-0717
Categories: 11(writing)-47-59

Mail Order Catalogs That Feature Books

A Child's Collection
Robert Fisher, President
611 Broadway, Room 708
New York NY 10012
800-652-2665
Categories: 21-31-76-89

A Photographer's Place
P O Box 274
133 Mercer Street
New York NY 10012
212-431-9358
Categories: 11(photography)

American Express Catalog
Travel Related Services Company
American Express Plaza
New York NY 10004
Categories: 99

Angel Book Distribution Center
561 Tyler Street
Monterey CA 93940
408-372-1658
Categories: 37-53-99
books and tapes, 150 publishers

Animal City
8500 Alvarado Road
P O Box 1076
La Mesa CA 92041-0318
619-469-0188
Categories: 15
wholesale animal supplies

Animal Specialties
P O Box 531
Camden NJ 08101
609-662-8530
Categories: 15

Antheil Booksellers
2177 Isabelle Court
North Bellmore NY 11710
Categories: 55(military, naval)
            69(boating)

Aperture
Elm Street
Millerton NY 12546
Categories: 11(photography)

Asian Advertising & Marketing
Cynthia Caldwell, Business Mgr.
Travel Publishing Ltd
1801 World Trade Centre
Causeway Bay, Hong Kong
5-7903067
Categories: 19(marketing)

Asian World of Martial Arts
1917 Arch
Philadelphia PA 19103
Categories: 69(martial arts)

Aspen Cabin
5038 Sixth Avenue
Kenosha WI 53140
Categories: 29-51-69-71

Atlantic Book Service
P O Box 218
Charlestown MA 02129
Categories: 69(boating)

Audubon Workshop
1501 Paddock Drive
Northbrook IL 60062
312-729-6660
Categories: 11(birds)

Aviation Book Company
Walter Winner, Buyer
1640 Victory Boulevard
Glendale CA 91201
818-240-1771
Categories: 69(aviation)

Aviator's Supply House
113-15 Springfield Boulevard
Queens Village NY 11429
718-464-9300
Categories: 69(aviation)
aviation books and supplies

Banana Republic Travel Bookstore
Irma Zegas, General Manager
175 Bluxome Street
P O Box 7347
San Francisco CA 94120
800-527-5200; 415-777-0250
Categories: 69-71

The Baseball Advertiser
T.C.M.A.
P O Box 2
Amawalk NY 10501
Categories: 69(baseball)

Basic Crafts
1201 Broadway
New York NY 10001
212-679-3516
Categories: 29
craft wholesalers

Bicycle Posters & Prints
P O Box 7164
Hicksville NY 11802
Categories: 69(bicycling)
books, gifts, cards, posters

Boat Owners Association of U.S.
Book Department
880 S Pickett Street
Alexandria VA 22304
703-823-9550
Categories: 69(nautical,
            sailing)-71

Book Call
Thomas and Marguerite Whitney
New Canaan Bookshop
59 Elm Street
New Canaan CT 06840
203-966-5470; 800-255-2665
Categories: 99

Book Order Service
Science News
1719 N Street NW
Washington DC 20036
202-785-2255
Categories: 23-51-57-59-67

Boycan's Crafts
P O Box 897
Sharon PA 16146
Categories: 29

Buckley-Little Book Catalog
P O Box 512
Canal Street Station
New York NY 10013
Categories: 99(remainders)
remainders from authors

Bud Lilly's Trout Shop
P O Box 698
West Yellowstone MT 59758
406-646-7801
Categories: 69(fishing)

Builder's Booksource
George Kiskaddon
1801 4th Street
Berkeley CA 94710
415-845-6874
Categories: 11(architecture)
            29-43

The Butterfly Company
51-17 Rockaway Beach Boulevard
Far Rockaway NY 11691
212-945-5400
Categories: 15(butterflies)

BWD's Giftshelf
P O Box 110
Marietta OH 45750
614-373-5285
Categories: 15(birds)

Cabela's
812 - 13th Avenue
Sidney NE 69160
Categories: 15-69(fishing)

Caldwell Industries
603-909 E Davis Street
P O Box 170
Luling TX 78648
512-875-2654
Categories: 29

Mail Order Catalogs That Feature Books

California Crafts Supply
1096 N Main Street
Orange CA 92667
714-633-8891
Categories: 29

Cat Book Center
P O Box 112, Wykagyl Station
New Rochelle NY 10804
Categories: 15(cats)-75(cats)

Charter Oaks Distributors
50 Walnut Street
Middletown CT 06457
203-347-6995
Categories: 69

Chewnings Auto Literature
Route 1, Box 12A
Weyers Cave VA 24486
703-234-8968
Categories: 43(automobiles)

Childcraft
Susan Metcalfe, Buyer
Childcraft Education Corporation
20 Kilmer Avenue
Edison NJ 08818
201-572-6100
Categories: 21-31-76-89

Children's Book & Music Center
5373 W Pico Boulevard
Los Angeles CA 90019
213-937-1825
Categories: 11-21-31-76-89

Chinaberry Book Service
Ann S Ruethling
3160 Ivy Street
P O Box 167
San Diego CA 92104
619-284-0902
Categories: 21-31-76-89

Chosen Books
P O Box 05007
Detroit MI 48205
Categories: 37-73

Classic Motor Books
729 Prospect Avenue
P O Box 1
Osceola WI 54020
Categories: 43(automobiles)

Clifton Associates
349 E Cooke Road
Columbus OH 43214
614-268-8028
Categories: 33-69(magic,
         gambling)

Colonial Crafts
Book Division
P O Box 345
Sturbridge MA 01566
Categories: 29

Commodore Nautical Supplies
396 Broadway
New York NY 10013
212-226-1880
Categories: 69(boating)

Computer Book Store
796 Navy Street
Fort Walton Beach FL 32548
Categories: 23

Computer Museum Store
Museum Wharf
300 Congress Street
Boston MA 02210
617-426-2800
Categories: 23

Cotton Patch
1025 Brown Avenue
Lafayette CA 94549
Categories: 29(cross-stitch)

CraftsWoman Catalog
Anne Patterson Dee, Buyer
815 Hawthorne Lane
Libertyville IL 60048-0848
312-362-9186
Categories: 19-23

Crawford-Peters Aeronautica
James P Peters, Buyer
3702 Nassau Drive
San Diego CA 92115
619-287-3933
Categories: 69(aviation)

Creative Craft House
P O Box 1386
Santa Barbara CA 93102
716-325-5547
Categories: 29

Creative Needle
109 Ridge Road
Littleton CO 80120
Categories: 29(needlework)

Cruising World Bookshelf
524 Thames Street
Newport RI 02840
401-847-1588
Categories: 69(nautical,
         sailing)-71

Daedalus Books
Helaine Harris & Robin Moody
Book Buyers
2260 25th Place NE
Washington DC 20018
202-526-0558
Categories: 11-17-27-47-65-75
literary books, also remainders

Dance Mart
P O Box 48
Brooklyn NY 11229
Categories: 11(dance)

Defender Industries
255 Main Street
P O Box 820
New Rochelle NY 10801
914-632-3001
Categories: 69(boating)

Dick Blick Company
P O Box 1267
Galesburg IL 61401
309-343-6181
Categories: 11
also PA and NV locations
art and graphic supplies

**Dictionaries and Encyclopedias
of the World**
Nick Caramihai, Pergamon Press
Maxwell House, Fairview Park
Elmsford NY 10523
914-592-7700
Categories: 59
5000 dictionaries, etc

Direct Marketing Library
Hoke Communications
224 Seventh Street
Garden City NY 11530
516-746-6700; 800-645-6132
Categories: 19(marketing,
         fundraising)

Discount Books
Daniel Martin
427 Ferry Street
Newark NJ 07105
Categories: 99
discount books, remainders, new

Don Brown Bookseller
Don Brown, Buyer
Leon IA 50144
Categories: 29(antiques,
         collectibles)

Doug Kibbe Natural History Books
Doug Kibbe, Owner
P O Box 34
Maryland NY 12116
Categories: 15(birds)-51

Drawing Board Computer Supply
Computer Supplies Division
P O Box 2995
Hartford CT 06104-2995
203-379-9961
Categories: 23

Duncraft
25 South Main Street
Penacook NH 03303
603-753-6341
Categories: 15(birds)

East West Market Exchange
5533 N Broadway
Chicago IL 60640
Categories: 69(martial arts)

Edmund Scientific
7880 Edscorp Building
Barrington NJ 08007
609-547-3488
Categories: 23-29-39-67-69
scientific items, some books

Edward R Hamilton
Bookseller
P O Box 358
Falls Village CT 06031-0358
Categories: 99(remainders)

Enchanted Unicorn
415 Tennessee #E
Redlands CA 92373
Categories: 29(cross-stitch)

Entrepreneur's Success Catalog
Janet Hansen, President
Koolewong Ltd
P O Box 283
Mount Prospect IL 60056
312-253-9357
Categories: 19(home businesses)
              29(crafts)

Especially Maine
U. S. Route 1
Arundel ME 04046
207-985-3749
Categories: 61(ME)
items from and about Maine

Exanimo Establishment
P O Box 448
Fremont NE 68025
Categories: 69(treasure hunting)

Executive Golf Collection
Golf Day Products
3015 Commercial Avenue
Northbrook IL 60062
Categories: 69(golf)

Farmstead Market Basket
Farmstead Magazine
P O Box 111
Freedom ME 04941
207-382-6200
Categories: 15-27-29-43-51

Fly Fisherman's Bookcase
3890 Stewart Road
Eugene OR 97402
503-484-0898
Categories: 69(fishing)

Fm. FIVE Catalog
Fm. FIVE Magazine
P O Box 882108
San Francisco CA 94188
Categories: 75-95

Forearmed Traveler
227 Scenic Avenue
Piedmont CA 94611
Categories: 71

Foster Trent
2345 Boston Post Road
Larchmont NY 10538
Categories: 99

Fox-Smith Books
Mark Fox, General Manager
915 King Street #B-38
Alexandria VA 22314
Categories: 98(genealogy)
            41-61(Americana)

Foxy Catalog
204 W Lawton Street
Edgerton WI 53534
608-884-3461
Categories: 15(foxes)

Frank Mittermeier Catalog
3577 E Tremont Avenue
Bronx NY 10465
212-828-3843
Categories: 43

Funny Side Up
425 Stump Road
North Wales PA 19454
Categories: 33-69(games,
              novelties)

The Game Room
P O Box 4290
Washington DC 20012
202-723-0201
Categories: 33-69(games)

Games Magazine
800 Morse Avenue
Elk Grove Villag IL 60007
800-833-1003
Categories: 33-69(games,
              novelties)

Gene's Tackle Shop
P O Box 7701
Rochester NY 14622
Categories: 69(fishing)

Genealogist's Bookshelf
343 East 85th Street
New York NY 10028
Categories: 35-98(genealogy)

Geode Industries
106 W Main Street
New London IA 52645
319-367-2286
Categories: 29(lapidary)

Goldbergs Marine
202 Market Street
Philadelphia PA 19106
800-523-2926
Categories: 69(boating)

Golden Earth Wholesale
512 E Lambert
Brea CA 92621

714-990-0681
Categories: 43(gardening)

Goodspeeds Book Shop
18 Beacon Street
Boston MA 01208
Categories: 35-98(genealogy)

Green River Tools
5 Cotton Mill Hill
P O Box 1919
Brattleboro VT 05301
802-254-2388
Categories: 29-43-51

H Kauffman & Sons Saddlery
139 - 141 East 24th Street
New York NY 10010
212-684-6060
Categories: 15(horses)

Hampton Books, Cinema 8
Route 1
Box 76
Newberry SC 29108
803-276-6870
Categories: 11-33

Hanover House
340 Poplar
Hanover PA 17331
Categories: 99
12 different catalogs

Health Research
P O Box 70
Mokelumne Hill CA 95245
Categories: 39-53

Healthbooks
Joanne G Angle, Buyer
1137 N Highland #7
Arlington VA 22201
202-363-8526
Categories: 39

Hearth Song Catalog
Barbara Kane
P O Box B
Sebastopol CA 95472
707-829-1550
Categories: 21-27-29-31-35-39
              43-57

Hemmings Bookshelf
P O Box 76
Bennington VT 05201
Categories: 43(automobiles)

Henry Brandt & Company
Evergreen Drive
Hollister MO 65672
Categories: 29

Hershey's Chocolate Catalog
P O Box 800
Hershey PA 17033-0800
Categories: 27(chocolate)

How-to-Do-Anything Bookstores
Sally L Lasater, President
2611 Garden Road
Monterey CA 93940
800-367-0432; CA: 800-345-1441
Categories: 11-19-27-29-39-43
              57-69-71

Indoor Gardening Supplies
P O Box 40567
Detroit MI 48240
Categories: 43(gardening)
gardening supplies and books

Insite Creations
Frank Oppedisano, President
37-40 - 98th Street
Flushing NY 11368
212-898-9656
Categories: 19(small business)

**International Center for
Photography**
Museum Book Shop
1130 Fifth Avenue
New York NY 10028
Categories: 11(photography)

International Imports
P O Box 2010
Toluca Lake CA 91602
213-761-3991
Categories: 53

International Marine Publishing
21 Elm Street
Camden ME 04843
207-236-4342
Categories: 69(nautical,
              sailing)-71

IPS Associates Catalog
Institute for Policy Studies
1901 Q Street NW
Washington DC 20009
202-234-9382
Categories: 11(media)-13-19
              55-98(farming)

J C Whitney & Company
1917 Archer Avenue
P O Box 8410
Chicago IL 60680
312-431-6102
Categories: 43(automobiles)
automobile supplies and books

J W Elwood Supply Company
1202 Howard Street
Omaha NE 68103
Categories: 15(taxidermy)

Jameco Electronics
1355 Shoreway Road
Belmont CA 94002
415-592-8097
Categories: 23-67
books, computer peripherals, etc.

James Bliss and Company
Route 128
Dedham MA 02026
617-329-2430
Categories: 69(boating)

Jessica's Biscuits
P O Box 301
Newtonville MA 02106
800-225-4264
Categories: 27

Johnson-Smith
35075 Automation
Mount Clemens MI 48043
Categories: 33-69(games,
              novelties)

Keepin' Track Library
P O Box 48
Spring Valley NY 10977
914-425-2649
Categories: 43(automobiles--
              Corvettes)

Ken Lange, Bookseller
6031 N 7th Street
Phoenix AZ 85014
602-266-5637
Categories: 49(Native American)
              78-79

KidsRight
Martin and Judith Foner
Mount Dora FL 32757
Categories: 21-31-35-76
specialty: child abuse issues

Kitchen Arts & Letters
N Waxman, Book Buyer
1435 Lexington Avenue
New York NY 10128
212-876-5550
Categories: 27

Krupp Mail Order
Boulder CO 80306
Categories: 33-69(games,
              novelty)
comics and books

Libertyville Saddleshop
P O Box M
Libertyville IL 60048
312-362-0570
Categories: 15(horses)

Light Impressions
439 Monroe Avenue
P O Box 940
Rochester NY 14603
Categories: 11(photography)

Loompanics Unlimited
Michael Hoy, Owner
P O Box 1197
Port Townsend WA 98368
Categories: 11-33-98(unusual)

Lotus Computer Catalog
Diane McCarthy
Lotus Development Corporation
55 Cambridge Parkway
Cambridge MA 02142
Categories: 23
computer software and books

Mail Box Marina
29-60 167th Street
Flushing NY 11358
Categories: 69(boating)

Management Contents
New Business Books
P O Box 1054
Skokie IL 60077
Categories: 19(management)
co-op sales of books reviewed

Marathon International
Jim Wortham, President
P O Box 33008
Louisville KY 40232
Categories: 27-29

Marine Press of Canada
95 Berkeley Street
Toronto M5A 2W8 ON Canada
416-366-7566
Categories: 69(nautical,
              sailing)-71

Maverick Mail Order Bookstore
Marilyn Ross, Buyer
Communication Creativity
P O Box 213
Saguache CO 81149
Categories: 11(writing)
              19(publishing)

Micro Center Computer Books
Micro Center
1555 W Lane Avenue
Columbus OH 43221
800-634-3478
Categories: 23

Miles Kimball
Alberta Kimball, Buyer
41 West 8th Avenue
Oshkosh WI 54906
Categories: 99
gifts, some books

Moonbooks Travel Catalog
Asha Johnson, Buyer
133 W Lindo Avenue
P O Box 1696
Chico CA 95927
916-345-5473
Categories: 71

Moor & Mountain
63 Park Street
Andover MA 01810
617-475-3665
Categories: 69-71

Museum of the American Indian
3753 Broadway
New York NY 10032
212-283-2420
Categories: 49(Native American)
78-79

Music Emporium USA
8101 Cessna Avenue
Gaithersburg MD 20879
301-869-5880
Categories: 11-23

My Child's Destiny
Ray Raymond
70 Grant Avenue
San Francisco CA 94107
415-861-3808
Categories: 21-31-76-89

Natural History Books
P O Box 1089
Lake Helen FL 32744-1089
904-228-3356
Categories: 15(birds)-51

Navigation Equipment Company
228 W Chicago Avenue
Chicago IL 60610
312-944-3634
Categories: 69(boating)

Needle People
2435 S Winchester Boulevard
Campbell CA 95008
Categories: 29(needlecraft)

Nervo Distributors
650 University Avenue
Berkeley CA 94710
415-848-6464
Categories: 11-29(stained glass)
stained glass craft distributors

New York Astrology Center
127 Madison Avenue
New York NY 10016
212-679-5676
Categories: 53(astrology)

Northwest Farms
P O Box 3003
Portland OR 97208
503-653-0344
Categories: 15

Nostalgia Station
901 W Pratt Street
Baltimore MI 21223
Categories: 29(railroads)

Nostalgic Aviator
Carol Heiderman, Owner
1215 Kint Street
Alexandria VA 22314
703-684-5118
Categories: 69(aviation,
flying)-71

Nova Winds
P O Box 271
55 McCaul Street
Toronto M5T 2W7 ON Canada
Categories: 86

Owen Davies Bookseller
1214 N LaSalle Street
Chicago IL 60610
312-642-6697
Categories: 29(railroads)

P C Products Book Mart
Parth Domke
Cahners Publishing
221 Columbus Avenue
Boston MA 02116
Categories: 23
monthly offerings in magazine

Paladin Press
P O Box 1307
Boulder CO 80306
Categories: 69(self defense,
martial arts)

Patricia Ledlie, Bookseller
P O Box 46
Buckfield ME 04220
207-336-2969
Categories: 15-51

Pedigrees - The Pet Catalog
P O Box 110
Spencerport NY 14559
Categories: 15(pets)

Pelanor Books
P O Box 3920
Styvesant Plaza
Albany NY 12203
Categories: 86

Pet Express
P O Box 5422
Scottsdale AZ 85261
Categories: 15

Photo-Eye Books
P O Box 2686
Austin TX 78768
Categories: 11(photography)

Pipestone Indian Shrine
P O Box 727
Pipestone MN 56164
Categories: 49(Native Americans)
78-79
Native American gifts and books

Platte Valley Books and Gifts
Virginia Sidlinger Foster, Buyer
The Meadows D-1
P O Box 756
Alliance NE 69301
308-762-6866
Categories: 98(genealogy)
books, gifts, supplies

Playing It Safe Catalog
LuAnn and Jack Elsinger
P O Box 968
Stevens Point WI 54481
715-346-1045
Categories: 21-75
books and safe toys for children

Plume Trading and Sales Company
P O Box 585
Monroe NY 10950
914-782-8594
Categories: 29-49(Native
American)

Print Book Store
6400 Goldsboro Road
Bethesda MD 20817-9969
301-229-9040
Categories: 11(graphics)
19(printing)
see Print/Graphic Arts Book Club

Printed Matter Catalog
Susan Wheeler, Director
7 Lispenard Street
New York NY 10013
212-925-0325
Categories: 11

Quill Corporation
100 S Schelter Road
P O Box 4700
Lincolnshire IL 60197-4700
312-634-4850
Categories: 19
office supplies & business books

Report Store
Krista Rogers, Managing Editor
Ergosyst Associates
910 Massachusetts Street #503F
Lawrence KS 66044-2975
913-842-7348
Categories: 23
books, reports, technical

Roberts Colonial House
570 West 167th Street
P O Box 308
South Holland IL 60473
312-331-6233
Categories: 21-27-76
wholesale and retail

S & C Huber Accoutrements
82 Plants Dam Road
East Lyme CT 06333
203-739-0772
Categories: 29
craft supplies and books

S & P of New York Budo
P O Box 2
Depew NY 14043
716-681-7911
Categories: 69(martial arts)
martial arts supplies and books

Mail Order Catalogs that Feature Books

Safari Enterprises
M Ngatia
2518 Lafayette Drive
Davis CA 95616
916-753-5838
Categories: 19-99

Sax Arts and Crafts
P O Box 2002
Milwaukee WI 53201
414-272-4900
Categories: 11-29

Sax Lewis Falken Inc
Eugene M Falken
180 Highfield Lane
Nutley NJ 07110
201-235-9444
Categories: 19(industrial
          safety)

Schweizer Aircraft Corporation
P O Box 147
Elmira NY 14902
607-739-3821
Categories: 69(aviation)

Self-Publisher's Bookstore
Jerry Buchanan, Owner
TOWERS Club
P O Box 2038
Vancouver WA 98668
Categories: 19(publishing,
          marketing)

Skipper's Bookshelf
P O Box 1328
Hightstown NJ 08520
Categories: 69(nautical,
          sailing)-71

Small Business Success Catalog
Jeffrey Lant, Owner
JLA Publications
50 Follen Street #507
Cambridge MA 02138
617-547-6372
Categories: 19

Smith & Hawken
Paul Hawken, Buyer
25 Corte Madera
Mill Valley CA 94941
415-383-4050
Categories: 43-51-71

Specialty Hobby & Needlecraft
4604 Idaho
Vancouver WA 98661
206-694-9519
Categories: 29-43(automobiles)

Spencer Gifts
590 Spencer Building
1601 Albany Avenue
Atlantic City NJ 08411
Categories: 99
mainly gifts, some books

Sporting Dog Specialties
P O Box 68
Spencerport NY 14559
Categories: 15(dogs)-69

The Storyteller
P O Box 1229
Boulder CO 80306-1229
Categories: 21-76-89

Sunset House
282 Sunset Building
Beverly Hills CA 90215
Categories: 99
mainly gifts, some books

Sydney B Vernon
P O Box 387
Baldwin NY 11510
516-536-5287
Categories: 55(military)

T B Hagstoz and Son
709 Sanson Street
Philadelphia PA 19106
Categories: 29(jewelry)

Talas
104 Fifth Avenue
New York NY 10011
212-675-0718
Categories: 11

TCMA Ltd
Jeanne and Michael Aronstein
1000 N Division Street
Peekskill NY 10566
914-739-0161
Categories: 69(baseball)

Teacher's Desk Catalog
RM Educational Service
27022 Mallorca Lane
Mission Viejo CA 92691
Categories: 31
a magazine sent to schools
150,000

Teacher-Parent Store
185 Main Street
Danbury CT 06810
203-794-0577
Categories: 21-31-76

The Nature Company
Elsie White, Book Buyer
750 Hearst Avenue
Berkeley CA 94710
415-524-9811
Categories: 15-51-69-71
also a chain of stores

The Professional's Bookshelf
Aames-Allen Publishing
1106 Main Street
Huntington Beach CA 92648
714-536-4926
Categories: 19

Tipi Shop
P O Box 1542
Rapid City SD 57709
605-343-7851
Categories: 49(Native Americans)
          78-79

Tools of the Trade
Miriam D Ross
Ross Book Service
3718 Seminary Road
Alexandria VA 22304-0993
703-823-1919
Categories: 11(writing)
          19(publishing)

Toys to Grow On
P O Box 17
Long Beach CA 90801
213-603-8890
Categories: 21-31-76
toys and books

Travel Quest
Richard A McBride, V.P.
20103 La Roda Court
Cupertino CA 95014
408-446-0600
Categories: 27-45-71-79-80
mail order book service

Traveler's Checklist
Cornwall Bridge Road
Sharon CT 06069
Categories: 71

Utrecht Linens Company
33 - 35th Street
Brooklyn NY 11232
212-768-2525
Categories: 11-29

Valiant Universal Micro
195 Bonhomme Street
P O Box 488
Hackensack NJ 07602
201-487-6340
Categories: 23

Video Schoolhouse
Sally L Lasater, President
2611 Garden Road
Monterey CA 93940
800-367-0432; CA: 800-345-1441
Categories: 99(videotapes only)

Village Store
Winemakers Ltd
999 Main Road, Box C51
Westport MA 02790
617-636-2572
Categories: 27(wine and herbs)

Walter Drake & Sons
Drake Building
Colorado Springs CO 80901
Categories: 99
low-priced gifts and novelties

Mail Order Catalogs That Feature Books

Wayfarer Publications
P O Box 26156
Los Angeles CA 90026
Categories: 69(martial arts)

The Whole Family
1085 West 21st Street
Upland CA 91786
714-946-7731
Categories: 21-31-35-76
books, toys, baby clothes

Whole Mirth Catalog
Allen Klein
1034 Page Street
San Francisco CA 94117
Categories: 33-69(novelty)

Whole Work Catalog
Tom and Sue Ellison
The New Careers Center
6003 N 51st Street, P O Box 297
Boulder CO 80306
303-530-1087
Categories: 19(careers,
              employment)

Wildcountry Books
236 S Third
Montrose CA 81401
Categories:51-69-71

Willis Mohr
24725 Butler Road
Junction City OR 97448
503-998-8233
Categories: 19

Wine and Food Library
1207 West Madison
Ann Arbor MI 48103
Categories: 27(wine, food)

Wings Inc
P O Box 430
Daleville AL 36322
205-598-4270
Categories: 69(aviation)

Wittenborn Art Books
1018 Madison Avenue
New York NY 10021
212-288-1558
Categories: 11

Woodworkers Store
21801 Industrial Boulevard
Rogers MN 55374
612-428-4101
Categories: 29(woodworking)

The Write Stuff
P O Box 475
Jamestown NC 27282
Categories: 69(aviation)

Yes Inc
1035 - 31st Street NW
Washington DC 20007
Categories: 39

Youngers Books and Reports
Wayne E Youngers
636 River Drive
P O Box 37
Princeton IA 52768
Categories: 19(opportunity)

Bookstore Catalogs

21st Century Bookstore Catalog
Tony Kainauskas
401 N 4th Street
Fairfield IA 52556
515-472-5105
Categories: 27-39-53-57

Abalone Books
Mildred Steiner, Buyer
15 Cottage
P O Box 61
Derby CT 06418
203-735-0701
Categories: 17-83-95

Agri Bookstore
Steven Breth, Manager
IADS Operations
1611 N Kent Street
Arlington Hall VA 22209
703-525-9455
Categories: 98(agriculture)-19
            15-51

Amazon Bookstore
1612 Harmon Place
Minneapolis MN 55403
612-338-6560
Categories: 73

Applause Theatre Books
Glenn Young, Owner
100 West 67th Street
New York NY 10023
212-496-7511
Categories: 11(performing arts)

Bank Street College Book Store
610 West 112th Street
New York NY 10025
201-663-7200
Categories: 21-31-76

Barbara Weindling, Bookseller
Barbara Weindling
69 Ball Pond Road
Danbury CT 06811
Categories: 21-27

Barnes & Noble
126 Fifth Avenue
New York NY 10011
Categories: 99
new and remainders

Book Passage
Elaine Petrocelli & Irma Zigas
51 Tamal Vista Boulevard
Corte Madera CA 94925
415-927-0960; 800-321-9785
Categories: 19(international)
            45-71
books and maps

Books of Wonder
Peter Glassman
464 Hudson Street
New York NY 10014
212-989-3270
Categories: 21-76
Wizard of Oz books and gifts

Bruner-Mazel
19 Union Square W
New York NY 10003
212-924-3344
Categories: 57

Complete Traveller
Harriet Greenberg
199 Madison Avenue
New York NY 10016
212-679-4339
Categories: 45-71

Cricket Craft Shop
152 Woodstock Avenue
Route 4 East
Rutland VT 05701
Categories: 29(needlework)

Drama Book Shop
150 West 52nd Street
New York NY 10019
212-582-1037
Categories: 11(performing arts)

Fairfield Book Company
Harold Kurfehs, President
42 N Obtuse Road
P O Box 289
Brookfield CT 06805
203-775-0053; 800-243-1318
Categories: 41-55(military)
            61(Western)-69

Fancywork
2708 Slaterville Road
Slaterville Spring NY 14881
Categories: 29(needlework)

Grolier Book Shop
Louisa Solano, Buyer
6 Plympton Street
Cambridge MA 02138
617-547-4648
Categories: 95

Merlyn's Science Fiction/Fantasy
Paul Wilson, Manager
621 W Mallon
Spokane WA 99201
509-325-3358
Categories: 33-39-61(Western)
            69-75-86
books, games, sidelines

Minnesota Bookline
Odegard Books
857 Grand Avenue
Saint Paul MN 55105
800-247-0635
Categories: 61(MN)-99

Paperback Catalog Service
Lake Shore Road
Roaring Brook Lake
Putnam Valley NY 10579
Categories: 99
independent bookstore catalogs

Sandmeyer's Bookstore
714 S Dearborn Street
Chicago IL 60605
312-922-2104
Categories: 45-71

Science Fiction Shop
Martin Last, Buyer
56 Eighth Avenue
New York NY 10014
212-741-0270
Categories: 86

Waldenbooks
Dan Krieger, Marketing Director
201 High Ridge Road
Stamford CT 06904
203-356-7500
Categories: 99
various catalogs

Remainder Dealers

American Media Library Books
219 N Milwaukee Street
Milwaukee WI 53202
414-272-3355
Categories: 21-76-89

B Dalton Bookseller
James Chandler, Buyer
Bargain Books
7505 Metro Boulevard
Minneapolis MN 55435
612-893-7000
Categories: 99

Book Bargains
164 Mill Street
Westwood NJ 07675
201-664-0577
Categories: 99

Book Sales Inc
110 Enterprise Avenue
Secaucus NJ 07094
201-864-6341
Categories: 99

Book Services International
Key Book Services
425 Asylum Street
Bridgeport CT 06610
203-334-2165
Categories: 99

Book World Promotions
Mark Adams, Book Buyer
87-93 Christie Street
Newark NJ 07105
201-589-7877
Categories: 99

Bookking International
16 rue des Gds Augustins
75006 Paris France
1-43542750
Categories: 99

Booksmith Promotional Company
432 Park Avenue South
New York NY 10016
212-782-0405
Categories: 11-21-76-89-99
juveniles their specialty

Bookthrift Marketing
45 W 36th Street
New York NY 10018
212-947-0909
Categories: 99

Cicero Bible Press
Industrial Park Road
P O Box 160
Harrison AR 72601
501-741-3400
Categories: 63-99

Daedalus Books
Helaine Harris & Robin Moody
2260 25th Place NE
Washington DC 20018
202-526-0558
Categories: 11-17-27-47-65-75
literary books, consumer catalog

East Coast Christian Distributor
35 Teadington Road
P O Box 4200
Somerville NJ 08876
201-722-5050
Categories:63-99

Edu-Tech Corporation
Robert Caston
65 Bailey Road
Fairfield CT 06430
203-372-3353
Categories: 10(adult non-fiction)

Fairmount Books
77 Milliken Boulevard #10
Scarborough M1V 2R4 ON Canada
416-298-6743
Categories: 11-17-41-59-75-99

Hispano-American Publications
45-57 Davis Street
Long Island City NY 11101
718-937-2330
Categories: 45(Spanish)-49-80

Horizon Book Promotions
William Holmes, President
230 Fifth Avenue #1808
New York NY 10001
212-696-9171
Categories: 99

International Service Company
333 4th Avenue
Indialantic FL 32903
305-724-1443
Categories: 99

Jean Karr & Company
5656 Third Street NE
Washington DC 20011
202-529-6789
Categories: 11-76-99

John K Sharpe Inc
Jack Sharpe, Book Buyer
P O Box 442
Wilmette IL 60091
312-256-2086
Categories: 99

Landmark Book Company
260 Fifth Avenue
New York NY 10010
212-696-5430
Categories: 99

Lescron Enterprises
Bert Rosenbaum, Book Buyer
80-90 Arch Street
P O Box B
Johnson City NY 13790
607-729-6281
Categories: 11-17-21-27-31
                39-59-65-75-99

Louis Goldberg Library Books
139 Main Street
Nazareth PA 18064
215-759-9458
Categories: 99

Louis J Martin & Associates
P O Box 247
Rye NY 10580
914-967-0979
Category: 11 (art books)

Marboro Books
205 Moonachie Road
Moonachie NJ 07074
212-924-8395
Categories: 11-17-41-47-75-99
hardcovers, import and export

Merchandise Dynamics
184 Fifth Avenue
New York NY 10010
212-929-0090
Categories: 99

Moneysworth Books
251 West 57th Street
New York NY 10019
212-581-2000
Categories: 19-29-39-99

Noontide Press
Thomas J Marcellus, Director
P O Box 1248
Torrance CA 90505
Categories: 41-61(Americana)-55

Ollis Book Corporation
Kenneth Ollis, Book Buyer
28 E 35th Street
Steger IL 60475
312-755-5151
Categories: 21-76

Outlet Book Company
Caryn Malitzky, Book Buyer
225 Park Avenue South
New York NY 10016
212-532-9200
Categories: 99

Overstock Book Company
120 Secatogue Avenue
Farmingdale NY 11735
516-293-6969
Categories: 99

Pen Notes
134 Westside Avenue
Freeport NY 11520
516-868-5753
Categories: 99

Promotional Book Company
510 Front Street West
Toronto M5V 1B8 ON Canada
416-596-8906
Categories: 99

Publishers Marketing Enterprises
PME Bargain Books
386 Park Avenue South
New York NY 10016
212-686-8000
Categories: 11-21-76-99

Regency Book Distributors
1341 Dayton Street
Salinas CA 93901
408-754-1416
Categories: 99

Roy Derstine Book Company
14 Birch Road
Kinnelon NJ 07405
201-838-1109
Categories: 99

Ruby's Book Sale
119 Chambers Street
New York NY 10007
212-732-8676
Categories: 99

S & L Sales
P O Box 2067
Waycross GA 31501
912-283-0210
Categories: 99
any subject, any quantity

School Aid Company
911 Colfax
Danville IL 61832
217-442-6855
Categories: 21-76-89-99

Seven Hills Books
519 W Third Street
Cincinnati OH 45202
513-381-3881
Categories: 11-21-59-76

Sunflower Books
c/o W H Smith Publishers
112 Madison Avenue
New York NY 10016
212-532-6600
Categories: 99

Texas Bookman
2730 Seelco Drive
Dallas TX 75235
214-350-6648
Categories: 99

Thames Book Company
34 Truman Street
P O Box 97
New London CT 06320
203-443-1293
Categories: 99

University Book Service
2436 W Granville Road
Worthington OH 43085
614-889-1855
Categories: 99

Victor Hotho & Company
P O Box 9738
Fort Worth TX 76107
817-335-1833
Categories: 99

Western Book Distributors
Deborah Phelps, Book Buyer
2970 San Pablo Avenue
Berkeley CA 94702
415-849-0100
Categories: 99
any quantity, any subject

World Wide Book Service
P O Box 544
New York NY 10010
212-673-6160
Categories: 99

X-S Books
725 Dell Road
Carlstadt NJ 07072
201-935-4493
Categories: 11-21-76-99

York Promotional Books
25-10 Connell Court
Etobicoke M8Z 1E8 ON Canada
416-252-2253
Categories: 99

Mailing List Sources for Book Publishers

Alvin B Zeller Inc
475 Park Avenue South
New York NY 10016
800-223-0814; 212-689-4900
Categories: 99
catalog available

American Business Lists
5707 S 86th Circle
Omaha NE 68127
402-331-7169
Categories: 19
compiled from yellow pages
catalog available

American List Counsel
88 Orchard Road
Princeton NJ 08540-8019
800-526-3973; 201-874-4300
Categories: 99
catalog available

Angelo R Venezian
10-64 Jackson Avenue
Long Island City NY 11101-5778
800-221-2270; NY: 718-784-0500
Categories: 19-99

AZ Marketing Services Inc
Judith Savio
31 River Road
Cos Cob CT 06807
203-629-8088
Categories: 99

Bernice Bush Company
15052 Springdale Street
Huntington Beach CA 92649
714-891-3344
Categories: 63-99

Booksellers List
Booksellers Association
254 Buckingham Palace Road
London SW1W 9TZ   England
Categories: 99
booksellers in United Kingdom

Bowker Mailing Lists
Jack Burns, Manager
R R Bowker & Company
205 East 42nd Street
New York NY 10017
212-916-1698
Categories: 99
bookstores/libraries/publishers

Business List Management
Direct Media List Management
70 Riverdale Avenue
P O Box 4565
Greenwich CT 06830
203-531-1091
Categories: 19-23-99

Business Mailers
640 N LaSalle Drive
Chicago IL 60610
312-943-6666
Categories: 39(doctors/dentists)

Catholic Lists
Charles J McNeill
10 Fiske Place
Mount Vernon NY 10550
914-668-7320
Categories: 63(Catholics)

CBS Magazines List Management
1515 Broadway
New York NY 10036
212-719-6677
Categories: 99

College Marketing Group
Fifth Cross Street
Winchester MA 01890
617-729-7865
Categories: 31-65-99
college faculty
catalog available

Command Productions
Radio/TV List
Warren Weagant
P O Box 26348
San Francisco CA 94126
415-332-3161
Categories: 99
radio/TV stations

Compilers Plus
2 Penn Place
Pelham Manor NY 10803
800-431-2914; 914-738-1520
Categories: 99
catalog available

Curriculum Information Center
1020 - 15th Street #42-C
Denver CO 80202
Categories: 21-31-76-89
school lists

Demographic Systems
325 Hudson Street
New York NY 10013
212-255-8707
Categories: 99
catalog available

Dependable Lists
33 Irving Place
New York NY 10003
212-677-6760

1825 K Street NW
Washington DC 20006
212-677-6760

Dependable Lists continued
215 S Northwest Highway
Barrington IL 60010
312-382-4501
Categories: 99
catalog available

Direct Marketing Services
Norman Lind or Sharon Rosen
144 West 27th Street
New York NY 10001
212-255-9404
Categories: 55-99

Direct Media List Management
220 Grace Church Street
Port Chester NY 10573
914-937-5600
Categories: 19-99

Directory of Special Libraries
Karen Wilhelm
Gale Research Company
Book Tower
Detroit MI 48226
800-223-gale, 313-961-2242
Categories: 99
special libraries

Doubleday Mailing Lists
501 Franklin Avenue
Garden City NY 11530
516-294-4065
Categories: 99
book buyer lists

Dun & Bradstreet Canada
415 Yonge Street #1107
Toronto M5B 2E7   ON Canada
416-925-2861
Categories: 19(Canada)
Canadian business lists

Dunhill International List
2340 W Oakland Park Boulevard
Fort Lauderdale FL 33311
305-484-8300
Categories: 19
international mailing lists

Dustbooks Mailing Lists
Dustbooks
P O Box 100
Paradise CA 95969
916-877-6110
Categories: 99(small press)
libraries/bookstores/publishers

Ed Burnett Company
99 W Sheffield Avenue
Englewood NJ 07631
201-871-1100; 800-223-7777
Categories: 99
business and general lists

Mailing List Sources for Book Publishers

Educational Directory
One Park Avenue
New York NY 10016
212-889-8455
Categories: 31-65-99
faculty & schools catalog

Encyclopedia of Associations
Karen Wilhelm
Gale Research Company
Book Tower
Detroit MI 48226
800-223-gale; 313-961-2242
Categories: 99(associations)
mailing lists available

Executive Services Companies
Consumer List Division
901 N International Parkway
Richardson TX 75081
800-527-3933; TX: 214-699-1271
Categories: 99

Floridata Inc
Pablo Glaser
Senior Account Executive
7101 Biscayne Boulevard
Miami FL 33138
800-882-5323; FL: 305-751-5323
Categories: 19(business and
           professionals)
compiled lists

Fred Woolf List Company
280 N Central Avenue
Hartsdale NY 10530
800-431-1557; 914-946-0336
Categories: 99
catalog available

George Madden and Associates
3101 Fourth Avenue
San Diego CA 92103
714-298-0202
Categories: 31-65-99
college faculty catalog

Hugo Dunhill Mailing Lists
Sal Buttaci
630 Third Avenue
New York NY 10017
800-223-6454; 212-682-8030
Categories: 19-99
catalog available

IBIS Information Services
215 Park Avenue #5
New York NY 10003-1603
212-505-7620
Categories: 99
foreign libraries & bookstores

JAMI
Lana Cardinale
2 Executive Drive
Fort Lee NJ 07024
201-461-8868
Categories: 99

The Kleid Company
200 Park Avenue
New York NY 10166
212-599-4140
Categories: 99
catalog available

Lakewood Publications
Direct Mail Lists
Paul Kolars
50 S Ninth Street
Minneapolis MN 55402
800-328-4329
Categories: 11-19-69-71

List Brokerage and Management
15 East 40th Street #702
New York NY 10016
212-481-9290
Categories: 19-99

Maclean-Hunter DM Services
481 University Avenue
Toronto M5W 1A7 ON Canada
Categories: 19-23-67
most professions

Mail Communications Inc
Charles B Parrish, President
721 Olive Street
St. Louis MO 63101
800-325-7942; 314-241-5408
Categories: 63

Mailing List Marketing
Medical Economics Company
680 Kinderkamack Road
Oradell NJ 07649
201-262-3030
Categories: 39-99
international mailing lists

Mal Dunn Associates
159 Madison Avenue
New York NY 10016
212-683-2032
Categories: 19(international)

Mardev S.A.
International Lists
9, rue Charles-Humbert
CH-1205 Geneva Switzerland
022/28 75 36
Categories: 19(international)

Market Data Retrieval
16 Progress Drive
Shelton CT 06484
800-624-5669; 203-926-4800
Categories: 21-31-63-76-89
schools and libraries

Media Horizons Inc
Phoebe Harnett
50 West 23rd Street
New York NY 10159-9990
212-645-1000
Categories: 11-19-23-99

Meredith List Marketing
Ron Davis, Director
Locust at 17th
Des Moines IA 50336
515-284-2891
Categories: 27-29-35-39-43-69
magazine subscribers, etc.

Micromedia Ltd
144 Front Street W
Toronto M5J 1G2 ON Canada
416-593-5211
Categories: 99
all kinds of Canadian libraries

MMS
Medical Marketing Lists
541 N Fairbanks Court #1910
Chicago IL 60611-3302
800-621-5073; 312-467-9540
Categories: 39(doctors)

NAM Mailing Lists
D K Khalsa
P O Box 1067
Berkeley CA 94701
415-644-3229
Categories: 27-39-53
bookstores, publishers, etc.

Names in the News
530 Bush Street
San Francisco CA 94108
415-989-3350
Categories: 55
political donors and others

National Women's Mailing List
P O Box 68
Jenner CA 95450
415-824-6800
Categories: 73-99
professional women, others

New Pages Mailing Lists
Casey Hill
New Pages Press
4426 S Belsay Road
Grand Blanc MI 48439
313-742-9583
Categories: 13-37-49-53-73-99
bookstores, libraries & others
  interested in alternative books

P & L Direct Marketing Group
9255 Sunset Boulevard #523
Los Angeles CA 90069
213-858-8875
Categories: 21-76
Muppet/Barbie/He-Man subscribers

ParaLists
Para Publishing
P O Box 4232
Santa Barbara CA 93140-4232
805-968-7277
Categories: 69(parachuting)-99
variety of lists

Mailing List Sources for Book Publishers

Professional Mailing Lists
170 Fifth Avenue
New York NY 10010
Categories: 19-99
professionals and libraries

Qualified Lists Corporation
135 Bedford Road
Armonk NY 10504
914-273-6700; 212-409-6200
Categories: 21-76-99
Weekly Reader book buyers, etc.

Radio Direct Lists
Kevin Collins, Publisher
Box 267, Kennett Pike
Chadds Ford PA 19317
215-388-7533
Categories: 99
radio station list rentals

Religious Booksellers List
Christian Booksellers Assn.
2031 W Cheyenne Road
Colorado Springs CO 80906
Categories: 63
religious bookstores

Religious Lists
Marty Sass
86 Maple Avenue
New City NY 10956
800-431-5303; NY: 914-634-8724
Categories: 63
religious book buyers, others

Research Projects Corporation
Pomperaug Avenue
Woodbury CT 06798
800-243-4360
Categories: 19-99
catalog available

Resources Mailing Lists
P O Box 134, Harvard Square
Cambridge MA 02238-0134
617-876-2789
Categories: 13-37-53-73
progressive and innovative lists

Rubin Response Services
3315 West Algonquin Road
Rolling Meadows IL 60008
312-394-3400
Categories: 99

School Lists Mailings Corp.
1710 Highway 35
Oakhurst NJ 07755
Categories: 21-31-76
school lists

Southam Direct Marketing Service
1408 Birchmount Road
Scarborough M5J 1G2   ON Canada
416-445-6641
Categories: 19-61(Canada)
catalog available

Special Libraries Association
235 Park Avenue
New York NY 10003
Categories: 19-39-65-67-99
special libraries

Steve Millard Inc
Ben Perez or Nancy Timko
Spring Hill Road - Sharon
Peterborough NH 03458
603-924-9421
Categories: 99

Talk Show Producer Mailing Lst
Mitchell P Davis
Broadcast Interview Source
2500 Wisconsin Avenue NW #930
Washington DC 20007-9990
202-333-4904
Categories: 99
radio/tv talk show producers

Teachers of Foreign Languages
Northeast Conference
P O Box 623
Middlebury VT 05753
802-388-4017
Categories: 31-45
foreign language faculty

Thomas Lists
One Penn Plaza
250 West 34th Street
New York NY 10119
Categories: 19-99
catalog available

Uni-Mail Commercial
Kay Cassidy
One Lincoln Plaza
New York NY 10023
800-223-1033; 212-362-8500
Categories: 99

Venture Communications
Erik Schonher
161 West 54th Street
New York NY 10019
212-245-6101
Categories: 19-99

Warren, Gorham & Lamont Inc
List Manager
210 South Street
Boston MA 02111
617-423-2020
Categories: 19(banking,
            real estate)
book and newsletter buyers

Willowood Lists
Willowood Press
P O Box 1846
Minot ND 58702
Categories: 31-99
libraries/schools/English Dept

World Innovators
Anne Peterson
72 Park Street
New Canaan CT 06840
203-966-0374
Categories: 11-19-23-67-99

Zeller & Letica Inc
15 East 26th Street
New York NY 10010
800-221-4112; 212-685-7512
Categories: 99
catalog available

Card Packs (or Decks)

BrownCor International Cards
Direct Media Card Decks
220 Grace Church Street
Port Chester NY 10573
914-937-5600
Categories: 19(purchasing)
office supply buyers

Business Buyers' Action Pack
Margaret MacGregor
The Economics Press
12 Daniel Road
Fairfield NJ 07006
800-526-2554
Categories: 19(employee training)

Business Management DR Cards
Market Direct Inc
1040 Bayview Drive #209
Fort Lauderdale FL 33304
305-563-5544
Categories: 19

Caddylak Systems Postcards
Direct Media Card Decks
220 Grace Church Street
Port Chester NY 10573
914-937-5600
Categories: 19

Corporate Executives MarketPlace
MarketPlace Publications
600 W Putnam Avenue
Greenwich CT 06830
203-661-0693
Categories: 19

CPA's MarketPlace
MarketPlace Publications
600 W Putnam Avenue
Greenwich CT 06830
203-661-0693
Categories: 19(accounting/finance)

Dentists MarketPlace
MarketPlace Publications
600 W Putnam Avenue
Greenwich CT 06830
203-661-0693
Categories: 39(dentists)

Doctor's Mart
Ray Hamel
Publisher
4 Tech Circle
Natick MA 01760
800-343-6969; 617-655-4600
Categories: 39(doctors)

Enterprise Action Pack
725 Market Street
Wilmington DE 19801
302-654-0110
Categories: 19

Esquire Card Pack
American List Counsel
88 Orchard Road
Princeton NJ 08540
201-874-4300
Categories: 19-75-99
Esquire subscribers

Executive Decision Card Deck
Names in the News
One Penn Plaza
New York NY 10119
212-279-0444
Categories: 19

Executive Management
Direct Media Card Decks
220 Grace Church Street
Port Chester NY 10573
914-937-5600
Categories: 19(small business
owners)

Executive Mart
Ray Hamel, Publisher
4 Tech Circle
Natick MA 01760
800-343-6969; 617-655-4600
Categories: 19-99

Executive Woman Card Pack
American List Counsel
88 Orchard Road
Princeton NJ 08540
201-874-4300
Categories: 19-73-99

Gardener's Marketplace
Storey Communications
Schoolhouse Road
Pownal VT 05261
802-823-5811
Categories: 43
Circulation: 750,000

Gordon Industrial Action Cards
Judd Bergenfeld, Director
P O Box 1952
Dover NJ 07801-0952
800-222-0289
Categories: 19(industrial)

Health Care Buyers Mart
SYCOM
P O Box 7947
Madison WI 53791-9956
800-356-8153
Categories: 39

High Tech Times
22-D West Micheltorena
Santa Barbara CA 93101-2856
805-687-8878
Categories: 19-23

Inc. Magazine Card Pack
American List Counsel
88 Orchard Road
Princeton NJ 08540
201-874-4300
Categories: 19
Inc. subscribers

Investment Action Cards
Direct Media Card Decks
220 Grace Church Street
Port Chester NY 10573
914-937-5600
Categories: 19(investment)

ITC Industrial Response Deck
ITC Publishers Service
63 Hemlock Drive
Hempstead NY 11550
516-485-1000
Categories: 19(industrial)

Lawyers MarketPlace
MarketPlace Publications
600 W Putnam Avenue
Greenwich CT 06830
203-661-0693
Categories: 19-55(law)

Main Deck
130 Quiqley Boulevard
P O Box 12446
Wilmington DE 19850-2446
302-322-9911
Categories: 19

Marketing Bulletin Board
22 W. Micheltorena #D
Santa Barbara CA 93101
800-687-3137
Categories: 19(sales/marketing)

Marketing Officers Information
Kevin Stevens
155 River Road, P O Box 520
North Arlington NJ 07032
800-526-1242; NJ: 201-997-0880
Categories: 19(sales & marketing)

Matthew Bender Card Decks
Patti Jupin
Matthew Bender & Company
1275 Broadway
Albany NY 12201
800-424-4200; NY: 518-462-3331
Categories: 19-55(law, taxes)

**McGraw-Hill Business Leaders
Direct Response Deck**
Abelow Response
430 W Merrick Road
Valley Stream NY 11580
800-845-5599; 516-825-0013
Categories: 19

Card Packs (and Decks)

Medical Exec-Cards
Frank Turner
221 W State Street
P O Box 197
Rockford IL 61105
800-435-2937; IL: 815-963-7771
Categories: 39(doctors)

Mellow Mail Card Pack
Leon Henry Inc
455 Central Avenue
Scarsdale NY 10583
914-723-3176
Categories: 11-33

Micro Computing Card Deck
Venture Communications
161 West 54th Street
New York NY 10019
212-245-6101
Categories: 19-23

National Pen Buyers Cards
Direct Media Card Decks
220 Grace Church Street
Port Chester NY 10573
914-937-5600
Categories: 19(marketings/sales)

NursePac
Venture Communications
161 West 54th Street
New York NY 10019
212-245-6101
Categories: 39(nurses)

One Minute Catalog for Dentist
SYCOM
P O Box 7947
Madison WI 53791-9956
800-356-8153
Categories: 39(dentists)

Organic Gardening Card Pack
Sisy Harrison, Coordinator
33 E Minor Street
Emmaus PA 18049
215-967-5171
Categories: 43(gardening)

Parade of Values Card Pack
Kathleen Ryan
National Syndications
230 Fifth Avenue
New York NY 10001
212-686-8680
Categories: 99
Parade magazine ad responders

PC/Pak
J F Glaser
800 Roosevelt Road
Building B #311
Glen Ellyn IL 60137
312-251-2541
Categories: 23 (IBM PC owners)

Photographer's Pro-Deck
Thom Reece, President
1750 Kalakaua #3-627
Honolulu HI 96826
808-942-3786
Categories: 11(photography)

Physicians MarketPlace
MarketPlace Publications
600 W Putnam Avenue
Greenwich CT 06830
203-661-0693
Categories: 39(doctors)

Potentials in Marketing
Idea File Card Deck
50 South 9th Street
Minneapolis MN 55402
Categories: 19(marketing)

Prentice-Hall Business Mgmt.
Venture Communications
161 West 54th Street
New York NY 10019
212-245-6101
Categories: 19

Prentice-Hall Educators
Venture Communications
161 West 54th Street
New York NY 10019
212-245-6101
Categories: 31

Prentice-Hall Law Card Deck
Venture Communications
161 West 54th Street
New York NY 10019
212-245-6101
Categories: 19(law)

Presidents Exec-Cards
Frank Turner
221 W State Street
P O Box 197
Rockford IL 61105
800-435-2937; IL: 815-963-7771
Categories: 19

Religious Bookseller Cards
Bill Burns
Resource Publications Inc
160 E Virginia Street #290
San Jose CA 95112
408-286-8505
Categories: 63

Sales & Marketing Exec-Cards
Frank Turner or Stan Smith
221 W State Street
P O Box 197
Rockford IL 61105
800-435-2937; IL: 815-963-7771
Categories: 19(marketing/sales)

Success Card Deck
Venture Communications
161 West 54th Street
New York NY 10019
212-245-6101
Categories: 19
Success magazine subscribers

Technology Hotlines
519 Cleveland Street #211
P O Box 719
Clearwater FL 33517
Categories: 19-23

Telecommunications Card Deck
610 Washington Street
Dedham MA 02026
617-326-8220
Categories: 19-23

Today's Business Woman Cards
Direct Media Card Decks
220 Grace Church Street
Port Chester NY 10573
914-937-5600
Categories: 19-73

U.S. Pencil & Stationery Cards
Direct Media Card Decks
220 Grace Church Street
Port Chester NY 10573
914-937-5600
Categories: 19(sales, marketing)

Venture Magazine Card Deck
Direct Media Card Decks
220 Grace Church Street
Port Chester NY 10573
914-937-5600
Categories: 19
Venture Magazine subscribers

Working Woman Card Deck
Venture Communications
161 West 54th Street
New York NY 10019
212-245-6101
Categories: 19-73
Working Woman subscribers

Foreign Sales Representatives and Exporters

Beijing Book Company
701 E Linden Avenue
Linden NJ 07036
201-862-0909
Categories: 45(Chinese)-99
US agents for China National
    Publications (see below)

China Book Import Centre
P O Box 399
Beijing China
Categories: 45(Chinese)-99
China sales agents

China National Publications
Import-Export Corporation
P O Box 50-A
Beijing China
Categories: 45(Chinese)-99
China sales agents

Contacto Editorial
Rafael Domingo, Editor
Cervantes International
1708 - 11th Avenue
Brooklyn NY 11218
718-768-0755
Categories: 45-80(Spanish)
paid ads for rights sales

Cypress Book Company
Paramus Place #225
205 Robin Road
Paramus NJ 07652
201-967-7820
Categories: 45(Chinese)-99
US agents for China Book Import
    Centre (see above)

East-West Export Books
Warren Iwasa
2840 Kolowalu Street
University of Hawaii Press
Honolulu HI 96822
808-948-8697
Categories: 99
export representatives
    for Asia & the Pacific

European Book Service
P O Box 124
1380 AC Weesp
The Netherlands
0-2940-14459
Categories: 99
English language distributor

Feffer & Simons
Donald Traynor
100 Park Avenue
New York NY 10017
212-686-0888
Categories: 99
export representatives

Kaiman & Polon
Kenneth L Kaiman
2175 Lemoine Avenue
Fort Lee NJ 07024
201-944-0500
Categories: 99
export representatives

Libros de Espana y America
Angel Capellan
170-23 83rd Avenue
Jamaica Hills NY 11432
718-291-9891
Categories: 45(Spanish)
              80(Spanish)-99
exports and imports

Lynn Franklin Agency
Lynn C Franklin
386 Park Avenue South #1903
New York NY 10016
212-689-1842
Categories: 99
foreign rights representative

Maydo Kooy
Literary Agent
Kerkstraat 321
1017 GZ
Amsterdam Netherlands
Categories: 99
foreign rights - Netherlands

Michelle Lapautre
Agent Litteraire
6, rue Jean Carries
75007
Paris France
Categories: 99
foreign rights - France

Monica Heyum Literary Agency
Monica Heyum
P O Box 3300
Vendelso S-136 03 Handen
Stockholm Sweden
Categories: 99
foreign rights - Sweden

Paul & Peter Fritz
Literary Agency
Jupiterstrasse I
8032
Zurich Switzerlnd
Categories: 99
foreign rights - Switzerland

Rights Unlimited
Bernie Kurman and Sue Herner
31 East 28th Street
New York NY 10016
212-889-3733
Categories: 99
foreign rights representative

Rogan-Pikarski Literary Agency
12 George Eliot Street
Tel Aviv Israel
Categories: 99
foreign rights - Israel

Second Back Row Press
P O Box 43
Leura NSW 2781 Australia
Categories: 99(small press)
Australian distributor

Shanghai Book Traders
P O Box 234
Shanghai China
Categories: 45(Chinese)-99
book distributors in China

The English Agency
305 Azabu Empire Mansion
4-11-28 Nishi Azabu
Minato-ku
Tokyo 106 Japan
Categories: 99
foreign rights - Japan

Worldwide Media Service
Shelley Sakolsky
386 Park Avenue South
New York NY 10016
212-686-1520
Categories: 99
export representatives

Book Fairs and Conventions

ABA Convention
American Booksellers Association
122 East 42nd Street
New York NY 10017
212-867-9060
Categories: 99
Attendance: 18,000
Dates: May

ALA Convention
American Library Association
50 East Huron Street
Chicago IL 60611
312-944-6780
Categories: 99
Attendance: 13,769
Dates: June

Arabic Book Exhibition
Kuwait International Fair
P O Box 656
Safat Kuwait, Kuwait
Categories: 99
Dates: November

Beijing International Book Fair
China National Publications
P O Box 88
Beijing, China
Categories: 99
Dates: September

Bologna Children's Book Fair
Luciano Chicchi, Director
Piazza Constituzione 6
Bologna 40128 Italia
051-28.21.11
Categories: 21-76-89
Dates: April
major children's book fair

Brasil Internacional do Livro
Camara Brasileira do Livro
Avenida Ipiranga 1267, 10' andar
Sao Paulo 01039 Brasil
Categories: 99
Dates: August, bienniel

Brussels International Book Fair
Willy Vandermeulen, Director
321 Avenue des Volontaires
Brussels B-1150 Belgium
Categories: 99
Attendance: 323,000
Dates: March

Cairo International Book Fair
General Egyptian Book Organ.
Corniche El Nil, Boulac
Cairo, Egypt
00202-775371
Categories: 99
Attendance: 2,150,000
Dates: January

Cairo Intl. Children's Book Fair
Samir Saad Khalil, Director
General Egyptian Book Organ.
Corniche El Nil, Boulac
Cairo Egypt
00202-775371
Categories: 21-31-76-89
Attendance: 680,000
Dates: November
open to the public

Canadian Booksellers Convention
Canadian Booksellers Association
49 Laing Street
Toronto M4L 2N4 ON Canada
Categories: 99
Dates: late June

CBA Convention
Christian Booksellers Association
2031 W Cheyenne Road
Colorado Springs CO 80906
Categories: 63-99
Dates: late July

Colombo Children's Book Fair
Children's Book Fair
415 Galle Road
Colombo 4 Sri Lanka
Categories: 21-76
Dates: December

Frankfurt Book Fair
Postfach 2404
Kleiner Hirschgraben 10/12
D-6000
Frankfurt am Main 1 W Germany
611-2102-225
Categories: 99
Attendance: 110,000
Dates: October
major foreign rights book fair

Ife Book Fair
University of Ife Bookshop
Ile-Ife
Oyo State Nigeria
Categories: 99
Dates: November

International Book Fair of Mexico
Victor Porras Silva, Director
Apartado Postal 20-515
01000
Mexico D.F. Mexico
905-512-8273
Categories: 99
Dates: March

Jerusalem International Book Fair
22 Jaffa Road
Jerusalem 91-000 Israel
Categories: 99

Liber '86 (Barcelona Book Fair)
Evelyne de Lepine, Director
Federation of Spanish Publishers
P. Castellana 82
Madrid 28046 Espana
341-411-5795
Categories: 99
Dates: September

London Book Fair
Katy James, Director
Oriel House, 26 the Quadrant
Richmond-Upon-Thames
Surrey TW9 1DL G. Britain
01-940-6065
Categories: 99
Dates: March

Manila International Book Fest
PHILCITE, CCP Complex
P O Box 598
Manila Philippine
Categories: 99
Dates: June

Miami Book Fair International
Books by the Bay
Miami Dade Community College
300 NE Second Avenue #1402
Miami FL 33132
305-347-3203
Categories: 99
Attendance: 80,000
Dates: November

Moscow International Book Fair
Directorate of Intl. Book Fair
C.C.C.P. Goskomisdat
16 Chekhov Street
Moscow 1003006 U.S.S.R.
Categories: 99

NACS Convention
National Assn. of College Stores
528 E Lorain Street
Oberlin OH 44074
216-775-7777
Categories: 99
Attendance: 4900
Dates: April

New York Book Fair
321 West 94th Street
New York NY 10025
Categories: 99

Quebec International Book Fair
M Lorenzo Michaud, Director
2590 Boulevard Laurier #860
Ste-Foy G1V 4M6 PQ Canada
418-658-1974
Categories: 99
Attendance: 83,800
Dates: April

Book Fairs and Conventions

Salon du livre de Montreal
Salon du Livre
1151 rue Alexandre de Seve
Montreal H2L 2T7 PQ Canada
Categories: 99
Dates: November

Singapore Festival of Books
Festival of Books Singapore
865 Mountbatten Road #05-28
Singapore 1543 Singapore
Categories: 99
Dates: September

Sofia International Book Fair
Department of Exhibitions
11 Slaveikov Square
Sofia Bulgaria
Categories: 99
Dates: June

Swedish Book Fair
Urban Hagman, Congress Center
Stockholmsmassan AB
S-125-80
Stockholm Sweden
Categories: 99

Tianjin International Book Fair
International Exhibits
57 Wyndham Street, 1st Floor
Central Hong Kong
Categories: 99
Dates: June

Warsaw International Book Fair
Wladyslaw Bienkowski, Director
Krakowskie Przedmiescie 7
P O Box 1001
Warsaw Poland
17-86-41
Categories: 99
Attendance: 50,000
Dates: May

===

Trade Show Directories

Directory of Conventions
Successful Meetings
633 Third Avenue
New York NY 10017
Categories: 99
trade conventions

Exhibits Directory
Assn. of American Publishers
One Park Avenue
New York NY 10016
212-689-8920
Categories: 99
library/bookseller/education

Exhibits Schedule
Successful Meetings
633 Third Avenue
New York NY 10017
Categories: 99
conventions

**Trade Shows & Professional
Exhibits Directory**
Gale Research Company
Book Tower
Detroit MI 48226
800-223-gale
Categories: 99
exhibits and conventions

Tradeshow Week Data Book
Tradeshow Week
P O Box 716
Back Bay Annex
Boston MA 02117
Categories: 19-99
U.S. tradeshows

Exhibit Services

Academia Book Exhibits
Emmy Jacobius
4036 Poplar Street
Fairfax VA 22030
703-691-1109
Categories: 65-67-99
academic conferences

Baker & Taylor Exhibit Service
Patricia Bostelman
Baker & Taylor
6 Kirby Avenue
Somerville NJ 08876
202-526-8000
Categories: 99
international exhibits

Center for Thanatology
Research and Education
Roberta Halporn
391 Atlantic Avenue
Brooklyn NY 11217
718-858-3026
Categories: 39(death)
meetings: death-related topics

Conference Book Service
Attn: Roseann Doyle
80 South Early Street
P O Box 298
Alexandria VA 22314
703-823-6966
Categories: 99-65
book fairs and conferences

COSMEP Exhibit Service
Richard Morris
P O Box 703
San Francisco CA 94101
415-921-6190
Categories: 99(small press)
small press publications

Exhibit Promotions Plus
Nadine Hines
10369 Currycomb Court
Columbia MD 21044
301-997-0763
Categories: 19-31-35-55-57-63
65-99

Independent Publishers Service
Ruth Gottstein
1027 Schrader Street
San Francisco CA 94117
415-664-5600
Categories: 99(small press)

Joint Promotions
17 Stanley Hill Avenue
Amersham, Bucks
HP7 PBB England
02403-7867
Categories: 99
international book fairs

New Pages Exhibiting Service
Casey Hill
4426 S Belsay Road
Grand Blanc MI 48439
313-742-9583
Categories: 13-37-49-53-73-99
library, bookseller, other fairs

Periodical Display Service
Turner Subscriptions
116 East 16th Street
New York NY 10003
Categories: 99(magazines)

PMA Display Service
Jan Nathan
2401 Pacific Coast Highway #206
P O Box 299
Hermosa Beach CA 90254
213-372-2732
Categories: 99

Publishers Book Display
John Money
Special Libraries Book Service
Old Malt House, St. Johns Road
Banbury OX16 8HX   England
1-0295-68301
Categories: 99
conferences in England

Publishers Book Exhibit
Jon E Malinowski
86 Millwood Road
Millwood NY 10546
914-762-2422
Categories: 99

Publishers Exposition Displays
235 Park Avenue
New York NY 10003
Categories: 99

Reed/Spelling Associates
315 N Sycamore Avenue
Los Angeles CA 90036
Categories: 99

Ross Book Service
Miriam D Ross, Director
3718 Seminary Road
Seminary P O
Alexandria VA 22304-0993
703-823-1919
Categories: 11-19(publishing,
        marketing, PR)
Printfest, ACRL convention

USA Book-Expo
Ed Malinowski
ABA Calendar Exhibit
86 Millwood Road
Millwood NY 10546
914-762-2422
Categories: 99(calendars)

Cooperative Book Marketing Programs

Author Interviews Mailing
Dan Poynter
Para Publishing
P O Box 4232
Santa Barbara CA 93140-4232
805-968-7277
Categories: 99
author interviews - radio/TV

Bloomsbury Review
The Catalog Bookshelf
P O Box 8928
Denver CO 80201
Categories: 99
book catalog advertising section

Books For Review
Jan Nathan
Publishers Marketing Association
2401 Pacific Coast Highway #206
P O Box 299
Hermosa Beach CA 90254
213-372-2732
Categories: 10
co-op mailing to book reviewers

Business Books Marketing Group
Tod J Snodgrass
Lowen Publishing
P O Box 6870
Torrance CA 90504-0870
213-831-2770
Categories: 19
co-op library mailings and more

Direct Mail Promotions
L J Morton
342 Madison Avenue
New York NY 10017
212-687-1910
Categories: 99
paid mailings to libraries

Focus on Books
7744 - 31st Avenue NE
P O Box 51103
Seattle WA 98113
206-527-2900
Categories: 99
co-op review sent to libraries

Game-Show Placements
7011 Willoughby Avenue
Hollywood CA 90038
213-462-2277
Categories: 99
paid game show placements

Harris Catalog Library
Warren Harris, President
6230 Rampart Drive #209
Carmichael CA 95608
916-966-9552
Categories: 99
catalog kiosks in libraries

Mothers' Mailpak
Georganne Fiumara, Director
Mothers' Home Business Network
P O Box 423
East Meadow NY 11554
516-997-7394
Categories: 19-73
inserts to homeworking mothers

National Syndications
Kathleen Ryan
Parade / USA Weekend
230 Fifth Avenue #2010
New York NY 10001
212-686-8680
Categories: 99
per inquiry listings

Nationwide Shopper Systems
144 S First Street
P O Box 3197
Burbank CA 91504
818-846-5576
Categories: 99
catalog requests in magazines

PMA Co-op Mailings
Jan Nathan
Publishers Marketing Association
2401 Pacific Coast Hiway #206
P O Box 299
Hermosa Beach CA 90254
213-372-2732
Categories: 10
co-op mailing to libraries

Radio Direct Co-op Mailings
Kevin Collins, Publisher
Box 267, Kennett Pike
Chadds Ford PA 19317
215-388-7533
Categories: 99
co-op mailing to radio reviewers

Resources Publications Inc
160 E Virginia Street #250
San Jose CA 85112
Categories: 63
co-op mailing to
religious bookstores

Sales Call in an Envelope
Peggy Glenn
Book Marketing Group
1106 Main Street
Huntington Beach CA 92648
714-536-4926
Categories: 99
co-op mailing to bookstores

Small Press Library Service
Bookworks
796 South 980 East
Pleasant Grove UT 84062
801-785-1578
Categories: 99(small press)
co-op library catalog mailing

Spotlight
7744 - 31st Avenue NE
P O Box 51103
Seattle WA 98113
206-527-2900
Categories: 99
author interviews - radio/TV

Fulfillment Services

Central Distribution Services
Steve Rudminas, Manager
J J Keller & Associates Inc
8261 U.S. Highway 45
Neenah WI 54956
414-722-2848

Fulfillment Unlimited
2727 Scioto Parkway
P O Box 16539
Columbus OH 43216
614-771-1876

Fulfillment Unlimited
200 Hembree Park Drive
Roswell GA 30076
404-442-8633

Georgetown Book Warehouse
Lois M Fraser, Director
34 Armstrong Avenue
Georgetown L7G 4R9 ON Canada
416-792-8806
fulfillment service, customs

J-V Corporation
11575 Linda Way
Sparks NV 89431

Mercedex Distribution Center
160 Imlay Street
Brooklyn NY 11231

National Fulfillment Services
Lois Bowman
Holmes Corporate Center
100 Pine Avenue
Holmes PA 19043
800-345-8112; PA:215-532-4700

Nationwide Distribution Service
41 Drexel Drive
Bayshore NY 11706
516-435-1077

WHSCO Distribution Services
John MacFarlane
4419 West 1980 South
Salt Lake City UT 84104
801-973-4660

==

Marketing Services

About Books
Marilyn Ross
P O Box 213
Saguache CO 81149-0213
303-655-2504

Grybauskas & Partners Marketing
Roland Grybauskas, President
96 Morton Street
New York NY 10014
212-645-4646
marketing, product development

**I.S.B.S. - International
Specialized Book Services**
Cliff Martin, Director
5602 NE Hassalo Street
Portland OR 97213-3640
marketing services and more

Publishers Marketing Services
Len Forman, President
11661 San Vicente Boulevard #206
Los Angeles CA 90049
213-820-8672
fulfillment, marketing

R L Silver Associates
Ronald Silver, President
384 Park Avenue
New York NY 10016
212-684-0560
pr, advertising, graphics

Rivendell Marketing Company
Joseph Di Sabato, President
666 Avenue of the Americas
New York NY 10010
212-242-6863
Category: 37

Sensible Solutions
Judith Appelbaum
14 East 75th Street #5C
New York NY 10021
212-861-3693
general marketing services

Susanne K Williams College Mktg.
49 Sidney Place
Brooklyn NY 11201
718-802-1407
Categories: 31-65-99
college adoptions

Publicity and Public Relations Services

Accent on Broadcasting
Randie Levine
165 West 66th Street
New York NY 10023
212-362-3616
author tours

Ad Systems
723 S Wells
Chicago IL 60607

All Florida News Service
P O Drawer 1774
Tallahassee FL 32302
904-878-2690
Categories: 61(Florida)-99
Florida newspapers

All Media Services
Terry Sherf
13415 Ventura Boulevard
Sherman Oaks CA 91423

American Media Escorts
Dick Brown, President
501 Knickerbocker Place
Kansas City MO 64111
816-931-8580
PR escort service

Anita Helen Brooks Associates
155 East 55th Street
New York NY 10022
212-755-4498
all publicity services

Associated Release Service
  221 Park Avenue South
  New York NY 10003

  1120 - 19th Street NW
  Washington DC 20036

  2 N Riverside Plaza
  Chicago IL 60606

  161 Peachtree Street
  Atlanta GA 30303

  2112 Strand
  Manhattan Beach CA 90266
news release distribution
to newspapers, TV, and radio

Audio Features
342 Madison Avenue
New York NY 10017
radio features

Bacon's Publicity Distribution
R H Bacon Company
14 E Jackson Boulevard
Chicago IL 60604
800-621-0561; 312-922-8419

Barbara J Hendra Associates
350 Fifth Avenue #1101
New York NY 10118
212-947-9898
full publicity services

Betsy Nolan Group
Betsy Nolan, President
215 Park Avenue South #1602
New York NY 10003
212-420-6000
specialize in cross country tours

Betty Marks, Publicist
176 East 77th Street
New York NY 10021
212-535-8388
book publicity

Book World
David Sittenfeld
Townley Associates
220 East 23rd Street #601
New York NY 10010
212-532-2185
paid television interviews

Bookers
Morton Wax
Morton D Wax & Associates
200 West 51st Street
New York NY 10019
212-247-2159
all media, author tours

Bruce Merrin Public Relations
Bruce Merrin, President
Warner Center
6400 Canoga Avenue #311
Woodland Hills CA 91367
213-887-5066
most media

Business Wire
44 Montgomery Street #2150
San Francisco CA 94104
800-227-0845
Category: 19
electronic transmission of news

Canaan Communications
Lee Canaan, President
310 East 44th Street
New York NY 10017
212-682-4030
all media

Carl Ruff Associates
280 Madison Avenue
New York NY 10016
212-889-3671
Categories: 11(design,
                architecture)-43
architecture specialists

Carolyn Anthony Public Relations
213 St Johns Place
Brooklyn NY 11217
718-638-1822
pr services, subsidiary rights

Cassidy Brown Public Relations
21 Middle Street
Gloucester MA 01930
617-281-3102
national publicity

Celebrity Guide of California
Darlene La Madrid, Director
2568 Albatross #3
San Diego CA 92101
619-233-1054
author tours, escort services

Chase Direct Mail Corporation
228 East 45th Street
New York NY 10017

Communications Channels
118 S Clinton Street
Chicago IL 60606

Continental Features
507 Fifth Avenue
New York NY 10017
Categories: 49-78
black newspapers

Derus Media Service
  119 West 57th Street
  New York NY 10019

  1090 NE 79th Street
  Miami FL 33138

  907 Wayne Towers
  Wayne MI 48184

  8 W Hubbard Street
  Chicago IL 60610

  4017 San Fernando Road
  Glendale CA 91204

Diane Glynn Publicity and PR
Diane Glynn, President
200 Madison Avenue
New York NY 10016
212-686-6950
full service

Drummond Associates
659 East 48th Street
Brooklyn NY 11234

Family Features
P O Box 8398
Shawnee Mission KS 66208
newspapers, color features

Publicity and Public Relations Services

Frank Promotions
Ben Frank, President
60 East 42nd Street #757
New York NY 10017
212-687-3383
Categories: 39-99

H Blacker Public Relations
Harriet Blacker
230 Park Avenue #552
New York NY 10169
212-697-6228

Jeff Herman Agency
166 Lexington Avenue
New York NY 10016
212-725-4660
new division for small press

Kim Freilich Publicity
Kim Freilich
8405 Lookout Mountain Avenue
Los Angeles CA 90046
213-650-5523

Martin Pine Associates
Martin Pine
Press News Syndicate
2073 Gerritsen Avenue
Brooklyn NY 11229
718-339-1417
radio/TV talk show arrangements

Media Distribution Services
Alan Lederman
Sales Representative
307 West 36th Street
New York NY 10018
212-279-4800
tv/radio/newspapers

Media Tours Northwest
Northgate Station
P O Box 7
Seattle WA 98126
tour service for publishers

Metro Associated Services
33 West 34th Street
New York NY 10001
newspaper features

Michael D Beinner Associates
342 Madison Avenue #2000
New York NY 10017
212-986-5758
national tours, 35 offices

Michael Druxman Public Relations
P O Box 8086
Calabasas CA 91302
818-992-0633
PR for books, businesses, movies

National Press Service
19 West 44th Street
New York NY 10036
newspaper features

North American Precis Syndicate
201 East 42nd Street
New York NY 10017
radio features and releases

On the Scene Productions
Sally Jewett
6363 Sunset Boulevard
Los Angeles CA 90028
213-461-8698
satellite and video interviews

Parkhurst Communications
William Parkhurst, President
461 Park Avenue
New York NY 10016
212-683-0506
electronic publicity

Paul Kelly, Publicist
14618 Tyler Foote Boulevard
Nevada City CA 95959
916-292-3316

Planned Communications Service
12 East 46th Street
New York NY 10017
radio

Planned Television Arts
Rich Frishman or Mike Levine
25 West 43rd Street
New York NY 10036
212-921-5111
TV/radio interviews

PR Data Systems
33 Danbury Road
Wilton CT 06897

Public Relations Aids
330 West 34th Street
New York NY 10001
212-947-7733

1620 I Street NW
Washington DC 20006
202-659-0627

161 Spring Street
Atlanta GA 30303
404-523-2512

24500 Southfield Road
Southfield MI 48075
313-557-7474

2100 Pillsbury Avenue S
Minneapolis MN 55404
612-871-7201

111 N Canal Street
Chicago IL 60606
312-454-0755

1801 S Hill Street
Los Angeles CA 90015
213-749-7383

Publicity Circuit Monthly
Bradley Communications
312l-B West Montgomery Avenue
P O Box 299
Haverford PA 19041
215-896-6146
paid listings of author tours

Radio & TV Roundup Productions
111 Maplewood Avenue
Maplewood NJ 07040
radio/TV

Richard Weiner Inc
Richard Weiner
888 Seventh Avenue
New York NY 10106
212-315-8000

S&S Public Relations
40 Skokie Boulevard #430
Northbrook IL 60062
312-291-1616

Savvy Management
80 Fourth Street
New York NY 10003
212-477-1717
all services

SCW Inc
20433 Nordhoff Street
Chatsworth CA 91311

Selma Shapiro Public Relations
501 Fifth Avenue #500
New York NY 10017
212-867-7038
book review media, radio/TV

Shapian and Associates
Betty Shapian, President
9110 Sunset Boulevard
Los Angeles CA 90069
213-276-1005
see also On the Scene Production

Sheridan-Elson Communications
355 Lexington Avenue
New York NY 10017
radio/TV

Sun Color Service
P O Box 2810
Newport Beach CA 92660
newspapers, color features

Susan Friedman Public Relations
107-18 70th Avenue
Forest Hills NY 11375
718-544-8210
PR for authors and publishers

Susan W Wood Escort Service
150 E Mission Lane
Bloomington MN 55420
612-888-5831
book marketing and promotion

VIP R
Public Relations & Advertising
1857 Phillips Drive
Pomona CA 91766
714-623-5399
all media - pay only for results

Washington News Service
908 National Press Building
Washington DC 20045
202-737-4434

Wendy Doremus Public Relations
Wendy Doremus, President
876 Broadway
New York NY 10003
212-673-3809
Categories: 27(food and wine)-55
all media

Zucker International
Irwin Zucker
6430 Sunset Boulevard
Hollywood CA 90028
213-461-3921
all media

Publicity and Marketing Directories

**Advertiser's Guide to
Scholarly Periodicals**
American University Presses
One Park Avenue
New York NY 10016
212-889-3510
Categories: 65

All-in-One Directory
Gebbie Press
P O Box 1000
New Paltz NY 12561
914-255-7560
Categories: 99
all media

Alternative Access Directory
Catalyst Press
P O Box 462
Kentfield CA 94904
Categories: 13-53
alternative organizations

Alternative Press Index
P O Box 7229
Baltimore MD 21218
Categories: 13-53
alternative publications

American Book Trade Directory
R R Bowker Company
205 East 42nd Street
New York NY 10017
212-916-1600
Categories: 99
bookstores/chains/wholesalers

American Library Directory
R R Bowker Company
205 East 42nd Street
New York NY 10017
212-916-1600
Categories: 99
public and private libraries

Anglo-Jewish Media List
R K Communications
98-15 65th Road
Rego Park NY 11374
212-275-2546
Categories: 63(Jewish)
publications

Associated Church Press
P O Box 306
Geneva IL 60134
312-232-1055
Categories: 63(Protestant)
religious magazines

Bacon's Publicity Checker
R H Bacon Company
14 E Jackson Boulevard
Chicago IL 60604

800-621-0561
Categories: 99
magazines/syndicates/newspapers

Black Media Directory
Burrelle's
75 E Northfield Avenue
Livingston NJ 07039
Categories: 49-99
all media, black and minority

Black Press Periodical Directory
Black Newspaper Clipping Bureau
68 East 121st Street
New York NY 10037
212-281-6000
Categories: 49-99
newspapers/radio/tv/magazines

**Broadcasting and
Cablecasting Yearbook**
Broadcasting Publications
1735 DeSales Street NW
Washington DC 20036
202-638-1022
Categories: 99
radio/TV stations, US and Canada

**Cable Services Report:
Local Programming**
National Cable TV Association
1724 Massachusetts Avenue NW
Washington DC 20036
202-775-3550
Categories: 99
cable TV stations

Cable TV Publicity Outlets
Public Relations Plus
P O Box 329
Washington Depot CT 06794
203-868-0200
Categories: 99
cable TV stations

Catholic Press Directory
Catholic Press Association
119 N Park Avenue
Rockville Centre NY 11570
516-766-3400
Categories: 63(Catholic)
newspapers/magazines

College Alumni Publications
Public Relations Publishing
888 Seventh Avenue
New York NY 10106
212-582-7373
Categories: 99
college alumni magazines

College Newspaper Sourcebook
Cass Communications
1633 Central Street

Evanston IL 60201
800-323-4044
Categories: 11-33-69-99
free catalog of college papers

College Student Press Directory
Oxbridge Communications
150 Fifth Avenue #301
New York NY 10011
212-741-0231
Categories: 11-33-69-99
college magazines and newspapers

Contact Book
Celebrity Service
171 West 57th Street
New York NY 10019
212-757-7979
Categories: 99
authors

The Corporate 1000
c/o The Washington Monitor
Suite 1000
1301 Pennsylvania Avenue NW
Washington DC 20004
202-347-7757
Categories: 19
corporations and officers

Direct Mail List Rates & Data
Standard Rate & Data Service
3004 Glenview Road
Wilmette IL 60091
800-323-4588
Categories: 19-99
sources of mailing lists

Direct Marketing Market Place
Hilary House Publishers
1033 Channel Drive
Hewlett Harbor NY 11557
516-295-2376
Categories: 99
resources, catalogs, etc.

**Directory of Arts, Crafts,
Gifts and Home Based
Business Publications**
Publishers Services
6318 Vesper Avenue
Van Nuys CA 91411-2378
818-785-8039
Categories: 11-19-29
magazines and newspapers

Directory of College Stores
Bernard Klein, Editor
B Klein Publications
P O Box 8503
Coral Springs FL 33065
305-752-1708
Categories: 11-33-69-99
college bookstores

Directory of Ethnic Periodicals
Oxbridge Communications
150 Fifth Avenue #301
New York NY 10011
212-741-0231
Categories: 49
minority magazines

Directory of Mailing Lists
B Klein Publications
P O Box 8503
Coral Springs FL 33065
305-752-1708
Categories: 99
sources of mailing lists

**Directory of Multiple Book
Store Owners**
Oldden Mercantile Corporation
31 Glen Head Road
Glen Head NY 11545
516-759-1200
Categories: 99
bookstore and other chains

**Directory of Southern California
Buyers, Retailers & Sales Cos.**
Publishers Services
6318 Vesper Avenue
Van Nuys CA 91411-2378
818-785-8039
Categories: 19
Southern California companies

Directory of Special Libraries
Gale Research Company
Book Tower
Detroit MI 48226
800-223-gale; 313-961-2242
Categories: 99
special libraries

Directory of Weekly Newspapers
National Newspaper Association
1627 K Street NW #400
Washington DC 20006
202-466-7200
Categories: 99
weekly newspapers

Directory of Women's Media
Women's Inst. for Freedom Press
3306 Ross Place NW
Washington DC 20008
Categories: 73
magazines/publishers/groups/books

Editor and Publisher Yearbook
575 Lexington Avenue
New York NY 10707
212-752-7050
Categories: 99
newspapers

Encyclopedia of Associations
Gale Research Company
Book Tower
Detroit MI 48226

800-223-gale; 313-961-2242
Categories: 99
associations

Family Page Directory
Public Relations Plus
P O Box 329
Washington Depot CT 06794
203-868-0200
Categories: 15-25-27-29-31
                35-39-43-73
newspaper editors

Gebbie House Magazine Directory
The Gebbie Press
P O Box 1000
New Paltz NY 12561
914-255-7560
Categories: 19-99
company magazines

Great Book of Catalogs
Pinkerton Marketing
209 Change Street
New Bern NC 28560
Categories: 99
consumer catalogs

Health Media Buyer's Guide
Nautillus Publishing Corporation
P O Box 4790
Stamford CT 06907
Categories: 39
health publications

Hispanic Media Directory
Burrelle's
75 E Northfield Avenue
Livingston NJ 07039
Categories: 49-78
Hispanic media

IMS Directory of Publications
IMS Press
426 Pennsylvania Avenue
Fort Washington PA 19034
215-628-4920
Categories: 99
magazines/newspapers

Internal Publications Directory
National Research Bureau
104 S Michigan Avenue
Chicago IL 60603
Categories: 19-99
company publications

**International Media Guide:
Business and Professional**
Directories International
150 Fifth Avenue
New York NY 10011
212-807-1660
Categories: 19

**International Media Guide:
Consumer Magazines**
Directories International

150 Fifth Avenue
New York NY 10011
212-807-1660
Categories: 99
consumer magazines around
the world

**International Media Guide:
Newspapers and News Magazines**
Directories International
150 Fifth Avenue
New York NY 10011
212-807-1660
Categories: 99
international news publications

Jewish Press in America
60 East 42nd Street
New York NY 10017
Categories: 63(Jewish)
publications

The Left Index
511 Lincoln Street
Santa Cruz CA 95060
Categories: 13
alternative newspapers

Literary Bookstores: A List
Poets and Writers
201 West 54th Street
New York NY 10019
212-757-1766
Categories: 83-95
bookstores

Mail Order Catalogs Directory
Grey House Publishing
Colonial Bank Building
Sharon CT 06069
Categories: 19-99
mail order catalogs

Military Publications
Richard Weiner, Editor
Public Relations Publishing Co
888 Seventh Avenue
New York NY 10106
212-582-7373
Categories: 55(military)
military publications

Minorty-Ethnic Media Guide
Directories International
150 Fifth Avenue
New York NY 10011
212-807-1660
Categories: 49-78
minority media

**National Directory of Newsletter
and Reporting Services**
Gale Research Company
Book Tower
Detroit MI 48226
313-961-2242
Categories: 99
newsletters & reporting services

Publicity and Marketing Directories

National Radio Publicity Directory
Peter Glenn Publications
17 East 48th Street
New York NY 10017
212-688-7940
Categories: 99
radio talk shows nationwide

National Survey of Newspaper Op-Ed Pages
Communication Creativity
P O Box 213
Saguache CO 81149-0213
303-589-8223
Categories: 99
newspapers with op-ed sections

National Trade & Professional Associations of the U.S.
Columbia Books
1350 New York Avenue NW #207
Washington DC 20005
202-737-3777
Categories: 19-99
associations

National Women's Organizations
Pattie Overstreet-Miller
UA Director
Allstate Insurance Company
Allstate Plaza F3
Northbrook IL 60062
Categories: 19-73
national women's organizations

Nationwide Black Radio Directory
CDE
P O Box 41551
Atlanta GA 30331
Categories: 49-78
black-owned radio stations

New Consciousness Source Book
Spiritual Community Publications
P O Box 1080
San Rafael CA 94902
415-644-3229
Categories: 53
yoga centers, natural foodstores
bookstores, and other resources

News Bureaus in the U.S.
Richard Weiner, Editor
Public Relations Publishing
888 Seventh Avenue
New York NY 10106
212-582-7373
Categories: 99
newspapers

Newsletter Yearbook Directory
The Newsletter Clearinghouse
44 West Market Street
Rhinebeck NY 12572
914-876-2081
Categories: 99
newsletters

Newsmaker Interviews
439 S La Cienega Boulevard #219
Los Angeles CA 90048
213-274-6866
Categories: 99
authors for radio/TV

North American Radio and TV Station Guide
Howard W Sams & Company
4300 West 62nd Street
Indianapolis IN 46206
317-298-5400
Categories: 99
radio/TV stations

Oxbridge Newsletter Directory
Oxbridge Communications
150 Fifth Avenue #301
New York NY 10011
212-741-0231
Categories: 99
newsletters

Radio Contacts
Larimi Communications
151 East 50th Street
New York NY 10022
212-935-9262
Categories: 99
radio programs with guests

Regional Publications Directory
Bradley Communications
3121-B West Montgomery Avenue
P O Box 299
Haverford PA 19041
215-896-6146
Categories: 61
city, state, regional magazines

Religious Broadcasting Directory
National Religious Broadcasters
38 Speedwell Avenue
Morristown NJ 07960
201-575-4000
Categories: 63
radio/tv/publishers/records

Religious Periodical Directory
Oxbridge Communications
150 Fifth Avenue #301
New York NY 10011
212-741-0231
Categories: 63
religious magazines

Standard Periodical Directory
Oxbridge Communications
150 Fifth Avenue #301
New York NY 10011
212-741-0231
Categories: 99
magazines and newsletters

Suburban Newspapers of America Membership Directory
111 E Wacker Drive #600

Chicago IL 60601
312-644-6610
Categories: 99
suburban newspapers

Syndicated Columnists
Richard Weiner, Editor
Public Relations Publishing
888 Seventh Avenue
New York NY 10106
212-582-7373
Categories: 99
columnists

Syndicated Features Directory
Editor and Publisher
575 Lexington Avenue
New York NY 10707
212-752-7050
Categories: 99

Talk Show Directory: Radio-TV
National Research Bureau
Automated Marketing Systems
310 S Michigan Avenue
Chicago IL 60604
312-663-5580
Categories: 99
radio/TV talk shows

Talk Show Guest Directory
Mitchell P Davis, Editor
Broadcast Interview Source
2500 Wisconsin Ave NW #930
Washington DC 20007-9990
202-333-4904
Categories: 99
authors available for interview

Television Contacts
Larimi Communications Associates
151 East 50th Street
New York NY 10022
212-935-9262
Categories: 99
TV stations

Television Factbook
Television Digest
1836 Jefferson Place NW
Washington DC 20036
202-872-9200
Categories: 99
worldwide TV contacts

Thomas Register of American Manufacturers
461 Eighth Avenue
New York NY 10001
Categories: 19
manufacturers by product

Trade Directories of the World
Croner Publications
211-03 Jamaica Avenue
Queens Village NY 11428
212-464-0866
Categories: 19

Publicity and Marketing Directories

Travel News & Publicity Directory
Discover America Travel
  Organization
1899 L Street NW
Washington DC 20036
Categories: 61-71
writers and publications

TV Publicity Outlets
Public Relations Plus
P O Box 329
Washington Depot CT 06794
203-868-0200
Categories: 99
TV stations

**U S Government Purchasing
and Sales Directory**
Department 36-PD
Superintendent of Documents
Washington DC 20402
Categories: 55
doing business with government

U S Publicity Directory
John Wiley & Company
605 Third Avenue
New York NY 10016
Categories: 99
all media

U S Industrial Directory
Cahners Publishing Company
270 Saint Paul Street
Denver CO 80206-9988
Categories: 19
46,000 manufacturers

**Ulrich's International
Periodicals Directory**
R R Bowker Company
205 East 42nd Street
New York NY 10017
212-916-1600
Categories: 99
magazines and other periodicals

Women's Media Directory
Burrelle's
75 E Northfield Avenue
Livingston NJ 07039
Categories: 73-99
all media

Working Press of the Nation
National Research Bureau
424 N Third Street
Burlington IA 52601
312-663-5580
Categories:
all media / 5 volumes

Bibliographies and Other Publisher Listings

ABA Book Buyer's Handbook
Mary Ann Tennenhaus, Editor
American Booksellers Association
122 East 42nd Street
New York NY 10168
212-867-9060
Categories: 99
for bookstore buyers

Alternative America
Resources
P O Box 134 Harvard Square
Cambridge MA 02238-0134
617-876-2789
Categories: 13-37-53
529 bookstores, 1717 publishers

**Alternative Press Publishers
of Children's Books**
Wendy Osterweil, Editor
Cooperative Children's Book Center
P O Box 5288
Madison WI 53705-0288
Categories: 13-21-76

American Reference Book Annual
Bohdan S Wynar, Editor
Libraries Unlimited
P O Box 263
Littleton CO 80160-0263
Categories: 59

**Annotated Bibliography of New
Publications in Performing Arts**
Ralph Schoolcraft, Editor
Drama Book Shop
723 Seventh Avenue
New York NY 10019
212-944-0595
Categories: 11(performing
          arts, dance)

Artist's Market
Writer's Digest Books
9933 Alliance Road
Cincinnati OH 45242
513-984-0717
Categories: 11

**Associations' Publications
in Print**
R. R. Bowker Company
205 East 42nd Street
New York NY 10017
212-916-1600
Categories: 19-99

Audio Video Market Place
R R Bowker Company
205 East 42nd Street
New York NY 10017
212-916-1600
Categories: 99
audio/video suppliers/publishers

**Bibliographic Guide to
Business and Economics**
G K Hall
70 Lincoln Street
Boston MA 02111
617-423-3990
Categories: 19

**Bibliography of Books for
Children**
Assn for Childhood Education
3615 Wisconsin Avenue NW
Washington DC 20016
202-363-6963
Categories: 21-31-76

Book Trade in Canada
Ampersand Communications Service
RR #1
Caledon L0N 1C0 ON Canada
519-927-3321
Categories: 61(Canada)-99
500 publishers, 2000 bookstores

Books in Print Database
ABI Information Office
R R Bowker Company
205 East 42nd Street
New York NY 10017
212-916-1600
Categories: 99
bibliographies for various areas

Canadian Books in Print
Marian Butler, Editor
University of Toronto Press
St. George Campus
Toronto M5S 1A6 ON Canada
416-978-8651
Categories: 99
books from Canadian publishers

Canadian Publishers Directory
Key Publishers
59 E Front Street
Toronto M5E 1B3 ON Canada
416-364-3333
Categories: 99

Catholic Book Annual
Thomas More Association
223 West Erie Street
Chicago IL 60610
312-951-2100
Categories: 99(Catholic)
Catholic books in print

Children's Authors/Illustrators
Gale Research Company
Book Tower
Detroit MI 48226
313-961-2242
Categories: 21-76
illustrators/authors

Children's Books of the Year
The Child Study Book Committee
Bank Street College
610 West 112th Street
New York NY 10025
212-667-7200
Categories: 21-76
features 500 titles

Children's Choices for 1985
International Reading Assn.
P O Box 8139
Newark DE 19714
Categories: 21-31-76
books selected by children

Children's Media Market Place
Neal-Schuman Publications
23 Cornelia Street
New York NY 10014
212-620-5900
Categories: 21-76
publishers, clubs, stores, etc.

Colorado Books in Print
Jende-Hagen Book Corporation
P O Box 177
Frederick CO 80530
303-833-2030
Categories: 61(Colorado)-71

Contemporary Authors
Gale Research Company
Book Tower
Detroit MI 48226
313-961-2242
Categories: 17-99
author biographies

**Directory of American Poets
and Fiction Writers**
Poets & Writers
201 West 54th Street
New York NY 10019
212-757-1766
Categories: 75-95
poets and fiction authors

Directory of Directories
Gale Research Company
Book Tower
Detroit MI 48226
313-961-2242
Categories: 59
directories, databases

Directory of Poetry Publishers
Len Fulton & Ellen Ferber
Dustbooks
P O Box 100
Paradise CA 95969
916-877-6110
Categories: 95
book and magazine publishers

Bibliographies and Other Publisher Listings

**Directory of Small Magazine /
Press Editors & Publishers**
Dustbooks
P O Box 100
Paradise CA 95969
916-877-6110
Categories: 99(small press)

Fiction Writer's Market
Writer's Digest Books
9933 Alliance Road
Cincinnati OH 45242
513-984-0717
Categories: 75
book and magazine publishers

Gayellow Pages
Renaissance House
P O Box 292, Village Station
New York NY 10014
Categories: 37
bookstores, publications, etc.

**Genealogical and Local History
Books in Print**
6818 Lois Drive
Springfield VA 22150
Categories: 35-98(genealogy)

Guide to American Directories
Bernard Klein, Editor
B Klein Publications
P O Box 8503
Coral Springs FL 33065
305-752-1708
Categories: 59

**Guide to Publishers & Distribu-
tors Serving Minority Languages**
National Clearinghouse for
  Bilingual Education
5555 Wilson Boulevard #605
Rosslyn VA 22209
Categories: 45-49
publishers and distributors

Information America
Neal-Schuman Publications
23 Cornelia Street
New York NY 10014
212-620-5990
Categories: 19-59-99

Information Sources
Information Industry Association
316 Pennsylvania Avenue SE #400
Washington DC 20003
202-544-1969
Categories: 19-59-99

**International Directory of
Children's Literature**
George Kurian Reference Books
P O Box 519
Baldwin Place NY 10505
914-962-3287
Categories: 21-76
bookclubs/stores/publishers/etc.

**International Directory of
Little Magazines & Small Press**
Dustbooks
P O Box 100
Paradise CA 95969
916-877-6110
Categories: 99(small press)

**International Directory of
Military Publications**
Sidney Allinson
24 Ravencliff Crescent
Scarborough M1T1R8 ON Canada
Categories: 55(military)

**International Science Fiction
Yearbook**
Big O Publishing Ltd
228 Fulham Road
London SW1 9NB England
Categories: 86
books, events, magazines, etc

Intl. Literary Market Place
R R Bowker Company
205 East 42nd Street
New York NY 10017
212-916-1600
Categories: 99
international publishing resources

**Irregular Serials and Annuals:
An International Directory**
R R Bowker Company
205 East 42nd Street
New York NY 10017
212-916-1600
Categories: 59
annuals and irregulars

Jewish Book Annual
Jewish Book Council of America
15 East 26th Street
New York NY 10010
212-532-4949
Categories: 63(Jewish)

Law Books in Print
Robert Buckwalter
Glanville Publications
75 Main Street
Dobbs Ferry NY 10522
914-693-5944
Categories: 19-55(law)

Literary Market Place
R R Bowker Company
205 East 42nd Street
New York NY 10017
212-916-1600
Categories: 99
publishers, suppliers, etc.

NACS Book Buyer's Manual
Brenda L Henderson, Editor
National Assn of College Stores
528 E Lorain Street
P O Box 58

Oberlin OH 44074
216-775-7777
Categories: 99
textbooks, college bookstores

New & Forthcoming Canadian Books
Key Publishers
59 Front Street East
Toronto M5E 1B3 ON Canada
416-364-3333
Categories: 61(Canada)-99
Canadian books in print

New Age Directory
Survival Foundation
P O Box 64
Woodstock Valley CT 06282
203-974-2440
Categories: 53
centers, publishers, etc.

New Jewish Yellow Pages
SBS Publishing
51 Railroad Avenue
Closter NJ 07624
201-767-9450
Categories: 63(Jewish)
products and services

New Scholarly Books in America
Norman Perle, Editor
University Press Book Service
302 Fifth Avenue
New York NY 10001
212-564-2048
Categories: 65

**New Scientific & Technical
Books in America**
University Press Book Service
302 Fifth Avenue
New York NY 10001
212-564-2048
Categories: 23-67

Notable Children's Books
ALA - Association for Library
Services to Children
50 E. Huron Street
Chicago IL 60611
312-944-6780
Categories: 21-76

**Paperback Books for Young
People: An Annotated Guide**
American Library Association
50 E Huron Street
Chicago IL 60611
312-944-6780
Categories: 21-76

Photographer's Market
Writer's Digest Books
9933 Alliance Road
Cincinnati OH 45242
513-984-0717
Categories: 11-99
photographers marketplace

Bibliographies and Other Publisher Listings

Poet's Market
Judson Jerome, Editor
Writer's Digest Books
9933 Alliance Road
Cincinnati OH 45242
513-984-0717
Categories: 95
book and magazine publishers

Poets Marketplace
Joseph J Kelly, Editor
Running Press
125 South 22nd Street
Philadelphia PA 19103
215-567-5080
Categories: 95

**Policies of Publishers: A
Handbook for Order Librarians**
Scarecrow Press
52 Liberty Street
Metuchen NJ 08840
201-548-8600
Categories: 99
for acquisition librarians

**Publishers and Producers in
Minnesota Annual Directory**
MORE Information
4717 - 12th Avenue S.
Minneapolis MN 55407
612-822-6167
Categories: 61(Minnesota)-99

Publishers Directory
Gale Research Company
150 East 50th Street
New York NY 10022
212-751-3033
Categories: 99
book publishers and others

**Publishers' International
Directory**
K G Saur Verlag KG
Postfach 148
D-8023 Pullach West Germany
Categories: 99
international book publishers

Reading Aloud with Children
The Child Study Book Committee
Bank Street College
610 West 112th Street
New York NY 10025
212-667-7200
Categories: 21-76

**Real Estate Books & Periodicals
in Print**
Real Estate Publishing Company
P O Box 41177
Sacramento CA 95841
Categories: 19(real estate)-43

**Reference Sources for Small
and Medium-Sized Libraries**
ALA Reference & Adult Services
50 E Huron Street
Chicago IL 60611
312-944-6780
Categories: 59
for libraries

Science Book List for Children
American Association for the
Advancement of Science
1515 Massachusetts Avenue NW
Washington DC 20005
202-467-4400
Categories: 21-67

**SIE Guide to Business and
Investment Books**
George H Wein, Editor
Select Information Exchange
2095 Broadway
New York NY 10023
212-874-6408
Categories: 19

**Small Press Record
of Books in Print**
Len Fulton, Editor
Dustbooks
P O Box 100
Paradise CA 95969
916-877-6110
Categories: 99(small press)

Source Directory
Nellie Connor, Editor
Predicasts Inc
11001 Cedar Avenue
Cleveland OH 44106
216-795-3000
Categories: 19
sources of business information

The Bookfinder
American Guidance Service
660 Publishers' Building
Circle Pines MN 55014-1796
612-786-4343
Categories: 21-31-76

Third World Resource Directory
Thomas Fenton & Mary Heffron
Orbis Books
Maryknoll NY 10545
Categories: 13-80
                55(international)
organizations, publications, etc

**Who's Who in U.S. Writers,
Editors & Poets**
December Press
P O Box 302
Highland Park IL 60035
312-432-6804
Categories: 75-95-99

Whole Again Resource Guide
Tim Ryan & Rae Jappinen
Sourcenet
P O Box 6767
Santa Barbara CA 93111
Categories: 13-49-53-73
directory of resources

Writer's Market
Writer's Digest Books
9933 Alliance Road
Cincinnati OH 45242
513-984-0717
Categories: 99
book and magazine publishers

Writer's Northwest Handbook
Media Weavers
P O Box 19755
Portland OR 97219
Categories: 61(northwest US)-99

How to Use the Review Files

DAILY AND WEEKLY NEWSPAPERS

All the major daily and weekly newspapers are listed in this file. Where known, we've listed the book review editor for the newspaper. For those newspapers which responded to our questionnaire in full, we are also able to list other editors who are responsible for special sections of the newspaper -- arts and entertainment, business, computer, cookbooks/diet, family, home and hobby, automotive, local and national news, science, sports, and travel.

We also indicate, where known, the paper's circulation, the number of book reviews they feature (either per issue, per week, or per year), and whether they buy first serial rights, second serial rights, or both--or don't buy rights at all.

MAGAZINES

Though we've tried to list all major magazines (especially those featuring book reviews or excerpts), we have undoubtedly missed a few. Besides the major magazines, we've also listed a good number of more limited circulation or specialized magazines. We hope to expand this category in future editions.

As with the newspapers, we've indicated, where known, the magazines circulation, frequency, number of book reviews per issue, and whether they buy serial rights.

RADIO AND TV

Where the radio or TV station did not respond to our survey, we are only able to list their name, address and phone number (and, in some cases, the general manager or news director). For those radio and TV stations and shows which responded to our survey, we've listed both the person to contact and the name of the host (these are usually not the same person).

Where known, we also indicate the format of the show-- whether live, taped, live with call-ins, and/or telephone interviews. We also list what the show features--whether interviews, news, features, book reviews, and/or book readings. Given this information, for example, you could target all those radio stations which do telephone interviews. You could, in effect, set up a national author tour from your living room or office.

Note also that many review media are only interested in certain categories of books or topics. Use the category codes to help you target those media which would be most interested in your books.

<u>**CATEGORIES**</u> -- coded by number

10 General Nonfiction
11 Art/Music/Photography/Dance
13 Alternative Issues
15 Animals/Pets
17 Biographies/Autobiographies
19 Business/Economics
21 Children's Books
23 Computers/Technology
25 Consumer Issues and Guides
27 Cookbooks/Nutrition
29 Crafts/Hobbies/How-to
31 Education/Child Development
33 Entertainment/Movies/Humor
35 Family/Marriage/Retirement
37 Gay/Lesbian
39 Health/Medicine/Diet/Exercise
41 History

43 House/Garden/Automobiles
45 Languages:________________
47 Literature/Humanities
49 Minority Studies
51 Nature/Ecology/Conservation
53 New Age/Astrology/Occult
55 Politics/Government/Military
57 Psychology/Self-Help
59 Reference Books
61 Regional Titles
63 Religions/Philosophy
65 Scholarly Titles
67 Science/Mathematics
69 Sports/Games/Recreation
71 Travel/Geography
73 Women's Issues

75 General Fiction
76 Children's Stories
77 Contemporary Novels
78 Ethnic/Minority Literature
79 Folklore/Fairy Tales
80 Foreign Literature
81 Historical
82 Horror/Occult

83 Literary
84 Mystery/Detective
85 Romance/Gothic
86 Science Fiction/Fantasy
87 Suspense/Adventure
88 Westerns
89 Young Adult
90 Short Stories/Anthologies

95 Poetry
97 News

98 Other:__________________
99 All subjects and categories

==

<u>**Radio**</u> / <u>**Television**</u> -- special codes

Formats: C = Live with Call-ins
           L = Live
           P = Telephone Interviews
           T = Taped

Features: B = Book Reviews
           F = Features
           I = Interviews
           N = News
           R = Book Readings

==

Daily Newspapers

ALABAMA

Birmingham News
Kenneth Shorey, Book Editor
2200 Fourth Avenue N
P O Box 2553
Birmingham AL 35202
205-325-2479
Category: 99
Circulation: 213,000

Birmingham Post Herald
Sarah Teague, Book Editor
2200 Fourth Avenue N
P O Box 2553
Birmingham AL 35202
205-325-2222
Category: 99
Circulation: 66,000
Reviews: some

Huntsville Times
Alan Moore, Book Editor
Susan Still, Business Editor
Judi Moon, Feature Editor
Mickey Ellis, Food Editor
Lee Roop, Local News Editor
Joe Duncan, National News Editor
Martin Burkey, Science Editor
John Pruett, Sports Editor
2317 Memorial Parkway S
Huntsville AL 35807
205-532-4000
Category: 11-19-25-27-29-31-33
35-39-43-57-67-71-97
(news)-99
Circulation: 74,000
Reviews: 260/year
Does not buy serial rights.

Mobile Press-Register
Gordon Tatum, Book Editor
304 Government Street
P O Box 2488
Mobile AL 36630
205-433-1551
Category: 99
Circulation: 105,000

Montgomery Advertiser
Jim Earnhardt, Book Editor
200 Washington Avenue
P O Box 1000
Montgomery AL 36192
205-262-1611
Category: 99

ATLANTA

Anchorage Daily News
Jim Macknicki, Book Editor
200 Potter Drive
Pouch 6616
Anchorage AK 99502

907-786-4200
Category: 99
Circulation: 63,000

Anchorage Times
Carmen Dybdahl, Book Editor
820 West 4th Avenue
Anchorage AK 99501
907-279-5622
Category: 99
Circulation: 52,000

Juneau Empire
Carl Sampson, Editor
235 Second Street
Juneau AK 99801
907-586-3740
Category: 99
Circulation: 8000

ARIZONA

Arizona Republic
Mike McKay, Book Editor
120 E Van Buren
Phoenix AZ 85001
602-271-8000
Category: 99
Circulation: 450,000

Phoenix Gazette
Kyle Lawson, Book Editor
120 E Van Buren
Phoenix AZ 85001
602-271-8602
Category: 99
Circulation: 115,000

Arizona Daily Star
June C Martin, Book Editor
Tony Tselentis, Business Editor
Maria Parham, Family Editor
John Peck, Feature Editor
Judy Ratliff, Food Editor
Tom Beal, Local News Editor
Don Bennett, National News Editor
Jim Erickson, Science Editor
Chuck Kramer, Sports Editor
4850 S Park Avenue
Tucson AZ 85726
602-573-4111
Category: 11-19-23-25-27-29-31-33
35-39-43-57-67-69-71-97
Circulation: 160,000
Reviews: 175-200/year
Buys only 1st serial rights.

Tucson Citizen
Paul Allen, Book Editor
4850 S Park Avenue
Tucson AZ 85726
602-573-4561
Category: 99
Circulation: 67,000

ARKANSAS

Little Rock Arkansas Democrat
Meredith L Oakley, Book Editor
Sandy Miller Hays, Business Editor
Eric Harrison, Entertainment
Jame Dearing, Feature Editor
Helen Austin, Food Editor
Ray Hobbs, Local News Editor
Deidre Tucker, National News
Bobbi Ridlehoover, Science Editor
Wally Hall, Sports Editor
Betty Woods, Travel Editor
Capitol Avenue and Scott Street
P O Box 2221
Little Rock AR 72203
501-378-3400
Category: 11-19-23-25-27-29-31
33-35-39-43-57-67-69
71-97(news)-99
Circulation: 150,000
Reviews: varies
Buys 1st and 2nd serial rights.

Little Rock Arkansas Gazette
Willard Lewis, Book Editor
112 W Third Avenue
Little Rock AR 72203
501-371-3700
Category: 99
Circulation: 165,000

CALIFORNIA

Anaheim Bulletin
Karl Wray, Book Editor
Freedom Newspapers
1771 S Lewis Street
Anaheim CA 92805
714-634-1567
Category: 99
Circulation: 14,000

Bakersfield Californian
1707 Eye Street
Bakersfield CA 93302
805-395-7364
Category: 99
Circulation: 77,000

Corona-Norco Independent
Peter Fischetti, Managing Editor
823 S Main Street
Corona CA 91720
714-737-1234
Category: 99
Circulation: 7800

San Gabriel Valley Daily Tribune
Barbara Tarshes, Features Editor
P O Box 1259
Covina CA 91722

818-962-8811
Category: 99
Circulation: 65,000

Fresno Bee
Eddie Lopez, Book Editor
1626 E Street
Fresno CA 93786
209-441-6111
Category: 99
Circulation: 160,000

Glendale News-Press
Virgil Pinkley, Editor
111 N Isabel
P O Box 991
Glendale CA 91209
818-241-4141
Category: 99
Circulation: 11,000

Hayward Daily Review
P O Box 5050
Hayward CA 94540
415-783-6111
Category: 99
Circulation: 47,000

Daily Variety
Thomas Pryor, Editor
1400 N Cahuenga Boulevard
Hollywood CA 90028
213-469-1141
Category: 11-33
Circulation: 20,000

Hollywood Reporter
Book Editor
6715 Sunset Boulevard
Hollywood CA 90028
213-464-7411
Category: 11-33
Circulation: 18,000

Long Beach Press Telegram
Harold Glicken, Lifestyle Editor
604 Pine Avenue
Long Beach CA 90844
213-435-1161
Category: 11-27-29-33-39-43-71-99
Circulation: 136,000

Los Angeles Herald-Examiner
Digby Diehl, Editor
Book World
1111 S Broadway
Los Angeles CA 90015
213-744-8000
Category: 99
Circulation: 240,000

Los Angeles Times
Jack Miles, Book Editor
Times Mirror Square
Los Angeles CA 90053
213-972-5000
Category: 99
Circulation: 1,347,000

Modesto Bee
14th & H Streets
P O Box 3928
Modesto CA 95352
209-578-2000
Category: 99
Circulation: 75,000

Oakland Tribune
Diane Ketcham, Book Editor
409 13th Street
P O Box 24424
Oakland CA 94623
415-645-2000
Category: 99
Circulation: 158,000

Oceanside Blade-Tribune
1722 S Hill
P O Box 90
Oceanside CA 92054
619-433-7333
Category: 99
Circulation: 32,000

Palm Springs Desert Sun
Beth Harris, Book Reviews
P O Box 190
Palm Springs CA 92263
619-325-8666
Category: 99
Circulation: 29,000

Antelope Valley Press
Dale Brown, Automotive Editor
Steve Hendrickson, Book Editor
Katie Corbett, Business Editor
Darlene Phillips, Family Editor
Bill MacKenzie, Features Editor
Lynn DuPratt, Food Editor
Jackie Greer, Home Editor
Linda Warner, National News
Larry Grooms, News Editor
Mik Peck, Sports Editor
Linda Lee, Travel Editor
P O Box 880
Palmdale CA 93550
805-273-2700
Category: 11-19-23-25-27-31-33
        35-39-43-57-67-69-71
        97(news)-99
Circulation: 50,000
Reviews: 52/year
Does not buy serial rights.

Peninsula Times Tribune
Jean Griffin, Book Editor
Marlene Somsak, Business Editor
Paul Savoia, Feature Editor
Lou Pappas, Food Editor
Don Thornton, Local News Editor
Leanne McLaughlin, National News
Anne Gibbons, Science Editor
Karen Smith, Travel Editor
245 Lytton Avenue
P O Box 300
Palo Alto CA 94301
415-853-5219

Category: 11-19-23-25-29-33-35-39
        43-67-69-71-97(news)-99
Circulation: 60,000
Reviews: 70/year
Buys 1st and 2nd serial rights.

Pasadena Star News
Kathy Register, Book Editor
525 E Colorado Boulevard
Pasadena CA 91109
818-578-6300
Category: 99
Circulation: 50,000

Pinole West County Times
Carol Fowler, Book Editor
P O Box 128
Pinole CA 94564
415-724-7171
Category: 99
Circulation: 53,000

Pomona Progress Bulletin
L T Rogers, Book Editor
P O Box 2708
300 S Thomas Street
Pomona CA 91766
714-622-1201
Category: 99
Circulation: 44,000

Riverside Press Enterprise
Joel Blain, Book Editor
3512 14th Street
P O Box 792
Riverside CA 92502
714-684-1200
Category: 99
Circulation: 132,000

Sacramento Bee
Paul Craig, Book Editor
21 and Q Streets
P O Box 15779
Sacramento CA 95813
916-446-9211
Category: 99
Circulation: 261,000

Sacramento Union
Colleen Hilker, Book Editor
301 Capitol Mall
Sacramento CA 95812
916-442-7811
Category: 99
Circulation: 107,000

San Bernardino Sun
399 D Street
San Bernardino CA 92401
714-889-9666
Category: 99
Circulation: 90,000

San Diego Tribune
Lois Horowitz, Book Editor
350 Camino de La Reina
San Diego CA 92112

619-299-3131
Category: 99
Circulation: 131,000

San Diego Union
Ed Hutsching, Book Editor
350 Camino De La Reina
San Diego CA 92112
619-299-3131
Category: 99
Circulation: 350,000

San Francisco Chronicle
William German, Book Editor
Peter Sinton, Business Editor
Kenneth E Wilson, Computer Editor
Robert Graham, Entertainment
Iris Frost, Feature Editor
Rosalie M Wright, Home Editor
Alan Mutter, Local News Editor
Jack Breibart, National News
Dan McGrath, Sports Editor
901 Mission Street
San Francisco CA 94103
415-777-1111
Category: 11-19-23-25-27-29-31-33
     35-43-57-69-71-97(news)-99
Circulation: 545,600
Reviews: 700/year
Buys 1st and 2nd serial rights.

San Francisco Examiner
Pamela Brunger, Book Editor
P O Box 7260
110 Fifth Street
San Francisco CA 94120
415-777-2424
Category: 99
Circulation: 155,000

San Jose Mercury/News
Constance Casey, Book Editor
750 Ridder Park Drive
San Jose CA 95190
408-920-5000
Category: 99
Circulation: 300,000

San Mateo Times
Jack Russell, Book Editor
1080 S Amphlett Boulevard
San Mateo CA 94402
415-348-4321
Category: 99
Circulation: 50,000

San Rafael Independent Journal
Barbara Morgan, Book Editor
P O Box 330
San Rafael CA 94915
415-883-8600
Category: 99
Circulation: 40,000

Orange County Register
Steve Plesa, Book Editor
625 N Grand Avenue
Santa Ana CA 92711

714-835-1234
Category: 99
Circulation: 325,000

Santa Barbara News Press
Joan Crowder, Book Editor
P O Drawer NN
De La Guerra Plaza
Santa Barbara CA 93102
805-966-3911
Category: 99
Circulation: 58,000

Santa Cruz Sentinel
Chris Watson, Book Editor
207 Church Street
Santa Cruz CA 95061
408-423-4242
Category: 99
Circulation: 32,000

Santa Monica Evening Outlook
Greg Davy, Feature Editor
1920 Colorado Avenue
Santa Monica CA 90406
213-829-6811
Category: 99
Circulation: 27,000

Santa Rosa Press Democrat
Sophia Annan, Feature Editor
472 Mendocino Avenue
P O Box 569
Santa Rosa CA 95402
707-546-2020
Category: 11-27-29-33-35-39-43-71
Circulation: 83,000

Stockton Record
530 E Market Street
Stockton CA 95202
209-943-6397
Category: 99
Circulation: 54,000

Torrance Daily Breeze
5215 Torrance Boulevard
Torrance CA 90509
213-540-5511
Category: 99
Circulation: 130,000

Van Nuys Daily News
Bruce Cook, Book Editor
Jane Amari, Features Editor
14539 Sylvan Street
Van Nuys CA 91411
213-997-4111
Category: 11-27-29-33-35-39-43-71
Circulation: 165,000

Contra Costa Times
Carol Fowler, Book Editor
P O Box 5088
Walnut Creek CA 94596
415-935-2525
Category: 99
Circulation: 92,000

Watsonville Register-Pajaronian
Ward Bushee, Book Editor
1000 Main Street
Watsonville CA 95076
408-724-0611
Category: 99
Circulation: 14,000

<u>COLORADO</u>

Colorado Springs Sun
Victoria Makings, Book Editor
Colorado Springs CO 80901
303-633-3881
Category: 99
Circulation: 80,000

Gazette Telegraph
Linda Navarro, Book Editor
30 S Prospect Street
Colorado Springs CO 80901
303-632-5511
Category: 99
Circulation: 107,000

Denver Post
Clarus Backes, Book Editor
650 15th Street
Denver CO 80201
303-820-1010
Category: 99
Circulation: 344,000

Rocky Mountain News
Marge Carlin, Book Editor
400 West Colfax Avenue
Denver CO 80204
303-892-5000
Category: 99
Circulation: 386,000

Grand Junction Daily Sentinel
David McLean, Managing Editor
730 S Seventh Street
Grand Junction CO 81501
303-242-5050
Category: 99
Circulation: 35,000

Pueblo Chieftain
Bob Thomas, Book Editor
825 West 6th Street
Pueblo CO 81002
303-544-3520
Category: 99
Circulation: 52,000

<u>CONNECTICUT</u>

Bridgeport Post-Telegram
Patrick Pallotto, Editor
   Sunday Book Section
Vicki Epstein, Business Editor
Henry Fountain, Computer Editor
Helen Jankoski, Feature Editor
Charles Walsh, Feature Editor
Michael Joseph, Local News Editor
Stephen Winters, Managing Editor

Daily Newspapers

Mary Moran, National News Editor
Emmett Spillane, Sports Editor
410 State Street
Bridgeport CT 06604
203-333-0161
Category: 11-19-23-25-27-29-31
33-35-43-57-67-69-71
97(news)-99
Circulation: 95,000
Reviews: 500/year
Does not buy serial rights.

Hartford Courant
Garret Condon, Book Editor
285 Broad Street
Hartford CT 06115
203-241-3743
Category: 99
Circulation: 297,000

Meriden Record-Journal
Barbara White, Book Editor
11-19 Crown Street
Meriden CT 06450
203-235-1661
Category: 99
Circulation: 30,000

Middletown Press
Russell D'Oench Jr, Book Editor
2 Main Street
Middletown CT 06457
203-347-3331
Category: 99
Circulation: 22,000

New Haven Register
Don Rabin, Book Editor
40 Sargent Drive
New Haven CT 06511
203-562-1121
Category: 99
Circulation: 142,000

Stamford Advocate
Book Editor
75 Tresser Boulevard
Stamford CT 06901
203-964-2200
Category: 99
Circulation: 31,000

Waterbury Republican
Joseph O'Donovan, Book Editor
389 Meadow Street
P O Box 2090
Waterbury CT 06722
203-574-3636
Category: 99
Circulation: 73,000

DELAWARE

Delaware State News
Ron Stevens, Editor
P O Box 737
New Burton Road
Dover DE 19901

302-674-3600
Category: 99
Circulation: 32,000

Wilmington News Journal
Gary Mullinax, Book Editor
831 Orange Street
P O Box 1111
Wilmington DE 19899
302-573-2000
Category: 99
Circulation: 124,000
Reviews: some

DISTRICT OF COLUMBIA

Legal Times
Larry Lempert, Editor
1666 Connecticut Avenue NW
Washington DC 20009
202-797-9600
Category: 19-55(law)
Circulation: 7000

USA Today
John C Quinn, Editor
Robert Wilson, Book Editor
P O Box 500
Washington DC 20044
800-368-3024
Category: 99
Circulation: 1,450,000
Reviews: 3-4/week
See also USA Weekend (magazines)

Washington Post
Leonard Downie Jr, Mng Editor
1150 15th Street NW
Washington DC 20071
202-334-6000
Category: 99
Circulation: 1,067,000
Buys 1st and 2nd serial rights.

Washington Post Book World
Alice Digilio, Book Editor
1150 15th Street NW
Washington DC 20071
202-334-6000
Category: 99
Circulation: 1,067,000
Reviews: 50/issue
Does not buy serial rights.

Washington Times
Colin Walters, Book Editor
3600 New York Avenue NE
Washington DC 20002
202-636-8220
Category: 99
Circulation: 76,000

FLORIDA

Cocoa Today
Betty Shyimabukuro, Book Editor
308 Forest Avenue
Cocoa FL 32922

305-632-8700
Category: 99
Circulation: 80,000

Daytona Journal-News
Dick Dunkel, Book Editor
901 Sixth Street
P O Box 431
Daytona Beach FL 32015
904-252-1511
Category: 99
Circulation: 62,000

Fort Lauderdale Sun-Sentinel
Paulette Everett, Book Editor
101 N New River Drive E
P O Box 14430
Fort Lauderdale FL 33302
305-761-4000
Category: 99
Circulation: 248,000

Fort Myers News Press
2442 Anderson Avenue
Fort Myers FL 33902
813-335-0200
Category: 99
Circulation: 81,000

Florida Times Union
Phil Kloer, Book Editor
1 Riverside Avenue
Jacksonville FL 32231
904-359-4111
Category: 99
Circulation: 215,000

Jacksonville Journal
Charlie Patton, Book Editor
1 Riverside Avenue
Jacksonville FL 32231
904-359-4111
Category: 99

Lakeland Ledger
Mark Mathes, Book Editor
P O Box 408
Lakeland FL 33802
813-687-7000
Category: 99
Circulation: 80,000
Buys 1st and 2nd serial rights.

Marietta Daily Journal
Bobby Newbitt, Editor
580 Fairground Street
Marietta FL 30060
404-428-9411
Category: 99
Circulation: 27,000

Miami Herald
William Robertson, Book Editor
One Herald Plaza
Miami FL 33101
305-350-2111
Category: 99
Circulation: 512,000

Daily Newspapers

Miami News
One Herald Plaza
P O Box 615
Miami FL 33152
305-350-2200
Category: 99
Circulation: 65,000

Orlando Sentinel
Nancy Pate, Book Editor
Manning Pym, Business Editor
Dennis Moore, Entertainment
Dana Eagles, Lifestyle Editor
Steve Doyle, Sports Editor
Mary Beth Davies, Travel Editor
633 N Orange Avenue
Orlando FL 32801
305-420-5000
Category: 11-19-25-27-29-31-33
        35-39-43-57-69-71-99
Circulation: 350,000
Reviews: 500/year
Does not buy serial rights.

Pensacola News Journal
Pat Lloyd, Book Editor
Charlotte Wittwer, Business
Tom Kerr, Feature Editor
Ginny MacDonald, Feature Editor
Dave Richardson, Local News
John MacDonald, National News
Jeff Hand, Sports Editor
1 News Journal Plaza
P O Box 12710
Pensacola FL 32571
904-433-0041
Category: 11-19-23-21-25-29-33-35
        43-57-67-69-71-97(news)-99
Circulation: 72,000
Reviews: 156/year
Does not buy serial rights.

Sarasota Herald Tribune
Joan Cullers, Book Editor
P O Box 1719
Sarasota FL 33578
813-953-7755
Category: 99
Circulation: 133,000

Saint Petersburg Times
Malcolm Jones, Book Editor
Elizabeth Whitney, Business
Neville Green, Feature Editor
Janis Froelich, Food Editor
Susan Martin, Local News Editor
Mike Moscardini, National News
Duke Mass, Sports Editor
Cindy McGrath, Travel Editor
490 First Avenue S
Saint Petersburg FL 33731
813-893-8111
Category: 11-19-23-25-27-29-31
        33-35-39-43-57-67-69
        71-97(news)-99
Circulation: 350,000
Reviews: 500-600/year
Buys 1st and 2nd serial rights.

Tallahassee Democrat
Martha Gruender, Book Editor
277 N Magnolia Drive
P O Box 990
Tallahassee FL 32302
904-599-2100
Category: 99
Circulation: 63,000

Tampa Tribune
Holmes Alexander, Book Editor
Jim Kennedy, Business Editor
Frank Ruiz, Computer Editor
Judy Hamilton, Feature Editor
Ann McDuffie, Food Editor
Dave Nicholson, Home Editor
Joe Registrato, Local News Editor
Denise Costa, National News
Alan Sverdlik, Science Editor
Tom McEwen, Sports Editor
Dorothy Smiljanich, Travel Editor
202 S Parker Street
P O Box 191
Tampa FL 33606
813-272-7711
Category: 11-19-23-25-27-29-31
        33-35-39-43-57-67-69
        71-97(news)-99
Circulation: 271,618
Reviews: 7/week
Buys only 2nd serial rights

Palm Beach Post/Times
Carolyn Jack, Book Editor
2751 S Dixie Highway
P O Drawer T
West Palm Beach FL 33402
305-837-4100
Category: 99
Circulation: 125,000

GEORGIA

Atlanta Journal & Constitution
Don O'Briant, Book Editor
72 Marietta Street NW
P O Box 4689
Atlanta GA 30302
404-526-5440
Category: 99
Circulation: 550,000

Augusta Chronicle & Herald
Dahlia Wren, Book Editor
725 Broad Street
P O Box 1928
Augusta GA 30913
404-724-0851
Category: 99
Circulation: 85,000

Columbus Ledger & Enquirer
Priscilla Black, Book Editor
17 West 12th Street
Columbus GA 31994
404-324-5526
Category: 99
Circulation: 68,000

Macon Telegraph & News
R L Day, Book Editor
120 Broadway
P O Box 4167
Macon GA 31213
912-744-4200
Category: 99
Circulation: 90,000

Savannah News-Press
Larry Powell, Book Editor
P O Box 1088
105 W Bay Street
Savannah GA 31402
912-236-9511
Category: 99
Circulation: 75,000

HAWAII

Honolulu Advertiser
Mike Middlesworth, Managing Ed.
605 Kapiolani Boulevard
P O Box 3080
Honolulu HI 96813
808-525-8640
Category: 99
Circulation: 82,000

Honolulu Star-Bulletin/Advertiser
Charles Frankel, Book Editor
605 Kapiolani Boulevard
Honolulu HI 96813
808-525-8640
Category: 99
Circulation: 200,000

IDAHO

Idaho Statesman
1200 N Curtis Road
Boise ID 83707
208-377-6400
Category: 99
Circulation: 75,000

Lewistown Tribune
Ladd Hamilton, Book Editor
505 C Street
Lewiston ID 83501
208-743-9411
Category: 99
Circulation: 26,000

Idaho State Journal
Lyle Olson, Managing Editor
305 S Arthur Street
Pocatello ID 83204
208-232-4161
Category: 99
Circulation: 21,000

ILLINOIS

Paddock Publications
Anna Madrzyk, Book Editor
P O Box 280
217 W Campbell Street

Arlington Heights IL 60006
312-870-3600
Category: 99
Circulation: 70,000

Bloomington Pantagraph
301 W Washington
P O Box 2907
Bloomington IL 61701
309-829-9411
Category: 99
Circulation: 53,000

Champaign News Gazette
Doug Royalty, Book Editor
Don Dodson, Business Editor
Heidi Myers, Feature Editor
John Foreman, Local News Editor
John Beck, National News Editor
Jean McDonald, Sports Editor
15 Main Street
P O Box 677
Champaign IL 61820
217-351-5252
Category: 11-19-23-25-27-29-31
        33-35-39-43-57-67-69
        71-97(news)-99
Circulation: 50,000
Reviews: 50/year
Does not buy serial rights.

Chicago Sun-Times
Henry Kisor, Book Editor
Carol Stoner, Feature Editor
401 N Wabash
Chicago IL 60611
312-321-3000
Category: 99
Circulation: 690,000

Chicago Tribune
Diane Donovan, Book Editor
Terry Brown, Business Editor
James Squires, Editor
Ron Kotulak, Science Editor
435 N Michigan Avenue
Chicago IL 60611
312-222-3232
Category: 19-23-67-99
Circulation: 1,140,000

Daily Southtown Economist
L Gary Thorne, Book Editor
Harry Gamble, Business Editor
George Haas, Entertainment Editor
Joyce Macey, Food Editor
McGurk, Feature Editor
John Hector, Sports Editor
Gordon Quarnstrom, Travel Editor
5959 S Harlem
Chicago IL 60638
312-586-8800
Category: 11-19-25-27-29-31
        33-35-39-43-57-69
        71-97(news)-99
Circulation: 40,000
Reviews: 20/year
Does not buy serial rights.

Decatur Herald & Review
Rob Strabala, Computer Editor
Carol Alexander, Feature Editor
Mike Carr, Feature Editor
Roger D Hughes, Local News Editor
Dana M Ewell, National News
Robert L Fallstrom, Sports Editor
601 E Williams Street
Decatur IL 62525
217-429-5151
Category: 11-19-23-25-27-29-31
        33-35-39-43-57-69-71
        97(news)-99
Circulation: 56,400
Reviews: none
Does not buy serial rights.

Galesburg Register-Mail
Robert Harrison, Editor
140 S Prairie Street
Galesburg IL 61401
309-343-7181
Category: 99
Circulation: 22,000
Reviews: some

Peoria Journal Star
M Ganning, Managing Editor
1 News Plaza
Peoria IL 61643
309-686-3000
Category: 99
Circulation: 118,000
Reviews: none

Rockford Register-Star
Lark Borden, Book Editor
99 E State Street
Rockford IL 61105
815-987-1200
Category: 99
Circulation: 85,000

State Journal-Register
Mike Kienzler, Book Editor
330 S 9th Street
Springfield IL 62705
217-788-1303
Category: 99
Circulation: 72,000

INDIANA

Bloomington Herald-Times
Elizabeth Winkler, Book Editor
19000 S Walnut Street
Bloomington IN 47402
Category: 99
Circulation: 42,000

Evansville Press
Larry Duhe, Book Editor
P O Box 454
201 NW Second Street
Evansville IN 47702
812-424-7711
Category: 99
Circulation: 42,000

Fort Wayne Journal-Gazette
Allan McMahan, Book Editor
600 W Main Street
Fort Wayne IN 46802
219-461-8333
Category: 99
Circulation: 108,000

Fort Wayne News-Sentinel
Nancy Vendrely, Feature Editor
600 W Main Street
Fort Wayne IN 46802
219-461-8333
Category: 99
Circulation: 71,000
Reviews: some

Gary Post-Tribune
Bonnie Rubin, Book Editor
1065 Broadway
Gary IN 46402
219-886-5000
Category: 99
Circulation: 90,000

Hammond Times
William Chapman, Book Editor
417 Lafayette Street
Hammond IN 46320
219-933-3200
Category: 99
Circulation: 80,000

Indianapolis News
Marion Garmel, Arts Editor
L T Brown, Book Editor
Edward Lawler, Business Editor
Shirley Roberts, Family Editor
Marge Hanley, Foods Editor
Wendell Trogdon, National News
David McCarty, Science Editor
Lyle Mannweiler, Sports Editor
Kathy Short, Travel Editor
307 Pennsylvania Street
Indianapolis IN 46206-0145
317-633-9070
Category: 11-19-25-27-29-31-33
        35-39-43-57-67-69-71
        97(News)-99
Circulation: 135,000
Reviews: 200/year
Does not buy serial rights.

Indianapolis Star
Donna Fry, Book Editor
307 Pennsylvania Street
Indianapolis IN 46206
317-633-1240
Category: 25-29-43-97(News)-99
Circulation: 395,000

Lafayette Journal & Courier
Robert Kriebel, Editor
217 N Sixth Street
Lafayette IN 47901
317-423-5511
Category: 99
Circulation: 37,000

Muncie Star / Evening Press
Harold Trulock, Book Editor
125 S High Street
Muncie IN 47302
317-747-5700
Category: 99
Circulation: 35,000

South Bend Tribune
Walter Collins, Book Editor
223 W Colfax Avenue
South Bend IN 46626
219-233-6161
Category: 99
Circulation: 126,000

IOWA

Cedar Rapids Gazette
Bridget Janus, Book Editor
John Robertson, Managing Editor
500 Third Avenue SE
Cedars Rapids IA 52406
319-398-8211
Category: 99
Circulation: 80,000

Council Bluffs Nonpareil
John Skipper, Managing Editor
117 Pearl Street
Council Bluffs IA 51501
712-328-1811
Category: 99
Circulation: 21,000

Quad City Times
Debroah Brasier, Book Editor
Randy Heuston, Business Editor
Dan Foley, News Editor
Don Doxsie, Sports Editor
Shirley Davis, Travel Editor
124 East 2nd Street
P O Box 3828
Davenport IA 52808
319-383-2200
Category: 11-19-23-25-27-29-31
        33-35-39-43-57-69-71
        97(news)-99
Circulation: 65,000
Reviews: 50/year

Des Moines Register
Joan Bunke, Book Editor
James P Gannon, Editor
715 Locust Street
Des Moines IA 50309
515-284-8065
Category: 99
Circulation: 385,000
Reviews: 5-10/week

Iowa City Press-Citizen
James Kaufman, Editor
428 Clark Street
Iowa City IA 52240
319-337-3181
Category: 61(IA)-99
Reviews: some

Minneapolis Star and Tribune
James Kaufman, Crime Corner
428 Clark Street
Iowa City IA 52240
319-337-3181
Category: 84
Circulation: 587,000

Sioux City Journal
Bruce Miller, Living Editor
Sixth and Pavonia Streets
Sioux City IA 51102
712-279-5075
Category: 99
Circulation: 60,000

Waterloo Daily Courier
P O Box 540
Waterloo IA 50704
319-291-1400
Category: 99
Circulation: 55,000

KANSAS

Emporia Gazette
Mrs W L White, Editor
517 Merchant Street
Emporia KS 66801
316-342-4800
Category: 99
Circulation: 12,000

Topeka Capital-Journal
Jacalyn Midell, Arts Editor
Gene Smith, Book Editor
Anita Miller, Business Editor
Don Marker, City Editor
Ann Hungerford, Family Editor
Merle Bird, Foods Editor
Bob Hentzen, Sports Editor
Dick King, Travel Editor
Stauffer Communications
616 Jefferson
Topeka KS 66607
913-295-1111
Category: 11-19-23-31-33-35-57
        69-71-97(news)-99
Circulation: 68,000
Reviews: 150/year
Does not buy serial rights.

Wichita Eagle Beacon
Chuck Potter, Book Editor
825 East Douglas Street
Wichita KS 67201
316-268-6000
Category: 99
Circulation: 185,000

KENTUCKY

Kentucky Post
421 Madison Avenue
Covington KY 41011
606-292-2642
Category: 99
Circulation: 50,000

Frankfurt State Journal
Carl West, Editor
P O Box 368
321 W Main Street
Frankfurt KY 40601
502-227-4556
Category: 99
Circulation: 11,000

Kentucky New Era
Cecil Herndon, Editor
1618 E Ninth Street
Hopkinsville KY 42240
502-886-4444
Category: 99
Circulation: 6000

Lexington Herald-Leader
John Carroll, Editor
Ed Newman, Book Editor
Jim Jordan, Business Editor
Jim Durham, Lifestyle Editor
Main and Midland
Lexington KY 40507
606-231-3100
Category: 11-19-27-29-33
        35-39-43-71-99
Circulation: 120,000

Louisville Courier-Journal
Shirley Williams, Book Editor
525 West Broadway
Louisville KY 40202
502-582-4011
Category: 99
Circulation: 176,000

Louisville Times
Rob Deckard, Book Editor
525 W Broadway
Louisville KY 40202
502-582-4641
Category: 99
Circulation: 135,000

Louisiana

Baton Rouge Advocate
Charles Lindsay, Book Editor
525 Lafayette Street
P O Box 588
Baton Rouge LA 70821
504-383-1111
Category: 99
Circulation: 134,000

Lake Charles American Press
Ward Threatt, Book Editor
327 Broad Street
Lake Charles LA 70602
318-439-2781
Category: 99
Circulation: 42,000

Monroe News-Star-World
Jarry Pittman, Editor
P O Box 1502
411 N Fourth Street

Monroe LA 71201
318-322-5161
Category: 99
Circulation: 46,000

Times-Picayne/States-Item
Mable Simmons, Book Editor
Times-Picayune Publishing Co.
3800 Howard Avenue
New Orleans LA 70140
504-826-3448
Category: 99
Circulation: 321,000

Shreveport Times/Journal
Charlotte Burrows, Book Editor
Orland Dodson, Business Editor
Raymond McDaniel, Editor
P O Box 222
222 Lake Street
Shreveport LA 71130
318-459-3200
Category: 19-99
Circulation: 110,000

MAINE

Bangor Daily News
V Paul Reynolds, Managing Editor
491 Main Street
Bangor ME 04401
207-942-4881
Category: 99
Circulation: 91,000

Lewiston Daily Sun
Kent Foster, Managing Editor
P O Box 4400
104 Park Street
Lewiston ME 04240
207-784-5411
Category: 99

Lewiston Journal
Sue Dillingham, Managing Editor
P O Box 4400
104 Park Street
Lewiston ME 04240
207-784-5411
Category: 99
Circulation: 36,000

Maine Sunday Telegram
Don King, Book Editor
George Weir, Auto Editor
  also Business Editor
John Halvorsen, Entertainment
Rik O'Neal, Feature Editor
P O Box 1460
390 Congress Street
Portland ME 04104
207-775-5811
Category: 11-19-23-25-27-29-31
        33-35-39-43-57-67-69
        71-97(news)-99
Circulation: 130,000
Reviews: 60/year
Does not buy serial rights.

Portland Evening Express
George Weir, Business Editor
Bob Niss, Entertainment Editor
390 Congress Street
Portland ME 04104
207-775-5811
Category: 11-19(local only)-33
Circulation: 28,000

MARYLAND

The Capital
Edward Casey, Editor
Capital-Gazette Newspapers
213 West Street
Annapolis MD 21404
301-268-5000
Category: 99
Circulation: 37,000

Baltimore News-American
Scott Lebar, Book Editor
David Postal, Business Editor
Thomas White, Editor
301 E Lombard Street
Baltimore MD 21203
301-528-8000
Category: 19-99
Circulation: 145,000

Baltimore Sun
John Kelly, Book Review Editor
Phillip Moeller, Business Editor
Eric Seigel, Entertainment Editor
Jan Warrington, Family Editor
Eizabeth Lorge, Food Editor
Carol Frey, Local News Editor
Frank Starr, National News Editor
Albert Selstedt, Science Editor
Marty Kaiser, Sports Editor
501 N Calvert Street
Baltimore MD 21278
301-332-6000
Category: 11-19-27-31-33-35-39
        57-67-69-71-97(news)
Circulation: 408,000
Reviews: 10-16/week
Buys only 1st serial rights.

MASSACHUSETTS

Boston Globe
Mark Feeney, Book Editor
135 Morrissey Boulevard
Boston MA 02107
617-929-2785
Category: 99
Circulation: 803,000

Boston Herald
Steve Morgan, Book Editor
Lynn Kettelson, Business Editor
Joe Robinowitz, Editor
One Herald Square
Boston MA 02106
617-426-3000
Category: 19-99
Circulation: 368,000

Christian Science Monitor
Tom D'Evelyn, Book Editor
Rushworth Kidder, Features
1 Norway Street
Boston MA 02115
617-262-2300
Category: 11-17-29-33-35
        39-43-71-99
Circulation: 141,000

Brockton Enterprise
Steve Austen, Book Editor
60 Main Street
Brockton MA 02403
617-586-6200
Category: 99
Circulation: 62,000

Fall River Herald-News
Paul Beriner, Managing Editor
207 Pocasset Street
Fall River MA 02722
617-676-8211
Category: 99
Circulation: 40,000

Middlesex Daily News
Dave Funkhouser, Book Editor
33 New York Avenue
Framingham MA 01701
617-872-4321
Category: 99
Circulation: 50,000

Holyoke Transcript-Telegram
Kay Manning, Managing Editor
120 Whiting Farms Road
Holyoke MA 01040
413-536-2300
Category: 99
Circulation: 29,000

Cape Cod Times
John Johnson, Business Editor
William Breisky, Editor
Ann Farrow, Features Editor
319 Main Street
Hyannis MA 02106
617-775-1200
Category: 11-17-19-27-29-33
        35-39-43-71-75-99
Circulation: 53,000

Lawrence Eagle Tribune
Daniel J Warner, Book Editor
P O Box 100
Lawrence MA 01842
617-685-1000
Category: 99
Circulation: 60,000
Reviews: 250/year
Buys 1st and 2nd serial rights.

Lowell Sun
Kendall Wallace, Book Editor
15 Kearney Square
P O Box 1477
Lowell MA 01852

617-458-7100
Category: 99
Circulation: 55,000

Malden News
David Brickman, Editor
Malden Publications
277 Commercial Street
Malden MA 02148
617-321-8000
Category: 99
Circulation: 7,000

New Bedford Standard Times
John Ackerman, Book Editor
BowSprit Magazine
555 Pleasant Street
New Bedford MA 02742
617-997-7411
Category: 99
Circulation: 52,000

Daily News
Calhoun Killeen, Managing Editor
23 Liberty Street
Newburyport MA 01950
617-462-6666
Category: 99
Circulation: 12,000

Daily Hampshire Gazette
Marietta Pritchard, Book Editor
P O Box 299
115 Conz Street
Northampton MA 01060
413-584-5000
Category: 99
Circulation: 20,000
Reviews: Some

Quincy Patriot Ledger
Paul A Williams, Book Editor
Jack Hoey, Business Editor
William B Kotter, Editor
13 Temple Street
Quincy MA 02169
617-786-7000
Category: 19-99
Circulation: 100,000
Reviews: 1-3/issue
Does not buy serial rights.

Salem Evening News
James Stommen, Editor
155 Washington Street
Salem MA 01970
617-744-0600
Category: 99
Circulation: 31,000

Springfield Union News
Arnold Friedman, Editor
The Republican Company
1860 Main Street
Springfield MA 01101
413-788-1200
Category: 99
Circulation: 153,000

Waltham News-Tribune
Thomas Neville, Managing Editor
P O Box 69
18 Pine Street
Waltham MA 02254
617-893-1670
Category: 99
Circulation: 13,000

Worcester Evening Gazette
Diane Benison, Managing Editor
20 Franklin Street
Worcester MA 01613
617-793-9100
Category: 99
Circulation: 97,000

Worcester Telegram
Nicholas Basbanes, Book Editor
20 Franklin Street
Worcester MA 01613
617-793-9100
Category: 99
Circulation: 138,000

MICHIGAN

Ann Arbor News
Jeff Mortimer, Book Editor
340 E Huron Street
Ann Arbor MI 48106
313-994-6870
Category: 99
Circulation: 50,000

Battle Creek Enquirer
David Smith, Managing Editor
155 W Van Buren
Battle Creek MI 49016
616-964-7161
Category: 99
Circulation: 38,000
Reviews: 2-4/week

Bay City Times
Wallace Town, Book Editor
Robert Longstaff, Editor
311 Fifth Street
Bay City MI 48706
517-895-8551
Category: 99
Circulation: 45,000
Reviews: 2-4/week

Detroit Free Press
Bob McKelvey, Book Editor
321 W Lafayette
Detroit MI 48231
313-222-6400
Category: 99
Circulation: 778,000

Detroit News
Pam Schermeyer, Arts Editor
Ruth Coughlin, Book Editor
Liz Spayd, Business Editor
Eric Wujick, Computers Editor
Sue Wyland, Family Editor

Andrea Wojack, Foods Editor
Dick Wright, Hobby Editor
Mark Hass, Local News Editor
Mary Swanton, National News
Alan Stamm, Science Editor
Rick Sayers, Sports Editor
Larry Sullivan, Travel Editor
615 Lafayette
Detroit MI 48231
313-222-2300
Category: 11-19-23-25-27-29-31
33-35-39-43-57-67-69
71-97(news)-99
Circulation: 860,000
Reviews: 120/year
Buys 1st and 2nd serial rights.

Flint Journal
James Harvey, Book Editor
Bob Sherefkin, Business Editor
Alfred Peloquin, Editor
Lee Morrissey, Science Editor
200 E First Street
Flint MI 48502
313-767-0660
Category: 19-23-67-99
Circulation: 120,000

Grand Rapids Press
Wes Wietsma, Book Editor
Patrick Shellenbarger, Business
Michael Lloyd, Editor
Press Plaza
155 Michigan Avenue NW
Grand Rapids MI 49503
616-459-1400
Category: 19-23-99
Circulation: 172,000

Kalamazoo Gazette
Kathy Doud, Book Editor
P O Box 2007
Kalamazoo MI 49003
616-345-3511
Category: 99
Circulation: 72,000

Lansing State Journal
120 E Lenawee Street
Lansing MI 48919
517-377-1000
Category: 99
Circulation: 81,000

Macomb Daily
Mitch Kehetian, Book Editor
67 Cass Avenue
Mount Clemens MI 48043
313-469-4510
Category: 99
Circulation: 58,000

Oakland Press
Bobby Mather, Book Editor
David Versical, Business Editor
Kenn Jones, Entertainment Editor
Annemarie Schiavi-Pedersen,
Feature Editor

Sybil Little, Food Editor
Susan Belniak, Local News Editor
Garry Gilbert, National News
Don Frost, Sports Editor
Dolly Moseeff, Travel Editor
48 W Huron
P O Box 9
Pontiac MI 48056
313-332-8181
Category: 11-19-25-27-29-31-33
        35-39-43-57-67-69-71
        97(news)-99
Circulation: 80,000
Reviews: 100/year
Does not buy serial rights.

Port Huron Times Herald
Susan Burzynski, Managing Editor
911 Military Street
Port Huron MI 48060
313-985-7171
Category: 99
Circulation: 34,000

Daily Tribune
John Schultz, Business Editor
Bob Ball, Computer Editor
Mike Beeson, Entertainment Editor
Jana Goldman, Feature Editor
Randy Bawkon, News Editor
Steve Stein, Sports Editor
210 E 3rd Street
Royal Oak MI 48067
313-541-3000
Category: 11-19-23-27-31-33-35
        39-57-69-71-97(news)
Circulation: 42,000
Reviews: none

Saginaw News
Fred Garrett, Book Editor
203 S Washington Avenue
Saginaw MI 48605
517-752-7171
Category: 99
Circulation: 57,000

MINNESOTA

News-Tribune & Herald
Sylvia Wier, Book Editor
M L Levandowski, Business Editor
Thomas Daly, Executive Editor
424 W First Street
Duluth MN 55802
218-723-5281
Category: 19-99
Circulation: 83,000
Reviews: 5-10/week

Minneapolis Star and Tribune
David Wood, Book Editor
425 Portland Avenue
Minneapolis MN 55488
612-372-4141
Category: 99
Circulation: 587,000
Reviews: 10-20/week

St Paul Pioneer Press & Dispatch
Mary Ann Grossman, Book Editor
David Beal, Business Editor
Deborah Howell, Executive Editor
Russell Johnson, Feature Editor
345 Cedar Street
Saint Paul MN 55101
612-222-5011
Category: 11-17-19-29-33-35-39
        43-71-99
Circulation: 249,000

MISSISSIPPI

Delta Democrat-Times
Ken Cazalas, Managing Editor
P O Box 1618
988 N Broadway
Greenville MS 38701
601-335-1155
Category: 99
Circulation: 17,000
Reviews: some

Clarion Ledger/Daily News
Nell Thames, Book Editor
Leisure Section
311 E Pearl Street
Jackson MS 39205
601-961-7000
Category: 99
Circulation: 117,000

McComb Enterprise-Journal
Patsy Brumfield, Managing Editor
129 N Broadway
McComb MS 39648
601-684-2421
Category: 99
Circulation: 13,000
Reviews: some

MISSOURI

Columbia Missourian
Steve Weinberg, Book Editor
Brian Brooks, Managing Editor
P O Box 917
Columbia MO 65202
314-442-3161
Category: 99
Circulation: 6000

Independence Examiner
Dan Potter, Editor
410 S Liberty Street
Independence MO 64051
816-254-8600
Category: 99
Circulation: 16,000

Jefferson City News & Tribune
Richard McGonegal, Editor
210 Monroe Street
Jefferson City MO 65102
314-636-3131
Category: 99
Circulation: 22,000

Joplin Globe
Irene Wilkins, Feature Editor
117 E Fourth Street
Joplin MO 64801
417-623-3480
Category: 99
Circulation: 62,000

Kansas City Star
Betsy Klein, Book Editor
Jerry Heaster, Business Editor
David Zeeck, Managing Editor
1729 Grand Avenue
Kansas City MO 64108
816-234-4300
Category: 19-99
Circulation: 399,000

Kansas City Times
Monroe Dodd, Managing Editor
1729 Grand Avenue
Kansas City MO 64108
816-234-4300
Category: 99
Circulation: 290,000

St Joseph Gazette/News Press
Robert Waldrop, Book Editor
Preston Filbert, Business Editor
Don Thornton, Entertainment
Phyllis Wright, Feature Editor
Bob Martin, Sports Editor
9th & Edmond Streets
Saint Joseph MO 64502
816-279-5671
Category: 11-19-23-25-27-29-31
        33-35-39-43-57-67-69
        71-97(news)-99
Circulation: 44,500
Does not buy serial rights.

Saint Louis Globe-Democrat
Brenda Murphy, Book Editor
Patrick Gauen, Managing Editor
Roger McGrath, Business Editor
710 N Tucker Boulevard
Saint Louis MO 63101
314-342-1212
Category: 19-99
Circulation: 225,000

Saint Louis Post-Dispatch
Clarence E Olson, Book Editor
900 N Tucker Boulevard
Saint Louis MO 63101
314-622-7000
Category: 99
Circulation: 495,000

Springfield News-Leader
Bill Southerland, Editor
Bill Tatum, Feature Editor
651 Boonville Avenue
Springfield MO 65801
417-836-1100
Category: 11-17-29-33-35
        39-43-71-99
Circulation: 87,000

Daily Newspapers

MONTANA

Billings Gazette
Richard Wesnick, Book Editor
Paul Holley, Business Editor
Joyce Michels, Feature Editor
401 Broadway
Billings MT 59103
406-657-1200
Category: 11-17-19-29-33
        35-39-43-71-99
Circulation: 65,000

Bozeman Daily Chronicle
Joan Haines, Book Editor
Rob Dean, Editor
P O Box 1188
32 S Rouse Street
Bozeman MT 59771
406-587-4491
Category: 99
Circulation: 13,000

Helena Independent Record
Dave Fuselier, Managing Editor
P O Box 4249
317 Allen Street
Helena MT 59601
406-442-7190
Category: 99
Circulation: 14,000

NEBRASKA

Lincoln Journal-Star
Herb Hyde, Book Editor
Dick Piersol, Business Editor
Joe Seacrest, Editor
926 P Street
P O Box 81689
Lincoln NE 68501
402-475-7222
Category: 19-99
Circulation: 71,000

Omaha World Herald
Carol Bicak, Book Editor
Alan Gersten, Business Editor
Tim Sacco, Feature Editor
Pat Wolfe, Feature Editor
Jane Palmer, Food Editor
Larry King, Local News Editor
Bob Pearman, National News Editor
Larry Lough, Science Editor
Mike Kelly, Sports Editor
World Herald Square
Omaha NE 68102
402-444-1000
Category: 11-19-25-27-29-31-33
        35-39-43-57-67-69-71
        97(news)-99
Circulation: 290,000
Reviews: 50/year
Does not buy serial rights.

NEVADA

Nevada Appeal
Sue Morrow, City Editor
Done Ham, Editor
P O Box 2288
200 Bath Street
Carson City NV 89702
702-882-2111
Category: 11-17-27-29-35
        39-43-71-99
Circulation: 10,000
Reviews: some

Las Vegas Review-Journal
Joe Kirby, Book Editor
1111 W Bonanza Road
P O Box 70
Las Vegas NV 89125
702-385-4241
Category: 61(Southwest)-99
Circulation: 114,000

Las Vegas Sun
Dick Maurice, Arts Editor
Tom Bruny, Business Editor
Jerry Ralya, City Editor
Sandy Thompson, Family Editor
Tom Shannon, Hobby Editor
Jim Barrows, Managing Editor
Mary Manning, Science Editor
Mike Fitzgerald, Sports Editor
Les Ritchie, Travel Editor
P O Box 4275
121 S Highland Drive
Las Vegas NV 89127
702-385-3111
Category: 11-19-23-25-27-29-31
        33-35-39-43-57-67-69
        71-97(news)-99
Circulation: 107,000
Reviews: 200-300/year
Does not buy serial rights.

Reno Gazette Journal
Tonia Cunning, Book Editor
Susan Voyles, Business Editor
Guy Richardson, Entertainment
Sandra Marcias, Food Editor
Cory Farley, Home Editor
Joe Howry, Local News Editor
Ev Landers, National News Editor
Mike Blackwell, Sports Editor
Alan Risdon, Travel Editor
955 Kuenzli
P O Box 22000
Reno NV 89520-2000
702-788-6397
Category: 11-19-25-27-29-31-33
        35-39-43-57-67-69-71
        97(news)-99
Circulation: 70,000
Reviews: 150/year
Does not buy serial rights.

NEW HAMPSHIRE

Claremont Times
Bertha Edmonds, Book Editor
19 Sullivan Street
Claremont NH 03743
603-542-5121
Category: 99
Circulation: 11,000

Concord Monitor
Mike Pride, Editor
3 N State Street
Concord NH 03301
603-224-5301
Category: 99
Circulation: 21,000
Reviews: 5-10/week

Manchester Union Leader
Dirk Ruemenapp, Book Editor
35 Amherst Street
P O Box 780
Manchester NH 03105
603-668-4321
Category: 99
Circulation: 87,000
Reviews: 200/year
Does not buy serial rights.

New Hampshire Sunday News
Charles Perkins, Editor
Harvey Dodd, Business Editor
Paul Lacaillade, Entertainment
Meg Geraghty, Family Editor
Alan Jahn, Home Editor
C. J. McCarth, Sports Editor
John Stith, Travel Editor
Manchester Union Leader
35 Amherst Street
Manchester NH 03105
603-668-4321
Category: 11-19-23-25-27-29-31
        33-35-39-43-57-69-71
        97(news)-99
Circulation: 87,000
Frequency: 52
Reviews: 200/year
Does not buy serial rights.

Monadnock Ledger
E R Leach, Editor
24 Main Street
Peterborough NH 03458
603-924-7171
Category: 99
Circulation: 6000
Reviews: 2-3/month

NEW JERSEY

Atlantic City Press
Paul Merkoski, Book Editor
1900 Atlantic Avenue

===

133

Daily Newspapers

Atlantic City NJ 08401
609-345-1234
Category: 99
Circulation: 84,000

Bridgewater Courier-News
Gary Mayk, Lifestyle Editor
1201 Route 22
P O Box 6600
Bridgewater NJ 08807
201-722-8800
Category: 99
Circulation: 126,000

Camden Courier-Post
Carl Winter, Book Editor
Stan Goldstein, Feature Editor
301 Cuthbert Boulevard
Cherry Hill NJ 08002
609-663-6000
Category: 11-17-29-33-35
        39-43-71-99
Circulation: 108,000

The Record
Ann Podd, Business Editor
Virginia Lambert, Entertainment
Paul Schulman, Computer Editor
Miriam Taylor, Family Editor
Jim McGarvey, Local News Editor
Dick Benfield, National News
Don Sherlock, Sports Editor
Judy Dash, Travel Editor
150 River Street
Hackensack NJ 07601
201-646-4360
Category: 11-19-23-31-33-35
        57-69-71-97(news)
Circulation: 225,000

Jersey Journal
August Lockwood, Book Editor
Steve Newhouse, Editor
Harvey Zucker, Science Editor
30 Journal Square
Jersey City NJ 07306
201-653-1000
Category: 23-67-99
Circulation: 64,000
Reviews: 5-10/week

Morristown Daily Record
Richard Bigelow, Magazine Editor
55 Park Place
Morristown NJ 07960
201-538-3030
Category: 99
Circulation: 70,000

Asbury Park Press
Myrna Lippman, Book Editor
David McDaniel, Business Editor
Thomas Jobson, Managing Editor
3601 Highway 66
Neptune NJ 07754
201-992-6000
Category: 19-99
Circulation: 190,000

New Brunswick Home News
Helen Schwartz, Book Editor
123 How Lane
P O Box 551
New Brunswick NJ 08903
201-246-5500
Category: 99
Circulation: 72,000

Newark Star Ledger
Roger Harris, Book Editor
Star Ledger Plaza
Newark NJ 07101
201-877-4141
Category: 99
Circulation: 661,000

Passaic Herald News
Editor
988 Main Avenue
P O Box 1019
Passaic NJ 07055
201-365-3000
Category: 99
Circulation: 75,000

Paterson News
Maureen Urbanowitz, Editor
1 News Plaza
Paterson NJ 07509
201-684-3000
Category: 99
Circulation: 49,000

The Times
Linda Cunningham, Editor
500 Perry Street
P O Box 847
Trenton NJ 08605
609-396-3232
Category: 99
Circulation: 78,000

Trentonian
William Dwyer, Book Editor
600 Perry Street
Trenton NJ 08602
609-989-7800
Category: 99
Circulation: 64,000

The Record
Mark Howat, Book Editor
41 Beech Street
Westwood NJ 07605
201-646-4360
Category: 27-39-99
Circulation: 225,000
Reviews: 6-7/week
Buys only 1st serial rights.

Woodbridge News Tribune
Charles Paolino, Book Editor
1 Hoover Way
Woodbridge NJ 07095
201-442-0400
Category: 99
Circulation: 57,000

<u>**NEW MEXICO**</u>

Albuquerque Journal
Bruce Daniels, Book Editor
P O Drawer J
717 Silver Avenue SW
Albuquerque NM 87103
505-842-2300
Category: 99
Circulation: 134,000

**Albuquerque Journal
Impact Magazine**
Tom Mayer, Book Editor
Harold Cousland, Business Editor
Tom Harmon, City Editor
David Steinberg, Entertainment
Steve Hallock, Features Editor
Susan Stiger, Food/Fashion Editor
Byron Spice, Science Editor
Dennis Latta, Sports Editor
Roger Ruvolo, Travel Editor
P O Drawer J
Albuquerque NM 87103
505-823-3880
Category: 11-19-25-27-29-31-33
        35-39-43-57-67-69-71
        97(news)-99
Circulation: 140,000
Reviews: 260+/year

Albuquerque Tribune
Ollie Reed, Book Editor
P O Drawer T
17777 Jefferson NE
Albuquerque NM 87109
505-842-2371
Category: 99
Circulation: 46,000

Santa Fe New Mexican
Larry Sanders, Editor
202 E Marcy Street
Santa Fe NM 87501
505-983-3303
Category: 99
Circulation: 20,000
Reviews: 3-5/week

<u>**NEW YORK**</u>

Albany Times-Union
Fred LeBrun, Book Editor
645 Albany Shaker Road
P O Box 15000
Albany NY 12212
518-454-5420
Category: 99
Circulation: 168,000

Knickerbocker News
William Dowd, News Editor
News Plaza
P O Box 15000
Albany NY 12212
518-454-5420
Category: 99
Circulation: 36,000

Daily Newspapers

Binghamton Press
Mike Doll, Book Editor
Vestal Parkway East
P O Box 1270
Binghamton NY 13902
607-798-1234
Category: 99
Circulation: 85,000

Binghamton Sun-Bulletin
Gene Grey, Book Editor
Vestal Parkway East
P O Box 1270
Binghamton NY 13902
607-798-1234
Category: 99
Circulation: 30,000

New York Daily Challenge
1368 Fulton Street
Brooklyn NY 11216
718-636-9500
Category: 99
Circulation: 72,000

Buffalo Evening News
Dave White, Book Editor
1 News Plaza
P O Box 100
Buffalo NY 14240
716-849-4444
Category: 99
Circulation: 320,000

Newsday
Nina King, Book Editor
Gary Hoenig, Business Editor
Suzanne Curley, Children's Books
Anthony Insolia, Editor
235 Pinelawn Road
Long Island NY 11747
516-454-2020
Category: 19-21-76-89-99
Circulation: 600,000

Times Herald-Record
40 Mulberry Street
Middletown NY 10940
914-343-2181
Category: 99
Circulation: 83,000

New York Daily News
Susan Toepfer, Book Editor
Steve Yahn, Business Editor
R B Plunkett Jr, Consumer Editor
Spencer Gilman, Editor
Patricia Crain, Romance Books
220 East 42nd Street
New York NY 10017
212-210-2100
Category: 19-25-85-99
Circulation: 1,888,000

New York Daily News
Carol McGuirk, Science Fiction
City Lights Section
22030 Boca Place Drive

Boca Raton FL 33433
212-210-2100
Category: 86
Circulation: 1,888,000

New York Post
Gerard Bray, Business Editor
Roger Wood, Executive Editor
Diane Reid, Feature Editor
210 South Street
New York NY 10002
212-815-8000
Category: 19-99
Circulation: 960,000
Buys 1st and 2nd serial rights.

New York Times
C Gerald Fraser, Book Editor (PB)
Mitchel Levitas, Book Editor (HC)
Eden Ross Lipson, Children's Book
229 West 43rd Street
New York NY 10036
212-556-1234
Category: 21-76-89-99
Circulation: 1,700,000
Reviews: many
Buys 1st and 2nd serial rights.

New York Times Book Review
Rebecca Sinkler, Deputy Editor
229 West 43rd Street
New York NY 10036
212-556-1234
Category: 99
Circulation: 1,700,000
(See also those listed above.)

New York Tribune
Thomas Clifford, Feature Editor
401 Fifth Avenue
New York NY 10016
212-532-8300
Category: 99
Circulation: 70,000

Wall Street Journal
Claudia Rosett, Book Editor
Robert Bartley, Editor
200 Liberty Street
New York NY 10281
212-285-5000
Category: 19-99
Circulation: 1,960,000
Reviews: 2/issue

Women's Wear Daily
7 East 12th Street
New York NY 10003
212-741-4000
Category: 99
Circulation: 75,000

Poughkeepsie Journal
85 Civic Center Plaza
Poughkeepsie NY 12602
914-454-2000
Category: 99
Circulation: 55,000

Rochester Democrat-Chronicle
Andy Smith, Book Editor
David Dorsey, Business Editor
Robert Giles, Editor
Phil Fuhrur, Feature Editor
55 Exchange Street
Rochester NY 14614
716-232-7100
Category: 11-17-19-29-33
        35-39-43-71-99
Circulation: 247,000

Rochester Times-Union
Patrick Farrell, Book Editor
55 Exchange Street
Rochester NY 14614
716-232-7100
Category: 99
Circulation: 132,000

Schenectady Gazette
Shirley Peterson, Book Editor
332 State Street
Schenectady NY 12301
518-374-4141
Category: 99
Circulation: 70,000

Staten Island Advance
Robert Raymond, Book Editor
Charles Schmidt, Business Editor
Les Trautmann, Editor
Wendy Greenfield, Science Editor
950 Fingerboard Road
Staten Island NY 10305
718-981-1234
Category: 19-23-67-99
Circulation: 82,000

Syracuse Herald-Journal
William Robinson, Book Editor
Clinton Square
P O Box 4915
Syracuse NY 13221
315-470-0011
Category: 99
Circulation: 237,000

Syracuse Post Standard
Jerod Rosen, Business Editor
Pamm Higgins, Feature Editor
Mark Libbou, Local News Editor
Jinx Johnstone, National Editor
Tom Boll, Sports Editor
Clinton Square
P O Box 4818
Syracuse NY 13208
315-470-2146
Category: 11-19-22-33-27-29-31-33
        35-39-43-69-97(news)-99
Circulation: 90,000
Reviews: 100/year
Does not buy serial rights.

Watertown Daily Times
Patience O'Riley, Feature Editor
260 Washington Street
Watertown NY 13601

315-782-1000
Category: 99
Circulation: 29,000

Westchester-Rockland Newspapers
Evelyn McCormack, Book Editor
Liesure Section
One Gannett Drive
White Plains NY 10604
914-694-9300
Category: 99
Circulation: 195,000

<u>NORTH</u> <u>CAROLINA</u>

Asheville Citizen-Times
Bill Moore, Book Editor
David Nivens, Business Editor
James Wilson, Editor
P O Box 2090
140 Henry Avenue
Asheville NC 28802
704-252-5611
Category: 19-99
Circulation: 72,000

Charlotte Observer
Dannye Romine, Book Editor
600 S Tryon Street
Charlotte NC 28232
704-379-6300
Category: 99
Circulation: 255,000

Durham Morning Herald
Ed Hodges, Book Editor
115 Market Street
P O Box 2092
Durham NC 27702
919-682-8181
Category: 99
Circulation: 70,000
Reviews: 250/year
Does not buy serial rights.

Fayetteville Observer & Times
Roy Parker Jr, Editor
458 Whitfield Road
Fayetteville NC 28302
919-323-4848
Category: 99
Circulation: 62,000

Greensboro News & Record
Robert Gingher, Book Editor
Ned Cline, Managing Editor
Van King, Business Editor
Larry Spohn, Science Editor
200 E Market Street
Greensboro NC 27402
919-373-7000
Category: 19-23-67-97(News)-99
Circulation: 118,000

High Point Enterprise
Meg Gunkel, Book Editor
210 Church Avenue
High Point NC 27261

919-885-2161
Category: 99
Circulation: 32,000

Raleigh News & Observer
Guy Munger, Book Editor
John Byrd, Business Editor
Claude Sitton, Editor
Monte Basgall, Science Editor
215 S McDowell Street
Raleigh NC 27602
919-829-4500
Category: 19-23-67-99
Circulation: 167,000

Rocky Mount Telegram
Carl Worsley, Editor
150 Howard Street
Rocky Mount NC 27801
919-446-5161
Category: 99
Circulation: 16,000

Statesville Record & Landmark
Jerry Josey, Editor
220 E Broad Street
Statesville NC 28677
704-873-1451
Category: 99
Circulation: 18,000

Winston-Salem Journal
Dick Creed, Arts Editor
Linda C Brinson, Book Editor
Floyd Rogers, Business Editor
Tom Travin, Entertainment Editor
Elizabeth Sparks, Food Editor
Nell Perry, Family Editor
Jim Laughrun, News Editor
Terry Oberle, Sports Editor
P O Box 3159
418 N Marshall Street
Winston-Salem NC 27102
919-727-7394
Category: 11-19-27-31-33-35-39
         57-69-71-97(news)-99
Circulation: 120,000
Reviews: 400-500/year
Does not buy serial rights.

<u>NORTH</u> <u>DAKOTA</u>

Bismarck Tribune
George Moore, Managing Editor
P O Box 1498
Seventh and Front Streets
Bismarck ND 58501
701-223-2500
Category: 99
Circulation: 29,000

Fargo Forum
Joseph Dill, Book Editor
Phil Matthews, Business Editor
Kathy Freise, Entertainment
Syb Gullickson, Feature Editor
Terry Devine, News Editor
Curt Monson, Sports Editor

Janna Q Anderson, Travel Editor
101 N Fifth Street West
P O Box 2020
Fargo ND 58107
701-235-7311
Category: 11-19-23-25-27-29-31
         33-35-39-43-57-67-69
         71-97(news)-99
Circulation: 57,000
Reviews: 50/year
Does not buy serial rights.

Grand Forks Herald
Gail Hand, Editor
Books and Entertainment
114 N Fourth Street
Grand Forks ND 58201
701-775-4211
Category: 11-17-33-99
Circulation: 39,000

<u>OHIO</u>

Akron Beacon Journal
James Toms, Business Editor
Barbara Griffin, Feature Editor
Paul A Poorman, Editor
Peter Geiger, Science Editor
44 E Exchange Street
Akron OH 44328
216-375-8111
Category: 11-17-19-23-27-29-33
         35-39-43-67-71-99
Circulation: 232,000

Canton Repository
Michael Hanke, Book Editor
500 Market Avenue S
Canton OH 44702
216-454-5611
Category: 99
Circulation: 80,000

Cincinnati Enquirer
Alice Hornbaker, Book Editor
Kerry Klumpe, Business Editor
Jim Delaney, City Editor
John Bryan, Computer Editor
Sara Pearce, Food Editor
Linda Cagnetti, Features Editor
Jim Smith, National News
Greg Noble, Sports Editor
John Menzies, Travel Editor
617 Vine Street
Cincinnati OH 45201
513-721-2700
Category: 11-19-23-25-27-29-33
         31-35-39-43-57-67-69
         71-97(news)
Circulation: 300,000
Reviews: 5-10/week

Cincinnati Post
Thomas Dunning, Book Editor
Dan Andriacco, Business Editor
Steve Burke, Feature Editor
800 Broadway
Cincinnati OH 45202

513-352-2000
Category: 11-19-29-33-39-71-99
Circulation: 130,000

Cleveland Plain Dealer
Walter Berkov, Book Editor
Thomas Vail, Editor
Karen Long, Science Editor
1801 Superior Avenue NE
Cleveland OH 44114
216-344-4500
Category: 23-67-99
Circulation: 543,000

Columbus Citizen-Journal
Rebecca Teagarden, Book Editor
Richard Campbell, Editor
34 S Third Street
Columbus OH 43216
614-461-5000
Category: 99
Circulation: 122,000

Columbus Dispatch
George Myers Jr, Book Editor
Peter Franklin, Business Editor
Luke Feck, Editor
David Lore, Science Editor
34 S Third Street
Columbus OH 43216
614-461-8837
Category: 19-23-67-99
Circulation: 350,000

Dayton Daily News
Betty Krebs, Book Editor
Brad Tillson, Editor
37 S Ludlow Street
Dayton OH 45401
513-225-2335
Category: 99
Circulation: 116,000

Dayton Journal Herald
Trudy Krisher, Book Editor
37 S Ludlow Street
Dayton OH 45401
513-225-2335
Category: 99
Circulation: 225,000

Toledo Blade
Tom Gearhart, Arts Editor
Fred Lutz, Book Editor
Home Brickey, Business Editor
Gretchen Ziems, Family Editor
Mary Alice Powell, Food Editor
Mike Tressler, Hobby Editor
Larry Keeler, News Editor
Michael Woods, Science Editor
John Hannen, Sports Editor
Fred Nofziger, Travel Editor
The Toledo Blade Company
541 Superior Street
Toledo OH 43660
419-245-6000
Category: 11-19-23-25-27-29-31
33-35-39-43-57-67-69

Category (cont.): 71-97(news)
Circulation: 216,000
Reviews: 250/year

Youngstown Vindicator
Ann Przelomski, Book Editor
David Wolf, Business Editor
Tom Williams, Feature Editor
Vindicator Square
P O Box 780
Youngstown OH 44501
216-747-1471
Category: 11-17-19-29-33
35-39-43-71-99
Circulation: 151,000

OKLAHOMA

Ada Evening News
P O Box 489
120 N Broadway
Ada OK 74820
405-332-4433
Category: 99
Circulation: 10,000
Reviews: some

Oklahoman
Ivy Coffey, Book Editor
500 N Broadway
P O Box 25125
Oklahoma City OK 73125
405-232-3311
Category: 99
Circulation: 320,000

Tulsa Tribune
Tim Morris, Book Editor
P O Box 1770
Tulsa OK 74102
918-581-8412
Category: 99
Circulation: 79,000

Tulsa World
Ken Jackson, Book Editor
Bob Bonebrake, Business Editor
Bob Haring, Executive Editor
P O Box 1770
Tulsa OK 74102
918-581-8300
Category: 19-99
Circulation: 240,000

OREGON

Eugene Register Guard
Dean Rea, Oregon Life Editor
975 High Street
Eugene OR 97440
503-485-1234
Category: 61(OR)-99
Circulation: 73,000

Medford Mail Tribune
Eric Allen Jr, Editor
Lifestyle Section
33 N First Street

Medford OR 97501
503-776-4411
Category: 99
Circulation: 31,000

Portland Oregonian
Paul Pintarich, Book Editor
Steve Carter, Business Editor
William Hilliard, Editor
1320 SW Broadway
Portland OR 97201
503-221-8327
Category: 19-99
Circulation: 397,000

Salem Statesman-Journal
John Goddard, Book Editor
Marc Faulconer, Feature Editor
John Ericksen, Managing Editor
Oregon Territory Magazine
280 Church Street NE
Salem OR 97309
503-399-6611
Category: 11-17-29-33-39-71-99
Circulation: 56,00U

PENNSYLVANIA

Allentown Morning Call
Paul Willistein, Book Editor
Ray Holton, Business Editor
Polly Rayner, Family Editor
Diane Stoneback, Feature Editor
John Grim, Local News Editor
Eric Chiles, National News
Randy Kraft, Science Editor
Paul Reinhard, Sports Editor
Jane Koch, Travel Editor
101 N 6th Street
P O Box 1260
Allentown PA 18105-1260
215-820-6546
Category: 11-19-23-25-27-29-31
33-35-39-43-57-67-69
71-97(news)-99
Circulation: 175,000
Reviews: 150/year
Buys 1st and 2nd serial rights.

Beaver County Times
P O Box 400
Beaver PA 15009
412-775-3200
Category: 99
Circulation: 53,000

Easton Express
Robert K Hays, Book Editor
P O Box 391
Easton PA 18042
215-258-7171
Category: 99
Circulation: 48,000

Erie Times-News
Ed Wellejus, Book Editor
205 W 12th Street
Erie PA 16534

814-456-8531
Category: 99
Circulation: 101,000

Greensburg Tribune-Review
Sue Schantz, Book Editor
Cabin Hill Drive
Greensburg PA 15601
412-834-1151
Category: 99
Circulation: 53,000

Harrisburg Patriot-News
James Beidler, Book Editor
812 Market Street
P O Box 2265
Harrisburg PA 17105
717-255-8100
Category: 99
Circulation: 163,000

Johnstown Tribune Democrat
Harold Barkhimer, Feature Editor
425 Locust Street
P O Box 340
Johnstown PA 15907
814-536-0711
Category: 99
Circulation: 52,000

Lancaster New Era
8 West King Street
Lancaster PA 17603
717-291-8811
Category: 99
Circulation: 138,000

Bucks County Courier Times
Liz Fisher, Book Editor
8400 Route 13
Levittown PA 19057
215-752-6701
Category: 99
Circulation: 69,000

Philadelphia Daily News
Rick Selvin, Book Editor
400 N Broad Street
P O Box 7788
Philadelphia PA 19101
215-854-5887
Category: 99
Circulation: 315,000

Philadelphia Inquirer
Carlin Romano, Book Editor
Larry Williams, Business Editor
Gene Roberts, Executive Editor
400 N Broad Street
Philadelphia PA 19101
215-854-2000
Category: 19-99
Circulation: 1,035,000

Pittsburgh Post Gazette
George Anderson, Book Editor
John Bronson, Business Editor
Dick Hellmann, Computer Editor

Susan Puskar, Lifestyle Editor
David Warner, Local News Editor
Paul Ayars, National News Editor
50 Boulevard of the Allies
Mark Roth, Science Editor
John Clendenon, Sports Editor
Mike Kalina, Travel Editor
50 Boulevard of the Allies
Pittsburgh PA 15222
412-263-1601
Category: 11-19-23-25-27-29-31
33-35-39-43-57-67-69
71-97(news)-99
Circulation: 180,000
Reviews: 150-200/year
Does not buy serial rights.

Pittsburgh Press
Sylvia Sachs, Book Editor
Ann Job, Business Editor
Ed Plank, Entertainment Editor
Marilyn Rubin, Food Editor
Mark Lett, Local News Editor
Carl Apone, Music Editor
George Pupik, National News
Jeffrey Fraser, Science Editor
Russ Brown, Sports Editor
Ruth Heimbuccher, Travel Editor
34 Boulevard of the Allies
Pittsburgh PA 15230
412-263-1519
Category: 11-19-23-27-33-39-67
69-71-97(news)-99
Circulation: 600,000
Does not buy serial rights.

Reading Eagle & Reading Times
Karen Miller, Book Editor
Edward Shultz, Business Editor
Roger Ulrich, Computer Editor
George Hatza, Entertainment
Nora Coyne, Feature Editor
Mary Jo Fox, Food Editor
John Koehler, Local News
Frank Mazurkiewicz, National News
Bruce Posten, Science Editor
John Ernesto, Sports Editor
P O Box 582
Reading PA 19603
215-373-4221
Category: 11-19-23-25-27-29-31
33-35-39-43-57-67-69
71-97(news)-99
Circulation: 116,000
Reviews: 520-560/year
Does not buy serial rights.

Scranton Tribune
Hal Lewis, Book Editor
338 N Washington Avenue
Scranton PA 18505
717-344-7221
Category: 99
Circulation: 50,000

Scrantonion
Edwin Rogers, Book Editor
338 N Washington Avenue

Scranton PA 18501
717-344-7221
Category: 99
Circulation: 56,000

York Dispatch
Editor
15 E Philadelphia Street
York PA 17401
717-854-1575
Category: 99
Circulation: 51,000
Reviews: Some

<u>RHODE ISLAND</u>

Providence Journal-Bulletin
Elliot Krieger, Book Editor
75 Fountain Street
Providence RI 02902
401-277-7000
Category: 99
Circulation: 255,000

<u>SOUTH CAROLINA</u>

Charleston Evening Post
Warren Ripley, Book Editor
134 Columbus Street
Charleston SC 29402
803-577-7111
Category: 99
Circulation: 40,000

Charleston News & Courier
P Manigault, Book Editor
134 Columbus Street
Charleston SC 29402
803-577-7111
Category: 99
Circulation: 117,000

Columbia State Newspaper
William W Starr, Book Editor
Fred Monk, Business Editor
Margaret Bauknight, Feature
Mary Terry, Food Editor
Herman Helms, Sports Editor
P O Box 1333
1103 George Rogers Boulevard
Columbia SC 29202
803-771-6161
Category: 11-19-23-25-27-29-31
33-35-39-43-57-69-71
99
Circulation: 140,000
Reviews: 300-400/year
Does not buy serial rights.

Greenville News-Piedmont
John Pittman, Editor
Sharon Todd, Feature Editor
P O Box 1688
305 S Main Street
Greenville SC 29602
803-298-4110
Category: 99
Circulation: 120,000

Daily Newspapers

SOUTH DAKOTA

Pierre Capitol Journal
John Hipple, Managing Editor
404 E Sioux
Pierre SD 57501
605-224-7301
Category: 99
Circulation: 4000

Argus Leader
Mary Lochridge, Book Editor
P O Box 5034
200 S Minnesota
Sioux Falls SD 57102
605-331-2200
Category: 99
Circulation: 57,000
Reviews: 12/week

TENNESSEE

Chattanooga News-Free Press
Helen Hexum, Book Editor
400 E 11th Street
Chattanooga TN 37401
615-756-6900
Category: 99
Circulation: 108,000

Chattanooga Times
Wes Hasden, Book Editor
117 E Tenth Street
Chattanooga TN 37402
615-756-1234
Category: 99
Circulation: 45,000

Cleveland Banner
Beecher Hunter, Editor
1505 - 25th Street NW
Cleveland TN 37311
615-472-5041
Category: 99
Circulation: 17,000

Jackson Sun
Michael Craft, Editor
245 W Lafayette
Jackson TN 38301
901-427-3333
Category: 99
Circulation: 37,000

Johnson City Press-Chronicle
Elaine Goller, Book Editor
P O Box 1717
Johnson City TN 37601
615-929-3111
Category: 99
Circulation: 31,000

Kingsport Times-News
701 Lynn Garden Drive
Kingsport TN 37662
615-246-8121
Category: 99
Circulation: 46,000

Knoxville Journal
Tom Sweeten, Book Editor
Joe Krakoviak, Business Editor
Ron McMahon, Editor
Randall Beck, Science Editor
210 W Church Avenue
Knoxville TN 37901
615-522-4141
Category: 19-23-67-99
Circulation: 60,000

Knoxville News-Sentinel
Bill Dockery, Book Editor
204 W Church
P O Box 80
Knoxville TN 37901
615-523-3131
Category: 99
Circulation: 163,000

Maryville Daily Times
Elizabeth Bradford, Features
P O Box 568
Maryville TN 37803
615-981-1100
Category: 99
Circulation: 21,000

Memphis Commercial Appeal
Tom Fox, Book Editor
Bob Hetherington, Business Editor
Michael Grehl, Editor
495 Union Avenue
Memphis TN 38101
901-529-2211
Category: 19-99
Circulation: 289,000

Nashville Banner
Jim Ewing, Book Editor
1100 Broadway
Nashville TN 37202
615-259-8800
Category: 99
Circulation: 73,000

Nashville Tennessean
Robert Wyatt, Book Editor
1100 Broadway
Nashville TN 37202
615-259-8095
Category: 61(TN)-99
Circulation: 242,000

TEXAS

Abilene Reporter-News
William Whitaker, Arts Editor
Larry Lawrence, Book Editor
Douglas Williamson, Business
Merle Watson, Family Editor
Karen Reese, Food Editor
Larry Zelisko, News Editor
Rebecca Harris, Science Editor
Bill Hart, Sports Editor
Bob Bruce, Travel Editor
101 Cypress Street
P O Box 30

Abilene TX 79604
915-673-4271
Category: 11-19-23-25-27-29-31-33
    35-39-43(automobiles)
    57-67-69-71-75(news)-99
Circulation: 60,000
Reviews: 250/year
Does not buy serial rights.

Amarillo Globe-News
Mary Kate Tripp, Book Editor
Phillip Fiorini, Business Editor
Beth Duke, Feature Editor
Kay Mohr, Feature Editor
David Stevens, Home Editor
Dennis Spies, Local News
Dorsey Wilmarth, National News
Al Lewis, Science Editor
Kenneth Tidmore, Sports Editor
900 Harrison
Amarillo TX 79166
806-376-4488
Category: 11-19-25-27-29-31-33
    35-39-43-57-67-69-71
    97(news)-99
Circulation: 82,000
Reviews: 4-6/week
Does not buy serial rights.

Austin American-Statesman
Mike Cox, Book Editor
Kirk Ladendorf, Business Editor
Arnold Rosenfeld, Editor
166 E Riverside Drive
Austin TX 78767
512-445-3500
Category: 19-99
Circulation: 191,000

Beaumont Enterprise
Lela Davis, Book Editor
Jon Talton, Business Editor
June Smith, Lifestyles Editor
Rick Smith, Local News Editor
William Mock, Managing Editor
Joe Heiling, Sports Editor
380 Walnut
P O Box 3071
Beaumont TX 77701
409-838-2803
Category: 11-19-23-25-27-29-31
    33-35-39-43-57-67-69
    71-97(news)-99
Circulation: 74,000
Reviews: 150-200/year
Does not buy serial rights.

Corpus Christi Caller-Times
Eric Whittington, Business Editor
Gretchen Ray, Feature Editor
John Thomas, Managing Editor
P O Box 9136
820 Lower Broadway
Corpus Christi TX 78469
512-884-2011
Category: 11-17-19-29-33
    35-39-43-71-99
Circulation: 87,000

Dallas Morning News
Robert Compton, Book Editor
Si Dunn, Paperback Editor
Cherie Clodfelter, Children's
Cheryl Hall, Business Editor
Communications Center
P O Box 225237
Dallas TX 75265
214-977-8222
Category: 19-21-31-76-89-99
Circulation: 454,000
Reviews: every week

Dallas Times Herald
Jeff Unger, Book Editor
Herald Square
1101 Pacific
Dallas TX 75202
214-744-6111
Category: 99
Circulation: 364,000

El Paso Herald-Post
Stephen Owens, Book Editor
Comment Page
401 Mills Avenue
El Paso TX 79999
915-546-6349
Category: 99
Circulation: 34,000
Reviews: 4-5/week

El Paso Times
Josie Weber, Book Editor
Neal Templin, Business Editor
Barbara Funkhouse, Editor
401 Mills Avenue
El Paso TX 79999
915-546-6100
Category: 19-99
Circulation: 86,000
El Paso TX 79999
915-546-6100
Category: 19
Circulation: 86,000

Fort Worth Star-Telegram
Harriet Simpson, Arts Editor
Larry Swindell, Book Editor
Mike Norman, Business Editor
Dan Reed, Computer Editor
Linda Gandy, Family Editor
JoAnn Vachule, Food Editor
Carol Nuckols, Hobby Editor
Gene Zipperlen, National News
James Walker, News Editor
Anita Baker, Science Editor
Bruce Raben, Sports Editor
Jerry Flemmons, Travel Editor
400 W 7th Street
Fort Worth TX 76102
817-390-7000
Category: 11-19-25-27-29-31-33
        35-39-43-57-67-69-71
        97(news)-99
Circulation: 300,000
Reviews: 400/year
Does not buy serial rights.

Houston Chronicle
George Christian, Book Editor
Susan Bischoff, Business Editor
Philip Warner, Editor
Tony Pederson, Managing Editor
Jack Rickman, Feature Editor
P O Box 4260
801 Texas Street
Houston TX 77002
713-220-7171
Category: 11-17-19-29-33
        35-39-43-71-99
Circulation: 547,000

Houston Post
Peter Wyckoff, Book Editor
4747 SW Freeway
Houston TX 77001
713-840-5600
Category: 99
Circulation: 367,000

Lubbock Avalanche-Journal
Bill Kerns, Book Editor
P O Box 491
Lubbock TX 79408
806-762-8844
Category: 11-33-99
Circulation: 81,000
Reviews: few

San Angelo Standard-Times
Kandis Gatewood, Book Editor
P O Box 5111
San Angelo TX 76902
915-653-1221
Category: 99
Circulation: 41,000

San Antonio Express News
Craig Kibler, Book Editor
David St Mary, Business Editor
Bert Wise, Executive Editor
Mildred Whitaker, Science Editor
Avenue E and 3rd Street
P O Box 2171
San Antonio TX 78297
512-225-7411
Category: 19-23-67-99
Circulation: 205,000

San Antonio Light
John Cochran, Entertainment Ed.
420 Broadway
P O Box 161
San Antonio TX 78291
512-226-4271
Category: 11-33-99
Circulation: 202,000

Tyler Courier-Times/Telegraph
Everett Taylor, Book Editor
P O Box 2030
410 W Erwin Street
Tyler TX 75710
214-597-8111
Category: 99
Circulation: 49,000

Waco Tribune Herald
Robert Darden, Book Editor
900 Franklin Street
P O Box 1100
Waco TX 76703
817-753-1511
Category: 99
Circulation: 64,000

Wichita Falls Record-News/Times
Louise Gregg, Book Editor
Joe Lackey, Business Editor
Bruce Fisher, Editor
1301 Lamar
P O Box 120
Wichita Falls TX 76307
817-767-8341
Category: 19-99
Circulation: 50,000

<u>UTAH</u>

Ogden Standard-Examiner
Cliff Thompson, Business Editor
Holly Mullen, Feature Editor
Phil Jensen, Local News
Tom McEachin, National News
Ensign Ritchie, Sports Editor
455 23rd Street
P O Box 951
Ogden UT 84401
801-394-7711
Category: 11-19-23-25-27-29
        35-39-43-57-69-71
        97(news)-99
Circulation: 56,000
Reviews: 3/week
Buys only 1st serial rights.

Desert News
Jerry Johnston, Book Editor
30 East 1st South Street
Salt Lake City UT 84111
801-237-2100
Category: 99
Circulation: 64,000

Salt Lake Tribune
Harold Schindler, Book Editor
Robert Woody, Business Editor
Will Fehr, Executive Editor
Eric McMullin, Science Editor
143 S Main Street
P O Box 867
Salt Lake City UT 84110
801-237-2011
Category: 23-67-99
Circulation: 130,000

<u>VERMONT</u>

Barre Times-Argus
Elaine Harrington, Features
540 N Main Street
Barre VT 05641
802-479-0191
Category: 99
Circulation: 13,000

Burlington Free Press
Rob Eley, Business Editor
Stephen M Mease, Feature Editor
Stephen Hemingway, Local News
David Herd, National News
Ted Ryan, Sports Editor
191 College Street
P O Box 10
Burlington VT 05401
802-863-3441
Category: 11-19-23-25-27-29-31
          33-35-39-43-57-69-71
          97(news)-99
Circulation: 50,000
Reviews: 50-75/year
Does not buy serial rights.

Rutland Daily Herald
S K Wild, Editor
27 Wales Street
Rutland VT 05701
802-775-5511
Category: 99
Circulation: 20,000

VIRGINIA

Daily Press/Times-Herald
Will Molineux, Book Editor
David Parsons, Business Editor
Carolyn West, Feature Editor
Karen Walker, Food Editor
Myrtle Barnes, News Editor
Jay Hancock, Science Editor
Skip Miller, Sports Editor
7505 Warwick Boulevard
Newport News VA 23607
804-247-4627
Category: 11-19-23-25-29-27-31
          33-35-39-43-57-67-69
          71-97(news)-99
Circulation: 110,000
Reviews: 8-10/week
Buys 1st and 2nd serial rights.

Virginian Pilot/Ledger-Star
Ruth Walker, Book Editor
150 W Brambleton Avenue
Norfolk VA 23501
804-446-2000
Category: 99
Circulation: 225,000

Richmond News Leader
Ann L Merriman, Book Editor
Steve Row, Business Editor
Jerald Finch, Managing Editor
Dawn Chase, Science Editor
333 E Grace Street
Richmond VA 23293
804-649-6000
Category: 19-23-67-99
Circulation: 112,000

Richmond Times-Dispatch
Robert Merrit, Book Editor
Marvin Garrette, Managing Editor
333 E Grace Street

Richmond VA 23293
804-649-6000
Category: 99
Circulation: 225,000

Roanoke Times & World-News
Mike Mayo, Book Editor
201 Campbell Avenue SW
Roanoke VA 24010
703-981-3000
Category: 99
Circulation: 127,000

Springfield Journal
6885 Commercial Drive
Springfield VA 22151
703-750-2000
Category: 99
Circulation: 61,000

WASHINGTON

Bremerton Sun
Gene Gisley, Feature Editor
P O Box 259
545 Fifth Street
Bremerton WA 98310
206-377-3711
Category: 99
Circulation: 38,000

Everett Herald
Nancy Erickson, Book Editor
Grand & California Avenues
P O Box 930
Everett WA 98206
206-339-3000
Category: 99
Circulation: 56,000

The Olympian
Jim Casey, Feature Editor
1268 Fourth Avenue E
Olympia WA 98507
206-754-5400
Category: 99
Circulation: 29,000

Seattle Post-Intelligencer
Michael Conant, Book Editor
James Rennie, Managing Editor
6th & Wall Streets
P O Box 1909
Seattle WA 98111
206-628-8000
Category: 99
Circulation: 465,000

Seattle Times
Donn Fry, Book Editor
Stephen Dunfey, Business Editor
James B King, Editor
Fairview Avenue and John Street
P O Box 70
Seattle WA 98111
206-464-2111
Category: 19-99
Circulation: 473,000

Spokesman-Review/Chronicle
Dan Webster, Arts Editor
Kathryn J DeLong, Feature Editor
Cheryl Ernst, Food Editor
Chris Peck, Managing Editor
Jeff Jordan, Sports Editor
927 W Riverside
Spokane WA 99210
509-459-5413
Category: 11-25-27-29-31-33
          35-39-43-57-67-69
          71-97(news)-99
Circulation: 135,000
Reviews: 200-300/year
Does not buy serial rights.

Tacoma News Tribune
Charles Rice, Feature Editor
1950 S State Street
Tacoma WA 98411
206-597-8563
Category: 99
Circulation: 118,000

Vancouver Columbian
P O Box 180
Vancouver WA 98666
206-694-3391
Category: 99
Circulation: 50,000

Walla Walla Union-Bulletin
Rick Doyle, Managing Editor
Weekend Magazine
First & Poplar Streets
Walla Walla WA 99362
509-525-3300
Category: 99
Circulation: 16,000

WEST VIRGINIA

Charleston Daily Mail
Nanya Gadd, Book Editor
Bill Virgin, Business Editor
David Greenfield, Editor
Susan Jones, Entertainment
Julie Kemp, Feature Editor
Bill Byrd, Local News Editor
Richard Grimes, Science Editor
Don Hager, Sports Editor
1001 Virginia Street E
Charleston WV 25301
304-348-4870
Category: 11-19-23-25-27-29-31
          33-35-39-43-57-67-69
          71-97(news)-99
Circulation: 55,000
Reviews: 20-30/year
Does not buy serial rights.

Charleston Gazette
Don Marsh, Editor
1001 Virginia Street E
Charleston WV 25301
304-348-5140
Category: 99
Circulation: 108,000

Herald-Disptach
James Casto, Book Editor
P O Box 2017
946 Fifth Avenue
Huntington WV 25720
304-696-5678
Category: 99
Circulation: 49,000

Wheeling News Register
1500 Main Streets
Wheeling WV 26003
304-233-0100
Category: 99
Circulation: 65,000

WISCONSIN

Appleton Post Cresent
306 W Washington Street
Appleton WI 54912
414-733-4411
Category: 99
Circulation: 60,000

Green Bay Press-Gazette
Editor
435 E Walnut
Green Bay WI 54305
414-435-4411
Category: 99
Circulation: 70,000

Madison State Journal
Don Davies, Feature Editor
1901 Fish Hatchery Road
P O Box 8058
Madison WI 53708
608-252-6100
Category: 11-17-29-33
           39-43-71-99
Circulation: 127,000

Milwaukee Journal
Robert Kenyon, Book Editor
333 W State Street
P O Box 661
Milwaukee WI 53201
414-224-2000
Category: 99
Circulation: 513,000

Milwaukee Sentinel
Kevin Keefe, Arts Editor
Larry Engel, Automotive Editor
Ernst Franzen, Book Editor
John Torinus, Business Editor
Marilyn Kucer, Family Editor
Lee Aschoff, Food Editor
Sandy Wilson, Hobby Editor
Tom Mueller, National News
Gerry Hinkley, News Editor
Joe Manning, Science Editor
Joe Karius, Sports Editor
Dean Jensen, Travel Editor
P O Box 371
918 N Fourth Street
Milwaukee WI 53201

414-224-2142
Category: 11-19-25-27-29-31
          33-35-39-43-57-67
          69-71-97(news)-99
Circulation: 186,000
Reviews: 150/year
Buys 1st and 2nd serial rights.

WYOMING

Wyoming Tribune-Eagle
Frances Hardy, Book Editor
110 E 17th Street
Cheyenne WY 82001
307-634-3361
Category: 99
Circulation: 21,000

ALBERTA, CANADA

Calgary Herald
Kevin Peterson, Managing Editor
Ken McGoohan, Book Editor
Gary Park, Business Editor
Michael Burn, Entertainment
P O Box 2400
215 - 16th Street SE
Calgary T2P 0W8   AB Canada
403-235-7100
Category: 11-19-33-99
Circulation: 137,000

Calgary Sun
Stephani Keer, Book Editor
Ron Stewart, Business Editor
John Coulhourn, Entertainment
Mary-Jane Kletke, Feature Editor
Robb Fergusson, Feature Editor
John Gradon, Local News Editor
Mike Strobel, National News
Peter Menzies, Sports Editor
2615 12th Street NE
Calgary T2E 7W9   AB Canada
403-250-4200
Category: 11-19-25-27-29-31
          33-35-39-43-57-69
          71-97(news)-99
Circulation: 90,000
Reviews: varies
Does not buy serial rights.

Edmonton Journal
James Adams, Book Editor
10006 - 101st Street
Edmonton T5J 2S6   AB Canada
403-429-5100
Category: 99
Circulation: 213,000

BRITISH COLUMBIA, CANADA

Vancouver Province
G T Molyneux, Book Editor
2250 Granville Street
Vancouver   BC Canada
604-732-2222
Category: 99
Circulation: 155,000

Vancouver Sun
Leslie Peterson, Book Editor
Bruce Larsen, Managing Editor
Paul Musgrove, Science Editor
2250 Granville Street
Vancouver V6H 3G2   BC Canada
604-732-2121
Category: 23-67-99
Circulation: 278,000

Victoria Times-Colonist
Gordon Bell, Managing Editor
P O Box 300
2621 Douglas
Victoria V8W 2N4   BC Canada
604-382-7211
Category: 99
Circulation: 76,000

MANITOBA, CANADA

Winnipeg Free Press
Tom Oleson, Book Editor
Murray Burt, Managing Editor
Phil Anwyl, Business Editor
Doug MacKay, Science Editor
300 Carlton Street
Winnipeg R3C 3C1   MB Canada
204-943-9331
Category: 19-23-67-99
Circulation: 240,000

NEW BRUNSWICK, CANADA

Daily Gleaner
Stanley Kneebone, Book Editor
P O Box 3370
Fredericton E3B 5A2   NB Canada
506-452-6671
Category: 99
Circulation: 27,000

Telegraph-Journal/Times-Globe
Fred Hazel, Editor
Crown & Union Streets
P O Box 2350
St Johns E2L 3V8   NB Canada
506-657-1230
Category: 99
Circulation: 68,000

NEWFOUNDLAND, CANADA

St John's Evening Telegram
S X Finn, Editor
P O Box 5970
400 Topsail Road
St John's A1C 5X7   NF Canada
709-364-6300
Category: 99
Circulation: 51,000
Reviews: few

NOVA SCOTIA, CANADA

Chronicle-Herald/Mail-Star
Lorna Innes, Book Editor
1650 Argyle Street

Daily Newspapers

P O Box 610
Halifax B3J 2T2 NS Canada
902-426-2811
Category: 99
Circulation: 79,000

ONTARIO, CANADA

Brockville Recorder & Times
Perry Beverley, Editor
23 King Street W
Brockville K6V 5T8 ON Canada
613-342-4441
Category: 99
Circulation: 14,000

Cornwall Standard-Freeholder
D H Tomchick, Book Editor
44 Pitt Street
Cornwall K6J 3P3 ON Canada
613-933-3160
Category: 99
Circulation: 18,000

Hamilton Spectator
Ken Kilpatrick, Book Editor
44 Frid Street
Hamilton L8N 3G3 ON Canada
416-526-3333
Category: 99
Circulation: 75,000

Peterborough Examiner
G F Toner, Managing Editor
P O Box 389
Peterborough K9J 6Z4 ON Canada
705-745-4641
Category: 99
Circulation: 24,000

Kingston Whig-Standard
Larry Scanlan, Book Editor
306 King Street
Kingston K7L 4Z7 ON Canada
613-544-5000
Category: 99
Circulation: 42,000

Waterloo Record
Lynda Coates, Book Editor
William Dunfield, Managing Editor
Bob Porteous, Business Editor
Philip Bast, Science Editor
225 Fairway Road S
Kitchener N2G 4E5 ON Canada
519-894-22
Category: 19-23-67-99
Circulation: 75,000

London Free Press
Norman Ibsen, Book Editor
W I Morley, Editor
James Tost, Business Editor
369 York Street
London N6A 4G1 ON Canada
519-679-1111
Category: 19-99
Circulation: 126,000

Ottawa Citizen
Burt Heward, Book Editor
Deborah Dowling, Business Editor
Jay Stone, Entertainment Editor
Kathy Walker, Food Editor
Ros Guggi, Feature Editor
Tom Hill, Local News/Computers
Graham Parley, National News
April Lindgren, Science Editor
Alje Kaminga, Sports Editor
1101 Baxter Road
Ottawa K2B 7G8 ON Canada
613-829-9100
Category: 11-19-23-25-27-29
         31-33-35-43-57-67
         69-71-97(news)-99
Circulation: 180,000
Reviews: 20/week
Buys only 2nd serial rights.

St Thomas Times-Journal
L J Beavis, Book Editor
Garnet Cowsill, Managing Editor
16 Hincks Street
St Thomas N5P 3W6 ON Canada
519-631-2790
Category: 99
Circulation: 10,000

Toronto Sun
Yvonne Crittenden, Book Editor
Pat Job, Book Editor
Garth Turner, Business Editor
Peter Brewster, Managing Editor
333 King Street E
Toronto M5A 3X5 ON Canada
416-947-2222
Category: 19-99
Circulation: 450,000

Toronto Star
Lew Gloin, Book Editor
John Honderich, Business Editor
Raymond Timson, Managing Editor
Jack Miller, Science Editor
1 Yonge Street
Toronto M5E 1E6 ON Canada
416-869-4479
Category: 19-23-67-99
Circulation: 526,034
Reviews: 30-35/week
Buys only 1st serial rights.

Toronto Globe & Mail
William French, Book Editor
444 Front Street W
Toronto M5V 2S9 ON Canada
416-585-5319
Category: 99
Circulation: 328,000

Welland Evening Tribune
James Middleton, Managing Editor
228 E Main Street
Welland L3B 3W8 ON Canada
416-732-2411
Category: 99
Circulation: 19,000

Windsor Star
Marty Gervais, Book Editor
Bill Shields, Business Editor
Carl Morgan, Editor
167 Ferry Street
Windsor N9A 4M5 ON Canada
519-255-5711
Category: 19-99
Circulation: 94,000

QUEBEC, CANADA

Le Journal de Quebec
Pierre Nadeau, Book Editor
450 rue Bechard
Ville Vanier G1M 2E9 PQ Canada
418-683-1573
Category: 99
Circulation: 100,000

Montreal La Presse
Reginald Martel, Book Editor
7 Ouest rue St Jacques
Montreal H2Y 1K9 PQ Canada
514-285-7272
Category: 99
Circulation: 280,000

Montreal Gazette
Heather Hill, Book Editor
Richard Conrad, Business Editor
Mel Morris, Managing Editor
250 St Antoine Street W
Montreal H2Y 3R7 PQ Canada
514-282-2899
Category: 19-99
Circulation: 276,000

Le Journal de Montreal
Louise Blanchard, Book Editor
155 Port Royal West
Montreal H3L 2B1 PQ Canada
514-521-4545
Category: 99
Circulation: 326,000

Quebec Le Soleil
Jacques Samson, Book Editor
390 St Vallier E
Quebec G1K 7J6 PQ Canada
418-647-3233
Category: 99
Circulation: 145,000

Sherbrooke Record
Charles Bury, News Editor
2850 Delorme
Sherbrooke J1K 1A1 PQ Canada
819-569-9526
Category: 99
Circulation: 6,000

SASKATCHEWAN, CANADA

Regina Leader Post
Pat Williams, Book Editor
Bruce Johnstone, Business Editor
John Swan, Managing Editor

1964 Park Street
P O Box 2020
Regina S4P 3G4 SK Canada
306-565-8211
Category: 19-99
Circulation: 70,000

Saskatoon Star-Phoenix
Wilfred Petro, Editor
Wilfred Popoff, Book Editor
Nancy Russell, Business Editor
204 Fifth Avenue N
Saskatoon S7K 2P1 SK Canada
306-652-9200
Category: 19
Circulation: 56,000

CALIFORNIA

Azusa Herald
234 E Foothill Boulevard
Azusa CA 91702
818-969-1711
Category: 99
Circulation: 30,000
Frequency: 52

Beverly Hills Courier
8840 Olympic Boulevard
Beverly Hills CA 90211
213-278-1322
Category: 99
Circulation: 46,000
Frequency: 52

La Puente West Covina Highlander
Highlander Publications
19331 E Walnut Drive
City of Industry CA 91744
714-595-3263
Category: 99
Frequency: 52

San Jose Sun
Meredith Papers
P O Box 368
Cupertino CA 95015
408-255-7500
Category: 99
Frequency: 52

Sherman Oaks Sun
Associated Valley Publications
P O Box 257
Encino CA 91316
818-907-5449
Category: 99
Frequency: 52

Huntington Beach Independent
West Orange Publishing
13261 Century Boulevard
Garden Grove CA 92643
714-537-7510
Category: 99
Frequency: 52

Hermosa Beach Argonaut
P O Box 728
Hermosa Beach CA 90254
213-372-2155
Category: 99
Frequency: 52

Hollywood Citizen News
1550 Wilcox Avenue
Hollywood CA 90028
213-463-3400
Category: 99
Circulation: 100,000
Frequency: 52

Irvine World News
P O Box 19512
Irvine CA 92713
714-261-2435
Category: 99
Circulation: 40,000
Frequency: 52

Long Beach Marina News
P O Box 7097
Long Beach CA 90807
213-426-3294
Category: 99
Circulation: 34,000
Frequency: 52

Los Alamitos News Enterprise
P O Box 38
Los Alamitos CA 90720
213-431-1397
Category: 99
Circulation: 30,000
Frequency: 52

L.A. Weekly
2140 Hyperion Avenue
Los Angeles CA 90027
213-667-2620
Category: 99
Circulation: 135,000
Frequency: 52

Los Angeles Reader
Harry N Jigamian, Book Editor
8471 Melrose Avenue
Los Angeles CA 90069
213-655-8810
Category: 99
Circulation: 90,000
Frequency: 52
Reviews: 25-50/year
Does not buy serial rights.

Los Angeles Wilshire Press
1660 Beverly Boulevard
Los Angeles CA 90026
213-484-2840
Category: 99
Frequency: 52

West L.A. Pico Post
P O Box 35447
Los Angeles CA 90035
213-552-3370
Category: 99
Frequency: 52

Pacific Sun
21 Corte Madera Avenue
Mill Valley CA 94942
415-383-4500
Category: 99
Circulation: 31,000
Frequency: 52

Costa Mesa News
883 Production Place
Newport Beach CA 92663
714-631-8120
Category: 99
Frequency: 52

Palo Alto Weekly
Charlotte Muse, Editor
Title Pages
P O Box 1610
Palo Alto CA 94302
415-326-8210
Category: 99
Circulation: 42,000
Frequency: 52

San Francisco Today
San Mateo Times Group
P O Box 2527
South San Francisco CA 94083
415-952-4109
Category: 99
Frequency: 52

San Fernando Valley Sun
314 Chatsworth Drive
San Fernando CA 91340
818-365-3111
Category: 99
Frequency: 52

San Francisco Bay Guardian
Book Editor
2700 19th Street
San Francisco CA 94110
415-824-7660
Category: 99
Circulation: 40,000
Frequency: 52

San Francisco Progress
851 Howard Street
San Francisco CA 94103
415-982-8022
Category: 99
Circulation: 220,000
Frequency: 52

Culver City Goodlife
P O Box 1260
Santa Monica CA 90401
213-393-0601
Category: 99
Frequency: 52

Seal Beach Journal
Editor
P O Box 755
Seal Beach CA 90740
213-430-7555
Category: 99
Circulation: 30,000
Frequency: 52

Weekly Newspapers

Southeast News Signal
8088 National Avenue
South Gate CA 90280
213-927-8681
Category: 99
Frequency: 52

Sunnyvale Valley Journal
298 Sunnyvale Avenue #104
Sunnyvale CA 94086
408-736-9090
Category: 99
Circulation: 31,000
Frequency: 52

COLORADO

Sentinel Newspapers
3501 E 46th Avenue
Denver CO 80216
303-292-5551
Category: 99
Frequency: 52

CONNECTICUT

Advocate Publishing
30 Arbor Street
Hartford CT 06016
203-232-4501
Category: 99
Frequency: 52

Norwalk Fairpress
Deborah Grahame-Smith, Editor
  (also reviews books)
Robert Viagas, Arts Editor
Elizabeth Payne, Business Editor
Marilyn Grogins, Family Editor
Janike Bruce, Metro Editor
Sue Walionis, Science Editor
P O Box 5700
200 Westport Avenue, County Mall
Norwalk CT 06856
203-846-3451
Category: 11-19-27-31-33-35-39
        57-67-97(news)-99
Circulation: 63,000
Frequency: 52
Reviews: 24/year
Does not buy serial rights.

Village Gazette
182 Sound Beach Avenue
Old Greenwich CT 06870
203-637-1774
Category: 99
Circulation: 34,000
Frequency: 52

Stamford Mail
Editor
P O Box 2220
Stamford CT 06906
203-327-2550
Category: 99
Circulation: 36,000
Frequency: 52

DISTRICT OF COLUMBIA

Human Events
Thomas S Winter, Editor
422 First Street SE
Washington DC 20003
202-546-0856
Category: 41-55-97(news)-99
Circulation: 48,000
Frequency: 52
Reviews: few

Washington Capital Spotlight
1158 National Press Building
Washington DC 20045
202-628-0700
Category: 99
Circulation: 60,000
Frequency: 52

Washington Informer
3117 ML King Jr Avenue SE
Washington DC 20032
202-561-4100
Category: 99
Circulation: 35,000
Frequency: 52

Washington New Observer
811 Florida Avenue NW
Washington DC 20001
202-232-3060
Category: 99
Circulation: 25,000
Frequency: 52

DELAWARE

Wilmington Dialogue
P O Box 2208
Wilmington DE 19899
302-573-3109
Category: 99
Circulation: 41,000
Frequency: 52

FLORIDA

Broward Tribune
Gloria Katz, General Editor
Bob Freund, Entertainment Editor
Jeff Harrell, Sports Editor
Arline Horne, Travel Editor
P O Box 23909
Fort Lauderdale FL 33307
305-563-3311
Category: 11-33-69-71-99
Circulation: 40,000
Frequency: 52
Reviews: 2-4/year
Does not buy serial rights.

Hallandale Digest
P O Box 785
Hallandale FL 33009
Category: 99
Circulation: 44,000
Frequency: 52

Jensen Beach Mirror
Editor
P O Box 787
Jensen Beach FL 33457
305-334-4333
Category: 99
Circulation: 56,000
Frequency: 52

Lake Worth Coastal Observer
Editor
P O Box 191
Lake Worth FL 33460
305-585-9387
Category: 99
Circulation: 37,000
Frequency: 52

National Enquirer
Iain Calder, Editor
Lantana FL 33464
Category: 99
Circulation: 4,500,000
Frequency: 99
Buys 1st and 2nd serial rights.

Melbourne Times
P O Box 1870
Melbourne FL 32901
305-723-7661
Category: 99
Circulation: 45,000
Frequency: 52

Miami Beach Sun
Editor
P O Box 390420
Miami Beach FL 33139
305-532-4531
Category: 99
Circulation: 45,000
Frequency: 52

Tampa Metro Neighbor
109 Brush Street
Tampa FL 33602
813-223-9711
Category: 99
Circulation: 140,000
Frequency: 52

Sun Coast Media
Editor
200 E Miami Avenue
Venice FL 33595
813-488-2611
Category: 99
Frequency: 52

GEORGIA

Decatur News Publishing
Editor
739 Dekalb Industrial Way
Decatur GA 30033
404-292-3536
Category: 99
Frequency: 52

Weekly Newspapers

ILLINOIS

Belleville Journal
219 N Illinois
Belleville IL 62222
618-277-7000
Category: 99
Circulation: 37,000
Frequency: 52

Chicago Downtown
Linda Pratico, Editor
17 E Monroe #200
Chicago IL 60603
312-346-6884
Category: 99
Circulation: 100,000
Frequency: 52

Chicago Good News
4710 Lincoln Avenue
Chicago IL 60625
312-878-7334
Category: 99
Circulation: 35,000
Frequency: 52

Chicago Northwest Press
4941 N Milwaukee Avenue
Chicago IL 60630
312-286-6100
Category: 99
Circulation: 35,000
Frequency: 52

Chicago Reader
Robert Roth, Editor
11 E Illinois
Chicago IL 60611
312-828-0350
Category: 11-33-99
Circulation: 125,000
Frequency: 52

Chicago Sunday Star
Myers Publishing
7519 N Ashland Avenue
Chicago IL 60626
312-761-7200
Category: 99
Frequency: 52

Peoria Observer
Editor
100 Detroit Avenue
Morton IL 61550
309-263-2211
Category: 99
Circulation: 70,000
Frequency: 52

Palos Heights Regional News
Editor
12243 S Harlem
Palos Heights IL 60463
312-448-4000
Category: 99
Frequency: 52

INDIANA

Highland Calumet Press
8411 Kennedy Avenue
Highland IN 46322
219-838-0717
Category: 99
Frequency: 52

MASSACHUSETTS

Boston Phoenix
Richard Gaines, Editor
100 Massachusetts Avenue
Boston MA 02115
617-536-5390
Category: 99
Circulation: 135,000
Frequency: 52

Boston Ledger
P O Box 481
Brookline MA 01246
617-232-7000
Category: 99
Frequency: 52

Fitchburg Montachusett Review
P O Drawer A
Fitchburg MA 01420
617-342-8064
Category: 99
Circulation: 48,000
Frequency: 52

Ipswich North Shore
P O Box 192
Ipswich MA 01938
617-356-5141
Category: 99
Circulation: 111,000
Frequency: 52

Marlboro Compass
250 Maple Street
Marlboro MA 01752
617-485-5200
Category: 99
Circulation: 36,000
Frequency: 52

Rockland South Shore News
65 Grove Street
Rockland MA 02370
617-878-5100
Category: 99
Circulation: 68,000
Frequency: 52

MARYLAND

Gaithersburg Gazette
P O Box 606
Gaithersburg MD 20760
301-948-3120
Category: 99
Circulation: 51,000
Frequency: 52

Rockville Montgomery Sentinel
9030 Comprint Court
Gaithersburg MD 20767
301-948-1500
Category: 99
Circulation: 48,000
Frequency: 52

Glen Burnie Gazette
P O Box 567
Glen Burnie MD 21061
301-766-3700
Category: 99
Circulation: 32,000
Frequency: 52

MICHIGAN

Clarkston Reminder
6569 Dixie Highway
Clarkston MI 48106
313-625-9346
Category: 99
Circulation: 35,000
Frequency: 52

Fenton Independent
111 River Street
Fenton MI 49430
313-629-2203
Category: 99
Circulation: 53,000
Frequency: 52

Mount ClemensCommunity News
Mitch Kehetian, Editor
67 Cass Avenue
Mount Clemens MI 48043
313-469-4510
Category: 99
Circulation: 41,000
Frequency: 52

Sterling Heights Advisor
45184 Cass Avenue
Utica MI 48087
313-731-1000
Category: 99
Circulation: 38,000
Frequency: 52

MINNESOTA

Twin Cities Sun Newspapers
7401 Bush Lake Road
Edina MN 55435
612-831-1200
Category: 99
Frequency: 52

Minneapolis City Pages
Phil Davies, Editor
100 N 6th Street
Minneapolis MN 55403
612-375-1015
Category: 99
Circulation: 100,000
Frequency: 52

Minneapolis Skyway News
2104 Park
Minneapolis MN 55404
612-871-3333
Category: 99
Circulation: 50,000
Frequency: 52

MISSOURI

Affton South
Saint Louis County News
9111 Gravois
Affton MO 63123
314-638-1222
Category: 99
Circulation: 60,000
Frequency: 52

Kansas City Dispatch
P O Box 12338
Kansas City MO 64116
816-454-9660
Category: 99
Circulation: 52,000
Frequency: 52

St Louis Naborhood Link
416 Lemay Ferry Road
Saint Louis MO 63125
314-631-4321
Category: 99
Circulation: 40,000
Frequency: 52

St Louis Suburban Papers
7020 Chippewa
Saint Louis MO 63119
314-481-1111
Category: 99
Circulation:
Frequency: 52

NEW JERSEY

Dateline Journal
296 Clifton Avenue
Clifton NJ 07011
201-773-5010
Category: 99
Circulation: 33,000
Frequency: 52

North Jersey Suburbanite
50 Piermont Road
Cresskill NJ 07626
201-567-4880
Category: 99
Circulation: 45,000
Frequency: 52

Mid Jersey News
P O Box 219
Dunellen NJ 08812
201-469-2255
Category: 99
Circulation: 65,000
Frequency: 52

Shopper Newspapers, Week Ahead
Midge Boardman, Editor
12-38 River Road
Fair Lawn NJ 07410
201-791-8400
Category: 99
Circulation: 93,000
Frequency: 52
Reviews: 4/year
Does not buy serial rights.

Suburban News
795 Susquehanna Avenue
Franklin Lakes NJ 07417
201-891-6400
Category: 99
Circulation: 95,000
Frequency: 52

Hacketstown Forum
P O Box 500
Hacketstown NJ 07840
201-852-1212
Category: 99
Circulation: 73,000
Frequency: 52

Hillside Citizen
1 Evans Terminal
Hillside NJ 07205
201-352-0800
Category: 99
Circulation: 60,000
Frequency: 52

Criterion News Advertiser
P O Box 768
Metuchen NJ 08840
201-548-8300
Category: 99
Circulation: 42,000
Frequency: 52

Middletown Advisor
915 Highway 35
Middletown NJ 07748
201-671-5300
Category: 99
Circulation: 80,000
Frequency: 52

Essex Journal
Worral Publications
P O Box 849
Orange NJ 07051
201-767-4800
Category: 99
Circulation: 45,000
Frequency: 52

Bergen News
Editor
P O Box 616
Palisades Park NJ 07650
201-947-5000
Category: 99
Circulation: 55,000
Frequency: 52

Atom Tabloid
P O Box 1061
Rahway NJ 07065
201-574-1200
Category: 99
Circulation: 65,000
Frequency: 52

South Bergenite
Patricia White, Editor
39 Meadow Road
Rutherford NJ 07070
201-933-2700
Category: 99
Circulation: 36,000
Frequency: 52

Ship Bottom Beachcomer
P O Box 119
Ships Bottom NJ 08008
609-494-5444
Category: 99
Circulation: 45,000
Frequency: 52

Toms River Reporter
P O Box 908
Toms River NJ 08753
201-270-1300
Category: 99
Circulation: 82,000
Frequency: 52

Suburban Life
Editor
1661 Route 23
Wayne NJ 07470
201-696-3000
Category: 99
Circulation: 62,000
Frequency: 52

Aquarian
P O Box 716
West Caldwell NJ 07007
201-575-3310
Category: 99
Circulation: 150,000
Frequency: 52

Suburban News
P O Box 2309
Westfield NJ 07091
201-232-3800
Category: 99
Circulation: 102,000
Frequency: 52

NEW YORK

Babylon Beacon
Editor
P O Box L
Babylon NY 11702
516-587-5612
Category: 99
Circulation: 30,000
Frequency: 52

Brooklyn Paper Publications
Ann V Bollinger, Editor
26 Court Street
Brooklyn NY 11242
718-834-9161
Category: 99
Circulation: 46,000
Frequency: 52
Reviews: 25/year
Buys 1st and 2nd serial rights.

Brooklyn Times
8723 Third Avenue
Brooklyn NY 11209
718-238-6600
Category: 99
Circulation: 30,000
Frequency: 52

Jewish Press
Yehuda Schwartz, Editor
338 Third Avenue
Brooklyn NY 11215
718-858-3300
Category: 63(Jewish)-99
Circulation: 210,000
Frequency: 52

Phoenix Newspaper
Michael A Armstrong, Book Editor
395 Atlantic Avenue
Brooklyn NY 11217
718-643-1400
Category: 99
Circulation: 15,000
Frequency: 52
Reviews: 30-40/year
Does not buy serial rights.

Prospect Press
Mike Stein, Editor-in-Chief
Susan Fleminger, Arts Editor
529 Carroll Street
Brooklyn NY 11215
718-788-4111
Category: 11-33-99
Circulation: 34,000
Frequency: 26
Reviews: 6-10/year
Does not buy serial rights.

Queens Tribune
Editor
4625 Kissina Boulevard
Flushing NY 11355
718-359-7777
Category: 99
Circulation: 75,000
Frequency: 52

Trader Newspaper
Editor
275 Long Beach Road
Island Park NY 11558
516-431-8781
Category: 99
Circulation: 85,000
Frequency: 52

South Bay's Papers
150 W Hoffman Avenue
Lindenhurst NY 11757
516-226-2636
Category: 99
Circulation: 55,000
Frequency: 52

Long Island Journal
Editor
P O Box 697
Long Beach NY 11561
516-889-1822
Category: 99
Circulation: 65,000
Frequency: 52

Manhattan East
Editor
2973 Bond Drive
Merrick NY 11566
516-546-6633
Category: 99
Circulation: 60,000
Frequency: 52

Action Newspaper
David O'briab, Book Editor
M T Mehdi, Editor
American-Arab Relations Committee
P O Box 416
New York NY 10017
212-972-0460
Category: 97(news)-98(Arab)-99
Circulation: 15,000
Frequency: 52

Downtown Manhattan
Paulett Shapiro, Editor
496 La Guardia Place #240
New York NY 10012
212-219-8629
Category: 25-27-29-39-43-75-99
Circulation: 50,000
Frequency: 52
Reviews: 1-2/issue
Does not buy serial rights.

Herald Newspaper Group
Suzanne Jobes, Book Editor
William Vanderdam, Arts Editor
Bonnie Bantavolglio, Business
Constance Preggors, Family Editor
Mary Vann, Feature Editor
Richard Bettis, Food Editor
Michael Schoen, News Editor
David Alden, Science Editor
Harriet Freedman, Travel Editor
30 Irving Place
New York NY 10003-2303
212-777-6810
Category: 11-19-23-25-27-29-31
            33-35-39-43-57-67-69
            71-97(news)-99
Circulation: 110,000
Frequency: 52
Reviews: 4/issue
Does not buy serial rights.

Manhattan News/Pennysaver
Dotti Evans, Editor
106 Fulton Street
New York NY 10038
212-962-1715
Category: 99
Circulation: 100,000
Frequency: 52
Reviews: 1/issue
Does not buy serial rights.

New York Calendar
Gary Bouton, Editor
2067 Broadway
New York NY 10023
212-870-0901
Category: 11-33-75-99
Circulation: 65,000
Frequency: 52

NY Talk
1133 Broadway
New York NY 10010
212-206-1661
Category: 99
Circulation: 55,000
Frequency: 52

Reform Judaism
Steven Schnur, Editor
838 Fifth Avenue
New York NY 10021
212-249-1000
Category: 63(Jewish)-99
Circulation: 276,000
Frequency: 52
Reviews: 2/issue

Village Voice
David Schneiderman, Editor
842 Broadway
New York NY 10003
212-475-3300
Category: 75-77-83-95-99
Circulation: 165,000
Frequency: 52
Reviews: many

Voice Literary Supplement
M Mark, Editor
The Village Voice
842 Broadway
New York NY 10003
212-475-3300
Category: 47-75-77-83-95-99
Circulation: 165,000
Frequency: 12
Reviews: many

Yankee Trader
Editor
1110 Hallock Avenue
P O Box N
Point Jefferson NY 11776
516-331-3300
Category: 99
Circulation: 45,000
Frequency: 52

Riverhead Suffolk Life
Editor
P O Box 167
Riverhead NY 11901
516-369-0800
Category: 99
Circulation: 200,000
Frequency: 52

New Times
Editor
406 S Franklin Street
Syracuse NY 13202
315-422-7011
Category: 99
Circulation: 42,000
Frequency: 52

<u>OHIO</u>

Cincinnati Suburban Press
Editor
1329 Arlington Street
Cincinnati OH 45225
513-542-8833
Category: 99
Circulation: 32,000
Frequency: 52

Sun Newspapers
Editor
5510 Cloverleaf Parkway
Cleveland OH 44125
216-524-0830
Category: 99
Circulation: 38,000
Frequency: 52

<u>OREGON</u>

Portland Week
Editor
320 SW Stark Street
Portland OR 97204
503-243-2122
Category: 99
Circulation: 50,000
Frequency: 52

Willamette Week
Ronald Buel, Editor
320 SW Stark Street
Portland OR 97204
503-243-2122
Category: 99
Circulation: 20,000
Frequency: 52

<u>PENNSYLVANIA</u>

King of Prussia Today's Post
Montgomery Publishing
P O Box 188
Fort Washington PA 19034
215-337-1700
Category: 99
Circulation:
Frequency: 52

Media Town Talk
Editor
P O Box 110
Media PA 19063
215-566-6755
Category: 99
Circulation: 50,000
Frequency: 52

Philadelphia Northeast Times
Editor
8033 Frankford Avenue
Philadelphia PA 19120
215-332-3300
Category: 99
Circulation: 117,000
Frequency: 52

West Oak Lane Leader
Editor
6220 Ridge Avenue
Philadelphia PA 19128
215-483-7300
Category: 99
Circulation: 30,000
Frequency: 52

Pittsburgh Green Sheet
Editor
404 North Avenue
Pittsburgh PA 15209
412-821-4100
Category: 99
Circulation: 90,000
Frequency: 52

Grit
Editor
208 W Third Street
Williamsport PA 17701
717-326-1771
Category: 99
Circulation: 625,000
Frequency: 52

<u>TEXAS</u>

Pleasanton Express
Michelle Pfeil, Book Editor
1301 W Ben White #208
Austin TX 78704
Category: 99
Circulation: 6000
Frequency: 52

Houston Community Papers
Editor
P O Box 280
Channelview TX 77530
713-452-0530
Category: 99
Frequency: 52
Reviews: some

Pasadena Citizen
Reg Noble, Editor
P O Box 6192
Pasadena TX 77506
713-477-0221
Category: 99
Circulation: 8500
Frequency: 99

Universal City Herald News
Editor
P O Box 2789
Universal City TX 78148
512-658-7424
Category: 99
Circulation: 38,000
Frequency: 52

<u>VIRGINIA</u>

USA Weekend
Ron Schoolmeester, Book Editor
John C Quinn, Editor-In-Chief
Marcia Bullard, Managing Editor
1000 Wilson Boulevard
Arlington VA 22209
(P O Box 500
Washington DC 20044)
703-276-3400
Category: 99
Circulation: 22,000,000
Frequency: 52
Buys 1st and 2nd serial rights.

<u>WASHINGTON</u>

Seattle Herald
Editor
3500 SW Alaska Street
Seattle WA 98126
206-932-0300
Category: 99
Circulation: 32,000
Frequency: 52

The Weekly
Rebecca Boren, Senior Editor
Sasquatch Publishing Company
1931 Second Avenue
Seattle WA 98101
206-441-5555
Category: 61(Seattle,WA)-99
Circulation: 31,500
Frequency: 99

<u>GREAT BRITAIN</u>

Times Literary Supplement
Alan Hollinghurst, Deputy Editor
Priory House, St John's Lane
London EC1M 4BX England
01-253-3000
Category: 99
Frequency: 52
Reviews: 50/issue

Magazine Editors and Book Reviewers

A+ Magazine
Maggie Canon, Editor-in-Chief
11 Davis Drive
Belmont CA 94002
415-598-2290
Category: 23(Apple specific)
Issues per year: 12

AB Bookman's Weekly
Jacob L Chernofsky, Editor
P O Box AB
Clifton NJ 07015
201-772-0020
Category: 99(reprints)
Circulation: 8000
Issues per year: 52
Reviews: 4-5/issue
Does not buy serial rights.

ABA Banking Journal
William Streeter, Editor
345 Hudson Street
New York NY 10014
212-620-7200
Category: 19(banking)

Aboriginal SF
Charles Ryan, Editor
P O Box 2449
Woburn MA 01888-0849
Category: 86
Circulation: 24,000
Issues per year: 6

Abraxas
Warren Woessner, Editor
2322 Rugby Row
Madison WI 53705
Category: 83-95

Academe
Jonathan Knight, Editor
Bulletin of the AAUP
1012 14th Street NW
Washington DC 20005
202-737-5900
Category: 31
Circulation: 55,000
Issues per year: 6
Reviews: 3/issue
Does not buy serial rights.

Access Newsletter
Association of Black
  Women Entrepreneurs
P O Box 1375
Detroit MI 48231
Category: 19(small business)
             49-73

Access: Apple
Jeffrey Tarter, Editor
306 Dartmouth Street
Boston MA 02116

617-267-7100
Category: 19-23(Apple specific)
Issues per year: 12

Across the Board
Howard Muson, Editor
Hal Goodman, Books Editor
Nancy Boas, Feature Editor
845 Third Avenue
New York NY 10022
212-759-0900
Category: 11-19-23-33-67-99
Circulation: 35,000
Issues per year: 12
Reviews: 1-3/issue
Buys only 2nd serial rights.

Administrative Digest
Elizabeth Schwartz, Editor
1450 Don Mills Road
Don Mills M3B 2X7 ON Canada
416-445-6641
Category: 19(administration)

Adventure Road
Deborah Thompson, Editor
641 Lexington Avenue
New York NY 10022
Category: 71

Advertising Age
Fred Danzig, Editor
740 Rush Street
Chicago IL 60611
312-649-5200
Category: 19(advertising)
Circulation: 85,000
Issues per year: 26

Advocate
Advocates of Literature
3331 Windermere Street
Columbus GA 31904
Category: 21-31-76-89
Issues per year: 3
Reviews: many
Does not buy serial rights.

Adweek
Thomas Forbes, Editor
820 2nd Avenue
New York NY 10017
212-661-8080
Category: 19(advertising)
Circulation: 53,700
Issues per year: 52

Adweek Midwest
Mary Connors, Editor
435 N Michigan Avenue #1333
Chicago IL 60611
312-467-6500
Category: 19(advertising)
Issues per year: 52

Adweek West
Jon Berry, Bureau Manager
440 Pacific
San Francisco CA 94133
415-788-1924
Category: 19(advertising)
Issues per year: 52

Adweek West
Jack Feuer, Editor
514 Shatto Place
Los Angeles CA 90020
213-384-7100
Category: 19(advertising)
Issues per year: 52

Aerospace America
John Newbauer, Editor
1633 Broadway
New York NY 10019
212-581-1004
Category: 69(airplanes)

Afro-Hispanic Review
Afro-Hispanic Institute
3306 Ross Place NW
Washington DC 20008
Category: 49-78
Issues per year: 3

After Dark
Lee Swanson, Editor
P O Box 1693
Burbank CA 91507
212-674-5200
Category: 11-33

Afterimage
Nathan Lyons, Editor
Visual Studies Workshop
31 Prince Street
Rochester NY 14608
716-442-8676
Category: 11(photography)
Circulation: 4,200

Agricultural Marketing
Marsha Mauzey, Editor
5520-G Touhy Avenue
Skokie IL 60077
Category: 19(marketing,
            agriculture)

Air and Space
George Larsen, Editor
National Air and Space Museum
Smithsonian Institution
Washington DC 20560
Category: 23-55-67-99(flying)
Issues per year: 6

Air Cal
Steve Winston, Editor
12955 Biscayne Boulevard #202

North Miami FL 33181
305-893-1520
Category: 71

Air Force Magazine
John Correll, Editor
1501 Lee Highway
Arlington VA 22209
703-247-5800
Category: 55(military)

Air Force Times
Bruce Callander, Editor
475 School Street SW
Washington DC 20024
202-554-7113
Category: 55(military)

Airline Executive
Communication Channels
6255 Barfield Road
Atlanta GA 30328
404-256-9800
Category: 19-71
Circulation: 46,000
Issues per year: 12

Alaska Airlines
1932 First Avenue #503
Seattle WA 98101
206-441-5871
Category: 61(AK)-71
Issues per year: 12

Albuquerque Living
P O Box 3767
Albuquerque NM 87190
505-242-5985
Category: 11-33-39-55
          61(Albuquerque NM)
Circulation: 16,000
Issues per year: 12

Alliance Quarterly
Wendy Lazar, Editor
National Alliance of Homebased
Businesswomen -- P O Box 95
Norwood NJ 07648
Category: 19(small business)-73
Issues per year: 4

Alternative Media
Antonio Huneeus, Editor
P O Box 1347
Ansonia Station
New York NY 10023
Category: 13

AMA Journal
George D Lundberg, Editor
535 N Dearborn Street
Chicago IL 60610
312-751-6000
Category: 39

Amazing Stories
Robert Coulson, Book Reviewer
John Gregory Betancourt, Reviewer

TSR Inc, P O Box 110
201 Sheridan Springs Road
Lake Geneva WI 53147
Category: 86
Circulation: 40,000
Issues per year: 6
Reviews: 12/issue
Buys only 1st serial rights.

American Agent & Broker
David Baetz, Editor
408 Olive Street
St Louis MO 63102
314-421-5445
Category: 19(insurance)

American Artist
M Stephen Doherty, Editor
1515 Broadway
New York NY 10036
212-764-7300
Category: 11-29
Circulation: 167,000
Issues per year: 12

American Baby
Judith Nolte, Editor
575 Lexington Avenue
New York NY 10022
212-752-0775
Category: 21-31-35-76-79
Circulation: 1,000,000
Issues per year: 12

American Bar Association Journal
Linda Castle, Books Editor
750 N Lakeshore Drive
Chicago IL 60611
312-988-5000
Category: 19-55(law)

American Book Review
Rochelle Ratner, Editor
Box 188, Cooper Union Station
New York NY 10003
212-749-1251
Category: 47-75-95
Issues per year: 6
Reviews: 25-50/issue

American Bookseller
Ginger Curwen, Editor
American Booksellers Association
122 East 42nd Street #1410
New York NY 10168
212-867-9060
Category: 99
Circulation: 8,000
Issues per year: 12

American Business
Joe Queenan, Editor
1775 Broadway
New York NY 10019
212-581-2000
Category: 19
Circulation: 228,000
Issues per year: 12

American Chiropractor
3401 Lake Avenue
Fort Wayne IN 46805
Category: 39(chiropractry)

American City & County
Ken Anderberg, Editor
6255 Barfield Road
Atlanta GA 30328
404-256-9800
Category: 55(city government)
Circulation: 56,000

American Collectors Journal
Dennis Sullivan, Editor
P O Box 707
Kewanee IL 61443
Category: 29(collectibles)

American Craft
Lois Moran, Editor
American Craft Council
401 Park Avenue South
New York NY 10016
212-696-0710
Category: 29
Circulation: 44,000
Issues per year: 6

American Demographics
Bickley Townsend, Books Editor
Cheryl Russell, Editor
127 W State Street
Ithaca NY 14850
607-273-6343
Category: 19(marketing)-99
Circulation: 9,000
Issues per year: 12
Reviews: 2/issue

American Export Market
Joel S Nadel, Editor
10076 Boca Entrada Boulevard
P O Box 3007
Boca Raton FL 33431-0907
Category: 19(marketing, exports)
Issues per year: 12

American Film
Ann Martin, Editor
MD Publications
3 East 54th Street, 9th Floor
New York NY 10022
212-355-5432
Category: 11-33
Issues per year: 12
Buys 1st and 2nd serial rights.

American Health
George Harris, Editor
80 Fifth Avenue #302
New York NY 10011
212-242-2460
Category: 39

American Hockey
U S Amateur Hockey Association
2997 Broadmoor Valley Road

Colorado Springs CO 80906
303-576-4990
Category: 69(hockey)
Issues per year: 12

American Import/Export
Toni Lamber, Editor
North American Publishing
401 N Broad Street
Philadelphia PA 19108
215-238-5300
Category: 19(marketing, exports)
Circulation: 10,600
Issues per year: 12

American Industry
Jack S Panes, Editor
21 Russell Woods Road
Great Neck NY 11021
516-487-0990
Category: 19(industry)
Circulation: 25,000
Issues per year: 12

American Journal of Nursing
Patricia Brider, Editor
Pricila Scherer, Computer Editor
Jeanne D Fonseca, Features Editor
Mary Mallison, Science Editor
Janet Dyer, Travel Editor
555 West 57th Street
New York NY 10019
212-582-8820
Category: 19-23-35-39(nursing)
          67-71-97(news)
Circulation: 300,000
Issues per year: 12
Reviews: 50/year
Does not buy serial rights.

**American Journal of Occupational
Therapy**
Elaine Viseltear, Editor
1383 Piccard Drive
Rockville MD 20850
301-948-9626
Category: 39
Circulation: 43,000
Issues per year: 12
Reviews: 2-6/year

American Legion Magazine
Daniel Wheeler, Editor
700 N Pennsylvania Street
P O Box 1055
Indianapolis IN 46206
Category: 99
Issues per year: 12

American Libraries
Gordon Flagg, Editor
The Source Department
50 E Huron Street
Chicago IL 60611
312-944-2117
Category: 59(bibliographies)
Issues per year: 11
Reviews: some

American Literature
Edwin H Cady, Editor
Duke University
P O Box 6697 College Station
Durham NC 27708
Category: 47-65-75-95

American Medical News
Dick Walt, Editor
535 N Dearborn
Chicago IL 60610
312-751-6633
Category: 39

American Notes and Queries
Lawrence Thompson, Books Editor
Erasmus Press
225 Culpepper
Lexington KY 40502
Category: 41-47-79
Circulation: 1,000
Issues per year: 10

American Photographer
Sean Callahan, Editor
1515 Broadway
New York NY 10036
212-719-6265
Category: 11(photography)
Circulation: 285,000
Issues per year: 12

American Poetry Review
Stephen Berg, Book Editor
1616 Walnut Street #405
Philadelphia PA 19103
Category: 47-95
Circulation: 24,000
Issues per year: 6

American Printer
E G Berglund, Editor
Mac-Lean-Hunter Publishing
300 W Adams Street
Chicago IL 60606
312-726-2802
Category: 19(printing)
Circulation: 88,000
Issues per year: 12

American Scientist
Michelle Press, Editor
345 Whitney Avenue
New Haven CT 06511
203-624-2566
Category: 67
Issues per year: 12

American Spectator
R Emmett Tyrrell, Jr, Editor
1101 N Highland Street
P O Box 10448
Arlington VA 22210
703-243-3733
Category: 41-55(conservative)-99
Issues per year: 12
Reviews: 8-10/issue
Buys 1st and 2nd serial rights.

American Teacher
Roger Newell, Editor
555 New Jersey NW
Washington DC 20001
202-879-4400
Category: 31

American West
Mae Reid-Bills, Managing Editor
Attn: Western Books in Brief
3033 N Campbell Avenue
Tucson AZ 85719
602-881-5850
Category: 61(western America)
Circulation: 125,000
Issues per year: 6
Reviews: 15-20/issue

Americana
Michael Durham, Editor
29 West 38th Street
New York NY 10018
212-398-1550
Category: 27-29(antiques)
Circulation: 320,000

Amtrak Express
Christopher Podgus, Editor
P O Box O
140 E Main Street
Huntington NY 11743
516-427-3345
Category: 71

Analog
Tom Easton, Book Reviewer
The Reference Library
380 Lexington Avenue
New York NY 10017
212-557-9100
Category: 86
Circulation: 110,000
Issues per year: 13
Reviews: 12/issue
Buys only 1st serial rights.

Animal Husbandry Journal
George Frangoulis, Editor
Farmstead Publications
P O Box 111
Freedom ME 04941
207-382-6200
Category: 15
Issues per year: 6

Antiques & Collecting Hobbies
Frances L Graham, Editor
1006 S Michigan Avenue
Chicago IL 60605
312-939-6747
Category: 29(antiques)
Circulation: 40,000
Issues per year: 12

Antiques Dealer
Nancy Adams, Editor
1115 Clifton Avenue
P O Box 2147

Clifton NJ 07013
201-779-1600
Category: 29(antiques)
Circulation: 7,000
Issues per year: 12

Apothecary
Janet Goodman, Editor
P O Box AP
Los Altos CA 94023
Category: 19
Issues per year: 6

Architectural Digest
Debra Bond, Books Editor
5900 Wilshire Boulevard
Los Angeles CA 90036
213-937-4740
Category: 11(architecture)-43
Issues per year: 12

Architectural Record
Mildred Schmertz, Editor
1221 Avenue of the Americas
New York NY 10020
212-997-2593
Category: 11-19(architecture
          building)

Architectural Technology
Mitchell Rouda, Editor
1735 New York Avenue
Washington DC 20006
202-626-7590
Category: 11-19(architecture
          building)

Architecture
Michael Hanley, Editor
Architecture Institute
1735 New York Avenue NW
Washington DC 20006
202-626-7300
Category: 11-19(architecture
          building)

Arizona Highways
Merril Windsor, Editor
2039 W Lewis
Phoenix AZ 85009
602-258-6641
Category: 61(AZ)-71

Army Magazine
James Binder, Editor
2425 Wilson Boulevard
Arlington VA 22201
703-841-4300
Category: 55(military)

Art Forum
Ingrid Sischy, Editor
205 Mulberry Street
New York NY 10012
212-925-4000
Category: 11
Circulation: 25,000
Issues per year: 12

Art in America
Elizabeth C Baker, Editor
850 Third Avenue
New York NY 10222
212-593-2100
Category: 11
Circulation: 48,000
Issues per year: 12

Art Material Trade News
Communication Channels
6255 Barfield Road
Atlanta GA 30328
404-256-9800
Category: 11-19(retail marketing)
Circulation: 11,500

Art News
Milton Esterow, Editor
5 West 37th Street
New York NY 10018
212-398-1690
Category: 11
Circulation: 74,000
Issues per year: 12

Art Product News
Nancy Aldrich-Ruenzel, Editor
One Plaza Place NE
P O Box 117
St Petersburg FL 33731
813-821-6064
Category: 11
Circulation: 47,000
Issues per year: 12

Artist's Magazine
Michael Ward, Editor
9933 Alliance Road
Cincinnati OH 45242
513-984-0717
Category: 11
Circulation: 160,000
Issues per year: 12

Arts & Activities
591 Camino De La Reina #200
San Diego CA 92108
714-297-8522
Category: 11-29-31
Circulation: 24,000

Arts & Crafts Newsletter
50 West Oak Hill Road
Williston VT 05495
Category: 11-29
Issues per year: 4

Arts Magazine
23 East 26th Street
New York NY 10010
212-685-8500
Category: 11
Circulation: 29,000
Issues per year: 12

ASHA Magazine
10801 Rockville Pike

Rockville MD 20852
301-897-5700
Category: 39

Asian Advertising & Marketing
Susan P Girdwood, Editor
Travel Publishing Ltd
1801 World Trade Centre
Causeway Bay Hong Kong
5-7903067
Category: 19(marketing)-99(Asia)
Circulation: 10,000
Issues per year: 12

Asiaweek
16th Floor, Caxton House
1 Duddell Street
Central Hong Kong
5-214555-8
Category: 19(marketing)-99(Asia)
Issues per year: 52

Association of Research Library
Editor, Newsletter
1527 New Hampshire Avenue NW
Washington DC 20036
202-232-8656
Category: 59-99
Issues per year:

Association Trends
Frank Martineau, Editor
4948 St Elmo Avenue
Bethesda MD 20814
301-652-8666
Category: 19(associations)
Issues per year: 6

Atlanta
Neil Shister, Editor
6255 Barfield Road
Atlanta GA 30328
404-256-9800
Category: 61(Atlanta GA)-99
Circulation: 35,000
Issues per year: 12

Atlanta Business Chronicle
Dick Gentry, Editor
1740 Century Circle
Atlanta GA 30345
404-325-2442
Category: 19-61(GA)
Circulation: 16,900
Issues per year: 12

Atlanta Women's News
Rebecca Nash King, Editor
2810 New Spring Road #106
Atlanta GA 30339
404-434-5966
Category: 61(Atlanta GA)-73
Circulation: 40,000
Issues per year: 12

The Atlantic
Phoebe-Lou Adams, Editor
8 Arlington Street

Boston MA 02116
617-536-9500
Category: 75-95-99
Issues per year: 12
Buys 1st and 2nd serial rights.

Austin Magazine
P O Box 4368
Austin TX 78765
512-339-9955
Category: 19-61(Austin TX)-99
Issues per year: 12

Autonomy
Helen Borel, Book Columnist
200 West 79th Street #9L
New York NY 10024
212-362-7119
Category: 47-75-95

Autumn Leaves
Natl. Fed. of Grandmother Clubs
203 N Wabash Avenue
Chicago IL 60601
Category: 35-99

Avenue
Dan Flores, Editor
145 East 57th Street
New York NY 10022
212-758-9517
Category: 61(New York NY)

Aviation Week & Space Technology
Donald Fink, Editor
1221 Avenue of the Americas
New York NY 10020
212-512-4117
Category: 23-67(airplanes)
Issues per year: 52

AVMA Journal
Dr A Freeman, Editor
930 N Meacham Road
Schaumburg IL 60196
312-885-8070
Category: 39(veterinarian)

Baby Care
Evelyn Polsiadlo, Editor
685 Third Avenue
New York NY 10017
212-878-8700
Category: 21-31-35-76-79
Circulation: 800,000
Issues per year: 4

Baby Talk
185 Madison Avenue
New York NY 10016
212-679-4400
Category: 21-31-35-76-79
Circulation: 985,000
Issues per year: 12

Baltimore Business Journal
Jack Kramer, Editor
811 S Broadway

Baltimore MD 21231
301-268-5000
Category: 19-61(Baltimore MD)
Circulation: 12,500
Issues per year: 52

Baltimore Magazine
J. Stanley Heuisler, Editor
26 S Calvert Street
Baltimore MD 21202
301-752-7375
Category: 61(Baltimore MD)
Issues per year: 12

Bank Admininstration
R. Gerald Fox, Editor
60 Gould Center, East Tower
Rolling Meadows IL 60008
312-228-6200
Category: 19(banking)

Bank Marketing
Charles E Bartling, Editor
309 W Washington Street
Chicago IL 60606
Issues per year: 12

Bank Systems & Equipment
Joan Hyman, Editor
1515 Broadway
New York NY 10036
212-869-1300
Category: 19(banking)

Barron's
Alan Abelson, Editor
Richard Rescigno, News Editor
200 Liberty Street
New York NY 10281
Category: 19-97(news)
Circulation: 300,300
Issues per year: 52

Baseball History
Peter Levine, Editor
Meckler Publishing
11 Ferry Lane West
Westport CT 06880
203-226-6967
Category: 41-69(baseball)

Baseball Hobby News
Vivian and Frank Barning, Editors
4540 Kearney Villa Road #215
San Diego CA 92123
Category: 29-69(baseball)

Baton Rouge Magazine
5555 Hilton Avenue #203
Baton Rouge LA 70808
504-928-2525
Category: 61(Baton Rouge LA)

Bay Area Business
Dave Phinney, Editor
1410 62nd Street
Emeryville CA 94608
415-547-1963

Category: 19-61(San Francisco)
Circulation: 45,000
Issues per year: 12
Reviews: 2/issue
Does not buy serial rights.

BC Business
B Irving, Editor
200 - 550 Burrard Street
Vancouver V6C 2J6 BC Canada
604-669-1721
Category: 19-61(British Columbia)
Circulation: 26,000
Issues per year: 12
Reviews: 0
Buys 1st and 2nd serial rights.

Behind Small Business
Dona M Risdall, Editor
P O Box 27147
Minneapolis MN 55431
Category: 19(small business)
Issues per year: 12

Belles Lettres
Janet P Mullaney, Editor
P O Box 987
Arlington VA 22216
301-294-0278
Category: 17-47-73-73-95
Circulation: 10,000

Better Homes & Gardens
David Jordan, Editor
Joan McCloskey, Building Editor
Jean Lemmon, Crafts Editor
Shirley van Zante, Design Editor
Paul Krantz, Health/Education
Barbara Humeston, Pets/Travel
Margaret Daly, Features Editor
Nancy Byal, Food Editor
Douglas Jimerson, Garden Editor
1716 Locust Street
Des Moines IA 50336
515-284-3000
Category: 11(design)-15
        19(money)-23-27-29
        31-35-39-43-71-99
Issues per year: 12

Better Investing
Thomas O'Hara, Editor
1515 East 11 Mile Road
P O Box 220
Royal Oak MI 48068
313-543-0612
Category: 19(investment)

Beverly Hills 213
Susan Warner, Editor
9570 Wilshire Boulevard
Beverly Hills CA 90212
213-275-8850
Category: 61(Beverly Hills CA)

Bicycling
Rodale Press
33 E Minor Street

Emmaus PA 18049
215-967-5171
Category: 69-71
Issues per year: 12

Bird Watchers Digest
Mary Beacom Bowers, Editor
Attn: BWD Book Notes
P O Box 110
Marietta OH 45750
614-373-5285
Category: 15(birds)-29
       69(bird watching)
Circulation: 56,000
Issues per year: 6
Reviews: 15/issue
Buys only 2nd serial rights.

Black Careers
Emory Washington, Editor
P O Box 8214
Philadelphia PA 19101
215-387-1600
Category: 19(careers)-49

Black Enterprise
130 Fifth Avenue
New York NY 10011
212-242-8000
Category: 19

Black Scholar
P O Box 7106
San Francisco CA 94120
Category: 13-49-65-78

Bloomsbury Review
Tom Auer, Editor
Attn: Bibliofile
2933 Wyandot Street
Denver CO 80211
303-455-0593
Category: 99(small press)
Issues per year: 12

Boardroom Reports
Sam Edelston, Editor
500 Fifth Avenue
New York NY 10110
212-354-0005
Category: 19
Circulation: 180,000
Issues per year: 26

Book and Magazine Production
Virgil Busto, Editor
Innes Publishing Company
P O Box 368
Northbrook IL 60062
Category: 19(printing)

Book Forum
Marilyn Wood, Editor
The Hudson River Press
38 East 76th Street
New York NY 10021
212-861-8328
Category: 99

Book Review Digest
H W Wilson Company
950 University Avenue
Bronx NY 10452
Category: 99
Issues per year: 12

BookDealers World
Al Galasso, Editor
American Bookdealers Exchange
P O Box 2525
La Mesa CA 92041
Category: 99(small press)
Issues per year: 12

Booklist
Sally Estes, Editor
  Books for Young Adults
Barbara Elleman, Editor
  Children's Books
Bill Ott, Editor, Adult Books
American Library Association
50 East Huron Street
Chicago IL 60611
312-944-6780
Category: 21-31-76-89-99
Issues per year: 22
Reviews: many
Does not buy serial rights.

BookLover
Elizabeth Timmerman, Editor
Reading Rage Publishing
151 West 75th Street
New York NY 10023
212-362-8096
Category: 99
Circulation: 50,000
Issues per year: 6

Books and Records Reviews
M. G. Paregian, Review Editor
733 Childs Avenue
Drexel Hill PA 19026
Category: 11-99

Bookstore Journal
Dana Lowe, Editor
Michael Whiteman, Books Editor
2620 Venetucci Boulevard #200
Colorado Springs CO 80901
303-576-7880
Category: 63-99
Circulation: 8,000
Issues per year: 12

Boston Business Journal
393 D Street
Boston MA 02210
617-268-9880
Category: 19-61(Boston MA)

Boston Magazine
Ken Hartnett, Editor
300 Massachusetts Avenue
Boston MA 02116
617-357-4000
Category: 61(Boston MA)

Boston Phoenix
Kit Rachlis, Books Editor
100 Massachusetts Avenue
Boston MA 02115
617-536-5390
Category: 61(Boston MA)-99

Boy's Life
Bill Butterworth, Arts Editor
Jon C Halter, Books Editor
Scott Stuckey, Feature Editor
Boy Scouts of America
1325 Walnut Hill Lane
Irving TX 75038-3096
214-580-2366
Category: 11-23-29-33-35-43-51
      67-69-71
Circulation: 1,500,000
Issues per year: 12
Reviews: 5-10/issue
Buys 1st and 2nd serial rights.

Broker World
Sharon Chace, Assoc. Editor
2310 West 75th Street #201A
Prairie Village KS 66208
913-432-3880
Category: 19(insurance)
Issues per year: 12
Reviews: few

Buffalo Spree
Johanna Shotell, Editor
4511 Harlem Road
P O Box 38
Buffalo NY 14226
716-839-3405
Category: 61(Buffalo NY)

Building Design & Construction
1350 E Touhy Ave
Des Plaines IL 60017
312-635-8800
Category: 11-19(architecture)

Building Design Journal
6255 Barfield Road
Atlanta GA 30328
404-256-9800
Category: 11(architecture)
      19(building)
Circulation: 50,000
Issues per year: 12

Bull & Bear Financial Newspaper
David Robinson, Editor
Valerie Waters, Computer Editor
P O Box 4267
Winter Park FL 32793
305-677-7872
Category: 19-23
Circulation: 55,000
Issues per year: 12
Buys 1st and 2nd serial rights.

Bulletin of Science and Technology for the Handicapped
Sue Forman, Editor

1515 Massachusetts Avenue NW
Washington DC 20005
202-467-4400
Category: 39-67

Bulletin on Bibliography
Dean H Keller, Editor
Special Collections, Library
Kent State University
Kent OH 44242
Category: 59(bibliographies)

Business & Health
Jane Stein, Editor
229 1/2 Pennsylvania Avenue SE
Washington DC 20003
202-547-6644
Category: 19-39

Business & Society Review
Bruce Slater, Editor
870 Seventh Avenue
New York NY 10019
212-977-7436
Category: 19-55
Circulation: 3,000
Issues per year: 4
Reviews: 30-40/year
Does not buy serial rights.

Business Advocate
Michael Lewis, Editor
1615 H Street NW
Washington DC 20006
202-463-5663
Category: 19-55

Business Age
Rosanne M Bane, Editor
P O Box 11597
Shorewood WI 53211
414-332-7507
Category: 19-39
Circulation: 100,000
Issues per year: 6
Reviews: 3-4/issue

Business and Industry
James Snyder, Editor
1200 - 35th Street #300W
Des Moines IA 50265
515-225-2545
Category: 19
Issues per year: 6

Business Atlanta
Lu Ann Nelson, Editor
6255 Barfield Road
Atlanta GA 30328
404-256-9800
Category: 19-61(GA)
Circulation: 18,000
Issues per year: 12

Business Book Review
Jagdish Sheth, Editor
Corporate Support Systems
507 W Springfield

Urbana IL 61801
Category: 19
Issues per year: 6

Business Communications Review
Fred Knight, Editor
950 York Road
Hinsdale IL 60521
312-986-1432
Category: 19(communications)

Business Computing
Editor, New Products
119 Russell Street
Littleton MA 01460
Category: 19-23

Business Digest
Jerry Helzner, Editor
Tom Werner, Computer Editor
Mike Hughes, Feature Editor
P O Box 324
Bala Cynwyd PA 19004
215-477-8620
Category: 19-23-43-61(PA, NJ)
         69-71
Circulation: 80,000
Issues per year: 12
Reviews: 2/issue
Does not buy serial rights.

Business Direct to Business
Renee Rewiski, Editor
117 Fort Lee Road
Leonia NJ 07605
201-461-5503
Category: 19(marketing)-23
Circulation: 45,000
Issues per year: 12
Reviews: 6/year
Does not buy serial rights.

Business Education Forum
Dr O J Byrnside Jr, Director
1914 Association Drive
Reston VA 22091
Category: 19-31
Circulation: 22,000

Business Education World
Maria Mangieri, Editor
1221 Avenue of the Americas
New York NY 10020
212-997-2057
Category: 19-31

Business First Buffalo
Monica Roland, Magazine Editor
361 Delaware Avenue #200
Buffalo NY 14202
716-852-6200
Category: 19-61(Buffalo NY)
Circulation: 14,000
Issues per year: 52

Business Forms and Systems
Norman Adams, Editor
North American Publishing

401 N Broad Street
Philadelphia PA 19108
215-238-5300
Category: 19(office)

Business Insurance
James Burcke, Assistant Editor
740 N Rush Street
Chicago IL 60611
312-649-5398
Category: 19(insurance)
Issues per year: 12

Business Journal of New Jersey
Cathy Barry, Editor
CN - 2
Jamesburg NJ 08831
Category: 19-61(NJ)

Business Library Newsletter
Jonathan Pond, Editor
Investment Mgmt. Information
127 Mount Auburn Street
Cambridge MA 02138
617-876-9688
Category: 19
Circulation: 750
Issues per year: 6

Business Marketing
Bob Donath, Editor
740 Rush Street
Chicago IL 60611
312-649-5260
Category: 19(marketing)
Circulation: 34,000
Issues per year: 12

Business North Carolina
James Duff, Editor
212 S Tryon Street #1450
Charlotte NC 28281
704-372-9794
Category: 19-61(NC)

Business Opportunities Digest
Jim Straw, Editor
301 Plymouth Avenue NE
Dalton GA 30720
Category: 19(opportunities)
Issues per year: 12

Business Opportunities Journal
John R Brooker, Editor
Business Bookshelf
1021 Rosecrans
San Diego CA 92106
Category: 19(opportunities)
Issues per year: 12

Business Software
James E Fawcette, Editor
M & T Publishing
501 Galveston Drive
Redwood City CA 94063
415-366-3600
Category: 19-23
Issues per year: 12

Business Times
544 Tolland Street
East Hartford CT 06108
Category: 19

Business to Business
Byron De Arakal, Editor
3740 Campus Drive
Newport Beach CA 92660
714-852-9300
Category: 19(marketing)

Business Today
Alan Pardee, Editor
Found. for Student Communication
Aaron Burr Hall
Princeton NJ 08540
609-921-1111
Category: 19
Circulation: 200,000
Issues per year: 3

Business Travel
Editor
6 East 46th Street
New York NY 10017
Category: 19-71

Business Week
William Wolman, Editor
Morton Reicheck, Books Editor
Catherine Harris, Computer Editor
Paul Brown, Marketing Editor
Mark Vamos, Media Editor
Sarah Bartlett, Money/Banking
Ellyn Spragins, Real Estate
Emily T Smith, Science Editor
McGraw-Hill Building
1221 Avenue of the Americas
New York NY 10020
212-512-2000
Category: 19-23-67
Circulation: 775,000
Issues per year: 52
Reviews: 2/issue

Business Woman
Carole Holcomb, Editor
5755 Cohasset Way
P O Box 23276
San Jose CA 95193
408-226-3311
Category: 19-73

The Business Writer
Patrick Williams, Editor
Lawrence Ragan Company
407 S Dearborn Street
Chicago IL 60605
312-922-8245
Category: 11(writing)-19

BYTE
What's New Department
70 Main Street
Peterborough NH 03458
Category: 23
Issues per year: 12

Byways Magazine
11961 Tech Road
Silver Spring MD 20904
301-622-5100
Category: 35(retirement)-71
Circulation: 50,000R

CA Magazine
Nelson Luscombe, Editor
150 Bloor Street W
Toronto M5S 2Y2 ON Canada
416-962-1242
Category: 19

California Business
Michael Harris, Editor
4221 Wilshire Boulevard #400
Los Angeles CA 90010
213-653-9340
Category: 19-61(CA)

California Lawyer
Jonathan Maslow, Editor
555 Franklin Street
San Francisco CA 94102
415-561-8280
Category: 19-55(law)-61(CA)

California Magazine
Greil Marcus, Editor
Kenneth Turan, Books Editor
11601 Wilshire Boulevard #1800
Los Angeles CA 90025
213-479-6511
Category: 61(CA)-99

California Real Estate
Patricia McLean, Editor
525 S Virgil Avenue
Los Angeles CA 90020
213-739-8200
Category: 19(real estate)-61(CA)
Circulation: 105,000
Issues per year: 12
Reviews: none
Does not buy serial rights.

Call APPLE
Don Elman, Managing Editor
290 SW 43rd Street
Renton VA 98055
206-251-5222
Category: 23(Apple specific)
Issues per year: 12

Canadian Banker
Brian O'Brien, Editor
2 First Canadian Place
Toronto M5X 1E1 ON Canada
416-362-6092
Category: 19(banking)-61(CN)

Canadian Business
Charles Davies, Editor
70 The Esplanade
Toronto M5E 1R2 ON Canada
416-364-4266
Category: 19-61(CN)

Canadian Electronics Engineering
Peter Thorne, Editor
777 Bay Street
Toronto M5W 1A7 ON Canada
416-596-5729
Category: 19-23(electronics)-61(CN

Canadian Living
Judy Brandow, Editor
50 Holly Street
Toronto M4S 3B3 ON Canada
416-482-8600
Category: 61(CN)-99

Canadian Printer and Publisher
Jack Homer, Editor
MacLean-Hunter Publishing
481 University Avenue
Toronto M5W 1A7 ON Canada
416-596-5000
Category: 19(printing, publishing)
Circulation: 8,000
Issues per year: 12

Candlelighter
Shirley Caplin, Editor
Intl. Guild of Candle Artisans
9248 Brush Run
Columbia MD 21045
Category: 29(candles)
Issues per year: 12

Capital District Business Review
Richard Landers, Editor
76 Exchange
Albany NY 12205
518-458-7000
Category: 19-61(Albany NY)
Circulation: 12,500

Car Collector and Car Classics
Peterson, Donald R, Editor
Classic Publishing
8601 Dunwoody Place #144
Atlanta GA 30338
404-998-4603
Category: 43(automobiles)
Circulation: 70,000
Issues per year: 12
Reviews: 5-6/issue

Career Woman
Ann Kelly, Editor
Equal Opportunity Publications
44 Broadway
Greenlawn NY 11740
516-261-8917
Category: 19(career guidance)-73
Circulation: 10,500
Issues per year: 3
Buys only 2nd serial rights.

Careers & The Handicapped
Ann Kelly, Editor
Equal Opportunity Publications
44 Broadway
Greenlawn NY 11740
516-261-8917

Category: 19(career guidance)
          39(handicap)
Circulation: 5,000
Issues per year: 3
Buys only 2nd serial rights.

Catalog Age
Charles I Tanner, Editor
125 Elm Street
P O Box 4006
New Canaan CT 06840-4006
203-972-0761
Category: 19(marketing)
Issues per year: 12

Catholic Library World
Mary Mills, Adult Books
Sally Ann Thompson, Children
Julie Cunningham, Professional
Paul Chervenie, Religious Books
461 W Lancaster Avenue
Haverford PA 19041
215-649-5250
Category: 23-31-59-63(Catholic)
          76-89-99
Circulation: 3,000
Issues per year: 6

Cats Magazine
Linda J Walton, Editor
Attn: Cats Bookshelf--What's New
P O Box 37
Port Orange FL 32029
904-788-2770
Category: 14(cats)
Circulation: 115,000
Issues per year: 12
Reviews: 2/issue

CCLM News
Ken Duffy, Editor
CCLM
2 Park Avenue
New York NY 10016
212-481-5245
Category: 19(publishing)
Issues per year: 12

Center for Research Libraries
Susan Vankamen, Editor
Newsletter
5721 S Cottage Grove Avenue
Chicago IL 60637
312-955-4545
Category: 23-59-67
Circulation: 3,300

Ceramic Arts & Crafts
Bill Thompson, Editor
30595 West 8 Mile Road
Livonia MI 48152
313-477-6650
Category: 29(ceramic)
Circulation: 51,000

Ceramic Hobbyist
Joy Nelson, Editor
2175 Sheppard Avenue E. #110

Willowdale M2J1W8 ON Canada
Category: 29(ceramics)
Issues per year: 6

Ceramic Scope
Joyce Fiske, Publisher
5208 West Pico Boulevard
Los Angeles CA 90019
213-835-1121
Category: 29(ceramics)
Circulation: 7,800
Issues per year: 12

Ceramic Scope
Michael Scott, Editor
700 Orange Street
Wilmington DE 19801
Category: 29(ceramics)
Issues per year: 12

Ceramic World
Barbara Campbell, Editor
Daisy Publishing
429 Boren Avenue N
Seattle WA 98109
Category: 29(ceramics)
Circulation: 55,000
Issues per year: 12

Ceramics Monthly
William C Hunt, Editor
1609 Northwest Boulevard
Columbus OH 43212
Category: 29(ceramics)
Issues per year: 10

CFO
Julia Homer, Editor
268 Summer Street
Boston MA 02210
617-542-0660
Category: 19(financial)

Chain Store Age Executive
Stanley Slom, Editor
425 Park Avenue
New York NY 10022
212-371-9400
Category: 19(retail marketing)

Changing Times
Marjorie White, Editor
1729 H Street NW
Worth Getting Department
Washington DC 20006
202-887-6400
Category: 99

Chatelaine
Mildred Istona, Editor
777 Bay Street
Toronto M5W 1A7 ON Canada
416-596-5425
Category: 73-99

Chicago
Christine Newman, Books Editor
303 E Wacker Drive

Chicago IL 60601
312-565-5100
Category: 61(Chicago IL)

Chicago Lawyer
Sheldon T Zenner, Editor
208 S LaSalle Street #1200
Chicago IL 60604
Category: 19-55(law)

Chicago Literary Review
Ida Noyes Hall, Editor
1212 East 59th Street
Chicago IL 60637
Category: 47-75-95

Chip Chats
Edward F Gallensten, Editor
National Wood Carvers Assn.
7424 Miami Avenue
Cincinnati OH 45243
513-561-9051
Category: 29(woodcarving)
Circulation: 25,500
Issues per year: 6

Choice
Patricia E Sabosik, Book Reviews
100 Riverview Center
Middletown CT 06457
203-347-6933
Category: 99
Issues per year: 10
Reviews: 6000/year

Choices
American Entrepreneurs Assn.
2311 Pontius Avenue
Los Angeles CA 90064-1894
213-477-1011
Category: 19(small business)-73
Issues per year: 2

Christian Bookseller & Library
Karen M Ball, Editor
Christian Life Missions
396 E Saint Charles Road
Wheaton IL 60187
312-653-4200
Category: 63-99
Circulation: 10,000
Issues per year: 12

Chronicle of Higher Education
Ellenn Coughlin, Books Editor
1255 23rd Street NW
Washington DC 20037
202-466-1000
Category: 31-65
Circulation: 70,000
Issues per year: 52

Church and Synagogue Libraries
William H Gentz, Editor
Church & Synagogue Libraries Asn
P O Box 1130
Bryn Mawr PA 19010
Category: 63

Church Media Library Magazine
Jacqulyn Anderson, Books Editor
Sunday School Board
127 Ninth Avenue N
Nashville TN 37234
615-251-2751
Category: 63
Circulation: 16,000
Issues per year: 4

Church Newsletter News
Nathan Neibauer, Editor
Louis Neibauer Company
20 Industrial Drive
Ivyland PA 18974
Category: 63

Cincinnati Business Scene
Lisa Phillips, Editor
2055 Reading Road
Cincinnati OH 45202
Category: 19-61(Cincinnati OH)
Circulation: 10,000

Civil Engineering
Howard Smallowitz, Editor
345 East 47th Street
New York NY 10017
212-705-7507
Category: 19-23(engineering)

Clergy Journal
Manfred Holck Jr, Editor
6311 Shoal Creek West Drive
P O Box 1625
Austin TX 78767
Category: 63

Cleveland
Michael Roberts, Editor
1621 Euclid Avenue
Cleveland OH 44115
216-771-2833
Category: 61(Cleveland OH)

Club Management
Eldon Miller, Editor
Commerce Publishing
408 Olive Street
St. Louis MO 63102
Category: 99
Issues per year: 12

Coast Magazine
W A Marjenhoff, Editor
5 Kings Highway N
P O Drawer 2448
Myrtle Beach SC 29578
803-449-7121
Category: 11-27-33-61(SE US)-71
Circulation: 1,050,000
Issues per year: 52
Reviews: 35/year
Does not buy serial rights.

College & Research Libraries
Charles Martell, Editor
200 Jed Smith Drive

California State University
Sacramento CA 95819
916-454-6444
Category: 99
Circulation: 12,000
Issues per year: 6

College Store Executive
Catherine Orobona, Editor
825 Old Country Road/P O Box 1500
Westbury NY 11590
516-334-3030
Category: 19(retail marketing)-99
Circulation: 7,600
Issues per year: 10
Does not buy serial rights.

College Store Journal
Russell Reynolds, Editor
528 E Lorain Street
P O Box 58
Oberlin OH 44074
216-775-7777
Category: 19(retail marketing,
          colleges)
Issues per year: 12

Colorado Business
Jim Craig, Editor
P O Box 5400
Denver CO 80217
303-573-1433
Category: 19-61(CO)

Columba: Midwest Review of Books
Jeanne Bonham, Co-Editor
101 E Wilson Bridge Road
Columbus OH 43085
614-885-1031
Category: 75-76-84-89

Columbia Journalism Review
Gloria Cooper, Books Editor
700 Journalism Building
Columbia University
New York NY 10027
212-280-5595
Category: 19(journalism
          publishing)
Circulation: 33,000
Issues per year: 6

Commentary
Neal Kozodny, Books Editor
165 East 56 Street
New York NY 10022
212-751-4000
Category: 41-55

Common Sense Press
John A Pugsley, Editor
711 W 17th Street
Costa Mesa CA 92627
Category: 19

Commonweal
David Toolan, Books Editor
232 Madison Avenue

New York NY 10016
212-683-2042
Category: 63

Communication Briefings
Frank Grazian, Editor
Encoders Inc
806 Westminster Boulevard
Blackwood NJ 08012
609-589-3503
Category: 19(communication)
Circulation: 1,500
Issues per year: 12

Communication Concepts
Editor
P O Box 1608
Springfield VA 22151-0608
Category: 19(communication)

Communication World
Cliff McGoon, Editor
Assn of Business Communicators
870 Market Street #928
San Francisco CA 94102
Category: 19(communication)

Communications Arts
Richard Coyne, Editor
410 Sherman Avenue
P O Box 10300
Palo Alto CA 94303
415-326-6040
Category: 11-19(graphics)

Communications Illustrated
Joe Williams, Editor
P O Box 924
Bartlesville OK 74005
Category: 11(graphics)
          19(communications)

Communications News
Donald Wiley, Editor
124 S First Street
Geneva IL 60134
312-232-1400
Category: 19
          23(telecommunications)

Communications Week
Paul Travis, Editor
600 Community Drive
Manhasset NY 11030
516-365-4600
Category: 19(communication)

Communicator's Journal
P O Box 602
Omaha NE 68101
Category: 19(publicity
          marketing)

Compute!
Kathleen Martinek, Editor
324 W Wendover Avenue
Greensboro NC 27408

313-545-6779
Category: 23
Issues per year: 12

Computer & Electronics Marketing
Ronald Karjian, Editor
1050 Commonwealth Avenue
Boston MA 02215
617-739-4750
Category: 19(marketing)-23

Computer Graphics World
Randall Stickrod, Editor
1714 Stockton Street
San Francisco CA 94133
415-398-7151
Category: 11(graphics)-23

Computer Marketing Newsletter
Gerard Guyod, Editor
1000 Quail #120
Newport Beach CA 92660
714-752-0271
Category: 19(marketing)-23
Circulation: 4,000
Issues per year: 12

Computerworld
John Whitmarsh, Editor
375 Cochituate Road, Route 30
Framingham MA 01701
617-879-0700
Category: 23

Concerned Asian Scholars Bull.
P O Box R
Berthoud CO 80513
Category: 55-65(Asia)
Issues per year: 4

Connecticut
Sara Cuneo, Editor
636 Kings Highway/P O Box 907
Fairfield CT 06430
203-576-1205
Category: 61(CT)

Connecticut Business Review
Gerald Brittle, Editor
595 Franklin Avenue
Hartford CT 06114
203-278-3800
Category: 19-61(CT)

Connexions Digest
Ulli Diemer, Editor
427 Bloor Street W
Toronto M5S 1X7 ON Canada
416-960-3903
Category: 19(publishing
          marketing)-23-59
Issues per year: 4

Constantine's Woodworking
2050 Eastchester Road
Bronx NY 10461
212-792-1600
Category: 29(woodworking)

Consultants Newsletter
James H Kennedy, Editor
Templeton Road
Fitzwilliam NH 03447
Category: 19(consulting)
Issues per year: 12

Consulting Opportunities Journal
J Stephen Lanning, Editor
P O Box 17674
Washington DC 20041
304-725-8726
Category: 19(consulting)
Circulation: 7,000
Issues per year: 12

Consumer Electronics
Richard Ekstract, Editor
345 Park Avenue South
New York NY 10010
212-686-7744
Category: 23-29

Consumers Digest Magazine
Frank Bowers, Editor
5705 N Lincoln
Chicago IL 60659
312-275-3590
Category: 25
Issues per year: 12

Consumers Research
Maureen Bozell, Editor
517 Second Street NE
Washington DC 20002
202-546-1710
Category: 25

Contact II
Maurice Kenny, Editor
A Bimonthly Poetry Review
P O Box 451, Bowling Green
New York NY 10004
Category: 75-83-95

Contemporary Christian
Editor
P O Box 6300
Laguna Hills CA 92654
714-951-9106
Category: 11-33-63(Christian)
Issues per year: 12

Control Engineering
Edward Kompass, Editor
1301 S Grove Avenue
P O Box 1030
Barrington IL 60010
312-381-1840
Category: 19-23(engineering)

Cornell Quarterly
H. Louise Ahl, Editor
Cornell University
327 Statler Hall
Ithaca NY 14863
Category: 31
Issues per year: 4

Corporate Communications Report
Courtenay Beinhorn, Editor
112 East 31st Street
New York NY 10016
212-889-2450
Category: 19(communications)
Circulation: 1,250

Corporate Design
Roger Yee, Editor
850 Third Avenue
New York NY 10022-6222
212-949-4400
Category: 19(design)
Circulation: 25,000
Issues per year: 6

Corporate Director
Thomas J Goff IV, Editor
P O Box 10133
Beverly Hills CA 90213
Category: 19(management)

Corporate Report, Kansas City
Jane Mobley, Editor
4149 Pennsylvania Avenue
Kansas City MO 64111
816-931-4541
Category: 19-61(Kansas City KS/MO)
Circulation: 22,000

Corporate Report, Minnesota
Jay Novak, Editor
7831 E Bush Lake Road
Minneapolis MN 55435
612-835-6855
Category: 19-61(MN)
Circulation: 26,000
Issues per year: 12
Does not buy serial rights.

Corporate Travel
Gordon Harrington, Editor
25 Penn Boulevard
Scarsdale NY 10583
914-472-3040
Category: 19-71
Issues per year: 12

Cosmopolitan
Carol E Rinzler, Book Columnist
Betty Kelly, Book Editor
Barbara Creaturo, Editor
  Cosmo Tells All
224 West 57th Street
New York NY 10019
212-262-7417
Category: 73-99
Issues per year: 12
Buys 1st and 2nd serial rights.

Cost and Management
Jacqueline Hewer, Editor
154 Main Street E
P O Box 176
Hamilton L8N 3C3 ON Canada
416-525-4100
Category: 19(financial)

Counselors Information Service
S Norman Feingold, Editor
Bellman Publishing Company
P O Box 34937
Bethesda MD 20817
Category: 19-31(careers)

Counted Thread
Elizabeth Stears, Editor
3305 S Newport Street
Denver CO 80224
Category: 29(needlework)
Circulation: 8,000
Issues per year: 4

Country Cooking
Rachael Newman, Editor
959 Eighth Avenue
New York NY 10019
Category: 27-39

Country Home
Meredith Corporation
Locust at 17th
Des Moines IA 50336
515-284-3000
Category: 27-29-43
Circulation: 600,000

Country Journal
110 Sutter Street #608
San Francisco CA 94104
415-982-7981
Category: 27-29-43
Circulation: 320,000

Country Living
Hearst Corporation
224 West 47th Street
New York NY 10019
212-262-5700
Category: 27-29-43
Circulation: 800,000
Issues per year: 12

Crafts
Judith Brossart, Editor
PJS Publications
P O Box 1790
Peoria IL 61656
309-682-6626
Category: 29
Circulation: 525,000
Issues per year: 12

Crafts 'N Things
Editor
Clapper Publishing Company
14 Main Street
Park Ridge IL 60068
312-825-2161
Category: 29
Circulation: 300,000
Issues per year: 6

Crafts Report
Michael Smith, Editor
3632 Ashworth N

Seattle WA 98103
206-632-7222
Category: 29-43

CraftsWoman Magazine
Anne Patterson Dee, Editor
Daedalus Publications
P O Box 848
Libertyville IL 60048
312-945-1769
Category: 19-29
Issues per year: 6

Crain's Chicago Business
Dan Miller, Editor
740 N Rush Street
Chicago IL 60611
312-649-5200
Category: 19-61(Chicago IL)
Circulation: 45,000
Issues per year: 12

Crain's Cleveland Business
Brian Tucker, Editor
140 Public Square #412
Cleveland OH 44114
216-522-1383
Category: 19-61(Cleveland OH)
Circulation: 25,000
Issues per year: 12

Crain's New York Business
Robert Harris, Editor
220 East 42nd Street
New York NY 10017
212-210-0294
Category: 19-61(New York NY)
Circulation: 80,000
Issues per year: 12

Creative Computing
Ziff-Davis Publications
One Park Avenue
New York NY 10016
212-503-5255
Category: 23
Issues per year: 12

Creative Crafts and Miniatures
Rebecca L Carstens, Editor
Carstens Publications
P O Box 700
Newton NJ 07860
201-383-3355
Category: 29
Issues per year: 6

Creative Loafing
1011 West Peachtree Street
Atlanta GA 30308
404-873-5623
Category: 29-69
Circulation: 52,000
Issues per year: 52

Creative Marketing
George Meredith, Editor
Assn of Retail Marketing Service

412 Ocean Avenue
Seabright NJ 07760
201-842-5070
Category: 19(retail marketing)
Circulation: 3,700

Creative Products News
Linda McKee Lewis, Editor
P O Box 584
Lake Forest IL 60045-0584
312-234-5052
Category: 19-29

Credit & Financial Management
Constance Clark, Editor
475 Park Avenue South
New York NY 10016
212-578-4410
Category: 19(financial)

Credit Union Magazine
Paul Butler, Editor
P O Box 431
Madison WI 53701
608-231-4000
Category: 19(banking)

Crochet World
House of White Birches
P O Box 337
Seabrook NH 03874
603-474-3587
Category: 29(crochet)
Circulation: 160,000
Issues per year: 4

Cross Country Skier
33 E Minor Street
Emmaus PA 18049
215-967-5171
Category: 69-71

Cruising World
George Day, Editor
524 Thames Street
Newport RI 02840
401-847-1588
Category: 69(nautical, sailing)
Circulation: 120,000
Issues per year: 12

Cruising World
Herb McCormick, Books Editor
524 Thames Street
Newport RI 02840
401-847-1588
Category: 69(nautical, sailing)
Circulation: 120,000
Issues per year: 12
Reviews: 13/issue

Current Science
Vincent Marteka, Editor
245 Long Mill Road
Middletown CT 06457
203-347-7251
Category: 67

Magazine Editors and Book Reviewers

Curriculum Product Review
Bobit Publishing
2500 Artesia Boulevard
Redondo Beach CA 90278
213-376-8788
Category: 31
Circulation: 50,000
Issues per year: 9
Does not buy serial rights.

Cycling USA
Diane Fritschner, Editor
United States Cycling Federation
1750 E Boulder Street
Colorado Springs CO 80909
Category: 69(bicycling)
Circulation: 20,000
Issues per year: 12
Does not buy serial rights.

Cyclist Magazine
20916 Higgins Court
Torrance CA 90501
213-328-5700
Category: 39
Circulation: 100,000
Issues per year: 10

D Magazine
Ruth Fitzgibbons, Editor
3988 N Central Expressway #1200
Dallas TX 75204
214-827-5000
Category: 11-61(Dallas TX)
Issues per year: 12

D&B Reports
Patricia Hamilton, Editor
299 Park Avenue
New York NY 10171
212-593-6723
Category: 19(financial)

Dakota Family
Doug Busselman, Editor
North Dakota Farm Bureau
P O Box 2064
Fargo ND 58107
701-237-9717
Category: 19(farming)-61(ND)
Circulation: 21,000
Issues per year: 11

Dallas
D. Ann Shiffler, Editor
1507 Pacific Avenue
Dallas TX 75201
214-655-1430
Category: 11-61(Dallas TX)
Issues per year: 12

Dallas/Ft Worth Living
Karen Colbert, Editor
5757 Alpha Road #400
Dallas TX 75240
214-239-2399
Category: 11-61(Dallas TX)
Issues per year: 12

Decor
William M Humberg, Editor
408 Olive Street
St Louis MO 63102
319-421-5445
Category: 11
Circulation: 20,500
Issues per year: 13

Defense Electronics
Kelly Braniff, New Products
EW Communications
1170 E Meadow Drive
Palo Alto CA 94303
415-494-2800
Category: 19-23(electronics)
        55(military)
Circulation: 41,500
Issues per year: 12
Reviews: None
Does not buy serial rights.

Delta Sky
Lidia De Leon, Editor
12955 Biscayne Boulevard
North Miami FL 33181
305-893-1520
Category: 71
Issues per year: 12

Denver
Seymour Epstein, Books Editor
899 Logan #307
Denver CO 80203
303-832-5400
Category: 11-61(Denver CO)
Issues per year: 12

Denver Business
Terry Vitale, Editor
899 Logan Street #307
Denver CO 80203
303-832-5400
Category: 19-61(Denver CO)

Department Store Economist
Murray Furer, Editor
48 East 43rd Street
New York NY 10017
212-687-6190
Category: 19(retail marketing
        financial)

Design Graphics World
James J Maivald, Editor
6255 Barfield Road
Atlanta GA 30328
404-256-9800
Category: 11(graphics)-19-23
Circulation: 36,000
Issues per year: 12

Design News
Lars Soderholm, Editor
275 Washington Street
Newton MA 02158
617-964-3030
Category: 19-23(design)

=================================

<u>CATEGORIES</u> -- coded by number

10 General Nonfiction

11 Art/Music/Photography/Dance
13 Alternative Issues
15 Animals/Pets
17 Biographies/Autobiographies
19 Business/Economics
21 Children's Books
23 Computers/Technology
25 Consumer Issues and Guides
27 Cookbooks/Nutrition
29 Crafts/Hobbies/How-to
31 Education/Child Development
33 Entertainment/Movies/Humor
35 Family/Marriage/Retirement
37 Gay/Lesbian
39 Health/Medicine/Diet/Exercise
41 History
43 House/Garden/Automobiles
45 Languages:_______________
47 Literature/Humanities
49 Minority Studies
51 Nature/Ecology/Conservation
53 New Age/Astrology/Occult
55 Politics/Government/Military
57 Psychology/Self-Help
59 Reference Books
61 Regional Titles
63 Religions/Philosophy
65 Scholarly Titles
67 Science/Mathematics
69 Sports/Games/Recreation
71 Travel/Geography
73 Women's Issues

75 General Fiction

76 Children's Stories
77 Contemporary Novels
78 Ethnic/Minority Literature
79 Folklore/Fairy Tales
80 Foreign Literature
81 Historical
82 Horror/Occult
83 Literary
84 Mystery/Detective
85 Romance/Gothic
86 Science Fiction/Fantasy
87 Suspense/Adventure
88 Westerns
89 Young Adult
90 Short Stories/Anthologies

95 Poetry

97 News
98 Other:____________________

99 All subjects and categories

=================================

Design News
Lyle McCarty, Editor
3031 Tisch Way #100
San Jose CA 95128
408-243-8838
Category: 19-23(design)

Desktop Publishing
Tony Bove, Editor
2055 Woodside Road #180
P O Box 5245
Redwood City CA 94061
415-364-0108
Category: 19(publishing)-23
Issues per year: 12

The Desktop
342 E Third Street
Loveland CO 80537
303-663-1724
Category: 11(graphics)-23
Issues per year: 12
Does not buy serial rights.

Detroit Monthly
John Barron, Editor
Crain Communications
1400 Woodbridge
Detroit MI 48207
313-446-0340
Category: 19
Circulation: 80,000
Issues per year: 12
Reviews: 60-70/year
Buys 1st and 2nd serial rights.

Diabetes Self-Management
Betty Marks, Editor
176 East 77th Street
New York NY 10021
212-535-8388
Category: 27-39(diabetes)
Issues per year: 6

Dial
Jane Ciabattari, Editor
34 East 51st Street
New York NY 10022
212-888-5900
Category: 11-33

Direct Marketing
Raymond Roel, Editor
Attn: New Books
224 Seventh Street
Garden City NY 11530
516-746-6700
Category: 19(marketing)
Circulation: 30,000
Issues per year: 12
Reviews: 1/issue
Buys only 2nd serial rights.

Directions
Vicki L Hanson, Editor
Baker & Taylor
6 Kirby Avenue
Somerville NJ 08876

201-526-8000
Category: 19-31-41-47-55-57-59
63-65-67
Issues per year: 12
Reviews: 2500/month
Does not buy serial rights.

Discover
Gil Rogin, Editor
Time and Life Building
1271 Avenue of the Americas
New York NY 10020
212-586-1212
Category: 23-67
Issues per year: 12

Distribution
Jay Gordon, Editor
Bruce Heydt, Computer Editor
Chilton Way
Radnor PA 19089
215-964-4385
Category: 19-23
Circulation: 70,000
Issues per year: 12
Reviews: 8-10/year
Does not buy serial rights.

DM News
Joe Fitz-Morris, Editor
Michele Whitney, Book Reviews
DM News Corporation
19 West 21st Street
New York NY 10010
212-741-2095
Category: 19(marketing)
Issues per year: 26
Reviews: 2/issue
Does not buy serial rights.

Dog Fancy
Moira Anderson, Managing Editor
Fancy Publications
P O Box 6050
Mission Viejo CA 92690
714-240-6001
Category: 15
Issues per year: 12

Doll Directory
117 F Riverside Avenue
Newport Beach CA 92663
Category: 29(dolls, collectibles)

Doll Times
Aubrey Lovell, Editor
1675 Orchid Avenue
Aurora IL 60505
312-820-0019
Category: 29(dolls, collectibles)
Circulation: 25,000

Doll World
P O Box 428
Seabrook NH 03874
Category: 29(dolls, collectibles)
Circulation: 67,000
Issues per year: 6

Dollars and Sense
Editor, Book Reviews
38 Union Square
Somerville MA 02143
Category: 13-19-55
Issues per year: 12

Dolls
Collector Communications Corp.
170 Fifth Avenue
New York NY 10010
212-989-8700
Category: 29(dolls, collectibles)

Dow Jones Online Book Reviews
Christopher Keledjian, Editor
Salem Press
150 S Los Robles Avenue #720
Pasadena CA 91101
818-584-0106
Category: 75-99

Down East Magazine
Davis Thomas, Editor
P O Box 679
Camden ME 04843
207-594-9544
Category: 61(ME)-99
Circulation: 70,000
Issues per year: 12

Dun's
875 Third Avenue
New York NY 10022
212-605-9400
Category: 19

Dynamic Years
Lorena Farrell, Editor
3200 E Carson Street
Lakewood CA 90712-4096
Category: 35(retirement)-99

Eagle Magazine
Robert Hansen, Editor
Fraternal Orders of Eagles
2401 W Wise Avenue
Milwaukee WI 53233
Category: 99
Issues per year: 12

Early Childhood Special Educ.
Rebecca R Fewell, Editor
Pro-Ed
5341 Industrial Oaks Boulevard
Austin TX 78735
512-892-3142
Category: 31
Circulation: 2,000
Issues per year: 4

East West Journal
Mark Mayell, Editor
17 Station Street
P O Box 1200
Brookline MA 02147
617-232-1000
Category: 53-57-63

Circulation: 70,000
Issues per year: 12
Reviews: 6/issue
Buys 1st and 2nd serial rights.

Eastern Review
John Atwood, Editor
34 East 51st Street
New York NY 10022
212-888-5900
Category: 61(eastern US)-71

Ebony
Lerone Bennett, Books Editor
820 S Michigan Avenue
Chicago IL 60605
312-322-9250
Category: 49-99
Issues per year: 12

Economic World
Yoshimasa Takagi, Editor
60 East 42nd Street #734
New York NY 10165
212-986-1588
Category: 19(financial)

Editor & Publisher
John Consoli, News Editor
11 West 19th Street
New York NY 10011
212-752-7050
Category: 19(publishing)

Editorial Eye
Priscilla Taylor, Editor
85 S Bragg Street
Alexandria VA 22312
703-823-3223
Category: 19(communications
        publishing)
Issues per year: 12

Education Digest
Alan H Jones, Editor
416 Longshore Drive/P O Box 8623
Ann Arbor MI 48107
313-769-1211
Category: 31
Circulation: 35,000
Issues per year: 9
Reviews: 5-6/year
Does not buy serial rights.

Education Week
1255 23rd Street NW #775
Washington DC 20037
202-466-5190
Category: 31
Circulation: 55,000
Issues per year: 40

Educational Dealer
Kevin Fahy, Editor
P O Box 526
Dansville NY 14437
716-335-2530
Category: 31

EE Product News
Ed Walter, Editor
707 Westchester Avenue
White Plains NY 10604
914-949-8500
Category: 19-23(engineering)

Electron
Richard Westfall, Editor
4781 East 355 Street
Willoughby OH 44094
216-781-9400
Category: 23(electronics)

Electronic Business
Andrea Ovans, Book Editor
275 Washington Street
Newton MA 02158
617-964-3030
Category: 23
Circulation: 60,000
Issues per year: 24
Reviews: 12/year
Does not buy serial rights.

Electronic Buyers News
Paul Hyman, Editor
600 Community Drive
Manhasset NY 11030
516-365-4600
Category: 23(electronics)

Electronic Design
David Bursky, Editor
Steve Orr, Editor
Hayden Publishing
1307 S Mary Avenue #210
Sunnyvale CA 94087
408-736-6667
Category: 11-23-67
Circulation: 138,000
Issues per year: 30
Reviews: 50/year
Does not buy serial rights.

Electronic Engineering Times
Girish Mhatre, Editor
600 Community Drive
Manhasset NY 11030
516-365-4600
Category: 23(engineering)

Electronic Office
Jan Wright, Editor
Auerbach Publishers
6560 N Park Drive
Pennsauken NJ 08109-4374
609-662-2070
Category: 19-23
Issues per year: 12
Does not buy serial rights.

Electronic Products
Al Rosenblatt, Editor
645 Stewart Avenue
Garden City NY 11530
516-222-2500
Category: 19(electronics)

Electronics
Steve Zollo, New Products Ed
1221 Avenue of the Americas
New York NY 10020
212-512-2685
Category: 23(electronics)

Electronics for Kids
Rick Anguilla, Editor
11 West 19th Street
New York NY 10011
212-741-7210
Category: 21-23-29
Issues per year: 12

Elks Magazine
Donald Stahl, Managing Editor
425 W Diversey Place
Chicago IL 60614
Category: 99
Issues per year: 12

EM: Ebony Man
Alfred Fornay, Editor
Johnson Publishing Company
1270 Avenue of the Americas
New York NY 10020
212-586-2911
Category: 11-39-49-99(fashion,
        grooming)
Issues per year: 12

Engineering Digest
H W Meyfarth, Editor
Canadian Engineering Publication
111 Peter Street #411
Toronto ON Canada
416-596-1624
Category: 19-23-67
Circulation: 70,000
Issues per year: 10
Reviews: 10+/issue
Does not buy serial rights.

Engineering News-Record
Editor
1221 Avenue of the Americas
New York NY 10020
212-997-3242
Category: 23(engineering)

Engineering Times
Mary Paris, Editor
1420 King Street
Alexandria VA 22314
703-684-2875
Category: 23(engineering)

Entrepreneur
Ronald J Smith, Editor
David C Lustig, Features Editor
American Entrepreneurs Assn.
2311 Pontius Avenue
Los Angeles CA 90064-1894
213-477-1011
Category: 19(small business)
Issues per year: 12
Entrepreneur

Entrepreneur Clubletter
Darryl E Ruff, Editor
Magnum Group
P O Box 692
Kelowna V1Y 7P4 BC Canada
604-764-7536
Category: 19(small business)
Issues per year: 6

Entrepreneurial Manager
Joseph Mancuso, Director
Center for Entrepreneurial Mgmt.
83 Spring Street
New York NY 10012
212-925-7304
Category: 19(small business)
Issues per year: 6

Entrepreneurial Women
Miriam Walton, Editor
Sunshine Press
3221 Bloomfield Park Drive
West Bloomfield MI 48033
Category: 19-73

EPB Electronic Publishing and
Sandra Paul, Editor
Bookselling
2214 N Central #103
Phoenix AZ 85004-1483
602-254-6156
Category: 99(publishing)
Issues per year: 12

Episcopalian
Judy Mathe Foley, Books Editor
Janette Pierce, News Editor
1201 Chestnut Street
Philadelphia PA 19107
215-564-2010
Category: 23-63(Episcopalian)-99
Circulation: 300,000
Issues per year: 12
Reviews: 100/year
Buys 1st and 2nd serial rights.

Equal Opportunity
Ann Kelly, Editor
Equal Opportunity Publications
44 Broadway
Greenlawn NY 11740
516-261-8917
Category: 19(career guidance)-49
Circulation: 16,000
Issues per year: 3
Buys only 2nd serial rights.

Esquire
Jenny Gleich, Books Editor
2 Park Avenue
New York NY 10016
212-561-8100
Category: 33-99(men's)
Issues per year: 12

Executive
Patricia Anderson, Editor
2973 Weston Road

Weston M9N 3R3 ON Canada
416-741-1112
Category: 19(adminstrative)

Executive Female
Mary Tervella, Editor
Natl Assn of Female Executives
1041 Third Avenue
New York NY 10021
212-371-0740
Category: 19-73
Circulation: 160,000
Issues per year: 8
Reviews: 2/issue
Does not buy serial rights.

Executive Fitness Newsletter
Rodale Press
33 E Minor Street
Emmaus PA 18049
215-967-5171
Category: 19-27-39-69

Explorer
Museum of Natural History
Wade Oval, University Circle
Cleveland OH 44106
216-231-4600
Category: 21-51

Exploring Magazine
Scott Daniels, Editor
1325 Walnut Hill Lane
Irving TX 75062
214-659-2365
Category: 15-29-43-51-69

Facilities Design & Management
Anne Fallucchi, Editor
1515 Broadway
New York NY 10036
212-869-1300
Category: 11-19(office)

Fact Magazine
Daniel Kehrer, Editor
305 E 46th Street
New York NY 10017
212-319-6868
Category: 19
Circulation: 150,000
Issues per year: 12

Family Business Forum
Editor
National Family Business Council
3916 Detroit Boulevard
West Bloomfield MA 48033
313-553-1000
Category: 19(small business)

Family Circle
Gay Bryant, Editor
Nicole Gregory, Book Reviews
Molly Sinclair, Money Editor
488 Madison Avenue
New York NY 10022
212-593-8000

Category: 19(money)-25-27-29-35
  43-73
Issues per year: 17
Buys 1st and 2nd serial rights.

Family Handyman
Joe Provey, Editor
1999 Shepard Road
St Paul MN 55116
612-690-7534
Category: 29-43
Circulation: 1,100,000
Issues per year: 6

Family Magazine
Mary Jane Ryan, Editor
9 East 41st Street #300
New York NY 10017
212-661-6550
Category: 35-55(military)

Family Weekly
Thomas Plate, Editor
1515 Broadway
New York NY 10036
212-719-6900
Category: 27-29-33-35-43-73
Issues per year: 52

Farm Futures
Editor
330 E Kilbourn Avenue
Milwaukee WI 53202
414-278-7676
Category: 19(farming)
Circulation: 160,000

Farm Journal
Marcia Taylor, Editor
230 W Washington Square
Philadelphia PA 19105
215-574-1200
Category: 19(farming)
Issues per year: 14

Farmer-Stockman
Ernest Shiner, Editor
P O Box 25125
Oklahoma City OK 73125
214-363-7651
Category: 19(farming)

Farmstead
Heidi Brugger, Managing Editor
Attn: Country Ways Department
P O Box 111
Freedom ME 04941
207-382-6200
Category: 19(farming)-29-43-51
Circulation: 150,000
Issues per year: 6
Reviews: 2/issue

Feminist Bookstore News
Susanna J Sturgis, SF Editor
P O Box 39
West Tisbury MA 02575
Category: 73-86

Magazine Editors and Book Reviewers

Feminist Bookstore News
Carol Seajay, Books Editor
P O Box 882554
San Francisco CA 94188
Category: 73

Feminist Review
Editor, Book Reviews
804 Meigs Street
Rochester NY 14620
Category: 73

Fessenden Review
Douglas Cruickshank, Editor
P O Box 7272
San Diego CA 92107
415-327-6121
Category: 99
Issues per year: 4

Fiction Monthly
Anthony Caqvellin, Books Editor
24234 Durant Avenue
Berkeley CA 94704
Category: 75-83-95
Issues per year: 12

Financial Analysts Journal
Judith Kimball, Editor
1633 Broadway
New York NY 10019
212-957-2866
Category: 19(financial)

Financial Post
777 Bay Street
Toronto M5W 1A7 ON Canada
416-596-5632
Category: 19(financial)

Financial Times of Canada
Terence Corcoran, Editor
920 Yonge Street #500
Toronto M4W 3L5 ON Canada
416-922-1133
Category: 19(banking, financial)

Financial World
Douglas A McIntyre, Editor
P O Box 10745
Des Moines IA 50349
Category: 19

Financial World
Peter Hall, Editor
1450 Broadway
New York NY 10018
212-869-1616
Category: 19(financial)
Circulation: 165,000
Issues per year: 26
Reviews: 1-2/issue
Buys only 2nd serial rights.

Fine Homebuilding
John Lively, Editor
The Taunton Press
63 S Main Street

Newton CT 06470
203-426-8171
Category: 29(woodworking)-43
Issues per year: 6
Reviews: 6/issue

Fine Print
Sandra Kirshenbaum, Editor
P O Box 3394
San Francisco CA 94119
415-776-1530
Category: 11(book arts)
            19(printing)
Circulation: 3,500
Issues per year: 4

Fine Woodworking
John Kelsey, Editor
63 S Main Street
Newton CT 06470
203-426-8171
Category: 29(woodworking)-43
Circulation: 240,000
Issues per year: 6

Florida Gulf Coast
Milana Petty, Editor
Baker Publications
1311 N Westshore #109
Tampa FL 33607
813-879-1177
Category: 43(home)-61(FL)
Circulation: 70,000
Issues per year: 7
Reviews: 1-7/year

Florida Trend
Richard Edmonds, Editor
440 1st Avenue South
P O Box 611
Saint Petersburg FL 33731
813-821-5800
Category: 19-61(FL)

Flying
Richard Collins, Editor-In-Chief
One Park Avenue
New York NY 10016
212-503-4200
Category: 69(aviation, flying)
Circulation: 332,000
Issues per year: 12

Flying Around the World
Rafael Trujillo, Editor
P O Box 738
Miami Beach FL 33139
305-361-8369
Category: 71
Circulation: 23,000
Issues per year: 12

Focus New York
Kristine Schein, Editor
375 Park Avenue
New York NY 10022
212-628-2000
Category: 11-33-61(New York NY)

Folio Magazine
Tania Hall, Asst Editor
Resources Department
125 Elm Street
New Canaan CT 06840-4006
203-972-0761
Category: 19(publishing)-99
Circulation: 10,000
Issues per year: 12

Food & Beverage Marketing
US Business Press
11 West 19th Street
New York NY 10011
212-741-7210
Category: 19(marketing)-27
Issues per year: 12

Food & Wine
American Express Publishing Co.
1120 Avenue of the Americas
New York NY 10036
212-382-5600
Category: 27
Circulation: 700,000
Issues per year: 12

Forbes
Stephen Kindel, Senior Editor
60 Fifth Avenue
New York NY 10011
212-620-2200
Category: 19
Circulation: 720,000

Ford Times
Arnold Hirsch, Editor
P O Box 1899
Dearborn MI 48121
313-322-9321
Category: 43-71
Issues per year: 12

Forecast
Vicki L Hanson, Editor
Baker & Taylor
6 Kirby Avenue
Somerville NJ 08876
201-526-8000
Category: 99
Issues per year: 12
Reviews: many
Does not buy serial rights.

Fortune
Edward P Lenahan, Editor
1271 Avenue of the Americas
New York NY 10020
212-586-1212
Category: 19
Circulation: 625,000

Foundation News
Arlie Schardt, Editor
Council on Foundations
1828 L Street NW
Washington DC 20036
202-466-6512

Category: 19(foundations)
Circulation: 14,300
Issues per year: 6

Free Enterprise
Kay Mancini DeGiorgi, Editor
P O Box 9663
Arlington VA 22209-9990
Category: 19(small business)

Freebies
P O Box 20283
Santa Barbara CA 93120
Category: 99
Circulation: 500,000
Issues per year: 12

FRI Portfolio
William F Balthaser, Editor
Fund Raising Institute
P O Box 365
Amber PA 19002-0365
215-628-8729
Category: 19(fundraising)
Circulation: 3,000
Issues per year: 6

Friendly Exchange
Adele Malott, Editor
Respectfully Yours
Meredith, Locust at 17th
Des Moines IA 50336
515-284-3000
Category: 99
Circulation: 4,500,000
Issues per year: 4

Front Room News
Adele Patti, Editor
63 Starmond Avenue
P O Box 1541
Clifton NJ 07015-1541
201-773-4215
Category: 19(small business)-29
        73

Fulfill Magazine
Robert Moore, Publisher
8701 Georgia Avenue #800
Silver Spring MD 20910
301-589-8875
Category: 19(marketing)
Issues per year: 26

Fund Raising Management
William Olcott, Editor
Hoke Communications
224 Seventh Avenue
Garden City NY 11530
516-746-6700
Category: 19(fundraising)
Circulation: 4,000
Issues per year: 12

Future
Brian Burnett, Books Editor
4 West 21st Street
P O Box 7

Tulsa OK 74121
918-584-2481
Category: 23-67-99(future)
Issues per year: 12

Futurific
Bailint Szent-Miklosy, Editor
280 Madison Avenue
New York NY 10016
212-684-4913
Category: 23-67-86
Circulation: 10,000
Issues per year: 12
Reviews: 1/issue
Does not buy serial rights.

Gallagher Report
Cynthia Billings, Editor
230 Park Avenue
New York NY 10169
212-661-5000
Category: 19(communications
        publicity)
Issues per year: 52

Gallery
Marc Lichter, Editor
800 Second Avenue
New York NY 10017
212-986-9600
Category: 11-33-99(men's)
Circulation: 500,000
Issues per year: 12
Buys 1st and 2nd serial rights.

Gallery
Tom Seligson, Arts Editor
Barry Janoff, Sports Editor
Chris Dubbs, Travel Editor
800 Second Avenue
New York NY 10017
212-986-9600
Category: 11-33-69-71-99(men's)
Circulation: 500,000
Issues per year: 12

Games
Burt Hochberg, Editor
Stephanie Spadaccini, Feature
Curtis Slepian, News Editor
R Wayne Schmittberger, Science
1350 Avenue of the Americas
16th Floor
New York NY 10019
212-246-4640
Category: 11-23-29(hobby)-33-67
        69(sports)-71-97(news)
Circulation: 650,000
Issues per year: 12
Reviews: 15/year
Does not buy serial rights.

Genealogical Library Quarterly
Patricia Kirkwood, Editor
1510 Cravens Avenue
Torrance CA 90501
Category: 35(genealogy)
Issues per year: 4

Genealogy Today
Diane Dieterle, Editor
2815 Clearview Place
Atlanta GA 30340
404-457-7801
Category: 35(genealogy)

Georgia Business
Dick Gentry, Editor
1800 Water Place NW #100
Atlanta GA 30339
404-952-6397
Category: 19-61(GA)

Geyer's Office Dealer
Robert Rauch, Editor
51 Madison Avenue
New York NY 10010
212-689-411
Category: 19(office)

Gift and Decorative Accessories
Patricia Corwin, Editor
Resource Letter
51 Madison Avenue
New York NY 10010
Category: 19(retail marketing)
        27-33
Issues per year: 12

Gift Reporter
Randy Richards, Editor
1785 The Exchange #300
Atlanta GA 30339
Category: 19(retail marketing)-33
Issues per year: 12
Does not buy serial rights.

Glamour
Laura Mathews, Book Editor
350 Madison Avenue
New York NY 10017
212-880-8800
Category: 39-73(fashion/beauty)
Issues per year: 12
Buys 1st and 2nd serial rights.

Golden Triad Magazine
Susan B Allen, Editor
Piedmont Impressions
311-K S Westgate Drive
Greensboro NC 27407
919-854-5500
Category: 61(NC)-99
Circulation: 20,000
Issues per year: 6

Golf Digest
5520 Park Avenue
P O Box 395
Turnbull CT 06611-0395
203-373-7000
Category: 69(golf)

Golf Illustrated
Al Barkow, Editor
Family Media
3 Park Avenue

New York NY 10016
212-340-9200
Category: 39-69(golf)
Circulation: 100,000
Issues per year: 12

Good Housekeeping
Erika Reider Mark, Editor
Leonard Dowty, Books Editor
959 Eighth Avenue
New York NY 10019
212-262-5700
Category: 27-29-35-43-73
Issues per year: 12

Good Toys
Rodale Press
33 E Minor Street
Emmaus PA 18049
215-967-5171
Category: 21-25-31-69-76
Circulation: 200,000+
Issues per year: 2

Gossage Regan Manager's Memo
Gordon Associates
118 West 74th Street #2B
New York NY 10023
212-787-8930
Category: 19(personnel
          management)
Issues per year: 4
Does not buy serial rights.

Gourmet Retailer
Editor
1545 NE 123rd Street
Miami FL 33161
305-893-8775
Category: 19(retail marketing)
          27
Circulation: 16,000

Government Executive
Carl White, Editor
1725 K Street NW
Washington DC 20006
202-785-2593
Category: 55

Government Product News
Leslie Drahos, Editor
1100 Superior Avenue
Cleveland OH 44114
216-696-7000
Category: 19-55
Circulation: 85,000
Issues per year: 12
Reviews: dozens/year
Does not buy serial rights.

GQ
Editor
350 Madison Avenue
New York NY 10017
212-880-8800
Category: 11-33-99(men's)
Issues per year: 12

Graduate Woman
Karen Johnson, Editor
2401 Virginia Avenue NW
Washington DC 20037
202-785-7734
Category: 31-73

Grain Age
Bruce Smith, Editor
Deborah Drilias, Business Editor
Alice Olsen, Family Editor
450 N Sunny Slope South #120
Brookfield WI 53005
414-786-7540
Category: 19(agriculture)-35-71
Circulation: 9,500
Issues per year: 6
Reviews: 8-12/year
Does not buy serial rights.

Grandparents
George Bush, Editor
Meredith Corporation
Locust at 17th
Des Moines IA 50336
515-284-3000
Category: 21-31-35-76
Circulation: 400,000

Graphic Arts Buyer
Kurt Wilner, Editor
Advertising Trade Publications
10 East 39th Street
New York NY 10016
212-889-6500
Category: 11(graphics)
Circulation: 9,500
Issues per year: 12

Graphic Arts Journal
Kay Leftwich, Editor
Attn: Reading Department
P O Box 6099
Salt Lake City UT 84106
Category: 11(graphics)
Circulation: 12,000
Issues per year: 4

Graphic Arts Monthly
Bert Chapman, Editor
875 Third Avenue
New York NY 10022
212-605-9400
Category: 11(graphics)
Circulation: 87,000
Issues per year: 12

Graphic Communicator
William Moody, Editor
1900 L Street NW
Washington DC 20036
202-872-7952
Category: 11-19(graphics
          publishing)

Graphic Informer
Bernice H Haug, Editor
3601 Edison Place

Rolling Meadows IL 60008
312-392-1476
Category: 11(graphics)
Circulation: 50,000
Issues per year: 4
Reviews: 1-2/issue

Graphic International
O Fichera, Editor
P O Box 4639
Margate FL 33063
305-971-4360
Category: 11(graphics)
          19(management)
Circulation: 29,000
Issues per year: 12

Graphic USA
Milton Kaye, Editor
120 East 56th Street
New York NY 10022
212-759-8813
Category: 11(graphics)
          19(advertising)
Issues per year: 12

Greater Philadelphia Economist
Raymond Berens, Editor
Land Title Building #802
Philadelphia PA 19110
215-569-4056
Category: 19-61(Philadelphia PA)

Gulfshore Life
Jan Gregory Frazer, Editor
P O Box 368
Naples FL 33939
813-262-6425
Category: 99
Issues per year: 12
Reviews: 4-6/issue

Hadassah
Alan Tigay, Editor
50 West 58th Street
New York NY 10019
212-355-7900
Category: 63(Jewish)

Handicap News
Phyllis Burns, Editor
272 N 11th Court
Brighton CO 80601
Category: 39(handicapped)

Handmade
Theresa Gaffey, Editor
50 College Street
Ashville NC 28801
Category: 29
Issues per year: 6

Happy Hobbies
Pam Myers, Editor
P O Box 862
Columbia MO 65205-0862
Category: 29
Issues per year: 6

Harper's
Lewis H Lapham, Editor
666 Broadway
New York NY 10012
212-614-6500
Category: 11-75-99
Issues per year: 12
Buys only 2nd serial rights.

Harper's Bazaar
Woody Hochswender, Features Editor
1700 Broadway
New York NY 10019
212-903-5000
Category: 73(beauty and fashion)
Issues per year: 12

Harrowsmith
Wayne Grad, Managing Editor
7 Queen Victoria Road
Camden East K0K1S0 ON Canada
Category: 27-29-45-51
Issues per year: 6

Hartford Woman
Joy Esterson, Managing Editor
595 Franklin Avenue
Hartford CT 06114
203-278-3800
Category: 19-61(CT)-73
Circulation: 40,000
Issues per year: 12

Harvard Business Review
Lynn Salerno, Editor
Teele Hall
Soldiers Field
Boston MA 02163
617-495-6800
Category: 19

Harvard Magazine
John Bethell, Books Editor
7 Ware Street
Cambridge MA 02138
617-495-5746
Category: 31

Health
Hank Herman, Editor
Family Media
3 Park Avenue
New York NY 10016
212-340-9200
Category: 39
Issues per year: 12

Health Foods Business
Editor
567 Morris Avenue
Elizabeth NJ 07208
Category: 19(retail marketing)
          27-39

Health Foods Retailing
Communication Channels
6255 Barfield Road
Atlanta GA 30328

404-256-9800
Category: 19(retail marketing)
          27-39
Circulation: 11,000

Health/Wealth
Hank Hudson, Editor
2720 NE 9th Terrace
Pompano Beach FL 33064
Category: 19-39

Healthcare Financial Management
Ronald Keener, Editor
1900 Spring Road #500
Oak Brook IL 60521
312-655-4600
Category: 19(financial)-39

Helicon Nine
P O Box 22412
Kansas City MO 64113
Category: 73-75-95
Issues per year: 3

High Technology
Robert Haavind, Editor
Sarah Glazer, Business Editor
Cary Lu, Computer Editor
38 Commercial Wharf
Boston MA 02110
617-227-4700
Category: 19-23-67
Circulation: 300,000
Issues per year: 12

High Volume Printing
Bill Esler, Editor
425 Huehl Road
P O Box 368
Northbrook IL 60062
Category: 19(printing)

Hiram Poetry Review
Carol Donley, Editor
Co-Editors
P O Box 162
Hiram OH 44234
Category: 47-95

Hispanic American Historical Rev
Neill Macaulay, Book Reviews
Grinter Hall
University of Florida
Gainesville FL 32611
Category: 41-49(Hispanics
          Latin America)
Circulation: 2,300
Issues per year: 4

Hispanic Business
Bonnie Chavarria, Editor
4672 Via Huerto
Santa Barbara CA 93110
Category: 19-49(Hispanics)

Hispanic USA
Maggie Aguilar, Editor
230 N Michigan Avenue #2112

Chicago IL 60601-5910
312-427-4045
Category: 19-49(Hispanic)-99

History
Heldref Publications
4000 Albemarle Street NW
Washington DC 20016
Category: 41-65
Issues per year: 10
Reviews: 500/year
Does not buy serial rights.

History of Political Economy
S. Todd Lowry, Book Reviews
Department of Economics
Washington and Lee University
Lexington VA 24450
Category: 19-41-55-65
Circulation: 1,500
Issues per year: 4

Hobby Merchandiser
Jack Harris, Editor
490 Route 9
P O Box 420
Englishtown NJ 07726
201-972-1022
Category: 19(retail marketing)-29
Issues per year: 12

Hombre de Mundo
Santiago Villazon, Editor
Editorial America
6355 NW 36th Street
Miami FL 33166
305-871-6400
Category: 49-78-80-99
Circulation: 130,000
Issues per year: 12
Reviews: 3/issue
Buys 1st and 2nd serial rights.

Home
Editor
140 East 45th Street
New York NY 10017
212-682-4040
Category: 43
Issues per year: 12

Home Business
Elliott Starkman, Editor
MAS Communications
1200 Hempstead Turnpike
Franklin Square NY 11010
516-328-6222
Category: 19(small business)
Circulation: 100,000
Issues per year: 12

Home Computer Magazine
Editor
HCM Product News
1500 Valley River Drive #250
Eugene OR 97401
503-485-8796
Category: 23

Home Entertainment
Judith Morrison, Editor
220 Westbury Avenue
Carle Place NY 11514
516-334-7880
Category: 11-29-33
Issues per year: 12

Home Mecahnix
Joseph Provey, Editor-in-Chief
1515 Broadway
New York NY 10036
212-719-6574
Category: 29-43
Issues per year: 12

Home Mecahnix
Don Chaikin, Auto Editor
Nancy Cooper, Consumer Editor
Michael Morris, House Editor
1515 Broadway
New York NY 10036
212-719-6574
Category: 25-29-43(automobiles)
Issues per year: 12

Home Office
Susan Grimbly, Editor
1271 Avenue of the Americas
New York NY 10020
Category: 19(home office)
Circulation: 35,000

Homebased Entrepreneur
Joanne Esters-Brown, Editor
JEB Publications
P O Box 19036
Chicago IL 60619
Category: 19(small business)
　　　　35-73

Homemakers Magazine
Jane Gale, Editor
2300 Yonge Street
Toronto M4P 1E4 ON Canada
416-482-8260
Category: 27-29-35-43

Homeworking Mothers
Georganne Fiumara, Editor
Mothers' Home Business Network
P O Box 423
East Meadow NY 11554
516-997-7394
Category: 19(small business)
　　　　35-73
Issues per year: 4

Honolulu
Dan Boylan, Editor
Debra Thomas, Arts Editor
Bill Wood, Business Editor
John Heckathorn, Computer Editor
Jim Hackleman, Sports Editor
36 Merchant Street
Honolulu HI 96813
808-524-7400
Category: 11-19-23-33

61(Honolulu HI)-69
Circulation: 38,000
Issues per year: 12
Reviews: 10/year
Does not buy serial rights.

Horn Book Magazine
Anita Silvey, Editor
31 St James Avenue
Boston MA 02116-4167
617-482-5198
Category: 21-76-89
Circulation: 20,000
Issues per year: 6
Reviews: many
Does not buy serial rights.

Horse Digest
Patterson House
4 Loudown Street SE
Leesburg VA 22075
703-777-6508
Category: 15(horses)
　　　　69(horseback riding)
Circulation: 20,000
Issues per year: 12

Horticulture
Thomas H Cooper, Editor
755 Boylston Street
Boston MA 02116
617-247-4100
Category: 43(gardening)
Circulation: 136,000
Issues per year: 12

Hospital Fund Raising
Robert Jenkins, Editor
Health Resources Publishing
P O Box 1442
Wall Township NJ 07719
Category: 19(fundraising)

Hospital Giftshop Magazine
7628 Densmore Avenue
Van Nuys CA 91406
Category: 19(retail marketing)
　　　　39-99

Hospital Practice
Samuel Bukantz, Editor
575 Lexington Avenue
New York NY 10022
212-421-7320
Category: 39

Hotline
Fred Goss, Editor
The Newsletter Association
1341 G Street NW #700
Washington DC 20005
202-347-5220
Category: 19(publishing)
Issues per year: 12

House & Garden
Shelley Wanger, Editor
350 Madison Avenue

New York NY 10017
212-880-8800
Category: 43
Circulation: 850,000
Issues per year: 12
Reviews: 5/issue
Buys 1st and 2nd serial rights.

House Beautiful
JoAnn R Barwick, Editor
Susan Zevon, Building Editor
Sarah Belk, Food Editor
Ken Druse, Garden Editor
Elizabeth Hunter, Travel Editor
1700 Broadway
New York NY 10019
212-903-5000
Category: 11(architecture)-27
　　　　43-71
Issues per year: 12

Household
SunBelt Publications
3001 Redhill Avenue, Bldg I-206
Costa Mesa CA 92626
714-521-4283
Category: 35-43
Circulation: 750,000
Issues per year: 12
Does not buy serial rights.

Houston
Richard Stanley, Editor
1100 Milam Building #2580
Houston TX 77002
713-651-1313
Category: 19-61(Houston TX)

Houston Business Journal
Bill Schadewald, Editor
5314 Bingle Road
P O Box 10973
Houston TX 77092
713-688-8811
Category: 19-61(Houston TX)
Circulation: 25,000
Issues per year: 12

Houston City Magazine
Fred Rhodes, Editor
1800 W Loop #1450
Houston TX 77027
214-850-7600
Category: 61(Houston TX)
Issues per year: 12

Houston Monthly
Roger Arnhart, Arts Editor
Jo Ann Horton, Food Editor
Janet Henke, Managing Editor
Sheila Keranen, Travel Editor
8313 Southwest Freeway #220
Houston TX 77074
713-772-1039
Category: 11-27-33-39
　　　　61(Houston TX)-71
Circulation: 55,000
Issues per year: 12

Humber Magazine World
205 Humber College Boulevard
Rexdale M9W 5L7 ON Canada
Category: 19(publishing)-99

Hungry Mind Review
Bart Schneider, Editor
1648 Grand Avenue
St. Paul MN 55105
612-699-0587
Category: 11-43-55-57-61(MW)-75
95-99
Issues per year: 4
Reviews: many
Does not buy serial rights.

I Know You Know
Jernan Ltd
5335 N Tacoma #14
Indianapolis IN 46220
Category: 37-73
Issues per year: 12

ID (International Design)
Chee Pearlman, Editor
330 West 42nd Street
New York NY 10036
212-695-4955
Category: 19-23(design
engineering)
Circulation: 13,000
Issues per year: 6
Reviews: 1-10/issue
Does not buy serial rights.

Ideas for Better Living
Susan W Mulgrew, Editor
1755 Northwest Boulevard
Columbus OH 43212
614-488-8252
Category: 27-43
Circulation: 450,000

Illinois Writers Review
Curtis White, Editor
Illinois Writers Inc
P O Box 562
Macomb IL 61455
Category: 61(IL)

Impact Newsletter
Robert L Baker, Editor
Baker & Bowden
P O Box 1896
Evanston IL 60204-1896
Category: 19(communications
publicity)
Issues per year: 12

In Business
Jerome Goldstein, Editor
18 S 17th Street
P O Box 351
Emmaus PA 18049
215-967-4135
Category: 19(marketing)
Circulation: 70,000
Issues per year: 6

In Tech
Charles Robinson, Product Editor
67 Alexander Drive
P O Box 12277
Research Triangle NC 27709
919-549-8411
Category: 19-23(design
engineering)

In-Register Newsletter
Richard Michaels, Editor
1485 Bayshore Boulevard
San Francisco CA 94124
415-467-8760
Category: 11(graphics)
Issues per year: 12

Inc Magazine
Sara Noble, Managing Editor
38 Commercial Wharf
Boston MA 02110
617-227-4700
Category: 19
Circulation: 600,000
Issues per year: 12

Income Opportunity
Jo Daffron, Editor
380 Lexington Avenue
New York NY 10017
212-557-9100
Category: 19(opportunities)
Circulation: 421,000
Issues per year: 12

Independent Agent
Stuart D'Adolf, Editor
100 Church Street
New York NY 10007
212-285-4250
Category: 19(insurance)
Issues per year: 12
Reviews: 2/month

Indiana Business
Joan Marie, Editor
1200 Waterway Boulevard
Indianapolis IN 46200
317-631-5645
Category: 10-61(IN)

Industrial World
J Fuentecilia, Editor
386 Park Avenue South
New York NY 10016
212-689-0120
Category: 19(industrial)-23-67
Circulation: 66,000
Issues per year: 9
Reviews: 10-12/year

Industry
Angelo Alabiso, Editor
462 Boylston Street
P O Box 763
Boston MA 02117
617-262-1180
Category: 19(industrial)

Industry Week
John Carson, News Editor
1111 Chester Avenue
Cleveland OH 44114
216-696-7000
Category: 19(industrial)
Issues per year: 52

Information Marketing Letter
Mark Nolan, Editor
139 G Street #162
Davis CA 95616
916-758-1379
Category: 19(marketing)
Circulation: 1,500
Issues per year: 12

Information Strategy
Ray Slater, Editor
Auerbach Publishers
6560 N Park Drive
Pennsauken NJ 08109-4374
609-662-2070
Category: 19-23(information
management)
Issues per year: 4
Does not buy serial rights.

Information Technology & Library
Editor
American Library Association
50 E Huron Street
Chicago IL 60611
312-944-6780
Category: 23-99

Information Week
Editor
CMP Publications
333 East Shore Road
Manhasset NY 11030
Category: 19-23
Issues per year: 52

Infoworld
Rory J O'Connor, News Editor
1060 Marsh Road #C-200
Menlo Park CA 94025
Category: 23
Issues per year: 52

Inkling
John Hall, Publisher
Books on Review
P O Box 128
Alexandria VA 56308
Category: 11(writing)-19
(publishing)
Issues per year: 12

Inside Bookselling
Brock Brower, Editor
Lebhar-Friedman
425 Park Avenue
New York NY 10022
212-371-9400
Category: 19(publishing)
Issues per year: 52

Magazine Editors and Book Reviewers

Instructor & Teacher
Leanna Landsmann, Editor
545 Fifth Avenue
New York NY 10017
212-888-3400
Category: 31

International Business Monthly
T George Pratt, Publisher
George's Publishing
P O Box 87339
Houston TX 77287-7339
713-641-0201
Category: 11-19-23-33
       42(automotive)-67-71
Circulation: 130,000
Issues per year: 12
Reviews: 10/issue
Buys only 1st serial rights.

International Jewish Monthly
Marc Silver, Editor
1640 Rhode Island Avenue NW
Washington DC 20036
202-857-6645
Category: 63(Jewish)
Issues per year: 12

International Publishing
K S Giniger, Editor
K S Giniger Company
1133 Broadway #1301
New York NY 10010
212-645-5150
Category: 19(publishing)
Issues per year: 12

Interview
Gael Love, Editor
19 East 32nd Street
New York NY 10016
212-685-1800
Category: 11-17-33
Issues per year: 12

Intl. Rehabilitation Review
Barbara Duncan, Editor
25 East 21st Street
New York NY 10010
212-869-0460
Category: 39

Intl. Social Science Review
Dr Panos D Bardis, Editor
University of Toledo
Toledo OH 43606
Category: 55(social studies)-65

Iowa Commerce
Thomas P Gale, Editor
Bolger Publications
3301 Como Avenue SE
Minneapolis MN 55414
612-645-6311
Category: 19-61(IA)
Issues per year: 6
Reviews: 2-3/year

Iris: A Journal about Women
Karen Whitehall, Books Editor
c/o Women's Studies Department
B5 Garrett Hall, Univ of VA
Charlottesville VA 22903
804-924-8979
Category: 73-75-95

Irish America
34 East 29th Street
New York NY 10016
212-725-2993
Category: 99(Irish American)

Isaac Asimov Science Fiction
Baird Searles, Book Editor
c/o The Science Fiction Shop
56 Eighth Avenue
New York NY 10014
Category: 86
Circulation: 100,000
Issues per year: 13
Reviews: 7-8/issue
Buys 1st and 2nd serial rights.

IWI Monthly
Deborah Bosley, Editor
Illinois Writers Inc
P O Box 562
Macomb IL 61455
Category: 99-61(IL)
Issues per year: 12

Jewelry & Gem Business
Linda Couch, Editor
P O Box 687
El Sobrante CA 94804
Category: 19(retail marketing)
       29(jewelry)
Circulation: 50,000
Issues per year: 6

Jewish Exponent
Sara Butler, Librarian
226 S 16th Street
Philadelphia PA 19102
Category: 63(Jewish)
Issues per year: 12

Jewish Press
Sholom Klass, Editor
338 Third Avenue
Brooklyn NY 11215
212-858-3300
Category: 63(Jewish)

Journal of Academic Libraries
Ann P Dougherty, Editor
P O Box 8330
Ann Arbor MI 48107
313-662-3925
Category: 59-65
Circulation: 2,700
Issues per year: 6

Journal of Accountancy
Barbara Shildneck, Editor
1211 Avenue of the Americas

New York NY 10036
212-575-6200
Category: 19(financial)

Journal of Accounting & EDP
Ray Slater, Editor
Auerbach Publishers
6560 N Park Drive
Pennsauken NJ 08109-4374
609-662-2070
Category: 19(accounting)-23
Circulation: 10,000
Issues per year: 4
Reviews: 2-4/issue
Does not buy serial rights.

**Journal of Information and
Image Management**
Ellen T Meyer, Editor
8719 Colesville Road
Silver Spring MD 20910
Category: 19-23

Journal of Learning Disabilities
Gerald M Senf, Editor
Profession Press
11 East Adams Street
Chicago IL 60603
312-922-5959
Category: 31-39

Journal of Marketing
Roger Kerin, Books Editor
Marketing Department
Southern Methodist University
Dallas TX 75275
312-648-0536
Category: 19(marketing)
Circulation: 10,000
Issues per year: 4

Journal of Marketing Research
Department of Marketing
University of Texas
Austin TX 78712
Category: 19(marketing)

Journal of Petroleum Technology
Jim McInnis, Editor
Society of Petroleum Engineers
P O Box 833836
Richardson TX 75083-3836
214-669-3377
Category: 23
Circulation: 59,000
Issues per year: 12
Reviews: 50-75/year
Does not buy serial rights.

Journal of Planning Literature
Editor
Ohio State University Press
1050 Carmack Road
Columbus OH 43210
614-422-6930
Category: 55(city planning)
Circulation: 2,000
Issues per year: 4

Journal of Rehabilitation
Dick Dietl, Editor
633 S Washington Street
Alexandria VA 22314
703-836-0850
Category: 39

Journal of Taxation
Ronald Klinger, Editor
1633 Broadway
New York NY 10019
212-977-7400
Category: 19-55(taxes)

Journalism Quarterly
Donald Shane and Jane Brown,
Book Review Editors
U of NC, School of Journalism
Chapel Hill NC 27514
Category: 19(journalism)
Issues per year: 4

JRG Newsletter
Jessyca Russell Gaver, Editor
167 Center Street
Metchen NJ 08840
201-549-7338
Category: 19(publishing)
Issues per year: 20

Junior Scholastic
Lee Baier, Editor
730 Broadway
New York NY 10003
212-505-2307
Category: 31

Just CrossStitch Magazine
Phyllis Hoffman, Editor
Symbol of Excellence Publishing
P O Box 76091
Birmingham AL 35213
205-967-8402
Category: 29(cross stitch)
Issues per year: 6

Kansas Business News
Dan Bearth, Editor
3601 SW 29th Street #124
P O Box 511
Topeka KS 66614
913-273-3010
Category: 19-61(KS)

Kansas City Business
Mark Pawlosky, Editor
3527 Broadway #500
Kansas City MO 64111
816-561-5900
Category: 19-61(KS/MO)
Circulation: 17,000
Issues per year: 12

Kirkus Reviews
Joanna Rudge Long, Children
Ann Larsen, Fiction
Ron De Paolo, Non-Fiction
200 Park Avenue

New York NY 10003
212-777-4554
Category: 10-21-31-75-76-89
Circulation:
Issues per year: 12
Does not buy serial rights.

Kiwanis Magazine
Scott Pemberton, Editor
Kiwanis International
3636 Woodview Terrace
Indianapolis IN 46268
Category: 99
Issues per year: 12

Kobrin Letter
732 N Greer Road
Palo Alto CA 94303
Category: 21-76-89
Issues per year: 8

L'Actualite
Jean Pare, Editor
1001 Maisonneuve Boulevard
Montreal H3A 3E1 PQ Canada
514-845-5141
Category: 61(Montreal CN)
Issues per year: 12

L.A. Business Journal
David Yochum, Editor
3727 West 6th Street
Los Angeles CA 90020
213-385-9050
Category: 19-61(Los Angeles CA)

Ladies Home Journal
Myrna Blyth, Editor-in-Chief
Mary Lou Mullen, Books Editor
Marilyn Glass, Design Editor
Lois Johnson, Fashion Editor
Jan Hazard, Food Editor
3 Park Avenue
New York NY 10016
212-340-9200
Category: 11(design)-27-29-35
          39-43-73-75-95
          98(beauty and fashion)
Issues per year: 12
Buys 1st and 2nd serial rights.

Lake Superior Port Cities
325 Lake Avenue South
Duluth MN 55802
Category: 61(MN, WI)
Issues per year: 6

Law Enforcement Technology
Doug Neiss, Editor
50 West 23rd Street
New York NY 10010-5205
212-725-2300
Category: 23-55

Learning 86
Susan Oranian, Editor
Springhouse Corporation
1111 Bethlehem Pike

Springhouse PA 19477
215-646-8700
Category: 31-41-55
Circulation: 200,000
Issues per year: 9
Reviews: 10+/issue

Learning for All Seasons
Susan B Capon, Editor
P O Box 579
Lexington MA 02173
617-861-0379
Category: 19(marketing)-31

Legal Systems Letter
William E Owens, Editor
3637 N Peachtree Road
Atlanta GA 30341
Category: 19-55(law)

Leisure Time Electronics
Dan Shannon, Editor
US Business Press
11 West 19th Street
New York NY 10011
212-741-7210
Category: 23-29-69
Issues per year: 12

Lens Magazine
Barry Tanenbaum, Editor
Hearst Business Publishing
645 Stewart Avenue
Garden City NY 11530
516-227-1300
Category: 11(photography)
Issues per year: 6
Reviews: 2-3/issue

Lens On Campus
Barry Tanenbaum, Editor
Attn: At Last Department
645 Stewart Avenue
Garden City NY 11530
516-227-1300
Category: 11(photography)-31
Circulation: 90,000
Issues per year: 6

Library Hi Tech
Edward Wall, Editor
P O Box 1808
Ann Arbor MI 48106
313-434-5530
Category: 23-99

Library Journal
Janet Fletcher, Books Editor
205 East 42nd Street
New York NY 10017
212-916-1927
Category: 99
Circulation: 28,000
Issues per year: 20

Library Quarterly
Mary Biggs, Editor
Graduate Library School

1100 E 57th Street
Chicago IL 60637
312-962-8266
Category: 99
Circulation: 3,000
Issues per year: 4

Life
Judith Daniels, Managing Editor
Jeff Wheelwright, Science Editor
Time-Life Building
Rockefeller Center
New York NY 10020-1393
212-586-1212
Category: 17-23-67-99
Issues per year: 12
Buys 1st and 2nd serial rights.

Lifestyle
Patricia Kimball, Editor
2194 Palou Avenue
San Francisco CA 94124
415-824-2900
Category: 11-33
        61(San Franisco CA)
Issues per year: 12

Lifestyle Guide
Gillian Bell, Editor
1909 N Enterprise Street
Orange CA 92665
714-921-0624
Category: 11-33-61(Orange Cty CA)
Issues per year: 12

Lilith
Editor, Book Reviews
250 West 57th Street #1328
New York NY 10019
212-757-0818
Category: 83(Jewish)-73

Lion Magazine
Robert Kleinfelder, Editor
Intl Association of Lions Clubs
300 - 22nd Street
Oak Brook IL 60570
Category: 99
Issues per year: 12

Literary Magazine Review
G. W. Clift, Editor
English Department, Denison Hall
Kansas State University
Manhattan KS 66506
Category: 83-95
Issues per year: 4

Locus
Charles Brown, Editor
P O Box 13305
34 Ridgewood Lane
Oakland CA 94611
415-339-9196
Category: 86
Circulation: 8,000
Issues per year: 12
Reviews: 12/issue

Los Angeles
Geoff Miller, Editor
1888 Century Park East
Los Angeles CA 90067
213-557-7569
Category: 11-33
        61(Los Angeles CA)
Issues per year: 12

Lotus Magazine
Editor, Book Reviews
Lotus Publishing Corporation
55 Cambridge Parkway
Cambridge MA 02142
617-494-1192
Category: 23(Lotus software)

Louisiana Life
Paul Stahls, Editor
P O Box 308
Matairie LA 70004
504-456-2220
Category: 61(LA)-75(LA)
Circulation: 50,000
Issues per year: 6
Reviews: 50/year
Does not buy serial rights.

Lutheran
Edgar Trexler, Editor
2900 Queen Lane
Philadelphia PA 19129
215-438-6580
Category: 63(Lutheran)

M-Gentle Men for Gender Justice
Feminist Men's Publications
306 N Brooks Street
Madison WI 53715
Category: 13-37-73

MACazine
Barbara J Chan, Editor
ICon Concepts Corporation
P O Box 1936
Athens TX 75751
214-677-2793
Category: 23(Macintosh)

Macintosh Connection
Russell Mareno, Editor
Hi-Tek Publishers
P O Box 99
North Salem NH 03073
603-893-2485
Category: 23(Macintosh)
Issues per year: 12

Maclean's Magazine
Kevin Doyle, Editor
777 Bay Street
Toronto M5W 1A7 ON Canada
416-596-5000
Category: 19-61(CN)

Macworld
Jerry Borrell, Editor
PC World Communications

555 De Haro Street
San Francisco CA 94107
415-861-3861
Category: 23(Macintosh)
Issues per year: 12

Mademoiselle
Carol Rinzler, Editor
    Dollars & Sense
350 Madison Avenue
New York NY 10017
212-880-8800
Category: 39-73-99(fashion and
        beauty)
Issues per year: 12

Madison Avenue Magazine
John Chervokas, Editor
369 Lexington Avenue
New York NY 10017
212-972-0600
Category: 19(advertising
        marketing)
Issues per year: 12

Magazine & Bookseller
Michele M Marini, Editor
North American Publishing
322 Eighth Avenue
New York NY 10001
212-620-7330
Category: 19(publishing
        retail marketing)
Circulation: 30,000
Issues per year: 12
Reviews: none
Does not buy serial rights.

Magazine Age
Alfred B Lee, Editor
225 Park Avenue
New York NY 10169
Category: 19(publishing)-99

Magazine Design and Production
Michael Scheibach, Editor
4551 S 107th Street #210
Overland Park KS 66207
913-642-6611
Category: 11(graphics)
        19(publishing)
Issues per year: 6

Magazine of Bibliographies
Lalla C Critz, Editor
1209 Clover Lane
Fort Worth TX 76107
Category: 59(bibliographies)
Issues per year: 6

Mail Order Digest
Paul Muchnick, Editor
National Mail Order Association
5818 Venice Boulevard
Los Angeles CA 90019
Category: 19(marketing)
Issues per year: 12
Reviews: 1/issue

Management Accounting
Erwin S Koval, Editor
Al King, Computer Editor
10 Paragon Drive
Montvale NJ 07645
201-573-6000
Category: 19(financial)-23
Circulation: 90,000
Issues per year: 12
Reviews: 8-10/issue
Does not buy serial rights.

Management Contents
2265 Carlson Drive #5000
Northfield IL 60062
Category: 19(management)
Issues per year: 26

Management Review
George Miliute, Book Editor
American Management Association
135 West 50th Street
New York NY 10020
212-568-8100
Category: 19(management)
Circulation: 83,000
Issues per year: 12

Management World
Jeffrey Long, Editor
2360 Maryland Road
Willow Grove PA 19090
215-659-4300
Category: 19(management)
Circulation: 13,000
Issues per year: 12

Manhattan
Rick Bard, Books Editor
158 West 81st Street #91
New York NY 10024
212-362-1260
Category: 11-33-61(New York NY)
          99
Circulation: 50,000
Issues per year: 4
Reviews: 3-8/issue
Does not buy serial rights.

Marketing & Media Decisions
Sandra Rifkin, Editor
1140 Avenue of the Americas
New York NY 10036
212-391-2155
Category: 19(advertising
          marketing)

Marketing Communications
Aimmee Stern, Editor
475 Park Avenue South
New York NY 10016
212-725-2300
Category: 19(advertising
          marketing)

Marketing Times
Roy Alexander, Editor
330 West 42nd Street

New York NY 10036
212-339-1919
Category: 19(marketing)
Circulation: 25,000
Issues per year: 6

Maryland
Bonnie Joe Ayers, Editor
45 Calvert
Annapolis MD 21401
301-269-3507
Category: 61(MD)

Maryland Business and Living
Joni Le Sage, Editor
1 E Chase Street
Baltimore MD 21202
301-234-0996
Category: 19-61(MD)

McCall's
A Elizabeth Sloan, Editor
Mary Clarke, Beauty Editor
Helen DelMonte, Book Editor
Ann Arnott, Business Editor
Ann Cassidy, Family Editor
David Denley, Feature Editor
Marianne Langer, Food Editor
Sid Wood, Home Editor
Denise Hatfield, Science Editor
Andrea Thompson, Senior Editor
Katy Koontz, Travel Editor
230 Park Avenue
New York NY 10169
212-551-9500
Category: 11-19-27-29-31-33-35
          39-43-67-73-75-90-98
          (beauty and fashion)
          99
Issues per year: 12
Reviews: varies
Buys 1st and 2nd serial rights.

MD Magazine
Barbara Guidos, Editor
30 East 60th Street
New York NY 10022
212-355-5432
Category: 39
Circulation: 155,000
Issues per year: 12

Mechanix Illustrated
Joseph Provey, Editor
1515 Broadway, 12th Floor
New York NY 10036
212-719-6626
Category: 23-29-43-67
Circulation: 800,000
Issues per year: 12

Media & Methods
Michele Sokoloff, Book Editor
American Society of Educators
1511 Walnut Street
Philadelphia PA 19102
215-563-3501
Category: 11-22-31

Circulation: 40,000
Issues per year: 6
Reviews: 4/issue

Media Magazine
Sheri Craig, Editor
Michael Rechtshaffen, Arts Editor
Jim McElgunn, Business Editor
Werner Bartsch, Computer Editor
Crailer Communications
643 Yonge Street
Toronto M4Y 1Z9 ON Canada
416-927-7200
Category: 11-19(advertising)-23
          33
Circulation: 10,000
Issues per year: 12
Does not buy serial rights.
Reviews: 3/issue

Media People
Gene Williamson, Editor
P O Box 3905
Grand Central Station
New York NY 10163
212-573-8582
Category: 19(advertising)

Medical Economics
Don Berg, Editor
680 Kinderkamack Road
Oradell NJ 07649
201-262-3030
Category: 19-39

Medical Electronics
Milton Aronson, Editor
2994 W Liberty
Pittsburgh PA 15216
412-343-9666
Category: 23-39

Medical Reference Services
Sandra M Wood, Editor
Harrell Library, Hershey Center
Pennsylvania State University
Hershey PA 17033
212-228-2800
Category: 39-59
Circulation: 800
Issues per year: 4

Medical Self-Care
P O Box 717
Inverness CA 94937
Category: 39
Issues per year: 4

Medical Tribune
Abraham Jacobson, Editor
257 Park Avenue South
New York NY 10010
212-674-8500
Category: 39

Medical World News
Mal Mander, Books Editor
211 East 43rd Street

New York NY 10017
212-490-7800
Category: 39

Memphis
Kenneth Neill, Editor
David Dawson, Books Editor
460 Tennessee Street
P O Box 256
Memphis TN 38101
901-521-9000
Category: 61(Memphis TN)-99
Circulation: 28,000
Issues per year: 12
Reviews: 2-3/issue

Men's Health
Editor, Special Interest,
Rodale Press
33 E Minor Street
Emmaus PA 18049
215-967-5171
Category: 39-69
Issues per year: 2

Merchandising
1515 Broadway
New York NY 10036
212-869-1300
Category: 19(retail marketing)

Merchant Magazine
Anita M Mumm, Editor
4500 Campus Drive #480
Newport Beach CA 92660
Category: 19(retail marketing)

Metro Newark
Robert England, Editor
338 Montgomery Street
P O Box 442
Jersey City NJ 07302
210-433-3133
Category: 19-61(Newark NJ)

Metro Toronto Business
Alan Morantz, Editor
3 First Canadian Place
P O Box 60
Toronto M5X 1C1 ON Canada
416-366-6811
Category: 19-61(Toronto CN)

Metropolitan Detroit
Kirk Cheyfitz, Editor
Paul Eisenstein, Business Editor
Dan Acosta, Medical Editor
422 W Congress
Detroit MI 48226
313-963-8500
Category: 19-29-61(Detroit MI)
Circulation: 90,000
Issues per year: 12

Metropolitan Home
Dorothy Kalins, Editor
Colin Andrews, Feature Writer
  Word of Mouth Department

Michael Walker, Senior Editor
  Hot Properties
750 Third Avenue
New York NY 10017
212-557-6600
Category: 43
Circulation: 715,000
Issues per year: 12
212-557-6600
Category: 27
Circulation: 715,000
Issues per year: 12
Reviews: 4-6/year
Does not buy serial rights.

Miami / South Florida
Erica Ravzin, Editor
75 SW 15 Road
Miami FL 33134
305-374-5011
Category: 61(Miami FL)
Issues per year: 12

Michigan Business
Ron Garbinski, Editor
30161 Southfield Road #302
Southfield MI 48076
313-647-0111
Category: 19-61(MI)
Circulation: 28,000
Issues per year: 12
Reviews: 1-3/issue
Does not buy serial rights.

Michigan Living
Leonard Barnes, Editor
17000 Executive Plaza Drive
Dearborn MI 48126
313-336-1211
Category: 61(MI)
Issues per year: 12

Micro Money Newsletter
Harry Wahl, Editor
P O Box 218
Washington IL 61571
Category: 19(marketing)-23

Microcomputing
Sheila Wright, Editor
80 Pine Street
Peterborough NH 03458
603-924-9471
Category: 23

Midwest Bookwatch
James Cox, Editor
Midwest Book Reviews
278 Orchard Drive
Oregon WI 53575
608-835-7937
Category: 99-61(MN, WI, IA, IL)
Circulation: 3,000
Issues per year: 6

Milwaukee
Charles J Sykes, Editor
312 E Buffalo

Milwaukee WI 53202
414-273-1101
Category: 61(Milwaukee WI)-99
Circulation: 44,000
Issues per year: 12
Buys 1st and 2nd serial rights.

Ministers Library
Cyril J Barbar, Editor
P O Box 5181
Hacienda Heights CA 91745-0181
Category: 63

Minneapolis City Business
John Kostouros, Editor
Gail E MarksJarvis, Managing Ed
600 First Avenue N #600
Minneapolis MN 55403
612-333-3717
Category: 19-23-61(Minneapolis MN)
  99
Circulation: 45,000
Issues per year: 6
Reviews: 5/year
Does not buy serial rights.

Minnesota Business Journal
Don Nelson, Editor
Dorn Communications
7831 E Bush Lake Road
Minneapolis MN 55435
612-835-6855
Category: 19-61(MN)
Circulation: 26,000
Does not buy serial rights.

Minnesota Review
Department of English
Oregon State University
Corvallis OR 97331
Category: 47-75-95
Issues per year: 2

Minnesota Reviews
Nancy Alsop, Editor
701 - 11th Street N
Virginia MN 55792
Category: 61(Minnesota)-99

Minorities and Women in Business
James Everett, Editor
Marion Pierre, Arts Editor
1701 Link Road
Winston-Salem NC 27103
919-722-3927
Category: 11-19-33-49-73
Circulation: 53,000+
Issues per year: 6
Does not buy serial rights.

Minority Engineer
Ann Kelly, Editor
Equal Opportunity Publications
44 Broadway
Greenlawn NY 11740
516-261-8917
Category: 19(career guidance)
  23-49

Circulation: 16,000
Issues per year: 4
Buys only 2nd serial rights.

Missouri Life
Debra Gluck, Editor
710 N Tucker
St Louis MO 63101
314-342-1281
Category: 61(MO)
Issues per year: 12

Modern Maturity
Ian Ledgerwood, Editor
215 Long Beach Boulevard
Long Beach CA 90801
212-432-5781
Category: 99(retirement)
Issues per year: 12

Modern Office Technology
Lura K Romei, Editor
1111 Chester Avenue
Cleveland OH 44144
216-696-7000
Category: 19(office)-23
Circulation: 156,000
Issues per year: 12
Reviews: 1/issue
Buys only 1st serial rights.

Modern Photography
Julia Scully, Editor
825 Seventh Avenue
New York NY 10019
212-265-8360
Category: 11(photography)
Issues per year: 12

Money
Gus Hedberg, Editor
1271 Avenue of the Americas
New York NY 10020
212-586-1212
Category: 19-99(money)
Issues per year: 12

Moneysworth
Susan Rogers, Editor
1775 Broadway, 26th Floor
New York NY 10019
212-581-2000
Category: 19-99(money)
Circulation: 1,000,000
Issues per year: 12

Montana Magazine
Carolyn Cunningham, Editor
3020 Bozeman Avenue
P O Box 5630
Helena MT 59604
406-443-2842
Category: 61(MT)
Circulation: 85,000
Issues per year: 6
Reviews: 4-5/issue
Does not buy serial rights.

Monthly Detroit
Don Kubit, Books Editor
1400 Woodward #1123
Detroit MI 48207
313-962-2350
Category: 61(Detroit MI)
Issues per year: 12

Moose Magazine
R Dickow, Managing Editor
Loyal Order of Moose
Mooseheart IL 60539
Category: 99
Issues per year: 12

Morrow Owner's Review
Spyko Andreae, Editor
P O Box 5487
Berkeley CA 94705
415-644-2638
Category: 23(CPM specific)
Issues per year: 6

Mother Earth News
Bruce Woods, Editor
Access Department
P O Box 70
Hendersonville NC 28791
Category: 13-15-19-27-29-39-43
        51-53-71
Issues per year: 6

Mother Jones
Bruce Dancis, Managing Editor
Attn: Books in Brief
1663 Mission Street
San Francisco CA 94103
415-558-8881
Category: 13-99
Issues per year: 10
Reviews: 3/issue
Buys 1st and 2nd serial rights.

Mothering
Mothering Publications
P O Box 8410
Santa Fe NM 87504
Category: 13-35-73

Mothers Today
Janet King, Editor
441 Lexington Avenue
New York NY 10017
212-867-4820
Category: 21-31-35-76-79
Circulation: 900,000
Issues per year: 6

Motorland
John Holmgren, Editor
150 Van Ness Avenue
San Francisco CA 94101
415-565-2620
Category: 43-71

Mpls-St Paul
Brian Anderson, Editor
12 S 6th Street #1030

Minneapolis MN 55402
612-339-7571
Category: 61(Minneapolis
          St Paul MN)
Issues per year: 12

Ms.
Ruth Sullivan, Books Editor
119 West 40th Street
New York NY 10018
212-719-9800
Category: 73
Issues per year: 12

Nashville's BookTalk
Roger Bishop, Editor
3823 Green Hills Village Drive
Nashville TN 37215
615-298-3357
Category: 99
Issues per year: 11
Reviews: many
Does not buy serial rights.

The Nation
Victor Navasky, Editor
72 Fifth Avenue
New York NY 10011
212-242-8400
Category: 55
Issues per year: 12

Nation's Business
Robert T Gray, Editor
1615 H Street NW
Washington DC 20062
202-659-6010
Category: 19-55
Circulation: 765,000
Issues per year: 12

National Business Woman
Leah Glasheen, Editor
2012 Massachusetts Avenue NW
Washington DC 20036
202-293-1100
Category: 19-73

National Catholic Register
Fran Maier, Editor
6404 Wilshire #900
Los Angeles CA 90048
213-653-2200
Category: 63(Catholic)

National Home Business Report
Barbara Brabec, Editor
P O Box 2137
Naperville IL 60566
Category: 19(small business)-29
Issues per year: 4

National Lampoon
Larry Sloman, Editor
635 Madison Avenue
New York NY 10022
212-688-4070
Category: 33

Circulation: 300,000
Issues per year: 12
Reviews: none
Buys 1st and 2nd serial rights.

National Law Journal
Steve Bauman, Editor
111 Eighth Avenue
New York NY 10011
212-741-8300
Category: 19-55(law)

National Parks
Michele Strutin, Senior Editor
National Parks and Conservation
1701 - 18th Street NW
Washington DC 20009
202-265-1717
Category: 51-69-71
Circulation: 100,000
Issues per year: 12

National Productivity Review
Myrna Leboy, Editor
33 West 60th Street
New York NY 10023
212-489-2670
Category: 19
Circulation: 5,000
Issues per year: 4

National Public Accountant
Stanley Stearman, Editor
1010 N Fairfax Street
Alexandria VA 22314
703-549-6400
Category: 19(financial)

National Real Estate Investor
Editor
Communication Channels
6255 Barfield Road
Atlanta GA 30328
404-256-9800
Category: 19(real estate)
Circulation: 28,000

National Review
William F Buckley Jr, Editor
254 Fifth Avenue
New York NY 10001
212-684-5500
Category: 41-55
Issues per year: 12

Natural Foods Merchandiser
Editor
328 S Main
New Hope PA 18938
Category: 19(retail marketing)
        27-39

Naval Affairs
Robert Nolan, Editor
1303 New Hampshire Avenue NW
Washington DC 20036
202-785-2768
Category: 55(military)

NEA Today
Ann Kurzius, Editor
1201 16th Street NW
Washington DC 20036
202-822-7200
Category: 31

Needle & Thread
Margaret Dittman, Editor
Bassion Publishing Company
4949 Byers
Ft Worth TX 76107
Category: 29(needlecraft)
Issues per year: 6

Needle People News
Margaret Fredericks, Editor
P O Box 115
Syosset NY 11791
Category: 29(needlecraft)

Needlecraft for Today
Charlie E Davis, Editor
Bassion Publishing Company
4949 Byers
Ft Worth TX 76107
Category: 29(needlecraft)
Issues per year: 6

Needlepoint Bulletin
Sharelen Weldon Weldon, Editor
P O Box 1585
Jupiter FL 33468-1585
Category: 29(needlecraft)
Issues per year: 12

Needlepoint News
Carol LaBranche, Editor
Wildflower Publications
P O Box 668
Evanston IL 60204
312-929-5000
Category: 29(needlecraft)
Circulation: 15,000
Issues per year: 6

Nevada Magazine
Jim Crandall, Editor
State of Nevada
Capitol Complex
Carson City NV 89710
702-885-5416
Category: 11-10-33-35-61(NV)
           69-71
Circulation: 75,000
Issues per year: 6
Reviews: 12/year
Does not buy serial rights.

New Age
Ruth Sullivan, Editor
Rising Star Associates
342 Western Avenue
Brighton MA 02135
617-787-2005
Category: 39-53
Issues per year: 12
Reviews: 2/issue

New Age Book Review
Douglas Aronson, Editor
Four Park Avenue
New York NY 10016
Category: 39-53-57-63

New Cleveland Woman
Jean Linderman, Editor
104 E Bridge Street
Berea OH 44017
216-243-3740
Category: 19-73
Circulation: 82,000
Issues per year: 12

New Dimensions
Tim Coffey, Editor
1908 Association Drive
Reston VA 22091
703-860-5000
Category: 31

New Directions for Women
Elizabeth Ann Sachs, Editor
17 Spruce Mountain Road
Danbury CT 06810
Category: 21-73-76-89
Issues per year: 6

New England Adweek
Charles Jackson, Editor
100 Boylston Street #735
Boston MA 02116
617-482-0876
Category: 19(advertising)

New England Business
Jane Adams, Books Editor
33 Union Street
Boston MA 02108
617-723-4300
Category: 19-61(New England)

New England Journal of Medicine
Arnold Relman, Editor
1440 Main Street
Waltham MA 02254
617-893-3800
Category: 39
Issues per year: 12

New England Living
Anne Marie Rafferty, Editor
Piper Street Inc
P O Box 725
Worcester MA 01613
617-892-4979
Category: 11-27-33-35-61(New
           England)-71
Circulation: 80,000
Issues per year: 6
Reviews: 30/year
Does not buy serial rights.

New Equipment Digest
Robert F King, Editor
Penton Publications
1111 Chester Avenue

Cleveland OH 44114
216-696-7000
Category: 19(purchasing
        industrial)
Circulation: 205,000
Issues per year: 12
Reviews: 14/issue
Does not buy serial rights.

New Home
Laurence E Oberwager, Editor
Village West, Country Club Road
P O Box 2008
Laconia NH 03247
Category: 29-43
Circulation: 200,000
Issues per year: 12

New Magazine Review
G. William Ludwig, Editor
P O Box 3699
Kachina Village
North Las Vegas NV 89030
Category: 75-95

New Mexico
V.B. Price, Editor
Bataan Memorial Building
Santa Fe NM 87503
505-827-6180
Category: 61(NM)
Issues per year: 12

New Orleans
Sandy Shilstone, Editor
6666 Morrison Road
P O Box 26815
New Orleans LA 70186
504-246-2700
Category: 61(New Orleans LA)
Issues per year: 12

New Orleans City Business
John Powers, Editor
111 Veterans #750
Metairie LA 70003
504-834-9292
Category: 19-61(New Orleans LA)
Circulation: 24,000

New Pages
Casey Hill, Editor
4426 S Belsay Road
Grand Blanc MI 48439
313-742-9583
Category: 13-37-53-73
Issues per year: 3

New Republic
Michael Kinsley, Editor
Steve Wasserman, Books Editor
1220 19th Street NW #200
Washington DC 20036
202-331-7494
Category: 55-99
Circulation:
Issues per year: 52
Reviews: 5-6/issue

New Shelter
John Viehman, Exec. Editor
Rodale Press
33 E Minor Street
Emmaus PA 18049
215-967-5171
Category: 43
Issues per year: 9

New Texas
Steven Dodds, Editor
P O Box 12165
Austin TX 98711
512-453-0515
Category: 19-61(Austin TX)
Issues per year: 12

New Woman
Sarah H Medford, Book Editor
215 Lexington Avenue
New York NY 10016
212-685-4790
Category: 39-73
Issues per year: 12
Buys 1st and 2nd serial rights.

New Women's Times
804 Meigs Street
Rochester NY 14620
716-271-5523
Category: 11-29
Issues per year: 11

New York
Deborah Harkins, Editor
755 Second Avenue
New York NY 10017
212-880-0700
Category: 11-33-61(New York NY)

New York Review of Books
Robert Silvers, Editor
250 West 57th Street
New York NY 10107
212-757-8070
Category: 99

New York Teacher
Ted Bleecker, Editor
260 Park Avenue South
New York NY 10010
212-254-7660
Category: 31-61(NY)

New Yorker
George Steiner, Book Editor
25 West 43rd Street
New York NY 10036
212-840-3800
Category: 75-95-99
Issues per year: 52
Reviews: 6/issue
Buys 1st and 2nd serial rights.

Newport Beach 714
883 Production Place
Newport Beach CA 92663-2809
Category: 61(Newport Beach CA)

News Basket
Shereen LaPlantz, Editor
Press de LaPlantz
899 Bayside Cutoff
Bayside CA 95524
Category: 29
Issues per year: 6

Newsletter on Newsletters
Howard Hudson, Editor
Newsletter Clearinghouse
44 W Market Street, P O Box 311
Rhinebeck NY 12572
914-876-2081
Category: 19(publishing
        marketing)
Issues per year: 12

Newsweek
Robert M Smith, Editor-in-Chief
Peter S. Prescott, Books Editor
444 Madison Avenue
New York NY 10022
212-350-4000
Category: 99
Issues per year: 52
Reviews: 3/issue
Buys 1st and 2nd serial rights.

Nightclub & Bar
Nancy Z Spillman, Editor
7618 Gazette Avenue
Canoga Park CA 91306
Category: 19-33

Nightlife
Rick Bard, Books Editor
158 West 81st Street #91
New York NY 10024
212-362-1260
Category: 11-33
Circulation: 90,000
Issues per year: 6
Reviews: 60/year
Does not buy serial rights.

Nit & Wit
Harrison McCormack, Editor
P O Box 627
Geneva IL 60134
312-232-9496
Category: 11-47-75-83

NJ Monthly
Larry Marscheck, Editor
7 Dumont Place
Morristown NJ 07960
201-539-8230
Category: 61(NJ)
Issues per year: 12

NJEA Review
Martha De Blieu, Editor
180 W State Street
P O Box 1211
Trenton NJ 08607
609-599-4561
Category: 31

No Apologies
Bryan R Monte, Editor
P O Box 1852
Brown University
Providence RI 02912
Category: 37-47-65-75-95
Circulation: 1,000
Issues per year: 3
Does not buy serial rights.

Nob Hill Gazette
Kathy Cole Manace, Editor
Pier 5
San Francisco CA 94111
415-788-3120
Category: 61(San Francisco CA)
Circulation: 55,000
Issues per year: 12
Reviews: 8-14/year
Does not buy serial rights.

Nolo News
Carol Pladsen, Editor
Nolo Press
950 Parker Street
Berkeley CA 94710
415-549-1976
Category: 19(accounting)-55(law)
Circulation: 45,000
Issues per year: 4

Non-Credit Learning News
Susan B Capon, Editor
Learning for All Seasons
P O Box 579
Lexington MA 02173
Category: 19(marketing
        management)-31
Does not buy serial rights.

Non-Foods Merchandising
US Business Press
11 West 19th Street
New York NY 10011
212-741-7210
Category: 19(marketing)
Issues per year: 12

NonProfit Executive
Susan Kalish, Editor
Taft Corporation
5125 MacArthur Boulevard NW
Washington DC 20016
Category: 19(fundraising)

Northwest Review of Books
Editor
P O Box 45593
Seattle WA 98145-0593
Category: 61-99(northwest OR
        WA, ID)

Nova Information Services
Louise Mazzalonga
Acquisitions Manager
6090 Jericho Turnpike
Commack NY 11725
Category: 23-55-67

Nursing 86
Jeanmarie Coogan, Editor
1111 Bethlehem Pike
Springhouse PA 19477
215-646-8700
Category: 39(nursing)
Issues per year: 12

Off Duty
Bruce Thorstad, Editor
Gail Perkins, Feature Editor
Mike Michaels, Tech Editor
3303 Harbor Boulevard #C-2
Costa Mesa CA 92626
714-549-7172
Category: 11-19-23-27-33-35-39
        43(automotive)
        55(military)-69-71-99
Circulation: 500,000
Issues per year: 12
Reviews: 10-12/year
Does not buy serial rights.

Off Our Backs
Editor, Book Reviews
Off Our Backs Collective
1841 Columbia Road NW #212
Washington DC 20009
Category: 13-55-73

Office Systems '86
William M Hogan, Editor
Attn: Reading Room
941 Danbury Road / P O Box 150
Georgetown CT 06829
203-544-9526
Category: 19(office)-23
Issues per year: 12
Reviews: 4-5/issue

Officer
Norman Burzynski, Editor
1 Constitution Avenue NE
Washington DC 20002
202-479-2200
Category: 55(military)

Ohio Business
Robert Gardner, Editor
1720 Euclid
Playhouse Square Building
Cleveland OH 44115
216-621-1644
Category: 19-61(OH)

Ohio Magazine
Ellen Stein, Editor
40 S Third Street
Columbus OH 43215
614-461-5083
Category: 61(OH)-99
Circulation: 119,000
Issues per year: 12
Buys 1st and 2nd serial rights.

Ohio Review
Editor, Book Reviews
Ellis Hall, Room 320

Ohio University
Athens OH 45701
Category: 47-75-95
Issues per year: 3

Oklahoma Business
J P Ulman, Editor
2525 NW Expressway #406
Oklahoma City OK 73112
405-943-3006
Category: 19-61(OK)

Oklahoma Living
Lu Hollander, Editor
P O Box 76179
Oklahoma City OK 73147
405-943-4289
Category: 61(OK)
Issues per year: 12

Old-House Journal
Patricia Poore, Editor
69A Seventh Avenue
Brooklyn NY 11217
Category: 43(house & home)

Omni
Gurney Williams III, Editor
1965 Broadway
New York NY 100235965
212-469-6100
Category: 12-23-53-67-86
Circulation: 600,000
Issues per year: 12
Buys only 1st serial rights.

On Cable Magazine
Peter Funt, Editor
25 Van Zant Street/P O Box 239
Norwalk CT 06855
203-866-6256
Category: 33

1001 Decorating Ideas
Evan B Frances, Editor
149 Fifth Avenue
New York NY 10010
Category: 29-43
Circulation: 750,000

1001 Home Ideas
Ellen Frankel, Editor
Lynne Cusack, Senior Editor
Phyllis M Kohn, Food Editor
3 Park Avenue
New York NY 10016
212-340-9200
Category: 27-29-43
Circulation: 1,500,000
Issues per year: 12
Buys only 2nd serial rights.

Ontario Craft & CraftNews
Susan Eckenwalder, Editor
346 Dundas Street W
Toronto M5T 1G5 ON Canada
Category: 29
Issues per year: 4

Ontario Living
Liz Primeau, Editor
2300 Yonge Street #401
Toronto M4P 1E4 ON Canada
416-482-8260
Category: 61(ON)

Orange Coast
Katherine Tomlinson, Editor
18200 W McDermott Street #C
Irvine CA 92714
714-966-1688
Category: 61(CA)
Issues per year: 12

Orange County Business Journal
Vickora Clepper, Editor
1112 E Chestnut
Santa Ana CA 92701
714-835-9692
Category: 19-61(Orange County CA)
Circulation: 20,000
Issues per year: 6
Does not buy serial rights.

Orange County South
Editor
31064 Via San Vicente
San Juan Capostran CA 92675-2237
Category: 61(Orange County CA)

Oregon
Lydia Lipman, Editor
208 SW Stark #500
Portland OR 97204
503-223-0304
Category: 61(OR)
Issues per year: 12

Oregon Business
Robert Hill, Editor
208 SW Stark #500
Portland OR 97204
503-228-0304
Category: 19-61(OR)

Organic Gardening
Stevie O Daniels, Exec. Editor
Rodale Press
33 E Minor Street
Emmaus PA 18049
215-967-5171
Category: 43
Issues per year: 12

Ottawa
Louis Valenzuela, Editor
340 MacLaren Street
Ottawa K2P 0M6 PQ Canada
613-234-7751
Category: 61(Ottawa CN)

Our Town
Edward Kayatt, Editor
435 East 86th Street
New York NY 10028
212-289-8700
Category: 61(New York NY)

Outdoor Life
Clare Conley, Editor
380 Madison Avenue
New York NY 10017
212-687-3000
Category: 15-29-39-51-69-71

P & I M Review
Raymond Feldman, Editor
Production and Inventory Mgmt.
2021 Coolidge Street
Hollywood FL 33020-2427
305-925-5900
Category: 19(management)
Circulation: 70,000
Issues per year: 12
Reviews: 24/year
Does not buy serial rights.

Pacific Book Reviews
Douglas Jones, Editor
3217 Johnson #30
San Luis Obispo CA 93401
Category: 99

Pacific Northwest
Peter Potterfield, Editor
222 Dexter Avenue
Seattle WA 98109
206-682-2704
Category: 61(WA)
Issues per year: 12

Pacific Purchaser
Jeanne Vlasny, Editor
6090 W Pico Boulevard
Los Angeles CA 90035
Category: 19(purchasing)

Palm Beach Life
Ann Wolf, Editor
265 Royal Poinciana Way
Palm Beach FL 33480
305-655-5755
Category: 61(Palm Beach FL)
Issues per year: 12

Palm Springs Life
Robert Mamis, Business Editor
303 N Indian Avenue
Palm Springs CA 92262
619-325-2333
Category: 61(Palm Springs CA)
Issues per year: 12

Pan Am Clipper
R.A. Kagan, Editor
34 East 51st Street
New York NY 10022
212-888-5900
Category: 71
Issues per year: 12

Paperback Rack
Henry Lash, Editor
10501 Wilshire Boulevard #2211
Los Angeles CA 90024
Category: 19(publishing)

Parade
Fran Carpentier, Editor
750 Third Avenue
New York NY 10017
212-573-7000
Category: 11-17-33-39-69-99
Issues per year: 52

Parents Magazine
Elizabeth Crow, Editor
685 Third Avenue
New York NY 10017
212-878-8700
Category: 21-31-35-76-89
Issues per year: 12

Parnassus: Poetry in Review
Herbert Leibowitz, Editor
205 West 89th Street
New York NY 10024
Category: 47-75-95

PC Magazine
Bill Machrone, Editor
Ziff-Davis Publications
David Obregon, Feature Editor
  New on the Market
One Park Avenue
New York NY 10016
212-503-5255
Category: 23(IBM specific)
Issues per year: 24

PC Perspective
Emanuel Katzin, Editor
Norman H Associates
5718 Birdwood
Houston TX 77096
713-774-1042
Category: 23
Issues per year: 12
Does not buy serial rights.

PC Productivity Digest
Lawrence C Oakley, Editor
Newsletter Management Corp
10076 Boca Entrada Boulevard
Boca Raton FL 33433-5897
305-483-2600
Category: 19-23
Circulation: 125,000
Issues per year: 12

PC Products
Tim Scannel, Editor
275 Washington Street
Newton MA 02158
617-964-3030
Category: 23
Issues per year: 12

PC Tech Journal
Ziff-Davis Publications
One Park Avenue
New York NY 10016
212-503-5255
Category: 23(IBM specific)
Issues per year: 12

PC World
Harry Miller, Editor
Attn: New Products
555 De Haro Street
San Francisco CA 94107
415-861-3861
Category: 23
Issues per year: 12

Pencil Press Quarterly
Angela R Dickey, Editor
P O Box 536177
Orlanda FL 32853
Category: 99(writing)
Issues per year: 4
Does not buy serial rights.

Pension World
Communication Channels
6255 Barfield Road
Atlanta GA 30328
404-256-9800
Category: 19(investing)
Circulation: 28,000

Penthouse
Peter Bloch, Editor
1965 Broadway
New York NY 10023
496-6100
Category: 11-33-69-99(men's)
Issues per year: 12

People
1271 Avenue of the Americas
New York NY 10020
212-586-1212
Category: 11-17-33-55-69-99
Issues per year: 52

Personal Composition Report
Michael Kleper, Editor
Graphic Dimensions
8 Frederick Road
Pittsford NY 14534
Category: 11(graphics)-23
Issues per year: 12

Personal Computer News
K Reed Huegel, Editor
P O Box 848
Pt. Reyes Station CA 94956-0848
415-669-7554
Category: 23
Circulation: 10,000
Issues per year: 12

Personal Computing
Hayden Publishing
10 Mulholland Drive
Hasbrouck Heights NJ 07604
201-393-6000
Category: 23
Issues per year: 12

Personal Finance
Richard Band, Editor
1300 N 17th Street #1660

Arlington VA 22209
703-528-1100
Category: 19(financial, money)
Circulation: 125,000
Issues per year: 26

Personal Publishing
Terry Ulick, Editor
245 S Parkside
P O Box 390
Itasca IL 60143
312-250-8900
Category: 19(publishing)-23
Circulation: 30,000
Issues per year: 12

Personnel Administrator
Lynne Chiara, Editor
606 N Washington Street
Alexandria VA 22314
703-548-3440
Category: 19(personnel)

Perspective
Heldref Publications
4000 Albemarle Street NW
Washington DC 20016
Category: 55-65
Issues per year: 10
Reviews: 400/year
Does not buy serial rights.

Pet Health News
Moira Anderson, Managing Editor
Fancy Publications
P O Box 6050
Mission Viejo CA 92690
714-240-6001
Category: 15
Issues per year: 12

Philadelphia
Ron Javers, Editor
1500 Walnut Street
Philadelphia PA 19102
215-545-3500
Category: 61(Philadelphia PA)
Issues per year: 12

Philadelphia Business Journal
Brian Sullivan, Editor
2401 Market Street
Philadelpia PA 19103
215-569-0202
Category: 19-61(Philadelphia PA)
Circulation: 15,500

Philadelphia Review
Jim Nelson, Editor
P O Box 2089
Philadelphia PA 19103
Category: 99-61(Philadephia PA)
Issues per year: 12

Phoenix
Fern Welch, Editor
4707 N 12th Street
Phoenix AZ 85014

602-248-8900
Category: 61(Phoenix AZ)
Issues per year: 12

Photo/Design
Joe Migliore, Editor
50 S Ninth Street
Minneapolis MN 55402
612-333-0471
Category: 11(graphics
              photography)
Issues per year: 6
Does not buy serial rights.

Physician's Financial News
Noreen Perrotta, Editor
800 Second Avenue
New York NY 10017
212-599-3400
Category: 19(financial)-39

Physician's Management
Mel Winters, Editor
120 W Second Street
Duluth MN 55802
Category: 19(management)-39

Physics Today
Gloria Lubkin, Editor
335 East 45th Street
New York NY 10017
212-661-9404
Category: 67(physics)

Pittsburgh
Bruce Van Wyngarden, Editor
4802 Fifth Avenue
Pittsburgh PA 15213
412-662-1360
Category: 61(Pittsburgh PA)
Issues per year: 12

Pittsburgh Business Times
Steven Czetli, Editor
10 N Two Gateway Center
Pittsburgh PA 15222
412-922-2404
Category: 19-61(Pittsburgh PA)
Circulation: 12,500

Plan and Print
James C Vebeck, Editor
Janet Thill, Computer Editor
9931 Franklin Avenue
Franklin Park IL 60131
312-671-5356
Category: 19(printing)-23
Circulation: 28,000
Issues per year: 12
Reviews: 1-3/year
Does not buy serial rights.

Playboy
John Rezek, Articles Editor
Barbara Nellis, Books Editor
David Stevens, Senior Editor
919 N Michigan Avenue
Chicago IL 60611

312-751-8000
Category: 11-19-23-29-33-39-43
        55-57-67-69-71
        99(men's)
Circulation: 4,500,000
Issues per year: 12
Reviews: 8-10/issue
Buys 1st and 2nd serial rights.

Poetry
The Modern Poetry Association
P O Box 4348
Chicago IL 60680
Category: 47-95
Issues per year: 12

Poetry Flash
P O Box 4172
Berkeley CA 94704
Category: 95-61(SF Bay area)
Issues per year: 12

Poetry Project Newsletter
Greg Masters, Editor
St Marks Church
Second Avenue & 10th Street
New York NY 10003
Category: 75-95

Popular Ceramics
Terry O'Neill, Editor
3639 San Fernando Road
Glendale CA 91205
213-246-8141
Category: 29(ceramics)
Circulation: 52,000
Issues per year: 12

Popular Computing
McGraw-Hill Publications
70 Main Street
Peterborough NH 03458
603-924-9281
Category: 23
Issues per year: 12

Popular Mechanics
Joe Oldham, Editor-in-Chief
Wade Hoyt, Auto Editor
Steve Booth, Computer Editor
Steve Willson, Home/Shop Editor
Tim Cole, Outdoor Editor
Dennis Eskow, Science Editor
224 West 57th Street
New York NY 10019
212-262-5700
Category: 11(photography)
        23(technology)-29-43
        51(outdoors)-67
        69(boating)-71
Circulation: 1,650,000
Issues per year: 12
Reviews: 12/year
Does not buy serial rights.

Popular Photography
Arthur Goldsmith, Editor
One Park Avenue

New York NY 10016
212-725-3779
Category: 11(photography)
Issues per year: 12

Popular Science
C P Gilmore, Editor
William Hawkins, Computer Editor
Tom Wilkinson, Hobby Editor
Arthur Fisher, Science Editor
380 Madison Avenue
New York NY 10017
212-687-3000
Category: 23-29-43-67
Circulation: 1,800,000
Issues per year: 12

Portland
Rolv Schillios, Editor
824 SW Fifth Avenue
Portland OR 97204
503-228-9411
Category: 61(Portland OR)
Issues per year: 12

Potentials in Marketing
Bill Anderson, Editor
Lakewood Publications
50 S Ninth Street
Minneapolis MN 55402
612-333-0471
Category: 19(marketing)
Circulation: 67,000
Issues per year: 12

PR News
Danny Griswold, Editor
Public Relations News
127 East 80th Street
New York NY 10021
212-879-7090
Category: 19(communications
        publicity)
Issues per year: 52

PR Reporter
Patrick Jackson, Editor
P O Box 600
Exeter NH 03833
603-778-0514
Category: 19(publicity)

Practical Accountant
Alex Cohen, Editor
964 Third Avenue
New York NY 10155
212-935-9210
Category: 19(financial)

Premium/Incentive Business
Deborah Hauss, Editor
Gralla Publications
1515 Broadway
New York NY 10036
212-869-1300
Category: 19(marketing)
Circulation: 30,000
Issues per year: 12

Prevention
Robert Rodale, Editor
Rodale Press
33 E Minor Street
Emmaus PA 18049
215-967-5171
Category: 39
Issues per year: 12

Print Magazine
Martin Fox, Editor
6400 Goldsboro Road
Bethesda MD 20817
301-229-9040
Category: 11(graphics)
        19(advertising)
Circulation: 35,000
Issues per year: 6

Printed Circuit Fabrication
Dave Blanchard, Editor
PMS Industries
1790 Hembree Road
Alpharetta GA 30201
404-475-1818
Category: 19-23-67
Circulation: 25,000
Issues per year: 12
Reviews: 1/issue
Does not buy serial rights.

Printing Buyer's Adviser
Halls Ivy Press
4545 Industrial Street
Simi Valley CA 93063
Category: 11(graphics)
        19(printing)

Printing Impressions
Mark Michelson, Editor
North American Publishing
401 N Broad Street
Philadelphia PA 19108
215-238-5300
Category: 19(printing)
Issues per year: 12
Does not buy serial rights.

Printing News
Leo H Joachim, Editor
468 Park Avenue South
New York NY 10016
212-689-9690
Circulation: 8,600
Issues per year: 52

Printing Views
Len Berman, Editor
Midwest Publishing Company
8328 N Lincoln Avenue
Skokie IL 60076
312-539-8540
Category: 19(printing)

Private Practice
Brian Sherman, Editor
3535 NW 58th Street #470
Oklahoma City OK 73112

405-943-2318
Category: 39
Circulation: 200,000
Issues per year: 12

Pro / Comm
Gene T Krane, Editor
Women in Communications
P O Box 9561
Austin TX 78766
Category: 19(communications
       publicity)-73

**Process: Psychoanalysis and
Creativity**
Helen Borel, Book Reviews
200 West 79th Street #9L
New York NY 10024
212-362-7119
Category: 57-63-65

Product Design and Development
Robert R Bierwirth, Editor
Chilton Way
Radnor PA 19089
215-964-4000
Category: 19-23(design
       engineering)
Circulation: 150,000
Issues per year: 12

Product Marketing
US Business Press
11 West 19th Street
New York NY 10011
212-741-7210
Category: 19(marketing)
Issues per year: 12

Professional Builder
James Carper, Editor
William Lurz, Computer Editor
P O Box 5080
Des Plaines IL 60017-5080
312-635-8800
Category: 19(building)-23
       43(house)
Circulation: 140,000
Issues per year: 12
Reviews: 4/year

The Professional Report
John L Springer, Editor
TPR Publishing
81 Montgomery Street
Scarsdale NY 10583
914-472-0366
Category: 19(small business)

Profit Strategy
John V Holmes, Editor
1801 E 5th Street
Charlotte NC 28204
Category: 19

Progressive Grocer
Edgar Walzer, Editor
1351 Washington Boulevard

Stamford CT 06902
203-232-1985
Category: 19(retail marketing)

The Progressive
Mary Sheridan, Books Editor
409 E Main Street
Madison WI 53703
608-257-4626
Category: 13-55

PSA
Al Austin, Editor
5900 Wilshire Boulevard #800
Los Angeles CA 90036
213-937-5810
Category: 71
Issues per year: 12

Public Relations Business
John Brice, Editor
246 West 38th Street, 11th Floor
New York NY 10018
212-819-9310
Category: 19(communications
       publicity)

Public Relations Journal
Celia K Lerhman, Editor
Michael Winkelman, Editor
Public Relations Society of Amer
845 Third Avenue
New York NY 10022
212-826-1757
Category: 11-19(publicity
       advertising-23-33-43
       69-71-99
Circulation: 69,000
Issues per year: 12
Reviews: 10-15/year
Does not buy serial rights.

Publishers Weekly
Diane Roback, Children's Books
Sybil Steinberg, Fiction
Penny Kaganoff, How-To Books
Genevievie Stuttaford, NonFiction
John Mutter, Paperback
Joann Davis, Trade News Editor
205 East 42nd Street
New York NY 10017
212-764-5156
Category: 10-19(publishing)-21
       27-29-31-43-75-76-89
       99
Circulation: 45,000
Issues per year: 52

Publishing Northwest
Frank Walsh, Editor
5770 Franson Court
North Bend OR 97459
Category: 10(small press)
       61(OR, WA, ID)

Puget Sound Business Journal
Mike Flynn, Editor
1008 Western Avenue #415

Seattle WA 98104
206-583-0701
Category: 19-61(Seattle WA)
Circulation: 16,000
Issues per year: 12

Purchasing Digest
Lee Walcutt, Editor
Gordon Publications
P O Box 1952
Dover NJ 07801-0952
201-267-6040
Category: 19(purchasing)
Circulation: 90,000
Issues per year: 12

Purchasing Magazine
John O'Connor, Editor
275 Washington Street
Newton MA 02158
617-994-3030
Category: 19(purchasing)
Circulation: 96,000
Issues per year: 12

Purchasing Management
Maria Alena Castle, Editor
Bolger Publications
3301 Como Avenue SE
Minneapolis MN 55414
612-645-6311
Category: 19(purchasing)
Circulation: 9,000
Issues per year: 12

Purchasing World
James Lorincz, Editor
Huebner Publications
6521 Davis Industrial Parkway
Solon OH 44139
216-248-1125
Category: 19(purchasing)
Circulation: 91,000
Issues per year: 12

Quality Crafts Marketing
Editor, Book Reviews
15 West 44th Street
New York NY 10036
Category: 19(marketing)-29

Quick, Health Cooking
Editor
Rodale Press
33 E Minor Street
Emmaus PA 18049
215-967-5171
Category: 27-39
Issues per year: 2

Quill
Mike Moore, Editor
53 W Jackson Drive #731
Chicago IL 60604
312-649-0129
Category: 19(publishing)
Issues per year: 12

Quill & Quire
Ann Vanderhoof, Editor
Diane Turbide, Book Reviews
Hamish Cameron, Trade Editor
56 The Esplanade #213
Toronto M5E 1A7 ON Canada
416-364-3333
Category: 19(publishing)-99
Circulation: 10,000
Issues per year: 12
Reviews: 25-50/issue

Quilter's Newsletter
Bonnie Leman, Editor
Leman Publications
6700 West 44th Avenue
Wheatridge CO 80033
303-420-4272
Category: 29(quilts)
Issues per year: 10

Reader's Digest
Walter Hunt, Books Editor
Reader's Digest Corporation
Pleasantville NY 10570
914-769-7000
Category: 99
Issues per year: 12

The Reading Teacher
Editor
International Reading Assn.
P O Box 8139
Newark DE 19714
Category: 21-31-76

Real Estate Today
Rene Love, Books Editor
430 N Michigan Avenue
Chicago IL 60611
312-329-8436
Category: 19(real estate)

Redbook
Annette Capone, Editor
224 West 57th Street
New York NY 10019
212-262-8250
Category: 27-29-39-43-73-75
Circulation: 4,000,000
Issues per year: 12
Buys 1st and 2nd serial rights.

Reference and Research Book News
Editor
5606 NE Hassalo Street
Portland OR 97213
503-281-9230
Category: 59
Circulation: 8,000

Reference Book Review
Cameron Northouse, Editor
P O Box 190954
Dallas TX 75219
Category: 59
Circulation: 1,000
Issues per year: 2

Reference Books Bulletin
Sandy Whiteley, Editor
American Library Association
50 E Huron Street
Chicago IL 60611
312-944-2117
Category: 59
Issues per year: 26
Reviews: many
Does not buy serial rights.

Reference Books Bulletin
Josephine McSweeney, Reference
Pratt Institute Library
200 Willoughby Avenue
Brooklyn NY 11205
Category: 59
Issues per year: 26
Reviews: many

Reference Quarterly
Kathleen Heim, Editor
American Library Association
50 East Huron Street
Chicago IL 60611
312-944-6780
Category: 59
Issues per year: 4

Reference Sources
Mary Hashman, Managing Editor
P O Box 1808
Ann Arbor MI 48106
Category: 59

Reform Judaism
Aron Hirt-Manheimer, Book Editor
838 Fifth Avenue
New York NY 10021
212-249-0100
Category: 63(Jewish)
Circulation: 280,000
Issues per year: 4
Reviews: 3/issue

Rehabilitation Literature
Steven J Regnier, Editor
Jean Bartholomew, Computer Editor
National Easter Seals
2023 W Ogden Avenue
Chicago IL 60612
312-243-8400
Category: 23-39
Circulation: 30,000
Issues per year: 6
Reviews: 25/issue
Does not buy serial rights.

Rehabilitation World
John Moses, Editor
1123 Broadway
New York NY 10010
212-741-5160
Category: 39

Remedial and Special Education
James M Kauffman, Editor
Pro-Ed

5341 Industrial Oaks Boulevard
Austin TX 78735
512-892-3142
Category: 31
Circulation: 3,000
Issues per year: 6

Republic
Jerry Lazar, Editor
5900 Wilshire Boulevard #800
Los Angeles CA 90036
213-937-5810
Category: 71
Issues per year: 12

Research & Development
Robert Jones, Editor
P O Box 1030
Barrington IL 60010
312-381-1840
Category: 23-67

Resource-Mag
Lynn McFadgen, Editor
18 Van Dusen Boulevard
Toronto M8Z 3E5 ON Canada
Category: 11(graphics)
           19(publishing)

Resources Newsletter
Richard Gardner, Editor
P O Box 134
Harvard Square
Cambridge MA 02138
Category: 19(marketing)
Issues per year: 12

Retail Business Promotion
ELMA Communications
P O Box 1142
Orange Park FL 32067-1142
Category: 19(retail marketing)

Retired Officer
Nora J Tuggle, Managing Editor
Retired Officers Association
201 N Washington Street
Alexandria VA 22314
703-549-2311
Category: 55-98(retirement)-99
Circulation: 350,000
Issues per year: 12
Reviews: 15-18/issue
Buys only 1st serial rights.

ReVision Journal
Editor
Rudi Foundation
P O Box 316
Cambridge MA 02238
Category: 53
Issues per year: 2

RFD
Editor
Route 1, Box 127-E
Bakersville NC 28705
Category: 13-37

RN
James Reynolds, Editor
680 Kinderkamack Road
Oradell NJ 07649
201-262-3030
Category: 39(nursing)

Robotics World
Communication Channels
6255 Barfield Road
Atlanta GA 30328
404-256-9800
Category: 23
Circulation: 23,00C

Rolling Stone
745 Fifth Avenue
New York NY 10151
212-758-3800
Category: 11-33

Romantic Times
163 Joralemon Street
Brooklyn Heights NY 11201
718-237-1097
Category: 85

Rotarian
Willmon White, Editor
Rotary International
1600 N Ridge Avenue
Evanston IL 60201
Category: 99
Issues per year: 12

Runner's World
Rodale Press
33 E Minor Street
Emmaus PA 18049
215-967-5171
Category: 39-69
Issues per year: 12

Sacramento Magazine
Cheryl Romo, Editor
620 Bercut Drive/P O Box 2424
Sacramento CA 95811
916-446-7548
Category: 61(Sacramento CA)
Issues per year: 12

Sales and Marketing Management
Richard Kern, Books Editor
633 Third Avenue
New York NY 10017
212-986-4800
Category: 19(marketing)
Circulation: 47,000
Issues per year: 16

San Diego Business
John Woolard, Editor
3444 Camino del Rio #204
San Diego CA 92018
619-283-2271
Category: 19-61(San Diego CA)
Circulation: 15,000
Issues per year: 12

San Diego Magazine
K McCormick Price, Book Editor
27 Crestmoor Drive
Denver CO 80220
303-377-3838
Category: 61(San Deigo CA)-99
Circulation: 60,000
Issues per year: 12
Reviews: 12/issue

San Diego Magazine
P O Box 85409
San Diego CA 92138
619-225-8953
Category: 61(San Deigo CA)
Issues per year: 12

San Diego Woman
2171 India Street
San Diego CA 92101
619-234-3644
Category: 61(San Diego CA)-73
Circulation: 42,000
Issues per year: 12

San Francisco
Ronald Hagen, Editor
950 Battery
San Francisco CA 94103
415-777-5555
Category: 61(San Francisco CA)
Issues per year: 12

San Francisco Business Journal
Tom York, Editor
465 California #430
San Francisco CA 94104-1812
415-391-6400
Category: 19-61(San Francisco CA)
Circulation: 17,000
Issues per year: 12

San Francisco Focus
Mark Powelson, Editor
Alice Thibeau, Arts Editor
Jackie Killeen, Asst. Editor
Herb Gold, Books Editor
Richard Rawles, Computer Editor
Amy Rennert, Family Editor
Warren Sharpe, News Editor
680 Eighth Street
San Francisco CA 94118
415-553-2800
Category: 11-19-23-27-29-33-35
          39-43-61(SF CA)-67-69
          71-99
Issues per year: 12
Reviews: 36-50/year
Buys 1st and 2nd serial rights.

San Francisco Review of Books
Ron Nowicki, Editor
Arnold Williams, Paperback Books
725 Second Street
P O Box 330090
San Francisco CA 94133
415-777-2923
Category: 99

San Jose Business
Lee Butcher, Editor
80 S Market
San Jose CA 95113
408-295-3800
Category: 19-61(San Jose CA)
Circulation: 18,000
Issues per year: 12

Santa Clara County Business
Morine Myslinski, Editor
National Communications
450 E Trimble Road
San Jose CA 95131-1220
408-435-1170
Category: 61(Silicon Valley CA)
          19-71
Circulation: 16,000
Issues per year: 12
Reviews: 1/issue
Does not buy serial rights.

Saturday Evening Post
Patrick Perry, Editor
1100 Waterway Boulevard
Indianapolis IN 46202
371-634-1100
Category: 99

Saturday Review
William Cole, Editor
Trade Winds
201-West 54th Street #1C
New York NY 10019
Category: 99

Saturday Review
Frank Cannon, Editor
214 Massachusettts Avenue NE
P O Box 6024
Washington DC 20002
202-547-1106
Category: 11-33-47-75-99

Savings Institutions
Mary Nowensnick, Editor
111 E Wacker Drive
Chicago IL 60601
312-644-3100
Category: 19(banking)

Savvy
Editor
111 Eighth Avenue
New York NY 10011
Category: 19-73
Issues per year: 12

Scholarly Publishing
Mark Carroll, Books Editor
6302 Friendship Court
Bethesda MD 20817
Category: 19(publishing)-65

Scholarly Publishing Journal
Eleanor Harman, Editor
University of Toronto Press
Toronto M5S 1A6 ON Canada

416-677-7781
Category: 19(publishing)-65
Circulation: 1,200

School Library Journal
Travelyn Jones, Editor
Books for Review
205 East 42nd Street
New York NY 10017
212-916-1600
Category: 21-31-76-89-99
Circulation: 42,000
Issues per year: 12

School Library Media
Judith F Davie, Books Editor
School Media Programs
Greensboro Public Schools, Box V
Greensboro NC 27402
312-944-6780
Category: 11-23
Issues per year: 4
Reviews: 6-10/issue
Does not buy serial rights.

School Shop
Alan H Jones, Editor
Prakken Publications
P O Box 8623
Ann Arbor MI 48107
313-769-1211
Category: 29(woodworking)-31
Circulation: 45,000
Issues per year: 9
Reviews: 2-5/issue
Does not buy serial rights.

Science
Barbara Culliton, News Editor
1333 H Street NW
Washington DC 20005
202-326-6400
Category: 67
Issues per year: 12

Science & Technical Libraries
Ellis Mount, Editor
Butler Library
Columbia University
New York NY 10027
212-228-2800
Category: 23-67
Circulation: 1,100
Issues per year: 4

Science 86
Avery Comarow, Editor
1101 Vermont Avenue NW
Washington DC 20005
202-842-9500
Category: 23-67
Issues per year: 12

Science Books and Films
Kathleen Johnson, Editor
AAAS
1333 H Street NW
Washington DC 20005

202-326-6454
Category: 23-31-59-67
Circulation: 4,000
Issues per year: 5
Reviews: 200/issue
Does not buy serial rights.

Science Digest
Oliver Moore, Editor
888 Seventh Avenue
New York NY 10106
212-262-7990
Category: 23-67
Issues per year: 12

Science Fiction Chronicle
Don D'Ammassa, Books Editor
323 Dodge Street
East Providence RI 02914
718-643-9011
Category: 86
Circulation: 5,000
Issues per year: 12
Reviews: 20-30/issue
Does not buy serial rights.

Science Fiction Chronicle
Andrew Porter, Editor
P O Box 4175
New York NY 10163
718-643-9011
Category: 86
Circulation: 5,000
Issues per year: 12
Reviews: 20-30/issue

Science News
Joel Greenberg, Editor
Jane M Livermore, Books Editor
Bruce Bower, Behavioral Science
Joanne Silberner, Earth Science
Julie Ann Miller, Life Science
Dietrick Thomsen, Physical Science
Jonathan Eberhart, Space Science
1719 N Street NW
Washington DC 20036
202-785-2255
Category: 15-23-51-57-59-67
Issues per year: 52
Reviews: 7/issue

Science Teacher
Glenn O Blough, Books Editor
National Science Teachers Assn.
1742 Connecticut Avenue NW
Washington DC 20009
202-328-5800
Category: 23-31-67

Science World
730 Broadway
New York NY 10003
212-505-3000
Category: 23-67

Sciences
Paul Libassi, Editor
2 East 63rd Street

New York NY 10021
212-838-0230
Category: 23-67

Scientific American
Jonathan Piel, Editor
415 Madison Avenue
New York NY 10017
212-754-0550
Category: 23-67
Issues per year: 12

Scroll Newsletter
Editor
Word Processing Users' Group
P O Box 144
Malverne NY 11565
Category: 11(writing)-23

Sea
Duncan McIntosh, Editor
1760 Monrovia Avenue #C-2
Costa Mesa CA 92627
714-673-9360
Category: 69(boating)-71
Issues per year: 12

Secretary
Shirley Englund, Editor
301 E Amour Boulevard #200
Kansas City MO 64111
816-531-7010
Category: 19(office)

Self
Phyllis Wilson, Editor
350 Madison Avenue
New York NY 10017
212-880-8800
Category: 19(careers, money)-39
        57-73-99(beauty and
        fashion)
Issues per year: 12

Selling Direct
Editor
Communication Channels
6255 Barfield Road
Atlanta GA 30328
404-256-9800
Category: 19(sales and marketing)
Circulation: 275,000
Issues per year: 12
Reviews: 2-5/issue
Buys 1st and 2nd serial rights.

Semiconductor International
Don Swanson, Editor
Cahners Publishing
1350 E Touhy Avenue
Des Plaines IL 60018-3358
312-635-8800
Category: 23
Circulation: 35,000
Issues per year: 12
Reviews: 3-5/issue
Does not buy serial rights.

Serials Librarian
Peter Gellatly, Editor
P O Box 15680
Seattle WA 98115
Category: 75-95
Circulation: 1,750
Issues per year: 4

Serials Review
P O Box 1808
Ann Arbor MI 48106
Category: 75-95

Seventeen
Midge T Richardson, Editor
Kathy Rich, Business Editor
Olga Rigsby, Cookbook Editor
Susan Evans, Family Editor
Sarah Crichton, Feature Editor
Joan Downs, Feature Editor
Edwin Miller, Feature Editor
Bonni Price, Fiction Editor
Gayle Malles, Hobby Editor
Cathi Hanauer, Science Editor
Nina Combe, Sports Editor
Judith Parnes, Travel Editor
850 Third Avenue
New York NY 10011
212-759-8100
Category: 11-19-27-29-33-39-43
        67-69-71-75-73-89
        99(beauty and fashion)
Circulation: 1,850,000
Issues per year: 12
Reviews: 12/year
Buys only 2nd serial rights.

Sew Business
Christina Holmes, Editor
Gralla Publications
1515 Broadway
New York NY 10036
212-869-1300
Category: 29(sewing, quilting)
Circulation: 17,000
Issues per year: 12

Sew News
Barbara Weiland, Editor
PJS Publications
News Plaza, P O Box 1790
Peoria IL 61656
Category: 29(sewing)
Issues per year: 12

Seybold Report on Publishing
Seybold Publications
P O Box 644
Media PA 19063
215-565-2480
Category: 19(publishing)-23
Issues per year: 12
Does not buy serial rights.

Shopping Center World
Communication Channels
6255 Barfield Road
Atlanta GA 30328

404-256-9800
Category: 19(retail marketing)
Circulation: 27,000
Issues per year: 12

Shuttle, Spindle & Dyepot
Jane Bradley Sitko,
Handweavers Guild of America
65 La Salle Road
West Hartford CT 06107
203-233-5124
Category: 29(sewing, spinning)
Issues per year: 4

Signal
Daniel Marcus, Editor
Anne Mattheisen, Book Editor
AFCEA
5641 Burke Centre Parkway
Burke VA 22015
703-425-8575
Category: 19-23-69-99
Circulation: 30,000
Issues per year: 12
Reviews: 6/issue
Does not buy serial rights.

Signature
Horace Sutton, Editor
641 Lexington Avenue
New York NY 10022
212-888-9450
Category: 71
Issues per year: 12

SignCraft
P O Box 06031
Fort Meyers FL 33906
813-939-4644
Category: 11(graphics)
Issues per year: 6
Does not buy serial rights.

Silicon Valley
Norbert Stein, Editor
P O Box 60145
Sunnyvale CA 94088
408-249-8020
Category: 19-61(Sunnyvale CA)

Sinister Wisdom
Melanie Kaye/Kantrowitz, Editor
P O Box 1023
Rockland ME 04841
Category: 37-73-75-95
Issues per year: 4

Sipapu
Neal Peattie, Editor
Route 1, Box 216
Winters CA 95694
Category: 13-83-95
Circulation: 450
Issues per year: 2

Sixteenth Century Journal
Robert Schnucker, Book Editor
LB 115

Northeast Missouri State Univ.
Kirksville MO 63501
Category: 41

Small Business Clinic
Austin P Elliott, Editor
113 Vista Del Lago
Scotts Valley CA 95066
408-438-1411
Category: 19(small business)

Small Business Computers
Howard Falk, Editor
AHL Publishing
P O Box 789
Morris Plains NJ 07960
Category: 19(small business)-23
Circulation: 34,000
Issues per year: 12

Small Business Connection
Vernon C Bank, Editor
P O Box 4669
Racine WI 53404
Category: 19(small business)

Small Business Magazine
Richard Blair, Editor
P O Box 1
Richboro PA 18954
Category: 19(small business)

Small Business Newsletter
Don Ristow, Editor
7514 N 53rd Street
Milwaukee WI 53223
Category: 19(small business)

Small Business Systems
Charles Moore, Editor
P O Box 6
Southampton PA 18966
215-364-2212
Category: 19(small business)-23
Issues per year: 12

Small Businesswoman
Jackie Barlow, Editor
P O Box 66
Mount Dora FL 32778
Category: 19(small business)-73

Small Press Book Review
Henry Berry, Editor
P O Box 176
Southport CT 06490
Category: 75-95-99(small press)
Issues per year: 6

Small Press Magazine
Doris Grumbach, Book Editor
Meckler Publishing
11 Ferry Lane West
Westport CT 06880
203-226-6967
Category: 75-95-99(small press)
Circulation: 10,000
Issues per year: 6

Small Press News
Diane Kruchkow, Editor
Weeks Mills
New Sharon ME 04955
Category: 83-95
Circulation: 2,500

Small Press Review
Len Fulton, Editor
Dustbooks
P O Box 100
Paradise CA 95969
916-877-6110
Category: 75-83-95
Circulation: 2,500
Issues per year: 12

Smithsonian
Marlane Liddell, Excerpt Editor
Bennett Schiff, Review Editor
900 Jefferson Drive SW
Washington DC 20560
202-357-1612
Category: 23-41-51-55-67-71
Circulation: 2,000,000
Issues per year: 12
Buys only 1st serial rights.

Social Education
Charles Rivera, Editor
Natl. Council for Social Studies
3501 Newark Street NW
Washington DC 20016
202-966-7840
Category: 21-31-55(social studies)

Social Science History
Alan M Kraut, Book Reviews
History Dept., American Univ.
Nebraska & Massachusetts Ave NW
Washington DC 20016
Category: 55-65
Circulation: 900
Issues per year: 4

Social Science Microcomputer
Donald F Norris, Book Reviews
Center \ Applied Urban Research
U of NE - 1313 Farnam on Mall
Omaha NE 68182
Category: 23-55(social science)
Circulation: 550
Issues per year: 4

Sociological Abstracts
Leo P Chall, Editor
International Sociological Assn
P O Box 22206
San Diego CA 92122
619-565-6603
Category: 55-65
Circulation: 1,200
Issues per year: 4
Does not buy serial rights.

Sociology: Reviews of New Books
Heldref Publications
4000 Albemarle Street NW

Washington DC 20016
Category: 55(sociology)-65
Issues per year: 6
Reviews: 400-500/year
Does not buy serial rights.

Soldiers Magazine
Dave Wagner, US Army Publication
11000 Wilshire Boulevard #10104
Los Angeles CA 90024
213-209-7623
Category: 55(military)-99

Sourcefinder
Margaret A Boyd, Editor
Boyd's
P O Box 6232
Augusta GA 30906
Category: 29

South Atlantic Quarterly
Oliver W Ferguson, Editor
6697 College Station
Durham NC 27708
Category: 47-765-75
Circulation: 1,100
Issues per year: 4

South Florida Living
Marcy Jay, Editor
700 W Hillsboro #3
Deerfield Beach FL 33441
305-428-5602
Category: 61(FL)
Issues per year: 12

Southeast Librarian
Paul F Feehan, Editor
Box 24-8214
University of Miami Library
Coral Gables FL 33124
Category: 99

Southern Accents
Helen Griffith, Editor
1760 Peachtree Road NW
Atlanta GA 30357
404-874-4462
Category: 61(southern)
Issues per year: 12

Southern Economics Journal
Vincent Tarascio, Editor
300 Hanes Hall
University of North Carolina
Chapel Hill NC 27514
919-966-5261
Category: 19-65
Circulation: 3,900
Issues per year: 4

Southern Graphics
Don Dunham, Editor
Cody Publications
P O Box 2028
Kissimmee FL 32741
305-846-2800
Category: 11(graphics)

Southern Living
Tom Curl, Editor
820 Shades Creek Parkway
P O Box 523
Birmingham AL 35201
205-877-6000
Category: 27-43-61(southern)
Circulation: 2,150,000
Issues per year: 12
Reviews: 36-60/year
Does not buy serial rights.

Southern Magazine
Linton Weeks, Editor
P O Box 3418
Little Rock AR 72203
501-375-4114
Category: 61(Southern US)-75-99
Circulation: 200,000
Issues per year: 12
Reviews: 5-10/issue
Buys 1st and 2nd serial rights.

Southwestern Historical Quartrly
Editor
Texas State Historical Assn
2/306 Richardson Hall, Univ Sta.
Austin TX 78712
512-471-1525
Category: 41-65
Issues per year: 4

Special Collections
Lee Ash, Editor
66 Humiston Drive
Bethany CT 06525
212-228-2800
Category: 59(bibliographies)
Circulation: 200
Issues per year: 4

Special Libraries
Nancy Viggiano, Editor
Special Libraries Association
235 Park Avenue South
New York NY 10003
Category: 99

Specifying Engineer
Robert L Oliverson, Editor
Cahners Publishing Company
1350 E Touhy Avenue
Des Plaines IL 60018
312-635-8800
Category: 23(engineering)
Circulation: 40,000
Issues per year: 12
Reviews: 10/year

Sporting News
Tom Barnidge, Editor
Times Mirror Company
1212 N Lindbergh Boulevard
St Louis MO 63132
314-993-7767
Category: 69
Issues per year: 52

Sports Illustrated
Mark Mulvoy, Editor
1271 Avenue of the Americas
New York NY 10020
212-586-1212
Category: 51-69
Issues per year: 52

St Anthony Messenger
Barbara Beckwith, Books Editor
1615 Republic Street
Cincinnati OH 45210
513-241-5616
Category: 63(Catholic)
Circulation: 425,000
Issues per year: 12
Reviews: 6/issue
Buys 1st and 2nd serial rights.

St. Louis Magazine
Barry Murov, Editor
Charlie Leonard, Asst. Editor
Jon Meyers, Asst. Editor
Cynthia Pappas, Business Editor
712 N 2nd Street/P O Box 88908
St Louis MO 63188-1908
314-231-7200
Category: 11-19-23-27-29-33-39
        43-61(St Louis MO)-67
        69-71
Circulation: 28,000
Issues per year: 12
Reviews: 4/year
Does not buy serial rights.

Star
Leslie Hinton, Editor
660 White Plains Road
Tarrytown NY 10591
914-332-5000
Category: 11-17-33-35-39-43-53
        57-69-99
Issues per year: 52

Statement Newsletter
Vicki Glenn, Editor
Assn of Women Business Owners
500 N Michigan Avenue
Chicago IL 60611
Category: 19-73

Step-by-Step Graphics
6000 N Forest Park Drive
P O Box 1901
Peoria IL 61656-9979
Category: 11(graphics)
Issues per year: 6

Stitches Count
Suzanne R Weyer, Editor
8991 Jaen Road N
Lake Elmo MN 55042
Category: 29(sewing)
Issues per year: 4

Stock Market Magazine
Bruce W Marcus, Editor
333 West End Avenue

New York NY 10023
212-580-0703
Category: 19
Circulation: 58,000
Issues per year: 12
Reviews: 10/issue
Does not buy serial rights.

Strategies
Harold Simon, Editor
31 The Crescent
P O Box 838
Montclair NJ 07042
Category: 11(photography)
        19(marketing)
Issues per year: 12

Studio Photography
101 Crossways Park
Woodbury NY 11797
Category: 11(photography)

Stylepages
Editor, Book Reviews
Third Coast Publications
P O Box 358
Cary IL 60013
Category: 29(needlecraft)
Issues per year: 4

Success!
Tina Dorfman, Books Editor
Scott De Garmo, Editor
342 Madison Avenue
New York NY 10173
212-309-9896
Category: 19-57
Circulation: 300,000
Issues per year: 12
Buys 1st and 2nd serial rights.

Successful Cash Flow
Smith, Donn E, Editor
1111 E Putnam Avenue
Riverside CT 06878
Category: 19

Successful Woman
Hennie Shore, Editor
American Society of Professional
& Executive Women - 1511 Walnut
Philadelphia PA 19102
215-563-3501
Category: 19-73
Circulation: 20,000
Issues per year: 6
Reviews: 1/issue

Sunrise Book Review
Michael J Lowrey, Editor
1847 N Second Street
Milwaukee WI 53212
414-372-9745
Category: 99

Sunset
Bill Marken, Editor
80 Willow Road

Menlo Park CA 94025
415-321-3600
Category: 27-29-35-43-61(western)
Issues per year: 12

Sylvia Porter's Personal Finance
Patricia Estes, Editor
380 Lexington Avenue
New York NY 10017
212-490-8989
Category: 19-99(money, financial)
Issues per year: 12

Talent Company
P O Box 3145
Minot ND 58702
Category: 19(small business)-29

Tampa Bay Metro
Terry Hunter, Editor
405 Reo Street #210
Tampa FL 33609-1010
813-885-9855
Category: 61(Tampa FL)
Issues per year: 12

Technical Communication
Frank Smith, Editor
815 15th Street NW
Washington DC 20005
202-737-0035
Category: 19(communication)-23

Technology Review
Peg Kirkpatrick, Editor
John I Mattill, Editor
10-140 MIT
77 Massachusetts Avenue
Cambridge MA 02139
617-253-8250
Category: 23-31-67
Circulation: 75,000
Issues per year: 12
Reviews: 25-30/year
Buys only 1st serial rights.

Teen
Linda Watson, Books Editor
8490 Sunset Boulevard
Los Angeles CA 90069
213-657-5100
Category: 11-33-89-99
Issues per year: 12

Telecommunications
Charles White, Editor
610 Washington Street
Dedham MA 02026
617-326-8220
Category: 19(communications)-23

Telemarketing
Linda Driscoll, Editor
One Technology Plaza
Norwalk CT 06854-1924
203-852-6800
Category: 19(marketing)-23
Circulation: 60,000

Issues per year: 12
Reviews: 1-2/year
Does not buy serial rights.

Teleprofessional
Joseph Hauber, Editor
1049 Camino del Mar
P O Box 123
Del Mar CA 92014
Category: 19(marketing)
Issues per year: 4

Tennis
Shephard Campbell, Editor
5520 Park Avenue
P O Box 395
Turnbull CT 06611-0395
203-373-7000
Category: 69(tennis)
Issues per year: 12

Texas Books and Authors
Christopher Woods, Book Editor
2229 Mimosa I
Houston TX 77019
713-521-9965
Category: 61(TX)
Issues per year: 4
Reviews: many/issue
Does not buy serial rights.

Texas Business
5757 Alpha #400
Dallas TX 75240
214-239-4481
Category: 19-61(TX)

Texas Fisherman
Larry Bocka, Editor
5314 Bingle Road
P O Box 920973
Houston TX 77292-0973
713-688-8811
Category: 69(fishing)
Circulation: 59,000
Issues per year: 9

Texas Monthly
Gregory Curtis, Editor
P O Box 1569
Austin TX 78767
512-476-7085
Category: 61(TX)
Issues per year: 12

Texas Woman's News
15790 Dooley Road
Dallas TX 75244
214-960-news
Category: 61(TX)-73

Textile Booklist
Karen Buffington Buffington,
P O Box 4392
Arcata CA 95521
707-882-7716
Category: 29(textile)
Issues per year: 4

The Book Report
Carolyn Hamilton, Editor
Linworth Publishing Company
2950 N High Street
Columbus OH 43214
614-261-6584
Category: 21-31-76-89
Circulation: 10,000
Issues per year: 5

The Office
C T Veilleux, Senior Editor
P O Box 1231
1600 Summer Street
Stamford CT 06904
Category: 19(office management)
23
Issues per year: 12

The Runner
Marc A Bloom, Editor
Linda Villarosa, Assoc. Editor
Dr George Sheehan, Medical Editor
Dr David Costill, Science Editor
One Park Avenue
New York NY 10016
212-503-3500
Category: 27-39-67-69(running)
Circulation: 280,000
Issues per year: 12
Buys 1st and 2nd serial rights.

Third Woman
Editor
Chicano-Riqueno Studies
849 Ballantine, Indiana Univ.
Bloomington IN 47401
Category: 47-73-78-95

Time
Henry Grunwald, Editor-in-Chief
Leon Jaroff, Sciences Editor
Time-Life Building
Rockefeller Center
New York NY 10020-1393
212-586-1212
Category: 17-23-51-67-99
Issues per year: 52
Reviews: 3/issue

Today's CPA
Kathleen Y Klein, Editor
Texax Society of CPAs
1421 W Mockingbird Lane #100
Dallas TX 75247-4957
214-689-6000
Category: 19(financial)
Circulation: 27,000
Issues per year: 6
Reviews: none
Does not buy serial rights.

Today's Living
Jerelyn Jordan, Editor
390 Fifth Avenue
New York NY 10018
212-613-9700
Category: 39

Toronto Life
Marq De Villiers, Editor
59 Front Street E
Toronto M5E 1B3 ON Canada
416-364-3333
Category: 61(Toronto CN)

Town & Country
Wendy Noonan, Editor
1700 Broadway
New York NY 10019
212-903-5000
Category: 43-99

Toy and Hobby World
Rick Anguilla, Editor
11 West 19th Street
New York NY 10011
212-741-7210
Category: 29(hobbies)-69(toys
    games)
Issues per year: 12

Toys, Hobbies & Crafts
Toy Trade Publishing
545 Fifth Avenue
New York NY 10036
212-503-2990
Category: 29(hobbies)-69(toys
    games)
Circulation: 11,000
Issues per year: 12

Tradeshow Week
12233 W Olympic #236
Los Angeles CA 90064
Category: 19(marketing)
Issues per year: 52

Tradeswomen Magazine
Joss Eldrege, Publisher
Attn: Book Reviews
P O Box 40664
San Francisco CA 94140
415-989-1566
Category: 19-73

Training
Jack Gordon, Editor
50 S 9th
Minneapolis MN 55402
612-333-0471
Category: 19(personnel)

Travel and Leisure
Victor Lipari, Editor
1120 Avenue of the Americas
New York NY 10019
212-386-5600
Category: 69-71

Travel/Holiday
Scott Shane, Editor
Travel Building
51 Atlantic Avenue
Floral Park NY 11001
516-352-9700
Category: 71

Treadleart
Janet Stocker, Editor
25834 Narbonne Avenue
Lomita CA 90717
213-534-5112
Category: 29(spinning)
Issues per year: 29

TV Guide
David Sendler, National Editor
TV Guide Publications
Radnor PA 19088
215-293-8500
Category: 17-33-69
Issues per year: 52

TWA Ambassador
Bonnie Blodgett, Editor
Doug Tice, Managing Editor
Libby O'Brien, Senior Editor
289 E 5th Street #209
St Paul MN 55101
612-291-1720
Category: 11-19-23-29-33-43-67
        71-99
Circulation: 1,000,000
Issues per year: 12
Reviews: 12/year
Does not buy serial rights.

Typeworld
Frank Romano, Editor
Blum Publications
15 Oakridge Circle
Wilmington MA 01887
Category: 11(graphics)

Typographer
Geoff Lindsey, Editor
Typographers Intl. Association
2262 Hall Place NW
Washington DC 20007
Category: 11(graphics)

U&lc
Edward Gottschall, Editor
International Typeface
2 Hammarskjold P.aza
New York NY 10017
212-371-0699
Category: 11(graphics)
Circulation: 210,000
Issues per year: 4
Buys only 2nd serial rights.

U.S. Banker
1 River Road
Cos Cob CT 06807
203-869-8200
Category: 19(banking)

U.S. News and World Report
Walter Wingo, Business Editor
Lucia Solorzano, Education Dept.
Kathleen McAuliffe, Health Editor
David R Gerger, News Editor
Stanley Wellborn, Science Editor
2400 N Street NW

Washington DC 20037
202-955-2000
Category: 19-23-31-39-51-67
        97(news)
Issues per year: 50

United Magazine
Jonathan Black, Editor
34 East 51st Street
New York NY 10022
212-888-5900
Category: 71
Issues per year: 12

Us
Richard Sanders, Articles Editor
745 Fifth Avenue
New York NY 10151
212-340-7500
Category: 11-17-33-55-99

USA Weekend
Contance Kurz, Editor
Mary Ellin Barrett, Feature Editor
Phil Pruitt, Senior Editor
Gannett
P O Box 500W
Washington DC 20044
703-276-4526
Category: 11-19-23-27-29-33-39
        43-69-71-99
Circulation: 13.1MM
Issues per year: 52
Reviews: 7/month
Buys 1st and 2nd serial rights.

Utne Reader
Eric Utne, Editor
Helen Cordes, Book Editor
LENS Publishing
2732 West 43rd Street
Minneapolis MN 55410
612-929-2670
Category: 99
Issues per year: 6
Buys only 2nd serial rights.

Vanity Fair
Tina Brown, Editor
350 Madison Avenue
New York NY 10017
212-880-8800
Category: 39-99(beauty, fashion)
Issues per year: 12

Venture Magazine
Sharon Kahn, Editor
35 West 45th Street
New York NY 10036
212-869-1300
Category: 19
Circulation: 255,000
Issues per year: 12

Verbatim
Laurence Urdang, Editor
The Language Quarterly
P O Box 668

Essex CT 06426
203-767-8248
Category: 45(language)-59
Circulation: 12,000
Issues per year: 4

VFW Magazine
James Andersen, Editor
9 East 41st Street
New York NY 10017
Category: 99
Issues per year: 12

Video
Doug Garr, Editor
Ben Templin, Computer Editor
Lou Kesten, Feature Editor
460 West 34th Street
New York NY 10001
212-947-6500
Category: 11-23-29-33-43-67
Circulation: 340,000
Issues per year: 12
Reviews: 12-18/year
Buys only 1st serial rights.

Vista/USA
Kathleen M Caccavale, Editor
General Drafting Company
Canfield Road
Convent Station NJ 07961
201-538-7600
Category: 11-29-33-43-69-71
Circulation: 850,000
Issues per year: 4
Reviews: none
Buys only 2nd serial rights.

Vogue
Marion Asnes, Editor
Talking About Money
350 Madison Avenue
New York NY 10017
212-880-8800
Category: 73-99(beauty and fashion
Issues per year: 12

Voice of Youth Advocates
Editor, Book Reviews
3936 W Colonial Parkway
Virginia Beach VA 23452
Category: 21-31-76

Wall Street Review of Books
David O Whitten, Editor
380 Adams Street
Bedford Hills NY 10507
914-241-7100
Category: 19-99

Washington Book Review
Edward D Scullen, Editor
P O Box 42538
Washington DC 20015-0538
202-363-5019
Category: 99
Issues per year: 26
Reviews: 100/issue

Washington Journalism Review
Shelby Sadler, Editor
2233 Wisconsin Avenue NW #442
Washington DC 20007
202-333-6800
Category: 11-19(journalism
        publishing)-23
Circulation: 30,000
Issues per year: 12
Reviews: 3-4/issue
Buys 1st and 2nd serial rights.

Washington Magazine
David Fuller, Managing Editor
1500 Eastlake Avenue E
Seattle WA 98102
Category: 61(WA)-99
Issues per year: 12

Washington Monthly
Charles Peters, Editor
1711 Connecticut Avenue NW
Washington DC 20009
202-462-0128
Category: 55-61(Washington DC)-99
Circulation: 35,000
Issues per year: 12
Reviews: 6-10/issue
Buys 1st and 2nd serial rights.

Washingtonian
John Bass, Editor
1828 L Street NW #200
Washington DC 20009
202-296-3600
Category: 61(Washington DC)
Issues per year: 12

Wealth
Robert Meier, Book Editor
Gary Alexander, Managing Editor
4425 W Napoleon Avenue
Metaire LA 70001
504-456-0040
Category: 19(investment)
Circulation: 40,000
Issues per year: 4
Reviews: 6/issue

Weaver's Journal
Suzanne Baizermann, Editor
P O Box 14238
St Paul MN 55114
612-646-7445
Category: 29(weaving)
Issues per year: 4

Weight Watchers Magazine
Lee Haiken, Editor-in-Chief
360 Lexington Avenue
New York NY 10017
212-370-0644
Category: 27-39-69
Issues per year: 12

West Coast Review of Books
D David Dreis, Editor
Henry Zorich, Paperback Books

Rapport Publishing Company
6331 Hollywood Boulevard #1002
Hollywood CA 90028
213-464-2662
Category: 99
Circulation: 80,000
Issues per year: 4
Reviews: 100/issue
Does not buy serial rights.

Western Landscaping
Jan Kingaard, Editor
P O Box 19531
Irvine CA 92713
Category: 43

Western Office Dealer
Mary Petrosky, Editor
41 Sutter Street #300
San Francisco CA 94104
Category: 19(purchasing)

Westways
Mary Ann Fisher, Editor
Terminal Annex
P O Box 2890
Los Angeles CA 90051
213-741-4760
Category: 71

Wharton Journal
Paul Summer, Editor
Vance Hall
3733 Spruce Street
Philadelphia PA 19104
215-898-3435
Category: 19
Circulation: 4,000

Whole Earth Review
Steward Brand, Editor
Point Foundation
27 Gate Five Road
Sausalito CA 94965
Category: 11-13-23-25-29-31-39
        43-47-51-53
Issues per year: 6

Wildlife Photography
Wildlife Photography Association
P O Box 691
Greenville PA 16125
Category: 11(photography)-15-51
Issues per year: 6

Wilson Library Bulletin
Milo Nelson, Editor
H W Wilson Company
950 University Avenue
Bronx NY 10452
212-588-8400
Category: 99
Issues per year: 12

Wilson Quarterly
Peter Braestrup, Editor
Smithsonian Institute
600 Maryland Avenue SW #430

Washington DC 20560
202-287-3400
Category: 41-55-99
Circulation: 110,000
Issues per year: 4
Reviews: 10/issue

Woman
Sherry Anatenstein, Editor
1115 Broadway
New York NY 10010
212-807-7100
Category: 73

Woman Engineer
Ann Kelly, Editor
Equal Opportunity Publications
44 Broadway
Greenlawn NY 11740
516-261-8917
Category: 19(career guidance)
        23-73
Circulation: 16,000
Issues per year: 4
Buys only 2nd serial rights.

Woman's Day
Eileen H Jordan, Book Editor
1515 Broadway
New York NY 10036
212-719-6000
Category: 73-99(fashion, beauty)

Woman's Review of Books
Woman's Resource Center
Wellesley College
Wellesley MA 02187
Category: 73-99
Issues per year: 12
Reviews: many

Woman's World
177 N Dean Street
P O Box 671
Englewood NJ 07631
Category: 27-29-35-39-43-73

Women Artists News
Rena Hansen, Editor
Midmarch Associates
P O Box 3304, Grand Central St
New York NY 10163
Category: 11-73

Women in Business
Margaret Horan, Editor
9100 Ward Parkway
P O Box 8728
Kansas City MO 64114
916-361-6621
Category: 19-73
Circulation: 110,000
Issues per year: 6

Women's Health
Rodale Press
33 E Minor Street
Emmaus PA 18049

215-967-5171
Category: 39-73
Issues per year: 2

Women's Record
Helen Borel, Book Reviews
200 West 79th Street #9L
New York NY 10024
212-362-7119
Category: 73

Women's Sports and Fitness
Martha Nelson, Editor
310 Town and Country Village
Palo Alto CA 94301
Category: 39-69-73
Issues per year: 12

Woodsmith
Donald B Peschke, Editor
2200 Grand Avenue
Des Moines IA 50312
Category: 29(woodworking)
Issues per year: 6

Woodworker's Journal
James J McQuillan, Editor
P O Box 1629
New Milford CT 06776
203-355-2694
Category: 29(woodworking)
Circulation: 120,000
Issues per year: 6

Words
Samuel Dickey, Editor
Intl Word-Processing Association
1015 N York Road
Willow Grove PA 19090
215-657-6300
Category: 19(office)-23
Circulation: 15,500
Issues per year: 6

Workbasket
Roma Jean Rice, Editor
4251 Pennsylvania Avenue
Kansas City MO 64111
Category: 29
Issues per year: 10

Workbench
Jay W Hedden, Editor
Modern Handcraft
4251 Pennsylvania Avenue
Kansas City MO 64111
Category: 29-43
Issues per year: 6

Working Mother
Karen Pritzker, Business Editor
Bulletin Board
230 Park Avenue
New York NY 10169
212-551-9412
Category: 19-35-73
Issues per year: 12

Working Parents
Janet Spencer King, Editor
441 Lexington Avenue
New York NY 10017
212-867-4820
Category: 19-35-73
Circulation: 500,000
Issues per year: 6

Working Woman
Julia Gray, Editor
342 Madison Avenue
New York NY 10173
212-309-9800
Category: 19-73
Circulation: 770,000
Issues per year: 12

Worksteader News
Lynie Arden, Editor
2396 Coolidge Way
Ranch Cordova CA 95670
Category: 19(small business)

Worlds of If
Orson Scott Card, Book Reviews
P O Box 93
Hicksville NY 11802
Category: 86
Issues per year: 6

The Writer
Sylvia K Burack, Editor
120 Boylston Street
Boston MA 02116
617-423-3157
Category: 11(writing)
Circulation: 57,000
Issues per year: 12
Reviews: 60/year

Writer's Digest
Sharon Rudd, Books Editor
Trends/Topics Department
9933 Alliance Road
Cincinnati OH 45242
513-984-0717
Category: 11(writing)
Circulation: 200,000
Issues per year: 12

Writer's Digest
Judson Jerome, Poetry Editor
917 Xenia Avenue
Yellow Springs OH 45387
Category: 95

Writing
Alan Lenhoff, Editor
3500 Western Avenue
Highland Park IL 60035
312-432-2700
Category: 11(writing)
Issues per year: 9

Yale Scientific Magazine
Sarah Fishman, Editor
P O Box 244A

Yale Station
New Haven CT 06520
203-436-3222
Category: 67
Circulation: 7,000
Issues per year: 4
Reviews: 10/issue
Does not buy serial rights.

Yard & Garden
Rod Dickens, Editor
Johnson Hill Press
P O Box 500
Fort Atkinson WI 53538
414-563-6388
Category: 19(marketing)
          43(garden)
Issues per year: 10
Does not buy serial rights.

Yoga Journal
California Yoga Teachers Assn.
2054 University Avenue
Berkeley CA 94704
Category: 53(yoga)

Your Church
Phyllis Rice, Editor
198 Allendale Road
King of Prussia PA 19406
215-265-9400
Category: 63

Your Money
Penny Williams, Editor
56 Esplanade
Toronto M5E 1A7 ON Canada
416-364-4266
Category: 19-99(money)

ZIP Target Marketing
Ernest E Schell, Editor
401 N Broad Street
Philadelphia PA 19108
212-574-9600
Category: 19(marketing)
Circulation: 38,000
Issues per year: 12

<u>CATEGORIES</u> -- coded by number

10 General Nonfiction
11 Art/Music/Photography/Dance
13 Alternative Issues
15 Animals/Pets
17 Biographies/Autobiographies
19 Business/Economics
21 Children's Books
23 Computers/Technology
25 Consumer Issues and Guides
27 Cookbooks/Nutrition
29 Crafts/Hobbies/How-to
31 Education/Child Development
33 Entertainment/Movies/Humor
35 Family/Marriage/Retirement
37 Gay/Lesbian
39 Health/Medicine/Diet/Exercise
41 History

43 House/Garden/Automobiles
45 Languages:_______________
47 Literature/Humanities
49 Minority Studies
51 Nature/Ecology/Conservation
53 New Age/Astrology/Occult
55 Politics/Government/Military
57 Psychology/Self-Help
59 Reference Books
61 Regional Titles
63 Religions/Philosophy
65 Scholarly Titles
67 Science/Mathematics
69 Sports/Games/Recreation
71 Travel/Geography
73 Women's Issues

75 General Fiction
76 Children's Stories
77 Contemporary Novels
78 Ethnic/Minority Literature
79 Folklore/Fairy Tales
80 Foreign Literature
81 Historical
82 Horror/Occult

83 Literary
84 Mystery/Detective
85 Romance/Gothic
86 Science Fiction/Fantasy
87 Suspense/Adventure
88 Westerns
89 Young Adult
90 Short Stories/Anthologies

95 Poetry
97 News

98 Other:_______________
99 All subjects and categories

==

<u>Radio</u> / <u>Television</u> -- special codes

Formats: C = Live with Call-ins
           L = Live
           P = Telephone Interviews
           T = Taped

Features: B = Book Reviews
           F = Features
           I = Interviews
           N = News
           R = Book Readings

==

Books with Eric Griffel
WKXL-FM
Eric Griffel
Apple Tree Book Shop
24 Warren Street
Concord NH 03301
603-228-8451
Category: 99
Host: Eric Griffel
Format: -- FM

CBL
News Director
P O Box 500, Station A
Toronto M5W 1E6   ON Canada
416-925-3311
Category: 99
Format: -- AM/FM

CFCF
John Oakley
Mid-morning
405 Ogilvy Avenue
Montreal H3N 1M4   PQ Canada
514-273-5141
Category: 99
Host: John Oakley
Format: C -- AM/FM
Features: I-N-F

CFCF
Frank W McCormick, News Director
Rod MacDonald, Research Director
405 Ogilvy Avenue
Montreal H3N 1M4   PQ Canada
514-273-5141
Category: 99
Format: -- AM/FM

CFCF
Mark Burns
Morning Program
405 Ogilvy Avenue
Montreal H2X 3R4   PQ Canada
514-274-5141
Category: 99
Host: Mark Burns
Format: L -- AM/FM
Features: I-N-F

CFRB
Program Director
2 St Clair Avenue West
Toronto M4V 1L6   ON Canada
416-924-5711
Category: 99
Format: -- AM

CFTR
25 Adelaide Street
Toronto M5C 1H3   ON Canada
416-864-2000
Category: 99
Format: -- AM

CHFI
25 Adelaide Street E
Toronto M5C 1H3   ON Canada
416-842-2070
Category: 99
Format: -- FM

CHOM
1355 Greene Avenue
Westmount H3Z 2A5   PQ Canada
514-935-2425
Category: 99
Format: -- FM

CHQM
Producer, Business Analysis
1134 Burrand
Vancouver V6Z 148   BC Canada
604-660-1320
Category: 19
Format: -- AM

CHUM
1331 Yonge Street
Toronto M4T 1Y1   ON Canada
416-925-6666
Category: 99
Format: -- AM/FM

CJAD
1411 Fort Street
Montreal H3H 2R1   PQ Canada
514-989-2523
Category: 99
Format: -- AM

CJCL
464 Yonge Street
Toronto M4Y 1W9   ON Canada
416-923-0921
Category: 99
Format: -- AM

CKEY
1 Yonge Street
Toronto M5E 1G1   ON Canada
416-361-1281
Category: 99
Format: -- AM

CKFM
24 St Clair Avenue W
Toronto M4V 1L4   ON Canada
416-922-9999
Category: 99
Format: -- FM

CKO Network
Joe Solway
Spectrum
30 Carlton Street
Toronto M5B 2E9   ON   Canada
416-591-1222
Category: 10-75

Host: Al Michaels/Betty Harrison
Format: L-T-P -- FM
Features: I-N-F

CKO Network
Melanie Reffes, Features Producer
Peter Varley
30 Carlton Street
Toronto M5B 2E9   ON Canada
416-591-1222
Category: 10-75
Host: Peter Varley
Format: L-T-C-P -- FM
Features: I-N-F-B

CKY/CITI
David Spence, News Director
Connections
Polo Park
Winnipeg R3G 0L7   MB Canada
204-786-8613
Category: 10
Host: Charles Adler
Format: T -- AM/FM
Features: I-N-F

CKY/CITI
David Spence, News Director
Citylife Magazine
Polo Park
Winnipeg R3G 0L7   MB Canada
204-786-8613
Category: 10
Host: David Spence
Format: T -- AM/FM
Features: I-N-F

KABC-AM
3321 S La Cienega Boulevard
Los Angeles CA 90016
213-557-7234
Category: 99
Format: -- AM

KABL
1025 Battery
San Francisco CA 94111
415-788-5225
Category: 99
Format: -- FM

KADI
7530 Forsyth
St Louis MO 63105
314-721-2323
Category: 99
Format: -- FM

KAFM
12700 Park Central Drive #512
Dallas TX 75251
214-386-6100
Category: 99
Format: -- FM

KALW-FM
Alan Farley
People, Places, and Ideas
2905 21th Street
San Francisco CA 94110
415-648-1177
Category: 99
Host: Alan Farley & N Schafler
Format: T -- FM
Features: I-F-B-R

KALW-FM
Julia Randall, Operations Manager
2905 21st Street
San Francisco CA 94110
415-648-1177
Category: 99
Format: -- FM

KAMT
P O Box 1277
Tacoma WA 98401
206-927-1360
Category: 99
Format: -- AM

KAMU
Texas A&M University
College Station TX 77840
409-845-5613
Category: 99
Format: -- FM

KANU-FM
Darrell Brogdon, Program Director
Morning Edition
Broadcasting Hall, U of KS
Lawrence KS 66045
913-864-4444
Category: 99
Host: Darrell Brogdon
Format: L -- FM
Features: I-N-F-B

KANU-FM
Rachel Hunter, Voices
Broadcasting Hall
University of Kansas
Lawrence KS 66045
913-864-4530
Category: 99
Host: Rachel Hunter
Format: T -- FM
Features: I

KAOK
P O Drawer S
Lake Charles LA 70602
318-436-7541
Category: 99
Format: -- AM

KARN-AM
P O Box 4189
Little Rock AR 72214
501-661-7500
Category: 99
Format: -- AM

KASU-FM
P O Box 2160
Arkansas State University
Jonesboro AR 72467
501-972-3070
Category: 99
Format: -- FM

KATZ
1139 Olive Street
St Louis MO 63101
314-241-6000
Category: 99
Format: -- AM

KBAY
Robin Rockwell, Public Affairs
P O Box 6616
San Jose CA 95150
408-370-7377
Category: 99
Format: -- FM

KBCQ
9416 Mission Gorge Road
Santee CA 92071
619-286-1170
Category: 99
Format: -- FM

KBEA
P O Box 1347
Mission KS 66222
913-432-1480
Category: 99
Format: -- AM

KBEQ-FM
Nancy Werner, Public Affairs
Community Concerns
4710 Pennsylvania
Kansas City MO 64112
816-531-2535
Category: 19-23-25-31-33-37-39
          43-49-55-57-69-71-73
Host: Nancy Werner
Format: T -- FM
Features: I-N-F-B

KBEQ-FM
Nancy Werner, Public Affairs
For Your Information
4710 Pennsylvania
Kansas City MO 64112
816-531-2535
Category: 19-23-25-31-33-37-39
          43-49-55-57-69-71-73
Host: Nancy Werner
Format: T -- FM
Features: I-N-F-B

KBIA
News Director
P O Box 758
Columbia MO 65205
314-882-3431
Category: 99
Format: -- FM

KBIG
Rob Edwards, Program Director
7755 Sunset Boulevard
Los Angeles CA 90046
213-874-7700
Category: 99
Format: -- FM

KBLX
Keith Jenkins, News Director
601 Ashby
Berkeley CA 94710
415-848-7713
Category: 99
Format: -- FM

KBOO
Ross Reynolds, News Director
Radio Zine
20 SE 8th Street
Portland OR 97214
503-231-8032
Category: 11-13-17-19-23-25-33
          35-37-39-41-47-49-51
          53-55-59-61-63-73
Host: Ross Reynolds
Format: L-T-C-P -- FM
Features: I-N-F-B-R

KBPI
Jo Myers, News Talent
KBPI Morning Show
1200 17th Street #2300
Denver CO 80201
303-572-6200
Category: 11-15-25-33-39-47-53
          55-57-61-69-73-77-79
          83-85-86-87-88-89
Host: Alan Dumas
Format: L -- FM
Features: I-N-F

KBPS-AM/FM
Tania D Thompson, Producer
Pastiche
546 N E 12th Avenue
Portland OR 97232
503-280-5828
Category: 11-33-47-75
Host: Tania Thompson
Format: T -- AM/FM
Features: F

KBRT
News Director
1888 Century Park East #208
Los Angeles CA 90067
213-277-9785
Category: 99
Format: -- AM

KBUR
Public Affairs Director
P O Box 70
Burlington IA 52601
319-752-2701
Category: 99
Format: -- AM

Local Radio Stations and Shows

KBVL-FM
P O Box 146
Boulder CO 80306
303-444-1490
Category: 99
Format: -- FM

KBZT
Donna Lum, Producer
California Conference Call
3580 Wilshire Boulevard
Los Angeles CA 90266
213-318-1666
Category: 10
Host: Mike Carruthers
Format: L-T-C-P -- FM
Features: I

KCBS
Steve Boffrey
KCBS News Magazine
One Embarcadero Center
San Francisco CA 94111-3602
415-982-7000
Category: 10
Format: I-P -- AM

KCBS
Andrew Finlayson, Associate
Jan Black's Journal
1 Embarcadero Center
San Francisco CA 94111
415-765-4121
Category: 99
Host: Jan Black
Format: C -- AM
Features: I-N-F

KCBS
Narsai David
Narsai and Company
1 Embarcadero Center
San Francisco CA 94111
415-527-7900
Category: 27-33-43-61-69-71
        98(wine)
Host: Narsai David
Format: L -- AM
Features: I-N-F

KCBX
1026 Chorro Street
San Luis Obispo CA 93401
805-541-1295
Category: 99
Format: -- FM

KCCK
6301 Kirkwood Blvd SW
P O Box 2068
Cedar Rapids IA 52406
319-398-5446
Category: 99
Format: -- FM

KCFR
Lee Frank, News Director
KCFR's Morning Edition

2249 S Josephine
Denver CO 80210-4805
303-871-9191
Category: 61
Host: Ms Penny Dennis
Format: L -- FM
Features: I-N-F-B

KCFR Radio
Robert Johnson, Book Reviewer
KCFR's Morning Edition
2249 South Josephine
Denver CO 80210-4805
303-871-9191
Category: 99
Format: L-T -- FM
Features: B

KCHO-FM
California State University
Chico CA 95929
Category: 99
Format: -- FM

KCMO
4500 Johnson Drive
Fairway KS 66205
913-677-7362
Category: 99
Format: -- AM/FM

KCNW
David Baldwin, Operations Manager
Christian Kansas City
4535 Metropolitian Avenue
Kansas City KS 66106
913-236-5269
Category: 21-35-63
Host: David Baldwin
Format: L-C-P -- AM
Features: I

KCOH
5011 Almeda
Houston TX 77004
713-522-1001
Category: 99
Format: -- AM

KCOK
717 N Mooney Boulevard
Tulare CA 93274
209-686-5265
Category: 99
Format: -- AM

KCSB-FM
P O Box 13401
Santa Barbara CA 93101
Category: 99
Format: -- FM

KCSM
1700 W Hillsdale Boulevard
San Mateo CA 94402
415-574-6427
Category: 99
Format: -- FM

KCSN
18111 Nordhoff Street
Northridge CA 91330
213-885-3090
Category: 99
Format: -- FM

KCUR
Laura Ziegler, News Director
Morning Edition
5100 Rockhill Road
Kansas City MO 64112
816-276-1551
Category: 99
Format: T-P -- FM
Features: I-N-F-B-R

KCUR
Laura Ziegler, News Director
Local Considerations
5100 Rockhill Road
Kansas City MO 64112
816-276-1551
Category: 99
Format: T -- FM
Features: I-N-F-B-R

KDB-AM
Cliff Marshall, News Director
23 W Micheltorena Street
Santa Barbara CA 93101
805-966-1490
Category: 99
Format: -- AM

KDEN
David Tanin, Program Director
5660 S Syracuse Circle
Englewood CO 80110
303-771-1500
Category: 99
Format: -- AM

KDFC
2822 Van Ness Avenue
San Francisco CA 94109
415-441-5332
Category: 99
Format: -- FM

KDKA
Judy Yanke, Producer
John Cigna Show
1 Gateway Center
Pittsburgh PA 15222
412-392-3261
Category: 99
Host: John Cigna
Format: L-P -- AM

KDKA
Producer
Perry Marshall Show
1 Gateway Center
Pittsburgh PA 15222
412-392-2556
Category: 99
Format: -- AM

Local Radio Stations and Shows

KDKA
Allan Jennings
Jennings Journal
1 Gateway Center
Pittsburgh PA 15222
412-392-3261
Category: 99
Host: Allan Jennings
Format: L-T -- AM
Features: N-F

KDKB
Pat Powers, News Director
1167 W Javelina
Mesa AZ 85202
602-897-9300
Category: 99
Format: -- FM

KDPS-FM
1800 Grand Avenue
Des Moines IA 50307
515-284-7723
Category: 99
Format: -- FM

KDSU
Ceres Hall
North Dakota State University
Fargo ND 58105
701-237-8329
Category: 99
Format: -- FM

KDTH
Don Hess, Program Director
8th & Bluff Streets
Dubuque IA 52001
319-588-5700
Category: 99
Format: -- AM

KDWB
Linda Hutchinson-Evans
News Director
Buck & O'Connor Morning Zoo
P O Box 19551
St Paul MN 55119
612-739-4000
Category: 11-15-17-19-21-25-33
        35-39-61-69-73
Host: Linda Evans
Format: L -- AM/FM
Features: I-N-F

KDWN
1 Main Street
Las Vegas NV 89101
702-385-7212
Category: 99
Format: -- AM

KDYL
57 W South Temple #800
Salt Lake UT 84101
801-524-2600
Category: 99
Format: -- AM

KEBC
P O Box 94580
Oklahoma City OK 73143
405-631-7501
Category: 99
Format: -- FM

KEGL
Terri Barrett, Public Affairs
5915 W Pioneer Parkway
Arlington TX 76013
817-457-9700
Category: 99
Format: -- FM

KENZ-AM/KSAC-FM
Mark Vandervelden, News Director
620 Bercut
P O Box 2424
Sacramento CA 95814
916-446-5769
Category: 99
Format: -- AM/FM

KERA
3000 Harry Hines Boulevard
Dallas TX 75201
214-744-1300
Category: 99
Format: -- FM

KESD
Pugsley Center
Brookings SD 57007
605-688-4191
Category: 99
Format: -- FM

KEST
1231 Market Street
San Francisco Ca 94103
415-626-5585
Category: 99
Format: -- AM

KEX 1190
Don Wright
North West at Night
4949 SW Macadam Avenue
Portland OR 97223
503-225-1190
Category: 10
Host: Don Wright
Format: L-P -- AM
Features: I-N-F-B

KEZO
11128 J Galt Boulevard
Omaha NE 68137
402-592-4048
Category: 99
Format: -- FM

KEZX
Alice Porter, News Director
Focal Point
3876 Bridgeway N
Seattle WA 98105
206-633-5590
Category: 25-33
Host: Alice Porter
Format: T -- FM
Features: I-N-F-B

KEZY-AM
1190 E Ball Road
Anaheim CA 92805
714-776-1191
Category: 99
Format: -- AM

KFAB-AM
5010 Underwood Avenue
Omaha NE 68132
402-556-8000
Category: 99
Format: -- AM

KFAC
6735 Yucca
Hollywood CA 90028
213-466-9566
Category: 99
Format: -- AM/FM

KFAX-AM
Tom Walles, Station Manager
KFAX - Talk
3106 Diablo Avenue
Hayward CA 94545
415-673-4148
Category: 10
Format: -- AM

KFBK-AM
Norm Woodruff, News Director
1440 Ethan Way #200
Sacramento CA 95825
916-929-5325
Category: 99
Format: -- AM

KFDI
P O Box 1402
Wichita KS 67201
316-838-3771
Category: 99
Format: -- AM/FM

KFH
Michael Dean, News Director
104 S Emporia
Wichita KS 67202
316-262-5791
Category: 99
Format: -- AM

KFI-AM
Sharon Doyle
Street Side
610 S Ardmore, P O Box 76860
Los Angeles CA 90005
213-385-0101
Category: 10
Format: C -- AM
Features: I

KFJC-FM
Don Surath
People in Peninsula Politics
12345 El Monte Road
Los Altos Hills CA 94022
415-960-4260
Category: 13-25-51-55
Host: Don Surath
Format: C -- FM
Features: I-N

KFJC-FM
Dave Emory
One Step Beyond
12345 El Monte Road
Los Altos Hills CA 94022
415-960-4260
Category: 13-17-19-41-55
Host: Dave Emory
Format: C -- FM
Features: N-R

KFJC-FM
John Porter
Brainwaves
12345 El Monte Road
Los Altos Hills CA 94022
415-960-4260
Category: 11-13-17-19-23-25-41
47-55-57-61-65-67-82
84-86
Host: John Porter
Format: C -- FM
Features: I-F-R

KFJM
News Director
P O Box 8116
University of North Dakota
Grand Forks ND 58202
701-777-2577
Category: 99
Format: -- AM/FM

KFMB
Producer
Bill Balance Show
7677 Engineer Road
San Diego CA 92111
619-292-7600
Category: 99
Format: -- AM/FM

KFMK
Chuck Shramek, News Director
6420 Richmond #600
Houston TX 77057
713-978-7328
Category: 99
Format: -- FM

KFOG
Scoop Nisker, News Director
900 North Point
San Francisco CA 94109
415-885-1045
Category: 99
Format: -- FM

KFOR
Producer, All About Books
P O Box 80209
Lincoln NE 68501
402-475-6606
Category: 99
Format: -- AM

KFOR
Dale Johnson, News Director
P O Box 80209
Lincoln NE 68501
402-475-6606
Category: 19-25-31-35-39
51-53-57-73
Format: -- AM

KFOX-FM
Mark Henry, News Director
123 W Torrance Boulevard #C-2
Redondo Beach CA 90277
213-374-9797
Category: 99
Format: -- FM

KFRC
Jaonne Greene, Director
Bottom Line
500 Washington Street
San Francisco CA 94111
415-986-6100
Category: 19
Host: Joanne Green
Format: T-C -- AM
Features: I-F

KFRC
Joanne Greene, Director
Body Talk
500 Washington Street
San Francisco CA 94111
415-986-6100
Category: 39-69-57
Host: Joanne Green
Format: T -- AM
Features: I-F

KFSD
1540 6th Street
San Diego CA 92101
619-239-9091
Category: 99
Format: -- FM

KFUO
Jerry Housholder, Director
THIS DAY
85 Founders Lane
St Louis MO 63105
314-725-3030
Category: 99
Host: Jerry Housholder
Format: L-T-C-P -- AM
Features: I-N-F-B

KFWB
6230 N Yucca Street
Los Angeles CA 90028

213-462-5392
Category: 99
Format: -- AM

KFYI
John Wheeling, News Director
100 Swan Way
Oakland CA 94621
415-430-9100
Category: 99
Format: -- AM

KGGO-FM
10880 Wilshire Boulevard
Los Angeles CA 90024
213-475-8525
Category: 99
Format: -- FM

KGIL
Tim Regan, Producer
Dick Whittington Show
14800 Lassen Street
San Fernando CA 91345
818-894-9191
Category: 10
Format: -- FM
Features: I

KGMI
Shawn Hansen, Public Affairs
2214 Yew Street
Bellingham WA 98225
206-734-9790
Category: 99
Format: -- AM

KGNR
Producer
Fred Hoffman Show
2225 19th Street
Sacramento CA 95818
916-441-5272
Category: 99
Format: -- AM

KGO
Producer, Sunday Morning
with Rabbi Bernstein
900 Front Street
San Francisco CA 94111
415-863-0077
Category: 63
Host: Rabbi Bernstein
Format: I -- AM

KGO
Cindy Slay
California Weekend
900 Front Street
San Francisco CA 94111
415-863-0077
Category: 69-29
Format: -- AM

KGO
Mikel Cleland, Producer
The Ronn Owens Show

900 Front Street
San Francisco CA 94111
415-954-8140
Category: 99
Host: Ronn Owens
Format: L-P -- AM
Features: I-N-F-B

KGON-FM
15351 SE Johnson Road
Clackamas OR 97015
503-655-9181
Category: 99
Format: -- FM

KGOU
780 Van Vleet Oval
Norman OK 73109
405-325-3388
Category: 99
Format: -- FM

KGU
Ellen Pelissero, Director
Ron Jacobs Show
2255 Kuhio Avenue #1201
Honolulu HI 96815
808-923-7600
Category: 99
Host: Ron Jacobs
Format: L-C-P -- AM
Features: I-N-F-B

KGU
Ellen Pelissero, Director
Mike Buck Show
2255 Kuhio Avenue #1201
Honolulu HI 96815
808-923-7600
Category: 99
Host: Mike Buck
Format: L-C-P -- AM
Features: I-N-F-B

KGW-AM
1501 SW Jefferson Street
Portland OR 97201
503-226-5095
Category: 99
Format: -- AM

KHCC
Patsy Terrell, News Director
KHCC Midday
815 N Walnut #300
Hutchison KS 67501
316-665-3555
Category: 11-15-17-19-25-31-33
        35-39-41-43-47-51-57
        61-67-71-73
Host: Patsy Terrell & Dan Skinner
Format: L-T-P -- FM
Features: I-N-F-B

KHEP
Will Ray, Program Director
Topic
3883 N 38th Avenue

Phoenix AZ 85019
602-278-5555
Category: 11-13-15-19-21-25
        17-29-31-35-39-43
        51-59-63-69-73
Host: Will Ray
Format: P -- AM
Features: I

KHFM
Mike Langner, Station Manager
Arts and Public Affairs
5900 Domingo Road NE
Albuquerque NM 87108
505-262-2631
Category: 11-47-83
Host: Mike Langner
Format: T -- FM
Features: I

KHJ
5515 Melrose
Hollywood CA 90038
213-462-2133
Category: 99
Format: -- AM

KHOW
Dee Ann Metzger, Director
Know Good Health & Fitness
8975 E Kenyon Avenue
Denver CO 80237
303-694-6300
Category: 39
Host: Laura Blackman
Format: T -- AM
Features: I

KHOW
Dee Ann Metzger, Director
Perspective
8975 E Kenyon Avenue
Denver CO 80237
303-694-6300
Category: 11-13-19-25-31-35-37
        39-49-51-55-75-77
Host: Dee Ann Metzger
Format: T -- AM
Features: I-N

KHPR
Bob Miller
Morning Edition
1335 Lower Campus Drive
Honolulu HI 96822
808-955-8821
Category: 10
Host: Bob Miller
Format: L-T -- FM
Features: I-N-F-B

KHTR
Kevin McCarthy, News Director
1 Memorial Drive
St Louis MO 63102
314-444-3269
Category: 99
Format: -- FM

KHTT
1420 Koll Circle
San Jose CA 95112
408-279-1738
Category: 99
Format: -- AM

KHVH
Julie Tavares, Newsroom Manager
1001 Bishop Street
Honolulu HI 96813
808-524-3111
Category: 99
Format: -- AM

KIEV-AM
Producer
George Putnam: Talk Back
104 N Glendale
Glendale CA 91206
213-245-2388
Category: 55
Format: -- AM
Features: N

KIEV-FM
Tania McKnight
Tania McKnight's World
4322 Wilshire Boulevard #604
Los Angeles CA 90010
213-933-8261
Category: 99
Format: -- FM
Features: I

KIIS
6255 Sunset Boulevard
Hollywood CA 90028
213-466-8381
Category: 99
Format: -- FM

KIKK
6306 Gulfton Drive
Houston TX 77081
713-772-4433
Category: 99
Format: -- FM

KILT-FM
500 Lovett Boulevard
Houston TX 77006
713-526-3461
Category: 99
Format: -- FM

KIMN
1095 S Monica Parkway
Denver CO 80224
303-234-9500
Category: 99
Format: -- AM

KING
Jessica Baldwin, Producer
Stacy Taylor Show
333 Dexter Avenue N
Seattle WA 98109

Local Radio Stations and Shows

206-343-3640
Category: 19-23-25-31-33-35
          37-41-49-51-55-57
          63-69-71-73
Host: Stacy Taylor
Format: L-T-C-P -- AM
Features: I-N-F

KING
Karen Williams, Producer
The Jim Althoff Show
333 Dexter Avenue N
Seattle WA 98109
206-448-3640
Category: 19-23-25-31-33-35
          37-41-49-51-55-57
          63-69-71-73
Host: Jim Althoff
Format: L-T-C-P -- AM
Features: I-N-F

KING
Frank Catalano, Producer
Healthtalk
333 Dexter Avenue N
Seattle WA 98109
206-448-3640
Category: 39
Host: Frank Catalano
Format: L-T-C-P -- AM
Features: I-N-F

KINK
1501 SW Jefferson
Portland OR 97201
503-226-5080
Category: 99
Format: -- FM

KINQ
Gary Dian, News Director
1975 Diamond Boulevard
Concord CA 94520
415-684-9919
Category: 10-77-81-83-84-86
Format: L -- FM
Features: N

KIOI-AM/FM
700 Montgomery Street
San Francisco Ca 94111
415-956-5101
Category: 99
Format: -- AM/FM

KIOS
3219 Cuming Street
Omaha School District
Omaha NE 68131
402-556-2770
Category: 99
Format: -- FM

KIQQ
Peter B Bie, News Director
6430 Sunset Boulevard #1102
Hollywood CA 90028
213-469-1631

Category: 17-19-21-23-25-33
          35-39-41-55-73
Host: Peter Bie
Format: T -- FM
Features: I-F-B

KIRO
2807 3rd Street
Seattle WA 98121
206-624-7077
Category: 99
Format: -- AM

KISS
1100 N Main
San Antonio TX 78212
512-223-6211
Category: 99
Format: -- FM

KISW
712 Aurora Avenue N
Seattle WA 98109
206-285-7625
Category: 99
Format: -- FM

KJOI
2555 Briarcrest Road
Beverly Hills CA 90210
213-278-5990
Category: 99
Format: -- FM

KJQY
Larry Frankel, Producer
Perspective
625 Broadway #1200
San Diego CA 92101
619-238-1037
Category: 13-19-25-55
          98(public affairs)
Host: Larry Frankel
Format: T -- FM
Features: I

KJR
P O Box 3726
Seattle WA 98124
206-937-5100
Category: 99
Format: -- AM

KKBQ
Jackie Robbins, News Director
11 Greenway Place #2022
Houston TX 77046
713-961-0092
Category: 99
Format: -- FM

KKEY-AM
Ralph Weagent, Program Director
P O Box 5757
Portland OR 97228
503-222-1150
Category: 99
Format: -- AM

KKHI
1410 St Francis Hotel
335 Powell Street
San Francisco CA 94102
415-986-2151
Category: 99
Format: -- AM

KKHR
Lou Simon
After Midnight
6121 Sunset Boulevard
Los Angeles CA 90028
213-460-3657
Category: 11-33
Host: Lou Simon
Format: T -- FM
Features: I

KKHR
Jim Chenevey, News Director
Free Forum
6121 Sunset Boulevard
Hollywood CA 90028
213-460-3657
Category: 19-23-25-31-35-39
          49-51-55-57-67-73
Host: Jim Chenevey
Format: T -- FM
Features: I

KKJY-FM
Producer
Sunday Morning Gallery
5000 Marble NE
Albuquerque NM 87110
505-262-1866
Category: 99
Format: -- FM

KKUA
Austin Vail, Program Director
765 Amana Street
Honolulu HI 96814
808-955-7795
Category: 99
Format: -- AM

KKYX
Steve Warren, Program Director
Perspective San Antonio
8401 Datapoint Drive #900
San Antonio TX 78229
512-690-1925
Category: 11-17-25-27-33-35-37
          39-49-51-73-81-88
Host: Steve Warren
Format: T -- AM
Features: I

KLAC-AM/KZLA-FM
Dean Sander, News Director
4000 W Alameda
Burbank CA 91510
818-842-0500
Category: 10
Format: T -- AM/FM
Features: I-N-F

KLAC-AM/KZLA-FM
Gene Ferguson
The Sunday Show
4000 W Alameda
Burbank CA 91510
818-842-0500
Category: 10
Host: Gene Ferguson
Format: T -- AM/FM
Features: I-N-F

KLBJ
Pat Overton, Coordinator
Talk of Austin
P O Box 1209
Austin TX 78767
512-474-6543
Category: 11-13-21-31-35-37-43-73
Host: Kathy Cronkite
Format: L-C-P -- AM
Features: I-N-F-B

KLBJ-AM
Pat Overton, Coordinator
The Olin Murrell Show
P O Box 1209
Austin TX 78767
512-474-6543
Category: 37-41-49-55-65
Host: Olin Murrell
Format: L-C-P -- AM
Features: I-N-F

KLCC-FM
Lois Wadsworth, Sunday Morning
659 W 25th Place
Eugene OR 97405
503-343-7508
Category: 77
Host: Steve Katz
Format: T-P -- FM
Features: I-N-F-B

KLCC-FM
Lois Wadsworth
Morning Edition - Local
659 W 25th Place
Eugene OR 97405
503-343-7508
Category: 77
Host: Barbara Dellenback
Format: T -- FM
Features: I-N-F-B

KLCC-FM
Don Hein, News Director
4000 East 30th Avenue
Eugene OR 97405
503-726-2212
Category: 99
Format: -- FM

KLEF
5353 W Alabama #410
Houston TX 77056
713-622-5533
Category: 99
Format: -- FM

KLIF
Karen Bloom, Producer
The David Gold Show
411 Ryan Plaza Drive
Arlington TX 76011
817-461-0995
Category: 11-13-17-25-27-33-35-37
39-49-55-61-65-69-73
Host: David Gold
Format: L-C-P -- AM
Features: I-N-F-B

KLIF
Karen Bloom, Producer
At Your Service
411 Ryan Plaza Drive
Arlington TX 76011
817-461-0995
Category: 15-19-23-27-39
43-53-75-77
Host: Karen Bloom and Art Snow
Format: L-C-P -- AM
Features: I

KLIQ-AM
Oaks Park
Portland OR 97202
503-234-8448
Category: 99
Format: -- AM

KLOL
Linda Silk, Public Affairs
P O Box 1520
Houston TX 77001
713-526-4591
Category: 99
Format: -- FM

KLON
Henry Glenn, News Director
1250 Bellflower Boulevard
Long Beach CA 90804
213-597-9441
Category: 99
Format: -- FM

KLOS-FM
Producer, Telephone Talk
3321 S La Cienega Boulevard
Los Angeles CA 90016
213-557-7243
Category: 99
Format: -- FM

KLRE-FM
7701 Scott Hamilton Drive
Little Rock AR 72209
501-562-5573
Category: 99
Format: -- FM

KLTR
10333 Richmond Avenue
Houston TX 77042
713-780-0937
Category: 99
Format: -- FM

KLUB
1550 West 22nd North
Salt Lake City UT 84110
801-359-7794
Category: 99
Format: -- AM

KLUC/KMJJ
Bob Beers, News Director
Action Line
P O Box 14805
Las Vegas NV 89114
702-739-9383
Category: 10
Host: Bob Beers
Format: T -- AM/FM
Features: I

KLVU
5217 Ross Avenue
Dallas TX 75243
214-826-8760
Category: 99
Format: -- AM

KLYD
924 Truxton Avenue
Bakersfield CA 93302
805-327-5772
Category: 99
Format: -- AM

KMAX
3844 E Foothill Boulevard
Pasadena CA 91107
213-681-2486
Category: 99
Format: -- FM

KMBZ-AM
4935 Belinder
Shawnee Mission KS 66205
913-236-9800
Category: 99
Format: -- AM

KMCR-FM
1435 S Dodson Road
Mesa AZ 85202
602-969-9099
Category: 99
Format: -- FM

KMEL
Producer, Bytes
2430 Curtis Street
Berkeley CA 94702
415-391-9400
Category: 23-99
Format: -- FM

KMET
Mike Harrison, Program Director
5746 Sunset Boulevard
Hollywood CA 90028
213-464-5638
Category: 99
Format: -- FM

KMFA
3001 N Lamarr #100
Austin TX 78705
512-476-5632
Category: 99
Format: -- FM

KMGG
6430 Sunset Boulevard #418
Los Angeles CA 90028
213-468-0007
Category: 99
Format: -- FM

KMGL
James Banzer, News Director
P O Box 14806
Oklahoma City OK 73114
405-478-2223
Category: 99
Format: -- FM

KMJ-AM
3636 N 1st Street
Fresno CA 93726
209-224-5734
Category: 99
Format: -- AM

KMJQ
3100 Richmond Avenue #210
Houston TX 77098
713-527-9545
Category: 99
Format: -- FM

KMOD/KBBT
Matt Skinner, News Director
Radio Free Tulsa
5801 E 41st Street #900
Tulsa OK 74135
918-664-2810
Category: 13-17-19-25-31-35-39
        55-67-103-115
Host: Matt Skinner
Format: T-P -- AM/FM
Features: I-N-B

KMOX-AM
1 Memorial Drive
St Louis MO 63102
314-621-2345
Category: 99
Format: -- AM

KMPC
5858 Sunset Boulevard
Los Angeles CA 90028
213-460-5628
Category: 99
Format: -- AM

KMUW
3317 E 17th Street
Wichita KS 67208
316-682-5737
Category: 99
Format: -- FM

KNBR-AM
Ginny Park Li, Public Affairs
Gene D'Accardo, News Director
1700 Montgomery Street #400
San Francisco CA 94111
415-546-2200
Category: 99
Format: -- AM

KNDI-AM
Mary Harbold, Program Director
1734 S King
Honolulu HI 96826
808-946-2844
Category: 99
Format: -- AM

KNEW
Rita Cohen, Public Affairs
P O Box 910
Oakland CA 94604
415-836-0910
Category: 99
Format: -- AM

KNPR
John Stark, Program Director
Library Reports
5151 Boulder Highway
Las Vegas NV 89122
702-456-6695
Category: 99
Host: Teresa Rogers
Format: T -- FM
Features: F-B

KNST
Mark Gilman, Producer
Mark Gilman Show
P O Box 3068
Tucson AZ 85702
602-624-2431
Category: 99
Host: Mark Gilman
Format: L-C-P -- AM
Features: I-N-F

KNST
Toni Stanton, Producer
Toni Stanton Show
P O Box 3068
Tucson AZ 85702
602-624-2431
Category: 99
Host: Toni Stanton
Format: L-C-P -- AM
Features: I-N-F

KNUS-AM
Jill Genser, Producer
Woody Paige Show
4450 Morrison Road
Denver CO 80219
303-937-1200
Category: 99
Host: Woody Paige
Format: L -- AM
Features: I-N-F

KNUS-AM
Producer, Mornings
Producer, Money Talks
Producer, Wehner & Co
4450 Morrison Road
Denver CO 80219
303-937-1200
Category: 19-25-99
Format: -- AM

KNUU (K-NEWS Radio)
Steve Kindred, News Director
Collage
2001 E Flamingo Road
Las Vegas NV 89119
702-735-8644
Category: 10
Host: Dawn Kamber
Format: P -- AM

KNWZ
Mel Hill, Station Manager
Newstalk
43-100 Cook Street
Palm Desert CA 92260
619-346-1270
Category: 10-77
Host: Mary Neiswender
Format: L-C-P -- AM
Features: I-N-F-B

KNWZ
Nick La Caprita
Sportstalk
43-100 Cook Street
Palm Desert CA 92260
619-346-1270
Category: 69
Host: Nick La Caprita
Format: L-C-P -- AM
Features: I-N

KNX
6121 Sunset Boulevard
Los Angeles CA 90028
213-460-3341
Category: 99
Format: -- AM

KOA
Susan Reiman, Program Director
P O Box 85
Denver CO 80236
303-893-8500
Category: 99
Format: -- AM

KOAC
Covell Hall
Oregon State University
Corvallis OR 97331
503-754-4311
Category: 99
Format: -- AM

KOAP
2828 SW Front Avenue
Portland OR 97201

503-229-4880
Category: 99
Format: -- FM

KOB
93 Broadcast Place SW
Albuquerque NM 87103
505-243-4411
Category: 99
Format: -- AM/FM

KODA
4810 San Felipe Road
Houston TX 77056
713-622-1010
Category: 99
Format: -- FM

KOGO
8665 Gibbs Drive #201
San Diego CA 92123
619-565-6006
Category: 99
Format: -- AM

KOH-AM
P O Box 2271
Reno NV 89505
702-356-8000
Category: 99
Format: -- AM

KOIT AM/FM
Bonnie Chastain, News Director
Today's World
77 Maiden Lane
San Francisco CA 94108
415-434-0965
Category: 17-25-27-31-35-37-39
        57-59-61-73
Host: Bonnie Chastain
Format: T -- AM/FM
Features: I-N-F-B

KOMA
P O Box 1520
Okla City OK 73101
405-794-5565
Category: 99
Format: -- AM

KOMO
100 4th Avenue N
Seattle WA 98109
206-223-4107
Category: 99
Format: -- AM

KOMP-FM/KENO-AM
P O Box 26629
Las Vegas NV 89126
702-876-1460
Category: 99
Format: -- AM/FM

KOOL AM/FM
Bobbe Clark, News Director
2196 E Camelback

Phoenix AZ 85016
602-956-9696
Category: 99
Format: -- AM/FM

KOOL AM/FM
Joe Kennedy
Close-up
2196 E Camelback
Phoenix AZ 85016
602-956-9696
Category: 19-25-31-37-51-55-59-73
Host: Joe Kennedy
Format: T -- AM/FM
Features: N

KOOL-AM/FM
Mike Sauceda
Focus
2196 E Camelback
Phoenix AZ 85003
602-956-9696
Category: 19-25-31-37-51-55-59-73
Host: Mike Sauceda
Format: T -- AM/FM
Features: N

KOST-FM
David Blake, News Director
610 S Ardmore
Los Angeles CA 90005
213-385-0101
Category: 99
Format: -- FM

KOST-FM
Producer, KOST Lines
610 S Ardmore Avenue
Los Angeles CA 90005
213-385-0101
Category: 10
Host: Sharon Dale and Bob Kerr
Format: -- FM

KOSU
Esta Wolfram, Producer
Book Hustler
Oklahoma State University
Stillwater OK 74078
405-624-6352
Category: 99
Format: -- FM

KPAC
Cosimo Lucchese, Program Director
8401 Data Point Drive #1050
San Antonio TX 78229
512-696-5722
Category: 99
Format: -- FM

KPBS-FM
San Diego State
5300 Campanile
San Diego CA 92182
619-265-6431
Category: 99
Format: -- FM

KPBX
2319 Monroe Street
Spokane WA 99205
509-328-5729
Category: 99
Format: -- FM

KPCC
Larry Mantle, News Director
Larry Mantle's AirTalk
1570 E Colorado Boulevard
Pasadena CA 91106
818-578-7231
Category: 10
Host: Larry Mantle
Format: C -- FM
Features: I-N-F

KPDQ-FM Radio
Lew Davies, Producer
Liveline
5110 SE Stark Street
Portland OR 97215
503-231-7800
Category: 13-17-31-35-39-41
        55-57-59-63-65-67
Host: Lew Davies
Format: L-C-P -- FM
Features: I-N-F-B

KPEL-AM
Kenny Hazelett, Producer
Morning Report
P O Box 52046
Lafayette LA 70505
318-233-7003
Category: 10-77
Host: Kenny Hazelett
Format: L-P -- AM
Features: I-N-F-B

KPEL-AM
Ken Lorman, Producer
Afternoon Journal
P O Box 52046
Lafayette LA 70506
318-233-7003
Category: 10
Host: Ken Lorman and Don Allen
Format: L-C-P -- AM
Features: I-N-F-B

KPFA-FM
Eric Bauersfeld, Producer
Bay Area Arts
220 Shattuck Avenue
Berkeley CA 94707
415-848-6767
Category: 11-33
Format: -- FM

KPFA-FM
Will Nofke
New Horizons
2207 Shattuck Avenue
Berkeley CA 94704
415-845-2216
Category: 10

Host: Will Nofke
Format: -- FM
Features: I

KPFK-FM
3729 Cahuenga
N Hollywood CA 91604
818-985-2711
Category: 99
Format: -- FM

KPFT
419 Lovett Boulevard
Houston TX 77006
713-526-4000
Category: 99
Format: -- FM

KPLU
Pacific Lutheran University
Tacoma WA 98447
206-535-7758
Category: 63-99
Format: -- FM

KPMC-AM
P O Box 1736
Bakersfield CA 93302
805-327-5121
Category: 99
Format: -- AM

KPOF
Donald Wolfram, NewsDirector
3455 West 83rd
Denver CO 80030
303-428-0910
Category: 99
Format: -- AM

KPOO
P O Box 11008
San Francisco CA 94101
415-346-5373
Category: 99
Format: -- FM

KPRO-AM
P O Box 1440
Riverside CA 92502
714-683-1440
Category: 99
Format: -- AM

KPSI-AM
Lisa Whitlock, Producer
The Morning Show
2100 Tahquitz-McCallum Way
Palm Springs CA 92262
619-325-2582
Category: 99
Host: Sheri Inglis & Mike Meenan
Format: P -- AM
Features: I-N-F

KPSI-AM
Mike Meenan, Producer
Mikeside

2100 E Tahquitz-McCallum Way
Palm Springs CA 92262
619-325-2582
Category: 99
Host: Mike Meenan
Format: C -- AM
Features: I-N-F

KQED-FM
Chuck Finney, Producer
Your Legal Rights
500 Eighth Street
San Francisco CA 94103
415-553-2129
Category: 25-55(law)
Format: -- FM
Features: I

KQED-FM
Victor Vedin, Music Director
500 Eighth Street
San Francisco CA 94103
415-553-2129
Category: 11-71
Format: -- FM

KQED-FM
Producer, Moneyline
500 Eighth Street
San Francisco CA 94110
415-553-2129
Category: 19
Format: -- FM

KQRS FM/AM
Dan Culhane, News Director
Morning Show
917 N Lilac Drive
Minneapolis MN 55442
612-545-5601
Category: 10-75
Host: Tom Barnard & Dan Culhane
Format: L-C-P -- AM/FM
Features: I-N-F-B

KQV
Eric Mathis, Producer
The Doug Hoerth Show
411 7th Avenue
Pittsburgh PA 15219
412-562-5960
Category: 11-13-15-17-19-33-37
         41-53-55-59-61-67-71
Host: Doug Hoerth
Format: L-T-C-P -- AM
Features: I-N-F-B

KRAE
2109 E 10th Street
P O Box 189
Cheyenne WY 82003
307-638-8921
Category: 99
Format: -- AM

KRAV-FM
P O Box 746
Tulsa OK 74101

918-582-9696
Category: 99
Format: -- FM

KRBE-AM
9801 Westheimer Road #700
Houston TX 77042
713-266-1111
Category: 99
Format: -- AM

KREX-AM
P O Box 789
Grand Junction CO 81502
303-242-5000
Category: 99
Format: -- AM

KRIG-AM
Jim Drachus, Director
News and Information
P O Box 4312
Odessa TX 79760
915-332-6871
Category: 11-13-23-25-29-33-53
         55-59-67-69-84-86-88
Host: Jim Drachus
Format: L-T -- AM
Features: I-N-F-B

KRIG-AM
Jim Williams
Energy and Economics
P O Box 4312
Odessa TX 79760
915-332-6871
Category: 19-23-25-51-55-59-65-67
Host: Jim Williams
Format: L-P -- AM
Features: I-F-B

KRLA
Donna Lum, Producer
California Conference Call
3580 Wilshire Boulevard
Los Angeles CA 90266
213-318-1666
Category: 10
Host: Mike Carruthers
Format: L-T-C-P -- AM
Features: I

KRLD News Radio
Alex Burton
Persons
1080 Metro Media Place
Dallas TX 75247
214-634-1080
Category: 99
Host: Alex Burton
Format: T -- AM
Features: I

KRMG
Joe Riddle
John Erling Show
7136 S Yale
Tulsa OK 74136

918-493-7400
Category: 19-25-33-55-29-31-53
Host: John Erling
Format: L -- AM
Features: I-F

KRMG
Sonny Daniels, Producer
Sonny Daniels Show
7136 S Yale
Tulsa OK 74136
918-493-7400
Category: 19-29-33-55-29-31-53
Host: Sonny Daniels
Format: L -- AM
Features: I-F

KRMG
Kelly Calls, News Director
7136 S Yale
Tulsa OK 74136
918-493-7400
Category: 99
Format: -- AM

KROQ
117 S Robles
Pasadena CA 91101
213-578-0830
Category: 99
Format: -- FM

KRQR
Chris Miller, Director
Contact
One Embarcadero Center #3200
San Francisco CA 94111
415-765-4035
Category: 11-15-25-39-69
Host: Michael Knight
Format: T -- FM
Features: I-N-F

KRSP
P O Box 7760
Salt Lake UT 84107
801-262-5541
Category: 99
Format: -- AM/FM

KRSS-AM
Richard Tiner, General Manager
KRSS-Talk
1406 N Ash
Spokane WA 99201
509-326-1699
Category: 11-17-19-21-31-33-35
        51-63-69-76-29
Host: Richard Tiner
Format: T-P -- AM
Features: I-F-B

KRTH
5901 Venice Boulevard
Los Angeles CA 90034
213-937-5230
Category: 99
Format: -- FM

KRWG
P O Box FM 91
New Mexico State University
Las Cruces NM 88003
505-646-4525
Category: 99
Format: -- FM

KS-95-FM
Michael O'Shea, Director
Twin Cities Insight
3415 University Avenue
Minneapolis MN 55414
612-642-4141
Category: 11-13-21-25-31-33
        39-51-59-61-69-71
Host: Michael O'Shea
Format: T -- FM
Features: I-N-F

KSAN
66 Jack London Square
Oakland CA 94604
415-836-0910
Category: 99
Format: -- FM

KSD
10155 Corporate Square
St Louis MO 63132
314-997-5594
Category: 99
Format: -- AM/FM

KSDO-AM/FM
3180 University Avenue
San Diego CA 92104
619-283-7121
Category: 99
Format: -- AM/FM

KSEA
2807 Third
Seattle WA 98121
206-382-5732
Category: 99
Format: -- FM

KSFM
500 Main Street
Woodland CA 95695
916-422-1025
Category: 99
Format: -- FM

KSFO
Adair Kaiser, Director
Sunday Morning Live
300 Broadway
San Francisco CA 94109
415-398-5600
Category: 10-77-78
Host: Jason Jennings
Format: C -- AM

KSHE-FM
Producer, St Louis Report
9420 Watson Road

Saint Louis MO 63126
314-842-1111
Category: 99
Format: -- FM

KSJN
45 East 8th Street
St Paul MN 55101
612-221-1500
Category: 99
Format: -- AM/FM

KSKA
4101 University Drive
Anchorage AK 99508
907-561-1161
Category: 99
Format: -- FM

KSL
Bob Lee, Program Director
Broadcast House
Salt Lake UT 84180
801-575-7768
Category: 99
Format: -- AM

KSLH
814 N Third Street
St Louis MO 63104
314-865-4550
Category: 99
Format: -- FM

KSON
Producer, Update
7520 El Cajon Boulevard
La Mesa CA 92041
619-589-1240
Category: 99
Format: -- AM/FM

KSRR-FM
Dean Hubbard, Production Manager
97 Rock Reviews
5401 Chimney Rock #218
Houston TX 77081
713-797-0097
Category: 11-17-19-25-41-43
        45(Spanish)-47-55-59
        61-65-71-80-83-84
Host: Dean Hubbard
Format: T -- FM
Features: B
Station: 1020 Holcombe, 70001

KSTP-AM
Producer, Dave Hillerman Show
2792 Maplewood Drive
Maplewood MN 55109
612-481-9333
Category: 99
Format: -- AM

KSTP-AM
Allison Brown, Producer
Mike Edwards Show
2792 Maplewood Drive

Maplewood MN 55109
612-481-9333
Category: 10
Host: Mike Edwards
Format: C-P -- AM
Features: I-B

KSTP-AM
Jean Bjorgen, Producer
Geoff Charles Show
2792 Maplewood Drive
Maplewood MN 55109
612-481-9333
Category: 99
Host: Goeff Charles
Format: C-I -- AM
Features: I-B

KSTP-AM
Dave Elvin, Producer
Don Vogel Show
2792 Maplewood Drive
Maplewood MN 55109
612-481-9333
Category: 13-25-17-33-61
Host: Don Vogel
Format: C-P -- AM
Features: I-F-B (M-F 3-6 pm)

KSTP-AM
Bruce Gordon, Producer
Twin Cities Weekend
2792 Maplewood Drive
Maplewood MN 55109
612-481-9333
Category: 39-33-25-73
Host: Bruce Gordon/Cathy Wurzer
Format: L-C-P -- AM
Features: I-B (Sat 6-8 am)

KSTP-AM
Robert C Pendleton, Producer
Home and Garden Show
2792 Maplewood Drive
Maplewood MN 55109
612-481-9333
Category: 29-39-43
Host: Bruce Gordon
Format: L-C-P -- AM
Features: I-B (Sat 8-10 am)

KSTP-AM
Robert C Pendleton, Producer
Auto Talk Show
2792 Maplewood Drive
Maplewood MN 55109
612-481-9333
Category: 25-43(automobiles)
Host: Paul Brand
Format: L-C-P -- AM
Features: I-F-B (Sat 12-3 pm)

KSTP-AM
Robert C Pendleton, Producer
Ask the Lawyer Show
2792 Maplewood Drive
Maplewood MN 55109
612-481-9333

Category: 19-25-41-49-55
          59-61-65-67
Host: John Murrin/Joel Fischer
Format: L-C-P -- AM
Features: I-F-B (Sat 3-5 pm)

KSTP-AM
Robert C Pendleton, Producer
Ask the Doctor Show
2792 Maplewood Drive
Maplewood MN 55109
612-481-9333
Category: 27-31-35-39-51-67
Host: Bob and Bill Drehmel
Format: L-C-P -- AM
Features: I-F-B (Sat 5-6 pm)

KSTP-AM
Robert C Pendleton, Producer
Religion on the Line
2792 Maplewood Drive
Maplewood MN 55109
612-481-9333
Category: 49-53-63
Host: Tom Di Nanni
Format: L-C-P -- AM
Features: I-F-B (Sun 8-9 am)

KSTP-AM
Robert C Pendleton, Producer
Marilyn Mason Show
2792 Maplewood Drive
Maplewood MN 55109
612-481-9333
Category: 13-21-37-53
          57-59-69-73
Host: Marilyn Mason
Format: L-C-P -- AM
Features: I-F-B
(Sun llam-1pm, psychology)

KSTP-AM
Robert C Pendleton, Producer
Jay Thomas Show
2792 Maplewood Drive
Maplewood MN 55109
612-481-9333
Category: 21-23-25-31-33-39-51
          53-57-69-71-73
Host: Jay Thomas
Format: L-C-P -- AM
Features: I-F-B (Sun 1-3 pm)

KSTP-AM
Robert C Pendleton, Producer
Ask the Realtor
2792 Maplewood Drive
Maplewood MN 55109
612-481-9333
Category: 19(real estate)
Host: Dan Coutelenc/Deb Sehrdoty
Format: L-C-P -- AM
Features: I-F-B (Sun 3-5 pm)

KSTP-AM
Robert C Pendleton, Producer
Money Talk
2792 Maplewood Drive

Maplewood MN 55109
612-481-9333
Category: 19-25-59
Host: Josh Arnold/Bob Markman
Format: L-C-P -- AM
Features: I-F-B (Sun 5-7 pm)

KSTP-AM
Bruce Gordon
Sports Talk
2792 Maplewood Drive
Maplewood MN 55109
612-481-9333
Category: 33-69
Host: Bruce Gordon
Format: L-C-P -- AM
Features: I-F-B (Sat 6-7 pm)

KSTP-AM
Karen Severson
Sunday Edition
2792 Maplewood Drive
Maplewood MN 55109
612-481-9333
Category: 11-17-21-25-31-33-39
          73-55-51
Host: Karen Severson
Format: L-C-P -- AM
Features: I-F-B (Sun 9-11 am)

KTAR
301 W Osborn Road
Phoenix AZ 85013
602-274-6200
Category: 99
Format: -- AM

KTEP
Cotton Memorial Building #206
University of Texas at El Paso
El Paso TX 79968
915-747-5152
Category: 99
Format: -- FM

KTFX
Kelly Lindholm, Public Affairs
Bill Payne Interview Show
8107 E Admiral Place
Tulsa OK 74115-8116
918-836-5512
Category: 11-15-19-23-25-27-31
          33-39-43-49-51-55-57
          69-73
Host: Bill Payne
Format: T -- FM
Features: I

KTHO-AM
P O Box AM
South Lake Tahoe CA 95705
916-544-6471
Category: 99
Format: -- AM

KTIS
3003 N Snelling
Roseville MN 55113

612-636-4900
Category: 99
Format: -- AM/FM

KTMS
Marc Bradley, Program Director
News Press Building
Drawer NN
Santa Barbara CA 93102
805-963-1975
Category: 99
Format: -- AM/FM

KTOK
Jackson Kane, Program Director
Marci Medford, Producer
P O Box 1000
Oklahoma City OK 73101
405-840-5271
Category: 10
Format: L-T-C-P -- AM
Features: I-N-F-B

KTOO-FM
Ed Schoenfeld, News Director
224 4th Street
Juneau AK 99801
907-586-1670
Category: 99
Format: -- FM

KTOW
5840 S Memorial Street
Tulsa OK 74145
918-224-2620
Category: 99
Format: -- AM

KTOX
Ron Grisham, General Manager
Talk of the Town
1002 W Frankin Street
Boise ID 83703
208-343-9393
Category: 10
Host: Keith Ashton
Format: L-C-P -- AM
Features: I-N-F

KTRH-AM
Laura Morris, Public Affairs
510 Lovett Boulevard
Houston TX 77006
713-526-4591
Category: 99
Format: -- AM

KTSA
Anne Schiller and Alan Redd,
Producers
Ricci Ware Show
P O Box 18128
4050 Eisenhauer
San Antonio TX 78218
512-655-5500
Category: 10
Format: L-C-P -- AM
Features: I

KTSA
Alan Redd and Anne Schiller
Producers
Talk San Antonio
P O Box 18128
4050 Eisenhauer
San Antonio TX 78218
512-655-5500
Category: 99
Format: L-C-P -- AM
Features: I
Anne Schiller, co-producer

KTSM
801 N Oregon
El Paso TX 79902
915-532-5421
Category: 99
Format: -- AM/FM

KTUC
76 S Stone Avenue
Tucson AZ 85717
602-622-1426
Category: 99
Format: -- AM

KTUH
Marsha Segawa, Program Director
2445 Campus Road #202
Honolulu HI 96822
Category: 99
Format: -- FM

KTXQ
3626 N Hall Street #910
Dallas TX 75219
214-528-5500
Category: 99
Format: -- FM

KUAT
Modern Languages Building
University of Arizona
Tucson AZ 85721
602-626-2334
Category: 99
Format: -- AM/FM

KUCR
691 Linden Street
Riverside CA 92507
714-787-3838
Category: 99
Format: -- FM

KUCV
3800 South 48
Union College
Lincoln NE 68506
402-488-0996
Category: 99
Format: -- FM

KUER
103 Kinsbury Hall
University of Utah
Salt Lake UT 84112

801-581-6625
Category: 99
Format: -- FM

KUGN
4222 Commerce Street
Eugene OR 97402
503-485-5846
Category: 99
Format: -- AM/FM

KUGS-FM
410 W Washington
Viking Union
Bellingham WA 98225
206-676-5847
Category: 19
Format: -- FM

KUHF
4600 Gulf Freeway #500
Houston University
Houston TX 77023
713-749-7186
Category: 99
Format: -- FM

KUMD
130 Humanities Building
University of Minnesota
Duluth MN 55812
218-726-7181
Category: 99
Format: -- FM

KUNI
University of Northern Iowa
Cedar Falls IA 50614
319-273-6400
Category: 99
Format: -- FM

KUNM
Campus and Girard NE
University of New Mexico
Albuquerque NM 87131
505-277-4806
Category: 99
Format: -- FM

KUOM-AM
David Lee Olson, News Director
Talking Sense
Rarig Center, Room 550
University of Minnesota
Minneapolis MN 55455
612-373-3812
Category: 10
Host: David Lee Olson
Format: L-C-P -- AM
Features: I-N-F-B-R
(2:30-3:30 pm)

KUOM-AM
Steve Davis
Talking Sense
Rarig Center Room 550, U of MN
Minneapolis MN 55455

612-373-3812
Category: 11-21-33-41-53-57
         65-67-69-71-75-95
Host: Steve Davis
Format: C-P -- AM
Features: I-N-F-B-R
(10:30-11:30 am)

KUOM-AM
Andy Marlow
Talking Sense
Rarig Center, Room 550
University of Minnesota
Minneapolis MN 55455
612-373-3812
Category: 13-19-23-35-49
         51-55-63-73
Host: Andy Marlow
Format: C-P -- AM
Features: I-N (11:30am-12:30pm)

KUOM-AM
Carol Robertshaw
Talking Sense
Rarig Center, Room 550
University of Minnesota
Minneapolis MN 55455
612-373-3812
Category: 13-17-21-25-31-35
         37-39-41-49-57-73
Host: Carol Robertshaw
Format: C-P -- AM
Features: I-N-F-B-R
(12:30-1:30 pm)

KUOM-AM
Steve Benson
Talking Sense
Rarig Center, Room 550
University of Minnesota
Minneapolis MN 55455
612-373-3812
Category: 15-25-27-31-35
         37-39-51-57-59
Host: Steve Benson
Format: C-P -- AM
Features: I-N (1:30-2:30 pm)

KUOP
3601 Pacific Avenue
Stockton CA 95211
209-946-2582
Category: 99
Format: -- FM

KUOW
325 Communications
University of Washington
Seattle WA 98195
206-543-2710
Category: 99
Format: -- FM

KUPD/KUKQ
Donna Castle, Assistant Director
Hour One
1900 W Carmen
Tempe AZ 85283

602-838-0400
Category: 10
Host: Donna Castle
Format: T -- AM/FM
Features: I-N-F

KUPL
6400 SW Canyon Court
Portland OR 97221
503-297-3311
Category: 99
Format: -- AM/FM

KUSD
310 E Clark Street
University of South Dakota
Vermillion SD 57069
605-677-5277
Category: 99
Format: -- FM

KUSF
2130 Fulton Street
University of San Francisco
San Francisco CA 94117
415-6666-206
Category: 99
Format: -- FM

KUSU
Lee Austin, News Director
Morning Edition and Noonview
Utah State University
Logan UT 84322-8505
801-750-3144
Category: 11-19-25-39-51-55-77
Host: Lee Austin
Format: L-T-P -- FM

KUT
Communications Center
University of Texas at Austin
Austin TX 78712
512-471-1631
Category: 99
Format: -- FM

KUTE-FM
1989 Riverside Drive
Los Angeles CA 90039
213-460-6464
Category: 99
Format: -- FM

KUWR
Mick McLean
Morning Edition
P O Box 3984, University Station
Laramie WY 82071-3984
307-766-6624
Category: 99
Host: Mick McLean
Format: T -- FM
Features: I-N-F-B

KUXL
John McCooley, General Manager
Consumer Update

5730 Duluth Street
Golden Valley MN 55422
612-544-3196
Category: 25
Host: Neil Wallace/Selma Kephart
Format: T-P -- AM
Features: I-N-F-B

KVCR
701 S Mount Vernon Avenue
San Bernardino CA 92410
714-888-6511
Category: 99
Format: -- FM

KVEN
3897 Market Street
Ventura CA 93002
805-642-8595
Category: 99
Format: -- AM

KVFM
University of Montana
Missoula MT 59812
406-243-4931
Category: 99
Format: -- FM

KVI
Tower Building
7th & Olive
Seattle WA 98101
206-223-5744
Category: 99
Format: -- AM

KVIL
Larry Dixon, Program Director
5307 E Mockingbird
Dallas TX 75206
214-647-9089
Category: 99
Format: -- AM/FM

KVLU
Darrell Brogdon, Program Director
P O Box 10064
Beaumont TX 77710
409-838-8164
Category: 99
Format: -- FM

KVNO
6625 Dodge Street
University of Nebraska
Omaha NE 68182
402-554-2701
Category: 99
Format: -- FM

KVOD
John Wolfe, Program Director
1601 W Jewell Avenue
Denver CO 80223
303-936-3428
Category: 99
Format: -- FM

KVON
P O Box 2250
Napa CA 94558
707-252-1440
Category: 99
Format: -- AM

KVOO
3701 S Peoria
Tulsa OK 74105
918-743-7814
Category: 99
Format: -- AM

KVOR
615 E Brookside
Colorado Springs CO 80901
303-632-3536
Category: 99
Format: -- AM

KVOV
P O Box 400
Henderson NV 89015
702-564-2591
Category: 99
Format: -- AM

KVPR
754 P Street
Fresno CA 93721
209-486-7710
Category: 99
Format: -- FM

KVSF
P O Box 2407
Santa Fe NM 87501
505-982-4455
Category: 99
Format: -- AM

KWAX
Villard Hall #341
University of Oregon
Eugene OR 97403
503-686-4239
Category: 99
Format: -- FM

KWBW
P O Box 1036
Hutchison KS 67501
316-662-4486
Category: 99
Format: -- AM

KWEN
1502 S Boulder Avenue
Tulsa OK 74119
918-587-9500
Category: 99
Format: -- FM

KWHO
Clate Holm, News Director
329 East 2nd Street S
Salt Lake City UT 84111

801-534-4105
Category: 99
Format: -- AM/FM

KWIX
P O Box 619
Moberly MO 65270
816-263-1230
Category: 99
Format: -- AM

KWJS
2216 S Cooper
Arlington TX 76013
817-265-3101
Category: 99
Format: -- FM

KWK
Beau Rains, Program Director
2360 Hampton Avenue
St Louis MO 63139
314-969-7625
Category: 99
Format: -- AM

KWMU
Lorin Cuoco, Operations Director
All Things Considered
8001 Natural Bridge Road
St Louis MO 63121
314-553-5968
Category: 11-37-39-47-51-53
         55-61-69-73-75-95
Host: Jim Dryden
Format: T -- FM
Features: I-N-F

KWMU
Eddith Dashiell, News Director
Morning Edition
8001 Natural Bridge
St. Louis MO 63121
314-553-5968
Category: 37-39-53-57-51-69-61-73
Host: Richard Green
Format: T -- FM
Features: I-N-F

KWMU-FM
Harry James Cargas, Professor
Booking Ahead
Webster University
St Louis MO 63119
314-968-7014
Category: 11-17-21-41-47-49-51
         55-57-59-63-67-69-95
         76-77-78-79-80-83
Host: Harry James Cargas
Format: T -- FM
Features: I-B

KXEG
Tim LaVigne, Director
Spotlight
1817 N 3rd Street #202
Phoenix AZ 85004
602-254-5333

Category: 17-21-25-31-35
         39-41-55-63
Host: Tim La Vigne
Format: T-P -- AM
Features: I-N-B

KXEG-AM
Tim LaVigne, Director
Contact Arizona
1817 N 3rd Street
Phoenix AZ 85004
602-254-5333
Category: 31-35-41-55-63-73
Host: Mark Buckley
Format: L-C-P -- AM
Features: I-N-F

KXEG-AM
Tim LaVigne, Director
Saturday Nite Alive
1817 N 3rd Street
Phoenix AZ 85004
602-254-5333
Category: 11-13-33-47-59-61
Host: Tim LaVigne
Format: L-C-P -- AM
Features: I-N-F

KXL
Brian Jennings, News Director
1415 SE Ankeny
Portland OR 97214
503-231-0750
Category: 99
Format: -- AM/FM

KXLR
77 Maiden Lane
San Francisco CA 94018
415-397-9696
Category: 99
Format: -- AM

KXLU-FM
Matt Matich, News Director
7101 W 80th Street
Los Angeles CA 90045
213-642-2866
Category: 99
Format: -- FM

KXLY
West 500 Boone Avenue
Spokane WA 99201
509-328-6292
Category: 99
Format: -- AM

KXOK-AM
7777 Bonhomme Avenue
St Louis MO 63105
314-727-6500
Category: 99
Format: -- AM

KXPR
6000 J Street
Sacramento CA 95819

916-454-6222
Category: 99
Format: -- FM

KXRB
3205 S Meadow Avenue
Sioux Falls SD 57106
605-336-7393
Category: 99
Format: -- AM

KXTR
Producer, Sounding Board
1701 S 55th Street
P O Box 1605
Kansas City KS 66106
913-432-1480
Category: 99
Format: -- FM

KXXO
5350 E 31st Street #200
Tulsa OK 74135
918-665-2810
Category: 99
Format: -- AM

KYA
Ken Dennis, Program Director
300 Broadway
San Francisco CA 94133
415-391-1260
Category: 99
Format: -- FM

KYNN
11128 John Galt Boulevard
Omaha NE 68137
402-592-3500
Category: 99
Format: -- AM

KYUU-FM
Gil Haar, News Director
530 Bush Street
San Francisco CA 94108
415-951-7200
Category: 99
Format: -- FM

KYW
Independence Mall East
Philadelphia PA 19106
215-238-4990
Category: 99
Format: -- AM

KYXI-AM
P O Box 22125
Portland OR 97222
503-656-1441
Category: 99
Format: -- AM

KYXY
Producer, San Diego Perspective
8033 N Linda Vista Road
San Diego CA 92111

619-571-7600
Category: 99
Format: -- FM

KZAP
Chris Davis, News Director
Sacramento People
P O Box 15985
Sacramento CA 95852-1985
916-925-3700
Category: 31-51-61
        98(public affairs)
Host: Chris Davis
Format: T -- FM
Features: I

KZEW
Communications Center
Dallas TX 75202
214-748-9898
Category: 99
Format: -- FM

KZIA
1309 San Pedro NE
Albuquerque NM 87110
505-262-1733
Category: 99
Format: -- AM

KZJO
3595 South 1300 West
Salt Lake UT 84119
801-263-0630
Category: 99
Format: -- AM

KZLA
5700 Sunset Boulevard
Los Angeles CA 90028
213-466-4123
Category: 99
Format: -- AM/FM

KZNG
600 W Main
Hot Springs AR 71901
501-624-5426
Category: 99
Format: -- AM

KZOK
200 W Mercer #304
Seattle WA 98119
206-281-5600
Category: 99
Format: -- FM

KZPS
Nancy Jay, News Director
Power Pages
15851 Dallas Parkway #1200
Dallas TX 75248
214-770-7777
Category: 99
Host: Nancy Jay
Format: T -- FM
Features: I

WAAM-AM
4230 Packard Road
Ann Arbor MI 48104
313-971-1689
Category: 99
Format: -- AM

WAAY-AM
P O Box 2041
Huntsville AL 35804
205-533-9190
Category: 99
Format: -- AM

WABC
Producer, Getting Together
Producer, Kathy Novak Show
1330 Avenue of the Americas
New York NY 10019
212-887-6778
Category: 99
Format: -- AM

WABX
20760 Coolidge Road
Detroit MI 48237
313-298-6060
Category: 99
Format: -- FM

WADK
140 Thomas Street
P O Box 367
Newport RI 02840
401-846-1540
Category: 99
Format: -- AM

WAEC
1420 W Peachtree Street #718
Atlanta GA 30309
404-875-7777
Category: 99
Format: -- AM

WAER-FM
Rick Mattioni, News Director
Syracuse Morning Edition
215 University Place
Syracuse NY 13244-2100
315-423-4046
Category: 11-19-23-25-33-39-43
         47-51-55-61-63-69
Host: Rick Mattioni
Format: L-T-C-P -- FM
Features: I-N-F

WAGC
Augusta College
Augusta GA 30910
404-828-3702
Category: 99
Format: -- FM

WAIV/WOKV
News Director
6869 Lenox Avenue
Jacksonville FL 32205

904-781-1820
Category: 99
Format: -- AM/FM

WAJC
Mary Spillman, Program Director
Indy Am on Fm
4600 Sunset Avenue
Indianapolis IN 46208
317-283-9500
Category: 99
Format: L-C -- FM
Features: I

WAKR
Bill Hart, Program Director
Bill Hart Show
P O Box 1590
Akron OH 44309
216-535-7831
Category: 19-25-27-29-33-39
        43-69-77-84-86-87
Host: Bill Hart
Format: L-P -- AM
Features: I-N-F

WALK
P O Box 230
Patchogue NY 11772
516-475-5200
Category: 99
Format: -- AM/FM

WAMC
P O Box 13000
Albany NY 12212
518-356-4310
Category: 99
Format: -- FM

WAMJ-AM
Michael Shannon, Director
Mark Murray Show
1129 N Hickory
South Bend IN 46615
219-234-1580
Category: 10
Host: Mark Murray
Format: L-T-C-P -- AM
Features: I-N-F-B-R

WAMJ-AM
Michael Shannon, Producer
Dugout
1129 N Hickory
South Bend IN 46615
219-234-1580
Category: 69
Host: Bud Bailey
Format: L-T-C-P -- AM
Features: I-F

WAMU-FM
American University
Washington DC 20016
202-885-1030
Category: 99
Format: -- FM

WAMU-FM
Diane Rehm, Producer
The Diane Rehm Show
The American University
Washington DC 20016
202-885-1030
Category: 99
Host: Diane Rehm
Format: C-P -- FM
Features: I-N-F-B

WANT
1101 Front Street
Richmond VA 23222
804-321-5662
Category: 99
Format: -- AM

WARA
Bonnie McNary, Producer
Kane and Company
8 N Main Street
Attleboro MA 02703
617-222-1320
Category: 13-15-17-25-31
        33-35-57-69-71
Host: Dave Kane
Format: L-C-P -- AM
Features: I-N-F-B-R

WARA
Bonnie McNary, Producer
Chuck Walen Show
8 N Main Street
Attleboro MA 02703
617-222-1320
Category: 27-31-39-43-71
Host: Chuck Walen
Format: L-C-P -- AM
Features: I-N-F-B-R

WARM
P O Box 590
Avoca PA 18641
717-346-4646
Category: 99
Format: -- AM

WASH
5151 Wisconsin Avenue NW
Washington DC 20016
202-244-9700
Category: 99
Format: -- FM

WATR-AM
Gary Peters, Program Director
Broadcast Lane
Waterbury CT 06706
203-755-1121
Category: 99
Format: -- AM

WAUK
Robert Cohen, News Director
1460 Whitehall Avenue
Waukesha WI 53186
414-544-6800

Category: 98(public service)
Format: T -- AM
Features: I-N

WBAI-FM
Larry Gutenberg
Gay New York
505 8th Avenue 19th Floor
New York NY 10018
212-734-6313
Category: 37
Format: -- FM

WBAI-FM
Rick Harris
Arts Extra
505 Eighth Avenue
New York NY 10018
212-279-0707
Category: 11-33
Format: -- FM

WBAL
Katherine McQuay, Producer
Joe Lombardo Show
3800 Hooper Avenue
Baltimore MD 21211
301-467-3000
Category: 19-25-33-35-37-49-55-57
Host: Joe Lombardo
Format: L-P -- AM
Features: I-N

WBAL
Katherine McQuay, Producer
Ron Smith Show
3800 Hooper Avenue
Baltimore MD 21211
301-467-3000
Category: 19-24-33-35-37-49-55-57
Host: Ron Smith
Format: L-C-P -- AM
Features: I-N

WBAP
Jon Holstead, News Director
1 Broadcast Hill
Fort Worth TX 76103
817-429-2330
Category: 99
Format: -- AM

WBBF
Ed Orenstein, Producer
Talknet
850 Midtown Tower
Rochester NY 14604
716-232-7550
Category: 99
Format: -- AM

WBBG-AM / WMJI-FM
David Popovich, Program Director
3940 Euclid Avenue
Cleveland OH 44115
216-391-1260
Category: 99
Format: -- AM/FM

WBBM-AM
Carleen Mosbach, Producer
Midday
630 N McClurg Court
Chicago IL 60611
312-951-3810
Category: 99
Host: Sherman Kaplan/Don Pearlman
Format: L-T-P -- AM
Features: I-N-F

WBBM-AM
Dick Helton, Afternoon Drive
630 N McClurg Court
Chicago IL 60611
312-951-3810
Category: 99
Host: Dick Helton
Format: L-T-P -- AM
Features: I-N

WBBM-AM
Carleen Mosbach, Producer
Nightime
630 N McClurg Court
Chicago IL 60611
312-951-3810
Category: 99
Host: Dale McCarren
Format: L-T-P -- AM
Features: I-N-F

WBBW
Helen Blasko, Operations Manager
Open Mike
418 Knox Street
Youngstown OH 44502
216-744-4421
Category: 19-33-39-55
Host: Steve Hook
Format: L-C-P -- AM
Features: I

WBBW
Helen Blasko, Operations Manager
Party Line
418 Knox Street
Youngstown OH 44502
216-744-4421
Category: 19-33-39-55
Host: Vince Camp
Format: L-C-P -- AM
Features: I

WBBW
Helen Blasko, Operations Manager
Electric Magazine
418 Knox Street
Youngstown OH 44502
216-744-4421
Category: 19-33-39-55
Host: Mike McKay
Format: L-C-P -- AM
Features: I

WBCB
200 Magnolia Drive
Levittown PA 19054

215-949-1490
Category: 99
Format: -- AM

WBCK-AM
390 Golden Avenue
Battle Creek MI 49015
616-963-5555
Category: 99
Format: -- AM

WBCN-FM
Mat Schaffer
Boston Sunday Review
1265 Boylston Street
Boston MA 02215
617-266-1111
Category: 99
Host: Mat Schaffer
Format: L-T-C-P -- FM
Features: I-N-F-B-R

WBCN-FM
1265 Boylston Street
Boston MA 02215
617-266-1111
Category: 99
Format: -- FM

WBEC
P O Box 958
Pittsfield MA 01202
413-499-3333
Category: 99
Format: -- FM

WBEN
2077 Elmwood Avenue
Buffalo NY 14207
716-876-1344
Category: 99
Format: -- AM/FM

WBET
60 Main Street
Brockton MA 02403
617-587-2458
Category: 99
Format: -- AM

WBEZ
Sondra Gair, Producer
Midday with Sondra Gair
1455 N Sandburg Terrace
Chicago IL 60610
312-372-0592
Category: 11-13-17-33-41-47
          49-55-59-65-73-77
          78-80-83-95
Host: Sondra Gair
Format: L-T-C-P -- FM
Features: I-N-F-B
312-372-0500

WBEZ
Ken Davis, Program Director
About Books
1455 N Sandburg Terrace

Chicago IL 60610
312-372-0500
Category: 99
Format: -- FM

WBEZ
Producer, Books & Writers
1455 N Sandburg Terrace
Chicago IL 60610
312-372-0500
Category: 99
Format: -- FM

WBFO
3435 Main Street
Buffalo NY 14214
716-831-2555
Category: 99
Format: -- FM

WBGO-FM
Wylie Rollins, Program Director
54 Park Place
Newark NJ 07102
201-624-8880
Category: 99
Format: -- FM

WBGO-FM
Mark Crumpton
Inside Newark
54 Park Place
Newark NJ 07102
201-624-8880
Category: 13-25-31-39-49-55-61-63
Host: Mark Crumpton
Format: T-I -- FM
Features: I-N-F-B

WBGO-FM
Bruce Anderson
Issues & People
54 Park Place
Newark NJ 07102
201-624-8880
Category: 10
Host: Bruce Anderson
Format: T-I -- FM
Features: I-F-B

WBHM
1028 - 7th Avenue S
Birmingham AL 35294
205-934-2606
Category: 99
Format: -- FM

WBJC
2901 Liberty Heights Avenue
Baltimore MD 21215
301-396-0404
Category: 99
Format: -- FM

WBJW-AM/FM
Rick Aguilar, Director
Community Tapestry
P O Box 8105

Winter Park FL 32790
305-629-5105
Category: 19-25-31-35-39
         51-57-61-73
Host: Dr Earl Scarbeary
Format: T -- AM/FM
Features: I

WBKV
Betty Christen-Nothem, Director
Experts on Call
303 East Decorah Road
West Bend WI 53095
414-334-2344
Category: 19-27-29-31-35
         39-43-53-73
Host: Steve Siegel
Format: L-C-P -- AM/FM
Features: I-F-B

WBKY
340 McVey Hall
University of Kentucky
Lexington KY 40506
606-257-3221
Category: 99
Format: -- FM

WBLS
801 Second Avenue
New York NY 10017
212-661-3344
Category: 99
Format: -- FM

WBSB
Linda Foy, Director
Baltimore's Best / Street Talk
7 E Lexington
Baltimore MD 21202
301-539-7808
Category: 11-25-27-33-35-39-49
Host: Linda Foy
Format: T -- FM
Features: I-N-F-B-R

WBSM
Marc Bernier, Program Director
Mac-in-the-Morning
220 Union Street
New Bedford MA 02740
617-993-1767
Category: 17-33-69
Host: Marc Bernier
Format: L-T-P -- AM
Features: I-N

WBSM
Mark Williams, Producer
Mark Williams Show
52 Temple Street #1
Boston MA 02114
617-723-2268
Category: 37-51-55-67-97(news)
Host: Mark Williams
Format: L-C-P -- AM
Features: I-N
New Bedford, MA station

WBST
M John Eiden, Manager
Something Extra
Ball State University
Muncie IN 47306
219-285-5888
Category: 99
Format: L-T -- FM
Features: I-N-F-B

WBT
Kathy L McKinna, Producer
The H A Thompson Show
1 Julian Price Place
Charlotte NC 28205
704-374-3575
Category: 15-17-19-25-27-33-35
         39-43-51-53-57-73
Host: H A Thompson
Format: C-P -- AM
Features: I-N

WBT
Kathy L McKinna, Producer
The Hello Henry Show
One Julian Price Place
Charlotte NC 28205
704-374-3575
Category: 15-17-19-25-27-33-35
         39-43-51-53-57-73
Host: Henry Boggan
Format: C-P -- AM
Features: I-N

WBUR
Producer, Morning Edition
Producer, Evening Edition
630 Commonwealth Avenue
Boston MA 02215
617-353-2790
Category: 99
Format: -- FM

WBVP-AM
Randy Buckwalter, News Director
P O Box 719
Beaver Falls PA 15010
412-846-4100
Category: 99
Format: -- AM

WBZ
Ellen T Sherman, Producer
Peter Meade Show
1170 Soldiers Field Road
Boston MA 02134
617-787-7395
Category: 10
Host: Peter Meade
Format: L-T-C-P -- AM
Features: I-N-F-B

WBZ
Ellen T Sherman, Producer
Larry Glick Show
1170 Soldiers Field Road
Boston MA 02134
617-787-7395

Category: 10-77-78-82-83
Host: Larry Glick
Format: L-C-P -- AM
Features: I-N

WBZZ
1715 Grandview Avenue
Pittsburgh PA 15211
412-381-8100
Category: 99
Format: -- FM

WCAI-AM
3448 Canal Street
Ft Myers FL 33901
813-334-1350
Category: 99
Format: -- AM

WCAU-AM
Producer, Ron Eisenberg Show
Producer, The Stan Gibell Show
Producer, The Maxine Schnall Show
Producer, Computer Talk
City Line & Monument Road
Philadelphia PA 19131
215-581-5839
Category: 23
Format: -- FM

WCAU-FM
Dave Solomon, News Director
98 Forum
City Line & Monument Road
Philadelphia PA 19131
215-581-5950
Category: 11-17-25-33-39-53
         57-77-82-84-86-87
Host: Dave Solomon
Format: T -- FM
Features: I-N-F

WCBE-FM
Marge Williams, Producer
Columbus Midweek
270 E State Street
Columbus OH 43215
614-225-2750
Category: 99
Host: Marge Williams
Format: T-P -- FM
Features: I-N-F-B

WCBM-AM
Producer, Morning News
68 Radio Place
Owings Mill MD 21117
301-363-2000
Category: 99
Format: -- AM

WCBS
Don Swaim, Producer
Book Beat
51 West 52nd Street 16th Floor
New York NY 10019
212-975-2127
Category: 47-75-95

Local Radio Stations and Shows

Format: T -- AM/FM
Features: I-N-F-B
CBS Radio Syndication

WCBU
Cheryl Corley, Public Affairs
1501 W Bradley Avenue
Peoria IL 61625
309-673-7100
Category: 99
Format: -- FM

WCCK
P O Box 1184
Erie PA 16512
814-456-7078
Category: 99
Format: -- FM

WCCO
Producer, Boone Erickson Show
625 Second Avenue S
Minneapolis MN 55402
612-370-0611
Category: 99
Format: -- AM/FM

WCFL
Edward Hyland, Producer
Reviewing Stand
1810 Hinman Avenue
Evanston IL 60201
312-491-5753
Category: 99
Format: -- AM

WCGO
Patty McDermott, Producer
Morning Show
3313 Chicago Road
Chicago Heights IL 60411
312-756-6100
Category: 99
Host: Patty McDermott
Format: I-C-P -- AM
Features: I-N-B

WCHS
1111 Virginia Street E
Charleston WV 25324
304-342-8131
Category: 99
Format: -- AM

WCKY
Producer, Computer Talk
219 McFarland Street
Cincinnati OH 45202
513-241-6565
Category: 23
Format: -- AM

WCLR-FM
Adrienne Kaplan, Director
Insight
8833 Grosspoint Road
Skokie IL 60077
312-677-5900

Category: 13-19-25-31-35
         39-53-55-73
Host: Adrienne Kaplan
Format: T -- FM
Features: I

WCLV
Robert Conrad, Program Manager
Arts Log
Terminal Tower
Cleveland OH 44113
216-241-0900
Category: 11-33
Host: Grace Mims
Format: T -- FM
Features: I

WCLV
Robert Conrad, Program Manager
Book Break
Terminal Tower
Cleveland OH 44113
216-241-0900
Category: 99
Host: Eugenia Thornton
Format: T -- FM
Features: B

WCMS-FM
Mike Meehan, Producer
In Touch with Tidewater
900 Commonwealth Place
Virginia Beach VA 23464
804-424-1050
Category: 11-19-23-69-84-85-87
Host: Mike Meehan
Format: T-P -- FM
Features: I-M-F-B

WCNN
1422 W Peachtree Road NE
Atlanta GA 30309
404-872-0068
Category: 99
Format: -- AM

WCNY
506 Old Liverpool Road
Syracuse NY 13088
315-457-0440
Category: 99
Format: -- FM

WCOS
2440 Milkwood
P O Box 748
Columbia SC 29202
803-256-7348
Category: 99
Format: -- FM

WCOZ-FM
Steve Hausmann, News Director
441 Stuart Street
Boston MA 02116
617-267-9090
Category: 99
Format: -- RF

WCPE
P O Box 828
Wake Forest NC 27587-0828
Category: 99
Format: -- FM

WCPN
3100 Chester Avenue
Cleveland OH 44114
216-621-0092
Category: 99
Format: -- FM

WCRB
Copley Plaza Hotel
Boston MA 02116
617-893-7080
Category: 99
Format: -- FM

WCSG
1001 E Beltline Avenue NE
Grand Rapids MI 49505
616-942-1500
Category: 99
Format: -- FM

WCTC
P O Box 100
New Brunswick NJ 08903
201-249-2600
Category: 99
Format: -- AM

WCXI
18900 James Couzens Highway
Detroit MI 48235
313-345-8600
Category: 99
Format: -- AM/FM

WCZE/WLOO
Hope Daniels, Director
Open Forum
875 N Michigan Avenue #3201
Chicago IL 60611
312-440-3100
Category: 13-17-19-23-25-41
         43-49-51-55-63-67
         69-71-73-77-81
Host: Hope Daniels
Format: T -- AM/FM
Features: I-N-F-B

WCZE/WLOO
Hope Daniels, Director
Human Nature
875 North Michigan #3201
Chicago IL 60611
312-440-3100
Category: 27-31-35-39-57-78
Host: Hope Daniels
Format: T -- AM/FM
Features: I-N-F-B

WCZY-FM
15401 W 10 Mile Road
Detroit MI 48237

313-967-3750
Category: 99
Format: -- FM

WDAF
Signal Hill
3020 Summit
Kansas City MO 64108
816-753-4567
Category: 99
Format: -- AM

WDAS
Belmont Avenue & Edgly Road
Philadelphia PA 19131
215-878-2000
Category: 99
Format: -- FM

WDBS-FM
P O Box 2126
Durham NC 27702
919-682-0318
Category: 99
Format: -- FM

WDCS-FM
P O Box 610
Scarborough ME 04012
207-883-9596
Category: 99
Format: -- FM

WDCU-FM
Ernest P White Jr, Producer
Cross Talk
4200 Connecticut Avenue NW
Washington DC 20008
202-282-7588
Category: 11-25-31-35-39-55-63-73
Host: Ernest P White Jr
Format: L -- FM
Features: I-F

WDET-FM
Jim Labadie, News Director
All Things Detroit
5057 Woodward
Detroit MI 48202
313-577-4146
Category: 13-17-19-31-35-39-41
         47-49-51-55-67-69
Host: Jim Labadie
Format: T -- FM
Features: I-N-F-B

WDGY
Gary Stone, Program Director
1300 N Country Drive
Minneapolis MN 55431
612-881-2633
Category: 99
Format: -- AM

WDJZ-AM
Russ Knight, Program Director
513 Boston Avenue
Bridgeport CT 06610

203-335-2544
Category: 99
Format: -- AM

WDMJ-AM
Patrick Dudley, News Director
WDMJ's Talkradio
845 W Washington
Marquette MI 49855
906-225-1313
Category: 99
Host: Patrick Dudley
Format: C-P -- AM
Features: I-N-F-B

WDOK
1250 Superior Avenue
Cleveland OH 44114
216-781-1100
Category: 99
Format: -- FM

WDRC-FM
169 Blue Hills Avenue
Bloomfield CT 06002
203-243-3984
Category: 99
Format: -- FM

WDRQ
Producer, Sunday Morning Live
20300 Civic Center Drive #300
Southfield MI 48076
313-354-9300
Category: 99
Format: -- FM

WDTR
John McArthur, Manager
9345 Lawton Street
Detroit MI 48206
313-494-1570
Category: 99
Format: -- FM

WDUQ
Kevin Gavin, Director
Between the Lines
Duquesne University
Pittsburgh PA 15282
412-434-6030
Category: 17-19-25-27-31-33-41
         43-55-69-71-77-81-84-87
Host: Kevin Gavin
Format: T -- FM
Features: I

WDVE
Greg Gillespi, Program Director
411 Seventh Avenue
Pittsburgh PA 15219
412-562-5959
Category: 99
Format: -- FM

WDVQ
Duquesne University
Duquesne PA 15219

412-434-6030
Category: 99
Format: -- FM

WDVT-AM
Julie Garberina, Producer
Carol Saline Show
2nd & Lombard Streets, Newmarket
Philadelphia PA 19147
215-238-3905
Category: 10
Host: Carol Saline
Format: L-C-P -- AM
Features: I-N-F-B

WDVT-AM
Julie Garberina, Producer
Frank Ford Show
2nd & Lombard Streets, Newmarket
Philadelphia PA 19147
215-238-3905
Category: 10
Host: Frank Ford
Format: L-C -- AM
Features: I-F-B

WDVT-AM
Julie Garberina, Producer
D I Strunk Show
2nd & Lombard Streets, Newmarket
Philadelphia PA 19147
215-238-3905
Category: 10
Host: D I Strunk
Format: C -- AM
Features: I-N-F-B

WDVT-AM
Julie Garberina, Producer
Grad Hospital Health Connection
2nd & Lombard Streets, Newmarket
Philadelphia PA 19147
215-238-3905
Category: 39
Host: Lulu Grant
Format: C -- AM
Features: I-N-F-B

WDVT-AM
Julie Garberina, Producer
Gardening with Ernesta Ballard
2nd & Lombard Streets, Newmarket
Philadelphia PA 19147
Category: 43(gardening)
Host: Ernesta Ballard
Format: C -- AM
Features: I-F

WDVT-AM
Julie Garberina, Producer
Food & Fine Living
2nd & Lombard Streets, Newmarket
Philadelphia PA 19147
215-238-3905
Category: 11-27
Host: Edward Bottone
Format: C -- AM
Features: I-F-B

Local Radio Stations and Shows

WDVT-AM
Julie Garberina, Producer
Travel
2nd & Lombard Streets, Newmarket
Philadelphia PA 19147
215-238-3905
Category: 71
Host: Bob & Paul Stalbaum
Format: C -- AM
Features: F-B

WDVT-AM
Julie Garberina, Producer
Singles on Saturday
2nd & Lombard Streets, Newmarket
Philadelphia PA 19147
215-238-3905
Category: 35-37-53
Host: Kiki Olson
Format: C -- AM
Features: F-B

WDVT-AM
Julie Garberina, Producer
Not For Men Only
2nd & Lombard Streets, Newmarket
Philadelphia PA 19147
215-238-3905
Category: 35-37
Host: Gerry Evans
Format: C -- AM
Features: I-F-B

WDVT-AM
Julie Garberina, Producer
Italy Today
2nd & Lombard Streets, Newmarket
Philadelphia PA 19147
215-238-3905
Category: 45(Italian)-78
Host: Dalmazio Dicristafaro
Format: L -- AM
Features: I-F

WDVT-AM
Julie Garberina, Producer
Opportunities in Business
2nd & Lombard Streets, Newmarket
Philadelphia PA 19147
215-238-3905
Category: 19
Host: Dan Goldberg
Format: C -- AM
Features: I-F-B

WDVT-AM
Julie Garberina, Producer
Let's Talk Law
2nd & Lombard Streets, Newmarket
Philadelphia PA 19147
Category: 19-55(law)
Host: Chuck Rabb
Format: C -- AM
Features: I

WDVT-AM
Julie Garberina, Producer
Let's Talk Real Estate

2nd & Lombard Streets, Newmarket
Philadelphia PA 19147
215-238-3905
Category: 19(real estate)
        43(home)
Host: Phil Mitsch
Format: C -- AM
Features: I-B

WDVT-AM
Julie Garberina, Producer
$mart Money
2nd & Lombard Streets, Newmarket
Philadelphia PA 19147
215-238-3905
Category: 19
Host: Ted Hechtman
Format: C -- AM
Features: I-F-B

WDVT-AM
Julie Garberina, Producer
Shape Up
2nd & Lombard Streets, Newmarket
Philadelphia PA 19147
215-238-3905
Category: 39
Host: Jim Schiller
Format: C -- AM
Features: I-F-B

WDVT-AM
Rich Ross
Peter Tolden's Morning Rush
2nd & Lombard Streets, Newmarket
Philadelphia PA 19147
Category: 10
Host: Peter Tilden
Format: L-C-P -- AM
Features: I-F-B

WDVT-AM
Julian Fox
All About Kids
2nd & Lombard Streets, Newmarket
Philadelphia PA 19147
Category: 21-31-76
Host: Millie Berg
Format: C-P -- AM
Features: I-F-N-B

WDVT-AM
Julian Fox
Holistic Hotline
2nd & Lombard Streets, Newmarket
Philadelphia PA 19147
215-238-3905
Category: 13-39-53
Host: Dr Tedd Koren
Format: C -- AM
Features: I-F-B

WDWS
P O Box 677
Champaign IL 61820
217-351-5300
Category: 99
Format: -- AM

WEAA
Morgan State University
Baltimore MD 21239
301-444-3564
Category: 99
Format: -- FM

WEAN
290 Westminster Mall
Providence RI 02903
401-277-7900
Category: 99
Format: -- AM

WEAZ
10 Presidential Boulevard
Bala Cynwyd PA 19004
215-667-8400
Category: 99
Format: -- FM

WEBN
2724 Erie Avenue
Cincinnati OH 45208
513-871-8500
Category: 99
Format: -- Rf

WEBR
Bruce Allen, Producer
Newsmaker Edition
23 North Street
Buffalo NY 14202
716-886-0970
Category: 19-25-39-51-55-69
Host: Scott Thomas
Format: C-P -- AM/FM
Features: N

WEBR
Bruce Allen, Producer
Weekend at Your Service
23 North Street
Buffalo NY 14202
716-886-0970
Category: 99
Host: Bruce Allen
Format: C-P -- AM/FM
Features: I-B

WEEI-AM
Michael McLean
Food News Hour
4450 Prudential Tower
Boston MA 02199
617-262-5900
Category: 27
Host: Lotte Mendelsohn
Format: L-C -- AM
Features: I-N-F-B

WEEI-AM
John Slack
Financial News Hour
4450 Prudential Tower
Boston MA 02199
617-262-5900
Category: 19

Host: John Slack
Format: L-C -- AM
Features: I-N-F

WEEI-AM
Doug Stephan
Personal Health & Medicine
4450 Prudential Tower
Boston MA 02199
617-262-5900
Category: 39
Host: Doug Stephan
Format: L-C-P -- AM
Features: I-N-F-B

WEEI-AM
Doug Stephan
Dining Guide
4450 Prudential Tower
Boston MA 02199
617-262-5900
Category: 27
Host: Doug Stephan
Format: L-C -- AM
Features: F

WEEI-AM
Avi Nelson, Producer
Avi Nelson Show
4450 Prudential Tower
Boston MA 02199
Category: 55-61
Host: Avi Nelson
Format: L-C-P -- AM
Features: I-N-F

WEEI-AM
Chuck Crouse, Producer
Bay State Forum
4450 Prudential Tower
Boston MA 02199
617-722-2377
Category: 19-25-55-61
Host: Chuck Crouse
Format: T -- AM
Features: I-N-F

WEEI-AM
Robert Ames, Producer
On the Line
4450 Prudential Tower
Boston MA 02199
Category: 13-25-31-33-35
        39-41-51-53-57
Host: Robert Ames
Format: T-P -- AM
Features: I-F-B

WEEI-AM
Annette Bosworth, Asst Director
Reporters' Journal
4450 Prudential Tower
Boston MA 02199
617-262-5900
Category: 13-25-31-33-35-39
        41-51-53-57-73
Format: T-P -- AM
Features: I-N-F

WEEI-AM
Jim Pansullo, Producer
Medical Journal
4450 Prudential Tower
Boston MA 02199
617-262-5900
Category: 39
Host: Jim Pansullo
Format: T-P -- AM
Features: I-N-F

WEEI-AM
Jim Pansullo, Producer
Topic Religion
4450 Prudential Tower
Boston MA 02199
617-262-5900
Category: 63
Host: Jim Pansullo
Format: T -- AM
Features: I-N-F

WELI-AM
Steven D Kalb, Producer
Art Barrett Show
P O Box 85
New Haven CT 06501
203-281-9600
Category: 15-23-25-33-41-47
        49-51-55-57-59
Host: Art Barrett
Format: L-C-P -- AM
Features: I-N

WELW
Joe Jastremski, News Director
Guest Time
36913 Stevens Boulevard
Willoughby OH 44094
216-946-1330
Category: 17-19-25-33-35-39
        43-55-59-69-73
Host: Joe Jastremski
Format: L-C-P -- AM

WERA
120 West 7th Street
Plainfield NJ 07060
201-755-1590
Category: 99
Format: -- AM

WERC
Tony Giles, Producer
Tony Giles Show
P O Box 10904
Birmingham AL 35202
205-591-7171
Category: 10
Host: Tony Giles
Format: C -- AM
Features: I-N

WERC
Bill Lawson, Producer
Bill Lawson Show
P O Box 10904
Birmingham AL 35202

205-591-7171
Category: 10
Host: Bill Lawson
Format: C -- AM
Features: I

WERE-AM
Ray Dorazewski
Cleveland Forum
1500 Chester Avenue
Cleveland OH 44114
216-696-1300
Category: 13-17-19-25-31-35
        39-43-49-51-55-73
Host: Bob Fuller
Format: L-C -- AM
Features: I-N-F

WERE-AM
Ray Dorazewski
Expanded News Hour
1500 Chester Avenue
Cleveland OH 44114
216-696-1300
Category: 13-17-19-25-31-35
        39-43-49-51-55-73
Host: Bob Fuller
Format: L-C-P -- AM
Features: I-N-F

WERI
19 Railroad Avenue
Westerly RI 02891
401-596-7728
Category: 99
Format: -- AM/FM

WEST
Producer, Be My Guest
436 Northampton Street
Easton PA 18042
215-250-9600
Category: 99
Format: -- AM

WETA/FM
Jeanette Bernay, P I Assistant
P O Box 2626
Washington DC 20013
202-998-2626
Category: 99
Format: -- FM

WEVD
Jonathan Schenker, Producer
Commentary
305 W 13th Street
New York NY 10014
212-243-1667
Category: 11-13-17-25-27-33-37
        39-41-53-57-63-71-73
Host: Jonathan Schenker
Format: T -- FM
Features: N-F-B-R

WEXI-AM
5621 Commerce
Jacksonville FL 32211

Local Radio Stations and Shows

904-744-1280
Category: 99
Format: -- AM

WEZB-FM
601 Loyola Avenue
New Orleans LA 70113
504-581-7002
Category: 99
Format: -- FM

WEZC-FM
137 S Kings Drive
P O Box 30247
Charlotte NC 28204
704-372-1106
Category: 99
Format: -- FM

WEZO-FM
360 East Avenue
Rochester NY 14604
716-232-3700
Category: 99
Format: -- FM

WEZW
Glenn Redd, Public Affairs
735 W Wisconsin
Milwaukee WI 53233
414-272-1040
Category: 99
Format: -- FM

WFAE
Kathy Merritt, News Director
Carolina Chronicle
University of North Carolina
Charlotte NC 28223
704-597-2555
Category: 11-19-25-39-47-55-77-95
Host: Kathy Merritt
Format: T-P -- FM
Features: I-N-F-B

WFAS
P O Box 551
White Plains NY 10602
914-693-2400
Category: 99
Format: -- AM/FM

WFBC-FM
Greg Anderson, Program Director
505 Rutherford Street
P O Box 1330
Greenville SC 29602
803-271-9200
Category: 99
Format: -- FM

WFBE
Board of Education
605 Crapo Street
Flint MI 48503
313-762-1148
Category: 99
Format: -- FM

WFBR
Alan Christian, Producer
Alan Christian Show
13 E 20th Street
Baltimore MD 21211
301-685-1300
Category: 10
Host: Alan Christian
Format: L -- AM
Features: I

WFCR
Hampshire House
University of Massachusetts
Amherst MA 01003
413-545-0100
Category: 99
Format: -- FM

WFDD
P O Box 7405
Winston-Salem NC 27109
919-761-5257
Category: 99
Format: -- FM

WFDU
795 Cedar Lane
Teaneck NJ 07666
201-692-2806
Category: 99
Format: -- FM

WFIL
440 Domino Lane
Philadelphia PA 19128
215-482-7000
Category: 99
Format: -- AM

WFIR-AM
Towers Mall
P O Box 150
Roanoke VA 24002
703-345-5955
Category: 99
Format: -- AM

WFIU
Radio/TV Building
Indiana University
Bloomington IN 47405
812-335-1357
Category: 99
Format: -- FM

WFLN
8200 Ridge Avenue
Philadelphia PA 19128
215-482-6000
Category: 99
Format: -- AM/FM

WFME-FM
Anita Karpathy, Program Director
Radio Reading Circle
289 Mount Pleasant Avenue
West Orange NJ 07052
201-736-3600
Category: 99
Format: -- FM

WFME-FM
Anita Karpathy, Program Director
Focus '86
289 Mount Pleasant Avenue
West Orange NJ 07052
201-736-3600
Category: 99
Format: -- FM
Features: I

WFMS-FM
Peter Miles, News Director
8120 Knue Road
Indianapolis IN 46250
317-842-9550
Category: 99
Format: -- FM

WFMT
Lois Baum, Producer
Writing & Writers
3 Illinois Center
Chicago IL 60601
312-565-5023
Category: 11-13-31-33-35-39-41-47
       49-55-61-77-78-81-82
Host: Herman Kogan
Format: T -- FM
Features: N-B-R

WFMT
Producer, Studs Terkel Show
3 Illinois Center
Chicago IL 60601
312-565-5000
Category: 99
Host: Studs Terkel
Format: -- FM

WFMT
Lois Baum, Producer
Arts & Artists
3 Illinois Center
Chicago IL 60601
312-565-5000
Category: 11-17
Format: -- FM

WFMT
Herman Kogan, Producer
Critic's Choice
3 Illinois Center
Chicago IL 60601
312-565-5000
Category: 11-33
Format: -- FM

WFMU
Prospect Street
Upsala College
East Orange NJ 07019
201-266-7900
Category: 99
Format: -- FM

WFNX-FM
Henry Santoro, Editor
Phoenix Features
25 Exchange Street
Lynn MA 01901
617-595-6200
Category: 99
Host: Henry Santoro
Format: L-T-C -- FM
Features: I-N-F-B

WFOG
Producer, Open Mind
330 W Brambleton Avenue
Norfolk VA 23510
804-622-6771
Category: 99
Format: -- FM

WFPL
York & 4th Streets
Louisville KY 40203
502-583-1864
Category: 99
Format: -- FM

WFRD-FM
P O Box 957
Hanover NH 07355
603-646-3313
Category: 99
Format: -- FM

WFSU
2561 Pottsdammer Road
Florida State University
Tallahassee FL 32306
904-644-6220
Category: 99
Format: -- FM

WFUV-FM
Robert Flaim, Producer
What's on Your Mind
Fordham University
Bronx NY 10458
212-365-8050
Category: 35-49-51-55-57-63
Host: Robert Flaim
Format: L-C-P -- FM
Features: I

WFYR-FM
Arcadia Letkemann, Director
Special Appeal
130 E Randolph Street #2303
Chicago IL 60601
312-861-8100
Category: 99
Format: T -- FM
Features: I-F
organizations needing volunteers

WFYR-FM
Arcadia Letkemann, Director
Money Talks
130 E Randolph Street #2303
Chicago IL 60601

312-861-8100
Category: 19-25
Host: Pat Finerty
Format: T-P -- FM
Features: I-F-B

WFYR-FM
Arcadia Letkemann, Director
Chicago Talk Exchange
130 E Randolph Street #2303
Chicago IL 60601
312-861-8100
Category: 11-33-69
Host: Jeff Blackman
Format: T-P -- FM
Features: I-F-B

WFYR-FM
Arcadia Letkemann, Director
Horizons
130 E Randolph Street #2303
Chicago IL 60601
312-861-8100
Category: 41-49-78-80
Host: Bill Zayas
Format: T-P -- FM
Features: I-F-B

WFYR-FM
Arcadia Letkemann, Director
Women at Work
130 E Randolph Street #2303
Chicago IL 60601
312-861-8100
Category: 19-73
Host: Carol Kleiman
Format: T -- FM
Features: I-F-B

WFYR-FM
Arcadia Letkemann, Director
Take 30
130 E Randolph Street #2303
Chicago IL 60601
312-861-8100
Category: 13-19-25-29-35-39
         43-53-55-57-71
Host: Tim Jackson
Format: T-P -- FM
Features: I-F-B

WFYR-FM
Arcadia Letkemann, Director
Straight Talk
130 E Randolph Street #2303
Chicago IL 60601
312-861-8100
Category: 11-13-17-19-23-25
         31-35-41-53-55
Host: Tim Jackson & Bruce DuMont
Format: L-C-P -- FM
Features: I-F-B

WFYR-FM
Arcadia Letkemann, Director
Conversations
130 E Randolph Street #2303
Chicago IL 60601

312-861-8100
Category: 49-78
Host: Arcadia Letkemann
Format: T -- FM
Features: I-F-B

WGAR
9446 Broadview Road
Cleveland OH 44147
216-526-6709
Category: 99
Format: -- AM

WGAY
Joan Henson, Public Affairs
8121 Georgia Avenue
Silver Spring MD 20910
301-587-4900
Category: 99
Format: -- AM/FM

WGBH
Ellen Kraft, Program Director
125 Western Avenue
Boston MA 02134
617-492-2777
Category: 99
Format: -- FM

WGBS-AM
Miriam De Wart, Producer
The Steve Kane Show
20450 NW Second Avenue
Miami FL 33169
305-653-8811
Category: 10
Host: Steve Kane
Format: -- AM

WGBS-AM
Miriam De Wart, Producer
The Shirley Peters Show
20450 NW Second Avenue
Miami Fl 33169
305-653-8811
Category: 10
Host: Shirley Peters
Format: -- AM

WGBS-AM
Miriam De Wart, Producer
The Allan Beschany Money Line
20450 NW Second Avenue
Miami Fl 33169
305-653-8811
Category: 10-19
Host: Allan Beschany
Format: C -- AM

WGBS-AM
Miriam De Wart, Producer
The Al Rantel Show
20450 NW Second Avenue
Miami Fl 33169
305-653-8811
Category: 10
Host: Al Rantel
Format: C -- AM

Local Radio Stations and Shows

WGBS-AM
Miriam De Wart, Producer
The Allan Burke Show
20450 NW Second Avenue
Miami Fl 33169
305-653-8811
Category: 10
Host: Allan Burke
Format: C -- AM

WGBS-AM
Miriam De Wart, Producer
The Bev Smith Show
20450 NW Second Avenue
Miami Fl 33169
305-653-8811
Category: 10
Host: Bev Smith
Format: C -- AM

WGCH
Bob McGonagle
People to People
P O Box 1490
Greenwich CT 06836
203-869-1490
Category: 25-27-29-33-35-39
        41-43-53-57-69-71
Host: Bob McGonagle
Format: C-P -- AM
Features: I-F

WGCI-FM
Graham Armstrong, Programing
6 N Michigan Avenue
Chicago IL 60602
312-984-1400
Category: 99
Format: -- FM

WGCL-FM
Gayle Pazderak, Public Affairs
1500 Chester Avenue
Cleveland OH 44114
216-861-0100
Category: 99
Format: -- FM

WGHQ
Hank Silverberg, News Director
82 John Street
P O Box 1880
Kingston NY 12401
914-331-8200
Category: 99
Format: -- AM

WGIR
Kevin Hamilton, News Director
AM Report
P O Box 610
Manchester NH 03105
603-625-6915
Category: 13-17-19-23-25-29
        33-35-39-41-55-61
Host: Kevin Hamilton
Format: L -- AM
Features: I-N-F

WGIR
Kevin Hamilton, News Director
PM Report
P O Box 610
Manchester NH 03105
603-625-6915
Category: 13-17-19-23-25-29
        33-35-39-41-55-61
Host: Amy Landsman
Format: L -- AM
Features: I-N-F

WGKA
Dianne Webb, Atlanta Arts
P O Box 52128
Atlanta GA 30355
404-231-1190
Category: 11-33
Format: L-T -- AM
Features: I-N

WGKA
Dianne Webb, Consumer Forum
P O Box 52128
Atlanta GA 30355
404-231-1190
Category: 25-27-39
Format: T -- AM
Features: N-F

WGLI-AM
1290 Peconic Avenue
Babylon NY 11704
516-661-1130
Category: 99
Format: -- AM

WGMS
11300 Rockville Pike
Rockville MD 20852
301-468-1800
Category: 99
Format: -- AM/FM

WGN-Radio
Lorna Gladstone
Assistant Program Director
2501 W Bradley Place
Chicago IL 60618
312-883-3362
Category: 99
Format: -- AM

WGN-Radio
Nina Newhousor
Roy Leonard Show
2501 W Bradley Place
Chicago IL 60618
312-883-3362
Category: 33
Host: Roy Leonard
Format: C -- AM
Features: I-N-B

WGR/WRLT
Tom Bauerle
Extension 55 (WGR)
464 Franklin Street

Buffalo NY 14202
716-881-4555
Category: 10
Host: Tom Bauerle
Format: L-P -- AM/FM
Features: I-N-F

WGR/WRLT
Sandy Kozel, News Director
464 Franklin Street
Buffalo NY 14202
716-881-4555
Category: 99
Format: -- AM/FM

WGST-AM
Mary Hylbock, Coordinator
Neal Boortz Program
550 Pharr Road #400
Atlanta GA 30363
404-231-0920
Category: 33-35-55-57-69-77
Host: Neal Boortz
Format: C-P -- AM

WGST-AM
Producer, Lifestyles
550 Pharr Road NE #400
Atlanta GA 30363
404-231-0920
Category: 99
Format: -- AM

WGTE
419 N St Clair
Toledo OH 43604
419-255-3330
Category: 99
Format: -- FM

WGTS
Producer, Talk It Over
7600 Flower Avenue
Takoma Park MD 20012
301-2891-420
Category: 99
Format: -- FM

WGUC University of Cincinnati
1223 Central Parkway
Cincinnati OH 45221
513-475-4444
Category: 99
Format: -- FM

WGVE
1800 E 35 Avenue
Gary IN 46409
219-962-7571
Category: 99
Format: -- FM

WGY
1410 Balltown Road
Schenectady NY 12309
518-385-1401
Category: 99
Format: -- AM

WHAG
Roger Keller, News Director
Viewpoint
1250 Maryland Avenue
Hagerstown MD 21740
301-797-7302
Category: 10
Host: Roger Keller
Format: L-C-P -- AM
Features: I-N-F-B

WHAS
520 W Chesnut Street
Louisville KY 40202
502-582-7814
Category: 99
Format: -- AM

WHB
106 West 14th Street
Kansas City MO 64105
816-221-8300
Category: 99
Format: -- AM

WHBQ-AM
483 South Highland
Memphis TN 38111
901-320-1356
Category: 99
Format: -- AM

WHBY
P O Box 1519
Appleton WI 54913
414-733-6639
Category: 99
Format: -- AM

WHCN
1039 Asylum Avenue
Hartford CT 06105
203-247-1060
Category: 99
Format: -- FM

WHDH-AM
Bruce Cornblatt, Producer
Paul Bencaquin Show
441 Stuart Street
Boston MA 02116-5019
617-267-1313
Category: 99
Format: -- AM

WHDH-AM
441 Stuart Street
Boston MA 02116
617-267-1313
Category: 99
Format: -- AM

WHEN
P O Box 6509
Syracuse NY 13217
315-457-6110
Category: 99
Format: -- AM

WHFM
259 Monroe Avenue
Rochester NY 14607-3632
716-454-3040
Category: 99
Format: -- FM

WHIO
1414 Wilmington
P O Box 1206
Dayton OH 45401
513-259-2111
Category: 99
Format: -- AM/FM

WHJJ
Mark Williams, Producer
Mark Williams Show
52 Temple Street #1
Boston MA 02114
617-723-2268
Category: 37-51-55-67-97(news)
Host: Mark Williams
Format: L-C-P -- AM
Features: I-N
Providence, RI station

WHLO
2650 W Market Street
Akron OH 44313
216-867-1650
Category: 99
Format: -- AM

WHN
400 Park Avenue
New York NY 10022
212-688-1000
Category: 99
Format: -- AM

WHO-AM
Lee Martin, Producer
The Lee Martin Show
1801 Grand Avenue
Des Moines IA 50308
515-242-3673; 515-242-3500
Category: 10
Host: Lee Martin
Format: L-C-P -- AM
Features: I

WHO-AM
Brian O'Brian, Producer
Brian O'Brian
1801 Grand Avenue
Des Moines IA 50308
515-242-3726; 515-242-3500
Category: 11-15-21-25-31-33
        35-39-43-51-53-57
        59-67-69-71-73-79
Host: Brian O'Brian
Format: L-C-P -- AM
Features: I

WHO-AM
Lee Kline
Midday Farm News

1801 Grand Avenue
Des Moines IA 50308
515-242-3551
Category: 98(agriculture)
Host: Lee Kline/Keith Kirkpatrick
Format: L -- AM

WHO-AM
Jim Zabel and Larry Cotlar
Sportsline
1801 Grand Avenue
Des Moines IA 50308
515-242-3500
Category: 69
Host: Jim Zabel
Format: L-C-P -- AM
Features: I

WHO-AM
Max Bennington, Producer
Cross Country America
1801 Grand Avenue
Des Moines IA 50308
515-242-3671
Category: 99
Host: Max Bennington
Format: L-C-I -- AM
Features: I

WHO-AM
John Kelling
Who Morning Team
1801 Grand Avenue
Des Moines IA 50308
515-242-3670
Category: 11-15-31-33-35
        39-43-69-71-86
Host: Jack Carey
Format: L-C-P -- AM
Features: I-N-F
515-242-3500

WHRB-FM
Harvard University
45 Quincy Street
Cambridge MA 02138
617-495-4818
Category: 99
Format: -- FM

WHRO
5200 Hampton Road
Norfolk VA 23508
804-489-9484
Category: 99
Format: -- FM

WHRS
505 S Congress Avenue
Boynton Beach FL 33435
305-732-7850
Category: 99
Format: -- FM

WHTT
Gordon Hill, News Director
4418 Prudential Tower
Boston MA 02199

617-262-5900
Category: 99
Format: -- FM

WHTX
400 Ardmore Boulevard
Pittsburgh PA 15230
412-244-4553
Category: 99
Format: -- FM

WHUE-AM
200 Clarendon Street
Boston MA 02116
617-267-0123
Category: 99
Format: -- AM

WHYI
2741 N 29th Avenue
Hollywood FL 33020
305-944-1956
Category: 99
Format: -- FM

WHYN-AM
Bob Johnson, Producer
Talking Sports
P O Box 9013
Springfield MA 01101
413-781-1011
Category: 69
Host: Bob Johnson
Format: C -- AM
Features: I-B

WHYN-AM
Cherie McBride, Producer
Cherie McBride Show
P O Box 9013
Springfield MA 01101
413-781-1011
Category: 99
Host: Cherie McBride
Format: C-P -- AM
Features: I-N-B

WHYT
2100 Fisher Building
Detroit MI 48202
313-875-4440
Category: 99
Format: -- FM

WHYY-FM
Danny Miller
Fresh Air
150 N 6th Street
Philadelphia PA 19106
215-351-9200
Category: 99
Host: Terry Gross
Format: L -- FM
Features: I

WHYY-FM
Marty Moss-Coane
Family Matters

150 N 6th Street
Philadelphia PA 19106
215-351-9200
Category: 35-57
Host: Dr Dan Gottlieb
Format: C -- FM
Features: I-F

WHYY-FM
Mark Vogelzang, Program Director
150 N 6th Street
Philadelphia PA 19106
215-351-9200
Category: 99
Format: -- FM

WIAN
931 Fletcher Avenue
Indianapolis IN 46203
317-266-4141
Category: 99
Format: -- FM

WIBA
P O Box 99
Madison WI 53701
608-274-5450
Category: 99
Format: -- AM/FM

WIBC
9292 N Meridian Street
Indianapolis IN 46260
317-844-7200
Category: 99
Format: -- AM

WIBX
P O Box 950
Utica NY 13503
315-736-9313
Category: 99
Format: -- AM

WICN Public Radio
Eugene R Petit, Director
Spectrum
P O Box 241
Worcester MA 01601
617-752-7517
Category: 11-13
Host: Eugene Petit
Format: L-T -- FM
Features: I

WIIN-AM
2707 Atlantic Avenue
Atlantic City NJ 08401
609-348-4646
Category: 99
Format: -- AM

WIL
300 N Tucker Street
St Louis MO 63101
314-436-1600
Category: 99
Format: -- AM/FM

WILL
Producer, Focus 580
810 S Wright Street
Urbana IL 61801
217-333-0850
Category: 99
Format: -- FM

WILM-AM
1215 French Street
Wilmington DE 19801
302-478-4572
Category: 99
Format: -- AM

WINA/WQMC
Patrick Wilson, Director
Patrick Wilson Show
P O Box 498
Charlottesville VA 22902
804-977-3030
Category: 23-25-29-33-43-53-57
          69-81-82-84-86-87-88
Host: Patrick Wilson
Format: L-C-I -- AM/FM
Features: I-N-F-B

WIND
Producer, Dave Baum Show
625 N Michigan Avenue
Chicago IL 60611
312-751-5560
Category: 99
Format: -- AM

WIND
David Graves, General Manager
The Carren Show
625 N Michigan Avenue
Chicago IL 60611-3110
312-751-5560
Category: 11-33
Format: C-P -- AM
Features: I

WIND
Producer, Clark Weber Show
625 N Michigan Avenue
Chicago IL 60611-3110
312-751-5560
Category: 99
Host: Clark Weber
Format: -- AM
Features: I

WING
717 E David Road
Dayton OH 45429
513-294-5858
Category: 99
Format: -- AM

WINS
90 Park Avenue
New York NY 10016
212-557-1010
Category: 99
Format: -- AM

WINZ-AM
Producer, Bill Calder Show
4330 NW 207 Drive
Miami FL 33055
305-624-6101
Category: 99
Format: -- AM

WINZ-AM
Chris Slogon
Bob Lassiter Show
4330 NW 207 Drive
Miami FL 33055
305-624-6101
Category: 99
Host: Bob Lassiter
Format: -- AM

WINZ-AM
Producer, Neil Rogert Show
4330 NW 207 Drive
Miami FL 33055
305-624-6101
Category: 99
Host: Neil Rogert
Format: -- AM

WIOD
Producer, Mark Pentrack Show
1401 N Bay Causeway
Miami FL 33141
305-759-4311
Category: 99
Host: Mark Pentrack
Format: -- AM

WIOQ Philadelphia
Juan Varleta, News Director
Horizons
Two Bala Cynwyd Place
Bala Cynwyd PA 19004
215-667-8100
Category: 13-19-21-25-31-37-61-67
Host: Juan Varleta
Format: T -- FM
Features: I-N-F

WIOQ, Philadelphia
Ed Orenstein,
Harvey in the Morning
Two Bala Cynwyd Place
Bala Cynwyd PA 19004
215-667-8100
Category: 33-69
Host: Harvey
Format: L-C -- FM
Features: I-N-F

WIP
19th & Walnut Streets
Philadelphia PA 19103
215-568-2900
Category: 99
Format: -- AM

WIS-AM
Thom Brabham, Producer
AM Magazine

P O Box 21567
Columbia SC 29221
803-772-5600
Category: 99
Host: Thom Brabham
Format: T-P -- AM
Features: I-N-F-B

WIS-AM
Don Mack, Program Manager
F.Y.I. (For Your Information)
P O Box 21567
Columbia SC 29221
803-772-5600
Category: 10
Host: Don Mack and Thom Brabham
Format: L-C -- AM
Features: I

WISN
Producer, Night Talk
759 N 19th Street
Milwaukee WI 53201
414-342-1111
Category: 99
Format: -- AM

WITF
Producer, Capitol Conversations
P O Box 2954
Harrisburg PA 17105
717-236-6000
Category: 99
Format: -- FM

WIVK
P O Box 10207
Knoxville TN 37939
615-588-6511
Category: 99
Format: -- AM

WIVS
300 Commerce Drive
Crystal Lake IL 60014
815-459-7000
Category: 99
Format: -- AM

WIXX
115 S Jefferson Street
Green Bay WI 54301
414-435-3771
Category: 99
Format: -- FM

WJBC
P O Box 8
Bloomington IL 61701
309-829-1221
Category: 99
Format: -- AM

WJCC
102 Pond Street
Norfolk MA 02056
617-384-2124
Format: -- AM

WJCT
100 Festival Park Avenue
Jacksonville FL 32233
904-359-9090
Category: 99
Format: -- FM

WJDX
P O Box 2171
Jackson MS 39205
601-982-1062
Category: 99
Format: -- AM

WJIB
68 Commercial Wharf
Boston MA 02110
617-523-6611
Category: 99
Format: -- FM

WJLK-AM
Annette Kaiser Haymon
Reaching Out
P O Box 880
Asbury Park NJ 07712
201-774-7700
Category: 13-39-49-57-63-73
Host: Annette K Haymon
Format: L-C-I -- AM
Features: I-N-B

WJMK-FM
Jay Congdon, Director
Colloquy
180 N Michigan Avenue
Chicago IL 60601
312-977-1800
Category: 10
Format: -- FM
Features: I

WJMO
11821 Euclid Avenue
Cleveland Heights OH 44106
216-795-1212
Category: 99
Format: -- AM

WJNO Newsradio
Frank Valente, Producer
Jack Cole's World Headquarters
P O Box 189
W Palm Beach FL 33402
305-838-4300
Category: 11-13-17-19-25-31-33
        35-47-49-51-55-57-67-69
Host: Jack Cole
Format: L-C-I -- AM
Features: I-N-F-B

WJOI
16550 West 9 Mile Road
P O Box 5005
Southfield MI 48086
313-222-2190
Category: 99
Format: -- FM

WJOL
601 Walnut Street
P O Box 430
Joliet IL 60434
815-726-4761
Category: 99
Format: -- AM

WJR Radio
Ms Terri Blatney, Producer
Warren Pierce Midday Magazine
2100 Fisher Building
Detroit MI 48202
313-875-4440
Category: 99
Host: Warren Pierce
Format: L-T-P -- AM
Features: I-N-F-B-R

WJR Radio
Bill Plegue II, Producer
Afternoon Music Hall
2100 Fisher Building
Detroit MI 48202
313-875-4440
Category: 11-17-19-27-29-33
        39-43-51-55-69
Host: Joel Alexander
Format: T-P -- AM
Features: I-N-F

WJR Radio
Sandra Knight, Producer
David Newman Show
2100 Fisher Building
Detroit MI 48202
313-875-4440
Category: 13-19-25-33-35
        37-39-55-57
Host: David Newman
Format: L-C -- AM
Features: I-N-F-B

WJW-AM
13461 Ridge Road
Cleveland OH 44133
216-237-8000
Category: 99
Format: -- AM

WJYW
101 N Tampa
Tampa FL 33602
813-229-1991
Category: 99
Format: -- FM

WKAT
1759 N Bay Road
Miami Beach FL 33139
305-538-7003
Category: 99
Format: -- AM

WKBN
Ron Verb, Producer
Nitetalk
3930 Sunset Boulevard

Youngstown OH 44501
216-782-1144
Category: 15-17-25-27-31-33-35-37
          39-43-51-53-55-57-63-73
Host: Ron Verb
Format: L-C-P -- AM/FM
Features: I

WKCN-AM
P O Box 5758
N Charleston SC 29406
803-747-0091
Category: 99
Format: -- AM

WKCR
Columbia University
208 Ferris Booth
New York NY 10027
212-280-5223
Category: 99
Format: -- FM

WKDA
506 S Second Avenue
Nashville TN 37210
615-244-9533
Category: 99
Format: -- AM

WKEE-FM
P O Box 2288
Huntington WV 25724
304-522-2000
Category: 99
Format: -- FM

WKGN
2900 Sutherland Avenue
Knoxville TN 37919
615-521-6220
Category: 99
Format: -- AM

WKHK
4130 - 58th Street
Woodside NY 11377
212-335-1700
Category: 99
Format: -- FM

WKHM
1700 Glenshire Drive
Jackson MI 49201
157-788-6360
Category: 99
Format: -- AM

WKIE
6001 Wilkinson Road
Richmond VA 23227
804-264-1540
Category: 99
Format: -- AM

WKIS-AM
P O Box 740
Orlando FL 32802

305-293-6397
Category: 99
Format: -- AM

WKKD-AM/FM
Mark Vasko, Producer
Sportswatch
P O Box C-1730
Aurora IL 60507
312-898-1580
Category: 69
Host: Mark Vasko
Format: L-T-P -- AM/FM
Features: I-N
312-898-6668

WKKD-AM/FM
Charlie Pajor, News Director
Insight(AM) / Viewpoint(FM)
P O Box C-1730
Aurora IL 60507
312-898-6668
Category: 13-15-17-19-23-25-27
          31-33-35-39-43-51-55
          69-77-81-84
Host: Charlie Pajor
Format: L-T-C-P -- AM/FM
Features: I

WKLS
1800 Century Boulevard #1200
Atlanta GA 30345
404-325-0960
Category: 99
Format: -- AM/FM

WKNO
Fred Willis, Program Director
P O Box 80000
Memphis TN 38152
901-458-2521
Category: 99
Format: -- FM

WKOX
100 Mount Wayne Avenue
Framingham MA 01701
617-879-2222
Category: 99
Format: -- AM

WKQX-FM
1700 Merchandise Mart Place
Chicago IL 60654
312-861-7940
Category: 99
Format: -- FM

WKRC-AM
1906 Highland Avenue
Cincinnati OH 45219
513-721-6397
Category: 99
Format: -- AM

WKRQ-FM
John Everett, Producer
Captions

1906 Highland Avenue
Cincinnati OH 45219
513-381-5500
Category: 99
Host: John Everett
Format: L -- FM
Features: I-N-F-B-R

WKRS
3250 Belvidere Road
Waukegan IL 60085
312-336-7900
Category: 99
Format: -- AM

WKRZ
P O Box 1600
Wilkes Barre PA 18702
717-823-5000
Category: 99
Format: -- AM

WKSI
Pam Conrad, Community Affairs
P O Box 19624
Greensboro NC 27416
919-275-9895
Category: 99
Format: -- FM

WKSI
Kim Roshelli, Producer
Kiss Close-up
P O Box 19624
Greensboro NC 27416
919-275-9895
Category: 13-15-25-31-35
          39-49-51-55
Host: Kim Roshelli
Format: T -- FM
Features: I-N-F

WKSS
60 Washington Street
Hartford CT 06106
203-243-9577
Category: 99
Format: -- FM

WKSU-FM
Kent State University
524 Wright Hall
Kent OH 44242
216-672-3114
Category: 99
Format: -- FM

WKTI
720 E Capitol Drive
Milwaukee WI 53201
414-332-9611
Category: 99
Format: -- FM

WKXL
Producer, Coffee Chat
P O Box 875
Concord NH 03301

603-225-5521
Category: 99
Format: -- AM

WKYS-FM
John Irving, News Director
4001 Nebraska Avenue NW
Washington DC 20016
202-686-6104
Category: 99
Format: -- FM

WKYS-FM
Bart Walsh, General Manager
The Sunday Morning Show
4001 Nebraska Avenue NW
Washington DC 20016
202-885-4554
Category: 99
Format: -- FM
Features: I-N-F

WKYU-FM
Mary Ann Jennings, News Director
Western Kentucky University
Bowling Green KY 42101
502-745-5384
Category: 99
Format: -- FM

WKZO
Ralph Grant, Program Director
590 W Maple Street
Kalamazoo MI 49008
616-345-2101
Category: 99
Format: -- AM

WKZO
John McKay, Producer
At Your Service
590 W Maple Street
Kalamazoo MI 49008
616-345-2101
Category: 11-25-27-31-33-35-39
          43-51-55-57-69-73
Host: John McKay
Format: L-C-T -- AM
Features: I-N

WLAC Radio
Bette Blackman, Coordinator
Teddy Bart Show
10 Music Circle East
Nashville TN 37203
615-748-8150
Category: 13-19-25-31-39-55
Host: Teddy Bart
Format: L-C-P -- AM
Features: I-N

WLAD-AM
Glenn O'Brien, Program Director
198 Main Street
Danbury CT 06770
203-744-4800
Category: 99
Format: -- AM

WLAD-AM
Bart Bustema, Producer
Sports 80
198 Main Street
Danbury CT 06770
203-744-4800
Category: 69
Host: Bart Bustema
Format: C -- AM
Features: I

WLAD-AM
Rhoda Daum
Dialogue 80
198 Main Street
Danbury CT 06770
203-744-4800
Category: 13-15-17-19-23-25-27
          29-31-33-35-39-51-53
          55-57-63-67-69-71-73
Host: Rhoda Daum
Format: C -- AM
Features: L-N-F

WLAK-FM
Carol Friar, Public Affairs
233 S Wacker Drive
Chicago IL 60606
312-329-8840
Category: 99
Format: -- FM

WLAV
101C Waters Building
Grand Rapids MI 49503
616-456-5461
Category: 99
Format: -- AM

WLGM
8th & Church Streets
Lynchburg VA 24504
804-847-1267
Category: 99
Format: -- AM

WLIB
David Lampell, Program Director
801 Second Avenue
New York NY 10017
212-661-3344
Category: 99
Format: -- AM

WLIK
Route 1
Newport TN 37821
615-623-3095
Category: 99
Format: -- AM

WLLZ-FM
Steve Monkiewicz, News Director
31555 14 Mile Road
Detroit MI 48018
313-855-5100
Category: 99
Format: -- FM

WLNR
2915 Bernice Road
Lansing IL 60438
312-895-1400
Category: 99
Format: -- FM

WLOL
Bob Berglund, News Director
716 N 1st Street
Minneapolis MN 55401
612-698-5566
Category: 99
Format: -- FM

WLRH
Jon Hicken, Director
Feedback
222 Holmes Avenue
Huntsville AL 35801
205-539-9405
Category: 11-13-19-23-25-31
        33-51-55-59-61-63
        65-67-73-80-81-86
Host: Jon Hicken
Format: L-C -- FM
Features: I-N-F-B-R

WLRN
1410 NE Second Avenue
Miami FL 33122
305-350-3228
Category: 99
Format: -- FM

WLS
Producer, Working
360 N Michigan Avenue
Chicago IL 60601
312-236-0507
Category: 19
Format: -- AM/FM

WLSU
University of Wisconsin
La Crosse WI 54601
608-785-8380
Category: 99
Format: -- FM

WLTF-FM/WRMR-AM
Tracy St John, News Director
One Radio Lane
Cleveland OH 44114
216-696-4444
Category: 99
Format: -- AM/FM

WLTF-FM/WRMR-AM
John Rehak,
Cleveland Conversation
One Radio Lane
Cleveland OH 44114
216-696-4444
Category: 99
Host: John Rehak
Format: T -- AM/FM
Features: I-F-B

WLTF-FM/WRMR-AM
Eric Brewer, Producer
Cleveland Perspective
One Radio Lane
Cleveland OH 44114
216-696-4444
Category: 99
Host: Eric Brewer
Format: T -- AM/FM
Features: I-N

WLTF-FM/WRMR-AM
John Rehak, Producer
New Age Cleveland
One Radio Lane
Cleveland OH 44114
216-696-4444
Category: 13-53-63
Host: John Rehak
Format: T -- AM/FM
Features: I-B-R

WLTF-FM/WRMR-AM
Mark Dougherty
Cleveland Conversations
One Radio Lane
Cleveland OH 44114
216-696-6999
Category: 13-19-25-27-31-35
        37-39-51-55-57
Host: Mark Dougherty
Format: T-P -- AM/FM
Features: N-F-B

WLTR/WEPR
P O Drawer L
2901 MIlkwood Avenue
Columbia SC 29205
803-758-2899
Category: 99
Format: -- AM/FM

WLTT-FM
5912 Hubbard Drive
Rockville MD 20852
301-984-6000
Category: 99
Format: -- FM

WLTW-FM
Sandy Jackson
Vista
140 West 43rd Street
New York NY 10036
212-382-6006
Category: 11-13-15-19-21-23-25
        29-31-33-35-39-43-51
        55-57-59-61-69-71-73
Host: Sandy Jackson
Format: T -- FM
Features: I-N-F

WLTW-FM
Rasa Kaye, News Director
Metro Monitor
140 West 43rd Street
New York NY 10036
212-382-6062

Category: 13-19-25-31-49-51-61-69
Host: Rasa Kaye
Format: T -- FM
Features: I-N-F

WLTY-FM
Jeanne Richards, News Director
Close-up
720 Boush Street
Norfolk VA 23510
804-446-2711
Category: 19-23-25-31-39-49-51-73
Host: Jeanne Richards
Format: T -- FM
Features: I-N

WLVQ-FM
Tom Thon, General Manager
Dr Hayes
42 E Gay Street
Columbus OH 43215
614-224-1271
Category: 10
Format: C -- FM
Features: I

WLW
3 East 4th Street #700
Cincinnati OH 45202
513-241-9597
Category: 99
Format: -- AM

WLYF
Producer, Life in South Florida
20450 NW Second Avenue
Miami FL 33169
305-653-8811
Category: 61(FL)-99
Format: -- FM

WMAL-AM
4400 Jennifer Street NW
Washington DC 20015
202-686-3020
Category: 99
Format: -- AM

WMAQ-AM
Merchandise Mart Place
Chicago IL 60654
312-861-8200
Category: 99
Format: -- AM

WMAR-FM
6400 York Road
Baltimore MD 21212
301-435-0106
Category: 99
Format: -- FM

WMAZ
1314 Gray Highway
Macon GA 31213
912-741-5799
Category: 99
Format: -- AM/FM

WMBM
Ron Lopez, Program Director
Spectrum
814 First Street
Miami Beach FL 33139
305-672-1100
Category: 13-19-25-33-41
         49-55-59-63
Host: Ron Lopez
Format: C-P -- AM
Features: I-N-B

WMBR-FM
Producer, Disability Directions
3 Ames Street
Cambridge MA 02142
617-494-8810
Category: 39
Format: -- FM

WMBR-FM
David E Moran
Temporarily Labelled
3 Ames Street
Cambridge MA 02142
617-494-8810
Category: 13-19-23-25-31-35
         39-47-49-55-57-75
Host: David E Moran
Format: C -- FM
Features: I-N-F

WMBW
P O Box 11127
Chattanooga TN 37401
615-266-2795
Category: 99
Format: -- FM

WMC-FM
Sandra Bray, Director
Impact AM79
1960 Union Avenue
Memphis TN 38104
901-726-0477
Category: 73-49-55-57-51
         76-78-89-82
Host: Sandra Bray
Format: T-P -- FM
Features: I-N-F-B

WMC-FM
Sandra Bray, Director
Memphis In Focus
1960 Union Avenue
Memphis TN 38104
901-726-0477
Category: 11-17-19-25-31
         33-35-37-61(TN)
Host: Sandra Bray
Format: T-P -- FM
Features: I-N-F-B

WMCA-AM
Scott Byrne, Producer
The Casper Citron Program
888 Seventh Avenue
New York NY 10019
212-586-5700
Category: 11-17-19-21-25-31-33
         37-39-41-47-49-51-55
         67-73-95-77-78-80-83
Host: Casper Citron
Format: T -- AM
Features: I-B

WMCA-AM
Tom Tradeup
Breakfast with Bob & Betty
888 Seventh Avenue
New York NY 10019
212-586-5700
Category: 99
Format: -- AM
Features: N

WMCA-AM
Producer, Barry Farber Show
Producer, Ralph & Ryan Show
Producer, Patricia McCann Show
888 Seventh Avenue
New York NY 10019
212-586-5700
Category: 99
Format: -- AM

WMCA-AM
Sue Bennet, Producer
John Scheuer, Your Money Man
888 Seventh Avenue
New York NY 10019
212-586-5700
Category: 19-25
Format: -- AM
Features: I

WMCA-AM
Sue Bennet, Producer
Barry Gray Show
888 Seventh Avenue
New York NY 10019
212-586-5700
Category: 10
Format: -- AM

WMFE
11510 E Colonial Drive
Orlando FL 32817
305-273-2300
Category: 99
Format: -- FM

WMFO-FM
Producer, Grassroots
P O Box 65, Tufts University

Medford MA 02153
617-381-3800
Category: 99
Format: -- FM

WMGK
1 Bala Cynwyd Place
Bala Cynwyd PA 19004
215-879-6000
Category: 99
Format: -- FM

WMHT
P O Box 17
Schenectady NY 12301
518-356-1700
Category: 99
Format: -- FM

WMIN
1995 S Century Avenue
Maplewood MN 55125
612-739-4433
Category: 99
Format: -- AM

WMJC-WHND
Producer, Community Report
One Radio Plaza
Detroit MI 48220
313-398-8190
Category: 99
Host: Barbara Kusak
Format: L-T-P -- AM/FM
Features: O-M-F-B

WMJC-WHND
Roberta Jasina, News Director
One Radio Plaza
Detroit MI 48220
313-398-8190
Category: 99
Format: -- AM/FM

WMJI-FM
3940 Euclid Avenue
Cleveland OH 44115
216-391-4400
Category: 99
Format: -- FM

WMJX
330 Stuart Street
Boston MA 02117
617-542-2749
Category: 99
Format: -- AM

WMMR-FM
Beverly Rohan, Director
Counterpoint Blank
19th & Walnut Streets

===

Format: L = Live   T = Taped   C = Live with Call-ins   P = Telephone Interviews

Features: I = Interviews   N = News   F = Features   B = Book Reviews   R = Book Readings

Philadelphia PA 19103
215-561-0933
Category: 13-17-19-25-27-35
          37-39-51-53-73
Host: Mark Drucker
Format: T -- FM
Features: I-N-F-B

WMMR-FM
Beverly Rohan, Director
Philadelphia Futures
19 & Walnut Streets
Philadelphia PA 19103
215-561-0933
Category: 21-31-47-49-61(PA)-67
Host: Peter Solomon
Format: T -- FM
Features: I-N-F-B

WMMS
John Gorman, Program Director
1200 Statler Office Tower
Cleveland OH 44115
216-781-5828
Category: 99
Format: -- FM

WMOC
Terry Smith, News Director
3661 Brainerd Road
Chattanooga TN 37411
615-629-1423
Category: 99
Format: -- AM

WMOT-FM
Randy O'Brien, News Director
Murfreesboro News in Review
P O Box 3 MTSU
Murfreesboro TN 37132
615-898-2300
Category: 77-80-81-83-84-86-87
Host: Randy O'Brien
Format: T -- FM
Features: I-N

WMOT-FM
Randy O'Brien, News Director
Morning Edition
P O Box 3 MTSU
Murfreesboro TN 37132
615-898-2300
Category: 11-19-23-31-35-41
          47-49-55-63-69
Host: Shawn Jacobs
Format: T-P -- FM
Features: I-N-F-B

WMRE
Leslie Bennett, News Director
WMRE Magazine
74 Lansdowne Street
Boston MA 02215
617-267-1510
Category: 25-33-57-61-82
Host: Leslie Bennett
Format: C -- AM
Features: I-F-B

WMRO
Joseph Collins, Talk Host
1280 Talk in the Afternoon
P O Box 2010
Aurora IL 60507
312-851-0100
Category: 10
Host: Joe Colliins
Format: L-C-P -- AM
Features: I-N-F-B

WMRO
Joseph Collins, Director
1280 Morning Show
P O Box 2010
Aurora IL 60507
312-851-0100
Category: 10
Host: P J Harrigan
Format: L-C-P -- AM
Features: I-N-F-B

WMSP-FM
Ray Lehman, Program Director
Opera Showcase
24 S Second Street
Harrisburg PA 17101
717-257-1300
Category: 11(opera/classical)
          17-33-41-45-59-95
Host: A J Moulfair
Format: L -- FM
Features: I-F-B-R

WMSP-FM
Ray Lehman, Program Director
Be My Guest
24 S Second Street
Harrisburg PA 17101
717-257-1300
Category: 99
Host: Pamela Knief
Format: T -- FM
Features: I-N-F-B-R

WMTR
Brian Emery, Program Director
P O Box 1250
Morristown NJ 07960
Category: 99
Format: -- AM

WMUK-FM
Garrard Macleod, General Manager
Spectator
Western Michigan University
Kalamazoo MI 49008
616-383-1921
Category: 11-17-23-29-33-41
          47-76-77-78-79-81
          84-85-86-87-95
Host: Garrard Macleod
Format: L-T -- FM
Features: I-N-F-B-R

WMUZ
12300 Radio Place
Detroit MI 48228

313-272-3434
Category: 99
Format: -- FM

WMYK/WZAM
168 Business Park Drive #100
Virginia Beach VA 23462-6523
804-461-1194
Category: 99
Format: -- AM/FM

WNAB
405 Tarrytown Road #395
White Plains NY 10607-1313
203-333-5551
Category: 99
Format: -- AM

WNBC Radio
Producer
Conversations with Joyce Hauser
30 Rockfeller Plaza
New York NY 10020
212-664-3159
Category: 99
Host: Joyce Hauser
Format: -- AM

WNCI
1 Nationwide Place #98
Columbus OH 43215
614-224-9624
Category: 99
Format: -- FM

WNCN
1180 Avenue of the Americas
New York NY 10036
212-730-9626
Category: 99
Format: -- FM

WNCT-AM
P O Box 7167
Greensville NC 27834
919-758-1070
Category: 99
Format: -- AM

WNED
23 North Street
Buffalo NY 14202
716-886-0970
Category: 99
Format: -- FM

WNEW-FM
655 Third Avenue
New York NY 10017
212-986-7000
Category: 99
Format: -- FM

WNIC
Jane London
Sunday Times
15001 Michigan Avenue
Dearborn MI 48126

313-846-8500
Category: 19-25-27-31-33
         35-39-51-55-57
Host: Dick Kernan
Format: C -- AM/FM
Features: I

WNIC
Tamara Nelson
Monitor 100
15001 Michigan Avenue
Dearborn MI 48126
313-846-8500
Category: 11-13-25-27-35
         39-51-57-71
Host: Tamara Nelson
Format: T-P -- AM/FM
Features: I-F

WNIC
Dave Lockhart, News Director
15001 Michigan Avenue
Dearborn MI 48126
313-846-8500
Category: 99
Format: -- AM/FM

WNIR-FM
P O Box 629
Kent OH 44240
216-673-2323
Category: 99
Format: -- FM

WNIS
1302 Ingleside Road
Norfolk VA 23502
804-857-6397
Category: 99
Format: -- AM

WNOG-AM
Ed Carroll, Producer
Talkback
333 8th Street S
Naples FL 33940
813-263-6592
Category: 18-19-23-25-33
         39-41-43-59
Host: Ed Carroll
Format: C -- AM
Features: I-N-F-B

WNOG-AM
Producer, The Morning Journal
333 8th Street S
Naples FL 33940
813-263-6597
Category: 99
Host: Brian Grineau
Format: -- AM

WNOR
700 Monticello Avenue
Norfolk VA 23510
804-623-9667
Category: 99
Format: -- FM

WNPR
Faith Middleton, News Director
24 Summit Street
Hartford CT 06106
203-527-0905
Category: 99
Format: -- FM

WNSC
P O Drawer L
2901 Milkwood Avenue
Columbia SC 29205
803-758-2899
Category: 19
Format: -- FM

WNTN
Syvil Tonkonogy, Director
143 Rumford Avenue
Newton MA 02166
617-969-1550
Category: 99
Format: -- AM

WNWK-FM
Margot Diekmann, Assistant
Le Bow at Large
515 Madison Avenue #1303
New York NY 10022
212-826-1059
Category: 10
Host: Guy LeBow
Format: T -- FM
Features: I-N-B

WNWS
Ms Marianne Deward, Producer
Steve Kane Show
20405 NW 2nd Avenue
Miami FL 33169
305-653-8811
Category: 13-19-25-27-31-33-35
         37-39-43-53-57-59-61
         63-65-67-71-73
Host: Steve Kane
Format: L-T-P -- AM
Features: I-N-F

WNWS
Ms Marianne Deward, Producer
Bev Smith Show
20405 NW 2nd Avenue
Miami FL 33169
305-653-8811
Category: 13-19-25-27-31-33-35
         37-39-43-53-57-59-61
         63-65-67-71-73
Host: Bev Smith
Format: L-T-P -- AM
Features: I

WNWZ
Robert Gilmore, News Director
4719 Nine Mile Road
Richmond VA 23223
804-222-7000
Category: 99
Format: -- AM

WNYC
Producer, Senior Edition
1 Center Street
New York NY 10007
212-566-1010
Category: 99
Format: -- AM/FM

WNYC-FM
Nancy Shear
Before Brunch with Nancy Shear
180 W End Avenue #28
New York NY 10023
Category: 99
Host: Nancy Shear
Format: C -- FM
Features: I

WNYM
News Director
7 Smyrna Avenue
Staten Island NY 10312
212-967-3800
Category: 99
Format: -- AM

WNYS
Mark Mobley, News Director
Buffalo Hilton
Church and Terrace
Buffalo NY 14202
716-854-1120
Category: 99
Format: -- AM/FM

WOAI-AM
Producer, Computer line
6222 NW I-H 10
San Antonio TX 78201
512-734-7301
Category: 23
Format: -- AM

WOC
Charles King, Program Director
805 Brady Street
Davenport IA 52808
319-383-7000
Category: 99
Format: -- AM

WOI
John Dougan, News Director
Iowa State University
Ames IA 50011
515-294-5067
Category: 99
Format: -- AM/FM

WOKI-FM
Jerry Howell, News Director
Lifestyle
P O Box 1010
Oak Ridge TN 37381
615-483-8451
Category: 99
Host: Jerry Howell
Format: T -- FM

WOKV
Kate Thompson, Producer
Affairs of the Air
7500 Powers Avenue #183
Jacksonville FL 32217
904-353-7770; 904-636-0386(home)
Category: 99
Host: Kate Thompson
Format: C-I -- AM
Features: I-B

WOMC-FM
Marie Osborne
WOMC Metro Magazine
2201 Woodward Heights Boulevard
Detroit MI 48220
313-546-9600
Category: 11-17-25-31-35-39-43
49-51-53-55-57-59-69-73
Host: Marie Osborne
Format: T -- FM
Features: I-N-F-B

WOMC-FM
Ed Richards, News Director
WOMC Sunday Chronicles
2201 Woodward Heights Boulevard
Detroit MI 48220
313-546-9600
Category: 11-17-25-31-35-39-43
49-51-53-55-57-59-69-73
Host: Ed Richards
Format: T -- FM
Features: I-N-F-B

WOMP-AM
Brant Newman
Newsday
P O Box 448
Bellaire OH 43906
614-676-5661
Category: 99
Host: Howard Monroe
Format: L -- AM
Features: N-F-B

WOMP-AM
Howard Monroe, News Director
The Party Line
P O Box 448
Bellaire OH 43906
614-676-5661
Category: 13-17-19-25-27-31
33-35-39-53-55-57
Host: Howard Monroe
Format: C-P -- AM
Features: I-N-F

WONN-AM
Laurie Krosney, Director
Lifestyle Lakeland
P O Box 2038
Lakeland FL 33806
813-682-8184
Category: 61(FL)-99
Host: Laurie Krosney
Format: L -- AM
Features: I-N-F-B

WONN-AM
Laurie Krosney, Director
Town Hall
P O Box 2038
Lakeland FL 33806
813-682-8184
Category: 99
Host: Laurie Krosney
Format: T -- AM
Features: I-N-F-B

WOOD
180 N Division
Grand Rapids MI 49503
616-459-1919
Category: 99
Format: -- AM/FM

WOOK
5321 First Place NE
Washington DC 20011
202-722-1000
Category: 99
Format: -- FM

WOPA
408 S Oak Park Avenue
Oak Park IL 60302
312-848-5760
Category: 99
Format: -- AM

WOR Radio
Producer, Ask Dr Blaker
1440 Broadway
New York NY 10018
212-642-4500
Category: 35-57
Host: Dr Karen Blaker
Format: L-C-P -- AM
Features: I

WOR Radio
Caryl Ratner, Producer
The Sherrye Henry Program
1440 Broadway
New York NY 10018
212-642-4500
Category: 19-51-55
Host: Sherrye Henry
Format: L -- AM
Features: I-N

WOR Radio
Producer, Design for Living
1440 Broadway
New York NY 10018
212-642-4500
Category: 39-77
Host: Dr Carlton Fredericks
Format: L-T-C -- AM
Features: I

WOR Radio
Cathy Shea, Producer
Joan Hamburg Program
1440 Broadway
New York NY 10018

212-642-4500
Category: 25-35-39-43-59
Host: Joan Hamburg
Format: L-T-C-P -- AM

WOR Radio
Susan Murphy, Producer
Rambling with Gambling
1440 Broadway
New York NY 10018
212-642-4500
Category: 98(offbeat & soft news)
Host: John Gambling
Format: L-T-P -- AM
Features: I-F

WOR Radio
Producer
Garden Hotline
1440 Broadway
New York NY 10018
212-642-4500
Category: 43(gardening)
Host: Ralph Snodsmith
Format: L-C- -- AM
Features: I

WOR Radio
Michael Castello, Producer
What's Your Problem
1440 Broadway
New York NY 10018
212-642-4500
Category: 25-35-43
Host: Bernard Meltzer
Format: L-T-C -- AM

WOR Radio
Producer
Life Extension
1440 Broadway
New York NY 10018
212-642-4500
Category: 39-69
Host: Dr Jeff Fisher
Format: L-C -- AM

WOSU
2400 Olentangy River Road
Columbus OH 43210
614-422-9678
Category: 99
Format: -- AM/FM

WOUB
Ohio University
9 South College
Athens OH 45701
614-594-5321
Category: 99
Format: -- AM/FM

WOWO-AM
203 W Wayne
Ft Wayne IN 46802
219-424-2400
Category: 99
Format: -- AM

WPAT
1396 Broad Street
Clifton NJ 07013
201-345-9300
Category: 99
Format: -- AM/FM

WPBN
Alumni Hall
Orono ME 04469
207-866-4493
Category: 99
Format: -- AM

WPBR
Valerie Aspinwall, Director
Palm Beach PM
3000 S Ocean Boulevard
Palm Beach FL 33480
305-582-7401
Category: 11-13-17-25-27-33-35
        39-41-43-47-55-57-59
        71-73-76-81-83-87
Host: Valerie & Everett Aspinwall
Format: L-C-P -- AM
Features: I-N-F-B-R

WPBR
Herbert Swope
Swope's Swope
3000 S Ocean Boulevard
Palm Beach FL 33480
305-582-7401
Category: 11-13-15-17-25-33-39
        41-49-55-57-69-95-81-87
Host: Herbert Bayard Swope, Jr
Format: L-C-P -- AM
Features: I-N-R

WPBR
Mark Scheinbaum
Let's Talk About Money
3000 S Ocean Boulevard
Palm Beach FL 33480
305-582-7401
Category: 19-23-25-51-55
        57-67-69-71
Host: Mark Scheinbaum
Format: L-C-P -- AM
Features: I

WPBR
Dan Gregory
Let's Talk
3000 S Ocean Boulevard
Palm Beach FL 33480
305-582-7401
Category: 13-15-25-39-41
        51-53-55-69-95
Host: Dan Gregory
Format: L-C -- AM
Features: I-N-R

WPCV
Laurie Krosney, Director
Winter Haven Forum
P O Box 2038
Lakeland FL 33806
813-682-8184
Category: 10
Host: Dick Eyrich & Shari Szabo
Format: T -- FM
Features: I-N-F

WPCV
Laurie Krosney, Director
Winter Haven Lifestyle
P O Box 2038
Lakeland FL 33806
813-682-8184
Category: 10
Host: Dick Eyrich
Format: T -- FM
Features: I-N-F

WPEN
1 Bala Cynwyd Place
Bala Cynwyd PA 19004
215-879-6000
Category: 99
Format: -- AM

WPEP
Patricia Riley, News Director
49 Broadway
Taunton MA 02780
617-824-7528
Category: 99
Format: -- AM

WPFW
Carol Jones, Program Director
700 H Street NW
Washington DC 20001
202-783-3100
Category: 99
Format: -- FM

WPGC/WCLY
Allan Hotlew, Program Director
Baker & Burd
P O Box 10239
Washington DC 20018
301-441-3500
Category: 10
Host: Jeff Baker and David Burd
Format: L -- AM/FM
Features: I-N-F

WPGC/WCLY
Lauri Butler
Contact
P O Box 10239
Washington DC 20018
301-441-3500

Category: 10
Host: Larui Butler
Format: L -- AM/FM
Features: I

WPIX-FM
Paul James, News Director
Dialogue 102
11 WPIX Plaza 28th Floor
New York NY 10017
212-949-2102
Category: 31-51-55-57-98(housing,
        transportation)
Host: Paul James
Format: T -- FM
Features: I-N

WPLJ-FM
Nicole Sandler, Producer
Jim Kerr & the Morning Crew
1330 Avenue of the Americas
New York NY 10019
212-887-6189
Category: 11-33
Host: Jim Kerr
Format: L -- FM
Features: I-N

WPLN-FM
Luanne Grandinetti, Director
5 min daily features
222 - 8th Avenue N
Nashville TN 37203
615-244-4700
Category: 97(news)
Format: T -- FM
Features: I-F-B

WPLN-FM
Producer, The Financial Report
222 - 8th Avenue N
Nashville TN 37203
Category: 19
Format: -- FM

WPLN-FM
Luanne Grandinetti, Director
Coffee Break
222 - 8th Avenue N
Nashville TN 37203
615-244-4700
Category: 99
Host: Rebecca Bain
Format: L-T -- FM
Features: I-F-B

WPLP
P O Box 570
Pinellas Park FL 33565
813-392-2215
Category: 99
Format: -- AM

==

Format: L = Live   T = Taped   C = Live with Call-ins   P = Telephone Interviews

Features: I = Interviews   N = News   F = Features   B = Book Reviews   R = Book Readings

WPNT
1051 Brinton Road
Pittsburgh PA 15221
412-244-7600
Category: 99
Format: -- FM

WPOC-FM
711 W 40th Street
Baltimore MD 21211
301-366-3693
Category: 99
Format: -- FM

WPOP
P O Box 11-1410
Hartford CT 06111
203-666-1411
Category: 99
Format: -- AM

WPRB
P O Box 342
Princeton University
Princeton NJ 08540
609-921-9287
Category: 99
Format: -- FM

WPRO
1502 Wampanoag Trail
E Providence RI 02915
401-433-4200
Category: 99
Format: -- AM/FM

WPTF-AM
P O Box 1511
410 S Salisbury Street
Raleigh NC 27602
919-832-8311
Category: 99
Format: -- AM

WPYX
1054 Troy-Schenectady Road
Schenectady NY 12110
518-785-9061
Category: 99
Format: -- FM

WQAL
1621 Euclid Avenue #1800
Cleveland OH 44115
216-696-6666
Category: 99
Format: -- FM

WQBK
Tom Mailey, Program Manager
Talk Radio
P O Box 1300
Albany NY 12201
518-462-5555
Category: 99
Host: Tom Mailey
Format: L-C-P -- AM
Features: I

WQDR-FM
410 S Salisbury Street
Raleigh NC 27602
919-832-8311
Category: 99
Format: -- FM

WQED-FM
Stephen Brown
Sunday Arts Magazine
4802 Fifth Avenue
Pittsburgh PA 15213
412-622-1546
Category: 11-33
Host: Ceci Sommers & Bill Homisak
Format: T -- FM
Features: I-F-B
412-622-1435

WQED-FM
Ceci Sommers, Station Manager
4802 Fifth Avenue
Pittsburgh PA 15213
412-622-1435
Category: 99
Format: -- FM

WQFM
606 W Wisconsin Avenue
Milwaukee WI 53203
414-276-2040
Category: 99
Format: -- FM

WQLN
8425 Peach Street
Erie PA 16509
814-864-3001
Category: 99
Format: -- FM

WQRS
500 Temple Avenue
Detroit MI 48201
313-833-6105
Category: 99
Format: -- FM

WQSA
Susan Loughren, Producer
Studio Three
P O Box 7700
Sarasota FL 33578
813-366-0424
Category: 11-13-15-25-27-29-33
           43-57-73-76-79-89
Host: Myron Thomas
Format: L-C-P -- AM
Features: I-F-B

WQSA
Ralph Janotti, Manager
Morning Desk
P O Box 7700
Sarasota FL 33578
813-366-0424
Category: 17-19-25-31-35-41-55
           59-61-63-69-81-84-86-87
Host: Ralph Janotti/Mike Edwards
Format: L-C-P -- AM
Features: I-N-F-B

WQUE-FM
1440 Canal Street #800
New Orleans LA 70112
504-581-1280
Category: 99
Format: -- FM

WQXI
3340 Peachtree Road NE #240
Atlanta GA 30326
404-261-6397
Category: 99
Format: -- AM

WQXR
229 West 43 Street
New York NY 10036
212-556-1144
Category: 99
Format: -- AM/FM

WQXT-AM/FM
Scott Byrne
Casper Citron Interviews
350 Central Park West
New York NY 10025
212-222-3333
Category: 99
Host: Caspar Citron
Format: -- AM/FM

WRAL
Bill Leslie, News Director
711 Hillsborough
Raleigh NC 27605
919-890-6101
Category: 99
Format: -- FM

WRBQ
Cat Lewis, Producer
Q Morning Zoo
5510 Gray Street
Tampa FL 33609
813-879-1420
Category: 11-13-33-69-77-82
Host: Cleveland Wheeler
Format: L-C -- FM
Features: I-N-F

WRC
Gordon Peil, Program Director
4001 Nebraska Avenue NW
Washington DC 20016
202-885-4000
Category: 99
Format: -- AM

WRCG-AM
P O Box 1537
Columbus GA 31906
404-327-1217
Category: 99
Format: -- AM

WREB-930 AM
Ron Chimelis
The Morning Show
1 Court Plaza
11 Suffolk Street
Holyoke MA 01040
413-536-3930
Category: 15-31-37-49-53
         55-63-69-73
Host: Ron Chimelis
Format: L-C-P -- AM
Features: I-N-F

WREB-930 AM
Mike Dobbs
Drive PM
1 Court Plaza
11 Suffolk Street
Holyoke MA 01040
413-536-3930
Category: 11-13-15-17-33-37-73
Host: Mike Dobbs
Format: L-C-P -- AM
Features: I-N-F-B

WREB-930 AM
Jonathan Evans, Director
Jonathan Evans Show
1 Court Plaza
11 Suffolk Street
Holyoke MA 01040
413-536-3930
Category: 13-17-19-21-23-31-35
         39-41-53-55-61-63
Host: Jonathan Evans
Format: L-C-P -- AM
Features: I-N-F-B

WREC
1385 Lamar
Memphis TN 38104
901-726-0060
Category: 99
Format: -- AM

WREN
P O Box 1280
1001 Filmore
Topeka KS 66604
913-232-9240
Category: 99
Format: -- AM

WRFG-FM
Mark Sheppard, News Director
P O Box 5332
1083 Austin Avenue
Atlanta GA 30307
404-523-3471
Category: 99
Format: -- FM

WRFK
Union Theological Seminary
Richmond VA 23227
804-264-2953
Category: 99
Format: -- FM

WRIF-FM
20777 W 10 Mile Road
Southfield MI 48037
313-827-1111
Category: 99
Format: -- FM

WRKC
Kings College
133 N Franklin Street
Wilkes Barre PA 18711
717-826-5821
Category: 99
Format: -- FM

WRKL
Morton M Siegel, Director
Hot Line
Route 20210
Pomona NY 10970
914-354-2000
Category: 19-23-25-31-35-39-43
         51-55-57-61-69-73
Host: Bobbi Lewis
Format: C -- AM
Features: I-N-F

WRKO
Mark Williams, Producer
Ten & Janet Show
52 Temple Street #1
Boston MA 02114
617-723-2268
Category: 19-37-55-97(news)
Host: Ted O'Brien/Janet Jeghelian
Format: L-C-P -- AM
Features: I-N

WRKS-FM
1440 Broadway
New York NY 10018
212-764-6613
Category: 99
Format: -- FM

WRNL
7100 Bethlehem Road
Richmond VA 23228
804-282-9731
Category: 99
Format: -- AM

WROL
Bill Porter, Director
Sherm Feller Show
312 Stuart Street
Boston MA 02116
617-423-0210
Category: 19-25-31-35-39-51-55
         41-61-67-71-73-81
Host: Sherm Feller
Format: C -- AM
Features: I-N-F
(May to September only)

WROL
Bill Porter, Director
Yankee Kitchen Program

312 Stuart Street
Boston MA 02116
617-423-0210
Category: 27
Host: Gus Saunders
Format: L-C -- AM
Features: I-F

WROQ-FM
400 Radio Road
Charlotte NC 28216
701-392-6191
Category: 99
Format: -- FM

WROR
3 Fenway Plaza
Boston MA 02215
617-236-6868
Category: 99
Format: -- FM

WRQC-FM
2156 Lee Road
Cleveland Heights OH 44118
216-371-3534
Category: 99
Format: -- FM

WRQX
David Page, News Director
Sundays
4400 Senifer Street NW
Washington DC 20015
202-686-3100
Category: 99
Host: David Page
Format: T -- FM
Features: I-N-F-B

WRQX
David Page, News Director
Call Page
4400 Senifer Street NW
Washington DC 20015
202-686-3100
Category: 99
Host: David Page
Format: C -- FM
Features: I-N-F-B

WRR
Fair Park Station
Dallas TX 75226
214-670-8888
Category: 99
Format: -- FM

WRR
7929 Meadow Park Drive #201
Dallas TX 75230
214-369-0904
Category: 99
Format: -- AM

WRSU
Rutgers University
126 College Avenue

New Brunswick NJ 08903
201-932-7800
Category: 99
Format: -- FM

WRTA Radio
Charlie Weston
Charlie Weston Talk Show
1417 12th Avenue
Altoona PA 16601
814-943-6112
Category: 13-19-23-25-31-35-39-55
Host: Charlie Weston
Format: L-C-P -- AM
Features: I-N

WRTH
7711 Carondelet #304
St Louis MO 63105
314-727-2160
Category: 99
Format: -- AM

WRTN-FM
Mime Gordon
Let's Talk
One Broadcast Forum
New Rochelle NY 10801
914-636-1460
Category: 99
Format: -- FM

WRUR
Producer, Dollars & Sense
P O Box 29068 (River Campus)
Rochester NY 14627
716-275-5967
Category: 19-25
Format: -- FM

WRUV
489 Main Street
Burlington VT 05405
802-655-9058
Category: 99
Format: -- FM

WRVA
Lou Dean, Program Director
P O Box 1516
Richmond VA 23234
804-643-6633
Category: 99
Format: -- AM

WRVQ-FM
P O Box 1394
Richmond VA 23211
804-649-9151
Category: 99
Format: -- FM

WRXL
7100 Bethlehem Road
Richmond VA 23228
804-282-9731
Category: 99
Format: -- FM

WSAR
P O Box 927
Fall River MA 02722
617-678-9727
Category: 99
Format: -- AM

WSB
Mariam Moad, Host
Womens World
1601 W Peachtree Street NE
Atlanta GA 30309
404-897-7594
Category: 19-25-31-35-39-49-57-73
Host: Mariam Moad
Format: T-P -- AM/FM
Features: I-N-F

WSB
Ricki Shaw, Operations Manager
Sound-off
1601 W Peachtree Street NE
Atlanta GA 30309
404-897-7594
Category: 13-19-25-37-55-63
Host: Bob Mohan/Dan Fitzpatrick
Format: L-P -- AM/FM
Features: I-N

WSBA-AM
P O Box 910
York PA 17045
717-764-1155
Category: 99
Format: -- AM

WSBY-AM
P O Box U
Salisbury MD 21801
301-742-1923
Category: 99
Format: -- AM

WSCI
Marcia Byars-Warnock
Coastal Nightline
P O Box 801
Mount Pleasant SC 29464
803-881-1160
Category: 99
Host: Keith Henty
Format: T -- FM
Features: I-F-R

WSGN
Ted Randall, News Director
Twin Towers East
236 Goodwin Crest
Birmingham AL 35209
205-942-0600
Category: 99
Format: -- AM

WSGW
1795 Tittabawassee Road
Saginaw MI 48605
Category: 99
Format: -- AM

WSHH
John Boyle, Public Affairs
Crane Avenue
Broadcast Plaza
Pittsburgh PA 15220
412-531-9500
Category: 99
Format: -- FM

WSIU
Southern Illinois University
Carbondale IL 62901
618-453-4343
Category: 99
Format: -- FM

WSJS/WTQR
Connie Elrod, News Editor
Forum
P O Box 3018
Winston-Salem NC 27102
919-727-8826
Category: 13-15-19-21-25-27-31
        35-37-39-43-49-51-55
        58-61-69-71-73
Host: Jim Steel
Format: T-C -- AM/FM
Features: I-N-F-B

WSJS/WTQR
Robert Owen, Operations Manager
P O Box 3018
Winston-Salem NC 27102
919-727-8826
Category: 99
Format: -- AM/FM

WSKG-FM
Julie Kramer, Producer
ArtScene
P O Box 3000
Binghamton NY 13902
607-755-0100
Category: 11-29-61(NY)-95
        75(regional only)
Host: Julie Kramer
Format: T -- FM
Features: I-F-R

WSKG-FM
Martin Murray
Direct Line
P O Box 3000
Binghamton NY 13902
607-755-0100
Category: 13-19-23-25-31-35
        39-51-55-59-73
Host: Martin Murray
Format: C -- FM
Features: I

WSM
Paul Dickerson, News Director
P O Box 100
Nashville TN 37202
615-889-0568
Category: 99
Format: -- AM/FM

WSMB-AM
13th Floor
Maison Blanche Building
New Orleans LA 70112
504-561-8111
Category: 99
Format: -- AM

WSNI-FM
Ruth Weisberg, News Director
Community Spotlight
One Bala Plaza
Bala Cynwyd PA 19004
215-668-0750
Category: 13-25-35-37-39-57-67-73
Host: Ruth Weisberg
Format: T -- FM
Features: I-F

WSOC
1901 N Tyron Street
Charlotte NC 28206
704-335-4889
Category: 99
Format: -- AM/FM

WSPD-AM
125 S Superior
Toledo OH 43602
419-244-8321
Category: 99
Format: -- AM

WSSJ
Courthouse Square
Camden NJ 08101
609-365-5600
Category: 99
Format: -- AM

WSSR
Sangamon State University
Springfield IL 62708
217-786-6516
Category: 99
Format: -- FM

WSUI
3300 Engineering Building
University of Iowa
Iowa City IA 52242
319-353-5665
Category: 99
Format: -- AM

WSWI
8600 University Boulevard
Evansville IN 47712
812-464-1836
Category: 99
Format: -- AM

WSYR/WYYY
John Butler, News Director
Noon Report and 4:30 Report
2 Clinton Square
Syracuse NY 13202
315-472-9797

Category: 13-19-25-27-29-31-43
51-55-59-61-69-71-73
77-83-84-87
Host: H Modell & Christine Rogers
Format: L-C -- AM/FM
Features: I-N-F-B

WTAD
P O Box 905
Quincy IL 62306
217-222-6200
Category: 99
Format: -- AM

WTAE
400 Ardmore Boulevard
Pittsburgh PA 15230
412-731-1250
Category: 99
Format: -- AM

WTAR-AM
720 Boush Street
Norfolk VA 23510
804-446-2700
Category: 99
Format: -- AM

WTAX/WDBR
Tim Schweizer, News Director
The Morning News
P O Box 2759
Springfield IL 62708
217-753-5400
Category: 13-19-23-25-31-35-39
41-43-55-59-61-67-69
Host: Bruce Bagg
Format: L-T-P -- AM/FM
Features: I-N-F

WTAX/WDBR
Patrick Gordon, News Director
P O Box 2759
Springfield IL 62708
217-753-5400
Category: 99
Format: -- AM/FM

WTCC-FM
P O Box 9000
1 Armory Square
Springfield MA 01101
413-736-8833
Category: 99
Format: -- FM

WTIC-AM
Producer, Dial Mark Davis
1 Financial Plaza
Hartford CT 06103
203-522-1080
Category: 99
Format: -- AM

WTIX
Ed Clancy
Morning Show
332 Carondelet Street

New Orleans LA 70130
504-561-0001
Category: 10
Host: Ed Clancy
Format: L-C-I -- AM
Features: I-N-F

WTIX
Brian Chase, Program Director
332 Carondelet Street
New Orleans LA 70130
504-561-0001
Category: 99
Format: -- AM

WTKN
1 Allegheny Square
Pittsburgh PA 15212
412-323-5300
Category: 99
Format: -- AM

WTKS
4646 40th Street NW
Washington DC 20016
301-364-5880
Category: 99
Format: -- FM

WTLB
Art Levy
TLB Live
P O Box 781
Utica NY 13503
315-797-1330
Category: 99
Host: Art Levy
Format: T -- AM
Features: I-N-F

WTMI
2951 S Bayshore Drive
Miami FL 33133
305-443-5251
Category: 99
Format: -- FM

WTMJ
Gus Gnorski
Gordon Hinkley Show
P O Box 620
Milwaukee WI 53201
414-332-9611
Category: 11-17-27-41-47-55
59-63-67-81-86
Host: Gordon Hinkley
Format: L-C-P -- AM
Features: I-F-B
414-223-5361

WTMJ
Virginia Duncan
Terry Meeuwsen Show
P O Box 620
Milwaukee WI 53201
414-332-9611
Category: 11-17-27-41-47-55
59-63-67-81-86

Host: Terry Meeuwsen
Format: L-C-P -- AM
Features: I-F

WTNT-AM
John Faulk, Program Director
P O Box 1047
Tallahassee FL 32302
904-386-6143
Category: 99
Format: -- AM

WTOP-AM
Jamie McIntyre
Issues
4646 - 40th Street NW
Washington DC 20016
202-364-5863
Category: 17-19-25-31-33-35
        41-49-55-61-69-73
Host: Jamie McIntyre
Format: T -- AM
Features: I

WTOP-AM
Bill Thompson
WTOP Sunday Morning
4646 - 40th Street NW
Washington DC 20016
202-364-5863
Category: 17-19-25-31-33-35
        41-49-55-61-69-73
Host: Bill Thompson
Format: T -- AM
Features: I-N-F

WTRY-AM
WTRY Road
Schenectady NY 12309
518-785-9061
Category: 99
Format: -- AM

WTTP
Diana Di Gioia, Public Affairs
24 W Central Street
Natick MA 02160
617-655-2500
Category: 99
Format: -- AM

WTVN-AM
Perry A Frey, General Manager
Dr Hayes
42 E Gay Street
Columbus OH 43215
614-224-1271
Category: 99
Format: -- AM
Features: I-C

WUFT
University of Florida
3100 Weimer Hall
Gainesville FL 32611
904-392-0771
Category: 99
Format: -- FM

WUHY
Independence Mall
Philadelphia PA 19106
215-351-9200
Category: 99
Format: -- AM

WUJC
20700 N Park Boulevard
Cleveland OH 44118
216-932-7946
Category: 99
Format: -- FM

WUNC
Swain Hall 004A
University of North Carolina
Chapel Hill NC 27514
919-966-5454
Category: 99
Format: -- FM

WUNH-FM
MUB #142
University of New Hampshire
Durham NH 03824
603-862-2222
Category: 99
Format: -- FM

WUOG-FM
Memorial Hall
P O Box 2065
Athens GA 30602
404-542-7100
Category: 99
Format: -- FM

WUOL
Stricker Hall
University of Louisville
Louisville KY 40292
502-588-6467
Category: 99
Format: -- FM

WUOM
5500 LSA Building
University of Michigan
Ann Arbor MI 48109
313-764-9210
Category: 99
Format: -- FM

WUOT
Ms Tinky Weisblat, Book Editor
232 Communications Building
University of Tennessee
Knoxville TN 37916
615-974-5375
Category: 11-21-27-33-47-65
        73-77-81-83-84-85
Format: T -- FM
Features: I-N-F-B

WUSB-FM
Norman Prusscin, General Manager
That's Television

SUNY
Stony Brook NY 11794
516-246-7900
Category: 11-33
Host: Mike Palmer
Format: T -- FM
Features: I

WUSB-FM
Norman Prusscin, General Manager
Poets Eye
SUNY
Stony Brook NY 11794
516-246-7900
Category: 95
Host: Sue Kain
Format: T -- FM
Features: R

WUSF
Producer, Tampa Bay Today
4202 Fowler Avenue
Tampa FL 33620
813-974-2215
Category: 61(FL)-99
Format: -- FM

WUSL-FM
440 Domino Lane
Philadelphia PA 19128
215-483-8900
Category: 99
Format: -- FM

WUTC
119 Race Hall, U of Tennessee
Chattanooga TN 37402
615-755-4346
Category: 99
Format: -- FM

WUWF
University of West Florida
Pensacola FL 32504
904-474-2327
Category: 99
Format: -- FM

WUWM
3223 N Downer Avenue
Milwaukee WI 53201
414-963-4664
Category: 99
Format: -- FM

WVAF
P O Box 4318
Charleston WV 25304
304-925-4947
Category: 99
Format: -- FM

WVCA
50 Maplewood Avenue
Gloucester MA 01930-2755
617-283-3700
Category: 99
Format: -- FM

WVIA
Public Broadcasting Center
Pittston PA 18640
717-655-2808
Category: 99
Format: -- FM

WVIK
Augustana College
639 38th Street
Rock Island IL 61201
309-794-7777
Category: 99
Format: -- FM

WVIP
Producer, Author Author
Radio Circle
Mount Kisco NY 10549
914-241-0552
Category: 99
Format: L-T-C-P -- AM/FM
Features: I-B

WVIP
Gerry Culliton, News Director
Periscope
Radio Circle
Mount Kisco NY 10549
914-241-0552
Category: 99
Host: Gerry Culliton
Format: T -- AM/FM
Features: I-N-B

WVLV
P O Box 940
Lebanon PA 17042
717-273-2611
Category: 99
Format: -- AM

WVOX-AM
Mime Gordon
Let's Talk
One Broadcast Forum
New Rochelle NY 10801
914-636-1460
Category: 99
Format: -- AM

WVPN
Building 6 #424, Capital Complex
Charleston WV 25305
304-348-3239
Category: 99
Format: -- FM

WVTF
Seth Williamson, Director
Virginia Bookshelf
4200 Avenham Avenue SW
Roanoke VA 24014
703-982-7397
Category: 11-33-99
Host: Seth Williamson
Format: T-P -- FM
Features: I-B

WVTF
Seth Williamson, Director
Morning Edition
4200 Avenham Avenue SW
Roanoke VA 24014
703-982-7397
Category: 99
Host: Rogert Fowler
Format: L-P -- FM
Features: I-N-F-B

WVXU
11 Alter Hall, Xavier University
Cincinnati OH 45207
513-745-3738
Category: 99
Format: -- FM

WWAM
P O Box 2026
Savannah GA 31402
912-232-4102
Category: 99
Format: -- AM

WWBA
9721 Executive Center Drive
St Petersburg FL 33702
813-576-1073
Category: 99
Format: -- FM

WWCN
P O Box 60
Glenmont NY 12077
518-439-1460
Category: 99
Format: -- AM

WWDB-FM
3930 Conshohocken Avenue
Philadelphia PA 19131
215-878-1500
Category: 99
Format: -- FM

WWDC-FM
Producer, DC 101 Report
1150 Connecticut Avenue NW
Washington DC 20036
202-828-9932
Category: 99
Format: -- FM

WWEE-AM
P O Box 17527
Memphis TN 38117
901-365-2032
Category: 99
Format: -- AM

WWFM
Steve Girone, Manager
P O Box B
Trenton NJ 08690
609-587-8989
Category: 99
Format: -- FM

WWFM
Nadia El-Meligi
Quarter Notes
P O Box B
Trenton NJ 08690
609-587-8989
Category: 11-17-39-41-47-49-53
          55-57-63-65-69-71-95
          76-78-80-81-83
Host: Nadia El-Meligi
Format: T-P -- FM
Features: I-F-R

WWJ-AM
P O Box 5005
16550 W 9 Mile Road
Southfield MI 48086
313-423-3311
Category: 99
Format: -- AM

WWL-AM
1024 N Rampart Street
New Orleans LA 70176
504-524-8787
Category: 99
Format: -- AM

WWNO-FM
Sarah Sherling
Gallery
University of New Orleans
Lakefront
New Orleans LA 70148
504-286-7000
Category: 11-33-47-49-65-73
Host: Sarah Sherling
Format: T-P -- FM
Features: I-F-B

WWNO-FM
Bill Zeeble, Program Director
University of New Orleans
Lakefront
New Orleans LA 70148
504-286-7000
Category: 99
Format: -- FM

WWSA/WCHY
Debbie Bolton, News Director
Savannah Supplement
P O Box 1247
Savannah GA 31402
912-964-7794
Category: 12-15-17-19-25-27-29
          31-33-35-39-43-49-53
          55-57-59-73-81-85
Host: Cindi Williams
Format: T-P -- AM/FM
Features: I-N-F-B

WWSH
555 City Line Avenue
Bala Cynwyd PA 19004
215-835-2350
Category: 99
Format: -- FM

Local Radio Stations and Shows

WWWE
1250 Superior Avenue
Cleveland OH 44114
216-781-1100
Category: 99
Format: -- AM/FM

WWWW-FM
2930 E Jefferson
Detroit MI 48207
313-259-4413
Category: 99
Format: -- FM

WXKW
700 Fenwick Street
Allentown PA 18103
215-434-4424
Category: 99
Format: -- FM

WXPN
Julie Drizin, News Director
Penumbra
3095 Spruce Street
Philadelphia PA 19104
215-386-0423
Category: 13-23-35-41-49-51
        55-63-73-77-78-95
Host: Julie Drizin
Format: L-T-P -- FM
Features: I-N-F

WXPN
Julie Drizin, News Director
Women's Consciousness Raising Hr
3095 Spruce Street
Philadelphia PA 19104
215-386-0423
Category: 13-37-55-73-95-77
Host: Julie Drizin
Format: T-P -- FM
Features: I-N-F-B-R

WXRK
655 Madison Avenue
New York NY 10021
212-750-0550
Category: 99
Format: -- AM

WXRT
4949 W Belmont
Chicago IL 60641
312-777-1700
Category: 99
Format: -- FM

WXXI-FM
P O Box 21
Rochester NY 14601
716-325-7500
Category: 99
Format: -- FM

WXYT-AM
Producer, Mark Scott Show
15600 West 12 Mile Road
Southfield MI 48076
313-569-8000
Category: 99
Format: -- AM

WYDD
810 Fifth Avenue
New Kensington PA 15068
412-362-2144
Category: 99
Format: -- FM

WYMS
Peter Zehren
Let's Talk Milwaukee
P O Drawer 10 K
Milwaukee WI 53201
414-475-8389
Category: 11-19-25-27-33
        35-39-55-57-69
Host: Peter Zehren
Format: L-T-C-P -- FM
Features: I-F

WYNY
30 Rockefeller Plaza #252
New York NY 10112
212-664-5295
Category: 99
Format: -- FM

WYSP
1 Bala Cynwyd Place
Bala Cynwyd PA 19004
215-688-9460
Category: 99
Format: -- FM

WYST
1111 Park Avenue Penthouse
Baltimore MD 21201
301-523-6900
Category: 99
Format: -- AM/FM

WZEE-FM
P O Box 8030
Madison WI 53708
608-274-1070
Category: 99
Format: -- FM

WZGC
603 W Peachtree Street NW
Atlanta GA 30379
404-881-0093
Category: 99
Format: -- FM

WZZK
530 Beacon Parkway West
Birmingham AL 35209
205-942-7800
Category: 99
Format: -- FM

WZZO
2285 Schoenersville Road #205
Bethlehem PA 18017
215-694-0511
Category: 99
Format: -- FM

==

Format: L = Live   T = Taped   C = Live with Call-ins   P = Telephone Interviews

Features: I = Interviews   N = News   F = Features   B = Book Reviews   R = Book Readings

==

Radio Networks and Network Shows

AB Newsamerica Satellite Newsnet
Program Director
309 National Press Building
Washington DC 20045
202-628-6397
Category: 99

ABC Info Radio
Business Report
125 West End Avenue
New York NY 10024
212-887-4138
Category: 19

ABC Radio
Rudd Awakening
1717 De Sales NW
Washington DC 20036
202-887-7777
Category: 99

ABC Radio
Direction Digest
1717 De Sales NW
Washington DC 20036
202-887-7613
Category: 99

ABC Radio
Producer
Business Directions
125 West End Avenue
New York NY 10024
212-887-4138
Category: 19

ABC Radio Network News
David R Alpert, Producer
Today's People
125 West End Avenue
New York NY 10024
212-887-4159
Category: 11-33-77
Host: Dave Alpert
Format: T-P
Features: I-N

ABC Radio Network News
David R Alpert, Producer
Young Adult Newscall
125 West End Avenue
New York NY 10024
212-887-4159
Category: 11-33-53-59-69-82-89
Host: David R Alpert
Format: T-P
Features: I-N-F

ABC Rock Radio
Producer, Lifelines
125 West End Avenue
New York NY 10023
215-667-8277
Category: 11-15-33

Africa News Service
Program Director
P O Box 3851
Durham NC 27702
919-286-0747
Category: 99(international)

AFRTS Programming Center
Program Director
1016 N McFadden Place
Los Angeles CA 90038
213-467-3561
Category: 99

American Forces Information
Program Director
1735 N Lynn Street
Arlington VA 22209
202-696-5284
Category: 98(military)-99

AP Radio
Consumer Editor
Business Editor
1825 K Street NW
Washington DC 20006
202-955-7210
Category: 19-25

AP Radio
Producer, Best Sellers
333 West 56 Street
New York NY 10019
Category: 99

Armed Forces Radio
Bonnie Mullins
AFSINC - IIBE
Kelly AFB TX 78241-5000
512-925-6261
Category: 10-98(military)

Associated Broadcast News Net
Robert C Cody, Managing Editor
Focal Point
1199 National Press Building
Washington DC 20045
202-628-6397
Category: 99
Host: Robert C Cody
301-320-4615

CBS Radio
Susan Monahan, Books Editor
524 West 57th Street
New York NY 10019
212-975-3615
Category: 99

CBS Radio
Producer, Business Update
Producer, Dateline America
Producer, Newsnotes
Producer, The Osgood File

Producer, Today in Business
524 West 57th Street
New York NY 10019
212-975-3615
Category: 19-99

CBS Radio Stations News Service
Chris Berry, Producer
Byline Magazine
2020 M Street NW
Washington DC 20036
202-457-4367
Category: 10
Contact: Nancy Johns
Format: T-P
Features: I-N-F

CKO Network
Melanie Reffes, Producer
30 Carlton Street
Toronto M5B 2E9   ON Canada
416-591-1222
Category: 99
Format: L-T-C-P
Features: I-N-F-B
Six shows daily

Copley Radio Network
P O Box 190
San Diego CA 92112
619-299-3131
Category: 99

Cox Communicaations
Program Director
P O Box 105357
Atlanta GA 30348
404-843-5000
Category: 99

Georgia Network
Producer, Business Report
683 Peachtree St NE
Atlanta GA 30308
404-875-8686
Category: 19

Georgia Radio Network
Richard Warner
Moneyline
110 Creekmont Way
Roswell GA 30076
404-231-1888
Category: 11-19-23-25-33
Host: Richard Warner
Format: T
Features: N-F

Group W
Program Director
90 Park Avenue
New York NY 10016
212-983-6500
Category: 99

Radio Networks and Network Shows

Linder Farm Network
Lynn Ketlesen, Farm Director
P O Box 838
Wilmar MN 56201
612-235-8695
Category: 98(agriculture)-99

Linder Farm Network
Gary Wilhelmi
Chicago Board of Trade
P O Box 838
Willmar MN 56201
612-235-8695
Category: 19-98(agriculture)
Host: Gary Wilhelmi
Format: I
Features: I-N

Linder Farm Network
Ron Michelson
Pro Farmer Audio
P O Box 838
Willmar MN 56201
612-235-8695
Category: 19-98(agriculture)
Host: Ron Michelson
Format: T
Features: F

Linder Farm Network
Jack Delaney
Jack Delaney Commentary
P O Box 838
Willmar MN 56201
612-235-8695
Category: 98(agriculture)-99
Host: Jack Delaney
Format: L
Features: Commentary

Maine Public Broadcasting
Keith McKeen, News Editor
Maine Things Considered
65 Texas Avenue
Bangor ME 04401
207-941-1010
Category: 97(news)-99
Host: Keith McKeen
Format: L-T-P
Features: I-N-F

Maine Public Broadcasting
Rufus Bisset, Producer
Focus on Art
65 Texas Avenue
Bangor ME 04401
207-941-1010
Category: 11
Host: Rufus Bisset
Format: T-P
Features: I-F-B

Mid-America Networks
Tony Purcell, News Director
Talk Line
P O Box 11705
Wichita KS 67202
316-267-0293

Category: 15-19-23-33-43-55-69
    98(agriculture)
Host: Tony Purcell
Format: C-P
Features: I-N-F

Mid-America Networks
Tony Purcell, News Director
KSN News
P O Box 11705
Wichita KS 67202
316-267-0293
Category: 15-19-23-33-43-55-69
    98(agriculture)
Host: Larry Steckline
Format: L
Features: N

Minnesota Public Radio
Marlene Reuber, Producer
Afterthoughts
45 East 8th Street
Saint Paul MN 55101
612-293-5438; 612-221-1500
Category: 99
Host: Tom Lijewski
Format: L-C
Features: I

Minnesota Public Radio
Marlene Reuber, Producer
Midday
45 E 8th Street
Saint Paul MN 55101
612-293-5438; 612-221-1500
Category: 10-95
Host: Bob Potter
Format: C
Features: I

Minnesota Public Radio
Mark Heistad, Producer
Weekend
45 E 8th Street
St Paul MN 55101
612-293-5443; 612-221-1500
Category: 99
Host: Mark Heistad
Format: T
Features: I-F-B

Minnesota Public Radio
Paula Drake and Jim Bickal
Producers
Morning Edition
45 E 8th Street
Saint Paul MN 55101
612-221-1502
Category: 99
Host: Loren Omoto
Format: L-T-P
Features: I-N-F

Minnesota Public Radio
Sara Meyer, Producer
MPR Journal
45 E 8th Street
Saint Paul MN 55101

612-293-5468
Category: 99
Host: Gary Eichten
Format: L-T
Features: I-N-F
612-221-1500

Missouri Network
Bob Pribby, News Director
Newscasts
216 E McCarty Street
Jefferson City MO 65101
314-634-3317
Category: 99
Format: T
Features: N

Mutual Broadcasting System
Program Director
708 3rd Avenue
New York NY 10017
Category: 99

Mutual Radio Network
Pat Piper, Producer
The Larry King Show
1755 S Jefferson Davis Highway
Arlington VA 22202
703-685-2000
Category: 99
Host: Larry King
Format: L
Features: I

Mutual Radio Network
Producer, Business Report
1755 S Jefferson Davis Highway
Arlington VA 22202
703-685-2000
Category: 19

Mutual Radio Network
Craig Warner, Producer
America in the Morning
1755 S Jefferson Davis Highway
Arlington VA 22202
703-685-2000
Category: 99

National Public Radio
Producer, All Things Considered
Producer, Let's Hear It
Producer, Morning Edition
2025 M Street NW
Washington DC 20036
202-822-2000
Category: 99
Features: I-N-F-B

NBC Radio
Producer, Source Report
Producer, Feedback
Producer, Money Memo
Producer, Bruce Williams Show
30 Rockefeller Plaza
New York NY 10020
212-664-4444
Category: 19-99

NBC Radio
Hank Miles, Science Editor
News Department
30 Rockefeller Plaza
New York NY 10020
212-664-2045
Category: 23-67

NBC Radio
Business Editor
News Department
4001 Nebraska NW
Washington DC 20016
202-686-4000
Category: 19

Progressive Radio Network
James Wynbrandt, Editor
P O Box 172
New York NY 10451
212-585-9400
Category: 11-15-23-25-29-33-39
        41-51-53-57-59-67-69
        71

Progressive Radio Network
Producer, Computer Program
P O Box 172
Bronx NY 10451
212-585-9400
Category: 23

Sheridan Broadcasting Network
James Hamlin, Editor
SBN News
411 Seventh Avenue #1500
Pittsburgh PA 15219
412-281-6756
Category: 17-25-19-33-49-55-59
        78
Format: L
Features: I-N-F-B

Texas State Agribusiness Network
Bob Cockrum, Associate Director
Gardener's Notebook
1080 Metromedia Place
Dallas TX 75247
214-688-1133
Category: 11(photography)-17-29
        41-43-51-61
Host: Bob Cockrum
Format: T
Features: I-F-B

Texas State Network
Mark Hallis, Producer
Financial/Business Review
1080 Metromedia Place
Dallas TX 75247
214-688-1133
Category: 19

Texas State Network
Tony Lawrence, Operations Manager
TSN Magazine
1080 Metromedia Place
Dallas TX 75247
214-688-1133
Category: 99
Host: Tony Lawrence
Format: T
Features: I-N-F-B

UPI Audio
Program Director
1400 Eye Street NW
Washington DC 20005
202-898-8120
Category: 23-67

UPI Radio Network
Bob Fuss, Bureau Manager
Reflection/View from the West
316 West 2nd Street 6th Floor
Los Angeles CA 90012
213-620-0977
Category: 10
Host: Bob Fuss
Format: T
Features: I-N-F

UPI Radio Network
Brian McFadden, Director
Reflections
220 East 42nd Street
New York NY 10017
212-850-8707
Category: 10
Format: T
Features: I-N-F

USRN Radio Network
1440 Broadway
New York NY 10018
212-575-6100
Category: 99

Voice of America
Program Director
330 Independence Avenue SW
Washington DC 20003
202-755-4754
Category: 99

Voice of America
Program Director
11000 Wilshire Boulevard #11221
Los Angeles CA 90024
213-209-7227
Category: 99

==

Format: L = Live   T = Taped   C = Live with Call-ins   P = Telephone Interviews

Features: I = Interviews   N = News   F = Features   B = Book Reviews   R = Book Readings

==

Radio Syndicates and Syndicated Shows

About Town/Focus
697 West End Avenue #6A
New York NY 10025
212-749-3647
Categories: 99

American Jewish Committee
Haina Just, Producer
Jewish Viewpoint
165 E 56th Street
New York NY 10022
212-751-4000
Categories: 11-17-27-31-35-73
63(Jewish)-59
Format: T
Features: I

American Jewish Committee
Haina Just, Producer
Present Tense
165 E 56th Street
New York NY 10022
212-751-4000
Categories: 13-17-55
98(mid-East affairs)
Format: T
Features: I

AMI Radio News
John Hamilton, Reporter
47 Kearney Street
San Francisco CA 94563
415-982-1441
Categories: 69-71
Format: T
Features: N-F-B

Author's Roundtable
Jim Pappas, Producer
20 West 37th Street 8th Floor
New York NY 10018
212-239-2000
Categories: 23-25-27-33-39-57-71
Host: Jim Pappas
Format: T
Features: I

Automotive Communication
Tech Talk
28450 Maitrott
Southfield MI 48034
313-358-2822
Categories: 43(automotive)

Better Business Bureau
Dianne M Skeltis, Director
Conversation for Consumers
1515 Wilson Boulevard #300
Arlington VA 22209
703-276-0100
Categories: 25-39-43-73
Host: Dianne M Skeltis
Format: T
Features: I-B

Books on Review
P O Box 5464
Richmond VA 23220
804-257-1260
Categories: 99

Books West
Sandra Dijkstra
1237 Camino Del Mar #515C
Del Mar CA 92104
619-755-3115
Categories: 98(issues)
Features: I

Bookshelf
Producer, Radio Show
135 Central Park West #5N
New York NY 10023
212-753-8151
Categories: 99

Broadcasting Foundation
International Science Report
P O Box 1805
Murray Hill Station
New York NY 10153
212-679-3388
Categories: 99

Bunchez & Associates
Mind Your Own Business
7730 Carondelet Street
St Louis MO 63105
314-862-5250
Categories: 19, 99

Business Week News
Producer, Radio Show
1221 Avenue of Americas
New York NY 10020
212-512-3280
Categories: 19

Computer Broadcasting Company
Ray Douglas, President
ComputerLine Radio Show
P O Box 21243
Minneapolis MN 55421
612-871-2608
Categories: 23
Host: Ray Douglas
Format: L-C-P
Features: I-N-F

Computer Connection Network
Sol Rosenberg, Producer
The Computer Connection
31 N Rigaud Road
Spring Valley NY 10977
914-425-3799
Categories: 23
Host: Sol Rosenberg, Pat Stanley
Format: T
Features: I-N-F-B

Computer Watch
1301 Pennsylvania Avenue NW #503
Washington DC 20004
202-393-6363
Categories: 23

Dow Jones
Barron's Investments
22 Cortlandt Street
New York NY 10007
212-285-8358
Categories: 19

Ethnic Press International News
Giorgio L Perna, Director
4710 Bethesda Avenue
Bethesda MD 20814-5219
301-986-1455
Categories: 11-17-27-41-45
55-71-78-80
Format: L-T
Features: I-N-F-B

Gamut's Living Archives
2 Spring Creek Road
Barrington IL 60010
312-381-3736
Categories: 99

Horn Book Radio Review
Amy Cohn, Producer
31 St James Avenue
Boston MA 02116
800-325-1170
Categories: 21-76
Host: Anita Silvey
Format: L-T
Features: I-F-B-R

Intermark Group
Book Ends
122 Park Avenue
New York NY 10708-1705
212-245-5098
Categories: 10
Host: Leslie Elish

Investors Club of the Air
Vera Gold, Director
KIEV-TV
P O Box 8039
Calabasas CA 91302
818-887-2347
Categories: 11-19(finance)-33-57
Host: Buz Schwartz
Format: L-C
Features: I-N-F

Jameson Broadcast
Online Computer Connection
P O Box 30964
Gahanna OH 43230
614-476-4424
Categories: 23-99

Joan Orth Syndicates
Joan Orth, Producer
Junior Book Beat
401 East 65th Street #145
New York NY 10021
212-734-9497
Categories: 21-76
Host: Joan Orth
Format: T
Features: I-B

Joan Orth Syndicates
Joan Orth, Producer
Business Topics by Joan Orth
401 East 65th Street #145
New York NY 10021
212-734-9497
Categories: 19-17-13-23-33-39
41-31-55-67
Host: Joan Orth
Format: T
Features: I-N-F-B

Joan Orth Syndicates
Joan Orth, Producer
Here Abouts with Joan Orth
401 East 65th Street #145
New York NY 10021
212-734-9497
Categories: 33-71
Host: Joan Orth
Format: T
Features: I-N-F-B

Joan Orth Syndicates
Joan Orth, Producer
Book Beat By Joan Orth
401 East 65th Street #145
New York NY 10021
212-734-9497
Categories: 99
Host: Joan Orth
Format: T
Features: I-B

John Austin's Hollywood Report
John Austin, Producer
KCRW-FM
P O Box 49957
Los Angeles CA 90049
714-678-6237
Categories: 11-17-33
Host: John Austin
Format: T-P
Features: I-N-B

Meredith Syndicate
Producer, Moneyline
550 Pharr Road
Atlanta GA 30363
404-261-2600
Categories: 19

More Than You Care to Know
John Austin, Producer
P O Box 49957
Los Angeles CA 90049
714-678-6237

Categories: 10
Host: John Austin
Format: T-L-P
Features: I-F-B

Narwood Productions
Producer, Minding Your Business
40 East 49th Street
New York NY 10017
212-755-3320
Categories: 19

Paul Harvey Show
360 N Michigan Avenue
Chicago IL 60601
312-750-7485
Categories: 99
Host: Paul Harvey

Radio America
Sarah Ban Breathnach, Editor
Mrs. Sharp's Traditions
906 Glaizewood Court
Tacoma Park MD 20912
301-270-0598
Categories: 21-31-35-76-89
Host: Sarah Ban Breathnach
Format: T-P
Features: F-B-R

Radio America
Sarah Ban Breathnach, Editor
Kaleidoscope
906 Glaizewood Court
Tacoma Park MD 20912
301-270-0598
Categories: 10-11-27-29-33-43-47
Host: Sarah Ban Breathnach
Format: T-P
Features: I-F-B

Radio New England
Barry Lunderville, Producer
Radio New England Magazine
75 Gardner Street
Hingham MA 02043
617-749-1304
Categories: 10
Host: Barry Lunderville
Format: T
Features: I

Radio Reader
Dick Estell, Book Review Editor
WKAR
MSU Communications Art Building
East Lansing MI 48824
517-355-2300
Categories: 17-33-41-47-69-71
77-81-83-87
Format: T
Features: B-R

Radio Works Inc
F London, Comptroller
Conozca a Las Estrellas
6363 Sunset Boulevard #520
Hollywood CA 90028

213-466-5128
Categories: 11-17-19-33-69
Latin celebrities and music
Host: Pepe Reyes
Format: T
Features: I

Radio Works Inc
Stacie Hunt
Some Kind of People
6363 Sunset #520
Hollywood CA 90028
213-466-5128
Categories: 99
Host: Stacie Hunt
Format: L-T-P
Features: I-N

Radio Works Inc
F London, Comptroller
Forbes Magazine Report
6363 Sunset Boulevard #520
Hollywood CA 90028
213-466-5128
Categories: 19
Features: N-I-F

Ralph Gardner's Bookshelf
Ralph Gardner, Producer
WVNJ
135 Central Park West
New York NY 10023
212-753-8151
Categories: 99
Host: Ralph Gardner
Format: T
Features: I-B

Rip 'N' Read News Service
Randy Alfred, Editor
88 First Street #302
San Francisco CA 94105
415-974-1622
Categories: 10
Format: P
Features: I-N-F-B

Sands Broadcast Productions
Alan Sands, President
Lively Arts
225 East 74th Street
New York NY 10021
212-697-6135
Categories: 11-17-19-27-29-33
39-47-57
Format: T
Features: F-B

Sands Broadcast Promotions
Alan Sands, President
Travel Talk
225 East 7th Street
New York NY 10021
212-697-6135
Categories: 71
Host: Alan Sands
Format: T
Features: F-B

Radio Syndicates and Syndicated Shows

SofTV Inc
Famous Computer Cafe
1322 Second Avenue
Santa Monica CA 90403
213-394-7242
Categories: 23

Strand Broadcast Services
Donna Lum, Producer
Something You Should Know
1117 11th Street #205
Manhattan Beach CA 90266
213-318-1666
Categories: 15-17-19-25-27-29-31
           33-35-39-43-55-57-69
           73-77-81-83-83
Host: Mike Carruthers
Format: T-P
Features: I

Talking Pictures
500 E Amado Drive
Palm Springs CA 92262
213-657-2024
Categories: 99

United Press International
Joe Fasbinder, Editor
Broadcast Book Corner
360 N Michigan Avenue
Chicago IL 60601
312-781-1632
Categories: 99
Host: Joe Fasbinder
Format: T
Features: B

US Chamber of Commerce
Producer, What's the Issue
1615 H Street NW
Washington DC 20001
202-659-6000
Categories: 19

Westwood One
Producer, Spaces and Places
9540 Washington Boulevard
Culver City CA 90230
213-204-5000
Categories: 99

Writing & Writers
Herman Kogan
Oak Lane
New Buffalo MI 49117
616-469-2360
Categories: 11-13-17-31-33-35
           39-41-47-49-55-61
           77-78-81-82
Host: Herman Kogan
Format: T
Features: N-B-R

WXYT/KMOX
Bill Cataldo, Producer
Autoshow/TechTalk
28450 Maitrott
Southfield MI 48034
313-582-2822
Categories: 19-23-29-43-65
Host: Howard Kenig
Format: L-C-P
Features: I-N-F-B

===

Format: L = Live   T = Taped   C = Live with Call-ins   P = Telephone Interviews

Features: I = Interviews   N = News   F = Features   B = Book Reviews   R = Book Readings

===

Radio Stations Sorted by State and City

ST	CITIES	RADIO STATIONS AND SHOWS
AK	Anchorage	KSKA
AK	Juneau	KTOO-FM
AL	Birmingham	WBHM
AL	Birmingham	WERC
AL	Birmingham	WSGN
AL	Birmingham	WZZK
AL	Huntsville	WAAY-AM
AL	Huntsville	WLRH
AL	Mobile	WKRG
AR	Hot Springs	KZNG
AR	Jonesboro	KASU-FM
AR	Little Rock	KARN-AM
AR	Little Rock	KLRE-FM
AZ	Mesa	KDKB
AZ	Mesa	KMCR-FM
AZ	Phoenix	KHEP
AZ	Phoenix	KOOL-AM/FM
AZ	Phoenix	KTAR
AZ	Phoenix	KXEG-AM
AZ	Tempe	KUPD/KUKQ
AZ	Tucson	KNST
AZ	Tucson	KTUC
AZ	Tucson	KUAT
CA	Anaheim	KEZY-AM
CA	Bakersfield	KLYD
CA	Bakersfield	KPMC-AM
CA	Berkeley	KBLX
CA	Berkeley	KMEL
CA	Berkeley	KPFA-FM
CA	Beverly Hills	KJOI
CA	Burbank	KLAC-AM/KZLA-FM
CA	Calabasas	Investors Club of the Air
CA	Chico	KCHO-FM
CA	Concord	KINQ
CA	Culver City	Westwood One
CA	Del Mar	Books West
CA	Fresno	KMJ-AM
CA	Fresno	KVPR
CA	Glendale	KIEV-AM
CA	Hayward	KFAX-AM
CA	Hollywood	KFAC
CA	Hollywood	KHJ
CA	Hollywood	KIIS
CA	Hollywood	KIQQ
CA	Hollywood	KKHR
CA	Hollywood	KMET
CA	Hollywood	Radio Works Inc
CA	La Mesa	KSON
CA	Long Beach	KLON
CA	Los Altos	KFJC-FM
CA	Los Angeles	AFRTS Programming Center
CA	Los Angeles	KABC-AM
CA	Los Angeles	KBIG
CA	Los Angeles	KBRT
CA	Los Angeles	KBZT
CA	Los Angeles	KCRW-FM
CA	Los Angeles	KFI-AM
CA	Los Angeles	KFWB
CA	Los Angeles	KGGO-FM
CA	Los Angeles	KIEV-FM
CA	Los Angeles	KKHR
CA	Los Angeles	KLOS-FM
CA	Los Angeles	KMGG
CA	Los Angeles	KMPC
CA	Los Angeles	KNX
CA	Los Angeles	KOST-FM
CA	Los Angeles	KRLA
CA	Los Angeles	KRTH
CA	Los Angeles	KUTE-FM
CA	Los Angeles	KXLU-FM
CA	Los Angeles	KZLA
CA	Los Angeles	National Public Radio
CA	Los Angeles	UPI Radio Network
CA	Los Angeles	Voice of America
CA	Manhattan Bch	Strand Broadcast Services
CA	N Hollywood	KPFK-FM
CA	Napa	KVON
CA	Northridge	KCSN
CA	Oakland	KFYI
CA	Oakland	KNEW
CA	Oakland	KSAN
CA	Palm Desert	KNWZ
CA	Palm Springs	KPSI-AM
CA	Palm Springs	Talking Pictures
CA	Pasadena	KMAX
CA	Pasadena	KPCC
CA	Pasadena	KROQ
CA	Redondo Beach	KFOX-FM
CA	Riverside	KPRO-AM
CA	Riverside	KUCR
CA	Sacramento	KENZ-AM/KSAC-FM
CA	Sacramento	KFBK-AM
CA	Sacramento	KGNR
CA	Sacramento	KXPR
CA	Sacramento	KZAP
CA	San Bernardino	KVCR
CA	San Diego	Copley Radio Network
CA	San Diego	KFMB
CA	San Diego	KFSD
CA	San Diego	KJQY
CA	San Diego	KOGO
CA	San Diego	KPBS-FM
CA	San Diego	KSDO-AM/FM
CA	San Diego	KYXY
CA	San Fernando	KGIL
CA	San Francisco	AMI Radio News
CA	San Francisco	KABL
CA	San Francisco	KALW-FM
CA	San Francisco	KCBS
CA	San Francisco	KDFC
Ca	San Francisco	KEST
CA	San Francisco	KFOG
CA	San Francisco	KFRC
CA	San Francisco	KGO
Ca	San Francisco	KIOI-AM/FM
CA	San Francisco	KKHI
CA	San Francisco	KNBR-AM
CA	San Francisco	KOIT AM/FM
CA	San Francisco	KPOO
CA	San Francisco	KQED-FM
CA	San Francisco	KRQR
CA	San Francisco	KSFO
CA	San Francisco	KUSF
CA	San Francisco	KXLR

Radio Stations Sorted by State and City

ST	CITIES	RADIO STATIONS AND SHOWS	ST	CITIES	RADIO STATIONS AND SHOWS
CA	San Francisco	KYA	FL	Boynton Beach	WHRS
CA	San Francisco	KYUU-FM	FL	Ft Myers	WCAI-AM
CA	San Francisco	Rip 'N' Read News	FL	Gainesville	WUFT
CA	San Jose	KBAY	FL	Hollywood	WHYI
CA	San Jose	KHTT	FL	Jacksonville	WAIV/WOKV
CA	SanLuisObispo	KCBX	FL	Jacksonville	WEXI-AM
CA	San Mateo	KCSM	FL	Jacksonville	WJCT
CA	Santa Barbara	KCSB-FM	FL	Jacksonville	WOKV
CA	Santa Barbara	KDB-AM	FL	Lakeland	WONN-AM
CA	Santa Barbara	KTMS	FL	Lakeland	WPCV
CA	Santa Monica	SofTV Inc	FL	Miami	WCMQ-AM/FM
CA	Santee	KBCQ	Fl	Miami	WGBS-AM
CA	S Lake Tahoe	KTHO-AM	FL	Miami	WINZ-AM/FM
CA	Stockton	KUOP	FL	Miami	WIOD
CA	Tulare	KCOK	FL	Miami	WLRN
CA	Ventura	KVEN	FL	Miami	WLYF
CA	Woodland	KSFM	FL	Miami	WNWS
CO	Boulder	KBVL-FM	FL	Miami	WTMI
CO	Colorado Sprgs	KVOR	FL	Miami Beach	WKAT
CO	Denver	KBPI	FL	Miami Beach	WMBM
CO	Denver	KCFR	FL	Naples	WNOG-AM
CO	Denver	KHOW	FL	Orlando	WKIS-AM
CO	Denver	KIMN	FL	Orlando	WMFE
CO	Denver	KNUS-AM	FL	Palm Beach	WPBR
CO	Denver	KOA	FL	Pensacola	WUWF
CO	Denver	KPOF	FL	Pinellas Park	WPLP
CO	Denver	KVOD	FL	Sarasota	WQSA
CO	Englewood	KDEN	FL	St Petersburg	WWBA
CO	Grand Junction	KREX-AM	FL	Tallahassee	WFSU
CT	Bloomfield	WDRC-FM	FL	Tallahassee	WTNT-AM
CT	Bridgeport	WDJZ-AM	FL	Tampa	WJYW
CT	Danbury	WLAD-AM	FL	Tampa	WRBQ
CT	Greenwich	WGCH	FL	Tampa	WUSF
CT	Hartford	WHCN	FL	W Palm Beach	WJNO Newsradio
CT	Hartford	WKSS	FL	Winter Park	WBJW-AM/FM
CT	Hartford	WNPR	GA	Athens	WUOG-FM
CT	Hartford	WPOP	GA	Atlanta	Cox Communicaations
CT	Hartford	WTIC-AM	GA	Atlanta	Georgia Network
CT	New Haven	WELI-AM	GA	Atlanta	Meredith Syndicate
CT	Waterbury	WATR-AM	GA	Atlanta	WAEC
DC	Washington	AB Newsamerica Satellite News	GA	Atlanta	WCNN
DC	Washington	ABC Radio	GA	Atlanta	WGKA
DC	Washington	AP Radio	GA	Atlanta	WGST-AM
DC	Washington	Associated Broadcast News	GA	Atlanta	WKLS
DC	Washington	CBS Radio Stations News	GA	Atlanta	WQXI
DC	Washington	Computer Watch	GA	Atlanta	WRFG-FM
DC	Washington	National Public Radio	GA	Atlanta	WSB
DC	Washington	NBC Radio	GA	Atlanta	WZGC
DC	Washington	UPI Audio	GA	Augusta	WAGC
DC	Washington	US Chamber of Commerce	GA	Columbus	WRCG-AM
DC	Washington	Voice of America	GA	Macon	WMAZ
DC	Washington	WAMU-FM	GA	Roswell	Georgia Radio Network
DC	Washington	WASH	GA	Savannah	WWAM
DC	Washington	WDCU-FM	GA	Savannah	WWSA/WCHY
DC	Washington	WETA/FM	HI	Honolulu	KGU
DC	Washington	WKYS-FM	HI	Honolulu	KHPR
DC	Washington	WMAL-AM	HI	Honolulu	KHVH
DC	Washington	WOOK	HI	Honolulu	KKUA
DC	Washington	WPFW	HI	Honolulu	KNDI-AM
DC	Washington	WPGC/WCLY	HI	Honolulu	KTUH
DC	Washington	WRC	IA	Ames	WOI
DC	Washington	WRQX	IA	Burlington	KBUR
DC	Washington	WTKS	IA	Cedar Falls	KUNI
DC	Washington	WTOP-AM	IA	Cedar Rapids	KCCK
DC	Washington	WWDC-FM	IA	Davenport	WOC
DE	Wilmington	WILM-AM	IA	Des Moines	KDPS-FM

Radio Stations Sorted by State and City

ST	CITIES	RADIO STATIONS AND SHOWS	ST	CITIES	RADIO STATIONS AND SHOWS
IA	Des Moines	WHO-AM	KY	Louisville	WFPL
IA	Dubuque	KDTH	KY	Louisville	WHAS
IA	Iowa City	WSUI	KY	Louisville	WUOL
ID	Boise	KTOX	LA	Lafayette	KPEL-AM
IL	Aurora	WKKD-AM/FM	LA	Lake Charles	KAOK
IL	Aurora	WMRO	LA	New Orleans	WEZB-FM
IL	Barrington	Gamut's Living Archives	LA	New Orleans	WQUE-FM
IL	Bloomington	WJBC	LA	New Orleans	WSMB-AM
IL	Carbondale	WSIU	LA	New Orleans	WTIX
IL	Champaign	WDWS	LA	New Orleans	WWL-AM
IL	Chicago	Paul Harvey Show	LA	New Orleans	WWNO-FM
IL	Chicago	United Press International	MA	Amherst	WFCR
IL	Chicago	UPI Audio	MA	Attleboro	WARA
IL	Chicago	WBBM-AM	MA	Boston	Horn Book Radio Review
IL	Chicago	WBEZ	MA	Boston	WBCN-FM
IL	Chicago	WCZE/WLOO	MA	Boston	WBSM
IL	Chicago	WFMT	MA	Boston	WBUR
IL	Chicago	WFYR-FM	MA	Boston	WBZ
IL	Chicago	WGCI-FM	MA	Boston	WCOZ-FM
IL	Chicago	WGN-Radio	MA	Boston	WCRB
IL	Chicago	WIND	MA	Boston	WEEI-AM
IL	Chicago	WJMK-FM	MA	Boston	WGBH
IL	Chicago	WKQX-FM	MA	Boston	WHDH-AM
IL	Chicago	WLAK-FM	MA	Boston	WHJJ
IL	Chicago	WLS	MA	Boston	WHTT
IL	Chicago	WMAQ-AM	MA	Boston	WHUE-AM
IL	Chicago	WXRT	MA	Boston	WJIB
IL	Chicago Hghts	WCGO	MA	Boston	WMJX
IL	Crystal Lake	WIVS	MA	Boston	WMRE
IL	Evanston	WCFL	MA	Boston	WRKO
IL	Joliet	WJOL	MA	Boston	WROL
IL	Lansing	WLNR	MA	Boston	WROR
IL	Oak Park	WOPA	MA	Brockton	WBET
IL	Peoria	WCBU	MA	Cambridge	WHRB-FM
IL	Quincy	WTAD	MA	Cambridge	WMBR-FM
IL	Rock Island	WVIK	MA	Fall River	WSAR
IL	Skokie	WCLR-FM	MA	Framingham	WKOX
IL	Springfield	WSSR	MA	Gloucester	WVCA
IL	Springfield	WTAX/WDBR	MA	Hingham	Radio New England
IL	Urbana	WILL	MA	Holyoke	WREB-930 AM
IL	Waukegan	WKRS	MA	Lynn	WFNX-FM
IN	Bloomington	WFIU	MA	Medford	WMFO-FM
IN	Evansville	WSWI	MA	Natick	WTTP
IN	Ft Wayne	WOWO-AM	MA	New Bedford	WBSM
IN	Gary	WGVE	MA	Newton	WNTN
IN	Indianapolis	WAJC	MA	Norfolk	WJCC
IN	Indianapolis	WFMS-FM	MA	Pittsfield	WBEC
IN	Indianapolis	WIAN	MA	Springfield	WHYN-AM
IN	Indianapolis	WIBC	MA	Springfield	WTCC-FM
IN	Muncie	WBST	MA	Taunton	WPEP
IN	South Bend	WAMJ-AM	MA	Worcester	WICN Public Radio
KS	Fairway	KCMO	MD	Baltimore	WBAL
KS	Hutchison	KHCC	MD	Baltimore	WBJC
KS	Hutchison	KWBW	MD	Baltimore	WBSB
KS	Kansas City	KCNW	MD	Baltimore	WEAA
KS	Kansas City	KXTR	MD	Baltimore	WFBR
KS	Lawrence	KANU-FM	MD	Baltimore	WMAR-FM
KS	Mission	KBEA	MD	Baltimore	WPOC-FM
KS	Shawnee Msn	KMBZ-AM	MD	Baltimore	WYST
KS	Topeka	WREN	MD	Bethesda	Ethnic Press International
KS	Wichita	KFDI	MD	Hagerstown	WHAG
KS	Wichita	KFH	MD	Owings Mill	WCBM-AM
KS	Wichita	KMUW	MD	Rockville	WGMS
KS	Wichita	Mid-America Networks	MD	Rockville	WLTT-FM
KY	Bowling Green	WKYU-FM	MD	Salisbury	WSBY-AM
KY	Lexington	WBKY	MD	Silver Spring	WGAY

Radio Stations Sorted by State and City

ST	CITIES	RADIO STATIONS AND SHOWS
MD	Tacoma Park	Radio America
MD	Takoma Park	WGTS
ME	Bangor	Maine Public Broadcasting
ME	Orono	WPBN
ME	Scarborough	WDCS-FM
MI	Ann Arbor	WAAM-AM
MI	Ann Arbor	WUOM
MI	Battle Creek	WBCK-AM
MI	Dearborn	WNIC
MI	Detroit	WABX
MI	Detroit	WCXI
MI	Detroit	WCZY-FM
MI	Detroit	WDET-FM
MI	Detroit	WDTR
MI	Detroit	WHYT
MI	Detroit	WJR Radio
MI	Detroit	WLLZ-FM
MI	Detroit	WMJC-WHND
MI	Detroit	WMUZ
MI	Detroit	WOMC-FM
MI	Detroit	WQRS
MI	Detroit	WWWW-FM
MI	East Lansing	Radio Reader
MI	Flint	WFBE
MI	Grand Rapids	WCSG
MI	Grand Rapids	WLAV
MI	Grand Rapids	WOOD
MI	Jackson	WKHM
MI	Kalamazoo	WKZO
MI	Kalamazoo	WMUK-FM
MI	Marquette	WDMJ-AM
MI	New Buffalo	Writing & Writers
MI	Saginaw	WSGW
MI	Southfield	Automotive Communication
MI	Southfield	WDRQ
MI	Southfield	WJOI
MI	Southfield	WRIF-FM
MI	Southfield	WWJ-AM
MI	Southfield	WXYT/KMOX
MN	Duluth	KUMD
MN	Golden Valley	KUXL
MN	Maplewood	KSTP-AM
MN	Maplewood	WMIN
MN	Minneapolis	Computer Broadcasting Company
MN	Minneapolis	KQRS FM/AM
MN	Minneapolis	KS-95-FM
MN	Minneapolis	KUOM-AM
MN	Minneapolis	WCCO
MN	Minneapolis	WDGY
MN	Minneapolis	WLOL
MN	Roseville	KTIS
MN	St Paul	KDWB
MN	St Paul	KSJN
MN	St Paul	Minnesota Public Radio
MN	Wilmar	Linder Farm Network
MO	Columbia	KBIA
MO	Jefferson City	Missouri Network
MO	Kansas City	KBEQ-FM
MO	Kansas City	KCUR
MO	Kansas City	WDAF
MO	Kansas City	WHB
MO	Moberly	KWIX
MO	St Louis	Bunchez & Associates
MO	St Louis	KADI
MO	St Louis	KATZ
MO	St Louis	KFUO
MO	St Louis	KHTR
MO	St Louis	KMOX-AM
MO	St Louis	KSD
MO	St Louis	KSHE-FM
MO	St Louis	KSLH
MO	St Louis	KWK
MO	St Louis	KWMU-FM
MO	St Louis	KXOK-AM
MO	St Louis	WIL
MO	St Louis	WRTH
MO	St Louis	KWMU
MS	Jackson	WJDX
MT	Missoula	KVFM
NC	Chapel Hill	WUNC
NC	Charlotte	WBT
NC	Charlotte	WEZC-FM
NC	Charlotte	WFAE
NC	Charlotte	WROQ-FM
NC	Charlotte	WSOC
NC	Durham	Africa News Service
NC	Durham	WDBS-FM
NC	Greensboro	WKSI
NC	Greensville	WNCT-AM
NC	Raleigh	WPTF-AM
NC	Raleigh	WQDR-FM
NC	Raleigh	WRAL
NC	Wake Forest	WCPE
NC	Winston-Salem	WFDD
NC	Winston-Salem	WSJS/WTQR
ND	Fargo	KDSU
ND	Grand Forks	KFJM
NE	Lincoln	KFOR
NE	Lincoln	KUCV
NE	Omaha	KEZO
NE	Omaha	KFAB-AM
NE	Omaha	KIOS
NE	Omaha	KVNO
NE	Omaha	KYNN
NH	Concord	Books with Eric Griffel
NH	Concord	WKXL
NH	Durham	WUNH-FM
NH	Hanover	WFRD-FM
NH	Manchester	WGIR
NJ	Asbury Park	WJLK-AM
NJ	Atlantic City	WIIN-AM
NJ	Camden	WSSJ
NJ	Clifton	WPAT
NJ	East Orange	WFMU
NJ	Morristown	WMTR
NJ	New Brunswick	WCTC
NJ	New Brunswick	WRSU
NJ	Newark	WBGO-FM
NJ	Plainfield	WERA
NJ	Princeton	WPRB
NJ	Teaneck	WFDU
NJ	Trenton	WWFM
NJ	West Orange	WFME-FM
NM	Albuquerque	KHFM
NM	Albuquerque	KKJY-FM
NM	Albuquerque	KOB
NM	Albuquerque	KUNM
NM	Albuquerque	KZIA
NM	Las Cruces	KRWG
NM	Santa Fe	KVSF
NV	Henderson	KVOV
NV	Las Vegas	KDWN

Radio Stations Sorted by State and City

ST	CITIES	RADIO STATIONS AND SHOWS	ST	CITIES	RADIO STATIONS AND SHOWS
NV	Las Vegas	KLUC/KMJJ	NY	New York	WPLJ-FM
NV	Las Vegas	KNPR	NY	New York	WQXR
NV	Las Vegas	KNUU (K-NEWS Radio)	NY	New York	WQXT-AM/FM
NV	Las Vegas	KOMP-FM/KENO-AM	NY	New York	WRKS-FM
NV	Reno	KOH-AM	NY	New York	WXRK
NY	Albany	WAMC	NY	New York	WYNY
NY	Albany	WQBK	NY	Patchogue	WALK
NY	Babylon	WGLI-AM	NY	Pomona	WRKL
NY	Binghamton	WSKG-FM	NY	Rochester	WBBF
NY	Bronx	Progressive Radio Network	NY	Rochester	WEZO-FM
NY	Bronx	WFUV-FM	NY	Rochester	WHFM
NY	Buffalo	WBEN	NY	Rochester	WRUR
NY	Buffalo	WBFO	NY	Rochester	WXXI-FM
NY	Buffalo	WEBR	NY	Schenectady	WGY
NY	Buffalo	WGR/WRLT	NY	Schenectady	WMHT
NY	Buffalo	WNED	NY	Schenectady	WPYX
NY	Buffalo	WNYS	NY	Schenectady	WTRY-AM
NY	Glenmont	WWCN	NY	Spring Valley	Computer Connection Network
NY	Kingston	WGHQ	NY	Staten Island	WNYM
NY	Mount Kisco	WVIP	NY	Stony Brook	WUSB-FM
NY	New Rochelle	WRTN-FM	NY	Syracuse	WAER-FM
NY	New Rochelle	WVOX-AM	NY	Syracuse	WCNY
NY	New York	ABC Info Radio	NY	Syracuse	WHEN
NY	New York	ABC Radio Network News	NY	Syracuse	WSYR/WYYY
NY	New York	ABC Rock Radio	NY	Utica	WIBX
NY	New York	About Town/Focus	NY	Utica	WTLB
NY	New York	American Jewish Committee	NY	White Plains	WFAS
NY	New York	AP Radio	NY	White Plains	WNAB
NY	New York	Author's Roundtable	NY	Woodside	WKHK
NY	New York	Bookshelf	OH	Akron	WAKR
NY	New York	Broadcasting Foundation	OH	Akron	WHLO
NY	New York	Business Week News	OH	Athens	WOUB
NY	New York	CBS Radio	OH	Bellaire	WOMP-AM
NY	New York	Dow Jones	OH	Cincinnati	WCKY
NY	New York	Group W	OH	Cincinnati	WEBN
NY	New York	Intermark Group	OH	Cincinnati	WGUC
NY	New York	Joan Orth Syndicates	OH	Cincinnati	WKRC-AM
NY	New York	Mutual Broadcasting System	OH	Cincinnati	WKRQ-FM
NY	New York	Narwood Productions	OH	Cincinnati	WLW
NY	New York	National Broadcasting Company	OH	Cincinnati	WVXU
NY	New York	National Public Radio	OH	Cleveland	WBBG
NY	New York	NBC Radio	OH	Cleveland	WCLV
NY	New York	NBC Talknet	OH	Cleveland	WCPN
NY	New York	Progressive Radio Network	OH	Cleveland	WDOK
NY	New York	Ralph Gardner's Bookshelf	OH	Cleveland	WERE-AM
NY	New York	Sands Broadcast Promotions	OH	Cleveland	WGAR
NY	New York	UPI Radio Network	OH	Cleveland	WGCL-FM
NY	New York	USRN Radio Network	OH	Cleveland	WJW-AM
NY	New York	WABC	OH	Cleveland	WLGF-FM
NY	New York	WBAI-FM	OH	Cleveland	WLTF-FM/WRMR-AM
NY	New York	WBLS	OH	Cleveland	WMJI-FM
NY	New York	WCBS	OH	Cleveland	WMMS
NY	New York	WEVD	OH	Cleveland	WQAL
NY	New York	WHN	OH	Cleveland	WUJC
NY	New York	WINS	OH	Cleveland	WWWE
NY	New York	WKCR	OH	Cleveland Hgts	WJMO
NY	New York	WLIB	OH	Cleveland Hgts	WRQC-FM
NY	New York	WLTW-FM	OH	Columbus	WCBE-FM
NY	New York	WMCA-AM	OH	Columbus	WLVQ-FM
NY	New York	WNBC Radio	OH	Columbus	WNCI
NY	New York	WNCN	OH	Columbus	WOSU
NY	New York	WNEW-FM	OH	Columbus	WTVN-AM
NY	New York	WNWK-FM	OH	Dayton	WHIO
NY	New York	WNYC-FM	OH	Dayton	WING
NY	New York	WOR Radio	OH	Gahanna	Jameson Broadcast
NY	New York	WPIX-FM	OH	Kent	WKSU-FM

ST	CITIES	RADIO STATIONS AND SHOWS
OH	Kent	WNIR-FM
OH	Toledo	WGTE
OH	Toledo	WSPD-AM
OH	Willoughby	WELW
OH	Youngstown	WBBW
OH	Youngstown	WKBN
OK	Norman	KGOU
OK	Okla City	KOMA
OK	Oklahoma City	KEBC
OK	Oklahoma City	KMGL
OK	Oklahoma City	KTOK
OK	Stillwater	KOSU
OK	Tulsa	KMOD/KBBT
OK	Tulsa	KRAV-FM
OK	Tulsa	KRMG
OK	Tulsa	KTFX
OK	Tulsa	KTOW
OK	Tulsa	KVOO
OK	Tulsa	KWEN
OK	Tulsa	KXXO
OK	Tulsa	WFMT-FM
OR	Clackamas	KGON-FM
OR	Corvallis	KOAC
OR	Eugene	KLCC-FM
OR	Eugene	KUGN
OR	Eugene	KWAX
OR	Portland	KBOO
OR	Portland	KBPS-AM/FM
OR	Portland	KEX 1190
OR	Portland	KGW-AM
OR	Portland	KINK
OR	Portland	KKEY-AM
OR	Portland	KLIQ-AM
OR	Portland	KOAP
OR	Portland	KPDQ-FM Radio
OR	Portland	KUPL
OR	Portland	KXL
OR	Portland	KYXI-AM
PA	Allentown	WXKW
PA	Altoona	WRTA Radio
PA	Avoca	WARM
PA	Bala Cynwyd	WEAZ
PA	Bala Cynwyd	WIOQ, Philadelphia
PA	Bala Cynwyd	WMGK
PA	Bala Cynwyd	WPEN
PA	Bala Cynwyd	WSNI-FM
PA	Bala Cynwyd	WWSH
PA	Bala Cynwyd	WYSP
PA	Beaver Falls	WBVP-AM
PA	Bethlehem	WZZO
PA	Duquesne	WDVQ
PA	Easton	WEST
PA	Erie	WCCK
PA	Erie	WQLN
PA	Harrisburg	WITF
PA	Harrisburg	WMSP-FM
PA	Lebanon	WVLV
PA	Levittown	WBCB
PA	New Kensington	WYDD
PA	Philadelphia	KYW
PA	Philadelphia	WCAU-AM
PA	Philadelphia	WDAS
PA	Philadelphia	WDVT-AM
PA	Philadelphia	WFIL
PA	Philadelphia	WFLN
PA	Philadelphia	WHYY-FM
PA	Philadelphia	WIP
PA	Philadelphia	WMMR-FM
PA	Philadelphia	WUHY
PA	Philadelphia	WUSL-FM
PA	Philadelphia	WWDB-FM
PA	Philadelphia	WXPN
PA	Pittsburgh	KDKA
PA	Pittsburgh	KQV
PA	Pittsburgh	Sheridan Broadcasting Network
PA	Pittsburgh	WBZZ
PA	Pittsburgh	WDUQ
PA	Pittsburgh	WDVE
PA	Pittsburgh	WHTX
PA	Pittsburgh	WPNT
PA	Pittsburgh	WQED-FM
PA	Pittsburgh	WSHH
PA	Pittsburgh	WTAE
PA	Pittsburgh	WTKN
PA	Pittston	WVIA
PA	Wilkes Barre	WKRZ
PA	Wilkes Barre	WRKC
PA	York	WSBA-AM
RI	E Providence	WPRO
RI	Newport	WADK
RI	Providence	WEAN
RI	Westerly	WERI
SC	Columbia	WCOS
SC	Columbia	WIS-AM
SC	Columbia	WLTR/WEPR
SC	Columbia	WNSC
SC	Greenville	WFBC-FM
SC	Mt Pleasant	WSCI
SC	N Charleston	WKCN-AM
SD	Brookings	KESD
SD	Sioux Falls	KXRB
SD	Vermillion	KUSD
TN	Chattanooga	WMBW
TN	Chattanooga	WMOC
TN	Chattanooga	WUTC
TN	Knoxville	WIVK
TN	Knoxville	WKGN
TN	Knoxville	WUOT
TN	Memphis	WHBQ-AM
TN	Memphis	WKNO
TN	Memphis	WMC-FM
TN	Memphis	WREC
TN	Memphis	WWEE-AM
TN	Murfreesboro	WMOT-FM
TN	Nashville	WKDA
TN	Nashville	WLAC Radio
TN	Nashville	WPLN-FM
TN	Nashville	WSM
TN	Newport	WLIK
TN	Oak Ridge	WOKI-FM
TX	Arlington	KEGL
TX	Arlington	KLIF
TX	Arlington	KWJS
TX	Austin	KLBJ-AM
TX	Austin	KMFA
TX	Austin	KUT
TX	Beaumont	KVLU
TX	College Stn	KAMU

Radio Stations Sorted by State and City

ST	CITIES	RADIO STATIONS AND SHOWS
TX	Dallas	KAFM
TX	Dallas	KERA
TX	Dallas	KLVU
TX	Dallas	KRLD News Radio
TX	Dallas	KTXQ
TX	Dallas	KVIL
TX	Dallas	KZEW
TX	Dallas	KZPS
TX	Dallas	Texas State Agribusiness
TX	Dallas	Texas State Network
TX	Dallas	WRR
TX	El Paso	KTEP
TX	El Paso	KTSM
TX	Ft Worth	WBAP
TX	Houston	KCOH
TX	Houston	KFMK
TX	Houston	KIKK
TX	Houston	KILT-FM
TX	Houston	KKBQ
TX	Houston	KLEF
TX	Houston	KLOL
TX	Houston	KLTR
TX	Houston	KMJQ
TX	Houston	KODA
TX	Houston	KPFT
TX	Houston	KPRC
TX	Houston	KRBE-AM
TX	Houston	KSRR-FM
TX	Houston	KTRH-AM
TX	Houston	KUHF
TX	Kelly AFB	Armed Forces Radio
TX	Odessa	KRIG-AM
TX	San Antonio	KISS
TX	San Antonio	KKYX
TX	San Antonio	KPAC
TX	San Antonio	KTSA
TX	San Antonio	KTSA
TX	San Antonio	WOAI-AM
UT	Logan	KUSU-FM
UT	Salt Lake	KDYL
UT	Salt Lake	KRSP
UT	Salt Lake	KSL
UT	Salt Lake	KUER
UT	Salt Lake	KZJO
UT	Salt Lake City	KLUB
UT	Salt Lake City	KWHO
VA	Arlington	American Forces Information
VA	Arlington	Better Business Bureau
VA	Arlington	Mutual Radio Network
VA	Charlottesville	WINA/WQMC
VA	Lynchburg	WLGM
VA	Norfolk	WFOG
VA	Norfolk	WHRO
VA	Norfolk	WLTY-FM
VA	Norfolk	WNIS
VA	Norfolk	WNOR
VA	Norfolk	WTAR-AM
VA	Richmond	Books on Review
VA	Richmond	WANT
VA	Richmond	WKIE
VA	Richmond	WNWZ
VA	Richmond	WRFK
VA	Richmond	WRNL

ST	CITIES	RADIO STATIONS AND SHOWS
VA	Richmond	WRVA
VA	Richmond	WRVQ-FM
VA	Richmond	WRXL
VA	Roanoke	WFIR-AM
VA	Roanoke	WVTF
VA	Virginia Beach	WCMS-FM
VA	Virginia Beach	WMYK/WZAM
VT	Burlington	WRUV
WA	Bellingham	KGMI
WA	Bellingham	KUGS-FM
WA	Seattle	KEZX
WA	Seattle	KING
WA	Seattle	KIRO
WA	Seattle	KISW
WA	Seattle	KJR
WA	Seattle	KOMO
WA	Seattle	KSEA
WA	Seattle	KUOW
WA	Seattle	KVI
WA	Seattle	KZOK
WA	Spokane	KPBX
WA	Spokane	KRSS-AM
WA	Spokane	KXLY
WA	Tacoma	KAMT
WA	Tacoma	KPLU
WI	Appleton	WHBY
WI	Green Bay	WIXX
WI	La Crosse	WLSU
WI	Madison	WIBA
WI	Madison	WZEE-FM
WI	Milwaukee	WEZW
WI	Milwaukee	WISN
WI	Milwaukee	WKTI
WI	Milwaukee	WQFM
WI	Milwaukee	WTMJ
WI	Milwaukee	WUWM
WI	Milwaukee	WYMS
WI	Waukesha	WAUK
WI	West Bend	WBKV
WV	Charleston	WCHS
WV	Charleston	WVAF
WV	Charleston	WVPN
WV	Huntington	WKEE-FM
WY	Cheyenne	KRAE
WY	Laramie	KUWR

CANADA

ST	CITIES	RADIO STATIONS AND SHOWS
BC	Vancouver	CHQM
MB	Winnipeg	CKY/CITI
ON	Toronto	CJCL
ON	Toronto	CKEY
ON	Toronto	CBL
ON	Toronto	CHUM
ON	Toronto	CKFM
ON	Toronto	CFRB
ON	Toronto	CKO Network
ON	Toronto	CFTR
ON	Toronto	CHFI
PQ	Montreal	CFCF
PQ	Montreal	CJAD
PQ	Montreal	CFCF
PQ	Westmount	CHOM

Local Television Stations and Shows

ALABAMA

WBIQ-TV
2101 Magnolia Avenue
Birmingham AL 35256
205-328-8756
Category: 99

WBMG-TV
Hoyle Broome Jr, General Manager
P O Box 6146
Birmingham AL 35209
205-322-4200
Category: 99

WBRC-TV
Nick Bolton, General Manager
Tom York Morning Show
P O Box 6
Birmingham AL 35201
205-322-6666
Category: 99
Host: Tom York

WVTM-TV
P O Box 10502
Birmingham AL 35202
205-933-2720
Category: 99

ALASKA

Channel 2 Broadcasting Company
P O Box 2880
Anchorage AK 99510
907-279-7477
Category: 99

ARIZONA

KPHO-TV
4016 N Black Canyon
Phoenix AZ 85017
602-264-1000
Category: 99

KPNX-TV
1101 N Central Avenue
P O Box 711
Phoenix AZ 85001
602-257-1212
Category: 99

KTSP-TV
511 W Adams
Phoenix AZ 85003
602-257-1234
Category: 99

KTVK-TV
3435 N 16th Street
Phoenix AZ 85016
602-266-5691
Category: 99

KAET-TV
Arizona State University
Tempe AZ 85281
602-965-3506
Category: 99

ARKANSAS

KETS-TV
350 S Donaghey
Conway AR 72032
501-329-3887
Category: 99

KARK-TV
201 W 3rd Street
Little Rock AR 72203
501-376-2481
Category: 99

KATV-TV
Eric Nelson, News Director
P O Box 77
Little Rock AR 72203
501-721-8372
Category: 99

KTHV-TV
P O Box 269
Little Rock AR 72203
501-376-1111
Category: 99

CALIFORNIA

KNOC, Group W
Mary Ellen Ritz, Librarian
Book Talk
7150 La Palma Avenue
Buena Park CA 90620
714-826-4100
Category: 99
Host: Mary Ellen Ritz
Format: T (cable TV)
Features: I-B

KNBC-TV
Tom Capra, News Director
3000 W Alameda
Burbank CA 91523
213-840-4444
Category: 99

KNBC-TV
Beth MacKenzie, Producer
Odyssey
3000 W Alameda
Burbank CA 91523
213-840-3388
Category: 63

KIEM-TV
5650 S Broadway
Eureka CA 95501
707-443-3123
Category: 99

KVIQ-TV
P O Box 1019
Eureka CA 95501
707-443-3061
Category: 99

KABC-TV
Terry Crofoot, News Director
Sherry A Weinman, Producer
4151 Prospect
Hollywood CA 90027
213-557-7777
Category: 99

KCBS-TV
Erik Sorenson, News Director
Joseph Dyer, Community Affairs
Joel Tator, 2 on the Town
6121 Sunset Boulevard
Hollywood CA 90028
213-460-3691
Category: 99

KCOP-TV
Ed Coghlan, News Director
915 N LaBrea Avenue
Hollywood CA 90038
213-851-1000
Category: 99

KHJ-TV
Willie Olmstead, Producer
Midmorning LA
5515 Melrose Avenue
Hollywood CA 90038
213-467-5459
Category: 99

KTLA-TV
Akila Gibbs, Consumer Affairs
5800 Sunset Boulevard
Hollywood CA 90028
213-460-5500
Category: 25

===

Format: L = Live;   T = Taped;   C = Live with call-ins;   P = Telephone interviews

Features: I = Interviews;   N = News;   F = Features;   B = Book reviews;   R = Readings from books

KTTV-TV
Don Tillman, Program Director
5746 Sunset Boulevard
Hollywood CA 90028
213-462-7111
Category: 99

KOCE-TV
P O Box 2476
Huntington Beach CA 92647
714-897-0302
Category: 99

KCET-TV
Tom Thompson, News Director
4401 Sunset Boulevard
Los Angeles CA 90027
213-666-6500
Category: 99

KWHY
Dick Spangler, Producer
Focus on Business
5545 Sunset Boulevard
Los Angeles CA 90028
213-466-5441
Category: 19

KTVU-TV
2 Jack London Square
Oakland CA 94623
415-834-1212
Category: 99

Money, Money, Money
Hal Morris
175 S Las Robles Avenue
Pasadena CA 91101
818-577-7444
Category: 19-25

KCRA-TV
Bill George, News Editor
Noon News
310 10th Street
Sacramento CA 95814
916-444-7316
Category: 99
Host: Mike Boyd
Format: L
Features: I-N-F-B

KOVR-TV
John VanOuwerkerk
Ask a Woman
1216 Arden Way
Sacramento CA 95815
916-927-1313
Category: 73
Format: T
Features: I-N

KOVR-TV
Michael Espinoza, Producer
Newswatch 13 at Noon
1216 Arden Way
Sacramento CA 95815
916-927-1313

Category: 99
Host: Don Wood & Jack Kavanaugh
Format: L-T
Features: I-N-F-B

KVIE-TV
P O Box 6
Sacramento CA 95801
916-929-5843
Category: 99

KXTV-TV
Jean LaMotte, Director
A New Morning
400 Broadway
Sacramento CA 95818
916-441-2345
Category: 99
Host: Jean LaMotte
Format: T
Features: I-F-B

KXTV-TV
Jean LaMotte, Director
Inside San Joaquin County
400 Broadway
Sacramento CA 95818
916-441-2345
Category: 61(CA)-99
Host: Jean LaMotte
Format: T
Features: I

KVCR-TV
Al Gondos, Producer
Dialogues
701 S Mount Vernon Avenue
San Bernardino CA 92410
714-888-6511
Category: 61(CA)-99
Host: Nancy Sidha & Chuck Palmer
Format: T
Features: I-F-B

KCST-TV
Ken Nelson, News Director
8330 Engineer Road
San Diego CA 92111
619-279-3939
Category: 99

KFMB-TV
News Director
Producer, Between the Lines
7677 Engineer Road
San Diego CA 92111
619-571-8888
Category: 99

KGTV-TV
Paul Sands, News Director
P O Box 85347
San Diego CA 92102
619-237-1010
Category: 99

KPBS-TV
San Diego State University

San Diego CA 92182
619-286-6415
Category: 99

KBHK-TV
News Director
Mary Lou Manalli, Weekday
420 Taylor Street
San Francisco CA 94102
415-885-3750
Category: 99
Host: Mary Lou Manalli

KGO-TV
Meg Conboy, Producer
AM San Francisco
900 Front Street
San Francisco CA 94111
415-954-7909
Category: 13-17-25-27-29-31-33
          35-37-39-43-53-57-69
          71-73
Host: Terry Lowry & Fred LaCosse
Format: L-T-C
Features: I-N-F-B-k

KGO-TV
Sylvia Ramirez, Producer
AM Weekend
900 Front Street
San Francisco CA 94111
415-954-7822
Category: 25-31-35-37-39-49
          55-57-73
Host: Sylvia Ramirez and
       Ray Taliaferro
Format: T
Features: I-N-F

KPIX-TV
Francee Covington, Producer
Pacific Currents
855 Battery Street
San Francisco CA 94111
415-765-8812
Category: 99
They do not handle book authors.

KPIX-TV
Linda Snyder, Producer
Noon News
855 Battery Street
San Francisco CA 94111
415-765-8688
Category: 99
Host: D Jackson and B Rodgers
Format: L
Features: I-N-F

KPIX-TV
Melanie Chilek
Evening Magazine
855 Battery Street
San Francisco CA 94111
415-765-8688
Category: 33-69
Format: T
Features: I-F

Local Television Stations and Shows

KQED-TV
Michael Tobias, Science Notes
500 8th Street
San Francisco CA 94103
415-864-2000
Category: 23-67-99

KRON-TV
Stephanie Noonan
Bay City Limits
1001 Van Ness Avenue
San Francisco CA 94109
415-441-4444
Category: 99

KICU-TV
1585 Schallenberger Road
San Jose CA 95131
408-298-3636
Category: 99

KCSM-TV
Sara O'Brien, Producer
Computer Chronicles
1700 W Hillsdale Boulevard
San Mateo CA 94402
415-574-6233
Category: 23-99

KTBN-TV
Vicki Davenpor, Joy
P O Box A
Santa Ana CA 92711
714-832-2950
Category: 63(Christian)

COLORADO

KBTV-TV
1089 Bannock Street
Denver CO 80204
303-825-5288
Category: 99

KCNC-TV
Marv Rockford, News Director
Roger L Odgen, General Manager
  Open Stage
1033 Lincoln Street
Denver CO 80203
303-861-4444
Category: 99

KMGH-TV
123 Speer Boulevard
Denver CO 80203
303-832-7777
Category: 99

KRMA-TV
Kaye Lavine
Conversations With...
1261 Glenarm Place
Denver CO 80204
303-892-6666
Category: 11-17-25-53-33-61(CO)
Format: T (Begins October 1986)
Features: I

KRMA-TV
Bob Bows
Senior Showcase
1261 Glenarm Place
Denver CO 80204
303-892-6666
Category: 29-35(retirement)
          39-55-57
Host: John Rayburn
Format: T
Features: I-F

KRMA-TV
Ronald K Salak, Program Director
1261 Glenarm Place
Denver CO 80204
303-892-6666
Category: 99

KUSA-TV
1089 Bannock Street
Denver CO 80217
303-893-4499
Category: 99

CONNECTICUT

WEDW-TV
N Benson Road
Fairfield CT 06430
203-255-4446
Category: 99

WEDH-TV
24 Summit Street
Hartford CT 06106
213-278-5310
Category: 99

WFSB-TV
3 Constitution Plaza
Hartford CT 06115
203-525-0801
Category: 99

WTNH-TV
Steve Sabato, News Producer
First Edition
8 Elm Street
New Haven CT 06508
203-787-3042
Category: 11-15-25-27-29-33-35
          43-51-53-55-69-71-73
Host: Diane Smith and Mark Davis
Format: L
Features: I-N-F

WVIT-TV
Carmen T Cordova, Director
Adelante
1422 New Britain Avenue
West Hartford CT 06110
203-521-3030
Category: 11-13-19-25-29-31-35
          37-41-45(Spanish)-49
          55-98(Latin American)
Format: T
Features: I-F

WVIT-TV
Anita Forb Saunders, Producer
Black Perspective
1422 New Britain Avenue
West Hartford CT 06110
203-521-3030
Category: 49(black)-99

WVIT-TV
Carmen Cordova, Director
What About Women
1422 New Britain Avenue
West Hartford CT 06110
203-521-3030
Category: 73-99
Format: T
Features: I-F-R

DISTRICT OF COLUMBIA

WTTG-TV
Jane Stoddard, Producer
Panorama
5151 Wisconsin Avenue NW
Washington DC 20016
202-244-5151
Category: 99

WDVM-TV
4001 Brandywine Street NW
Washington DC 20016
202-364-3900
Category: 99

WETA Channel 26
P O Box 2626
Washington DC 20013
202-998-2626
Category: 99

WHMM-TV
2222 4th Street NW
Washington DC 20008
202-686-3000
Category: 99

WJLA-TV
4461 Connecticut Avenue NW
Washington DC 20008
202-364-7777
Category: 99

WRC-TV
John McLaughlin
4001 Nebraska Avenue NW
Washington DC 20016
202-686-4000
Category: 99
Host: John McLaughlin

WRC-TV
Fred Demorco, General Manager
Live at Five
4001 Nebraska Avenue
Washington DC 20016
202-885-4095
Category: 99
Features: I

<u>CATEGORIES</u> -- coded by number

10 General Nonfiction
11 Art/Music/Photography/Dance
13 Alternative Issues
15 Animals/Pets
17 Biographies/Autobiographies
19 Business/Economics
21 Children's Books
23 Computers/Technology
25 Consumer Issues and Guides
27 Cookbooks/Nutrition
29 Crafts/Hobbies/How-to
31 Education/Child Development
33 Entertainment/Movies/Humor
35 Family/Marriage/Retirement
37 Gay/Lesbian
39 Health/Medicine/Diet/Exercise
41 History

43 House/Garden/Automobiles
45 Languages:_______________
47 Literature/Humanities
49 Minority Studies
51 Nature/Ecology/Conservation
53 New Age/Astrology/Occult
55 Politics/Government/Military
57 Psychology/Self-Help
59 Reference Books
61 Regional Titles
63 Religions/Philosophy
65 Scholarly Titles
67 Science/Mathematics
69 Sports/Games/Recreation
71 Travel/Geography
73 Women's Issues

75 General Fiction
76 Children's Stories
77 Contemporary Novels
78 Ethnic/Minority Literature
79 Folklore/Fairy Tales
80 Foreign Literature
81 Historical
82 Horror/Occult

83 Literary
84 Mystery/Detective
85 Romance/Gothic
86 Science Fiction/Fantasy
87 Suspense/Adventure
88 Westerns
89 Young Adult
90 Short Stories/Anthologies

95 Poetry
97 News

98 Other:_______________
99 All subjects and categories

===

<u>Radio</u> / <u>Television</u> -- special codes

Formats: C = Live with Call-ins
           L = Live
           P = Telephone Interviews
           T = Taped

Features: B = Book Reviews
            F = Features
            I = Interviews
            N = News
            R = Book Readings

===

Local Television Stations and Shows

<u>FLORIDA</u>

WTVJ-TV
Alan Mendelson
On the Money
316 N Miami Avenue
Miami FL 33128
305-579-1422
Category: 19

WTVJ-TV
Producer, AM South Florida
316 N Miami Avenue
Miami FL 33128
305-579-1422
Category: 99

WTVJ-TV
Alan Perris, Producer
Montage
316 N Miami Avenue
Miami FL 33128
305-579-1200
Category: 99

WCIX-TV
1111 Brickell Avenue
Miami FL 33131
305-377-0811
Category: 99

WLRN-TV
Producer, Something on 17
172 NE 15th Street
Miami FL 33132
305-372-5440
Category: 99

WPBT-TV
Producer, Nightly Business Rap
14901 NE 20th Avenue
Miami FL 33181
305-949-8321
Category: 19

WPLG-TV
3900 Biscayne Boulevard
P O Box 10
Miami FL 33128
305-576-1010
Category: 99

WSVN-TV
1401 79th Street Causeway
Miami FL 33141
305-751-6692
Category: 99

WCPX-TV
Michael Cerni, Producer
Newswatch Six...The Noon Report
P O Box 66000
Orlando FL 32804
305-291-6000
Category: 13-15-25-27-33-35
         37-39-53-57-73
Host: Carole Nelson
Format: L-T-C
Features: I-N

WESH-TV
Stacey Woelfel, Assignment Editor
NewsCenter 2
P O Box 7697
Orlando FL 32854
305-645-2222
Category: 11-19-33-69-82-86-87
Format: L
Features: I-N-F

WESH-TV
Michelle Vonderhaar
NewsCenter 2 Midday
P O Box 7697
Orlando FL 32854
305-645-2222
Category: 27-33-39-61-73
Host: Andrea Coudriet
Format: L
Features: I-N-F

WFTV-TV
Walter Windsor, President
Eyewitness News at Noon
639 W Central Boulevard
P O Box 999
Orlando FL 32802
305-841-9000
Category: 99
Format: L-T
Features: I

WMFE-TV
News Director
11510 E Colonial Drive
Orlando FL 32817
305-273-2300
Category: 99

WPTV-TV
622 N Flagler Drive
Palm Beach FL 33401
Category: 99

WTSP-TV
Michael Babich
Murphy In the Morning
P O Box 10000
Saint Petersburg FL 33733
813-577-1010
Category: 99
Host: Bill Murphy
Format: L-C-P
Features: I-F

WEDU-TV
1300 North Boulevard
Tampa FL 33607
813-253-2736
Category: 99

WTVT-TV
3213 JFK Boulevard
P O Box 22013
Tampa FL 33609
813-876-1313
Category: 99

WXFL-TV
Laurie Scollin, Producer
Newswatch 8
905 E Jackson Street
Tampa FL 33602
813-229-7781
Category: 99
Host: Jerry Firoe & Irene Mamer
Format: L
Features: I-N-F

WPEC-TV
Fairfield Drive
W Palm Beach FL 33407
305-844-1212
Category: 99

WXEL-TV
Andy Harper
Newsmakers
P O Box 6607
West Palm Beach FL 33405
305-732-7850
Category: 99
Host: Andy Harper
Format: C
Features: I-N

<u>GEORGIA</u>

WAGA-TV
Producer, PM Atlanta
P O Box 4207
Atlanta GA 30302
404-875-5551
Category: 99
Format: L-T
Features: N-F

WAGA-TV
Cathy Payen
Atlanta 730
P O Box 4207
Atlanta GA 30302
404-875-5551
Category: 99
Host: Cathy Payen
Format: L
Features: I-N-F

==

Format: L = Live; T = Taped; C = Live with call-ins; P = Telephone interviews

Features: I = Interviews; N = News; F = Features; B = Book reviews; R = Readings from books

Local Television Stations and Shows

WXIA-TV
Cindy Delv, Producer
Noon Day Show
1611 W Peachtree Street NE
Atlanta GA 30309
404-892-1611
Category: 99
Format: L-T
Features: N-F

WPBA-TV
740 Bismark Road NE
Atlanta GA 30324
404-873-4471
Category: 99

WSB-TV
1601 W Peachtree Road NE
Atlanta GA 30309
404-897-7500
Category: 99

WTBS-TV
1050 Techwood Drive NW
Atlanta GA 30318
404-892-1717
Category: 99

ILLINOIS

WTTW-TV
Todd Whitman, Kup's Show
233 N Michigan Avenue #1911
Chicago IL 60601
312-565-1012
Category: 99
Features: I

WBBM-TV
Beth Thomas, Two On Two
630 N McClurg Court
Chicago IL 60611
312-944-6000
Category: 99

WBBM-TV
Carolyn Miller, Producer
Different Drummers
630 N McClurg Court
Chicago IL 60611
312-565-1100
Category: 99

WBBM-TV
Aretha Marshall-Mills, Producer
Common Ground
630 N McClurg Court
Chicago IL 60611
312-944-6000
Category: 99

WBBM-TV
Lilly Eide, Director
Day Break
630 N McClurg Court
Chicago IL 60611
312-944-6000
Category: 99

WCIU-TV
Ben Larson, News Director
Business Newsmaker
141 W Jackson Boulevard
Chicago IL 60604
312-663-0260
Category: 17-19-23-25-35-39
          41-55-57-61-67-71
Format: L
Features: I

WFLD-TV
Rudy Guido, News Talk
300 N State Street
Chicago IL 60610
312-645-0300
Category: 99

WFLD-TV
Wanda Wells
Our People
300 N State Street
Chicago IL 60610
312-645-0300
Category: 99

WGN-TV
Paul Davis, News Director
2501 Bradley Place
Chicago IL 60618
312-528-2311
Category: 99

WLS-TV
Bonnie Kaplan
A M Chicago
190 N State Street
Chicago IL 60601
312-750-7777
Category: 99
Format: L-T
Features: I-N-F

WMAQ-TV
Dick Reingold, News Director
Merchandise Mart
111 E Wacker Drive #510
Chicago IL 60654
312-861-5555
Category: 99

WMAQ-TV
Bobbi Clark
Today in Chicago
111 E Wacker Drive #510
Chicago IL 60654
312-861-5409
Category: 99
Format: L
Features: I-N-F

WMAQ-TV
Lydia Talbot, Producer
Everyman
111 E Wacker Drive #510
Chicago IL 60601
312-565-1100
Category: 63

INDIANA

WFYI-TV
Terri Bertrand
Indiana Business Weekly
1401 N Meridian Street
Indianapolis IN 46202
317-636-2020
Category: 19-25-39-55
Host: Terri Bertrand
Format: T
Features: I-N-F

WFYI-TV
Kathy Miller, Director
Indiana Arts
1401 N Meridian Street
Indianapolis IN 46202
317-636-2020
Category: 11-47-95-75-77-81-83
Host: Bob Beckmann Jr
Format: T
Features: I-F-R

WISH-TV
Lee Giles, News Director
1950 N Meridian Street
Indianapolis IN 46207
317-924-4381
Category: 99
Format: L-T
Features: N-F

WRTV-TV
Bob Gamble, News Director
1330 N Meridian Street
Indianapolis IN 46206
317-635-9788
Category: 99

WTHR-TV
Debbie Wilson
AM Indiana, Track 13
1000 N Meridian Street
Indianapolis IN 46204
317-636-1313
Category: 99
Host: Dick Wolfsie
Format: C
Features: I-N-F-B

WTHR-TV
Bob Campbell, News Director
NewsCenter 13
1000 N Meridian Street
Indianapolis IN 46204
317-636-1313
Category: 99
Host: Bob Campbell
Format: L
Features: I-N-F-B

WTTV-TV
James Lockwood, News Director
3490 Bluff Road
Indianapolis IN 46217
317-787-2211
Category: 99

KANSAS

KAKE-TV
Robert E Dalton, General Manager
Kaleidoscope
P O Box 10
Wichita KS 67201
316-838-1212
Category: 99

KSNW-TV
R N Wilson, Assignment Manager
Scheduled Newcasts
833 N Main
Wichita KS 67201
316-265-5631
Category: 99
Format: L-T-C
Features: I-N-F

KWCH-TV
Ron Gergamo, General Manager
Noon News
P O Box 12
Wichita KS 67201
316-838-1212
Category: 99

KENTUCKY

WAVE-TV
Andy Coltpepper
Today in WAVE Country
P O Box 32970
Louisville KY 40232
505-585-2201
Category: 99
Host: Andy Coltpepper
Format: L
Features: I-N

WHAS-TV
P O Box 1084
Louisville KY 40201
502-582-7840
Category: 99

WKPC-TV
P O Box 37380
Louisville KY 40233
502-459-9572
Category: 99

WLKY-TV
1918 Mellwood Avenue
P O Box 6205
Louisville KY 40206
502-893-3671
Category: 99

LOUISIANA

WVUE-TV
1025 S Jefferson Davis Parkway
P O Box 13847
New Orleans LA 70125
504-486-6161
Category: 99

WWL-TV
Georgia Battlora, Producer
The Day Report
1024 N Rampart Street
New Orleans LA 70116
504-529-4444
Category: 99
Format: L-T
Features: N-I

WYES-TV
Gwynn Torres, Public Affairs
916 Navarre Avenue
New Orleans LA 70124
504-486-5511
Category: 99

WDSU-TV
Bob Raley
Breakfast Edition
520 Royal Street
New Orleans LA 70130
504-527-0666
Category: 99

KSLA-TV
P O Box 4812
Shreveport LA 71104
318-222-1212
Category: 99

KTBS-TV
312 E Kings Highway
P O Box 44227
Shreveport LA 71134
318-868-3644
Category: 99

MAINE

WLBZ-TV
Joan Grindel, Program Director
Mount Hope Avenue
P O Box 934
Bangor ME 04401
207-942-4822
Category: 99

WMTW-TV
Peter Weyl, News Director
P O Box 8
Poland Spring ME 04272
207-774-2100
Category: 99

WCSH-TV
Jeff Marks, News Director
1 Congress Square
Portland ME 04101
207-772-0181
Category: 99

WGME-TV
Dave Robinson, News Director
Northport Plaza
Portland ME 04104
207-797-9330
Category: 99

MARYLAND

WBAL-TV
Malcom D Potter, Manager
3800 Hooper Avenue
Baltimore MD 21211
301-467-3000
Category: 99

WJZ-TV
Kristin Leatherman, Director
People Are Talking
Westinghouse Broadcasting
TV Hill
Baltimore MD 21211
301-466-0013
Category: 99

WMAR-TV
Deb Yost Tewey, Producer
Channel 2 News at Noon
6400 York Road
Baltimore MD 21212
301-377-2222
Category: 11-25-27-29-31
          33-35-39-58-73
Host: Sloane Brown
Format: L
Features: I-N-F

WMAR-TV
Gail Bending
Newscope
6400 York Road
Baltimore MD 21212
301-377-2222
Category: 99

WDCA-TV
News Director
5202 River Road
Bethesda MD 20816
301-654-2600
Category: 99

WHAG-TV
Bob Borngesser, News Director
13 E Washington Street
Hagerstown MD 21740
301-797-4400
Category: 99

WMPB-TV
Michael Styer, Program Director
11767 Bonita Avenue
Owings Mills MD 21117
301-356-5600
Category: 99

MASSACHUSETTS

Nova
Paula Apsell
WGBH-TV
125 Western Avenue
Boston MA 02134
617-492-2777
Category: 67

WBZ-TV
Alan Schroeder, Producer
People are Talking
1170 Soldiers Field Road
Boston MA 01234
617-787-7109
Category: 25-35-37-39
        53-57-63-73
Host: Buzz Luttrell
Format: C
Features: I

WBZ-TV
Joseph Heston
Evening Magazine
1170 Soldiers Field Road
Boston MA 02134
617-787-7158
Category: 99
Format: L-T
Features: I-N-F

WBZ-TV
Bob Males, Producer
Live on 4
1170 Soldiers Field Road
Boston MA 02134
617-787-7144
Category: 11-17-33
Host: Joyce Kulhawtk
Format: L
Features: I-N

WCVB-TV
Lauren Griffiths, Publicist
Good Day!
5 TV Place, Needham Branch
Boston MA 02192
617-449-0400
Category: 99
Host: Eileen Prose & Tom Cottle
Format: T-C
Features: I-F-R

WCVB-TV
Lauren Griffiths, Publicist
Commentaries
5 TV Place, Needham Branch
Boston MA 02192
617-449-0400
Category: 99
Host: Chuck Kraemer
Format: T
Features: F

WGBH-TV
Steve Atlas, News Director
125 Western Avenue
Boston MA 02134
617-492-2777
Category: 99

WLVI-TV
Jack Fitzgerald, News Director
75 Morrissey Boulevard
Boston MA 02125
617-265-5656
Category: 99

WNEV-TV
Roni Goldbert, Producer
Morning Live
7 Bullfinch Place
Boston MA 02114
617-725-0777
Category: 99
Host: Susan Sikora
Format: L-C
Features: I

WSBK-TV
Eileen Cushing-Craig, Producer
Journal
83 Birmingham Parkway
Brighton MA 02135
617-783-3838
Category: 99
Host: Meg LaVigne
Format: L-C
Features: I-N-F

WSBK-TV
Eileen Cushing-Craig, Producer
Newsmakers
83 Birmingham Parkway
Brighton MA 02135
617-783-3838
Category: 17-19-33-31-55-67
Host: Meg LaVigne
Format: T
Features: I-N-F
national figures and celebrities

WLNE-TV
Carolyn Taylor
Trueman Taylor Talks To
430 Country Street
New Bedford MA 02741
617-992-6666
Category: 99
Host: Carolyn Taylor
Format: L-T
Features: I

MICHIGAN

WUHQ-TV
Sandy Swartz, Producer
5:30 News
5200 W Dickman Road
Battle Creek MI 49016
616-966-6841
Category: 99
Host: Trudy Yarnell
Format: L-C
Features: I-N-F

WUHQ-TV
Mark Crawford
6:00 News
5200 W Dickman Road
Battle Creek MI 49016
616-966-6841
Category: 99
Host: Mark Crawford/Jack Hawkins
Format: L
Features: I-N-F

WUHQ-TV
Jonathan Doonan, Assignments
5200 W Dickman Road
Battle Creek MI 49016
616-966-6841
Category: 99

WDIV-TV
Terri McCormick, Producer
Sonya
550 W Lafayette Boulevard
Detroit MI 48231
313-222-0689
Category: 99

WTVS-TV
Cheryl Head, News Director
7441 Second Boulevard
Detroit MI 48202
313-873-7200
Category: 99

WFUM-TV
University of Michigan
1321 E Court Street
Flint MI 48503
313-762-3028
Category: 99

WJRT-TV
2302 Lapeer Road
Flint MI 48503
313-233-3130
Category: 99

WZZM-TV
Dick Richards
Eyewitness News at Noon
P O Box Z
Grand Rapids MI 49501
616-784-4200
Category: 99
Format: L-T
Features: I-N

WOTV-TV
120 College Avenue SE
P O Box B
Grand Rapids MI 49501
616-459-4125
Category: 99

WKZO-TV
Della Di Pietro
Accent
590 W Maple Street
Kalamazoo MI 49008
616-345-2101
Category: 99
Host: Della Di Pietro
Format: L

WNEM-TV
P O Box 531
107 N Franklin
Saginaw MI 48606
517-755-8191
Category: 99

WJBK-TV
Denise Carmonia, Producer
Eyewitness News at Noon
2 Storer Place
P O Box 2000
Southfield MI 48124
313-552-5298
Category: 25-27-29-31-33-35-37
          39-43-53-55-57-73
Host: Virg Jacques/Sherry Margois
Format: L
Features: I-N-F

WJBK-TV
Beth Sosin
PM Magazine Detroit
2 Storer Place, P O Box 2000
Southfield MI 48124
313-557-2000
Category: 99

WKBD-TV
P O Box 50
Southfield MI 48037
313-444-8500
Category: 99

WXYZ-TV
Nancy Lenzen, Senior Producer
Kelly & Company
20777 W Ten Mile Road
Southfield MI 48018
313-827-9342
Category: 99
Host: John Kelly & Marilyn Turner
Format: L-C
Features: I

WXYZ-TV
Lori Weiss
Good Afternoon Detroit
20777 W Ten Mile Road
Southfield MI 48018
313-827-9333
Category: 99
Host: John Kelly & Marilyn Turner
Format: L-C
Features: I-N-F

WXYZ-TV
Claire Carmichael, Senior Producer
P O Box 789
Southfield MI 48037
313-827-9305
Category: 99

MINNESOTA

WUSA-TV
441 Boone Avenue N
Minneapolis MN 55427
612-546-1111
Category: 99

WCCO-TV
Lori Fink
PM Magazine
90 South 11th Street

Minneapolis MN 55403
612-333-2560
Category: 99
Format: L-T
Features: I-N-F

KSTP-TV
3415 University Avenue
Saint Paul MN 55114
612-646-5555
Category: 99

KTCA-TV
1640 Como Avenue
Saint Paul MN 55108
612-646-4611
Category: 99

MISSOURI

KCPT-TV
125 E 31 Street
Kansas City MO 64108
816-756-3580
Category: 99

KCTV-TV
Stan Carmack, Producer
Noon Edition
P O Box 5555
Kansas City MO 64109
913-677-5555; 913-677-7199
Category: 11-13-15-17-19-23-25
          33-39-57-73-77-84
Host: Stan Carmack
Format: L
Features: I-N-F

KMBC-TV
1049 Central Street
Kansas City MO 64105
816-221-9999
Category: 99

KSHB-TV
4720 Oak Street
Kansas City MO 64112
816-753-4141
Category: 99

WDAF-TV
Signal Hill
Kansas City MO 64108
816-753-4567
Category: 99

KTVI-TV
5915 Berthold Avenue
Saint Louis MO 63110
314-647-2222
Category: 99

KMOX-TV
Kathi McDonald, Business Editor
One S Memorial Drive
St Louis MO 63102
314-444-3371
Category: 19

KMOX-TV
Ellen Harris, Producer
One Memorial Drive
St Louis MO 63102
314-621-2345
Category: 99
Features: N

KSDK-TV
Burt Dubrow
Sally
1000 Market Street
St Louis MO 63101
314-444-5173
Category: 99

KETC-TV
Jeff Clarke, News Director
6996 Millbrook Road
St. Louis MO 63130
314-725-2460
Category: 99

KMOX-TV
Fred Burrows, News Director
One S Memorial Drive
St Louis MO 63102
314-621-2345
Category: 99

NEW JERSEY

WMGM-TV
Susan McLaughlin
Program Director
15 Shore Road
Linwood NJ 08221
609-927-4440

WOR-TV
Frank Anthony, News Director
43 Meadowlands Parkway
Secaucus NJ 07094
201-330-2100
Category: 99

NEW MEXICO

KGGM-TV
John Andrews, News Director
1414 Coal Street SW
P O Box 1294
Albuquerque NM 87103
505-243-2285
Category: 99

KNME-TV
1130 University Boulevard NE
Albuquerque NM 87102
505-277-2121
Category: 99

KOAT-TV
3801 Carlisle Boulevard NE
P O Box 25982
Albuquerque NM 87125
505-884-7777
Category: 99

KOB-TV
4 Broadcast Place SW
P O Box 1351
Albuquerque NM 87103
505-243-4411
Category: 99

NEW YORK

WNYT-TV
Stephen Baboulis, News Director
6:00 News
P O Box 4035
Albany NY 12204
518-436-4791
Category: 11-19-23-25-33-39-43
        55-57-59-69-71-73
Host: Ed Dague
Format: L
Features: I-N-F

WNYT-TV
Benita Zahn, 13 Forum
P O Box 4035
Albany NY 12204
518-436-4791
Category: 11-17-19-23-33-39
        43-55-57-61-71-73
Host: Benita Zahn
Format: T
Features: I

WTEN-TV
341 Northern Boulevard
Albany NY 12204
518-436-4822
Category: 99

WSKG-TV
Julie Kramer, Producer
ArtScene
P O Box 3000
Binghamton NY 13902
607-775-0100
Category: 11-29-61-95-11
Host: Julie Kramer
Format: T
Features: I-F-R

WGRZ-TV
Wayne Ludrey, Producer
Noon News
259 Delaware Avenue
Buffalo NY 14202
716-856-1414
Category: 99
Format: L
Features: I-N

WGRZ-TV
Stacey Roder, Producer
News Center at Noon
259 Deleware Avenue
Buffalo NY 14202
716-856-1414
Category: 99
Format: L
Features: I-N

WIVB-TV
2077 Elmwood Avenue
Buffalo NY 14207
716-874-4410
Category: 99

WKBW-TV
7 Broadcast Plaza
Buffalo NY 14202
716-845-6100
Category: 99

WNED-TV
P O Box 1263
Buffalo NY 14213
716-881-5000
Category: 99

WABC-TV
Delia Fine, Producer
The Morning Show
7 Lincoln Square
New York NY 10023
212-887-3054
Category: 99

WABC-TV
Producer, Eyewitness News
7 Lincoln Square
New York NY 10023
212-887-3100
Category: 99

WCBS-TV
Jim Zarchin, News Director
524 West 57th Street
New York NY 10019
212-975-4321
Category: 99

Group W Cable
Jim Carney, Producer
Manhattan Profile
5120 Broadway
New York NY 10034
212-304-3269
Category: 11-13-17-19-25-31-33
        49-55-61-73-77-78-83
Host: Bob Slade
Format: T
Features: I-F-B

Group W Cable Manhattan
Jim Carney, Producer
Community Watch
5120 Broadway
New York NY 10034
212-304-3269
Category: 11-13-17-19-25-31-33
        49-55-61-73
Host: Ada Alvarez
Format: T
Features: I-N-F

WNBC-TV
Bohdan Zachary
Live at Five
30 Rockefeller Plaza #724

New York NY 10010
212-664-2023
Category: 99
Format: L
Features: N-I

WNBC-TV
Christopher Salvador, Producer
The Prime of Your Life
30 Rockefeller Plaza
New York NY 10020
212-664-4765
Category: 35(retirement)

WNET-TV
Peter Foges, News Director
356 West 58th Street
New York NY 10019
212-560-2000
Category: 99

WNET-TV
Larry Lancit, Producer
Reading Rainbow
356 West 58th Street
New York NY 10019
212-560-2000
Category: 21-76
Features: B-R

WNEW-TV
Gwen Barret, Producer
Midday
205 East 67th Street
New York NY 10021
212-535-1000
Category: 99

WNEW-TV
Stephen Schwartz
PM Magazine
205 East 67th Street
New York NY 10021
212-535-1000
Category: 99
Format: L-T
Features: I-F

WOR-TV
Stanley Friedman, Producer
Straight Talk
1440 Broadway
New York NY 10018
212-767-7067
Category: 99
Format: L
Features: I

WOR-TV
Joe Franklin, Producer
Joe Franklin Show
1440 Broadway
New York NY 10018
212-221-1659
Category: 99
Host: Joe Franklin
Format: C
Features: I

Local Television Stations and Shows

WPIX-TV
Brooke Alwyn
Midday Edition
11 WPIX Plaza
New York NY 10017
212-949-1100
Category: 99

WPIX-TV
Iris Dudman
Wall Street Journal Report
11 WPIX Plaza
New York NY 10017
212-949-1100
Category: 19

WPIX-TV
Marianne Sankowski, Coordinator
The Open Mind
11 WPIX Plaza
New York NY 10017
212-949-1100
Category: 99
Features: I

WPIX-TV
Don Riggs
Starting Today Show
11 WPIX Plaza
New York NY 10017
212-949-1100
Category: 99
Host: Don Riggs
Features: I

WRGB-TV
1400 Balltown Road
Schenectady NY 12309
518-377-2261
Category: 99

WTVH-TV
980 James Street
Syracuse NY 13203
315-425-5555
Category: 99

WIXT-TV
P O Box 9
Syracuse NY 13214
315-446-4780
Category: 99

WSTM-TV
1030 James Street
Syracuse NY 13203
315-474-5000
Category: 99

NORTH CAROLINA

WLOS-TV
Mike Gehring, Manager
288 Macon Avenue
P O Box 2150
Asheville NC 28802
704-255-0013
Category: 99

WUNC-TV
910 Raleigh Road
P O Box 3508
Chapel Hill NC 27514
919-933-8191
Category: 99

WTVI-TV
42 Coliseum Drive
Charlotte NC 28205
704-372-2442
Category: 99

WBTV-TV
1 Julian Price Place
Charlotte NC 28208
704-374-3500
Category: 99

WPCQ-TV
Stanley Rudick, Manager
8036 Hood Road
P O Box 18665
Charlotte NC 28218
704-536-3636
Category: 99

WSOC-TV
Alan Battan, Book Reviews
Robin McCourt, Author Interviews
P O Box 34665
Charlotte NC 28215
704-335-4999
Category: 99
Features: I-B

WTVD-TV
Paul Bures, Manager
411 Liberty
P O Box 2009
Durham NC 27702
919-683-1111
Category: 99

WFMY-TV
Mike Conly, Manager
P O Box TV2
Greensboro NC 27405
919-379-9369
Category: 99

WGHP-TV
Gary Curtis, News Director
Eyewitness News
P O Box TV8
Greensboro NC 27420-6088
919-841-8888
Category: 99
Format: L
Features: I-N-F

WPTF-TV
Robert Butler, Manager
410 S Salisbury Street
P O Box 1511
Raleigh NC 27602
919-832-8311
Category: 99

WRAL-TV
Ron Price, News Director
2619 Western
Raleigh NC 27606
919-828-2511
Category: 99

WXII-TV
Reynard Corley, Manager
P O Box 11847
Winston-Salem NC 27106
919-721-9944
Category: 99

NORTH DAKOTA

KXMC-TV
Dean Thurow, Noon Show
P O Box 1686
Minot ND 58702
701-852-2104
Category: 29-43-69-71-87
Host: Dean Thurow
Format: L
Features: I-F-B

OHIO

WAKR-TV
Robert Bostian, Manager
853 Copley Road
Akron OH 44320
216-535-7831
Category: 99

WCET-TV
Joanne Grueter, News Director
1223 Central Parkway
Cincinnati OH 45214
513-381-4033
Category: 99

WCPO-TV
Charles Munro, News Director
500 Central Avenue
Cincinnati OH 45202
513-721-9900
Category: 99

WIW-TV
Mona Harrison, Producer
Midday
140 West 9th Street
Cincinnati OH 45213
513-352-5050
Category: 11-15-17-19-21-25-27
          31-33-35-39-43-55-69
          71-73-76-77-82-85-87
Host: Clyde Gray & Toria Hammil
Format: L
Features: I-N-F-B

WKRC-TV
John Rose, Manager
1906 Highland Avenue
Cincinnati OH 45219
513-651-1200
Category: 99

WLWT-TV
Producer, Braun & Company
140 W Ninth Street
Cincinnati OH 45202
513-352-5050
Category: 99

WXIX-TV
10490 Taconic Terrace
Cincinnati OH 45215
513-772-1919
Category: 99

WEWS-TV
Jane Temple
Morning Exchange
3001 Euclid Avenue
Cleveland OH 44115
216-431-5555
Category: 99

WEWS-TV
Gary Stark, Program Director
3001 Euclid Avenue
Cleveland OH 44115
216-431-5555
Category: 99

WJW-TV
Tony Ballew, News Director
Newscenter 8
5800 S Marginal Road
Cleveland OH 44103
216-431-8888
Category: 99
Format: L
Features: I-N-F-B

WJW-TV
David Whitaker, Vice President
Northcoast Magazine
5800 S Marginal Road
Cleveland OH 44103
216-431-8888
Category: 99

WKYC-TV
Producer, Sunday Magazine
1403 E 6th Street
Cleveland OH 44114
216-344-3365
Category: 99

WUAB-TV
8443 Day Drive
Cleveland OH 44129
216-845-6043
Category: 99

WVIZ-TV
4300 Brookpark Road
Cleveland OH 44134
216-398-2800
Category: 99

WBNS-TV
P O Box 1010
770 Twin Rivers Drive

Columbus OH 43216
614-460-3700
Category: 99

WCMH-TV
Ron Bilek, News Director
3165 Olentangy River Road
P O Box 4
Columbus OH 43202
614-263-4444
Category: 99

WOSU-TV
Howard Ornstein, News Director
2400 Olentangy River Road
Columbus OH 43210
614-422-9678
Category: 99

WTVN-TV
Joy Roller, Producer
Midday
P O Box 718
1261 Dublin Road
Columbus OH 43209
614-481-6666
Category: 99
Host: Tom Burris & Wendy Craver
Format: L
Features: I-N-F-B

WDTN-TV
4595 S Dixie Avenue
Dayton OH 45401
513-293-2101
Category: 99

WHIO-TV
Skip Hapner, News Director
1414 Wilmington
Dayton OH 45401
513-259-2111
Category: 99

WKEF-TV
Producer, Talk Back
1731 Soldiers Home Road
Dayton OH 45418
513-263-2662
Category: 99
Features: N

WPTD-TV
Judith Baker, Program Director
3440 Office Park Drive
Dayton OH 45439
513-298-9500
Category: 99

WDHO-TV
300 S Byrne Road
Toledo OH 43615
419-535-0024
Category: 99

WTOL-TV
Maria Morningstar, Director
One On One

730 N Summit Street
Toledo OH 43606
419-248-1150
Category: 99 (issues only)
Host: Elizabeth McGuire
Format: T
Features: pro/con discussions

WTOL-TV
Maria Morningstar, Director
Hotline
730 N Summit Street
Toledo OH 43606
419-248-1150
Category: 99
Host: Stuart Watson
Format: L-C
Features: I-N-F-B

WTOL-TV
Sharon Newsom
Community Showcase
730 N Summit Street
Toledo OH 43606
419-248-1150
Category: 99

WTVG-TV
Neil Carmean, News Director
4247 Dorr Street
Toledo OH 43607
419-531-1313
Category: 99

OKLAHOMA

KETA-TV
Tom Gilmore, News Director
7403 N Kelly Avenue
Oklahoma City OK 73114
405-848-8501
Category: 99

KOCO-TV
Producer, Saturday Review
Producer, Kaleidoscope
Perry Boxx, News Director
1300 E Britton Road
P O Box 14555
Oklahoma City OK 73113
405-478-3000
Category: 99

KTVY-TV
Bill Thrash, Program Manager
Ron Turner, News Director
500 E Britton Road
P O Box 14068
Oklahoma City OK 73114
405-478-1212
Category: 99

KWTV
7401 N Kelly
P O Box 14159
Oklahoma City OK 73113
405-843-6641
Category: 99

KJRH-TV
Tony Morino, News Director
3701 S Peoria
Tulsa OK 75105
918-743-2222
Category: 99

KOTV-TV
Bob Allen, Program Manager
James Morgan, News Director
302 S Frankfort
Tulsa OK 74120
918-582-6666
Category: 99

KTUL-TV
Tom Doerr, News Director
P O Box 8
Tulsa OK 74101
918-446-335
Category: 99

OREGON

KATU-TV
Alan Goldberg, News Director
2153 NE Sandy Boulevard
Portland OR 97208
503-231-4222
Category: 99

KGW-TV
Reagan Ramsey, News Director
1501 SW Jefferson Street
Portland OR 97201
503-226-5000
Category: 99

KOAP-TV
Thomas Doggett, Program Director
2828 SW Front Avenue
Portland OR 97201
503-229-4892
Category: 99

KOIN-TV
Ted Bryant, News Director
News Room Six at Noon
222 SW Columbia Street
Portland OR 97201
503-243-6666
Category: 99
Format: L-T
Features: I-N-F

KPTV-TV
P O Box 3401
Portland OR 97208
503-222-9921
Category: 99

PENNSYLVANIA

WNEP-TV
Wilkes-Barre/Scranton Airport
Avoca PA 18641
717-826-1616
Category: 99

WHP-TV
3300 N 6th Street
P O Box 1507
Harrisburg PA 17110
717-238-2100
Category: 99

WHTM-TV
P O Box 2775
Harrisburg PA 17105
717-236-2727
Category: 99

WITF-TV
Amy Gajda, News Anchor
33 Report
1982 Locust Lane
Harrisburg PA 17109
717-236-6000
Category: 99
Host: Amy Gajda
Format: L-T
Features: I-N-F

WJAC-TV
1949 Hickory Lane
Johnstown PA 15907
814-255-7600
Category: 99

WGAL-TV
Lincoln Highway West
Lancaster PA 17604
717-393-5851
Category: 99

WLYH-TV
Producer, Forum 15
1126 Park City Center
Lancaster, PA 17601
717-273-4551
Category: 99

WCAU-TV
Jay Newman, News Director
George Jason, Basically Economic
Dan Sitarski, Ten Around Town
City Avenue & Monument Road
Philadelphia PA 19131
215-581-5510
Category: 99

WPHL-TV
5001 Wynnefield Avenue
Philadelphia PA 19131
215-878-1700
Category: 99

WPVI-TV
Nancy Nolde, Producer
Dialogue
1501 Cherry Street
Philadelphia PA 19102
215-563-7854
Category: 63
Host: John Raines
Format: T
Features: I

WPVI-TV
Producer, AM Philadelphia
Producer, Prime Time
1501 Cherry Street
Philadelphia PA 19102
215-563-7854
Category: 99

WTAF-TV
Jill Chernekoff
Newsprobe
330 Market Street
Philadelphia PA 19106
215-925-2929
Category: 13-15-17-25-27-31-33
        35-39-51-55-73
Host: Jill Chernekoff
Format: T
Features: I-F-B-R

WTAF-TV
Roger LaMay, News Director
The Ten O'Clock News
330 Market Street
Philadelphia PA 19106
215-483-6387; 215-925-2929
Category: 11-13-19-23-25
        31-33-39-55-69
Host: Lee McCarthy & Howard Eskin
Format: L
Features: I-N-F

KYW-TV
Eileen Shaw, Research Director
Evening Magazine
Independence Mall East
Philadelphia PA 19106
215-238-4940
Category: 11-13-17-33-35-39-69
Host: Ray Murray and Nancy Glass
Format: T
Features: I-F

KYW-TV
Susan Roumelis, Producer
People Are Talking
Independence Mall East
Philadelphia PA 19106
215-238-4940
Category: 13-17-33-35-37
        39-53-57-73
Host: Richard Bey
Format: L
Features: I

KDKA-TV
Paul Kelvyn, Producer
Pittsburgh Today
1 Gateway Center
Pittsburgh PA 15222
412-392-2200
Category: 99

WPGH-TV
750 Ivory Avenue
Pittsburgh PA 15214
412-931-8600
Category: 99

WPXI-TV
10 TV Hill
P O Box 1100
Pittsburgh PA 15214
412-237-1100
Category: 99

WQED-TV
4802 Fifth Avenue
Pittsburgh PA 15213
412-622-1300
Category: 99

WTAE-TV
Jody Woznicki, Producer
Noon News
400 Ardmore Boulevard
Pittsburgh PA 15230
412-424-4300
Category: 99
Format: L
Features: N-I

WVIA-TV
Marianne Barret, Program Director
Public Broadcasting Center
Pittston PA 18648
717-826-6144
Category: 99

WDAU-TV
415 Lackawanna Avenue
Scranton PA 18503
717-961-2222
Category: 99

WBRE-TV
62 S Franklin Street
Wilkes-Barre PA 18773
717-823-3101
Category: 99

WPMT-TV
Don Travis, Manager
P O Box 1868
York PA 17405
717-843-0043

RHODE ISLAND

WJAR-TV
News Director
111 Dorrance Street
Providence RI 02903
401-751-5700
Category: 99

WPRI-TV
25 Catamore Boulevard
East Providence RI 02914
401-438-7200
Category: 99

WSBE-TV
24 Mason Street
Providence RI 02903
401-277-3636
Category: 99

SOUTH CAROLINA

WIS-TV
Diane Bagwell, Program Director
Carolina Today
1111 Bull Street
Columbia SC 29201
803-799-1010
Category: 99

WRLK-TV
2712 Milwood Avenue
Columbia SC 29205
803-242-4400
Category: 99

WYFF-TV
P O Box 788
Greenville SC 29602
803-242-4404
Category: 99

WNSC-TV
Larry Hall, Program Manager
P O Box 11766
Rock Hill SC 29731
803-324-3184
Category: 99

WNSC-TV
Elyse Williams, Upstate Tonight
P O Box 11766
Rock Hill SC 29731
803-324-3184
Category: 99
Host: Elyse Williams
Format: T-C
Features: I-F-R

WSPA-TV
Kevin Kelly, News Director
Eyewitness News at Noon
P O Box 1717
Spartanburg SC 29201
803-799-1010
Category: 99
Format: L-T
Features: N

TENNESSEE

WATE-TV
1306 NE Broadway
Knoxville TN 37901
615-637-9666
Category: 99

WBIR-TV
Producer, Early Morning
James Swinehart, News Director
1513 Hutchinson Avenue
Knoxville TN 37917
615-637-1010
Category: 99

WTVK-TV
Bill Eckstein
Focus
P O Box 1388
Knoxville TN 37901
615-687-2312
Category: 99
Host: Bill Eckstein
Format: L
Features: N-I

WHBQ-TV
Jack Moore, News Director
485 S Highland Avenue
Memphis TN 38111
901-320-1313
Category: 99

WKNO-TV
Fred Willis, Program Director
P O Box 80000
Memphis TN 38152
901-458-2521
Category: 99

WMC-TV
Edward Greaney, News Director
1960 Union Avenue
Memphis TN 38104
901-726-0555
Category: 99

WREG-TV
Walt Bolton, Producer
Good Morning with Memphis
803 Channel 3 Drive
Memphis TN 38103
901-577-0100
Category: 99

WDCN-TV
Mike Kroger
A Word on Words
P O Box 120609
Nashville TN 37212
615-259-9325
Category: 11(writing)-33

WKRN-TV
Michael Sullivan, News Director
441 Murfreesboro Road
Nashville TN 37210
615-259-2200
Category: 99

===

Format: L = Live; T = Taped; C = Live with call-ins; P = Telephone interviews

Features: I = Interviews; N = News; F = Features; B = Book reviews; R = Readings from books

Local Television Stations and Shows

WSMV-TV
Donna Smith, Producer
Channel 4 Magazine
5700 Knob Road
P O Box 4
Nashville TN 37202
615-749-2351
Category: 25-28-29-35
         39-43-57-73
Host: Charlie Chase
Format: L-C
Features: I-N-F

WTVF-TV
Debbie Allen
Talk of the Town
474 James Robertson Parkway
Nashville TN 37219
615-244-5000
Category: 99
Host: Debbie Allen and Joe Case
Format: L

TEXAS

KVUE-TV
News Director
P O Box 9927
Austin TX 78766
512-459-6521
Category: 99

KDFW-TV
Walter Evans, Producer
Crossroads of the 80's
400 N Griffin Street
Dallas TX 75202
214-744-4444
Category: 55-98(issues)
Host: Walter Evans
Format: T
Features: I

KDFW-TV
Walter Evans, Producer
Point of View
400 N Griffin Street
Dallas TX 75202
214-744-4444
Category: 55-98(issues)
Host: Walter Evans
Format: T
Features: I

KERA-TV
Michael Regunberg, News Director
3000 Harry Hines Boulevard
Dallas TX 75201
214-744-1300
Category: 99

WFAA-TV
Marty Haag, News Director
Beol Broadcasting Corporation
Communications Center
Dallas TX 75202
214-748-9631
Category: 99

KTSM-TV
Debby Roger
Emphasis El Paso
801 N Oregon
El Paso TX 79902
915-532-5421
Category: 19-25-39-41-43-49-51
         55-61-78-80-81-83
Host: Ralph Wilson Green
Format: T
Features: I-N-B

KTSM-TV
Ralph Wilson Green, News Director
801 N Oregon
El Paso TX 79902
915-532-5421
Category: 99

KTVT-TV
P O Box 2495
Fort Worth TX 76113
817-738-1951
Category: 99

KXAS
3900 Barnett Street
P O Box 1780
Fort Worth TX 76101
817-429-1550
Category: 99

Black Voice
Sonny Messiah
KRIV-TV
P O Box 8005
Houston TX 77288
713-663-7716
Category: 11-17-25-31-39
         49-61-69-71-73
Host: Sonny Messiah
Format: T
Features: I

KHOU-TV
1945 Allen Parkway
P O Box 11
Houston TX 77001
713-526-1111
Category: 99

KPRC-TV
P O Box 2222
Houston TX 77252
713-771-4631
Category: 99

KRIV-TV
Margo Kamin
Houston Live
P O Box 22810
Houston TX 77227
713-626-2610
Category: 17-19-23-25-31-35
         39-55-57-59-73-61
Host: Warner Roberts & Mike Lyons
Format: C
Features: I-F

KRIV-TV
Margo Kamin
Houston Kidtalk
P O Box 22810
Houston TX 77227
713-626-2610
Category: 15-21-33-69-76-79-89
Host: Josetta Jones & Tonya Lang
Format: T
Features: I-N-F-B

KRIV-TV
Allan Tudzin
The Midday News
P O Box 22810
Houston TX 77227
713-626-2610
Category: 17-19-23-25-33-39
         55-59-61-71-73
Format: L
Features: I-N-F

KRIV-TV
Shryl Smith
Herencia
P O Box 22810
Houston TX 77227
713-626-2610
Category: 11-17-49-61-78
Host: Marcello Marini
Format: T
Features: I-N

KRIV-TV
Aprille Meek, Producer
P O Box 22810
Houston TX 77227
713-626-2610
Category: 99

KTRK-TV
Kim Nordt, Producer
Good Morning Houston
3310 Bisonnet
P O Box 13
Houston TX 77005
713-666-0713
Category: 99

KUHT-TV
4513 Cullen Boulevard
Houston TX 77004
713-748-6814
Category: 99

KENS-TV
Bob Rogers, News Director
5400 Fredericksburg Road
P O Box TV5
San Antonio TX 78299
512-366-5000
Category: 99

KLRN-TV
P O Box 9
San Antonio TX 78291
512-222-8041
Category: 99

KMOL-TV
1031 Navarro Street
P O Box 2641
San Antonio TX 78299
512-226-4251
Category: 99

KSAT-TV
Producer, Noon Newscast
1408 N St Mary's
P O Box 2478
San Antonio TX 78215
512-226-7611
Category: 99

KTAL-TV
H Lee Bryand, General Manager
Texarkana Town Topic
3227 Summerhill Road
Texarkana TX 75501
214-793-1133
Category: 61(TX)-99

UTAH

KSL-TV
Broadcast House
#5 Triad Center
Salt Lake City UT 84180
801-575-5555
Category: 99

KSTU-TV
5020 W Amelia Earhart Drive
Salt Lake City UT 84104
801-972-1776
Category: 99

KTVX-TV
John Edwards, News Director
1760 Fremont Drive
Salt Lake City UT 84104
801-972-1776
Category: 99

KUED-TV
Maria Smith, Program Director
101 Gardner Hall
University of Utah
Salt Lake City UT 84112
801-581-7777
Category: 99

KUTV-TV
Michael Youngren, News Director
2185 South 3600 West
Salt Lake City UT 84119
801-973-3000
Category: 99

VIRGINIA

WHRO-TV
Patrick Arnoux, Program Director
5200 Hampton Boulevard
Norfolk VA 23508
804-489-9476
Category: 99

WTKR-TV
Joe Perkins, Program Director
613 Woodis Avenue
Norfolk VA 23510
804-446-1000
Category: 99

WVEC-TV
613 Woodis Avenue
Norfolk VA 23510
804-625-1313
Category: 99

WAVY-TV
Carol Hoffman, Producer
News at Noon
801 Wavy Street
Portsmouth VA 23704
804-393-1010
Category: 99
Host: Cathy Midkiff
Format: L
Features: I-N-F

WAVY-TV
Mac McManus, Producer
Tidewater Today
801 Wavy Street
Portsmouth VA 23704
804-393-1010
Category: 99
Host: Mac McManus
Format: T
Features: I-N-F

WCVE-TV
23 Sesame Street
Richmond VA 23235
804-320-1301
Category: 99

WTVR-TV
Jim Deschepper, Program Manager
Richmond Today
3301 W Broad Street
Richmond VA 23230
804-254-3600
Category: 99
Format: N-I

WWBT-TV
Norma Jean Blalock, Producer
The Weekend Edition
P O Box 12
Richmond VA 23201
804-233-5461
Category: 11-13-19-33-37
         39-41-53-73
Host: Norma Jean Blalock
Format: T
Features: I-N-F-B

WXEX-TV
James Abbott, News Director
21 Buford Road
Richmond VA 23235
804-733-8888
Category: 99

KCTS-TV
4045 Brooklyn Avenue NE
Seattle WA 98105
206-545-1808
Category: 99

KING-TV
Producer, King 5 News
333 Dexter Avenue N
Seattle WA 98109
206-448-3781
Category: 97-99

KING-TV
Andy Friedman, Good Company
333 Dexter Avenue N
Seattle WA 98109
206-448-3781
Category: 99
Host: Pat Finley and Cliff Lenz
Format: L-T-C
Features: I-F

KIRO-TV
3rd & Broad Streets
Seattle WA 98121
206-624-7077
Category: 99

KOMO-TV
Kathy Tolan, Associate Producer
Northwest Afternoon
100 Fourth Avenue North
Seattle WA 98109
206-443-4033
Category: 15-17-27-33-35-37-39
         53-57-73
Host: Dick Foley & Dana Middleton
Format: L
Features: I

KSTW-TV
P O Box 11411
Tacoma WA 98411
206-572-5789
Category: 99

WEST VIRGINIA

WCHS-TV
Roger Lyons
News 8 at Noon
1111 Virginia St E
Charleston WV 25301
304-345-4115
Category: 11-15-17-19-25-27
         29-33-35-39-43
Host: Jack Kane
Format: L
Features: I-N-F

WOWK-TV
625 4th Avenue
Huntington WV 25701
304-525-7661
Category: 99

Local Television Stations and Shows

WPBY-TV
Carol Brodtrick, Program Manager
3rd Avenue
Huntington WV 25701
304-696-6630
Category: 99
Do not have any shows.

WSAZ-TV
Leda Lewis
Newscenter 3 Early Morning
645 Fifth Avenue
Huntington WV 25721
304-697-4780
Category: 99
Host: Kathy Young
Format: L
Features: I-N-F

WSAZ-TV
Leda Lewis
Newscenter 3 at Midday
645 5th Avenue
Huntington WV 25721
304-697-4780
Category: 99
Host: Loren Tobia
Format: L
Features: I-N-F

WISCONSIN

New Tech Times
Jeff Clarke
WHA-TV
821 University Avenue
Madison WI 53706
608-263-6995
Category: 23

Public Conference (WITI-TV)
Gerald Peters, Producer
Milwaukee Public Library
814 W Wisconsin Avenue
Milwaukee WI 53233
414-278-3572
Category: 99

WISN-TV
759 N 19th Street
P O Box 402
Milwaukee WI 53233
414-342-8812
Category: 99

WITI-TV
Eric Anderson, News Director
9001 N Green Bay Road
Milwaukee WI 53209
414-355-6666
Category: 99

WMVS-TV
John Pushkash, Program Manager
1015 N 6th Street
Milwaukee WI 53203
414-271-1036
Category: 99

WTMJ-TV
720 E Capitol Drive
Milwaukee WI 53201
414-332-9611
Category: 99

BRITISH COLUMBIA

CBUT-TV
700 Hamilton Street
Vancouver V6B 2RS   BC Canada
604-665-8000
Category: 99

ONTARIO

CHCH-TV
163 Jackson Street W
Hamilton L8N 3A6   ON Canada
416-522-1101
Category: 99

CBMT-TV
1400 Dorchester Boulevard E
Montreal H3C 3A8   ON Canada
514-285-3211
Category: 99

CFCF-TV
405 Ogilvy Avenue
Montreal H3N 1M4   ON Canada
514-273-6311
Category: 99

CFMT-TV
Elena Caprile
Italianissimo
545 Lakeshore Boulevard West
Tornoto M5V 1A3   ON Canada
416-593-4747
Category: 99
Host: Laura Albanese/Cesare Pella
Format: L-T

CITY-TV
99 E Queen Street
Toronto M5C 2M1   ON Canada
416-367-5757
Category: 99

CBLT-TV
P O Box 500
Station A
Toronto M5W 1E6   ON Canada
416-925-3311
Category: 99

CFTO-TV
P O Box 9
Toronto M4A 2M9   ON Canada
416-299-2000
Category: 99

QUEBEC

CFCF-TV
Producer, As It Is
405 Ogilvy Avenue
Montreal H3N 1M4   PQ Canada
514-273-6311
Category: 99

===

Format: L = Live   T = Taped   C = Live with Call-ins   P = Telephone Interviews

Features: I = Interviews   N = News   F = Features   B = Book Reviews   R = Book Readings

===

Local Television Stations and Shows

(sorted alphabetically)

COMPANY	CITY	ST	COMPANY	CITY	ST
Black Voice	Houston	TX	KPBS-TV	San Diego	CA
CBLT-TV	Toronto	ON	KPHO-TV	Phoenix	AZ
CBMT-TV	Montreal	ON	KPIX-TV	San Francisco	CA
CBUT-TV	Vancouver	BC	KPNX-TV	Phoenix	AZ
CFCF-TV	Montreal	PQ	KPRC-TV	Houston	TX
CFMT-TV	Tornoto	ON	KPTV-TV	Portland	OR
CFTO-TV	Toronto	ON	KQED-TV	San Francisco	CA
Channel 2 Broadcasting	Anchorage	AK	KRIV-TV	Houston	TX
CHCH-TV	Hamilton	ON	KRMA-TV	Denver	CO
CITY-TV	Toronto	ON	KRON-TV	San Francisco	CA
Group W Cable	New York	NY	KSAT-TV	San Antonio	TX
KABC-TV	Hollywood	CA	KSDK-TV	St Louis	MO
KAET-TV	Tempe	AZ	KSHB-TV	Kansas City	MO
KAKE-TV	Wichita	KS	KSL-TV	Salt Lake City	UT
KARK-TV	Little Rock	AR	KSNW-TV	Wichita	KS
KATU-TV	Portland	OR	KSTP-TV	Saint Paul	MN
KATV-TV	Little Rock	AR	KSTU-TV	Salt Lake City	UT
KBHK-TV	San Francisco	CA	KSTW-TV	Tacoma	WA
KBTV-TV	Denver	CO	KTAL-TV	Texarkana	TX
KCBS-TV	Hollywood	CA	KTBN-TV	Santa Ana	CA
KCET-TV	Los Angeles	CA	KTCA-TV	Saint Paul	MN
KCNC-TV	Denver	CO	KTHV-TV	Little Rock	AR
KCOP-TV	Hollywood	CA	KTLA-TV	Los Angeles	CA
KCPT-TV	Kansas City	MO	KTRK-TV	Houston	TX
KCRA-TV	Sacramento	CA	KTSM-TV	El Paso	TX
KCSM-TV	San Mateo	CA	KTSP-TV	Phoenix	AZ
KCST-TV	San Diego	CA	KTTV-TV	Hollywood	CA
KCTS-TV	Seattle	WA	KTUL-TV	Tulsa	OK
KCTV-TV	Kansas City	MO	KTVI-TV	Saint Louis	MO
KDFW-TV	Dallas	TX	KTVK-TV	Phoenix	AZ
KDKA-TV	Pittsburgh	PA	KTVT-TV	Fort Worth	TX
KENS-TV	San Antonio	TX	KTVU-TV	Oakland	CA
KERA-TV	Dallas	TX	KTVX-TV	Salt Lake City	UT
KETA-TV	Oklahoma City	OK	KTVY-TV	Oklahoma City	OK
KETC-TV	St. Louis	MO	KUED-TV	Salt Lake City	UT
KETS-TV	Conway	AR	KUHT-TV	Houston	TX
KFMB-TV	San Diego	CA	KUSA-TV	Denver	CO
KGGM-TV	Albuquerque	NM	KUTV-TV	Salt Lake City	UT
KGO-TV	San Francisco	CA	KVCR-TV	San Bernardino	CA
KGTV-TV	San Diego	CA	KVIE-TV	Sacramento	CA
KGW-TV	Portland	OR	KVIQ-TV	Eureka	CA
KHJ-TV	Los Angeles	CA	KVUE-TV	Austin	TX
KHOU-TV	Houston	TX	KWCH-TV	Wichita	KS
KICU-TV	San Jose	CA	KWHY-TV	Los Angeles	CA
KIEM-TV	Eureka	CA	KWTV-TV	Oklahoma City	OK
KING-TV	Seattle	WA	KXAS-TV	Fort Worth	TX
KIRO-TV	Seattle	WA	KXMC-TV	Minot	ND
KJRH-TV	Tulsa	OK	KXTV-TV	Sacramento	CA
KLRN-TV	San Antonio	TX	KYW-TV	Philadelphia	PA
KMBC-TV	Kansas City	MO	Money, Money, Money	Pasadena	CA
KMGH-TV	Denver	CO	New Tech Times	Madison	WI
KMOL-TV	San Antonio	TX	Nova	Boston	MA
KMOX-TV	St Louis	MO	Public Conference (WITI)	Milwaukee	WI
KNBC-TV	Burbank	CA	WABC-TV	New York	NY
KNME-TV	Albuquerque	NM	WAGA-TV	Atlanta	GA
KNOC, Group W	Buena Park	CA	WATE-TV	Knoxville	TN
KOAP-TV	Portland	OR	WAVE-TV	Louisville	KY
KOAT-TV	Albuquerque	NM	WAVY-TV	Portsmouth	VA
KOB-TV	Albuquerque	NM	WBAL-TV	Baltimore	MD
KOCE-TV	Huntington Beach	CA	WBBM-TV	Chicago	IL
KOCO-TV	Oklahoma City	OK	WBIQ-TV	Birmingham	AL
KOIN-TV	Portland	OR	WBIR-TV	Knoxville	TN
KOMO-TV	Seattle	WA	WBMG-TV	Birmingham	AL
KOTV-TV	Tulsa	OK	WBNS-TV	Columbus	OH
KOVR-TV	Sacramento	CA	WBRC-TV	Birmingham	AL

Local Television Stations and Shows

(sorted alphabetically)

COMPANY	CITY	ST	COMPANY	CITY	ST
WBRE-TV	Wilkes-Barre	PA	WJZ-TV	Baltimore	MD
WBTV-TV	Charlotte	NC	WKBD-TV	Southfield	MI
WBZ-TV	Boston	MA	WKBW-TV	Buffalo	NY
WCAU-TV	Philadelphia	PA	WKEF-TV	Dayton	OH
WCBS-TV	New York	NY	WKNO-TV	Memphis	TN
WCCO-TV	Minneapolis	MN	WKPC-TV	Louisville	KY
WCET-TV	Cincinnati	OH	WKRC-TV	Cincinnati	OH
WCHS-TV	Charleston	WV	WKRN-TV	Nashville	TN
WCIU-TV	Chicago	IL	WKYC-TV	Cleveland	OH
WCIX-TV	Miami	FL	WKZO-TV	Kalamazoo	MI
WCMH-TV	Columbus	OH	WLKY-TV	Louisville	KY
WCPO-TV	Cincinnati	OH	WLNE-TV	New Bedford	MA
WCPX-TV	Orlando	FL	WLNE-TV	New Bedford	MA
WCSH-TV	Portland	ME	WLOS-TV	Asheville	NC
WCVB-TV	Boston	MA	WLRN-TV	Miami	FL
WCVE-TV	Richmond	VA	WLS-TV	Chicago	IL
WDAF-TV	Kansas City	MO	WLVI-TV	Boston	MA
WDAU-TV	Scranton	PA	WLWT-TV	Cincinnati	OH
WDCA-TV	Bethesda	MD	WLYH-TV	Lebanon	PA
WDCN-TV	Nashville	TN	WMAQ-TV	Chicago	IL
WDHO-TV	Toledo	OH	WMAR-TV	Baltimore	MD
WDIV-TV	Detroit	MI	WMC-TV	Memphis	TN
WDSU-TV	New Orleans	LA	WMFE-TV	Orlando	FL
WDTN-TV	Dayton	OH	WMPB-TV	Owings Mills	MD
WDVM-TV	Washington	DC	WMTW-TV	Poland Spring	ME
WEDH-TV	Hartford	CT	WMVS-TV	Milwaukee	WI
WEDU-TV	Tampa	FL	WNBC-TV	New York	NY
WEDW-TV	Fairfield	CT	WNED-TV	Buffalo	NY
WESH-TV	Orlando	FL	WNEM-TV	Saginaw	MI
WETA Channel 26	Washington	DC	WNEP-TV	Avoca	PA
WEWS-TV	Cleveland	OH	WNET-TV	New York	NY
WFAA-TV	Dallas	TX	WNEV-TV	Boston	MA
WFLD-TV	Chicago	IL	WNEW-TV	New York	NY
WFMY-TV	Greensboro	NC	WNSC-TV	Rock Hill	SC
WFSB-TV	Hartford	CT	WNYT-TV	Albany	NY
WFTV-TV	Orlando	FL	WOR-TV	Secaucus	NJ
WFUM-TV	Flint	MI	WOR-TV	New York	NY
WFYI-TV	Indianapolis	IN	WOSU-TV	Columbus	OH
WGAL-TV	Lancaster	PA	WOTV-TV	Grand Rapids	MI
WGBH-TV	Boston	MA	WOWK-TV	Huntington	WV
WGHP-TV	Greensboro	NC	WPBA-TV	Atlanta	GA
WGME-TV	Portland	ME	WPBT-TV	Miami	FL
WGN-TV	Chicago	IL	WPBY-TV	Huntington	WV
WGRZ-TV	Buffalo	NY	WPCQ-TV	Charlotte	NC
WHAS-TV	Louisville	KY	WPEC-TV	W Palm Beach	FL
WHBQ-TV	Memphis	TN	WPGH-TV	Pittsburgh	PA
WHIO-TV	Dayton	OH	WPHL-TV	Philadelphia	PA
WHMM-TV	Washington	DC	WPIX-TV	New York	NY
WHP-TV	Harrisburg	PA	WPLG-TV	Miami	FL
WHRO-TV	Norfolk	VA	WPRI-TV	East Providence	RI
WHTM-TV	Harrisburg	PA	WPTD-TV	Dayton	OH
WIS-TV	Columbia	SC	WPTF-TV	Raleigh	NC
WISH-TV	Indianapolis	IN	WPTV-TV	Palm Beach	FL
WISN-TV	Milwaukee	WI	WPVI-TV	Philadelphia	PA
WITF-TV	Harrisburg	PA	WPXI-TV	Pittsburgh	PA
WITI-TV	Milwaukee	WI	WQED-TV	Pittsburgh	PA
WIVB-TV	Buffalo	NY	WRAL-TV	Raleigh	NC
WIW-TV	Cincinnati	OH	WRC-TV	Washington	DC
WIXT-TV	Syracuse	NY	WREG-TV	Memphis	TN
WJAC-TV	Johnstown	PA	WRGB-TV	Schenectady	NY
WJAR-TV	Providence	RI	WRLK-TV	Columbia	SC
WJBK-TV	Southfield	MI	WRTV-TV	Indianapolis	IN
WJLA-TV	Washington	DC	WSAZ-TV	Huntington	WV
WJRT-TV	Flint	MI	WSB-TV	Atlanta	GA
WJW-TV	Cleveland	OH	WSBE-TV	Providence	RI

Local Television Stations and Shows

(sorted alphabetically)

COMPANY	CITY	ST	COMPANY	CITY	ST
WSBK-TV	Brighton	MA	WTVN-TV	Columbus	OH
WSKG-TV	Binghamton	NY	WTVR-TV	Richmond	VA
WSMV-TV	Nashville	TN	WTVS-TV	Detroit	MI
WSOC-TV	Charlotte	NC	WTVT-TV	Tampa	FL
WSPA-TV	Spartanburg	SC	WUAB-TV	Cleveland	OH
WSTM-TV	Syracuse	NY	WUHQ-TV	Battle Creek	MI
WSVN-TV	Miami	FL	WUNC-TV	Chapel Hill	NC
WTAE-TV	Pittsburgh	PA	WUSA-TV	Minneapolis	MN
WTAF-TV	Philadelphia	PA	WVEC-TV	Norfolk	VA
WTBS-TV	Atlanta	GA	WVIA-TV	Pittston	PA
WTEN-TV	Albany	NY	WVIT-TV	West Hartford	CT
WTHR-TV	Indianapolis	IN	WVIZ-TV	Cleveland	OH
WTKR-TV	Norfolk	VA	WVTM-TV	Birmingham	AL
WTMJ-TV	Milwaukee	WI	WVUE-TV	New Orleans	LA
WTNH-TV	New Haven	CT	WWBT-TV	Richmond	VA
WTOL-TV	Toledo	OH	WWL-TV	New Orleans	LA
WTSP-TV	Saint Petersburg	FL	WXEL-TV	West Palm Beach	FL
WTTG-TV	Washington	DC	WXEX-TV	Richmond	VA
WTTV-TV	Indianapolis	IN	WXFL-TV	Tampa	FL
WTTW-TV	Chicago	IL	WXIA-TV	Atlanta	GA
WTVD-TV	Durham	NC	WXII-TV	Winston-Salem	NC
WTVF-TV	Nashville	TN	WXIX-TV	Cincinnati	OH
WTVG-TV	Toledo	OH	WXYZ-TV	Southfield	MI
WTVH-TV	Syracuse	NY	WYES-TV	New Orleans	LA
WTVI-TV	Charlotte	NC	WYFF-TV	Greenville	SC
WTVJ-TV	Miami	FL	WZZM-TV	Grand Rapids	MI
WTVK-TV	Knoxville	TN			

A Better Way
Donald Elder, Producer
3321-B South Wakefield Street
Arlington VA 22206
202-447-7763
Category: 11-19-25-33-39-41-43
        47-51-55-69-71-77-8´-86
Host: Donald Elder
Format: T
Features: I-T-B

ABC After School Specials
Dolores Morris,
Director, Children's Programs
1330 Avenue of the Americas
New York NY 10019
212-887-6934
Category: 21-76

ABC News Nightline
7 West 66th Street
New York NY 10019
212-887-4995
Category: 55-97
Host: Ted Koppel
Format: L
Features: I-N-F

ABC Nightline
1717 DeSales Street NW
Washington DC 20036
202-887-7360
Category: 55-97(news)
Host: Ted Koppel
Format: L
Features: I-N-F

ABC Weekend Specials
Dolores Morris,
Director, Children's Programs
1330 Avenue of the Americas
New York NY 10019
212-887-6934
Category: 21-76
buy tv rights

ABC World News Tonight
7 West 66 Street
New York NY 10023
212-887-4993
Category: 97-99
Host: Peter Jennings
Format: L
Features: N-F

ABC-TV
1926 Broadway
New York NY 10023
212-887-4114
Category: 99

Adam Smith's Money World
Dan Preston
WNET-TV

45 West 45th Street, 15th Floor
New York NY 10019
212-221-6310
Category: 19-41-55
Host: Adam Smith
Format: T
Features: I-N-F

Affordable Computer
1182 N Capitola Avenue
San Jose CA 95132
408-251-0102
Category: 23

Agency for Instructional TV
Public Affairs Director
P O Box A
Bloomington IN 47402
812-339-2203
Category: 31

Alaska Television Network
1007 W 32nd Street
Anchorage AK 99503
907-561-4200
Category: 61(AK)-99

Alive and Well
Maryann Ridini
3211 Cahuenga Boulevard
Hollywood CA 90068
213-851-7801
Category: 39

American Almanac
NBC-TV
4001 Nebraska Avenue NW
Washington DC 20016
202-885-5000
Category: 99

American Business Network
1615 H Street NW
Washington DC 20062
202-463-5690
Category: 19

AP Broadcast Services
1825 K Street NW
Washington DC 20006-1253
202-955-7200
Category: 55-97(news)-99

AP News Cable
50 Rockefeller Plaza
New York NY 10020
212-621-1513
Category: 97-99

Arts and Entertainment Network
Producer, Daytime Show
555 Fifth Avenue
New York NY 10017
Category: 11-33

Assignment People
Ted White, Producer
P O Box 5464
Richmond VA 23220
804-257-1260
Category: 17-99
Features: I

Associated Broadcast News
Robert C Cody, Managing Editor
Focal Point
1199 National Press Building
Washington DC 20045
301-320-4615; 202-628-6397
Category: 99
Host: Robert C Cody
Format: T
Features: I-N-F-B

Audio-Video News
6130 Beachway Drive
Falls Church VA 22041
703-671-1049
Category: 97-99

Book of the Month Club
Robert P Riger, Coordinator
First Edition
485 Lexington Avenue
New York NY 10017
212-867-4300
Category: 99
Features: I-R

Bookends
Intermark Group
41 West 53rd Street #2A
New York NY 10019
212-245-5098
Category: 99
Features: I

Books & The World
Marian Vuilleumier
P O Box 111
West Hyannisport MA 02672
617-775-4811
Category: 99
Host: Marion Vuillemier
Format: T
Features: I

Broadcast News Service
P O Box 2360
New York NY 10116
212-223-0909
Category: 97-99

C-SPAN
Greg Barker, Guest Coordinator
National Viewer Call-In Program
400 North Capitol Street NW #155
Washington DC 20001
202-737-3220

Category: 19-41-55-63
Format: C
Features: N

Cable Health Network
Program Director
1211 Avenue of the Americas
New York NY 10036
212-719-7230
Category: 39

Cable News Network
Rod Foster, Producer
Newsnight
6290 Sunset Boulevard #600
Hollywood CA 90028
213-460-5000
Category: 99
Format: C
Features: N-B

Cable News Network
Hillary Hope
Showbiz Today
6290 Sunset Boulevard #600
Hollywood CA 90028
213-460-5000
Category: 11-33
Format: L
Features: I-F

Cable News Network
Roger Scott
Crossfire
6430 Sunset Boulevard
Hollywood CA 90028
213-460-5000
Category: 99

Cable News Network
Alice Glenn
Crossfire
2133 Wisconsin Avenue NW
Washington DC 20007
202-898-7900
Category: 99

Cable News Network
Gail Evans, Booking Director
Daybreak
1050 Techwood Drive NW
Atlanta GA 30348
404-827-1500
Category: 99
Host: P Greenlaw and Molly McCoy
Format: L
Features: I-N-F

Cable News Network
Gail Evans, Booking Director
Daywatch
1050 Techwood Drive NW
Atlanta GA 30348
404-827-1500
Category: 99
Host: Bob Cain/Mary Ann Loughlin
Format: L
Features: I-N-F

Cable News Network
Gail Evans, Booking Director
International Hour
1050 Techwood Drive NW
Atlanta GA 30348
404-827-1500
Category: 99
Host: Bernard Shaw
Format: L
Features: I-N-F

Cable News Network
Gail Evans, Booking Director
Take Two
1050 Techwood Drive NW
Atlanta GA 30348
404-827-1500
Category: 99
Host: Dave Walker and Lois Hart
Format: L
Features: I-N-F

Cable News Network
Michael Hessing
Crossfire
1050 Techwood Drive NW
Atlanta GA 30348
404-827-1307
Category: 99

Cable News Network
Program Director
Inside Business
5 Penn Plaza
New York NY 10001
212-839-6000
Category: 19

Cable News Network
Moneyline
5 Penn Plaza
New York NY 10001
212-839-6000
Category: 19(investing)

Cable News Network
Program Director
Business Morning
5 Penn Plaza
New York NY 10001
212-839-6000
Category: 19

Cable Satellite Public Affairs
400 N Capitol Street NW
Washington DC 20001
202-737-3220
Category: 55-97-99

Cablevision Systems
Patrick Dolan, Producer
Book Channel
One Media Crossways Drive
Woodbury NY 11797
Category: 99
Host: Chris Chase and Bill Small
Format: T
Features: I-B

California Farm Bureau
Ron Miller, Producer
Voice of Agriculture
1601 Exposition Boulevard
Sacramento CA 95815
916-924-4089
Category: 98(agriculture)
Host: Ron Miller
Format: T
Features: I-N-F

Canadian Broadcasting Corp.
P O Box 8478
1500 Bronson Avenue
Ottawa K1G 3J5 ON Canada
613-731-3111
Category: 99

Capital Broadcast News
Producer, Newscom
122 C Street NW #850
Washington DC 20001
202-638-6733
Category: 97-99

Capitol Connection News Service
3401 N Fairfax Drive
Arlington VA 22201
703-522-0026
Category: 97-99

CBS Evening News
CBS-TV
524 West 57th Street
New York NY 10019
212-975-3691
Category: 97-99
Host: Dan Rather

CBS Morning News
Roberta Dougherty, Producer
CBS-TV
524 West 57th Street
New York NY 10019
212-975-2824
Category: 97-99
Features: I-N-F

CBS Nightwatch
CBS-TV
2033 M Street NW
Washington DC 20036
202-775-6812
Category: 55-97-99

CBS Nightwatch
CBS-TV
524 West 57th Street
New York NY 10019
212-975-7997
Category: 97-99

CBS Reports
CBS-TV
2033 M Street NW
New York NY 10019
212-975-3076
Category: 97-99

Television Networks and Syndicated Shows

CBS Sunday Morning
Robert Northshield, Producer
CBS-TV
524 West 57th Street
New York NY 10019
212-975-6790
Category: 99
Host: Charles Kuralt

Chicago Tonight
John Callaway, News Director
WTTW-TV
5400 N St Louis Avenue
Chicago IL 60625
312-583-5000
Category: 99
Host: John Callaway
Format: L-T-C-P
Features: I-N-F-B

CKO Incorporated
30 Carlton Street
Toronto M5B 2E9   ON Canada
416-591-1222
Category: 99

Connie Martinson Talks Books
2288 Cold Water Canyon
Beverly Hills CA 90210
213-271-4127
Category: 99
Host: Connie Martinson
Format: T
Features: I-B

Cox Cable
1175 N Cuyumaca
El Cajon CA 92020
619-562-1180
Category: 99

CTV Television Network
42 Charles Street East
Toronto M4Y 1T5   ON Canada
416-928-6000
Category: 99

Dakota Giant Network
P O Box 1738
Bismarck ND 58501
701-223-0900
Category: 61(ND-SD)-99

David Letterman Show
Laurie Guthrie
NBC-TV
30 Rockefeller Plaza
New York NY 10112
212-664-5221
Category: 99
Host: David Letterman
Format: L
Features: I

David Susskind Show
Jean Kennedy, Producer
WNYW-TV
230 Park Avenue #963

New York NY 10169
212-818-1180; 212-535-1000
Category: 99
Host: David Susskind
Format: T
Features: I-N-F-B

Dial Magazine
Jane Ciabattari
34 East Street
New York NY 10022
212-888-5900
Category: 99

Discovery Computer Net
12401 W Olympic
Los Angeles CA 90064
213-820-2900
Category: 23

Dow Jones Cable News
P O Box 300
Princeton NJ 08540
609-452-2000
Category: 19-99

Dr Ruth Show
Ron Abbott
Lifetime Cable Network
1211 Avenue of the Americas
New York NY 10036
212-719-7198
Category: 99
Host: Ruth Westheimer
Format: L-T-C
Features: I-F-B
celebrity and expert interviews

Eastern Educational TV Network
120 Boylston Street
Boston MA 02116
617-338-4455
Category: 99

Ecumedia News Service
475 Riverside Drive #856
New York NY 10015
212-870-2255
Category: 99

Educational Broadcasting Corp.
356 West 58th Street
New York NY 10019
212-560-200
Category: 99

Entertainment Tonight
Sharon Smith
5555 Melrose Avenue
Hollywood CA 90038
213-468-4900
Category: 11-33

Eternal Word Television Network
Mary Ann Lollar, Asst Producer
Mother Angelica Live
5817 Old Leeds Road
Birmingham AL 35210

205-956-9537
Category: 63
Host: Mother Angelica
Format: C
Features: I

Ethnic Press International
Giorgio L Perna, Director
4710 Bethesda Avenue #917
Bethesda MD 20814
301-986-1455
Category: 11-17-27-41-45
        55-71-78-80-83
Host:
Format: L-T-C-P
Features: I-N-F-B

Evening Magazine
Ann Schultz, Producer
KDKA-TV
1 Gateway Center
Pittsburgh PA 15222
412-392-2578
Category: 11-15-17-33-35-41-45
        47-49-53-63-78-82-83
        86-87
Host: Jon Burnett and Liz Miles
Format: T
Features: N

Financial News Network
Debby Everett
2525 Ocean Park Boulevard
Santa Monica CA 90405
213-450-2412
Category: 19
Features: I-N

Financial News Network
Consumer Corner
2525 Ocean Park Boulevard
Santa Monica CA 90405
213-450-2412
Category: 25
Format: T
Features: I-N-F

Firing Line
Warren Steibel, Producer
PBS-TV
150 East 35th Street
New York NY 10020
212-679-7409
Category: 55
Host: William Buckley
Format: L
Features: (discussion)

Georgia Public Television
Keith Kozicki, Producer
Georgia Moneyline
1540 Steward Avenue SW
Atlanta GA 30310
404-656-5953
Category: 17-19-23-25-33-55-69
Host: Richard Warner
Format: T
Features: I-N-F

Global TV
81 Barber Green Road
Don Mills M3C 2A2 ON Canada
416-446-5311
Category: 99

Good Morning America
Phyllis McGrady, Producer
ABC-TV
1965 Broadway
New York NY 10023
212-580-6100
Category: 11-17-25-29-33-35-39
43-53-55-57-63-67-69
71-75-99
Host: David Hartman
Format: L
Features: I-N-F

Health Field
Pamela Field
CBS-TV
524 West 57th Street
New York NY 10019
212-975-5632
Category: 39

Hillier Productions
Erica Gerard, Producer
Epcot Magazine
15303 Ventura
Sherman Oaks CA 91403
818-990-4004
Category: 11-33-99

Home Box Office
1100 Avenue of the Americas
New York NY 10036
212-484-1100
Category: 11-33-99

Hour Magazine
Martin Berman, Producer
Group W Productions
5746 Sunset Boulevard
Hollywood CA 90028
213-460-5256
Category: 99
Host: Gary Collins
Format: L-T
Features: I-F

How About
Don Herbert, Producer
132 Stagecoach
Canoga Park CA 91307
818-703-1227
Category: 99

Hughes Television Network
4 Penn Plaza
New York NY 10001
212-563-8900
Category: 99

Inday News
Rita Baron-Faust, Producer
220 East 42nd Street

New York NY 10017
212-210-2474
Category: 97-99

Independent Television News
1705 DeSales Street #800
Washington DC 20036
202-429-9080
Category: 97-99

Information Age
Lea Nathans, Producer
Financial News Network
1 Liberty Place
New York NY 10038
Category: 19-99

International Business Network
Dan Sobol, Producer
575 Madison Avenue #1006
New York NY 10022
212-605-0426
Category: 19

KABC Hollywood Closeup
Pamela Hughes
4151 Prospect Avenue
Hollywood CA 90027
213-557-5911
Category: 11-17-33-77-81
Host: Steve Edwards
Format: T
Features: I-N-F-B
Hollywood entertainment only

Kansas Broadcasting System
Program Director
P O Box 12
Wichita KS 67201
316-838-1212
Category: 61(KS)-99

Kansas State Network
P O Box 333
Wichita KS 67201
316-265-5631
Category: 61(KS)-99

Keoland
KELO Building
Sioux Falls SD 57102
605-336-1100
Category: 99

KidVid
ARP Films
342 Madison Avenue
New York NY 10173
212-867-1700
Category: 21-31-76

KSTS Computer Show
Victoria Smith
Ocean Communications
3448 Mount Saint Helena
San Jose CA 95127
408-923-3917
Category: 23

Late Night America
Bill Pac, Producer
WTVS-TV
7441 Second Boulevard
Detroit MI 48202
313-873-7200
Category: 99
Format: L
Features: I

Lifetime Cable Network
Chuck Gingold, Programming
1211 Avenue of the Americas
New York NY 10036
212-719-7198
Category: 99

Lifetime Cable Network
Pam Burke, First Person
1211 Avenue of the Americas
New York NY 10036
212-719-7115
Category: 99
Format: T
Features: I

MacNeil-Lehrer Newshour
Gordon Earle, Producer
WNET-TV
356 West 58th Street
New York NY 10019
212-560-2000
Category: 99
Host: MacNeil and Lehrer
Format: L
Features: N

Maine News Service
P O Box 2043
Augusta ME 04330
207-582-6511
Category: 61(ME)-99

Meet the Press
Betty Dukert, Producer
NBC-TV
4001 Nebraska Avenue
Washington DC 20016
202-885-4598
Category: 99
Format: L
Features: I

Merv Griffin Show
Les Sinclair, Associate Producer
1541 N Vine Street
Hollywood CA 90028
213-461-4701
Category: 99
Host: Merv Griffin
Format: T
Features: I

Modern Satellite Network
45 Rockefeller Plaza
New York NY 10020
212-765-3100
Category: 99

Television Networks and Syndicated Shows

Montana Television Network
P O Box 2557
Billings MT 59103
406-256-0705
Category: 61(MT)-99

Nashville Network
News Director
2806 Opryland Drive
Nashville TN 37214
Category: 11-33

National Christian Network
1150 W King Street
Cocoa FL 32922
305-632-1000
Category: 63(Christian)

National Jewish Television
Palisades Avenue
Riverdale NY 10463
212-549-4160
Category: 63(Jewish)

Nemo News Service
7179 Via Maria
San Jose CA 95139
408-226-6339
Category: 99

News Information Weekly Service
15303 Ventura Boulevard Floor 11
Sherman Oaks CA 91403
Category: 99

Newsfile Inc
21 East 51st Street
New York NY 10022
Category: 99

Nickelodeon Livewire
Linda Kahn, Producer
1775 Broadway
New York NY 10019
212-713-6400
Category: 21-76

1986
Richard Harris, News Editor
NBC News
4001 Nebraska Avenue NW
Washington DC 20016
202-885-5019
Category: 99
Host: Mudd/Chung/Rabel
Format: T
Features: I-N-F

Phil Donahue Show
Gail Steinberg
NBC-TV
30 Rockefeller Plaza
New York NY 10112
212-664-6501
Category: 99
Host: Phil Donahue
Format: L
Features: I

Praise the Lord Network
PTL - The Inspirational Network
Charlotte NC 28279
704-542-6000
Category: 63(Christian)

Quality Parenting
Stephanie Borden
York Producing Group
4537 S 28th Avenue
Minneapolis MN 55406
612-722-0410
Category: 31-35

Regis Philbin Lifestyles
Pam Burke
Lifetime Cable Network
1211 Avenue of the Americas
New York NY 10036
212-719-7115
Category: 99
Host: Regis Philbin
Format: T
Features: I-F-B

Rip 'N' Read News Service
Randy Alfred, Editor
88 First Street #302
San Francisco CA 94105
415-974-1622
Category: 99
Format: P
Features: I-N-F-B

700 Club
Jackie Mitchum
Christian Broadcasting Network
CBN Center
Virginia Beach VA 23463
804-424-7777; 800-446-8272
Category: 99
Host: Pat Robertson
Format: L-T
Features: I

60 Minutes
Philip Sheffler, Producer
CBS-TV
524 West 57th Street
New York NY 10019
212-975-2009
Category: 99
Host: various
Format: L-T
Features: N-F-I

Standard Broadcast News
2 Saint Clair Avenue West
Toronto M4V 1L6 ON Canada
416-924-5711
Category: 99

Storybreak
40 West 57th Street, 16th Floor
New York NY 10019
212-975-2921
Category: 21-76
Host: Bob Keeshan

Strictly Business
Gay Rosenthal, Producer
WNBC-TV
30 Rockefeller Plaza
New York NY 10020
212-664-7872
Category: 19-23
Host: Jack Cafferty
Format: T
Features: I-N-F

Sun World Satellite News
444 N Capitol Street NW #6010
Washington DC 20001
202-783-7173
Category: 99
Features: N

The First Estate
Jerry Burke
NBC-TV
30 Rockefeller Plaza #1169
New York NY 10020
212-664-3097
Category: 63

The Kakeland Stations
P O Box 10
Wichita KS 67201
316-943-4221
Category: 99

The Learning Channel
Programing Director
1200 New Hampshire Ave NW #240
Washington DC 20036
202-331-8100
Category: 21-31-76
Features: F

The Newsfeed Network
90 Park Avenue
New York NY 10016
212-983-6513
Category: 99
Features: I-N

The World of Travel
Mike Michaels, Producer
Studio M Productions
8715 Waikki Street
Honolulu HI 96815
808-734-3345
Category: 71
Host: Martin Deutsch/Don Langley
Format: T
Features: I-N-F

This Week with David Brinkley
Veronique Rodman
ABC-TV
1717 DeSales Street NW
Washington DC 20036
202-887-7375
Category: 55-99
Host: David Brinkley
Format: L
Features: I

Television Networks and Syndicated Shows

Today Show
Emily Boxer or Marty Ryan
NBC-TV
30 Rockefeller Plaza
New York NY 10020
212-664-4444
Category: 99
Host: Bryant Gumbel
Format: L
Features: I-N-F

Tonight Show
Shirley Wood, Coordinator
NBC-TV
3000 W Alameda Avenue
Burbank CA 91523
818-840-4444
Category: 99
Host: Johnny Carson
Format: L
Features: I

TV-Airs
502 National Press Building
Washington DC 20045
202-628-6397
Category: 99

20/20
Victor Neufeld, Producer
ABC-TV News
157 Columbus Avenue
New York NY 10023
212-580-6061
Category: 97-99
Host: Barbara Walters/Hugh Downs
Format: L-T
Features: I-N-F

United Press International
Joe Fasbinder, Editor
Broadcast Book Corner
360 N Michigan Avenue
Chicago IL 60601
312-781-1632
Category: 99
Host: Joe Fasbinder
Features: B

UPI Cable News
220 East 42nd Street
New York NY 10017
212-850-8639
Category: 99

US Catholic Conference
1011 First Avenue #1300
New York NY 10022
212-644-1898
Category: 63(Catholic)-99

USA Cable Network
208 Harristown Road
Glen Rock NJ 07452
201-445-8550
Category: 99

USA Network
1230 Avenue of the Americas
New York NY 10020
212-408-9100
Category: 99

Vanguard News
P O Box 1240
Battleboro VT 05301
802-257-7131
Category: 99

Viewpoint on Nutrition
Dr Arnold Pike,
708 Katherine Drive
Montebello CA 90640
213-723-1516
Category: 27-39
Host: Dr Arnold Pike

Wally George Show
KDOC-TV
P O Box 787
Hollywood CA 90028
818-906-0860
Category: 99
Host: Wally George

Washington International Report
7245 Arlington Boulevard #200
Arlington VA 22042
703-573-7192
Category: 55-99

World Wide Information Services
360 First Avenue
New York NY 10010
212-677-6839
Category: 99

Television Networks and Syndicated Shows

(sorted by state and city)

ST	CITY	NETWORK OR SYNDICATED SHOW
AK	Anchorage	Alaska Television Network
AL	Birmingham	Eternal Word Television Network
CA	Beverly Hills	Connie Martinson Talks Books
CA	Burbank	Tonight Show
CA	Canoga Park	How About
CA	El Cajon	Cox Cable
CA	Hollywood	Alive and Well
CA	Hollywood	Cable News Network
CA	Hollywood	Entertainment Tonight
CA	Hollywood	Group W Productions
CA	Hollywood	Hour Magazine
CA	Hollywood	KABC Hollywood Closeup
CA	Hollywood	Merv Griffin Show
CA	Hollywood	Wally George Show
CA	Los Angeles	Discovery Computer Net
CA	Montebello	Viewpoint on Nutrition
CA	Sacramento	California Farm Bureau
CA	San Francisco	Rip 'N' Read News Service
CA	San Jose	Affordable Computer
CA	San Jose	KSTS Computer Show
CA	San Jose	Nemo News Service
CA	Santa Monica	Financial News Network
CA	Sherman Oaks	Hillier Productions
CA	Sherman Oaks	News Information Weekly Service
DC	Washington	ABC Nightline
DC	Washington	American Almanac
DC	Washington	American Business Network
DC	Washington	AP Broadcast Services
DC	Washington	AP News Cable
DC	Washington	Associated Broadcast News
DC	Washington	C-SPAN
DC	Washington	Cable News Network
DC	Washington	Cable Satellite Public Affairs
DC	Washington	Capital Broadcast News
DC	Washington	CBS Nightwatch
DC	Washington	Independent Television News
DC	Washington	Meet the Press
DC	Washington	NBC News
DC	Washington	Sun World Satellite News
DC	Washington	The Learning Channel
DC	Washington	This Week with David Brinkley
DC	Washington	TV-Airs
FL	Cocoa	National Christian Network
GA	Atlanta	Cable News Network
GA	Atlanta	Georgia Public Television
HI	Honolulu	The World of Travel
IL	Chicago	Chicago Tonight
IL	Chicago	United Press International
IN	Bloomington	Agency for Instructional TV
KS	Wichita	Kansas Broadcasting System
KS	Wichita	Kansas State Network
MA	Boston	Eastern Educational TV Network
MA	W Hyannisport	Books & The World
MD	Bethesda	Ethnic Press International
ME	Augusta	Maine News Service
MI	Detroit	Late Night America
MN	Minneapolis	Quality Parenting
MT	Billings	Montana Television Network
NC	Charlotte	Praise the Lord Network
ND	Bismarck	Dakota Giant Network
NJ	Glen Rock	USA Cable Network
NJ	Princeton	Dow Jones Cable News
NY	New York	ABC After School Specials
NY	New York	ABC News Nightline
NY	New York	ABC TV News
NY	New York	ABC Weekend Specials
NY	New York	ABC World News Tonight
NY	New York	Adam Smith's Money World
NY	New York	AP News Cable
NY	New York	Arts and Entertainment Network
NY	New York	Book of the Month Club
NY	New York	Bookends
NY	New York	Broadcast News Service
NY	New York	Cable Health Network
NY	New York	Cable News Network
NY	New York	CBS Evening News
NY	New York	CBS Morning News
NY	New York	CBS Nightwatch
NY	New York	CBS Reports
NY	New York	CBS Sunday Morning
NY	New York	David Letterman Show
NY	New York	David Susskind Show
NY	New York	Dial Magazine
NY	New York	Dr Ruth Show
NY	New York	Ecumedia News Service
NY	New York	Educational Broadcasting Corp.
NY	New York	Firing Line
NY	New York	Good Morning America
NY	New York	Health Field
NY	New York	Home Box Office
NY	New York	Hughes Television Network
NY	New York	Inday News
NY	New York	Information Age
NY	New York	International Business Network
NY	New York	KidVid
NY	New York	Lifetime Cable Network
NY	New York	MacNeil-Lehrer Newshour
NY	New York	Modern Satellite Network
NY	New York	NBC-TV
NY	New York	Newsfile Inc
NY	New York	Nickelodeon Livewire
NY	New York	Phil Donahue Show
NY	New York	Regis Philbin Lifestyles
NY	New York	Sixty 60 Minutes
NY	New York	Storybreak
NY	New York	Strictly Business
NY	New York	The First Estate
NY	New York	The Newsfeed Network
NY	New York	Today Show
NY	New York	United Press International
NY	New York	UPI Cable News
NY	New York	US Catholic Conference
NY	New York	USA Network
NY	New York	World Wide Information Services
NY	Riverdale	National Jewish Television
NY	Woodbury	Cablevision Systems
PA	Pittsburgh	Evening Magazine
SD	Sioux Falls	Keoland
TN	Nashville	Nashville Network
VA	Arlington	A Better Way
VA	Arlington	Capitol Connection News Service
VA	Arlington	Washington International Report
VA	Falls Church	Audio-Video News
VA	Richmond	Assignment People
VA	Virginia Beach	700 Club
VT	Battleboro	Vanguard News
ON	Don Mills	Global TV
ON	Ottawa	Canadian Broadcasting Corp.
ON	Toronto	CKO Incorporated
ON	Toronto	Standard Broadcast News

BIBLIOGRAPHY

Below are a few of the best books about publishing and self-publishing. For a complete bibliography of books, magazines, and other resources used in writing this book, see our 96-page bibliography, <u>The Independent Publisher's Bookshelf</u>.

American Association of University Presses, <u>One Book / Five Ways</u>
    (Los Altos, CA: William Kaufmann, 1978)
Bodian, Nat G., <u>Book Marketing Handbook, Volumes One</u>
    (New York: R. R. Bowker, 1980)
Bodian, Nat G., <u>Book Marketing Handbook, Volume Two</u>
    (New York: R. R. Bowker, 1983)
Bowker Company, R. R., <u>Literary Market Place 1986</u>
    (New York: R. R. Bowker, 1985)
Carter, Robert A., editor, <u>Trade Book Marketing</u>
    (New York: R. R. Bowker, 1983)
Corwin, Stanley J., <u>How to Become a Bestselling Author</u>
    (Cincinnati: Writer's Digest Books, 1984)
Glenn, Peggy, <u>Publicity for Books and Authors</u>
    (Huntington Beach, CA: Aames-Allen, 1984)
Gold, Ron, <u>The Personal Computer Publicity Book</u>
    (Santa Monica, CA: Gold, 1985)
Huenefeld, John, <u>The Huenefeld Guide to Book Publishing, 3rd Ed.</u>
    (Bedford: Huenefeld, 1986)
Jaques Cattell Press, <u>American Book Trade Directory, 31st Ed.</u>
    (New York: R. R. Bowker, 1985)
Kremer, John, <u>Book Marketing Made Easier</u>
    (Fairfield: Ad-Lib Publications, 1986)
Kremer, John, <u>Book Marketing Opportunities: A Database</u>
    (Fairfield: Ad-Lib Publications, 1986)
Kremer, John, <u>The Independent Publisher's Bookshelf</u>
    (Fairfield, Ad-Lib Publications, 1986)
Kremer, John, <u>101 Ways to Market Your Books</u>
    (Fairfield: Ad-Lib Publications, 1986)
Lant, Jeffrey, <u>The Unabashed Self-Promoter's Guide</u>
    (Cambridge, MA: JLA Associates, 1983)
McHugh, Jack, <u>McHugh Publishing Reports</u>
    (Framingham, MA: McHugh, 198-)
Parkhurst, William, <u>How to Get Publicity</u>
    (New York: Times Books, 1985)
Poynter, Dan, <u>Book Fairs: An Exhibiting Guide for Publishers</u>
    (Santa Barbara, CA: Para Publishing, 1986)
Poynter, Dan, <u>The Self-Publishing Manual, Third Edition</u>
    (Santa Barbara: Para, 1984)
Richards, Pamela, <u>Marketing Books and Journals to Western Europe</u>
    (Phoenix: Oryx Press, 1985)
Ross, Marilyn and Tom, <u>The Complete Guide to Self-Publishing</u>
    (Cincinnati: Writer's Digest Books, 1985)

Book Marketing Opportunities: A Database

To be quite honest, I don't know why anyone would want to use a printed directory when they could have the same information in database format. Databases allow you to make changes in the data, update as needed, sort by any criteria you like, print out labels and other reports and, in short, use the information more efficiently and effectively.

Yes, there are three drawbacks to many databases: 1) they are usually more expensive, 2) they may not work on your present computer, and 3) they may require too much training time for in-experienced users.

How does Book Marketing Opportunities: A Database measure up to these advantages and disadvantages of databases? Let's answer the objections first, and then we'll describe all the advantages.

BMO Database: Overcoming the Disadvantages

1)   While the BMO Database is more expensive than the Directory ($150.00 as compare to $19.95 plus $1.50 for shipping), the time it can save you will more than compensate for the additional cost. If you value your time at all (whether at minimum wage or at $50.00+ per hour), the Database will quickly repay your investment.

For example, to select out all the magazines which feature reviews of books on computers would take two minutes via computer but several hours by hand. In turn, the labels could be printed in ten minutes or less, while it might take another couple of hours to write out the labels. Total time savings for just one selection: 3-4 hours.

If you wanted to do a more complicated selection (for example, all the magazines featuring business articles or reviews located in a certain region), you could spend even more time.

2)   The BMO Database currently works only on the IBM-PC and highly compatibles. For example, it works on my Epson Equity I and my Standard Brands IBM compatible. It will not work on a CPM machine, Apple II computer, or Macintosh. Hence, to take full advantage of the database, you must own an IBM-PC or compatible.

As an alternative, we can also provide the database files as quote/comma-delimited ASCII files (in other words, files suitable for mail-merge) in most CPM formats as well as Macintosh format. You would then have to import the files into your own database program (if you have a database program, and if it is capable of importing such files [most newer programs are]).

Even then, it would not be ideal. The database files have
been specifically designed to work with our own proprietary
database program--which allows for some sophisticated tracking
mechanisms and allows us to provide updates to you without
affecting any changes you have made in the files. If you import
the files into a different database, these special features would
undoubtedly not be supported by your program.

If you do have an IBM-PC or compatible, however, this database program will undoubtedly be better than any system you now
have in place for doing your promotions and publicity.

3) While many database programs have a stiff learning curve
(which means that you spend more time learning the program than
it might save you), the BMO Database program is a menu-based
program that you should be able to use without ever having to
read the manual (though, of course, we do recommend that you read
the manual if you plan to use the program extensively).

You will not have to learn any sort of programming language
or complicated procedures. The BMO Database is a self-contained
program especially designed to be used for book marketing and
promotion. You'll be surprised at some of the things it will
allow you to do.

<u>BMO</u> <u>Database:</u> <u>Its</u> <u>Features</u> <u>and</u> <u>Advantages</u>

Here's just a few of the features of our new <u>Book Marketing
Opportunities: A Database</u>:

* Contains seven separate files
    * Radio Publicity File
    * TV Publicity File
    * Newspaper Publicity File
    * Magazine Publicity File
    * Wholesaler/Distributor File
    * Book Buyers File (Book Clubs, Chain Stores, Catalogs)
    * Miscellaneous File (Exhibits, Lists, Services, Etc.)

* Each file is selectable by any criteria you choose--city,
    state, address, company name, contact, category code or
    codes, phone numbers, zip codes, format, features,
    frequency, markets served; in other words, you can sort
    by any field in the file.

* Once you've selected the records you want, you can sort
    them either alphabetically or by zip code.

* Then you can send your records to your own self-designed
    list report, to mailing labels (of any size, and any
    number across), to disc, to screen, or to your printer.
    You can also send your reports to mail-merge files to be
    used with your word-processor for custom letters.

* The database also allows you to keep track of each time
  you contact someone or any group of records. (For you
  technical wizards, this is accomplished through repeating
  fields and a relational file; for you non-technical
  wizards, this is very easy to set up and use. Even I can
  use it.)

* As a result of the above point, you will be able to
  maintain your contact control cards, media activity
  records, and other files within the database. You'll
  have a record of each contact you've made (when, where,
  and results). From these records, you will even be able
  to set up a author tour schedule if you like.

* The BMO database allows you to add your own records,
  to change records as needed, to browse through the
  records, do scanning searches (for example, pick out all
  the radio records with ABC in them, whether KABC, WABC,
  ABC Sports, or whatever), and even do global updates
  where needed.

* Plus, the database will allow easy updating of records as
  we offer updates. At present we plan to offer updates
  every six months. With a few easy steps, these updated
  records (whether changes, additions, or deletions) will
  be added to your files quickly and painlessly--without
  changing any information you may have added to the file!

* Again, file updates will be available every six months.
  And, eventually, we hope, you'll be able to update any
  time you want via telephone (this service will, we hope,
  be available some time early in 1987).

* At present, updates will be available for the entire BMO
  Database or for portions of the database (that is, for
  any of the seven files currently available). Updates
  will cost $150.00 per year for the entire database, or
  $50.00 per file, for two updates each year.

* If you have any questions regarding this database, call
  our toll-free 800 number: 800-624-5893. We will also
  provide customer support via this toll-free number.
  Hence, if at any time while using the database, you have
  any problems, you can call us up direct (at no cost to
  you!) and we'll help clear up your problem.

* We will also be adding new files to the BMO database as
  we collect the information. For example, a file of over
  1000 specialty bookstores will be available in the fall.

* The cost for this service ($150.00 per year) for all
  updates and additions is less than the cost of one small
  list rental--and certainly less than you could do it
  yourself.

Book Marketing Opportunities: A Database

INFORMATION SUMMARY

Title: Book Marketing Opportunities: A Database

Author: John Kremer, with Marie Kiefer and Bob McIlvride

Publication Date: July 20, 1986

ISBN: 0-912411-12-0

Price: $150.00 before October 15, 1986
         $299.00 after October 15, 1986

         After October 15, 1986, the BMO Database will also
         include a new file, the Specialty Bookstore File of
         over 1000 specialty bookstores.

         Each database file will also be available separately
         at a cost of $50.00 per file after October 15, 1986.
         Hence, for example, you could buy the Radio Publicity
         File for $50.00, or the Wholesaler/Distributor File,
         or any of the other eight individual files (including
         the new Specialty Bookstore File).

Updates: Updates will be available every six months. The cost
         for these semi-annual updates will be $150.00 per year
         for the entire BMO Database or $50.00 per year for any
         individual files (such as the Radio Publicity File).

Requirements: IBM-PC or compatible computer
               PC-DOS or MS-DOS operating system
               512K RAM required
               5 1/4" floppy discs (hard disc recommended)

               The database files will also be available in
               comma-delimited ASCII format for use on most CPM
               systems (5 1/4" SS/DD or DS/DD floppy discs) as
               well as the Apple Macintosh (3 1/2" discs).

Documentation: The BMO Database comes with a printed copy of the
                BMO Directory, plus a separate manual describing
                how to make best use of the BMO Database software.

Demo Copy: A demo copy of the BMO Database with a special file
            of syndicated columnists (not included in the BMO
            Directory) is available for $10.00 postpaid. The
            $10.00 may be applied to your purchase of the full
            BMO Database by sending in the credit certificate
            which will be included with the demo copy.

==

INDEX

AN UNBEATABLE COMBINATION: SUPERB BOOKS AND A 30-DAY MONEY-BACK GUARANTEE

Please send me the following books. It is my understanding that if I am not completely satisfied with any book, I may return it within 30 days for a full refund. Thank you.

Quantity	Title of Book	Price	Total Amount
	Book Marketing Made Easier ISBN 0-912411-11-2	$14.95	
	101 Ways to Market Your Books -- For Publishers and Authors ISBN 0-912411-08-2	hc $19.95	
	101 Ways to Market Your Books -- For Publishers and Authors ISBN 0-912411-09-0	pb $14.95	
	Book Marketing Opportunities: A Directory ISBN 0-912411-10-4	$19.95	
	Book Marketing Opportunities: A Database ISBN 0-912411-12-0	$150.00	
	Directory of Short-Run Book Printers, Third Edition ISBN 0-912411-06-6	$12.00	
	Directory of Short-Run Book Printers, MailMerge Edition ISBN 0-912411-06-6	$30.00	
	The Independent Publisher's Bookshelf, Third Edition ISBN 0-912411-07-4	$3.95	
	FormAides for Direct Response Marketing: Mail Order Made Easy ISBN 0-912411-02-3	$9.95	
	TOTAL NUMBER OF BOOKS ORDERED	Subtotal =	
		Postage $1.00/book	
		TOTAL ORDER	

[ ] Check enclosed with order.
[ ] Please charge to my credit card number:
    [ ] American Express   [ ] Visa   [ ] MasterCard

Number___________________________ ________________

From:______________ To (Exp. Date):_______________

Name_________________________________ Signature_________________________________

Address______________________________ Company Name______________________________

____________________________________ Phone Number______________________________

AD-LIB PUBLICATIONS, P.O. BOX 1102, FAIRFIELD, IOWA 52556   (515) 472-6617